Selected Letters of Fyodor Dostoyevsky

SELECTED LETTERS OF

RUTGERS UNIVERSITY PRESS

New Brunswick and London

FYODOR DOSTOYEVSKY

EDITED BY *Joseph Frank and*
David I. Goldstein

Andrew R. MacAndrew, TRANSLATOR

Frontispiece: The closing lines and the postscript of
Dostoyevsky's letter of December 22, 1849 (Letter 18), written
from the Peter-and-Paul Fortress to his brother Mikhail.

Library of Congress Cataloging-in-Publication Data

Dostoyevsky, Fyodor, 1821–1881.
Selected letters of Fyodor Dostoyevsky.

Includes index.
1. Dostoyevsky, Fyodor, 1821–1881—Correspondence.
2. Novelists, Russian—19th century—Correspondence.
3. Dostoyevsky, Fyodor, 1821–1881—Translations,
English. I. Frank, Joseph, 1918– . II. Goldstein,
David I., 1924–1985 III. MacAndrew, Andrew Robert,
1911– . IV. Title.
PG3328.A3M27 1987   891.73'3 [B]   86–3861
ISBN 0–8135–1185–2

The publication of this book has been aided by the generous
support of the National Endowment for the Humanities
and the contributors to Rutgers University.

This volume is dedicated to the memory of
DAVID I. GOLDSTEIN (1924–1985)
who played a major part in preparing the letters
included here for publication.
He was a fine scholar; but his friends will
also remember the gentle, lovable, and delightful
companion, whose presence they will never cease
to miss.

CONTENTS

ACKNOWLEDGMENTS

The present volume is the culmination of a project that began many years ago at the initiative of the late William Sloane, then the director of the Rutgers University Press. He was enthusiastic about the idea of providing a reliable English translation of Dostoyevsky's letters, and he undertook to arrange the financing that allowed Andrew MacAndrew to proceed with the task. It is only fitting that his name appear at the head of all those who have been involved in helping to bring this volume to birth. The name of Helen Stewart, his assistant at the time, should also be recorded with gratitude.

David Goldstein lavished much of his time, energy, and abundant erudition on poring over the texts of the letters to make sure that no possible nuance of meaning had been slighted or overlooked. Unfortunately, he did not live to see the publication of the results of his labors. The book is dedicated to him with sadness, as a testimony to the years he devoted to its making. Words of thanks are also rightly due to Virginia Bennett, who aided the two editors in the early stages of work on the manuscript of the English version, and made many useful suggestions for its improvement.

In the final period of preparation, the editors were fortunate to have the collaboration of Robert Feldmesser, who took a very important part in getting the present volume ready for publication. He was, in particular, responsible for reducing the copious editorial annotations of the Russian edition to a more manageable form, and he brought his vigilance to bear as well on a wide range of other editorial problems. His role was really that of assistant editor, and he should be considered as such.

For reasons that need not be explained here, after William Sloane's death the Dostoyevsky project fell into abeyance for a number of years, and it was only when Kenneth Arnold became director of the Rutgers University Press that it was revived. To him, and to the driving energy of his senior editor, Leslie Mitchner, the idea owes its rebirth and reactivation. Without them this book would never have seen the light of day, and their staunch support of it should not be allowed to pass without a well-deserved tribute.

Joseph Frank
Stanford, California
July 1986

INTRODUCTION

The letters of any great personality or public figure would seem, at first sight, to offer the most direct access to the intimacy of their lives; but this is by no means always the case. Letters can be used to conceal rather than to disclose, to construct a social and public image that has little to do with the actual modalities of emotion and response. As Leon Edel has written of Henry James's voluminous correspondence, much of it tells us "very little about his art and indeed very little about the man who wrote [it] save that he possessed a verbal magic which he liked to wrap around friends and acquaintances the better to tie them—by those colored threads—to his lonely writing table." Such correspondences themselves become an art form, and the writers are much less concerned with direct communication than with suggesting or evoking some preconceived image of themselves that they desire to bring into existence in the mind of the recipient. This cannot help but be true of all correspondence, since the sending of any message is inevitably shaped by some knowledge of the receiver; but there are considerable degrees of difference in the extent to which such knowledge will dominate in any particular case. If one were to construct a scale, then Dostoyevsky's letters may be placed—with some notable exceptions inspired by special circumstances—among those least shaped by the effort to convey a particular image of the writer or to conform to established conventions of epistolary exchange.

Unlike Flaubert, who voluntarily turned to correspondence as a therapeutic release for an emotional afflatus that he carefully excluded from his books, Dostoyevsky had no taste at all for letter writing and made no bones about his aversion. Usually, he explained his dislike in terms of lack of ability. "Have I not already told you," he wrote his second wife in 1869, "that I do not know how to write letters, that I am just inept at doing so?" One should not take such a statement *too* literally because, as anyone who leafs through the present volume will see, Dostoyevsky was perfectly capable of writing letters skillfully crafted to obtain their desired effect. And from his brilliant use of letters in his novels (not only in his first work, *Poor Folk,* written in the form of an exchange of letters, but also in such inserted letters as that of Raskolnikov's mother to her son in *Crime and Punishment*), it is evident that the epistolary mode held no secrets from him and that he could manipulate it at will. But, in most instances, Dostoyevsky's own letters were torn out of him by the demands of the moment, by necessities so compelling that they completely overwhelmed all other considerations.

Dostoyevsky lived and worked under such continuous pressure that, for the greater part of his life, it was impossible for him to regard the time given to writing letters as anything but an intrusion and a waste. As a result, however, the letters that he threw off on the spur of the moment—often full of illegible words and spotted with inkblots, testifying to the haste with which they were written—bring us much closer to Dostoyevsky's true self than is normally the case even with relatively unbuttoned personalities whose lives were more serene. And perhaps, when read as a whole, they make him more available to us than he was even for those of his contemporaries who knew him personally but could view him only in one or another particular aspect or relation.

It is thus Dostoyevsky in all the many facets of his agitated life and volatile personality that the letters unroll before us with unexampled vividness. At first there is the young Romantic, enamored of Pushkin and the great European writers like Schiller and Hugo who first stir his literary ambitions. Consumed with the desire to become a writer, he stifled in the confines of the Academy of Engineers, which he entered only to satisfy his father's wishes; and his letters from there to his older brother Mikhail, once the two are separated, reveal all of his dissatisfaction and his desire for freedom. At the same time, his literary ambitions follow the trend of the period, and he trod in the footsteps of Gogol once Russian literature began to take this path. The great success of his first novel, *Poor Folk,* precipitates him into the ranks of the new young writers, and his letters now report, with naive vanity, on his new-found fame and social triumphs. For a brief moment he becomes the flattered favorite of the world and the protégé of the influential critic Vissarion Belinsky; but his prickly sensitivity and unconcealed vainglory soon lead to personal disaster, and his literary work also falls out of favor. The letters of the latter half of the 1840s furnish ample evidence of these personal difficulties, and also offer a glimpse into the inner workings of those Petersburg literary coteries in which, even much later in his life, Dostoyevsky never really felt at home.

For obvious reasons, his correspondence reveals no trace of the political activities in which he engaged between 1847 and 1849. He attended, as we know, the gatherings of socialist sympathizers at the home of Mikhail Butashevich-Petrashevsky and joined a small secret society—organized by the man he called his Mephistopheles, Nikolai Speshnev—whose purpose was to incite a peasant rebellion against serfdom. But, after his arrest with other members of the Petrashevsky circle, his letters from the Peter-and-Paul Fortress while awaiting trial show a remarkable fortitude and resilience of spirit as he struggles against depression and the despair induced by solitary confinement. And this series is crowned by one of the most revelatory documents ever to come from Dostoyevsky's pen—the missive he dashed off to Mikhail on returning to his prison cell just after being sentenced.

A mock execution had been staged by Nicholas I, and Dostoyevsky had believed, along with all the others, that he was just a moment or two away from death; it was only at the last instant that he heard the true sentence: exile at hard labor in Siberia for four years and then indefinite service in the Russian army. The words he wrote on this occasion spring straight from his very soul and take us into the most secret recesses of his feelings about life— his ecstatic apprehension of its infinite worth, the sense he was never to lose thereafter of the possibility of its moral transfiguration, the consolatory blessing of the last kiss of love and forgiveness he exchanged with his fellow prisoners on the scaffold. Nothing ever written about Dostoyevsky takes us so directly to the very heart of the values controlling his greatest work as does this unvarnished expression of his astonished joy at a resurrection from the grave.

The four years of Dostoyevsky's imprisonment constitute a gap in his correspondence, even though we know that he did write one or two lost letters to his brother Mikhail that remained unanswered. But the silence is amply compensated for by the long chronicle of his prison-camp years that he addresses to the same correspondent on his release. All the impressions he had stored up suddenly come tumbling out in a starkly graphic account of his lacerating but revelatory encounter with the Russian people in the shape of his peasant fellow prisoners. If the letter from the fortress had disclosed Dostoyevsky's new "metaphysical" grasp of human existence, then this breathless recital of his experiences in the strange society into which he was cast lays the foundation for his future views on the major problems confronting Russian society. For what really shocked him was to discover just how estranged he was, simply as a member of the educated class, from the mentality and world-view of his fellow Russians. All other social issues thus became subordinated for him to the well-nigh impossible task of bringing about a reconciliation between these two world-views without sacrificing what was valuable in each. The letters of these years of Siberian exile also contain the troubled history of his unhappy first marriage, and they detail his frantic efforts, with the help of his friend Baron Wrangel, to obtain promotion in the army and thus the freedom to resign and resume his literary career.

On returning to Petersburg in 1860, Dostoyevsky plunged again happily into the excitement of literary life, just then undergoing a period of dramatic upsurge as a result of the strong impetus provided by the liberation of the serfs and the movement for social reform initiated by Alexander II. Dostoyevsky now took active editorial charge of two monthly journals, first *Time* and then *Epoch,* and he was also the most prolific and important contributor to the first of these publications. His letters accordingly drop off in interest and importance, although the ones he wrote to the actress Aleksandra Shubert show him in the unaccustomed role of gallant and testify to his search for female companionship outside the domestic hearth. Several letters to Turgenev, with whom he was then on very good terms, initiate the most extensive correspondence he was to maintain with any of his great literary contemporaries. Dostoyevsky's letters from Europe during the summers of 1862 and 1863—the second voyage made in the tantalizing company of his young mistress, Apollinariya Suslova—contain some acerbic reactions to the splendors of European civilization; and such a reaction would continue to define his love-hate relationship to "the land of holy wonders."

When *Epoch* collapsed in 1865 for lack of funds, the occasion is marked by a copious letter-chronicle written over a period of two weeks and similar in importance to the one sent to Mikhail eleven years earlier. This time the recipient is Baron Wrangel, a friend from the years in Siberia, with whom Dostoyevsky had lost touch and for whose benefit he sums up much of the recent past. Dostoyevsky's letters now become preoccupied with the difficulties of his financial situation; and when he becomes stranded in Wiesbaden because of gambling losses, there is the first cycle of those numerous letters in which he is humiliatingly forced to plead for help from close friends and even from colleagues such as Turgenev and Herzen. It is in the throes of this situation that he writes the extremely valuable letter to M. N. Katkov, the editor of the *Russian Messenger,* outlining the first idea for the story that was soon to become *Crime and Punishment* and asking for an advance.

During the next five years, after marrying the young stenographer who enabled him to write *The Gambler* in record time while completing *Crime and Punishment,* Dostoyevsky fled to Europe to escape his creditors—or, rather, those of his older brother Mikhail, whose debts he had imprudently assumed. It was an act of desperation for Dostoyevsky, who found his self-imposed expatriation intolerable; he stifled in the solitude of separation from Russia, whose atmosphere was necessary both for his work and his psychic well-being. But what was a bane for Dostoyevsky is a benefit for posterity, since it led to a continual exchange of letters with literary friends like Apollon Maikov and Nikolai Strakhov as well as with editors from whom he was seeking advances. The result is that, during the period 1865– 1870, there is a steady supply of information about the major novels that Dostoyevsky was producing—*The Idiot* and *The Devils*—as well as a detailed explanation of his ideas for a never-written book, *The Life of a Great Sinner,* that he considered the most important of his whole creative career.

Also, his ever-present xenophobia now reaches a peak of exasperation, and he extends his hatred of life in Europe to Europeans and to those Russians, including old idols like Belinsky, who had infected Russia with the revolutionary virus by their admiration for Western culture. These letters exhibit Dostoyevsky in one of his least attractive moods; and his virulent anti-Westernism leads to the quarrel with Turgenev that he recounts in a letter which reads like a page from *The Devils*. Several of its details are, in fact, included in that novel along with a brilliant parody of the style of Turgenev's prose-poems.

These years also saw the sporadic flare-up of his gambling fever, and the numerous letters to his long-suffering young wife from various gambling spas make painful reading. Nowhere does Dostoyevsky reveal himself so unashamedly; nowhere does he resemble more closely those of his characters consumed by guilt and remorse. But all this should be seen against the background of his desperate desire to return to Russia and the irresistible feeling that an instant and miraculous solution to his financial predicament—the sole obstacle to his return—lay within his grasp if he could just manage to control his nerves. Like so many of his characters in the grip of obsessions, he became possessed by this dream and returned to the roulette tables again and again, always to suffer the same defeat and the same sense of self-abasement. It is all the more remarkable that he broke the spell in 1871, just before returning to Russia, and recorded this resolution in a letter describing how he entered a Jewish synagogue by mistake while roaming through the darkness of unfamiliar German streets in search of a Russian church. Dostoyevsky believed in omens, and there is probably a close connection between this seemingly insignificant incident and the definitive termination of his gambling mania.

The return to Russia marked the final triumphant phase of Dostoyevsky's career; by this time, as the author of three great novels, his position had been firmly established. He became the editor of a weekly, the *Citizen,* and somewhat later the owner, editor, and sole contributor to a unique monthly journal, *Diary of a Writer.* This publication played an enormous role in Russian public life and involved Dostoyevsky in a huge correspondence. Many letters of this period tend to be more perfunctory than personal; and if Dostoyevsky does not quite become the "smiling public man" of Yeats's famous poem (there are no pictures of him with a smile), he at least comes closer to this image than in any previous period.

Admirers of his work now began to flock around him, and he makes a whole circle of new acquaintances with exalted social connections but representing a broad range on the social-political spectrum. It is typical of his volatility that, just as he was attaining a new social respectability, his letters indicate that old friends such as Maikov and Strakhov were treating him coldly and distantly because the ferocious antinihilist who had written *The Devils* was now exhibiting an unexpected sympathy for the new type of radical Populism that had arrived on the Russian scene. This led to a suspicion that he was betraying his previous post-Siberian ideals and flirting with radicalism once again. The extensive correspondence with his wife, who successfully ran both his household and his business affairs, continued unabated during his voyages abroad for his health; but instead of frantic pleas for aid to cover gambling losses, his letters now are filled with an extreme nervous anxiety over the welfare of his family during his absence.

Dostoyevsky could not of course reply at length to all the letters addressed to him by strangers, but he made efforts to acknowledge them and sometimes wrote extensively when some issue was raised that touched him at a deeper level. Of particular interest is the reply to Arkady Kovner, a young Jewish journalist arrested for swindling a bank, who wrote from prison and accused Dostoyevsky of anti-Semitism. Another such letter was addressed to a group of progressive students (one of them being the young P. N. Milyukov, later a famous historian and head of the liberal Constitutional Democratic party) who had asked Dostoyevsky to comment on why the populace had brutally beaten a group of Moscow students come to greet others being sent into exile. Such a request indicates the special status Dostoyevsky had attained as someone standing above the battle of social-political factions and speaking as the voice of the Russian conscience.

During his last years, Dostoyevsky was engaged in the composition of *The Brothers Karamazov;* and many letters, to his editor as well as to friends and readers, are concerned with explaining and clarifying the aims of the novel. One agitated lady who could not wait for the next installment is reassured that Dmitry Karamazov is not the *real* murderer and is gently reprimanded for having failed to pick up the carefully planted clues that would indicate as much. K. P. Pobedonostsev, tutor to Crown Prince Alexander, is also reassured, though with some trepidation, that the chapter, "The Russian Monk," then being written would answer Ivan Karamazov's powerful revolt against the arrangements of God's world. Such letters form a more extensive corpus of commentary than is available for any other novel of Dostoyevsky's, and they are of inestimable value for the study and interpretation of this crowning and majestic creation.

A consecutive reading of the letters, as remarked earlier, allows the present-day observer to obtain a many-faceted image of Dostoyevsky that none of his contemporaries could possibly have commanded. Few writers have lived through such extreme changes of fortune as Dostoyevsky, and his correspondence allows us to participate equally in the misery and degradation of his prison-camp years and in the apotheosis depicted without exaggeration in the letter to his wife describing his triumph at the Pushkin festival in 1880. On that occasion, the political criminal once shunned and despised by peasant-convicts swept his distinguished audience away by his flaming words in praise of Pushkin and created an atmosphere of religious revivalism in which people weepingly embraced each other and hailed him as a prophet. This was the culmination of Dostoyevsky's entire existence, the momentary victory of the values of love and reconciliation that he had preached all through his lifetime in various forms and whose incarnation he had succeeded in discovering in those very peasant-convicts who had repulsed him so cruelly. Six months later he was dead.

Dostoyevsky's correspondence, precisely because of its uninhibited nature, conveys an extremely forceful impression of his difficult and tormented personality. It is impossible not to sympathize with him in certain situations and detest him in others; but whatever his weaknesses and failings—and they were, as Dostoyevsky himself was quite ready to acknowledge, all too many—the fact remains that he continually struggled to live up to the moral ideals in which he believed. And despite the many rumors of viciousness in Dostoyevsky's life, no convincing evidence for such gossip has ever been adduced. In the letters, if anywhere, we have the right to consider that we are seeing Dostoyevsky plain, and the erring but conscience-stricken man who wrote them hardly seems to justify the black legends that have accumulated around his name. Most of all, the letters portray a dedicated artist who never lost faith in his talent or its mission, and whose struggle to use his gifts properly—amidst personal crises that would have destroyed others, and though assailed by the crippling effects of an incurable illness that devastated his body and his mind—can only stimulate our admiration when we read the works he was creating despite all the travail recorded in these pages.

Joseph Frank

A NOTE
ON THE EDITION

Between 1928 and 1934, the Soviet publishing agency Academia published three volumes of the letters of Fyodor Dostoyevsky, copiously annotated by A. S. Dolinin (pen name of Arkady Iskoz), long one of the country's leading Dostoyevsky scholars. In 1959, after a hiatus caused by Dostoyevsky's disfavor with Soviet political authorities, the fourth and final volume appeared, similarly annotated (though published by a successor agency, Goslitizdat). These volumes constitute the basis of the present publication. From the 935 letters and other brief writings that they contain, most of them printed from the originals in Soviet archives, the editors of this volume have selected 152 of the most revealing, in terms of the author's literary career and personal fortunes, and to these have been added 4 others that have since come to light. All of them are given in their entirety.

The letters have been translated with the greatest possible fidelity to their published form, except in the following respects:

1. Dostoyevsky made numerous changes on the pages of his letters, replacing some words, crossing out others altogether, and adding still others between the lines or in the margins. Dolinin made scrupulous efforts to show all of these revisions on the printed page, but it would be impossible to do that in a translation. What is presented, then, is only what Dostoyevsky intended as the final form of each letter, except for indications (in brackets) of crossed-out or illegible words when their absence makes a sentence incomplete. There are also occasional bracketed insertions where they are needed to make Dostoyevsky's meaning clear.

2. Dostoyevsky frequently abbreviated the names of persons and publications. When it can reasonably be assumed that the reader will recognize the name because it has appeared in previous letters, the omitted portion is given in brackets at the first instance in a letter, and an abbreviation similar to Dostoyevsky's is then used at subsequent instances in the same letter. When that assumption cannot be made, Dostoyevsky's abbreviation is used from the start, and an explanation is provided in the note to the letter.

3. For the sake of clarity, the titles of publications have been set in italics, even though Dostoyevsky rarely underlined them. With that exception, only those words or names that Dostoyevsky *did* underline have been set in italics. It may be pointed out that he rarely underlined the French or German words that he used from time to time (and these have been given here in French or German rather than in English).

4. Dostoyevsky was not always clear about where he intended a new paragraph to begin; though he sometimes indented a line for that purpose, at other times he merely wrote one or two dashes when he was starting a new subject. Since not infrequently there may be no indentation for several successive pages, the editors have taken the liberty of starting a new paragraph wherever there is a hint of one, or where necessary for comprehension.

5. Erroneous or confusing dates in the headings have been corrected or clarified. This problem arose particularly with Old Style and New Style dates. At the time Dostoyevsky was writing, Russia had not adopted the Gregorian calendar and was thus twelve days "behind" Western Europe. In letters written from Western Europe to persons in Russia, he usually gave both the Old Style (Russian) and the New Style (European) dates, but sometimes in that order and sometimes reversed, and occasionally he got the two quite mixed up (e.g., giving the Old Style month with the New Style date of the month) or gave a date that was obviously wrong. Here, whenever Dostoyevsky does give two dates, the practice has been followed of giving (as nearly as can be determined) the correct Old Style date first and then the correct New Style date.

6. Several passages that had been published in earlier editions of the letters but were omitted from Dolinin's have been restored. These all occurred in the fourth volume (which covered the years from 1878 to 1881) and were expressions of Dostoyevsky's anti-Semitism.*

Dolinin's notes could not be reproduced in full in a work of this relatively modest size. They have thus been drastically condensed, preserving only those parts that seemed necessary to an understanding of the content of a given letter and that were judged to be of interest to present-day readers. This is one of the reasons why minor persons mentioned only in passing have not been identified; the other reason is that often Dolinin himself did not identify them, and it is impossible to find out anything about them now. Most of the members of Dostoyevsky's family, and other persons frequently mentioned in the letters, have been identified separately in a biographical list rather than being repeatedly identified in the notes, as Dolinin tended to do. The name "Dostoyevsky" is used in the notes to refer only to the author; other persons with the same surname are referred to either by their first name and patronymic (e.g., Anna Grigorevna, Dostoyevsky's second wife) or by their first name alone when their patronymic was the same as Dostoyevsky's (e.g., Mikhail, Dostoyevsky's older brother). Finally, some of

---

* For details, see David Goldstein, "Rewriting Dostoyevsky's Letters," *American Slavic and East European Review,* 20 (April 1961), pp. 279–288. Goldstein attributed these omissions not to Soviet censorship but to Dolinin's own reluctance to allow the subject of his life's work to appear to be anti-Semitic. A new edition of the letters is currently being issued in the Soviet Union, but since only the first three volumes have appeared, it cannot yet be said whether the missing passages will be included.

Dolinin's observations have been moved from one note to another where they are now more appropriate, and his observations in notes to letters not included in this edition at all have been inserted wherever they were pertinent. In a very few cases, new material has been added. No attempt has been made to annotate the pervasive and recurring references to famous literary figures such as Schiller, Byron, and Hugo; the letters themselves provide a context for understanding the influence that these writers had on Dostoyevsky's life and work.

For the transliteration of Russian names and words, this edition uses Shaw's System I, intended for use in publications of general readership.* The only important exception is that the names of the Russian tsars are spelled in the customary anglicized form (e.g., Peter rather than Pyotr).

Dostoyevsky frequently uses the term "printer's sheet" (*pechatny list*). This is what would today be called a "signature"—i.e., sixteen printed pages that make up the units that are then bound together in books or magazines. The printer's sheet was the unit by which writers were paid, and Dostoyevsky used it in writing to publishers about financial matters, as well as for a measure of the amount he planned to write or had written in a given period of time.

The names of various Russian and Western European monetary units appear quite often in the letters. The following table gives the approximate value of the most frequently mentioned units in terms of the currency of the United States at the time:

Denmark	rigsdaler	$ 0.54
Germany	gulden (=florin)	0.14
	mark	0.24
	thaler[a]	0.72
Russia	imperial	18.60
	paper ruble[b]	0.14
	silver ruble[b]	0.72
Switzerland	franc	0.19
	louis d'or	3.80

SOURCE: Hermann Schmidt, *Tate's Modern Cambist: A Manual of Foreign Exchanges and Bullion* . . . (London: Wilson, 1880), pp. 7, 35, 46, 49–51, 54, 73, 78, 83, 86, 97, 150.

[a] 1 thaler = 30 groschen.

[b] When Dostoyevsky speaks simply of "rubles," it can usually be assumed that he means silver rubles.

* J. Thomas Shaw, *The Transliteration of Modern Russian for English-Language Publications* (Madison: University of Wisconsin Press, for the Modern Language Association, 1967).

A Brief Chronology of Dostoyevsky's Life

The titles of Dostoyevsky's works are shown in the year of first publication or the start of publication.

1821
Born.

1837
Mother dies.

1838
Enters Academy of Military Engineering.

1839
Father dies.

1844
Leaves military service.

1846
Joins Petrashevsky circle.
Poor Folk (Bednye lyudi), *The Double* (Dvoinik),
Mr. Prokharchin (Gospodin Prokharchin).

1847
The Landlady (Khozyaika), *A Novel in 9 Letters*
(Roman v 9-i pismakh).

1848
An Honest Thief (Chestny vor), *White Nights*
(Belye nochi), *A Weak Heart* (Slaboye serdtse),
The Jealous Husband (Revnivy muzh), *A
Christmas Tree and a Wedding* (Yolka i svadba).

1849

Arrested and imprisoned for political activities. Death sentence commuted at last minute to exile in Siberia.
Netochka Nezvanova.

1850–1854

Serves sentence of hard labor in Omsk.

1854–1859

Posted to military battalion in Semipalatinsk, as continuation of his sentence.

1857

Marries Mariya Dmitriyevna Isayeva.
A Little Hero (Malenky Geroi).

1859

Permitted to return to European Russia; moves to Tver and then settles in St. Petersburg.
Uncle's Dream (Dyadyushkin son), *The Village of Stepanchikovo and Its Inhabitants* (Selo Stepanchikovo i yego obitateli).

1860

Begins publishing, with his brother Mikhail, the journal *Time* (Vremya).
Notes from the House of the Dead (Zapiski iz Myortvogo doma).

1861

The Insulted and Injured (Unizhonnye i oskorblyonnye).

1862

Makes first trip to western Europe.

1863

Time closed by censors.
Travels in Italy with Apollinariya Suslova.
Winter Notes on Summer Impressions (Zimniye zametki o letnikh vpechatleniyakh).

1864
Begins publishing, again with Mikhail, the
journal *Epoch* (Epokha), which is closed for lack
of funds early in 1865.
Mariya Dmitriyevna dies.
Mikhail dies.
Notes from Underground (Zapiski iz podpolya).

1865
Travels in western Europe.

1866
Crime and Punishment (Prestupleniye i
nakazaniye).

1867
Marries Anna Grigorevna Snitkina.
The Gambler (Igrok).

1867–1871
Lives in several cities of western Europe with
Anna Grigorevna.

1868
First child, Sonya, is born and dies.
The Idiot (Idiot).

1869
Second child, Lyubov, is born.

1870
The Eternal Husband (Vechny muzh).

1871
Returns to Russia.
Third child, Fyodor, is born.
The Devils (Besy).

1872
Spends first of several summers in Staraya Russa.

1873–1874
Serves as editor of the *Citizen* (Grazhdanin).

1874
Spends first of several summers in Ems for
treatment of emphysema.

1875
Fourth child, Aleksei, is born.
A Raw Youth (Podrostok).

1876–1878
Publishes the monthly journal *Diary of a Writer*
(Dnevnik pisatelya).

1878
Son Aleksei dies.

1879
The Brothers Karamazov (Bratya Karamazovy).

1880
Makes celebrated speech at dedication of
Pushkin monument.

1881
Dies.

SELECTED LETTERS
OF FYODOR DOSTOYEVSKY

PART

I

1821–
1859

FYODOR
Mikhailovich Dostoyevsky was born on October 20, 1821, the second son of Mikhail Andreyevich Dostoyevsky, a doctor on the staff of the Mariinsky Hospital in Moscow. A stern but conscientious father, Dr. Dostoyevsky's rigor was balanced by the more easygoing and charitable temperament of his wife, Mariya Fyodorovna, whom her second son remembered with love and devotion all his life. In 1831 Dr. Dostoyevsky purchased a small estate in the province of Tula, about a hundred miles south of Moscow, and Fyodor's first letters were written to his mother, who remained there when the father and elder children were forced to return to the city. Fyodor and his older brother Mikhail were carefully educated at home and then sent to a dayschool, reputed to be the finest in Moscow, run by a French émigré. Their father had decided—quite arbitrarily, but with the best interests of their financial future in mind—that his sons would become military engineers, even though both at an early age exhibited a marked taste for literature and dreamed of becoming writers. They were accordingly sent to St. Petersburg in 1837, the year of their mother's death, and placed in a preparatory school for the Academy of Engineers; five months later they took the examinations, and Fyodor was admitted. Mikhail, rejected on grounds of health, joined the Engineers' Cadet Corps instead.

The first correspondence printed in this volume, Fyodor's letters to his father and particularly to his brother, reveals the difficulties of his situation and his passionate involvement with literature despite his zealous efforts to keep up with the formidable engineering curriculum. References abound to Shakespeare, Schiller, E.T.A. Hoffmann, and Goethe, and also to Victor Hugo and Balzac; and Fyodor's Romantic proclivities were nurtured by his friendship with Ivan Nikolayevich Shidlovsky, a slightly older aspiring poet and "broad" Russian nature consumed by a hopeless Romantic passion and given both to strong drink and to religious mysticism.

Dostoyevsky's father died in June 1839, probably murdered by his peasants, and his estate was then administered by the husband of Dostoyevsky's younger sister Varvara, a solid and self-assured citizen named Pyotr Andreyevich Karepin. The impecunious but rather prodigal and spendthrift Fyodor soon came into conflict with Karepin over funds and his plans for a future as a writer.

On graduation from the Academy of Engineers in 1843, Dostoyevsky served as an army officer for a little over a year and then resigned to pursue his literary ambitions. Romanticism had now gone out of fashion in Russian literature, and the influential critic Vissarion Belinsky was calling for writers to follow the example of Gogol—to depict Russian life critically rather than soaring into the empyrean. Dostoyevsky's first novel, *Poor Folk*, fulfilled precisely this prescription, and it was clamorously hailed by Belinsky as a great work. Dostoyevsky thus enjoyed a brief moment of glory and was immediately taken into the intimacy of Belinsky's "pléiade," the group of young writers, including Turgenev, who clustered around the great critic. But his second work, *The Double*, was not so well received; and his pathologically suspicious nature, combined with an overweening vanity, soon led to quarrels with everyone, including Belinsky. From the fêted young hope of Russian literature, Dostoyevsky soon sank to the level of laughingstock, ridiculed and scorned by those who had previously praised him to the skies.

In 1847 Dostoyevsky began to associate with other groups and was led into the orbit of the circle that gathered weekly at the home of Mikhail Butashevich-Petrashevsky to discuss social-political issues. The revolutions of 1848 in Europe suddenly gave such discussions a burning actuality, and Dostoyevsky joined a secret society—organized by Nikolai Speshnev within the Petrashevsky circle—whose purpose was to set up a secret printing press and circulate propaganda aimed at stirring the enserfed Russian peasants to revolt. The government, however, succeeded in infiltrating the larger Petrashevsky group, and most of its members were arrested; the existence of the Speshnev secret society, and Dostoyevsky's adherence to it, were revealed only long after his death.

Trapped in the roundup of the Petrashevsky circle, Dostoyevsky spent a year in solitary confinement in the Peter-and-Paul Fortress. After an agonizing mock execution orchestrated by the tsar, he was sent to Siberia for a term of four years at hard labor in a camp and then indefinite service in the Russian army. Luckily, after his discharge from the camp in 1854 he met the young and influential Baron Wrangel, then serving as regional magistrate, who exercised his considerable prestige to ease Dostoyevsky's lot as a soldier and was instrumental in obtaining his promotion to the rank of officer. By this time Dostoyevsky had fallen in love with Mariya Dmitriyevna Isayeva, the wife of a ne'er-do-well friend; A. I. Isayev's death in 1855 cleared the way for Dostoyevsky's marriage with the widow, who became his first wife in 1857.

All Dostoyevsky's energies were now devoted to obtaining permission to retire from the army and return to St. Petersburg so as to resume his literary career. Two minor works, *Uncle's Dream* and *The Village of Stepanchikovo*, were written and published at this time but met a very lukewarm reception. Dostoyevsky was convinced, all the same, that his long ordeal had enormously enriched his sensibility and imagination and had provided him with a wealth of material that no other Russian writer could match. He finally obtained permission to resign his commission in the spring of 1859, and he traveled with his wife and stepson to the city of Tver, where he remained for several months. At last he received permission to reside in Petersburg, arriving there in mid-December 1859 ready to renew the struggle to advance to the front rank of Russian letters.

1. TO M. A. DOSTOYEVSKY
Petersburg, June 5, 1838

Dearest Papa!

My God, what a long time it's been since last I wrote you, since I last tasted those moments of true, heartfelt bliss, real, pure, and lofty, the bliss that is felt only by those who have someone with whom they can share their hours of exaltation and of disaster, who have someone they can trust with whatever may be going on in their souls. Ah, how keenly I am reveling in that bliss now.

I hasten to explain to you now the reasons for my long silence.

After that brief postscript that I added to my brother's letter, in which I sent you my good wishes for the Holy Days, I did not get another opportunity to do anything more for a long time. Our trimestrial examination, which lasts for at least a month, started just at that time. We had to work day and night, and it was the engineering drawings that finally broke our backs. We have four subjects involving drawing: (1) fortification design, (2) situation mapping, (3) architectural drawing, and (4) drawing from nature. And, as you know, I am a poor draftsman, and only in fortification design do I do quite well. But there was nothing I could do about it. And so it was my undoing. First of all, I am now ranked about in the middle of the class when I could have been first. Do you know that, in all the subjects requiring intelligence, I have top marks, so that I have five points more than the first-ranking student in all subjects that do not involve drawing? But they consider drawing more important than math. This disheartens me very much.

The second reason for my long silence is the field exercises. Just imagine this: five inspections by the Grand Duke and the Tsar—it completely exhausted us. We mounted guard, went to the manege with the guards, marched in parade, went through all sorts of drill formations, and before every inspection they tortured us with the company drill that prepared us for it. All these inspections were actually in preparation for the mammoth, brilliant, full-dress *May Parade,* which was attended by the entire Imperial Family, and in which 140,000 troops took part. That day exhausted us completely.

In the coming months we are going out on maneuvers. Because of my height, I have been placed in a reconnaissance company and so must go through a double training—that for the battalion and that for the reconnaissance unit. So I cannot help it if I don't have enough time to prepare for my classes. Well, these then are the reasons for my long silence.

Now, let me talk of something else. Yes, who would ever have thought that my brother would be sent off on detached service? But what can you do about it! That is God's will. And nothing in the world can alter His will. In general, fate plays with the world as with a toy. It distributes the parts people must play, but then fate is blind. But God will point out the path that will lead people out of every predicament. But my brother is still not disheartened. Of course, to witness the disappointment of such a father as you are is very painful to us. Our hearts bleed for you. But be reassured, dearest Papa, the place to which Brother has been sent and his service duties there have their own advantages. The most important thing for the engineering service is practical experience; he is getting it now. And there will always be an opportunity for him to study, wherever he is. So perhaps God has arranged everything for the best. I recently got a letter from my brother and, judging by his description, I dare say his life is quite enviable. But I suppose you must know all about it from his letter to you, because I feel certain that he has not failed to inform you of his news.

I suppose that now you are filling your lonely hours with running the estate and farming chores. And I wonder what this year will bring us and whether there will be much in it that will cheer us. Oh, may God send us happiness!

I continue to visit the Merkurovs. They are people who are worthy of friendship and respect. They receive me as though I were one of the family. May God grant happiness to every well-wisher of ours!

My present situation, as far as money goes, is a bit precarious. The trip to Revel cost my brother quite a bit, too! Moreover, of the money you sent me, I spent a tidy sum on things that are required by regulations. For I had to modify and supplement my uniforms and my equipment for the May Parade. All my new comrades, without exception, got themselves their own shakos, and the one that had been issued to me could very well have attracted the Tsar's attention. I had to buy myself a new one, and it cost me 25 rubles. And I spent the rest of the money on repairing my instruments and on paint and brushes. All these things are indispensable! But when the time comes for us to move out on maneuvers, I shall be in real trouble, because there it is really grim to be without money. If you can, dear Papa, please send me something. Address the letter directly to the Main Engineering School, because I am at a loss to explain to you the exact address of the Merkurovs. They have moved from their former apartment, and I have forgotten the name of their present landlord. Around June 12 we are moving out to maneuvers.

Farewell, dearest Papa, please kiss all my brothers and sisters for me. With sincere respect and filial devotion I remain.

F. Dostoyevsky

---

1. After joining the Engineers' Cadet Corps, Mikhail had been sent to a cadet company in Revel (now Tallinn).

The Merkurovs were a Petersburg family whom Dostoyevsky had met through Shidlovsky (see note to Letter 2).

2. TO M. M. DOSTOYEVSKY
Petersburg, August 9, 1838

Brother!

How surprised I was by your letter, dear brother; is it possible that you haven't received even half a line from me! I have sent you three letters since you left: one soon after your departure; I didn't answer your second letter because I was broke (I didn't borrow anything from the Merkurovs). This went on until July 20, when I received 40 rubles from Papa. And, finally, I recently sent you a third letter. And so you cannot boast of not having forgotten me and of writing me more often than I wrote you. And so I too have always been true to my word. True, I am lazy, very lazy. But what can I do when the only one thing left in the world for me is to take an uninterrupted siesta! I don't know whether these sad thoughts of mine will subside. Only one state is the lot of man: the atmosphere of his soul consists of a merging of the sky with the earth; what an unnatural creature man is, a breach of the law of nature—I believe that our world is a purgatory for heavenly spirits befogged by sinful thought. It seems to me that the world has acquired a negative signification and turned lofty, graceful spirituality into a satire. If an individual who shares neither the effect nor the thought with the whole, i.e., a complete outsider, comes into the picture, what will be the result? The picture will be spoiled and can no longer exist!

But to see only the hard shell in which the universe is languishing, to know that one single explosion of will would be sufficient to shatter it and to fuse it with eternity, to know that and to be like the last of the creatures— that is horrible! How cowardly is a man! Hamlet! Hamlet! When I think of those wild, stormy speeches which reverberate with the moans of the benumbed world, then neither mournful lamentation nor reproach constricts my breast—the soul is so weighed down by sorrow that it is afraid to acknowledge it lest it be torn to shreds. Pascal once said he who protests against philosophy is a philosopher himself. What a pitiful philosophy!

But I've lost myself in chatter. Of your letters, I received only two (besides the last one). Ah, brother, you complain of your poverty. Needless to say, I'm not so rich. Would you believe it that during all the time we were away from the camp and on the march, I didn't have one kopek. During the march I fell sick from the cold (it poured the whole day and we were in the open) and from hunger, and I didn't have a cent to buy a swallow of tea to wet my throat. I recovered, but back in camp I had a most awful time until I received that money from Papa. Then I paid back my debts and spent the rest.

But the description of your situation surpasses everything. Is it possible not to have five kopeks, to *feed* on God knows what, and to savor only with a gluttonous eye the delightful sweetness of the gorgeous berries that you are so fond of! How sorry I am for you! You will ask what happened to the Merkurovs and to your money. Well, here is what happened. I went to see them several times after you had left. Then I couldn't see them because I had to cram. When I was in desperate straits I sent someone to fetch some but they sent me so little that I was ashamed to ask them again. Then I received your letter to them addressed to me. I didn't have a kopek then, so I decided to send them a note, together with a letter for you, which I asked them to send on when they wrote to you. But apparently you did not receive either one or the other. So I suppose they didn't write you. Before going off on maneuvers (having no money to send off a letter I had written some time ago to Papa), I asked them to send me at least something. They sent me all our things, but not a single kopek nor a reply to my letter; so there I was like a stranded crayfish! From all this I concluded that they would like to be rid of our bothersome requests. I wanted to write them a letter about it, but I have been marking time since returning from maneuvers, and they have moved to another apartment. I know the house where they live now but do not have their exact address. I'll *notify* you of it later.

But it's high time I changed the topic of conversation. Well, you are bragging that you have read a lot, but don't imagine that I am envious of you. I myself did quite some reading in Peterhof, I suppose at least as much as you did. The whole of Hoffmann, some in Russian and some in German (i.e., the untranslated *Lebensansichten des Katers Murr*), almost all of Balzac (Balzac is great! His characters are the products of a universal mind! It is not the spirit of a period, but rather whole millennia that have, in their relentless strivings, gone to prepare this denouement in the soul of man); Goethe's *Faust* and his minor poems; Polevoi's *History* and *Ugolino, Undina* (I'll write you a few things about *Ugolino* later). Also Victor Hugo, other than *Cromwell* and *Hernani*. Now good-bye. But write, please, do me a favor, comfort me and write as often as possible. Answer this letter right away. I count on an answer from you in 12 days. That's at the latest! Write, or you'll make me miserable.

Your brother, F. Dostoyevsky

I have a plan: to become a madman. Let people get furious and put me under treatment, let them make me reasonable. If you have read the whole of Hoffmann, you certainly must remember the character called Alban. How do you like him? It is terrifying to find a man who has the inconceivable in his power, who does not know what to do, who plays with a toy that is— God!

Do you write often to the Kumanins? And let me know whether Kudryavtsev has told you anything about Chermak. For heaven's sake, write me about it. I am eager to have news of Andryusha.

But listen, brother, if our correspondence has to continue in this fashion, perhaps it would be better not to write at all. So let us agree to write every other Saturday. That would be better. I received another letter from Schrenk, and I owe him a letter for three months now. Frightful! This is what it means to be without money!

---

2. This letter may show the influence of Ivan Nikolayevich Shidlovsky (1816–1872), a volatile character whom Dostoyevsky and his brother had met in the spring of 1837. He had worked for a while on an ambitious project on the history of the church; the protagonist of Dostoyevsky's story *The Landlady* also worked on a history of the church and may have been partly suggested by Shidlovsky. At the time of this letter, Shidlovsky was going through a very depressed period and was contemplating suicide.

The authors mentioned in this letter all had an influence on Dostoyevsky's work. This was particularly true of Honoré de Balzac (1799–1850), who was very popular in Russia during the 1830s. Dostoyevsky's first literary work was a translation into Russian of Balzac's *Eugénie Grandet* (1833), and in his last work—his speech at the unveiling of the monument to Pushkin—he invoked the name of Rastignac, one of the main characters in Balzac's *Le père Goriot* (Father Goriot, 1835).

Nikolai Alekseyevich Polevoi (1796–1846) was a critic and writer and the chief editor of the *Moscow Telegraph* (Moskovsky telegraf), an important magazine of the 1820s and 1830s. His *History of the Russian People* (Istoriya russkogo naroda, 1829–1833) was directed primarily against N. M. Karamzin, whose *History of Russia* Dostoyevsky had admired as a boy. Polevoi sought to eliminate the personal and accidental in the history of Russia and to establish periods that followed each other in logical sequence. *Ugolino* (1838) was one of his early Romantic dramas.

"Undina" (1837) was a poem by Vasily Andreyevich Zhukovsky (1783–1852), based on the story *Undine* by Friedrich de La Motte-Fouqué. Zhukovsky was also the author of the words of the Russian national anthem, "God Save the Tsar" (Bozhe, tsarya khrani).

Alban is the hero of *Der Magnetiseur*, a novel by E.T.A. Hoffmann (1776–1822). He is depicted as a Romantic who despised the shackles of obsolete moral precepts.

Kudryavtsev had been a classmate of Dostoyevsky and his brother at Chermak's boarding school, which they had attended before going to the preparatory school for the military academy.

3. To M. M. Dostoyevsky
Petersburg, October 31, 1838

Oh, what a long, what a very long time it has been since I last wrote you, my dear brother—that miserable exam! It prevented me from writing to you and to Papa and from seeing Ivan Nikolayevich. And all that for what? I didn't pass. Oh, how awful; an extra year, a whole year more! I wouldn't be so furious if I didn't know that I was turned down just out of pure malice, nothing but that; I wouldn't feel so sorry about it if my poor father's tears were not searing my soul. Until now, I didn't know what wounded self-esteem could be like. I would have blushed had that feeling taken possession of me— But, do you know, I feel like crushing the whole world, just like that— I lost, I ruined so many days before the exams, I took sick, I lost weight, I came through the exam with flying colors in every sense of the term, and I was left back—that's the way one of the teachers (algebra) wanted it. I had been rude to him during the year and now he had the gall to bring it up to me when he was explaining why I had been left behind— My average was 9½ out of a possible 10, and I was left back— But to hell with it. If I have to take it, I'll take it— Why waste paper on it; as it is already, I'm seldom in touch with you.

My dear friend, you philosophize like a poet! And just as your soul bears the pitch of inspiration unevenly, so your philosophy is uneven and incorrect. That in order to *know* more you must *feel* less, and vice versa, is a rash formula, emotional raving coming from the heart. What do you mean by the word *know*? An understanding of nature, the human soul, God, love—that comes from the heart, not from the mind. If we were spirits, we would live and soar in the sphere of that thought over which our soul hovers when it wishes to fathom it. But since we are dust, men, we have to comprehend it, but we cannot embrace it all at once. It is *reason* that conducts thought through the frail membrane into the soul. Reason is a material faculty—the soul or the spirit lives by the idea that is whispered to it by the heart— An idea is born in the soul. Reason is the instrument, the machine that is set in motion by the fire of the soul— And so (this is the second point), human reason when it strays into the domain of knowledge operates independently of *feeling,* that is, of the *heart*. But if the goal is to understand love and nature, then a clear field is opened to the *heart*— I won't get into an argument with you, but let me tell you that I do not agree with you about poetry and philosophy— Philosophy should not be taken as an ordinary mathematical problem in which the unknown is nature— But note that a poet in a moment of inspiration perceives God; hence, he accomplishes the mission of philosophy. Hence, the poet's ecstasy is a philosophical ecstasy . . . Hence, philosophy is also poetry, only a higher degree of it! It strikes me as strange that you should reason in the spirit of today's philosophy. How many mixed-up philosophical systems have sprung up in ardent, intelligent minds. In order to obtain a reliable result from this diverse heap, you have to bring it under a mathematical formula. Such are the rules of today's philosophy— But I have let myself get carried away— Without accepting your feeble philosophy, I nevertheless do accept the existence of its feeble results, my comments on which I will spare you—

Brother, it is sad to live without hope— I look ahead and the future terrifies me— I am drifting around in some cold, polar atmosphere where no ray of sunshine has crept— It is long since I have experienced bursts of inspiration—on the other hand, I often find myself in the same state as the prisoner of Chillon, remember, after the death of his brothers in the dungeon— No poetic bird of paradise will ever fly in to visit me and warm my soul that has grown cold— You say I am secretive; but then my dreams of yesteryear have forsaken me, and those wonderful arabesques I once upon a time created have lost their golden luster. The thoughts whose rays used to set my heart and soul aglow have lost their fire and warmth, or else it is my heart that has hardened, or— I dare not go on—I am terrified by the idea that the whole past was nothing but a golden dream, luxuriant illusions—

Brother, I read your poem— It wrung a few tears from my soul, and for a moment the sweet whisper of memories lulled my spirit to sleep. You say you have an idea for a play— I am delighted— Write it— Oh, if you were deprived of the last crumbs of the feast of Paradise, what would there be left for you?—

It is a shame that I couldn't see Ivan Nikolayevich last week; I was sick. Listen! I believe that glory also contributes to the poet's inspiration. Byron was an egotist: his concept of glory was insignificant and vain— But only the thought that, at some time, a pure, beautiful, and lofty soul will tear itself from the dust to follow your ecstasy of a bygone day; the thought that inspiration, like a heavenly sacrament, will illumine the pages over which you have wept and posterity will weep, I cannot believe that this thought does not infuse the soul of the poet at the very moment of creation. But the empty clamor of the crowd is meaningless. Ah, that brings to my mind two lines of Pushkin in which he describes the poet and the crowd: "And crowds spit on the altar where your fire is lit, / And in their childish playfulness, your tripod shakes!"

Isn't that delightful? Good-bye. Your friend and brother,

F. Dostoyevsky

Ah yes! Write and tell me the central idea of Chateaubriand's *Le génie du christianisme*. Recently I read in *Son of the Fatherland* the article on Victor Hugo by the critic Nisard. Oh, how lowly Hugo is rated in the estimation of the French people. Nisard makes his plays and novels sound so insignificant. They are unfair to him, and Nisard (although he is an intelligent man) talks nonsense. One thing more: tell me the main idea of your play. I am sure it is marvelous, although ten years is precious little for molding the characters for a drama. Anyway, that is how I feel about it. Ah, brother, how sorry I am that you are short of money! Tears pour from my eyes. When has it ever been like this for us? Yes, by the way, I congratulate you on your name day and on your recent birthday.

In your poem "An Apparition of Mother" I do not understand the strange contours you have given to the soul of our late mother. That character from beyond the grave is not given adequate expression. But, on the other hand, the verses are good, although in one place there is a flaw. Don't be angry with me for this analysis. Write more often and I shall be more regular.

Ah, soon, very soon, I shall reread Ivan Nikolayevich's new poems. They are so full of poetry and so many inspired ideas! Oh yes, I almost forgot to tell you that Smirdin is preparing a book that will be the Pantheon of our Literature, portraits of one hundred men of letters, with a representative selection of the author's writing accompanying each portrait. And just imagine, Zotov (!?) and Orlov (Aleksandr Anfimovich) are included among them. What a joke! Listen, send me another poem. The other one is charming! The Merkurovs are leaving for Penza soon, if they haven't already left.

I pity poor father! What a strange character he has! How much he has had to suffer! I am so sorry that I could weep, because I can do nothing to console him. And, you know, Papa has absolutely no idea about the world; he has lived in it for fifty years and his opinion of people is just what it was thirty years ago. Blissful ignorance. But he is very disappointed in it. This seems to be our common lot. Good-bye once more. Yours.

---

3. The lines of Pushkin quoted here are from his sonnet, "To the Poet" (Poetu, 1830).

François René de Chateaubriand (1768–1848) was a forerunner of French Romanticism. His major work, *Le génie du christianisme* (The genius of Christianity, 1802), was both a defense of Christianity and a literary manifesto, summing up the literary trends of the late eighteenth century.

Son of the Fatherland (Syn otechestvo) was a magazine published from 1825 to 1839 by Nikolai Grech and Faddei Bulgarin. It campaigned against Romanticism in general and the "Frenetic" school of French Romanticism in particular, frequently running full translations of the articles of French critics. Desiré Nisard (1806–1888) was a French literary historian and a champion of classicism, who considered the era of Louis XIV to have been the high-water mark of French literature.

Mikhail's name day was November 8, his birthday October 13. His poem "An Apparition of Mother" (Videniye materi) has been lost, as have his other poems mentioned in Letter 5.

Aleksandr Filippovich Smirdin (1795–1857) was a well-known publisher in the first half of the nineteenth century. He published the collected works of Russian eighteenth- and nineteenth-century writers and the magazines *A Library for Reading* (Biblioteka dlya chteniya) from 1834 on and *Son of the Fatherland* from 1838 on, as well as various almanacs. *One Hundred Russian Men of Letters* (Sto russkikh literatorov) was to have been published in ten volumes, with ten authors in each volume. Volume 1 appeared in 1839, with "portraits" of Pushkin, Nikolai Polevoi (see note to Letter 2), Rafail Zotov (see below), and seven others.

Rafail Mikhailovich Zotov (1795–1871) was a translator and the author of many quasi-historical popular novels, which were frequently ridiculed by Belinsky.

Aleksandr Anfimovich Orlov (d. 1840) was a novelist whose most successful work was *The Death of Ivan Vyzhigin* (Smert Ivana Vyzhigina, 1831), a parody of Bulgarin's novel *Ivan Vyzhigin*. The critic Ksenofont Polevoi later called him "a cheap scribbler who turns out all sorts of disgusting booklets under various cynical titles." His portrait was not included in volume 1 of *One Hundred Russian Men of Letters*.

4. To M. M. Dostoyevsky
Petersburg, August 16, 1839

Yes, my dear brother, this is the way it always is with us: we promise ourselves to do things without knowing whether we can carry them out. A good thing that I never make rash promises. For instance, what do you say of my silence? that I am lazy, that I have forgotten you, etc. Not so! The whole trouble was that I didn't have a cent, but now I do have money and I cannot describe to you how welcome is this unaccustomed guest.

And so, here at long last is my letter!

Let's have a little talk, let's chat a bit!

My dear brother! I have shed many tears over our father's death, but now our situation is even worse than before, and I am not talking about myself but about our family. I am sending my letter to Revel without knowing whether it will reach you. I have the feeling it won't reach you in time— I hope to God you'll be in Moscow; then I wouldn't be so worried about our family. But tell me, please, is anyone in the world more miserable than our poor brothers and sisters? The thought that they will be brought up by strangers now kills me. And therefore your idea of going to live in the country once you get your officer's commission is an excellent one. There, my dear brother, you could see to their education, and being brought up there would be a happy thing for them. A harmonious development of the mind amidst one's own family, the cultivation of all faculties on Christian principles, pride in family virtues, a fear of vice and of dishonor—these would be the fruits of such an upbringing. And then, the bones of our parents will rest in peace in the damp earth. But you will have a lot to contend with, kind friend; you will have either to break off or fully reconcile yourself with our relatives. To sever relations would be disastrous; it would be fatal to our sisters. If you make up with them you will have to cater to them, and they are bound to accuse you of laziness for neglecting the service. But you will have to stick it out, my dear brother. Pay no attention to those petty, insignificant souls, and be the benefactor of your brothers. You alone will save them— I know that you have learned forbearance; so please, do carry out your plan. It is an excellent one. May God give you the strength you'll need for it! I declare in advance that I will be in agreement with you on everything.

I wonder what you're doing now. You are more sincere [with Ivan] Nikolayev[ich] than with me. [You told] him that you are weighed down with work and that you [have] no time, that being in the service is a hell[ish] job. [What is there] to do? Get out of it as soon as possible.

What can I tell you about myself?—I haven't had a sincere talk with you for a long time. I am not sure that I am in the right mood just now to speak to you about that. I don't know, but now, much more often than before, I am completely indifferent to everything around me. On the other hand, the moments of awakening are more violent. My one aim is to be free. I'd sacrifice everything for freedom. But often, often I wonder what freedom will give me—what will become of me all alone in a strange crowd? I will manage to get over it all but, I confess, it takes a strong faith in the future and a firm self-awareness to live by my present hopes. But what of it? It makes no difference whether they come true or not, I'll do what I have to do anyway. I bless those moments when I am reconciled with the present (and those moments now have become more frequent). During these moments, I am more clearly conscious of [my] situation, and I feel certain [that these] sacred hopes will come to pass.

[. . .] not tranquil now; but strong characters usually mature in this spiritual [struggle]; the befogged vision clears up and faith in life finds a purer and nobler source. My soul is no longer susceptible to its former violent impulses. Everything in it is as quiet as in the heart of a man who conceals a deep secret. I am learning a good deal about "what is man and what is life"; I can study human characters from writers with whom I spend the best part of my life, freely and joyfully. This is all I can say about myself. I have confidence in myself. Man is a mystery. It must be unraveled, and if it takes a whole lifetime, don't say that it's a waste of time. I am preoccupied by this mystery because I want to be a human being. Good-bye. Your friend and brother,

F. Dostoyevsky

[. . .] by favorite ideas every minute [. . .] in dreams and thoughts life less perceptively. One more thing—I know how to love and how to be a friend. Recently I [. . .] There are so many things that are sacred and great, pure [. . .] in this world. Moses and Shakespeare, all [. . .] only half-way.

Love! Love. You say that you pluck its flowers. I think that there is no man more saintly and altruistic than the poet. Can one possibly impart his exaltation to a piece of paper! The soul will always conceal more than can be expressed in words, in colors, and in sounds. That is why it is difficult to carry out the idea of a creation.

[. . .] when love links two hearts. Because [. . .] and so much the more does not show one's tears [. . .] but in the breast. One can cry [. . .] one must have Christ[ian] pride and faith [. . .] you something about M[. . .]

14

If a week from today I do not get an answer, I'll conclude that you are in Moscow, and I'll write you at the Kumanins' address. Write me at length what arrangements you have made and what arrangements the others have made. I await your answer impatiently. Now, my dear fellow, there will be no halt in our correspondence. Soon I'll send you a package of books. Write. I must stop now.

---

4. This letter contains the only known reaction of Dostoyevsky to the murder of his father.

In several places, pieces of the letter have been torn off. Along with the original there was a copy in an unknown hand; on this copy, the missing words were replaced by penciled-in words, which are here given in brackets. The passage that follows the signature was written on the margins of the first, second, and third pages of the letter, occupying a part of the torn-off edges; the missing words were not given in pencil on the copy and are indicated here by bracketed ellipses.

5. TO M. M. DOSTOYEVSKY
Petersburg, January 1, 1840

I thank you from the bottom of my heart, my kind brother, for your nice letter. No, I am not like you! You wouldn't believe how sweet is the tremor in my heart when I am handed a letter from you, and I have invented a new kind of delight for myself—a very bizarre one—to impose the agony of suspense upon myself. I take your letter and for several minutes I turn it this way and that in my hand, I feel whether it is heavy, and then, after examining and admiring it to my fill, I put the sealed letter in my pocket— You cannot believe what a voluptuous state of the soul, of the feelings, and of the heart it gives me! And I wait this way sometimes for a quarter of an hour. Then at last I greedily pounce upon the envelope, tear the seal, and devour your lines, your dear lines. Oh, what overwhelming emotions does my heart experience as I read them! All the sensations crowding in my soul, agreeable and unpleasant, sweet and bitter. Yes, dear brother, unpleasant and bitter too, because you cannot imagine how it feels when people don't fathom, don't understand you, when they put everything in a completely different way; not at all what I meant, but in a different, deformed way . . . When I read your last letter, I was un enragé, because I did not have you right here beside me: The best of all my heart's dreams, the most sacred rules of conduct acquired through hard, painful experience, have been twisted, distorted, and displayed in the most lamentable light. You write me yourself: "Write, object, argue with me," and you think some good will come of it! Nothing of the kind, my dear brother, absolutely nothing, except that your egotism (and all of us, sinners, suffer from it) will draw a conclusion that is *most advantageous* to yourself about your correspondent, about his opinions, principles, character, and simple-mindedness—and that is what hurts, brother! No! Polemics in friendly letters is sugar-coated poison. What will happen when we meet again? I believe it will be a constant source of discord between us— But I'll leave it at that! I may bring it up again in the last pages of my letter.

The Military Academy—c'est du sublime! Do you know that that is a most brilliant idea (?!) I have been giving a great deal of thought to your career and how to coordinate it with our circumstances, and I myself thought of the Military Academy. However, you beat me to it and I see you like it, too—But here's what: one must be in the service at least a year before entering the Military Academy, and so the best thing is to stick to your drafting board for one more year.

But what is this raving of yours about *notebooks,* when I don't even know what your curriculum is? So what should I send you? Artillery, I suppose, and a drill manual (I believe that is just what you need). I will send them to you without fail, as well as the notes on Major General Dyadin's course, since he is going to examine you in person. But, remember, I am sending you these notebooks for just one month. They don't belong to me and I had trouble getting them at all. You cannot have them one day longer than a month. Copy them or have them copied (Dyadin is a fussy man, you must either learn him by heart or, if you use your own words, they must sound as if they came out of the book). Field fortifications is so stupid that you can cram it in three days. Still, I'll send it to you in May, anyway. Permanent fortifications is quite a different matter; I'll see what I can do for you about it. We also have lithographed notes on analytic geometry but they are a word-for-word copy from Brashman and, of course, abridged. In short, we're using Brashman, so bone up on him yourself. Get yourself his book.

How are you in geodesy? We have a course in it (we use Bolotov). In physics, we are using Ozyomov. I will see what I can do about lithographed notes on differential calculus. Our history text is huge and very thick (lithographed) and I cannot get one. Russian language and literature—we have Plaksin's text and he is teaching it himself. Let me tell you that your exam for field engineers is very easy. They are not strict at all, and their policy is not to be too hard on their brother engineers. I have seen a number of examples that bear me out on this.

I have sent an extremely deferential letter to the Kumanins. So don't worry. I anticipate favorable results. I still haven't written to our guardian; God, I haven't had the time!

Best wishes for the New Year, dear one. What does it have in store for us? One thing for sure, the past five years have been terrible for our family. I have just read again your last year's New Year's greeting. The idea is good; the spirit and tone of the poem are strongly influenced by Barbier. By the way, his words about Napoleon were fresh in your memory at the time.

Now, about your poetry: Listen, dear brother, I believe that in the life of a man there are lots and lots of sadness and grief—but also much that gives joy. In the life of a poet there are both thorns and roses. Lyricism is the constant companion of the poet because he is a creature of words. Your lyric poetry was charming: "The Stroll," "Morning," "An Apparition of Mother," "The Rose" (was that the title?), "The Steeds of Phoebus," and many other delightful poems. They tell so many revealing things about you, my dear fellow! I feel them so intimately. I could understand you then, because those months were so memorable, so very memorable for me then. How many strange and wonderful things happened in my life at that time. It is a very long story, and I will tell it to no one—Shidlovsky showed me your poems then—you are so unfair to Shidlovsky. I don't want to defend those things in him that cannot be appreciated by someone who doesn't know him or his ideas or his rules of conduct and who is rather set in his opinions. If only you had seen him last year. He spent a whole year in Petersburg without having a post or employment. God only knows why he was living here; he was in no sense rich enough to lead a life of pleasure in Petersburg. But obviously he had come to Petersburg just to escape to some place. It was enough to take one look at him to see that he was suffering! He was very drawn, his cheeks were sunken, his eyes, once so moist, were dry and aflame; the spiritual beauty of his face had become enhanced by his physical decline. He suffered, suffered terribly! My God, how he loves a certain girl (I believe her name is Marie). She married somebody or other. Without that love, he couldn't have been the pure, lofty, unselfish priest of poetry he is—when I went to visit him in his poor lodgings on a winter's evening (e.g., just a year ago), I couldn't help thinking of the sad winter Onegin spent in Petersburg (chapter eight). But the difference was that before me was not a cold creature—an ardent dreamer in spite of himself—but a wonderful, noble person, a truly human being like those drawn by Shakespeare and Schiller, although, even then, he was ready to sink into the morose mania of Byronic characters. We often spent whole evenings together, talking about God knows what. What a pure and open soul! Tears gush from my eyes when I remember the past. He hid nothing from me, and what was I to him? He simply had to open himself up to someone. Ah, what a shame you weren't there with us! He wanted so much to see you! He wanted to tell you in person that you were his friend— a title that meant so much to him. I recall his reading your poems with tears running down his cheeks; he knew your poems by heart! And you had the audacity to say he was making fun of you! How miserable and pitiful he was! A pure angelic soul! And in that painful winter, he did not forget his love. Its flames burned brighter and brighter.

Then came the spring. It brought him back to life. His imagination began creating dramas, and what dramas they were, my brother. Your opinion of them would have changed if you had read *Mariya Simonova* when he had rewritten it. He had been rewriting it throughout the whole winter; the first draft he himself called ugly. And his lyric poetry! If only you had seen the poems he wrote last spring. For instance, the one in which he speaks of fame. I wish you'd read that one, brother!

After returning from camp, we spent little time together. During our last meeting we went for a walk in Yekaterinhof. Oh, what an evening we spent! We recalled those winter days when we talked about Homer, Shakespeare, Schiller, and Hoffmann, whom we read and discussed endlessly. We also talked about ourselves, about our past life, about the future, about you, my dear brother. But now, it has been a long time since he left, and I haven't heard a thing from or about him. I wonder whether he is still alive. He was in desperately bad health; do write him!

Last winter I was in some sort of exalted state. Shidlovsky gave me many of the best hours of my life, but that was not what caused it. Perhaps you have been and still are resentful of my not writing you. The reason for my silence was the stupid military routine. But is there really any need to tell you, my dear brother, that I have never been indifferent to you; that I loved you for your poems, for the poetry of your life, for your misfortunes—and no more than that; I did not love you as a brother and a friend—I had but one friend, one human being whom I loved that way. You said in your letter that I had not read Schiller. You are wrong, brother! I learned Schiller by heart, I talked Schiller, I dreamed Schiller; and I think nothing could have been more providential than my coming to know that great poet at that juncture of my life, for otherwise I should never have come to know him as I do now. Reading Schiller *with him*, I tested out *on him* the noble and ardent Don Carlos, Marquis Posa, and Mortimer. That friendship brought me so much sorrow and so much joy! Now, I shall keep eternal silence on that subject. But the name of Schiller has become a part of me, an enchanted sound that evokes a multitude of dreams that are now bitter to me. And that is why I didn't write to you about Schiller, brother, about the impressions he made on me. Even the sound of his name is painful to me.

I intended to reply at length to your attacks on me, to your erroneous interpretation of what I had written. I also wanted to talk about a few other things. But the letter I am now writing to you is giving me such delightful moments of reverie and recollection that I am unable to speak of anything else. I shall say only one thing in my defense: I never compared the great poets, especially since I didn't know them. I never drew parallels as, for example, between Pushkin and Schiller. I wonder what gave you that impression. Please copy down and send me my exact words, but I disavow any such comparison. Possibly in talking about something else, I mentioned Pushkin's and Schiller's names side by side but, even so, I would guess that there must have been a comma between the two names. There is no resemblance between them whatever. Pushkin and Byron, maybe. As to Homer and Victor

Hugo, I believe you have deliberately misinterpreted what I was trying to say. What I actually said was this: Homer (a legendary man, he was perhaps like Christ, an incarnation of God sent to us) can be compared only to Christ and not to Goethe. Try to understand him, brother, try to grasp the meaning of the *Iliad* (admit it—you haven't really read it, have you?). Don't you realize that in the *Iliad* Homer gave to the whole ancient world a scheme for spiritual and earthly life with the same force as Christ gave it to the modern world? Do you understand me this time? Now, as a lyricist with a purely angelic nature and with a Christian and childlike poetic spirit, Victor Hugo stands alone, and there is no one who can be compared to him in this, neither Schiller (Christian poet though he be), nor Shakespeare as a lyric poet—I have read his sonnets in French translation—nor Byron, nor Pushkin. Only Homer, who has the same unshakable belief in his vocation, with his childlike belief in the god of poetry whom he serves, draws his poetry from a source similar to Victor Hugo's, but only in his orientation and not in the idea, which he received from nature and to which he gave expression. But I am not even speaking of that. It seems to me that Derzhavin could be placed above either when it comes to lyricism. Good-bye, my dear fellow,

Your friend and brother,

F. Dostoyevsky

This letter has made me shed a few tears by reminding me of the past.

The subject of your play is charming, you demonstrate the truth of your idea, and I particularly like the idea of your hero who, in his search for the infinite and unencompassable, just like Faust, goes insane at the very moment he has found the infinite and unencompassable—at the moment he is loved. That is beautiful! I am delighted to see that Shakespeare has taught you something.

You are angry with me for not answering all your questions. I should have liked to oblige but it's impossible; I have neither time nor paper. But then, if I were to answer everything, including, for instance, such questions as "Do you have a moustache?" there would never be enough room to write something of greater interest. Farewell, my dear, good brother, farewell once more, and write.

And now I must take you to task: In speaking of form, you have almost gone out of your mind. I have suspected this slight mental disturbance of yours for a long time, and I am not joking. Recently you said something of the sort about Pushkin! I let it go, and I did so deliberately. I shall speak about your form in my next letter; now I have neither time nor space. But, please, do tell me: speaking of form, what made you say that we can like neither Racine nor *Corneille* (?!?) because their form isn't good. What a pitiful fellow you are! And then you go on to ask me such a clever question: *Is it possible that there is no poetry in them?* No poetry in Racine? In the fiery, passionate Racine, in love with his ideals—no poetry in him? You dare ask such a question? Have you ever read *Andromaque*? Have you, brother? Have you read *Iphigénie*? Can you possibly say that it isn't delicious? Is not Racine's Achilles worthy of Homer? To be sure, Racine stole him from Homer, but how wonderfully he stole him! And his women! Try to understand him. Racine was no genius, but what drama he could create! He could only imitate Corneille? And what about *Phèdre*? Ah, brother! God knows what will become of you if you don't admit that this is the highest, the purest nature and poetry. Why, it is an outline worthy of Shakespeare, although the final statue is of plaster rather than of marble.

Now, shall we talk about Corneille? Listen, brother, I don't know how to speak to you. I suppose the best thing would be to do so "having filled myself with peas," à la Ivan Nikiforovich. No, I just won't believe it, brother! You haven't read it, and that is why you are so far off the mark. Let me tell you, then, that with his monumental characters and his romantic spirit, he is almost Shakespeare's peer. My poor fellow! To everything you have just one set reply: "the classical form." But don't you realize, you poor devil, that Corneille appeared only 50 years after that pitifully sad mediocrity Jodelle and his wretched parody of *Cleopatra;* after Tredyakovsky's Ronsard; and after that cold rhymester Malherbe, who was almost his contemporary. So how could he possibly have invented the form of a play? It is a good thing that he took it from Seneca. Tell me, have you ever read his *Cinna*? Before this divine portrayal of Octavius, before whom [the corner of the page has been cut off here] Karl Moor, Fiesco, Tell, Don Carlos. They would have been a credit to Shakespeare. Poor fellow. If you haven't already done so, read it, especially the dialogue between Augustus and Cinna, where he forgives him his betrayal (but the way he forgives him (?)). You'll realize that only angels who have been offended talk like that. Especially the passage where Augustus says: "Soyons amis, Cinna." And have you read *Horace*? Where, except in Homer, can you find characters like those? The old Horace is a Diomedes; the young Horace—an Ajax Telamonide but with the spirit of Achilles; and Curiace—he is Patrocles, he is Achilles, he is everything that only the sadness of love and duty can express. What grandeur it possesses. And have you read *Le Cid*? Read it, miserable man, read it and fall on your face before Corneille. You have insulted him! Read him, read him. And what does Romanticism demand if its highest ideas are not developed in *Le Cid*? What characters, Don Rodrigue, his young son, and his paramour. And what an ending!

But don't get angry with me after all this for my offensive remarks. Don't be another Ivan Ivanovich Pererepenko.

---

5. Aleksei Vasilevich Dyadin (1791–1864) was an artillery specialist who served as an instructor for thirty-four years in the Army Engineers' School, where Dos-

toyevsky was a student. Nikolai Dmitriyevich Brashman (1796–1866) was a professor of mathematics and the author of *A Course in Analytic Geometry* (Kurs analiticheskoi geometrii, 1836). Aleksei Pavlovich Bolotov (1803–1853) was a geodesist and topographer, author of *A Course in Higher and Lower Geodesy* (Kurs vysshei and nizshei geodezii, 1837). Vasily Timofeyevich Plaksin (1796–1869) taught Russian language and literature and wrote *A History of Russian Literature* (Istoriya russkoi literatury, 1835).

Dostoyevsky's "deferential letter" to the Kumanins (not included in this collection) was an abject apology for not having written to them for so long. The Kumanins were the Dostoyevskys' wealthiest relatives and frequently came to their aid in financial difficulties. However, the estate they left was the subject of bitter arguments among the relatives during the last ten years of Dostoyevsky's life.

"Our guardian" was Karepin, the husband of Dostoyevsky's eldest sister, Varvara. He had been named family guardian upon the death of Dostoyevsky's father.

Henri Auguste Barbier (1805–1882) was a French satirical poet. His first collection, *Iambes*, made him famous overnight. He regarded Napoleon as an arrogant usurper.

The friend whom Dostoyevsky says he loved so much was probably Ivan Ignatevich Berezhetsky, one of his few friends at the engineering school.

Gavriil Romanovich Derzhavin (1743–1816) is often regarded as the greatest Russian poet before Pushkin. His "Ode to God" (Bog, 1784) was frequently read at family gatherings when Dostoyevsky was a child.

Ivan Nikiforovich and Ivan Ivanovich Pererepenko are the title characters of a story by Gogol, "How Ivan Ivanovich Quarreled with Ivan Nikiforovich" (Povest o tom, kak possorilsya Ivan Ivanovich s Ivanom Nikiforovichem, 1834).

Étienne Jodelle (1532–1573) was a French dramatist whose first play, *Cleopâtre captive*, was acclaimed by his contemporaries as a revival of ancient Greek tragedy. He was a member of the "Pléiade" formed about Pierre de Ronsard (1524–1585), the poet who created the lyrical form known as the Ronsard strophe. Vasily Kirillovich Tredyakovsky (1703–1796) was a Russian theoretician of poetry. François de Malherbe (1555–1628) was a French poet who wrote odes in the classical style.

In Corneille's play *Cinna*, Augustus discovers a plot against him by Cinna, but when he has Cinna at his mercy, he offers him his hand and says, "Soyons amis, Cinna" ("Let us be friends, Cinna").

6.   TO M. M. DOSTOYEVSKY
[Petersburg, September 30, 1844]

Dear brother,

I received *Don Carlos* and hasten to answer as quickly as possible (I don't have any time). The translation is quite good, in places remarkably good; some lines are bad, but that is because you were translating in a hurry. But there are, perhaps, five or six bad lines in all. I have taken the liberty of making some corrections here and there and also of making the rhyme sound better. The most annoying thing is your occasional use of foreign words such as *komplot*. That is inadmissible. Also (although I don't know how it is in the original) you use the word Sire. As far as I know, this term didn't exist in Spain but was used in Western Europe in countries of Norman origin. But that is of no importance whatsoever. The translation is surprisingly good. Better than I had expected. I'll take it to those fools at *Repertoire*. Let them gape open-mouthed. But if they already have Obodovsky's translation (which I fear they may have), I'll take it to *Notes of the Fatherland*. Don't worry, I won't sell it for a handful of change. I'll send you the money as soon as I have sold it. As to publishing a collection of Schiller's works, I am, of course, in full agreement with you and even wanted to suggest myself that it would be divided into three installments. We'll issue first *Die Räuber, Fiesco, Don Carlos, Kabale und Liebe*, the *Briefe über Carlos*, and *Über naive und sentimentalische Dichtung*. That would be very good. We'll decide about publishers later. But it would be best to publish it ourselves, because otherwise there's no money in it. You just keep translating and don't worry about money; we'll get it one way or another; it's not important how. But one thing, brother, we must see that this business is settled a month from now, i.e., a definite decision must be taken because the *announcement* will have to be made no later than that, and without the *announcement* we are lost. For this reason I'll see to it that a few words are placed in *Repertoire*. The translation will cause a sensation (and with the slightest success, the profits will be tremendous).

Well, brother, I am very well aware myself that I am in a hellish predicament. Here let me explain:

I resigned because I just had to resign, i.e., I swear I couldn't stand the service any longer. Life is bleak if one's best time is wasted. After all, I never intended to remain in the service for long and so why should I waste good years of my life? But the main reason is that they wanted to transfer me— and, please tell me, what would I do away from Petersburg? What use would I be? I wonder whether you fully understand me?

You need not worry about how I'll live now. I'll never go hungry. I'll work like a slave. Now I am a free man. But what shall I do right now, this very minute? That's the question. Imagine, brother, I owe 800 rubles, including 525 rubles in currency bills to my landlord (I wrote home asking for 1500 rubles, because I know their habit of sending one-third of the sum you ask for).

No one knows that I am leaving the service. If I leave right now, what shall I do? I haven't got one kopek to buy clothes. My resignation becomes effective October 14. If those Moscow pigs don't come through with the money in time, I'm done for. I shall be dragged off to jail for sure (no doubt about it). It's really comic. You speak about the division of the family estate. But do you know what I am asking for? Well, in exchange for my complete renunciation now of all claims on the estate and for forfeiting irrevocably my rights as soon as circumstances permit, i.e., ceding here and now all my rights to the estate, I am demanding a lump sum of 500 silver rubles plus another 500 to be paid to me in monthly installments of 10 silver rubles (and this is all I demand of them). You will have to agree that it isn't excessive and that I am not wronging anyone this way.

But they wouldn't even hear of it. I also am sure that you agree with me that it's not up to me now to repeat my offer. *They do not trust me.* They think I'll swindle them. Please, my boy, tell them that you are willing to vouch for me. Tell them exactly this: *that you are prepared to guarantee that I will make no further claims on them.* If they don't have that much money, in my situation, 700 or even 600 rubles would be very welcome; it would enable me to get along; and you can also guarantee them *that the sum in question will be deducted from the aggregate sum of 500 silver rubles and the 500 silver rubles that are to be paid in installments.*

You say that my salvation is in the drama. But you must understand that putting on a play takes time. And so does getting paid. And the date of my resignation is drawing close (but you must understand, my dear man, that if I hadn't sent in my resignation before, I would do it right now; I have no regrets.).

I have one hope. I am finishing a novel roughly the size of *Eugénie Grandet.* It is quite an original novel. I am already in the process of recopying it and, by the fourteenth, I hope to have an answer. I'll submit it to *Notes of the Fatherland.* (I am quite pleased with my work.) They'll pay me maybe 400 rubles or so for it. And this is my only hope. I should have liked to tell you more about my novel, but I have no time. (I shall stage my play without fail; it will be my means of support.)

That pig Kirstin is as stupid as an ass.

Those Muscovites are unspeakably vain, stupid, and quarrelsome. In his last letter, Karepin for some unearthly reason advised me not to get too enthusiastic about Shakespeare! He says that Shakespeare is just like a soap bubble. I wanted you to know about this idiotic resentment of Shakespeare. How in the world does Shakespeare come into the picture? You should have seen the letter I wrote him! In one word, it was a model piece of polemics. I really gave it to him. My letters are a chef d'oeuvre of lettristics.

Brother, please, in the name of the Creator Himself, write home as soon as you possibly can. I'm in terrible straits. The fourteenth is the absolute deadline—it's been six weeks since I handed in my resignation. In the name of God, ask them to send me that money! What worries me most is that I shan't have anything to put on. Khlestakov consented to go to jail only *if he looked respectable.* But what if I have no *trousers,* that won't be respectable, will it?

Karepin drinks, . . .* guzzles down vodka, has a rank, and *believes in God.* He figured it all out by himself.

---

* Several words are crossed out here, but apparently not by Dostoyevsky—Eds.

My address is Dostoyevsky, the Pryanishnikov House, Grafsky Alley by Saint Vladimir's Church.

I am extremely pleased with my novel. I couldn't be more so. This is probably the one that will bring me money, and after that—

Forgive me for this completely incoherent letter.

---

6. *Repertoire [and Pantheon]* (Repertuar i Panteon) was the magazine that had published Dostoyevsky's translation of Balzac's *Eugénie Grandet* in 1844. *Notes of the Fatherland* (Otechestvennye zapiski) was one of the most important magazines of the time; several of Dostoyevsky's works first appeared in it. Mikhail's translation of Schiller's *Don Carlos,* however, appeared in neither of these magazines but in *A Library for Reading* in 1848. No translations of other works by Schiller were ever published by either brother.

Platon Grigorevich Obodovsky (1805–1854) was an inspector of studies at a girls' school. He translated several German works, but his translation of *Don Carlos* was never published.

"The Moscow pigs" and "those Muscovites" are references to the Karepin family. Just prior to the writing of this letter, Dostoyevsky had exchanged acerbic letters with his brother-in-law Pyotr Andreyevich Karepin over Dostoyevsky's pleas for money and over the division of his father's estate. Karepin had sent him fifty (silver) rubles, but in an accompanying letter had vigorously objected to Dostoyevsky's resignation from the army, accusing him, among other things, of "indulging . . . in the abstract indolence and languor of Shakespearean dreams. . . . What is there to them besides an inflamed, inflated, swollen, enlarged but bubble-like shape?" Dostoyevsky's response had said, also among other things, "you . . . should not have expressed your feeling of superiority . . . with insolent and humiliating remarks . . . and with talk of Shakespearean soap bubbles. Strange, what did Shakespeare do to bring your displeasure down upon himself?" About a month after writing this letter to Mikhail, Dostoyevsky wrote another and much more submissive one to Karepin, as a result of which he did receive 500 rubles, half of what he was asking for as his share of his father's estate (see Letter 7).

The novel with which Dostoyevsky says he is "extremely pleased" was *Poor Folk,* which was completed in 1845 (see Letters 7–9).

Khlestakov is the main character in Gogol's *The Inspector General* (Revizor, 1836).

7.   To M. M. Dostoyevsky
[Petersburg] March 24 [1845]

Dear brother,

You've probably been waiting for my letter, my dear brother. But I was delayed by the instability of my situation. I am utterly incapable of concentrating on anything as long as I have nothing but the unknown and the undecided before my eyes. But since I still haven't got anything done about my private affairs, I am writing anyway, in fact I ought to have written long ago.

I received 500 silver rubles from the Muscovites. But I had so many debts, old and newly contracted, that there wasn't enough left to pay for the publishing. But that is not the worst of it. I could have arranged a loan with the press or not paid all of my personal debts, but I hadn't quite completed my novel. I had all but finished it back in November, but in December I suddenly felt I had to rewrite it entirely; so I rewrote it and recopied it. But then in February I began to clean it up again, to polish it, to add here and to take out there. Toward the middle of March, I was through and satisfied. But that isn't the end of it: censorship takes at least a month. It can't be done any quicker. The censors are supposedly swamped with work. I took my manuscript back, unable to decide what to do. Because, in addition to the four weeks it would be detained by the censors, the printing would eat up another three weeks or so. It would not come out until May. That would be too late! At this point people have begun urging me on all sides to turn over the affair to *Notes of the Fatherland*. Nonsense. I can give the manuscript to them, but no good will come of it. In the first place, they may not read it and, even if they do, it won't be for a good six months. They've got plenty of manuscripts without mine. Even if they did publish it, they wouldn't pay me a thing for it. It is some sort of oligarchy. And what is glory to me when I am writing to earn my bread? I have decided on a desperate leap: to hold back, to go into debt once more until September 1, when everyone will return to Petersburg and, like hunting dogs, will be sniffing around for something new; then I'll scrape the bottom of the barrel to publish my novel, although there may not be enough left for it. To hand over my novel to a magazine would be like indenturing myself not only to the head maitre d'hotel, but to all the sluts and kitchen boys who crowd the nests from which enlightenment is spread. There's not one—there are twenty dictators there. To have it published myself is like breaking open a path with my chest, and if the piece is good, not only will it not be wasted but it will free me from the shackles of debt and enable me to eat.

And now, speaking of food. Do you realize, brother, that in this respect I have been left to my own devices? But come what may, I have sworn to myself that even if I am driven to despair, I will stick it out and not write to order. Writing to order would crush me and destroy everything. I want everything I write to be distinctively good. Look at Pushkin, look at Gogol. Neither of them wrote a great deal, but posterity will remember them. Even now Gogol receives 1000 silver rubles per printer's sheet and, as you very well know, Pushkin received one gold ruble for a verse of poetry. But then their glory—Gogol's especially—was paid for by years of misery and hunger. The old schools are disappearing. The new schools scribble, they don't write. Their entire talent is spent in one broad sweep in which a freakish half-baked idea, a muscular sweep and only a tiny crumb of accomplishment can be recognized. Béranger has described today's French feuilletonists as "a bottle of Chambertin in a bucket of water." And they imitate them in this country. Raphael spent years on a painting, he polished it, improved on it, and the result was a miracle; gods came to life under his hand. Now Vernet turns out a painting every month, for which special large-sized rooms are built to order. His vision is rich, his drawings are ambitious, but the effect is not worth a kopek. Such people are nothing but decorators!

I am really pleased with my novel. It is a sober and well-constructed work. I must say, though, that it has some terrible shortcomings. The publication of it will compensate me for my efforts. Now, for the time being, I am drained dry. I am thinking of writing something to launch my career or just for money, but I don't feel like writing just rubbish, and trying to write something worthwhile would require a lot of time.

The time of my promised visit to you is drawing near, my dear friends, but I shan't have the means, i.e., the money, for it. I've decided to remain in my old apartment. Here, at least, I have a lease and don't have to worry for six months. So everything hinges on the publication of my novel. If the thing doesn't come off, I may hang myself.

I should like to save at least 300 rubles by August. Even 300 would make it possible to publish. But the money crawls away like crabs, scattering in all directions. I had about 400 silver rubles of debts (including my expenses and new clothes) but now, at least, I have all the clothes I need for two years. But I'll come to see you without fail. Let me know soon what you think of the way I handled my apartment. It was some decision to make, but there was no other choice.

You write that you're terrified at the prospect of the future without money. But Schiller will bail us all out and, furthermore, who knows how many copies of my novel will be sold? Farewell. Answer quickly. In my next letter, I'll inform you of all my decisions.

Your brother,
Dostoyevsky

Kiss the children, and my regards to Emiliya Fyodorovna. I often think of you all. Perhaps you want to know what I do with myself when I am not busy writing? Well, I read. I read an awful lot, and reading has a strange effect on me. When I reread something that I read a long time ago, I feel invigorated. I penetrate and keenly perceive the meaning of everything and derive from it the ability myself to create.

Write dramas—what are you talking about, brother? It would take years of labor and of tranquility, at least it would for me. Nowadays is a good time to be writing. The drama today has descended into melodrama. Shakespeare pales in the dusk and is seen like a god through the mists of purblind dramatists; he is like the apparition of a spirit on the Brocken or the Harz. Still, I may be writing in the summer. In two or three years, we shall see. But for now, let's wait.

Brother, when it comes to literature, *I am not the same* as I was two years ago. At that time it was childish nonsense. During these two years of study I have learned a great deal and unlearned a great deal.

I have just read an article in *Invalid* about German poets who died of starvation, of cold, or in lunatic asylums. There were about twenty of them, and what names! Even now, I still feel terrified. One has to be a fraud—

---

7. The novel that Dostoyevsky is writing about is, again, *Poor Folk.*

Pierre Béranger (1780–1857) was a French poet of liberal political sympathies who was widely known in Russia from translations published at the beginning of the nineteenth century. Belinsky declared him to be a "French Schiller," and Dostoyevsky himself later compared him to Pushkin. The Vernet mentioned here is presumably Horace Vernet (1789–1863), a French painter who was known both for his productivity and for the gigantic size of his canvases; his *La prise de la Smala d'Abd el-Kader,* for example, is seventy-two feet long.

Early in 1845 the magazine [*Russian*] *Invalid* (Russky invalid) carried an article entitled "Poets in Germany—Alexander Weiss's Article," in which a German newspaper was quoted as mentioning twenty German cultural figures who had come to painful ends during the previous half-century, including Lessing, Mozart, Beethoven, and Hölderlin. Since Dostoyevsky had recently resigned from the service and thus made his own future uncertain, the article may have made a great impression upon him.

8. To M. M. Dostoyevsky

[Petersburg] May 4, 1845

Dear brother,

Forgive me for not having written you all this time. I have been hellishly busy up till now. That novel of mine, which I am simply unable to extricate myself from, has given me so much work that, if I had realized it beforehand, I would never have got started on it at all. I decided to go over it once more, and I swear it was for the best—it's almost twice as good now. But I'm through with it; that revision was the final one. I have given myself my word not to touch it again. It is always the fate of first books to be corrected again and again, endlessly. I don't know whether *Atala* was the first thing Chateaubriand wrote, but I seem to remember that he rewrote it seventeen times. Pushkin made similar revisions even on his minor pieces of poetry. Gogol polished his wonderful works for two years. And if you happen to have read *Voyage Sentimental* [in French] by Sterne, which is a tiny book, you must remember what Valter [*sic*] Scott, in his Notice [in English] on Sterne, says, citing Sterne's servant La Fleur as his authority. La Fleur says that his master used up almost a hundred quires of paper on his voyage through France. One may wonder what happened to it? Well, it all went into the making of that little book which, had it been handled by a good scribbler like Plyushkin, for example, could have been done with just half a quire. What I don't understand is how this same Walter-Scott [*sic*] could, within the space of a few weeks, turn out such accomplished novels as *Mannering*, for instance! But perhaps it was because he was forty.

I don't know what will happen to me, brother! You are unfair when you say that I don't worry about my situation. I am worried sick, to the point of nausea. Often I cannot sleep whole nights on end because of such tormenting thoughts. Practical people tell me that I'm sealing my doom by trying to publish my novel on my own. They say, suppose the book is good, even very good. But you are no businessman. How will you publicize your novel? In the newspapers perhaps? You must absolutely have a book dealer at your disposal. But a book dealer is a shrewd individual, and he won't jeopardize himself by giving publicity to an unknown writer. He would lose the confidence of his pratiques. Every respectable book dealer is the owner of several periodicals and newspapers. The most outstanding authors—or those who claim to be—write for the periodicals and newspapers. The announcement of a new book carries the endorsement of the periodical, and that means a great deal. Therefore, when you approach a book dealer with your merchandise already printed, he will understand that he can squeeze you as hard as he pleases. That's how it is! And the book dealer is a venal soul; he'll certainly put on the squeeze, and I'll be left floundering; there's no doubt about it.

And so I've decided to turn to the periodicals and to give away my novel for a nominal fee—of course, to *Notes of the Fatherland*. It sells 2500 copies and, therefore, reaches at least 100,000 people. If they publish me, my future and my literary career are guaranteed. I shall have made it. The door to *Notes of the Fatherland* will always be open to me, and I'll always have money in my pocket. Moreover, assuming that my novel appears in the August or the September issue, I can have it reprinted in October at my own expense, this time with the full assurance that the novel will be sold out to those people who buy novels. Furthermore, I shan't have to spend a penny on advertising. So that is how things stand!

I cannot come to Revel before I have placed my novel, nor can I afford to waste any time now. It takes perseverance. I have a number of new ideas which, if my first novel is disposed of, will consolidate my literary reputation. These are all my hopes for the future.

As to money—alas! I don't have any. Damned if I know where it's gone. On the other hand, I have only a few debts. As to the apartment—in the first place I still owe something on it; and in the second, I am still uncertain whether I shall go to Revel or not, whether I shall place my novel or not. If I do go, then I'll arrange to vacate the apartment at that time, because the expenses and the trouble of moving would come to more than staying where I am, however cheap an apartment I might find. I have already made the calculation. The apartment, the novel, Revel—three fixed ideas. Ma femme et mon parapluie!

Farewell. Everything will be decided when I write to you next. Good-bye for now, and I wish you, your wife, and your children all the best.

Yours,
Dostoyevsky

The weather here is awful. The troughs of heaven have burst open, and Providence has visited thousands upon thousands of colds, coughs, consumption, and fevers, and other such benefactions upon Saint Palmyra. For we have sinned!

Have you read Weltman's *Yemelya* in the latest issue of *A Library for Reading*? What a delight! *Tarantas* is well written. But what revolting illustrations!

My deepest respects to Emiliya Fyodorovna. I should like so much to see you all.

If I manage to place my novel, it will be easy to place *Schiller,* too, or I don't know what I am talking about. *Le Juif errant* isn't bad. But as a matter of fact, Sue is quite limited.

Although I don't like to write about it, brother, I am so upset about your situation and about Schiller that I don't even think about myself, albeit my own situation is by no means an easy one.

And if I don't place my novel, I may jump into the Neva. What else is there? I've already given it a lot of thought. I couldn't survive the death of my idée fixe.

Answer quickly; it's so boring otherwise.

---

8. Sir Walter Scott (1771–1832) was very popular in Russia during the 1820s, when translations of his novels and poems appeared (often translated from French translations). His biographers have said that he wrote *Guy Mannering* in twenty-five days.

Plyushkin is the name of an extremely miserly character in Gogol's *Dead Souls.*

"Saint Palmyra" was an ironic term for St. Petersburg.

Aleksandr Fomich Weltman (1800–1870) was a novelist distinguished by the fact that he refused to join any of the warring literary groups. His *The New Yemelya, or The Transformation* (Novy Yemelya, ili Prevrashcheniye, 1845) was a parody of the Russian Romantic movement.

Tarantas (first seven chapters, 1840; complete book, 1845) was a novel by Count Vladimir Aleksandrovich Sollogub (1814–1882). The characters in it are traveling toward the village of Mordassy; the subtitle of Dostoyevsky's story *Uncle's Dream* is *From the Mordassy Chronicles.*

Le juif errant (The wandering Jew, 1844–1845), by Eugène Sue (1804–1857), was being published at the time of this letter in installments in the magazine *Le constitutionnel.*

9. To M. M. Dostoyevsky
[Petersburg] October 8 [1845]

Dear brother,

Thus far I have neither had the time nor been in the mood to inform you about anything that concerned me. Everything has gone so badly, so revoltingly that just to look at the world has made me sick. In the first place, my precious and one and only friend, I have been penniless all this time and living on credit, which is miserable. In the second place, I have been feeling somehow sad in general, so that I couldn't help getting discouraged. I stopped caring and became, not stupidly indifferent, but, what's worse, went beyond all limits and started raving and ranting.

At the beginning of the month, Nekrasov arrived and gave me back a part of the sum owed to me, and the balance is to come in a few days. I must tell you, too, that about two weeks ago Belinsky gave me a whole lecture on how to get on in our literary world and, in conclusion, explained to me that, for the salvation of my soul, I absolutely must charge at least 200 paper rubles a printer's sheet. That way, my Golyadkin would bring me at least 1500 paper rubles. Torn by pangs of conscience, Nekrasov came tearing over and promised me another 100 silver rubles by January 15 for the novel *Poor Folk,* which he had bought from me. For he honestly admitted himself that 150 silver rubles was not a Christian rate of pay. And so, to make amends, he was therefore adding an extra 100 silver rubles. So far so good. But here's something that isn't good: there's been absolutely no word from the censors about *Poor Folk.* An innocent novel like that is being dragged and dragged around, and I don't know what the outcome will be. And what if they forbid it? What if they make cuts in it from top to bottom? It would be a disaster, a pure and simple disaster, and Nekrasov tells me that then he won't be able to publish his *Almanac,* for which he has already laid out 4,000 paper rubles.

Yakov Petrovich Golyadkin remains absolutely true to his character. He is an awful scoundrel, impossible to get hold of him. He just refuses to budge, claims that he isn't ready yet, and that in the meantime he is just minding his own business, that he's just nothing in anybody's eyes, but that when it really comes down to it, why, he could do it too, and why couldn't he and why shouldn't he? He certainly is just like everyone else, he's just, you know—something or other, but otherwise he's just like everybody else. What is there to him? He's a scoundrel, a terrible scoundrel; he absolutely refuses to let me put an end to his career before mid-November, he won't hear of it. Now he is having things out with His Excellency and perhaps (why not?) is prepared to resign. And he is making my, his author's, situation extremely awkward.

I see Belinsky quite often. He is extremely well disposed toward me and seriously sees in me *a public vindication* of his opinions. A few days ago, I made the acquaintance of Kroneberg, the translator of Shakespeare (the son of Professor Kroneberg of Kharkov). Generally speaking, the future (and even the near future) could be good and it could be awfully bad. Belinsky is urging me to finish writing my Golyadkin. He has already announced it all over the literary world and has all but sold it to Krayevsky. As to *Poor Folk,* already half of Petersburg is talking about it. Grigorovich alone is worth a world! He tells me himself: "Je suis votre claqueur-chauffeur."

Nekrasov is a businessman by nature. He couldn't live without some business venture, because that's what he was born for. And so, on the very day of his arrival, he came to see me in the evening and explained his project for a *small fugitive miscellany* to which all the literary people will contribute what they can, but of which the chief editors will be Grigorovich, Nekrasov, and I. Nekrasov will foot the bill. The miscellany will consist of two printer's sheets and will come out *once* every two weeks—on the seventh and twenty-first of each month. It will be called *Jester,* and its aim is to be witty, to laugh at everything, to spare no one, to go after the theater, the press, society, literature, happenings in the street, the Exhibition, newspaper coverage of events both at home and abroad, in brief—to go after everything, and all that in the same spirit and from the same angle. Publication starts on November 7, and the issue promises to be beautiful. First of all, it will have illustrations. For our epigraph, we have taken Bulgarin's famous words from his article in the *Northern Bee.* "We are prepared to die for the truth; without truth we cannot live," etc., and Faddei Bulgarin will sign it. It will also be written up in an announcement that will appear on November 1. The first issue will include an article by Nekrasov, "On Some (of course, recent) Despicable Acts Committed in Petersburg." A future novel by Eugène Sue—*The Seven Deadly Sins* (the entire novel in just three pages). A review of all the periodicals. A lecture by Shevyryov about the harmony of Pushkin's verse being so great that, when he was in the *Coliseum* and read a few of *Pushkin's* verses aloud to two ladies in his company, *all the frogs and lizards present crawled out to listen to him.* (Shevyryov gave the lecture at Moscow University.) Then there will be the last meeting of the *Slavophiles* at which it is solemnly demonstrated that Adam was a Slav and had lived in Russia and therefore the tremendous importance and usefulness of solving this immense social problem for the good and welfare of the entire Russian nation will become manifest. Then in the section of the arts, *Jester* renders full justice to Kukolnik's *Illustration* and even refers to the passage where it says ysktgzeldtoomdudurn, etc., and a few lines in the same vein (*Illustration* is notorious for its poor proofreaders, and it thinks nothing of such things as running words back to front, switching letters, etc.). Grigorovich will write "The History of the Week" and will share some of his observations with the public. I shall contribute "A Lackey's Notes on His Master," etc. As you can judge from this, the magazine will be quite gay, something like Karr's *Guêpes*. It's a good business venture, for the very smallest estimate of my share of the profits ranges between 100 and 150 rubles a month. The magazine will sell. Nekrasov will also contribute his verse.

Well, good-bye, then, I'll write at greater length next time. I am awfully busy now, which hasn't prevented me, as you can see, from scribbling this full-length letter to you, while you won't write me even half a line unless you receive a letter from me. You keep count, like with official visits. You are just lazy, that's what you are, a real Fetyuk, just as lazy a lump as they come!

Read *Teverino* (by George Sand in *Notes of the Fatherland*). There hasn't been anything like it in our century. There are some real human prototypes for you!

Good-bye, my friend, give my regards to Emiliya Fyodorovna, I kiss her hands. Are the children in good health? Write me in greater detail.

Keep translating Schiller a little at a time, although I cannot tell you for certain when we'll be able to publish him. I'm now sniffing around, trying to find a translation for you. But, alas, there are three official translators attached to *Notes of the Fatherland*. But perhaps we'll manage something between the two of us, brother. But after all, everything is ahead of us. If my things sell, then *Schiller's Drama* will sell too—that's all I am sure of.

Yours,
F. Dostoyevsky

---

9. Golyadkin is the main character in Dostoyevsky's second novel, *The Double*, which was published in *Notes of the Fatherland* in 1846. Dostoyevsky writes of him here in the style of the novel. The scene with "His Excellency" takes place in the next-to-last chapter.

Poor Folk was in fact published in Nekrasov's magazine *Petersburg Miscellany* (Peterburgsky sbornik) in January 1846. This magazine was often referred to as the "Almanac" (Almanakh).

Andrei Ivanovich Kroneberg (d. 1885) had gained fame through his translations of several of Shakespeare's plays; his translation of *Macbeth* appeared in the same issue of *Petersburg Miscellany* as *Poor Folk*. His father, Ivan Yakovlevich (1788–1838), was a philologist, philosopher, and historian of literature, rector of Kharkov University, and compiler of a Latin-Russian dictionary.

Jester (Zuboskal) never materialized; it was forbidden by the censor. However, Nekrasov used some of the material in another miscellany, *First of April* (Pervoye aprelya), that came out in 1846. One of the pieces in it was evidently intended to be a parody of the huge novels of Eugène Sue; his *Les sept péchés capitaux* (The seven deadly sins), when published separately in 1848–1849, comprised sixteen volumes.

Faddei Venediktovich Bulgarin (1789−1859) had been an army officer, a thief, and an object of charity, but later turned to writing and magazine publishing. Among his popular historical novels were *Mazepa* (1833−1834) and *Ivan Vyzhigin* (1829), and the most important of his magazines was *Northern Bee* (Severnaya pchela, 1825−1859). He was almost implicated in the Decembrist plot, but he had protectors in high places and later apparently became an agent of the tsarist secret police.

Stepan Petrovich Shevyryov (1806−1864) was a professor at Moscow University and a literary historian, critic, and poet. He disapproved of Gogol and of the young Russian writers of the 1840s, including Turgenev and Dostoyevsky, and they in turn regarded him as a pompous pedant. Nestor Vasilevich Kukolnik (1809−1868) was an author, playwright, and publisher of several magazines, including *Illustration* (Illyustratsiya, 1845−1847).

Dmitry Vasilevich Grigorovich (1822−1900) was a novelist who wrote "naturalist" stories of ordinary life, of which the most successful was *The Village* (Derevnya, 1846). It was one of a series written in imitation of a popular French series entitled *Les français peints par eux-mêmes* (The French painted by themselves), each of which was described as a "physiology" of some aspect of Parisian life.

Dostoyevsky never wrote anything entitled "A Lackey's Notes on His Master."

Alphone Karr (1808−1890) was a French author of Romantic novels and short stories. In 1839 he published a satirical newspaper entitled *Guêpes* (Wasps).

"A real Fetyuk" was an expression of the character Nozdryov in Gogol's *Dead Souls*.

10. To M. M. Dostoyevsky

[Petersburg] November 16, 1845

Dear brother,

I'm writing this in haste, especially because I am not at all rich in time. I still haven't finished with Golyadkin, and I absolutely must finish him off by the twenty-fifth. You haven't answered my letters for a long time, and I was beginning to become very much worried about you. Write more often. Your excuse about having no time is just plain nonsense. It doesn't take much time. Provincial laziness is ruining you, my dear fellow, in the prime of your life, and that's that.

Well, let me tell you, brother, I don't believe that my fame will ever surpass the height it has now attained. Everywhere I am treated with incredible respect, and people are terribly curious about me. I've come to know a slew of the most respectable people. Prince Odoyevsky is begging me to honor him with a visit, and Count Sollogub is tearing out his hair in despair. Panayev announced to him that he had found a talent that would bury them all in the mud. Sollogub went running all around to everybody, and when he dropped in on Krayevsky he asked him abruptly: "Who is this Dostoyevsky? Where can I *get hold of Dostoyevsky?*" Krayevsky, who doesn't care a straw about anyone and cuts everyone down to size, retorted that "Dostoyevsky does not wish to honor you with a visit." And that is the truth; the miserable little aristocrat has got up on his high horse now and imagines that he is going to annihilate me with his condescending kindness. Everyone considers me a phenomenon. I cannot even open my mouth without people repeating in every corner that Dostoyevsky has said this or that, Dostoyevsky intends to do this or that. Belinsky could not be fonder of me. A few days ago the poet Turgenev (you surely have heard of him) returned from Paris and right away showed me such friendship and affection that Belinsky is persuaded he has fallen in love with me. But what a man he is, brother! I almost fell in love with him myself. He is a poet, a man of talent, an aristocrat, handsome, wealthy, intelligent, cultured, twenty-five years old; I doubt that nature has refused him anything. And, finally, his character is unstintingly straightforward, beautiful, formed in a good school. Read his novella *Andrei Kolosov* in *Notes of the Fatherland;* it is he himself, although he had no intention of putting himself on display in it.

When it comes to money, I still don't have much, although I am not really hard up. In the meantime, Nekrasov has been trying to launch *Jester,* a charming satirical miscellany; I wrote the announcement for it and it caused quite a sensation, because the miscellany is the first of its kind when it comes to lightness and humor. It reminded me of the first feuilleton of Lucien de Rubempré. My announcement has already been published in *Notes of the Fatherland* in the random-news column. I charged 20 silver rubles for it. Then, a few days ago, having no money, I went to see Nekrasov. As I was sitting with him, I conceived the idea of a novel in nine letters. When I got back home, I wrote the whole novel in one night; it is one-half a printer's sheet long. In the morning I took it to Nekrasov, and he gave me 125 paper rubles for it, i.e., a printer's sheet of mine is worth 250 rubles to *Jester.* In the evening my novel was read at Turgenev's before at least twenty members of our group, and it caused a furor. It will appear in the first issue of *Jester.* I'll send it to you toward December 1, and you'll judge for yourself whether it is worse than, say, Gogol's *Lawsuit.* Belinsky told me that he was now absolutely certain of me because I can take on completely different assignments. When, recently, Krayevsky heard that I had no money, he begged me humbly to allow him to lend me 500 rubles. I suppose I'll be selling to him at 200 rubles per printer's sheet.

I have an overflowing well of ideas, but I cannot talk about them to anybody, even, say, to Turgenev, or the next day it will be known in every corner of Petersburg that Dostoyevsky is writing such and such things.

Well, brother, if I attempted to enumerate all my achievements here, I shouldn't have enough paper. I believe that I'll have money. Golyadkin is coming off splendidly; it will be my chef d'oeuvre. Yesterday I went to see Panayev for the first time, and I think I have fallen in love with his wife. She is intelligent and pretty and, what's more, she's incredibly amiable and straightforward. I am having a very gay time. Our group is very large.

But I have been writing only about myself all this time; forgive me, my dear friend; let me tell you frankly, I am almost drunk with my fame right now. I'll send you *Jester* with my next letter. Belinsky says that I am cheapening myself by having my articles published in *Jester*.

Farewell, my boy. I wish you happiness. I congratulate you on your promotion. I kiss Emiliya Fyodorovna's hands and kiss your children. How are they?

Yours,
Dostoyevsky

Belinsky is guarding me from would-be managers. I have reread my letter and I have discovered that I am (1) illiterate and (2) a braggart.

Good-bye. For heaven's sake, write.

Our Schiller will certainly turn out all right. Belinsky is encouraging the publication of a *full edition*. I feel that in time we'll be able to sell it at a good price, perhaps to Nekrasov, for instance.

Good-bye.

The Minnas, the Klaras, the Mariannas, etc., have grown so much prettier that it is hard to believe, but they cost a frightful lot of money. A few days ago, Turgenev and Belinsky gave me hell for my disorderly life. These gentlemen don't know how to show their affection; they are all, to the last man, in love with me. My debts are still at the same point.

---

10. Prince Vladimir Fyodorovich Odoyevsky (1803–1869) was a Romantic writer and philosopher, a historian of music and a musicologist, and a prominent public figure. His main literary work was *Russian Nights* (Russkiye nochi, 1844), a collection of novellas and short stories. The epigraph of *Poor Folk* was drawn from Odoyevsky's story "The Martingale" (Martingal), which was published in the same issue of *Petersburg Miscellany* as Dostoyevsky's novel.

Ivan Ivanovich Panayev (1812–1862) was a short-story writer and, beginning in 1847, a co-editor of the *Contemporary* (Sovremennik). His column, "The New Poet," offered witty comments on current events. His wife, Yevdokiya Yakovlevna Golovachova-Panayeva (1820–1893), was also a writer, contributing novels and stories to the *Contemporary* under the pen name of N. Stanitsky and co-authoring several novels with Nekrasov that enjoyed considerable success.

Lucien de Rubempré is the main character in Balzac's *Illusions perdues* (Lost illusions), a writer whose first feuilleton brought him immediate fame.

Dostoyevsky's *Novel in Nine Letters* was published in the *Contemporary* in 1847.

"Our group" is an allusion to the group of writers that had formed around Belinsky—Turgenev, Nekrasov, Goncharov, Panayev, Grigorovich, and others.

"The Minnas, the Klaras, the Mariannas, etc.," were evidently "ladies of the evening," who in Russia took German and French names.

11. To M. M. Dostoyevsky
[Petersburg] February 1 [1846]

Dear brother,

First of all, do not be angry with me for not having written for so long. I swear I haven't had a moment to spare, and I'll prove it to you. Until very recently, i.e., until the 28th, the main thing that prevented me from writing was that I was finishing off my scoundrel Golyadkin. It's terrible! This is what happens to human calculations: I intended to finish before August, but it dragged on until February. I am sending you the *Almanac* now. *Poor Folk* came out on the 15th. Ah, brother! What fierce disparagement my novel met everywhere! What I read about it in *Illustration* sounded more like abuse than criticism. The *Northern Bee* printed God knows what. But I remember how they greeted Gogol's works, and we all know how Pushkin's were received. Even the public is in a frenzy: three-quarters of the readers abuse it, but the remaining quarter (or even fewer than that) praise it frantically. It has occasioned the most virulent *débats*. They abuse, abuse, and abuse, but they keep on reading. (The *Almanac* is selling unusually, fantastically well. There is the expectation that in 2 weeks there won't be a single copy left.) This is just the way it was with Gogol. They abused him and abused him, unremittingly abused him, but went on reading him just the same, and now they have become reconciled to him and have started praising him. I really gave it to them, like giving a bone to the dogs: let them snap and gnash at each other, the fools, as they build up my fame. The way *Northern Bee* brought shame upon itself with its review was a disgrace. Such fury—it's stupid! But to make up for it, what praise I hear, brother! Believe it or not, everybody in our group, even Belinsky, finds that I have left even Gogol far behind. In *A Library for Reading,* where Nikitenko does the literary criticism, there will be an exhaustive analysis of *Poor Folk* favorable to me. In March, Belinsky will ring the bells. Odoyevsky is writing a separate article on *Poor Folk,* and my friend Sollogub as well. I move in high society now, brother, and in three months or so I'll be able to tell you directly of all of my adventures.

Our public, like every crowd, has instinct, but not culture. They don't understand how it is possible to write in that style. They are accustomed to finding the author's mug in everything, whereas I don't show them mine. And they cannot grasp that it is Devushkin speaking and not me, and that there's no other way Devushkin can talk. They find my novel drawn out, when it doesn't contain one unnecessary word. Some (Belinsky and others) find a new and original streak in me in the fact that I proceed by Analysis rather than by Synthesis, i.e., that I go deep down and, digging it up, atom by atom, I uncover the whole; whereas Gogol takes the whole directly, and that's why he is not as profound as I am. When you read it, you'll see for yourself. But you know, brother, I have a most brilliant career ahead of me!

Today they are publishing Golyadkin. *Four days* ago I was still working on him. He's coming out in *Notes of the Fatherland,* where he'll occupy 11 printer's sheets. Golyadkin is ten times better than *Poor Folk.* Those in our group say that since *Dead Souls* there hasn't been anything like it in Russia, that it is a work of genius—and what don't they say! They are looking to me with such hopes! And, indeed, Golyadkin has come off incredibly well. I can't imagine anything you would like better! You, you'll like him better than *Dead Souls,* I know it. Can you get *Notes of the Fatherland* in your town? I am not certain whether Krayevsky will let me have a copy.

I haven't written you for such a long time, brother, that I cannot remember where I left off. So much water has flowed under the bridge since then! We'll soon get together. Next summer I'll join you, my dear friends, and I'll spend the whole time writing like mad— I have lots of ideas. I am writing now, too. Golyadkin brought me exactly 600 silver rubles. On top of that, I got a whole pile of money, which means that I've gone through 3 thousand since I left you. The trouble is I lead a disorderly life! I've moved from the apartment and am now renting two splendidly furnished rooms. It's very comfortable.

My address is: Merchant Kunchin's house, Apartment No. 9, corner of Grebetskaya Street and Kuznechny Lane, by Saint Vladimir's Church. Please, for God's sake, write. Write whether you liked *Poor Folk.* My regards to Emiliya Fyodorovna! Kiss the children. I had seriously fallen in love with Panayeva—I'm getting over it now, although I'm not quite sure yet. My health is in a frightful state: my nerves are a mess and I am very much afraid of nervous fever. I cannot lead a respectable life, because I am so dissolute. If I cannot take sea baths next summer, I'll be in real trouble. Good-bye; for God's sake, write. Forgive me for writing such a bad letter. I'm in a rush. I kiss you. Good-bye.

Yours,
Dostoyevsky

Well, brother, forgive me in the name of God for not having sent you anything up to now. I'll bring everything in the summer. Good-bye then for now; it is after two already.

I'll bring presents for everyone.

In the summer, my friend, the two of us will have ourselves a much better time than we're having now. I shan't be too well off in cash, but I hope to bring 800 or 1000 rubles with me. That should be enough for the summer.

Verochka is getting married. Did you know?

---

11. The reviews of *Poor Folk* had indeed been abusive, scoffing at it for its monotony, its "wealth of diminutives," and its "superficial imitation."

Aleksandr Vasilevich Nikitenko (1804–1877) was the son of a serf; he was freed in 1824, eventually received a doctorate from Petersburg University, and became a professor of literature there as well as a literary critic. He was appointed a censor in 1833, and in that capacity he often gave valuable assistance to writers, on several occasions even being put under house arrest for such indulgences. His review of *Poor Folk* did not turn out to be as favorable as Dostoyevsky thought it would be; he, too, criticized the abundance of diminutives and also the excessive sentimentality.

Belinsky's initial enthusiasm for *Poor Folk* had somewhat cooled by the time his article about it appeared in *Notes of the Fatherland,* in which he emphasized Dostoyevsky's indebtedness to Gogol and said nothing about a "new and original streak." Neither Odoyevsky nor Sollogub ever published anything about the novel.

12. To M. M. Dostoyevsky

[Petersburg] April 1, 1846

Dear brother,

I am sending you a helmet with all the trappings and a pair of epaulets. The shako has not been fixed to the helmet because they told me that it would get damaged on the way. I don't know whether I've done the right thing. If I haven't, it is really no fault of mine because I know absolutely nothing about these matters. I have lost touch with the times, my friend. Now, a second question: you may ask me why it took me so long to do what you asked, but the thing is, my good man, I am subjected to such hard labor that, incredible though it may seem to you, I couldn't find a spare moment to carry out your errand. It is true, though, that I missed two mails entirely through my own negligence. I am sorry. Don't be angry with me.

Now, something else. You must resent the fact that I haven't written to you for such a long time, but then, I completely agree with Gogol's *Poprishchin,* who says: "*Letters are nonsense, apothecaries write letters.*" What exactly was I to write to you? I should have had to fill volumes to tell you all the things I should have liked to. Every day in my life brings so much that is new, so many changes, so many impressions, so much that is pleasant and favorable and so much that is unpleasant and unfavorable, that I myself don't have the time to ponder about it all. To start with, I am frightfully busy. I have an inexhaustible fund of ideas and I never stop writing. Don't imagine that everything is roses. Nonsense! First of all I have gone through a lot of money, to be precise, 4,500 rubles in currency bills, since I saw you, plus a 1,000-ruble advance I received on my merchandise. And so, with my carefulness, which you know so well, I have completely robbed myself, and I don't have a kopek to my name, as before. But that's not important.

My fame has reached its apogee. In the past 2 months, by my own count, my name has been mentioned about 35 times in various publications. Some praise me to the skies, others entertain certain reservations, and still others cover me with undiluted abuse. What could be greater or better than that? But the painful and disgusting side of it is that my own group, our people,

Belinsky and all the rest, are displeased with Golyadkin. Their first reaction was one of unqualified enthusiasm, a lot of talk, noise, and chatter. Then— they criticized. That is to say, everyone agreed; i.e., *our* people and the public at large found Golyadkin so boring and dull and drawn-out that it was quite impossible to read. But the funniest thing of all is that all those who take me to task because the novel is so long gulp it down and then reread it again and again. And one of our group does nothing but reread a chapter of it every day, so as not to overtire himself, and he smacks his lips with sheer joy over it. Some members of the public vociferate that it is quite impossible, that it is stupid to write and publish such things; others that I copied and plagiarized from them; and I have heard such madrigals from still others that I am ashamed to repeat them.

As to myself, there was a moment when I was gripped by despair. I have a terrible weakness—a boundless pride and egotism. The idea that I had betrayed the expectations placed in me and spoiled something that could have been a major achievement just about killed me. I am sick of Golyadkin now. Much of it was written in a hurry and when I was tired. The first part is better than the last. Alongside of sparkling pages, there is rubbish and trash that turns the stomach and is painful to read. And this is what has made my life infernal for some time and made me sick with grief. I'll send you Golyadkin in a couple of weeks, brother, and you will read it. Then write me everything you think of it.

I'll skip writing about my life and my *apprenticeship* and tell you some of the news. First (a tremendous piece of news), *Belinsky* is leaving *Notes of the Fatherland*. His health is completely ruined and he is going to a spa, perhaps abroad. He won't take up literary criticism again for two years. But to shore up his finances, he is publishing an anthology of *titanic* proportions (60 printer's sheets). I am writing two stories for him: (1) "Shaved-Off Whiskers" and (2) "A Tale of Abolished Chancelleries," both pieces full of stunning, tragic interest, and—I guarantee in advance—as terse as can be. The public is waiting impatiently for something by me to appear. Both these stories will be quite short. On top of that, I must write something for Krayevsky and a novel for Nekrasov. All that should take me about a year. Now, I'm finishing "Shaved-Off Whiskers."

The second piece of news is that a whole host of new writers has come onto the scene. Some of them are my rivals. Among them, the most remarkable are Herzen (Iskander) and Goncharov. The former has already been published, the latter is a beginner as yet unpublished. Both are highly praised. For the time being, the primacy is mine, and I hope this will always be so. In general, the literary scene has never seethed with such activity as now. That is all to the good.

Number three. I may come over to visit you either very early in the season or very late, or not at all. I have debts, I shan't have any money (and I wouldn't think of coming without money, and thirdly I am buried in work; the future will tell).

Number four. Shidlovsky has shown signs of life. His brother came to see me. I am beginning to correspond with him.

Number five. If you want to earn something in the literary field, my beloved friend, there is an opportunity for you to sparkle and even to cause a stir with a translation. Translate Goethe's *Reinecke Fuchs*. I have even been solicited to ask you to do the translation, because it is needed for Nekrasov's anthology. If you feel like it, translate it. Don't hurry, though. And if I don't come by May 15 or June 1, send your translation here if you have it ready. Everyone will be leaving for the summer, but if I can manage it, I may be able to place it somewhere this spring and bring you the money when I come. And if not in the spring, then in the fall, *for sure*. You'll certainly get money for it. Nekrasov is a publisher—he will buy it; Belinsky will buy it; *Ratkov* will buy it. And as to Krayevsky, he is entirely at my disposal. It would be a profitable business. They have been talking about that translation around here. And so, start if you want to do it, and I vouch for its success with my life. If you translate three chapters or so, send them on to me, *I'll show* it to those gentlemen, and it is quite possible that they'll give you an advance.

Never have I been so rich in activity as I am now. Everything is seething, everything is on the march— Well, we'll see what comes of it. Good-bye, my beloved brother.

Good-bye, my dear fellow. Love to you all, and I wish you all the best. I kiss both of Emiliya Fyodorovna's hands. The children, too. How are you? Write about yourself. Ah, my friend, I do so long to see you. But what can I do?

Verochka has been married for three months now. I understand she's happy. Uncle gave her as much as he gave Varya. Write to Uncle. She married *Ivanov* (His Worship). He's 30 years old. He's a professor of chemistry somewhere or other. Verochka wrote me and said she'd written you, too.

> Yours alone,
> Dostoyevsky

---

12. The military accessories that Dostoyevsky sent to his brother were evidently cheaper in Petersburg than they were in Revel, where Mikhail was still stationed.

Poprishchin is the main character in Gogol's *Diary of a Madman* (Zapiski sumasshedshego, 1835).

Belinsky's "anthology of titanic proportions" never appeared, but all of its intended contents were eventually published in the *Contemporary*—except for the two stories Dostoyevsky was working on, "Shaved-Off Whiskers" (Sbritye bakenbardy) and "A Tale of Abolished Chancelleries" (Povest ob unichtozhennykh kantselyariyakh), which he never finished.

Aleksandr Ivanovich Herzen (1812–1870), who also wrote under the pen name of Iskander, was an essayist, social critic, and author, best known for his novel *Who Is to Blame?* (Kto vinovat?, 1847); his memoirs, *My Past and My Thoughts* (Byloye i dumy, 1861); and the magazine he published together with Nikolai Platonovich Ogaryov, the *Bell* (Kolokol). In the 1840s, he contributed a number of articles to *Notes of the Fatherland,* and he came to exercise an influence on Dostoyevsky comparable to that of Belinsky. Herzen left Russia in 1846 and thereafter lived chiefly in London (where Dostoyevsky visited him in 1862) and in Paris.

Ivan Aleksandrovich Goncharov (1812–1891) was a novelist and a member of the Belinsky circle. His "An Ordinary Story" (Obyknovennaya istoriya, 1847) was praised by Belinsky even before it was published, in the *Contemporary*. Dostoyevsky expressed respect for Goncharov's skill, and the two never clashed either in private life or in literature, but Dostoyevsky was nevertheless critical of Goncharov's "German" punctiliousness and seeming lack of passion.

Mikhail's translation of Goethe's *Reinecke Fuchs* was published in *Notes of the Fatherland* in 1849.

Contrary to what Dostoyevsky says, Ivanov taught not chemistry but physics.

13. To M. M. Dostoyevsky
[Petersburg] November 26, 1846

How could you, most precious friend, write that I was angry with you for not sending me the money and attribute my silence to that? How could you have imagined any such thing? And finally, what reason can I have given you for assuming anything of the sort? If you love me, do me a favor and dismiss any such ideas once and for all. Let's see to it that things are simple and straightforward between us. Let me declare aloud and emphatically that, as it is, I owe you a lot and that it would be ridiculous and despicably piggish on my part not to admit it. But enough of that for now. Better that I tell you of my present circumstances and do my best to give you as clear a picture of everything as possible.

First of all, all the publishing plans have burst like a bubble, and nothing has come of them. It wasn't worthwhile, it was taking up too much time, and it was not the right moment. The public maybe wouldn't have gone along with it. I'll put out an edition next fall. By that time, the public will have got to know me better, and my position will be more clear-cut. Furthermore, I am expecting to receive a few advances. Illustrations for *The Double* have already been done by a Moscow artist. Two others are now doing the illustrations for *Poor Folk*—we'll see which will be the better. Bernardsky says that he would like to start negotiating with me in February and to pay me a certain sum for the right to publish an illustrated edition. Until that time, he has his hands full with *Dead Souls*. In short, for the time being I have lost interest in publishing things on my own. Anyway, I have no time for it; I have a slew of work and of orders.

I must tell you that I have had the unpleasant experience of breaking off irrevocably with *Contemporary* in the person of Nekrasov. He was offended with me for going ahead and giving my stories to Krayevsky, to whom I owe money, and for refusing to declare publicly that I was not connected with *Notes of the Fatherland.* When he had lost hope of getting a story from me in the near future, he became rude and was unwise enough to demand that I return him the money. I took him at his word and gave him a note payable on December 15 for the sum in question. I want them to come crawling back to me. They are all despicable and envious. While I was giving Nekrasov a piece of my mind, he just kept squirming around, trying to wriggle out of the situation, like a Jew who is being robbed. To put it in a nutshell, it was quite an unsavory scene. And now, they are circulating rumors that I have become smitten with my own importance, that I fancy myself God knows what and that I am going over to Krayevsky because Maikov is enthusiastic about me. Even Nekrasov intends to disparage me. As to Belinsky, he is such a weak man that even when it comes to literary opinions he can come up with five Fridays in one week. However, I have maintained good relations with him. He is a noble person.

In the meantime, Krayevsky, taking advantage of the opportunity, gave me money, and, on top of that, promised to pay all my debts for me by December 15. In return, I'll be working for him until the spring.

Well, you see, brother, from all this I have deduced a wise precept: the most unprofitable course that a burgeoning talent can follow is to become friendly with the owners of publishing enterprises. For the inevitable consequence of it is familiarity, followed by various dirty tricks. What I need is an independent position and a chance to work with dedication for Holy Art in all the purity of my heart, a heart that has never before vibrated and throbbed within me the way it does now before the new images and characters that are springing up in my mind. Brother, I feel I have been reborn, and reborn not only in the spiritual but in the physical sense as well. There has never before been within me such richness and clarity, such evenness of character, such physical vigor. For all this, I owe much to my friends the Beketovs, to Zalyubetsky, and to the others with whom I am living; they are sensible people, intelligent, kindhearted, generous, and of strong character. Being in their company cured me and so, in the end, I suggested we live together. We found a large apartment, and all our expenses on board and lodging do not exceed 1200 rubles in currency bills a year per person. That is how great the advantages of association can be! I have my own room and I work there the whole day through. My new address, which I would like you to use when you write, is Apartment 26, Soloshich House, opposite the Lutheran Church, First Line on Bolshoi Prospect, Vasilevsky Island.

My congratulations, my dearest friend, on the arrival of my 3rd nephew. I wish all the best to him and to Emiliya Fyodorovna. I love you all three times as much now. And please don't be angry with me, my priceless brother, for writing you something that is less a letter than a piece of paper covered with scribbles: I am in a hurry, people are waiting for me. But I'll write again on Friday. You may consider this letter unfinished.

Your friend,

F. Dostoyevsky

---

13. About a month before this letter, Dostoyevsky had written to Mikhail enthusiastically about a proposal to put out a separate edition of *Poor Folk* on his own, in order to avoid being "swindled" by the book dealers. But he had no capital for the venture, and so he had asked Mikhail for a loan of 200 silver rubles.

Yevstafy Bernardsky (b. 1819) was a wood engraver who in 1846 produced the illustrations for Gogol's *Dead Souls*.

Valerian Nikolayevich Maikov (1823–1847) was one of the compilers of the *Pocket Dictionary of Foreign Words That Have Become Part of the Russian Language* (Karmanny slovar inostrannykh slov soshedshikh v sostav russkogo yazyka, 1845–1846), which was intended to play the same role in Russia that Voltaire's *Dictionnaire philosophique* had played in France; the book was severely criticized by the investigator of the Petrashevsky affair. Maikov was one of the few who admired the work that Dostoyevsky was publishing after *Poor Folk*. Dostoyevsky was very friendly with him, and his death at the age of 24 was a blow. Dostoyevsky transferred his affection to Valerian's older brother, Apollon, who became a lifelong friend.

The Beketovs were three brothers—Aleksei Nikolayevich (b. 1823), Andrei Nikolayevich (1825–1902), and Nikolai Nikolayevich (b. 1827)—with whom Dostoyevsky shared living quarters for about two years. The two younger brothers later become professors at Petersburg University.

---

14. To A. M. Dostoyevsky

[Peter-and-Paul Fortress, Petersburg] June 20, 1849

Dear brother Andrei Mikhailovich,

They gave me permission to write you a few lines, and I hasten to let you know that I am, thank God, in good health and that, although I feel a bit depressed, I am far from despairing. One can find some consolation in every situation. And so, do not worry about me. Please let me know about our brother's family—how is Emiliya Fyodorovna, how are the children? Do kiss them all on my behalf.

There is one favor I should like to ask you. All this time I have been in dire need of money and have been suffering great hardship. I suppose you did not know that it was possible to send me something to help me out, which explains your silence up to now. But now do not forget me. What I am asking of you is this—if that Moscow money business still has not been settled, write to Karepin in Moscow and ask him to send me, at once, 25 silver rubles on account of the sum that is coming to me. That is all I need for the time being.

If, on the other hand, the business has been settled, ask him to send me everything that I am entitled to. I assume that you yourself must have received something by now and that the matter is about to be wound up. Do not forget Mikhail's family either, and when you write to Moscow put in a word for him, too.

But, pending receipt of the money from Moscow, send me, if you can, 10 silver rubles. I have borrowed that sum here and must pay it back. You would greatly oblige me. So please, do it. Write to our sisters, give them my regards, and tell them that I am really quite all right, and don't frighten them. Give my regards to Uncle and especially to Auntie. Please, be sure not to forget about her.

I have another favor to ask of you. I don't know, however, whether it is feasible, i.e., whether they would allow you to do it, although I think they will. Mikhail has a coupon authorizing him to receive *Notes of the Fatherland,* and I don't think he has picked up the May number as yet. Ask Emiliya Fyodorovna to give you the coupon, pick up the magazine, and send it on to me. It contains the third installment of my novel, which they have published without me, without my checking— I didn't even see the proofs. I am worried about how much they have printed and whether they have distorted the novel. So, please send me that issue. Here is how you must address it: "To the Office of His Excellency, the Commandant of the Peter-and-Paul Fortress." Or it would be even better if you came and brought it in person.

I can just imagine how glad you must have been when they released you after having arrested you by mistake. Farewell, I wish you all the best. Wish me the same.

Your brother,
Fyodor Dostoyevsky

---

14. This is the first letter known to have been sent by Dostoyevsky after his arrest on April 23, 1849. Mikhail was supposed to have been arrested with him, but their brother Andrei had been arrested instead by mistake. When the error was discovered, Andrei was released and Mikhail was taken into custody.

The "Moscow money business" refers to the settlement of Dostoyevsky's father's estate. By this time, negotiations were under way for all the Dostoyevsky children to be bought out by one of their relatives, either Karepin or Ivanov. The latter did finally acquire the estate several years later.

Parts 1 and 2 of Dostoyevsky's novel *Netochka Nezvanova* had been published in *Notes of the Fatherland;* part 3 had been completed and submitted but not yet published when Dostoyevsky was arrested. The publisher, Krayevsky, applied to the Third Section for permission to print it, in view of the fact that it had already been approved by the censor. Permission was granted, but only on condition that the author's name not be printed.

15. TO M. M. DOSTOYEVSKY
[Peter-and-Paul Fortress, Petersburg] July 18, 1849

I cannot tell you how pleased I was to get your letter, my dear brother. I received it on July 11. So you are a free man at last, and I imagine what a joy it was for you to see your family again. How they must have been waiting for you! I see that you are settling down to a new life. What are you doing now and, more important, what are you living on now? Do you have some work, and exactly what is it that you are working on? Summers are oppressive in the city! Besides, you write that you have taken another apartment and you are probably even more crowded there. It is a shame you cannot spend the remainder of the summer out of town.

Thank you for your parcels. They were a great help and cheered me up a great deal. You write, my dear friend, that I should not despair. Well, I am not despairing. Of course, it is boring and depressing here, but how can it be helped? Actually it is not always boring. In general, my time passes very unevenly—at times too quickly, at others tediously. There are moments when you feel you've become used to such a life and it doesn't bother you one way or the other. Of course, I am chasing all the temptations of the imagination away, but sometimes you cannot contend with it and your former life comes bursting in, bringing along the old sensations, and the past surges up again. But I suppose that is in the order of things. Now the weather is nice, at least most of the time, and I have become a bit more cheerful. But in gloomy weather life becomes unbearable, and the casemate looks more forbidding. I have things to do, and I am not wasting my time doing nothing; I have thought up three stories and two novels. I am writing one of them now, but I don't dare to work on it too much.

This sort of work, especially if done with a will (and I have never worked as much con amore as now), has always exhausted me and affected my nerves. When I was working in freedom I felt the need to interrupt myself constantly and to do something distracting; whereas here, the state of agitation I get into after writing has to pass off by itself. My health is fine except perhaps for the hemorrhoids and the disorder of my nerves that goes in a *crescendo*. Now and then I have throat spasms like the ones I used to have before, I have little appetite, I sleep little, and when I do, I have bad nightmares. I sleep about five hours a day and wake up four times or so during the night. This is the most painful thing of all. The worst time is at dusk, and at nine it is already quite dark here. Sometimes I can't get to sleep until one or two in the morning, so that I must endure five hours or so of darkness. That, more than anything else, is ruining my health.

I cannot tell you anything about how soon our case will be settled, because I have lost all sense of time and merely keep a calendar on which I just passively tick off the days as they go by; one more gone—a good riddance!

I have not been reading much here: two accounts of travel to the Holy

Land and the works of St. Dmitry of Rostov. The latter held my interest; but such reading is just a drop in the ocean and I think I should be extraordinarily happy to get any kind of book, the more so because it would be salutary just to interrupt my own thoughts with someone else's or to re-fashion my own thoughts along new lines.

These are all the details of my existence, and that's all there is. I am very glad that you found your family in good health. Have you written to Moscow about your release? It is a shame that things there are not shaping up. How I should like to spend even just one day with you all! Do you remember how they used to take us out occasionally into the garden in May? Things were beginning to turn green even then, and it reminded me of Revel and the garden in the Engineering House there when I used to go to visit you at that time of the year. I kept imagining then that you, too, would make this association and it made me feel very sad.

There are others whom I should also enjoy seeing. Whom are you seeing now? I suppose everyone must be out of town. Our brother Andrei must surely be in town; and have you seen Nikolya? Give them my regards. Kiss all your children for me, give my regards to your wife, and tell her that I am very touched by her remembering me. And don't worry too much about me. All I ask is to remain in good health, for boredom is a passing thing and, anyway, keeping in good spirits depends on me alone. There are infinite reserves of vitality and adaptability in a man—more than I thought before I learned from experience. Well, good-bye now! I hope that these few words from me will cheer you up a bit. Give my best to everyone you see whom I used to know and don't leave anyone out. I have been thinking of everybody. What do the children think of me and, I wonder, what suppositions are they making about me: wherever can he have vanished to! Farewell, then. If it can be done, send me *Notes of the Fatherland*, so I'll be able to read something, at least. Also, write a few words. It would make me very happy.

So long. Your brother,

F. Dostoyevsky

---

15. Mikhail had been arrested on the night of May 5–6, and he was held in the Peter-and-Paul Fortress until June 24, when the police determined that he was "not only innocent of any crimes against the government, but even acted with a view to preventing them." He was cleared of all suspicion and received a grant of 200 rubles. At the time of his arrest, he had been working at *Notes of the Fatherland*, and Dostoyevsky was wondering whether he had been able to get his job back.

Of the "three stories and two novels" Dostoyevsky mentions, only the story "A Little Hero" is known to have been published—in *Notes of the Fatherland*, August 1857, over the signature "M—y."

St. Dmitry was Daniil Savvich Tuptalo (1651–1709), metropolitan of Rostov. His writings included *Lives of the Saints* (Minei-cheti) and several mystery plays with religious subjects.

16.   To M. M. Dostoyevsky
[Peter-and-Paul Fortress, Petersburg, August 27, 1849]

I am very glad that I can answer you, my dear brother, and thank you for sending me the books. I particularly appreciate *Notes of the Fatherland.* I am also delighted to hear that you are in good health and that imprisonment had no ill effects on your physical state. But you write so very little, and my letters are so much more detailed than yours. But let's leave that, you will make it up in time.

I cannot tell you anything definite about myself. There is still the same uncertainty about our whole case. My *private* life is just as monotonous as before, although they are again allowing me to go out into the little yard where there are almost seventeen trees. To me it is a whole great joyful event. Besides, I am now allowed to have a candle in the evenings, and this is another great joy. It would be a third one if you wrote me quickly and sent me *Notes of the Fatherland,* for I am in the position of an out-of-town subscriber waiting for it as for the millennium, waiting like a bored landowner in the provinces. You want to send me historical works? That would be fine. But it would be even better if you sent me the Bible (both Testaments). I need it. But if possible, send it in a French translation. And if you could, on top of that, send me one in Church Slavonic, that would be the height of perfection.

I have nothing very good to say about my health. For a whole month now, I have been swallowing castor oil and this is the only thing that keeps me going in this world. My hemorrhoids have become aggravated to the nth degree, and I have pains in my chest such as I have never experienced before. On top of that, my sensitivity increases, especially as night comes on, and during the night I have long, outlandish dreams and also, of late, I have been under the impression that the floor is swaying under me, so that I feel as if I were in a ship's cabin in my cell. All this leads me to conclude that my nerves are going to pieces. Before, when such a nervous state came over me, I took advantage of it to write—I could always write better and much more in this state; now, however, I restrain myself from writing so as not to do myself in completely. There was a spell of three weeks or so during which I didn't write at all. Now I have taken it up again. But all that is still of no consequence—life is still livable. Who knows, perhaps I'll manage to recover.

I was simply amazed to read in your letter that you think that our Moscow family know nothing about our mishap. I have given it some thought, made some deductions, and come to the conclusion that it is quite impossible. I am sure they know, and I can think of a quite different reason for their silence. But that was to be expected. It's all quite obvious.

How is Emiliya Fyodorovna's health? What bad luck, how hard it is on her! This is the second summer in a row that she has had to bear up under such adversity. Last year there was the cholera and the other things and, this year, it is already God knows what! Really, brother, it is a sin to slip into apathy; strenuous work con amore is the only true happiness. Work, write, what is there better than that?

You write that literature is sick. Still, the issues of *Notes of the Fatherland* are as rich in material as ever, although, of course, not when it comes to belles-lettres. I didn't find an article that I didn't read with pleasure. The science section is brilliant. "The Conquest of Peru" by itself is a whole *Iliad* and, I feel, is in no way inferior to last year's "The Conquest of Mexico." And so what if the article is a translation? I enjoyed immensely the second article analyzing the *Odyssey*, albeit this piece is much weaker than the first one, by Davydov, which was superb, especially the passage where he refutes Wolf; it was written with such profound understanding of the subject and with such enthusiasm that it struck me as rather surprising, coming from such an ancient professor. Even in this article he has managed to avoid the pedantry peculiar to scholars in general and to Moscow scholars in particular.

From all this you may conclude, brother, that your books afford me a great deal of pleasure and that I am infinitely grateful to you for them. Well, good-bye and I wish you every success. Write soon. It certainly would be a fine thing if you wrote our Moscow relatives about our affairs, and formally inquired about how things stand regarding the country estate. My kisses to all the children. I suppose they are being taken for walks in the Summer Garden. Give my regards to Emiliya Fyodorovna, and to any of my acquaintances whom you may see. You write that you'd like to see me— When will it be! Well, good-bye.

Yours,
Fyodor Dostoyevsky

Write and tell me who is the Mr. (Vl. Ch.) whose articles are appearing in *Notes of the Fatherland.* And, also, who is the author of the review of Shakhovskaya's poem in the July issue of the magazine? Find out if you can.

I shall run out of money between the tenth and the fifteenth of September. If you can, help me out once again. I don't need much. I have credit with Sorokin in connection with *Poor Folk;* I forget exactly how much there is, but the sum is quite insignificant—he had paid me almost everything.

Fyodor Dostoyevsky

---

16. Dostoyevsky's "Moscow family" consisted at this time of his married sisters, Varvara Karepina and Vera Ivanova, and the family of his Aunt Kumanina.

History of the Conquest of Peru (1847) and *History of the Conquest of Mexico* (3 vols., 1843) were by the American historian William Hickling Prescott (1796–1847), whose work was known in Europe as well as in America. *Conquest of Mexico* was carried in translation in *Notes of the Fatherland* in installments during 1848, *Conquest of Peru* in 1849.

Ivan Ivanovich Davydov (1794–1863) was a writer, an early follower of Schelling, and a lecturer on philosophy, algebra, and Russian literature at Moscow University. His 1849 article in *Notes of the Fatherland* was entitled "A Comparison of Zhukovsky's Translation of the *Odyssey* with the Original, Based on an Analysis of the Ninth Rhapsody" (Sravneniye perevoda "Odissei" Zhukovskogo s podlinnikom, na osnovanii razbora 9-oi rapsodii).

Friedrich August Wolf (1759–1824) was the author of *Prolegomena ad Homerum* (1795), in which he propounded the idea that the *Iliad* and the *Odyssey* in their present form were the work of many nameless authors rather than that of Homer alone.

The July 1849 issue of *Notes of the Fatherland* carried a story entitled "A Summer in Helsingfors in the Style of a Tale" (Leto v Gelsingforse v rode povesti), signed with the initials Vl. Ch.; a poem by Shakhovskaya entitled "The Lady of the World and the Woman Recluse" (Miryanka i otshelnitsa); and an unsigned review of the poem. The names of the author of the story and the poem's reviewer are not known.

17.   TO M. M. DOSTOYEVSKY
[Peter-and-Paul Fortress, Petersburg]
September 14, 1849

I have received, dear brother, your letter, the books (Shakespeare, the Bible, *Notes of the Fatherland*), and the money (10 silver rubles), for all of which I thank you. Things are still unchanged with me—the same diarrhea and hemorrhoids. I don't know when I shall ever get better. The troublesome fall months are coming on and, with them, my hypochondria. The sky is already frowning, whereas the bright patch of sky that I could see from my casemate was the guarantee of my health and good spirits. But, for the time being, I am still alive and healthy, and that's what counts. And so, please, don't be unduly concerned about me. For the moment, my health is fine. I expected it would be much worse, but now I see that I have so much vitality in reserve that it is virtually inexhaustible.

Once again, I thank you for the books. Whatever else, they are a source of distraction. For nearly five months now I've been living on my own resources, i.e., just out of my own head and nothing else. So far, the engine hasn't fallen apart and is still working. However, unending and solitary meditation, meditation totally unrelieved by outside impressions to renew and sustain the mind, is very oppressive! I feel as if I were under an air pump which is sucking away the air from around me. Everything inside me has flowed into my brain, and from my brain into thought, everything, absolutely everything, and this despite the fact that my work increases every day. Books, even though they are just a drop in the ocean, do help. But my own work alone seems to be squeezing out the last juices. However, I am satisfied with it.

I have been rereading the last batch of books you sent me. I am particularly grateful to you for the Shakespeare. What a great idea on your part! The English novel in *Notes of the Fatherland* is exceptionally good. But Turgenev's comedy is impermissibly bad. What's this affliction he is suffering from? Is the man really doomed to spoil everything he writes whenever it is more than one printer's sheet in length? I couldn't recognize him in this comedy. No originality whatever—the same old well-beaten path. All that has been said before him and much better. The closing scene leaves an impression of childish impotence. There are some flashes here and there, but they are only good for the lack of anything better. What an excellent article about the banks! And so easy to understand! I thank all those who have not forgotten me; give my regards to Emiliya Fyodorovna, to our brother Andrei, kiss the children—my special wish is for them to grow strong and healthy. Ah, brother, I wonder when we shall meet again! Farewell and please do not forget me. Write me even if only in two weeks or so.

Good-bye.

Yours,
F. Dostoyevsky

Please don't worry too much about me. If you find something to read, send it to me.

---

17. The "English novel" is *Jane Eyre* (1848), which appeared in Russian translation in *Notes of the Fatherland* during 1849. Its author, Charlotte Brontë (1816–1855), came to enjoy a reputation in Russia almost equal to that of Dickens and Thackeray.

Turgenev's comedy is *The Bachelor* (Kholostyak), which appeared in the September 1849 issue of *Notes of the Fatherland*. The relations between Moshkin and Masha in *The Bachelor* resemble those between Devushkin and Varenka in *Poor Folk*, and this may have been what Dostoyevsky was thinking of when he wrote that it had all "been said before . . . and much better."

18.　To M. M. DOSTOYEVSKY
[Peter-and-Paul Fortress, Petersburg]
December 22, 1849

Brother, my beloved friend!

It is decided! I have been sentenced to four years at hard labor in a fortress (I believe in the Orenburg Fortress), to be followed by service in the ranks. Today, this 22nd of December, they carted us off to Semyonovsky Square. There, they read us all our death sentence, allowed us to kiss the cross, broke a sword over each of our heads, and attired us for execution (white shirts). Then three of us were placed at the post for the execution to be carried out.

They were calling three names at a time. I was in the second group and so I had no more than one minute left to live. I thought of you, brother, of all your family; at the last moment you, you alone were in my mind, and it was only then that I realized how much I love you, my dear brother! I also had time to embrace Pleshcheyev and Durov, who were nearby, and to say good-bye to them.

Then they sounded retreat. Those who were tied to the post were led back, and they announced that His Imperial Majesty was granting us life. After that they read us our actual sentences. *Palm* alone was amnestied and returned to the army, retaining his former rank.

They have just informed me, my dear brother, that we are to set out on the march either today or tomorrow. I requested permission to see you, but I was told this was out of the question. All they would do is to allow me to write you this letter, which I should like you to answer right away. I am worried that you may have heard somehow about our being sentenced (to death). Out of the windows of the carriage in which I was being taken to Semyonovsky Square, I saw throngs of people; possibly the news had already reached you, too, and you were suffering for me. Now, you will feel easier about me. Brother, I have not lost courage and I do not feel dispirited. Life is life everywhere, life is within ourselves and not in externals. There will be people around me, and to be a *man* among men, to remain so forever and not to lose hope and give up, however hard things may be—that is what life is, that is its purpose. I have come to realize this. This idea has now become part of my flesh and blood. Yes, this is the truth! The head that created, that lived by the superior life of art, that recognized and became used to the highest spiritual values, that head has already been lopped off my shoulders. What is left is the memories and the images that I had already created but had not yet given form to. They will lacerate and torment me now, it is true! But I have, inside me, the same heart, the same flesh and blood that can still love and suffer and pity and remember—and this, after all, is life. On voit le soleil! Well, good-bye, brother, don't grieve for me!

Now some practical considerations. The books (I still have the Bible) and some manuscripts—rough sketches of a play and a novel (and a completed story, "A Child's Fairy Tale")—have been taken away from me and I suppose will be turned over to you. I am also leaving behind my overcoat and my old suit, and you can send someone to pick them up. And now, brother, I am faced with what may be a long journey to my place of deportation. I need money. As soon as you get this letter, my dear brother, get some money if you can and send it to me right away. Money is more important to me than the air I breathe just now (for a special reason). Also, write me a few lines. Then, if the Moscow money arrives, work on my case and don't abandon me. Well, that's that! There are the debts, but what can I do about them?—

Kiss your wife and the children. Remember me to them now and then, see to it that they do not forget me. Who knows, perhaps we'll meet again sometime?! Look after yourself and your family, brother, lead a quiet and provident life. Keep your children's future in mind— Lead a purposeful, useful life.

Never before have such rich and healthy reserves of spiritual life been seething in me as now. But will my body stand the ordeal?—that I do not know. I am setting out in poor health, I am suffering from scrofula. But who knows! I have been through so much in my life that there are few things left now that can frighten me. Come what may! Let me have news of you at the earliest opportunity. Give the Maikovs my final farewell regards. Tell them that I am grateful to them all for their unwavering concern for me. Say a few, particularly warm words for me—whatever your own heart dictates to you— to Yevgeniya Petrovna. I wish her much happiness, and shall always remember her with grateful respect. Shake the hands of Nikolai Apollonovich and Apollon Maikov for me, and also those of all the rest. Find Yanovsky. Thank him and shake his hand for me. And thank all those who have not forgotten me. And those who have—remember me to them. Give my love to our brother *Kolya*. Write to our brother *Andrei* and inform him about me. Write to our aunt and uncle. Do it on my behalf and give them my regards. Write to our sisters and tell them I wish them happiness!

And perhaps we'll meet again some day, brother. Take care of yourself and, for the sake of God, live to see me again. One day, we may yet hug each other and remember our young years, our bygone golden times, the dreams of our youth that at this instant I am tearing bleeding from my heart and burying.

Can it be that I shall never again take pen in hand? I hope that, in 4 years' time, it will be possible. I shall send you everything I write, if I write at all. My God! How many images to which I have given life and which are still alive will perish, will be snuffed out inside my head or will spread like poison in my blood! Yes, if I cannot write, I shall perish. Better fifteen years of confinement with a pen in my hand!

Write me more often, write me in greater detail, longer and fuller letters. Describe lengthily in every letter all the little things of family life, the trivia— and don't forget that. It will give me hope and life. If only you knew how much your letters sustained me in my casemate here. These (last) two and a half months, when we were not allowed to receive letters, were very painful to me. I was in poor health. The fact that at times you failed to send me money made me worry for you, because it meant that you yourself were in dire need! Once again kiss the children, I cannot get their lovely little faces out of my head. May they, at least, be happy! You, too, brother, I want you to be happy, too!

But, for heaven's sake, don't grieve over me! I want you to know that I am not discouraged, that hope has not abandoned me. In four years things will be a bit easier for me. I shall be an army private—that is already quite different from being a convict, and bear in mind that I will hug you one day. Why, didn't I face death for three-quarters of an hour today, live with this thought in my head, was I not a hairsbreadth away from death, and now I am living again!

If anyone remembers me unkindly and if I have quarreled with anybody or left him with an unpleasant impression of me, ask him to forget about it, if you happen to come across him. There is no bile or malice in my soul, and I should like so much, at this instant, to love and to press to my heart any of these former acquaintances. It is a joy; I experienced it today as I was taking leave of those who were dear to me before I was to die. At that moment I was thinking that when you heard about my execution the news would kill you. But now, I assure you that I am still alive and that I shall live in the future in the hope that one day I shall take you in my arms. That is all that I have in my mind right now.

I wonder what you're doing now? What have you been thinking about today? Did you know what happened to us? How cold it was today!

Ah, I hope my letter reaches you quickly. Otherwise I shall have to be some four months without news from you. I saw the packets in which you sent me the money during the past two months; the address was written in your own hand and I was so glad to see that you were well.

When I turn back to look at the past, I think how much time has been wasted, how much of it has been lost in misdirected efforts, mistakes, and idleness, in living in the wrong way; and, however I treasured life, how much I sinned against my heart and spirit—my heart bleeds now as I think of it. Life is a gift, life is happiness, each minute could be an eternity of bliss. Si jeunesse savait! Now, at this turning point in my life, I am being reborn in another form. Brother! I swear to you that I will not lose hope and will keep my spirit and my heart pure. I shall be reborn to something better. This is all my hope, my whole consolation!

Life in the casemate has already largely killed in me some demands of the flesh that were not quite pure; I hadn't guarded myself against them sufficiently before. Now, privations are nothing to me, and so do not be afraid that material hardship of some kind or another will kill me. Ah, if only I had my health!

Farewell, brother, farewell! When shall I be able to write to you again! You will get as detailed a report of my journey as feasible from me. If only I can manage to preserve my health, everything will be fine!

Well, good-bye, brother, good-bye now! I hug you hard and kiss you warmly. Remember me without heartache. Don't be sad, please don't be sad about me! In my very next letter I'll tell you how life is treating me. Never forget what I've told you: organize your life, don't waste it, plan your future, think of the children. Ah, when, when shall I see you again! Good-bye! I am tearing myself away now from everything that was dear to me, and it hurts to leave it! It is painful to break myself in two and to tear my heart in half. Farewell! Farewell! But I shall see you again, I hope; in fact, I feel sure, but don't change, don't stop loving me, don't let my memory grow dim, and the thought of your love will be the better part of my life. Farewell, once more, farewell! Farewell to all of you!

Your brother,
Fyodor Dostoyevsky

December 22, 1849

When they arrested me, they took some books away from me. Only two of them were illegal. Don't you want to take the others for yourself? But here is a service you could do for me: One of the books was *The Works of Valerian Maikov,* his critical articles; it belongs to Yevgeniya Petrovna. She gave it to me as one would give a treasured possession. When I was arrested I asked the officer of the security police to give her back the book, and gave him her address. Find out whether he did it! I don't want to deprive her of this memento. Good-bye, good-bye once more.

Yours,
F. Dostoyevsky

I don't know whether they will march or transport us there. I believe we shall be transported. Who knows?

Once again, shake Emiliya Fyodorovna's hand for me, kiss the children.

Give my regards to Krayevsky; perhaps—

Write to me in as much detail as possible about your arrest, imprisonment, and release.

---

18. This is the last letter Dostoyevsky wrote before leaving to serve his sentence at hard labor, which he did not in Orenburg but in Omsk. While in penal servitude, until 1854, he was not permitted to write any letters.

Aleksei Nikolayevich Pleshcheyev (1826–1897) was a poet and one of the first to attend Petrashevsky's weekly gatherings. He and Dostoyevsky probably met in 1846, either in the Beketov circle or at the Maikovs, and they soon became very close friends; *A Faint Heart* and *White Nights* were dedicated to him. Pleshcheyev did serve his sentence in Orenburg, and that may have been what led Dostoyevsky to think that he would be sent there as well. Pleshcheyev assisted Dostoyevsky with money, helped him to get a collection of his works published in 1860, and contributed to the periodicals that Dostoyevsky and his brother ran.

Sergei Fyodorovich Durov (1816–1869) was a writer and translator and one of the most assiduous participants in the Petrashevsky gatherings. When differences began to arise among members of the Petrashevsky group, Durov, Pleshcheyev, and Dostoyevsky formed their own little circle. Durov also served his sentence in Omsk, but he and Dostoyevsky had little to do with each other there. In 1857, Durov was permitted to return to European Russia because of illness; he lived for a time in Poltava with Palm, in whose house he died.

Aleksandr Ivanovich Palm (1822–1885), another member of the Petrashevsky circle, was the only one to be eventually pardoned. In 1872–1873 he published, under the pseudonym P. Alminsky, the novel *Aleksei Slobodin,* in which he portrays, under fictitious names, Dostoyevsky, Durov, Petrashevsky, and others, and describes one of their Friday gatherings.

"On voit le soleil!" is presumably an allusion to the words of the condemned man in Hugo's novel *Le dernier jour d'un condamné* (The last day of a condemned man, 1829). Eagerly hoping that his death sentence will be commuted to imprisonment, the convict exclaims: "Un forçat, cela marche encore, cela va et vient, cela voit le soleil!" ("A convict, that's someone who can still walk, someone who comes and goes, someone who sees the sun").

"A Child's Fairy Tale" was the story that was published in 1857 under the title of "A Little Hero." Ironically, when he learned of its publication from Mikhail, Dostoyevsky wrote to his brother that "the news . . . did not altogether fill me with joy. I had been thinking for a long time of reworking it. . . . But what can we do about it now?"

Yevgeniya Petrovna Maikova (1803–1880) was Valerian's and Apollon's mother, a poet and author in her own right; some of her work was published in *A Library for Reading* between 1841 and 1850. Nikolai Apollonovich Maikov (1794–1873) was their father; after service in the army, he took up painting and executed a series of ikons for the Holy Trinity Church in Petersburg. The *Works of Valerian Maikov* that Dostoyevsky mentions was perhaps printed privately by his parents, since no collection of his writings was published until 1891.

Stepan Dmitriyevich Yanovsky (1817–1897) was a physician in the Department of Government Medical Supplies of the Ministry of the Interior until his retirement in 1871; from 1877 until his death, he lived in Switzerland. He and Dostoyevsky had met in 1842 and became quite close friends.

19. To M. M. Dostoyevsky
[Omsk] February 22, 1854

At last, the moment seems to have come when I can speak with you at some length and a bit more reliably. But before I write anything at all, I must ask you: Tell me, in the name of the Lord God, why haven't you written me in all this time so much as a single line? How could have I expected that? Will you believe me that in my isolation and seclusion I succumbed a number of times to a feeling of genuine despair, thinking that you were no longer of this world? And then I worried nights on end about what would happen to your children, and damned my fate that made it impossible for me to help them. At other times, when I found out for sure that you were alive, I was gripped by anger (but this occurred during the painful hours, which were quite frequent with me), and I bitterly reproached you. But later that, too, passed—I forgave you, tried to think up all sorts of excuses for your behavior and, leaning on the best of them, calmed down, and never once lost faith in you; I knew you loved me and remembered me with affection.

I sent you a letter through the authorities, which you must have received. I waited for your answer but it never came. Did they really bar you from writing me? But even here it is authorized—all the political inmates receive several letters a year. Durov received several letters, and on the numerous occasions when we asked the penal authorities whether we had the right to receive letters, they said we could. I think I've guessed the real reason for your silence. Slow to move as you are, you wouldn't go around to ask the police authorities and, even if you did go, you contented yourself with the first unfavorable answer, which was, perhaps, given you by some official who wasn't even too sure of what he was talking about. This depressed me very much for quite selfish reasons. I thought to myself: If he cannot even manage to do what is necessary to get an authorization to write to me, how can I possibly rely on him to do some really important things for me! Write me an answer to this right away and through official channels, without waiting for some special occasion; and write as fully and in as much detail as possible. I feel now like a slice that has been lopped off from the rest of you; I should like to be grafted back on and become part of you all once again, but I cannot. Les absents ont toujours tort. Must that happen between us, too, then? But don't worry, I have faith in you.

It is now a week since I was released from the hard-labor camp. This letter is being sent to you in absolute secrecy, and you mustn't breathe a word about it. But I shall also send you an official letter through the headquarters of the Siberian Army Corps. You must answer my official letter right away, and wait for the first opportunity to answer this one. But in your official letter, too, you *must* give a highly detailed account of the most important things that have happened to you these last four years. And, for my part, I should be delighted to send you whole volumes; but since I have hardly enough time even for this letter, I shall tell you only about the most important things.

What is the most important? And what, exactly, is it that has been most important to me recently? When you come right down to it, what will probably happen is that I won't tell you a thing about it in this letter. Of course, how can I convey to you what is going on in my head, my idea of things, all I have lived through, the convictions I have gained and the conclusions I have arrived at during all this time? I am not setting out to do that. Such an effort would be quite unthinkable. I hate doing things halfway and to tell you just this or that at random would make no sense whatsoever. However, I shall now describe the essentials to you. Read and make out of it whatever you wish. I am obliged to do this and so I begin my reminiscences.

Do you remember how we parted, my dear, my good, my beloved brother? As soon as you left, they led away the three of us—Durov, Yastrzhembsky, and me—to shackle us with irons. At 12 o'clock sharp, that is, exactly in the first minute of Christmas, I had shackles put on me for the first time. They weighed 10 pounds or so and made walking extremely uncomfortable. Then they put us into open sleighs, each in a separate one with a guard, and so, on 4 sleds, with the state courier in the lead, we left Petersburg. My heart was heavy, and I felt confused and bewildered by a variety of sensations. My heart throbbed, and this made it ache and grieve dully. But the fresh air reinvigorated me and, since one always feels an influx of vitality and energy before every new turn in life, I was in reality very calm, and gazed intently at Petersburg as we drove past the houses, which were brightly lighted on this festive occasion; and I took leave of each of the houses, one by one. We drove past your apartment, and Krayevsky's place was all lit up. You had told me that he had a Christmas tree and that the children had gone over there with Emiliya Fyodorovna, and I felt a cruel pang of sadness as we passed by the house. It was as though I was saying good-bye to the children. I was terribly sorry for them and, years after that, how many were the times I thought of them almost with tears in my eyes. We were going toward Yaroslavl and so, toward morning, after we had passed three or 4 stations, we stopped at daybreak at an inn in Schlüsselburg. We pounced on the tea as though we hadn't eaten for a whole week. After 8 months of confinement, we were so starved after a 60-verst winter drive that it is a pleasure to remember it. I felt very cheerful, Durov chatted without letup, while Yastrzhembsky kept conjuring up awful visions of the future. We were all studying and sizing up our escort officer, and he turned out to be a nice, kind old man, as considerate with us as is possible to imagine; he had been around and seen things, traveled all over Europe as a courier carrying his messages. During the journey, he rendered us many services. His name was Kuzma Prokofevich Prokofev. By the way, he saw to it that we were transferred to covered sleighs, which was very helpful, because at times the cold was terrible. The next day being a holiday, the coachmen who drove us wore gray overcoats made of German cloth with crimson belts, and there was not a soul in the streets of the villages we passed through. It was a most marvelous winter day. They took us through deserted areas, along the Petersburg, Novgorod, and Yaroslavl roads, etc. The little towns along our way were few, and they were not much as towns go. But since we happened to have set out during the holiday time, there was plenty to eat and to drink everywhere. We were awfully cold. We were dressed warmly, but to sit for about 10 hours on end in a sleigh and cover 5 or 6 relays was just about unbearable. I would get frozen through all the way to my heart, and afterward barely managed to get myself warmed up again in the heated rooms. But—a strange thing—during the journey I completely recovered my health. In Perm Province, we had to weather a night when it was forty below. This is an experience I would not recommend to you. Quite unpleasant. The crossing of the Urals was a sad moment. The horses and covered sleighs got stuck in the snow drifts. There was a blizzard. It was night, and we got out and stood around waiting for the men to pull the sleighs free. There was snow all around us; the storm was raging. This was the boundary of Europe—ahead of us was Siberia and our mysterious destiny there, and behind was all our past. I felt sad and broke into tears.

Throughout the entire journey whole villages rushed out to watch us pass and, despite our shackles, we were charged three times the normal prices for refreshments at the stations. But Kuzma Prokofevich took care of about half our bills himself. He did so despite our protestations, and so we paid out only 15 silver rubles each while on the road.

We reached Tobolsk on January 11. There, we were handed over to the authorities, searched, and our money taken away from us. Then Durov, Yastrzhembsky, and I were taken to a special cell, while the others—and that included Speshnev and those who had arrived before us—were confined in another section; and so we hardly ever saw them during our stay there. I should like very much to dwell at some length on our six-day stopover in Tobolsk and on the impression it left on me, but this is not the place for it. I'll only say that from the compassion and deep sympathy we met with there we derived the reward of nearly complete happiness. The deportees of previous years (or their wives, rather than they themselves) looked after us as though we were part of their families. What magnificent souls, tested by 25 years of hardship and self-sacrifice. We only caught glimpses of them, because we were closely guarded. But they passed us food and clothes, consoled us, tried to cheer us up. I had been traveling light and had not even taken my own clothes with me, and regretted it. They even sent me some clothes.

At last we set out again, and three days later we arrived in Omsk. Back in Tobolsk I had obtained some information about our future immediate superiors. The commandant was a very decent man, but Drill Major Krivtsov was a scoundrel such as there are few of, a petty barbarian, a stickler for regulations, a drunk, and everything repulsive one can imagine. The first thing he did was to call Durov and me idiots and promise to subject us to corporal punishment the first time we got out of line. He had already been the major of the prison guard for two years then, and perpetrated the worst injustices. Two years later he was court-martialed and, thank God, I was rid of him. He always used to land on us when drunk (I never saw him sober), pick on some inmate who obviously hadn't had anything to drink, and beat him under the pretext that the man was dead drunk. Another time, while he was making his nightly rounds, he belabored one inmate for sleeping on his right side, another for crying or talking in his sleep—for anything that his drunken head could think up. And this was the sort of man with whom I had to try to live without getting hurt, the sort of man whose job it was to write reports about us and submit evaluations about us to Petersburg every month. I had already made the acquaintance of hard-labor camp elements back in Tobolsk, and in Omsk I prepared myself to live among them for the next four years. They are a coarse, irritated, and embittered lot. Their hatred for the gentry passes all limits, and for this reason they displayed hostility at the sight of us, along with a malicious joy at seeing us in such a sad plight. They would have devoured us if given the chance. But you can imagine for yourself how protected we were when we had to live, sleep, eat, and drink side by side with these people for several years, and when we didn't even have the time to complain about their insults of every shape and description, so numerous were they. "You of the gentry, you've pecked at us enough with your iron beaks. You used to be a gentleman and kick people around, and now you're lower than the lowest of us"—this was the theme played to us over and over again for 4 years. 150 enemies never tired of persecuting us; they enjoyed it, it was an occupation for them, a distraction, and the only way for us to avoid the worst of it was by meeting it with indifference, with a display of moral superiority that they couldn't fail to understand and respect in us, and by refusing to submit to their will. They were always conscious of the fact that we were above them. They had no conception of what crime we could have committed, and we ourselves kept silent about it. So they did not understand us any more than we understood them; and we had to bear the brunt of the desire to avenge, and to torment the gentry, by which these people breathe and live. Our life was very difficult. The military forced-labor camps are tougher than the civilian. I spent the entire four years within the confines of the penitentiary, behind walls, except when I was sent out to work. Although the work was not always unbearably hard, there were times in rough weather, on humid days, when the mud was deep, or in winter when the cold was excruciating, when I felt I was at the end of my strength. Once I spent four hours doing some emergency work when the mercury froze and it was perhaps 40 degrees below zero. My foot got frostbitten on that occasion.

We lived in a heap, all of us, in one barracks. Picture to yourself an old, ramshackle, wooden structure that should have been torn down long ago and that was no longer inhabitable. In the summer it was stuffy beyond description, in winter unbearably cold. All the floors were rotted through and covered with an inch-thick layer of filth, on which we slipped and fell. The windows, small as they were, would get so thickly covered with hoar frost that it was almost impossible to read even in the daytime. There was as much as an inch of ice on the glass. The ceiling dripped—there were cracks clean through it. And we were crowded in there like herring in a barrel.

They would light the stove and put half a dozen logs into it, but that didn't make it any warmer (the ice in the room would hardly even melt); the place got so full of smoke that it was hardly bearable—and so it went, the whole winter long. In that very barracks room the inmates did their laundry, splashing water all over the place. There wasn't room to turn around in. We couldn't go out to the latrines between dusk and dawn because the barracks was locked then; so during those hours a tub was placed by the door, and the stench was unspeakable. All the inmates reeked like pigs, and they would say: "A man can't help acting like a pig," since, as they put it, "he's alive, after all."

We slept on bare boards and were allowed only one pillow. We had only our half-length sheepskins to cover us, so our legs were exposed all night. All night we shivered. There were fleas and lice and cockroaches by the bucketful. In winter we wore ragged half-length sheepskins that gave us almost no warmth, and short boots—and that is how we had to go out in below-freezing temperatures. Our fare consisted of bread and cabbage soup, in which there was supposed to be 1/4 pound of beef per man; but they used chopped meat, and I never saw any of it. On holidays there was hardly any fat in our gruel, and during Lent we had hardly anything besides cabbage in water. I had terrible diarrhea, and several times was seriously ill. Judge for yourself whether it was possible to stay alive without money. Well, I can tell you that if I hadn't had any, I should certainly have died—no inmate could have stood the life. In fact, everyone worked, selling something to make himself a kopek. So I had my tea and a piece of meat to eat now and then, and that is what saved me. It was also impossible to do without some tobacco to smoke; otherwise you would have suffocated in that foul air. But it all had to be done on the sly.

Often I lay sick in the hospital. My unstrung nerves gave rise to epileptic attacks, although they were fairly rare. I am still troubled by rheumatism in my legs. Apart from that, I feel in quite good health. Add to all these niceties the fact that it was virtually impossible to get hold of a book and that, if you did, you could read it only on the sly; that you lived in the midst of relentless quarrels and hostility, foul abuse, shouting, noise, and din; that you were always under guard, never by yourself, and all that for four years without letup—well, one should really be excused for saying that it was bad. All of that, plus the awareness that at any moment you were answerable for the breach of some rule, the shackles, and the complete crushing of the spirit, gives you a picture of my daily life there. I shall not tell you what has happened to my soul, my beliefs, my intelligence, and my heart in these four years. It would be too long to tell. But the constant communion with my inner self, in which I took refuge from bitter reality, bore fruit. I now have many needs and hopes such as I had never thought of before. But I suppose this sounds mysterious, so let's drop it. One thing, though—don't forget me, and help me out. I must have books and money. Send me some, in the name of Christ.

Omsk is a nasty little town. It has hardly any trees. In summer there are scorching heat and winds loaded with sand, in winter—snowstorms. I haven't seen the countryside yet. The town itself is a grimy garrison town, debauched to the last degree. I am speaking about the uneducated masses. If I hadn't found some nice people here, I should have perished altogether. K. I. I—v treated me like his own brother. He did everything within his power to help me. I owe him some money. If you happen to see him in Petersburg, thank him. I owe him about 25 silver rubles. But how can I ever repay him for his hospitality, his constant readiness to respond to every request I might make, and for the care and concern he showed me, as though I were his own brother? And he was not the only one! There are very many noble people in the world, brother!

As I have already written you, your silence sometimes tortured me. Thank you for sending me money. Write me as fully as possible about everything to do with you in your very first letter (even if you send it through regular channels, because I am still not certain whether I am allowed to communicate with you). Write about Emiliya Fyodorovna, the children, about all our friends and relatives, about our Moscow family, let me know who is dead and who is still alive; tell me how your business is going and what capital you used to get started, whether it has been profitable, whether you have made something; and finally, whether you'll be able to help me out with money and how much you'll be able to send me every year. But don't send me any money in the official letter unless I fail to find myself another address. In the meantime, send it as from *Mikhail Petrovich* (you know what I mean). I still have some money, but no books. If you can, send me some magazines of the current year—*Notes of the Fatherland*, for instance. But here is something that is essential: I need (and need badly) historians of the ancient period (in French translation), and the new economists (Vico, Guizot, Thierry, Thiers, Ranke, and so forth), and the Church Fathers. Pick the cheapest and most compact editions. Send them right away. I am being sent to Semipalatinsk, which is almost all the way out in the Kirghiz Steppe. I shall send you my address later. In any case, here it is: *Private* [Dostoyevsky], *7th Battalion of the Siberian Regiment of the Line, Semipalatinsk.* Use this official address for letters. For the books I'll give you another. And in the meantime write as from Mikhail Petrovich. But understand—the book I need first of all is a German dictionary.

I don't know what there is in store for me in Semipalatinsk. And I am quite unconcerned about it, too. But here is something I am concerned about: get busy on my case; get someone to intercede for me. Find out whether it couldn't be arranged for me to be transferred to the Caucasus in a year or two—at least that's Russia! This is my fervent wish—do your utmost, in the name of Christ! Brother, don't forget me. Here I am writing to you and making disposition of everything, even of what you own. But my faith in you has not been extinguished. You are my brother, and you love me. I need money—I must live, brother. *These years will not be spent fruitlessly.* I need money and books. Whatever you spend on me will not be lost. You won't be despoiling your children if you give it to me. I'll make it up to them handsomely, if only I remain alive. Why, they are sure to allow me to publish in six years or so, and possibly even before that. You know many things can change, and now I won't write any trash. You'll hear of me.

We'll see each other very soon, brother. I'm as sure of it as I am of two times two. The outlook is bright. I see clearly before me my entire future and all the things I shall accomplish. I am satisfied with my life. There is only one thing to fear—men and their arbitrariness. If I fall into the hands of a superior who takes a dislike to me (and there are such people), he can find fault and spell my doom, or kill me with heavy work, and I am physically so weak as to be quite incapable of bearing all the hardships of a soldier's life. To cheer me up, people tell me, "Why, you'll meet nothing but simple folk there."

Yes, but I'm more apprehensive of a simple man than of a complicated one. Still, wherever they are, people are people. Even in penal servitude I learned, in those four years, to discern the human beings among the bandits. Believe me, there are profound, strong, beautiful natures among them, and what a pleasure it was to find gold under the rough cover. And I didn't find just one or two instances, but several of them. Some you cannot fail to respect, and others are positively admirable. There was a young Circassian (sent there for robbery) whom I taught to speak and write Russian. You should have seen all the marks of gratitude he showed me. Another inmate cried when he said good-bye to me on leaving. I had given him some money— but how much could it have been? Yet his gratitude was limitless. And this in spite of the fact that, my character having turned bad, I had often been ill-tempered and impatient with him. They respected my state of mind and bore everything uncomplainingly. A propos: how many types of the common people and characters did I carry away with me from the prison camp! I lived together with them, and so I think I know them quite well. I have heard so many stories of vagabonds and robbers and, in general, of their joyless and miserable lives. There's enough for volumes and volumes. What a wonderful people! On the whole, my time hasn't been wasted. I may not have seen Russia, but I got to know the Russian people well, as well, perhaps, as few know them. Well, this is a touch of vanity on my part, but I hope it is forgivable.

Brother, be sure to write me about the most important happenings in your life. Address your letters officially to *Semipalatinsk* and unofficially to you know where. Write about all our Petersburg acquaintances, write of literature (as specifically as possible) and, finally, write about our Muscovites. What is our brother Kolya doing? How is (and this is the most important) our little sister Sashenka? Is our uncle still alive? And how is our brother Andrei? I am writing to Auntie through our sister Verochka—I am taking advantage of a special opportunity to do so. That letter is being sent in secret. And, for heaven's sake, keep this letter a secret, too, and even burn it—don't endanger other people.

Don't forget to send me the books, my dear friend, above all, the historians, the economists, *Notes of the Fatherland,* the Church Fathers, and the history of the church. Send them at different times, but start sending them right away. I seem to be treating your pocket as if it were my own, but that's because I don't know what your financial situation is. Write me about that to give me a more accurate idea of how things stand. But understand, brother, that books mean life; they are my food and my future! So, in the name of God, don't forsake me. Please! Find out whether you can get permission to send me books officially. Still, you'd better be careful about it. If it is officially authorized, then send them. If not, send them through the brother of K. I., addressed to him, and they will be forwarded to me. But K. I. will be in Petersburg himself this year, he will tell you about everything. What a family he has! What a wife! She is a young lady, the daughter of the Decembrist Annenkov. What a heart, what a spirit, and how much they have had to bear!

I shall try to find you another address in Semipalatinsk where I am going in a week. I am still not quite well, and that is why my departure has been delayed for a while. Send me Carus, Kant's *Critique de raison pure* [*sic*] and, if there is any way of doing so unofficially, send me Hegel without fail, especially Hegel's *History of Philosophy*. My whole future is linked with it! But, in the name of God, do your best and petition them to transfer me to the Caucasus. Also, find out from people in the know whether there isn't some way for me to obtain permission to publish, and how one must go about it. I shall petition in two or three years. Until then, please feed me. Without money, soldiering will crush me. So don't fail! What about our other relatives? Don't you think they could help me out, if only to get me started? In that case, let them give you the money and you send it on to me. But in my letters to Auntie and Verochka, I didn't ask them for money. They'll guess by themselves if their hearts prompt them.

As he was leaving for Sevastopol, Filipov [*sic*] made a gift to me of 25 silver rubles. He left them with Commandant Nabokov and thus I didn't know anything about it. He thought I would be without money. He's such a kind soul. All our exiles manage to keep alive. Tol [*sic*] has finished his stretch in the prison camp; he is in Tomsk now and getting along quite well. Yastrzhembsky is finishing out his time in Tara. Speshnev is in Irkutsk Province, where he has gained the love and respect of everyone. This man's fate is extraordinary! Wherever and whenever he appears, the most spontaneous, the most unapproachable people surround him at once with veneration and respect. Petrashevsky still lacks common sense, as he always did. Mombelli and Lvov are in good health, and poor Grigorev has gone completely out of his mind and is in the hospital.

And what about yourself? Do you still see Mme Pleshcheyeva? How is her son? From exiles who were passing through here, I heard that he was in the *Orsk* Fortress, and Golovinsky has been in the Caucasus for a long time now. And what are you doing for literature, and how is literature treating you? Are you writing something? How is Krayevsky, and how are your relations with him? I don't think much of Ostrovsky, I haven't read any Pisemsky at all, and Druzhinin turns my stomach. Yevgeniya Tur aroused my enthusiastic admiration. I like Krestovsky, too.

I should have liked to write much more to you, but so much time has passed that I find myself having difficulty even with this letter. But we cannot, after all, have changed so much in the way we feel toward each other. Kiss the children. Do they still remember their Uncle Fedya? Give my regards to all our friends, but keep this letter strictly secret. Farewell, farewell, my dear fellow! You will hear about me, and maybe you will see me. Yes, we shall surely see each other. Farewell. Read carefully everything I have written. Write more often (even if only officially). I hug you and your whole family innumerable times.

Yours.

P.S. Did you receive my "Child's Fairy Tale" that I wrote in the Fortress? If you have it, don't do anything with it and don't show it to anyone. Who is this Chernov who wrote "The Double" in 1850?

Good-bye! Yours,

Dostoyevsky

February 22

I am almost sure that I shall be leaving tomorrow for Semipalatinsk. K. I. will remain here until May. If you do want to send me something—books, for example—I think that you can still send them, still addressing them to Mikhail Petrovich.

Perhaps I shall be able to give you another address (a non-official one) for Semipalatinsk. But be sure to write me as quickly and as often as you can officially. And, for God's sake, get busy on my case. Wouldn't it be possible for me to get to the Caucasus, or someplace outside of Siberia? Now I shall write novels and dramas, and I also have lots and lots of reading to do. So don't forget me, and, once again, good-bye.

Kiss all the children, yours,
Good-bye.

---

19. So far as is known, this letter is the first that Dostoyevsky wrote after his release from penal servitude on February 15, 1854. As part of his sentence, he was then required to serve as a private in the Seventh Line Battalion of the Siberian Army, stationed at Semipalatinsk (which he regularly misspelled as Semipolatinsk). He remained there until 1859, carrying on an active correspondence in two channels: an "official" one through the army, where the mail was censored, and an "unofficial" or secret one through various civilian acquaintances. Most of his letters to Mikhail were sent the second way.

In the letter, he mentions other members of the Petrashevsky circle, all of whom were sentenced to death along with him, had their sentences commuted to a period of hard labor, and (unlike Dostoyevsky) were granted amnesty in 1856. Ivan-Ferdinand Lvovich Yastrzhembsky (1814–1880s?) had taught political economy at institutions of technical higher education. Nikolai Aleksandrovich Speshnev (1821–1882) was one of the most radical members of the group. After the amnesty, he was assigned to forced residence in Siberia, where he edited the *Irkutsk Province Gazette* (Irkutskiye gubernskiye vedomosti). A man of strong will and great charm, he treated the other members of the circle with a shade of superiority. He made a deep impression on Dostoyevsky, who almost certainly used him as one source for the portrayal of Stavrogin in *The Devils*. Pavel Nikolayevich Filippov (1825–1855) was especially identified with the program of distributing articles on social problems; it was probably his idea to establish a secret printing press. He served his sentence not in Sevastopol but in Izmail; later, he served in the army and died of wounds received during the Crimean War. Feliks Gustavovich Toll (1823–1867) had taught Russian literature at the engineering school that Dostoyevsky had attended. He was assigned to forced residence in Tomsk, where he became friends with Mikhail Bakunin and produced a three-volume dictionary that was published between 1863 and 1866. Mikhail Vasilevich Butashevich-Petrashevsky (1821–1866) was the circle's founder. His orientation, influenced by Fourier and Feuerbach, was rationalist and positivist, rejecting nationalism, religion, and morality. It was a speech of his that drew the attention of the tsarist police to the group's Friday gatherings and led to the arrests. After the amnesty, he was assigned to forced residence in Irkutsk, where he was allowed to practice his profession as a lawyer. Nikolai Aleksandrovich Mombelli (1823–1891) had been a lieutenant in the Moscow Imperial Guards Regiment. After the amnesty, he served in the army in the Caucasus. Fyodor Nikolayevich Lvov (1823–1885) was trained as a chemist but had also been an officer in the Moscow Imperial Guards Regiment. He returned to European Russia in 1862, became secretary of the Russian Technical Society, and represented it at exhibitions in London and Brussels. Nikolai

Petrovich Grigorev (1822–1886) was a lieutenant in the Imperial Grenadier Guards. The mock execution triggered a mental disorder, and after the amnesty he was turned over to the care of his family in Nizhny Novgorod (now Gorky). Vasily Andreyevich Golovinsky (b. 1829) was a lawyer; he stood out in the group for his vehemence in advocating the emancipation of the serfs. He later entered government service in Simbirsk (now Ulyanovsk) and resumed the practice of the law.

"The deportees of previous years" were the Decembrists. Dostoyevsky later wrote about the meeting of the Petrashevtsy with the Decembrists' wives in *Diary of a Writer.*

The "very decent man" who was commandant of the Omsk prison was Major General de Gravé; he and Dostoyevsky became quite friendly, and he sometimes entertained Dostoyevsky at his home. Drill Major Krivtsov is portrayed in *House of the Dead* as a vicious and slovenly man.

"K. I. I—v" was Konstantin Ivanovich Ivanov (d. 1867), son-in-law of the Decembrist Annenkov (see below). He graduated from an engineering school, possibly the same one Dostoyevsky attended, and he then entered the army engineering corps. He served in western Siberia, perhaps in Omsk, and then was transferred to Petersburg, where he became adjutant to the inspector general of army engineers. He was in special favor with Eduard Ivanovich Totleben (see note to Letter 24), who was primarily responsible for bringing about the alleviation of Dostoyevsky's situation in Siberia.

Mikhail's business was a cigarette factory, which was doing well at the time. "Mikhail Petrovich" was a fictitious name used as a code between the two brothers.

Giovanni Battista Vico (1688–1744) was an Italian philosopher. François Guizot (1787–1874), Augustin Thierry (1795–1856), Adolphe Thiers (1797–1877), and Leopold von Ranke (1795–1886) were historians.

The "young Circassian" was Alei, who had been convicted of taking part, with his older brothers, in the robbery and murder of an Armenian merchant and his bodyguards. Dostoyevsky taught him to read Russian from the New Testament, and in *House of the Dead* he wrote that, although Alei was a Moslem, he had been strongly moved by the teachings of Jesus.

The inmate who cried when saying good-bye to Dostoyevsky is described in *House of the Dead* under the name of Sushilov; the leave-taking scene is in the last chapter.

Ivan Aleksandrovich Annenkov (1802–1874) was a Decembrist who had been sentenced to twenty years at hard labor for his part in that plot. He served his sentence in Chita and Tobolsk, where he remained until the 1856 amnesty. His daughter Olga was the wife of K. I. Ivanov.

Karl-Gustav Carus (1789–1869) was a German physician and philosopher, a follower of Schelling and Schopenbauer, and the author of *Psyche* (1846).

Ivan Aleksandrovich Nabokov (1787–1852) was the chairman of the committee that investigated the Petrashevsky affair. Most of the members of the group described him as a kind and compassionate man. In 1848 he was appointed a member of the Military Council and made commandant of the Peter-and-Paul Fortress.

Mme Pleshcheyeva was the mother of Aleksei Nikolayevich Pleshcheyev.

Aleksandr Vasilevich Druzhinin (1824–1864) was regarded for some time as

Russia's outstanding literary critic. He was a frequent contributor to the *Contemporary* and then wrote a regular column in the *Petersburg Gazette,* which he transferred to *A Library for Reading* upon becoming editor of that magazine in 1856.

For identification of Ostrovsky, Pisemsky, Yevgeniya Tur, and Krestovsky, see note to Letter 23.

The "Fortress" in which Dostoyevsky had written "A Child's Fairy Tale" was the Peter-and-Paul Fortress, where he had been held after his arrest in 1849.

Aleksandr Chernov was the pen name of Nikolai D. Akhsharumov. His short story, "The Double" (Dvoinik), was published in *Notes of the Fatherland* in 1859.

20. To N. D. Fonvizina
[Omsk, February 15–March 2, 1854]

At last, most gracious N. D., I am writing to you just after having left my former place of residence. The last time I wrote you I was sick in body and soul. I was devoured by gloom, and I believe I sent you a very confused letter indeed. My long and humdrum existence, both physically and morally oppressive, broke me down. At such moments I always feel too sad to write letters; and to thrust your sadness upon others then, even upon people very sympathetic toward you, is, I think, cowardly. Since I have a special opportunity to send this letter to you, I am as pleased as can be to have this chance to talk to you, the more so as I have been assigned to the Seventh Battalion in Semipalatinsk and, for that reason, don't yet know what the possibilities will be of writing you from there or receiving letters from you.

Quite some time ago you wrote me about my brother. At that time I prepared a letter for you, as well as one for my brother (enclosed in yours); but I didn't dare send it off, and I believe I did the right thing. I looked over all the addresses you gave in your letter to S. D., and I'll note them down for future reference. They may be reliable; however, your last letter arrived unsealed, and so we should take every precaution. So if it should be my pleasure to hear from you, it would be best to address your letters to my brother in Petersburg, or possibly (although this is by no means sure) he will see you in person in Petersburg or, perhaps, send someone to you who can be trusted. My brother now has a business, and so I suppose you could find his address quite easily—from the advertisements, for instance. I myself don't have his address. But, anyway, I wouldn't advise you to rely on the postal services. Since I can assume you do know persons traveling between Moscow and Petersburg, this would be the best way of getting a letter for me to him. Under this arrangement I shall be dealing only with my brother; it is much better under the circumstances to be in contact with one person than with two. It is safer. But, of course, if you can find some other foolproof way of reaching me, that will be fine, even preferable, since I still don't know myself how I shall write to my brother. I am basing myself on him only because, whomever else I write to, I shall certainly communicate with him. Moreover, you live in Marino, which is on the usual road from Moscow to our village in Tula Province. I have driven back and forth over that road at least twenty times, and so I can clearly picture for myself the place of your refuge or, to be more accurate, of your new confinement. With what delight do I read your letters, my most precious N. D.! Your letters are superb or, rather, I would say, they come straight from your kind, humane heart, easily and without any pretense. There are secretive, bilious natures rarely capable of experiencing the goodness of a brief moment of expansiveness. I know people like that. And still, they are not bad people by any means, even quite the contrary.

I am not sure, but your letter gives me the impression that you felt sadness upon returning to your native land. I understand that, for it has occurred to me several times that, if I ever return home, there will be more of pain in my impressions than joy. I have not lived your life, and there are many things in it that I know nothing of, for no one can know another person's life. However, human feeling is common to us all, and I believe that when an exile returns to his homeland he is bound to live his old sorrows all over again in his memory and his imagination. It is like a weighing machine—it weighs and tells you the true weight of what you have suffered, borne, and lost, and what the good people of this world have deprived you of. But may God grant you many, many years to come. I have heard from many, N. D., that you are a very religious woman. And not because you ate religious, but because I myself have experienced and felt it, I shall tell you that at such a time one thirsts for faith as "the withered grass" thirsts for water, and one actually finds it, because in misfortune the truth shines through. I can tell you about myself that I am a child of this century, a child of doubt and disbelief, I have always been and shall ever be (that I know), until they close the lid of my coffin. What terrible torment this thirst to believe has cost me and is still costing me, and the stronger it becomes in my soul, the stronger are the arguments against it. And, despite all this, God sends me moments of great tranquility, moments during which I love and find I am loved by others; and it was during such a moment that I formed within myself a symbol of faith in which all is clear and sacred for me. This symbol is very simple, and here is what it is: to believe that there is nothing more beautiful, more profound, more sympathetic, more reasonable, more courageous, and more perfect than Christ; and there not only isn't, but I tell myself with a jealous love, there cannot be. More than that—if someone succeeded in proving to me that Christ was ouside the truth, and if, *indeed,* the truth was outside Christ, I would sooner remain with Christ than with the truth.

But it is better to stop talking about this. Why is it, though, that certain topics of conversation are completely banned in society and, if they are broached, someone or other gives the impression of being shocked?

But let us leave that. I heard that you wish to go somewhere south? May it be God's will that you be granted the necessary permission. But when, please tell me, when will we be completely free, at least as free as other people are? Or will it only be when there is no longer any need to be free? As to me, I want either the best or nothing at all. In a soldier's uniform I am just as much a prisoner as I was before. And how happy I am that I still find in my soul enough patience to last me a long time, that I am not desirous of worldly blessings, and that all I need is books and the opportunity to write and to be alone every day for a few hours. It is this last point that worries me very much. Soon, it will be five years that I have been living under surveillance, in a crowd of men, never alone for a single hour. To be alone is a natural need, just like drinking and eating; otherwise, with this communism forced on him, man comes to hate mankind. The company of men becomes poison and contamination, and it was this unbearable scourge that made me suffer most of all during those four years. There were moments when I hated every man I met, whether innocent or guilty, and I regarded all of them as thieves who were stealing my life from me with impunity. There is no misfortune more abhorrent than when you yourself become unjust, evil, and wicked; you may realize it, even reproach yourself for it, but you are powerless to do anything about it. I have experienced that. But I am sure that God spared you from that. I think that you, as a woman, possessed much more fortitude, which enabled you to bear and to forgive.

Write me something, N. D. I am leaving for the wilds, deep into Asia, and once in Semipalatinsk, I think I'll be able to slough off for good all my impressions and memories, because I shall be leaving behind the last people whom I loved and who loomed before me like the shadows of bygone days. It is terrible, after I've acclimated myself, how attached I become to whatever is around me and how much it hurts me when I must tear myself away from it.

Live on, N. D., live a happy and long life! When we meet again we shall get to know one another again, and there may yet be many happy days in store for each of us.

I am living these days in a strange state of expectation; I feel as if I am still ill now, and I am under the impression that very soon, at any moment now, something very decisive is going to happen to me, that I am approaching the critical point of my whole life, that I have, as it were, matured for something or other, and that something, perhaps quiet and bright, perhaps dreadful but nonetheless inevitable, is about to happen. If it doesn't, my life will be wasted. But perhaps all this is nothing but the delirium of a sick man.

Farewell, farewell, N. D., or perhaps I should say, until we meet again, for let us trust that we shall meet again!

Yours, D.

In the name of the Lord our God, forgive me for sending you such messy, scribbled-over letters! But for the life of me, I cannot write without crossing out. Please don't hold it against me.

---

20. Natalya Dmitriyevna Fonvizina (1805–1869), née Apukhtina, was the wife of Mikhail Aleksandrovich Fonvizin. He had been arrested and exiled to Siberia for his part in the Decembrist plot; she followed him there and lived in Siberia for the twenty-five years of his sentence, during which time all her children died. She was one of the Decembrist wives who had treated the Petrashevtsy so kindly in the transit prison at Tobolsk. In *Diary of a Writer*, Dostoyevsky speaks of her as one of those women who had "sacrificed everything for a sublime moral duty, the freest duty that can exist." In 1853, she and her husband were allowed to return to European Russia, on condition that they not reside in an urban area; they settled in the village of Marino, about thirty miles from Moscow. Her husband became ill and died there the year after their arrival, which presumably accounts for the sadness of her letter.

"S. D." is Sergei Durov.

The potential antithesis between faith and truth that Dostoyevsky presents here reappears in *The Devils*.

21. To M. D. Isayeva
Semipalatinsk, June 4, 1855

I am infinitely grateful to you for your nice letter, written while you were on your journey, my dear and unforgettable friend, Mariya Dmitriyevna. I hope that you and Aleksandr Ivanovich will allow me to think of you both as my friends now. Indeed, we were friends here, and I hope we shall remain such. How could separation change us? It will not, judging by the strength of my attachment for you and how miserable I feel without you, my dear friends— Imagine, this is already the second letter I am writing to you. My answer to your kind, heartfelt letter was all ready to leave with the last mail, Mariya Dmitriyevna, but it didn't go out. Aleksandr Yegorych, with whom I wanted to send it to the post office, suddenly left for Zmiyev last Saturday, unbeknownst to me, and I found out about his departure only on Sunday. His servant also vanished for two days, and so the letter has remained in my pocket all this time. Such a pity! And as I write now, I am still uncertain whether I'll be able to send off this present letter. Al[eksandr] Yeg[orych] still isn't here, but they have sent a special messenger to get him.

We are expecting at any moment the visit of the governor general who, for all I know, may have arrived at this very minute. I understand he intends to remain here for five days. But enough of that. Tell me, rather, how you arrived in Kuznetsk and whether, God forbid, anything untoward happened during your journey. You wrote that you were upset and even felt ill. I am still terribly worried about you. Moving from one town to another in itself involves so much bother and unavoidable inconvenience, and when there is illness on top of it all, it becomes positively unbearable! I think of you all the time. Besides, you know what a worrier I am, so you can imagine my anxiety. My God, this fate, these trials and tribulations, and petty annoyances—is that what you deserve, you who could be the adornment of any society! Accursed fate! I am waiting impatiently for a letter from you. Ah, if only it would come with this mail; I went to find out, but Al. Yeg. still isn't here.

You write that you wonder how I am spending my time and that you don't know how I have organized the hours without you. Well, for two weeks now, I've been so sad that I don't know what to do with myself. If only you knew how bereaved I feel here now! Indeed, I feel these days very much the way I felt in 1849 when they arrested me for the first time and buried me in prison, after tearing me away from all that was near and dear to me. I became so accustomed to you. I never considered our acquaintance as just an ordinary one and now, having been deprived of you, I have to understand a great deal. For five years I literally lived alone, without having anyone to whom I could unburden my heart. And then you accepted me as one of your family. I remember feeling thoroughly at home in your house. Aleksandr Ivanovich could not have looked after his own brother better than he looked after me. I caused you so much unpleasantness because of my difficult character and, notwithstanding, you both loved me. And I do understand and appreciate it because, after all, even I have a heart. And you, you are a marvelous woman, your heart is full of marvelous childlike goodness, you were a true sister to me. The fact that a woman had offered me a helping hand was in itself a whole event in my life. The best man is, at certain moments, if you will allow me to say so, nothing but a stubborn fool. But a woman's heart, her compassion, her solicitude, her infinite kindness, such as we have no conception of and which, out of our stupidity, we often fail to notice, is irreplaceable. All that I discovered in you; my own sister could not have been kinder to me or more tolerant of my faults than you were. So that, even if there were flare-ups between us, it was, in the first place, because I was an ungrateful pig and, in the second, because you yourself were sick, irritated, and embittered over not being appreciated and understood by a society that is rotten, and a person of your energy cannot fail to become indignant at an injustice; that is noble and honorable. All this lies deep down in your character, but life and its sorrows have, of course, exaggerated and exacerbated some of these features in you; but, my God, you have enough in you to make up for it a hundredfold! And since I am not stupid all the time, I noticed and appreciated it. In brief, I couldn't help becoming attached to your household with all my heart, as if it were my own. I will never forget you two and will always be grateful to you. For I am convinced that neither of you understands what you have done for me and how much I needed people like you. You can't understand what I mean unless you've experienced it. If it hadn't been for you, I might have thoroughly petrified, but now I am a man once again. But enough of that; it cannot possibly be conveyed in a letter. A letter is an accursed thing, if only because it reminds one of separation, and in my case, everything reminds me of it.

In the evenings, at twilight, during those hours when I used to make my way to your house, an awful sadness comes over me; if tears were easy for me, I would weep, and you would probably laugh at me for it. My heart has always been that way—it grows onto things that are dear to it, so that when the time comes for me to tear it away from them, it bleeds.

Now I am completely alone; I have absolutely nowhere to go; I am fed up with everything here. Such emptiness! There's only Al. Yegorych left, but his presence is painful to me if only because I cannot help comparing his company with yours, and you can easily guess what the result is. And, besides, he is not even at home. In his absence, I went a few times to the Cossack Gardens, where he had moved, and it was so sad. When I recall last summer and remember how you, poor thing, were longing to go for a drive somewhere out of town to get a breath of fresh air, but couldn't, I feel so sorry for you and so bad about it. But do you remember once when we did succeed in driving out to the Cossack Gardens—you, Alek[sandr] Ivan[ovich], I, and Yelena. How vividly I recalled everything when I was in the gardens this time. Nothing was changed there, and there was the bench, the same one on which we sat— Ah, it was so very sad.

You write that I should move in with Wrangel, but I don't want to, for a number of important reasons. (1) *Money*. Living with him I should obviously have to spend more for lodgings, servants, and food, and it would be unpleasant for me to live at his expense. (2) My character. (3) His character. (4) I have noticed that people often come over to his place and hang around, lots of people. It would sometimes be impossible for me to avoid their company, and I cannot stand people I don't know. Finally, I like to be alone, I have become used to it, and habit is a second nature. But enough of that, I've told you scarcely anything yet. After I had seen you off as far as the forest and said good-bye under that pine tree (which I marked with a notch), I walked back with Wrangel arm-in-arm (he led his horse by the bridle) to the hospitable farmstead of the Peshekhonovs. And it was at this point that I felt so utterly forlorn. At first, we could still see your carriage, then we could only hear it and, finally, it was gone for good. We set out in our drozhky and

72

talked about you and how you would get to your destination. Mostly we spoke about you, Mariya Dmitriyevna, and then Wrangel quite casually told me something that made me very happy.

On the morning of the very day you left, Pyotr Mikhailovich had invited Wrangel somewhere for the whole evening. Wrangel said he couldn't come and, when asked why, explained that he was seeing the Isayevs off. There were some other people present. At once P. M. asked: "But didn't they say that you've only recently become acquainted?" Wrangel answered rather sharply that, although he hadn't known you for a very long time, yours was one of the houses in which he felt most comfortable and that the mistress of that house, i.e. you, was a woman such as he had never met in Petersburg and, indeed, did not expect to meet, a woman, he added, "such as you have probably never met and whom I consider it the greatest honor to know." I was very pleased with Wrangel's story. He is a man who certainly has met women of the highest society (for he was born into it) and has, I dare say, the right to speak out with authority on such matters.

Talking of these things and saying nasty things about the Peshekhonovs, we reached the town just before daybreak, and the coachman, to whom we had forgotten to give instructions, drove directly to my place. Thus, the tea that had been planned was out, and I was very pleased about it because I was terribly anxious to be alone. At home, it was a long time before I could get to sleep. I walked up and down my room, watched the sun come up, and called to mind the whole year that had passed so unnoticeably for me. I remembered everything, just everything, and as I thought about my fate, I felt very sad.

And ever since that day I have been roaming about aimlessly, a real Wandering Jew. I go practically nowhere. I am sick of it. I did go and see Grinenko, who has been assigned to Kopal and is leaving one of these days (he will also be in Verny); I saw Meder, who finds that I have lost weight; I went to Zhunechka (to congratulate her on her name day), and I met the Peshekhonovs there and had a chat with them; I sometimes visit Belikhov; and finally, I go to the camp for exercises. Now and then my health lets me down. I waited with great impatience for the Tartar coachmen. I went over and over again to see Ordynsky, and every evening Sivochka ran over to see whether there was any news. I went over to your apartment and picked up the ivy (it is at my place now); I saw poor abandoned Surka there—she rushed to greet me on all fours but she would not leave the house. At last the coachmen returned and I got the letter, for which I thank you endless times; it brought me great joy. I asked the Tartars about you and they told me many things. How they praised you (everyone praises you, Mariya Dmitriyevna)! I gave them some money. Next day I saw Koptev at Wrangel's. He also told me about your trip, but I couldn't very well ask him about what really interested me most—about the money to pay for your journey—it is a rather ticklish matter. I still can't imagine how you got to your destination!

What a nice letter you wrote me, Mariya Dmitriyevna! It was just the sort of letter I was hoping for—full of details, so keep it up in the future. I can picture your grandmother. Ah, the wretched old woman! She'll be the death of you yet. Let her stay alone with her lap dogs "unto her dying day." I hope that Aleksandr Ivanovich will manage to drag that will out of her without having to take her in to live with you. You must convince her that this will be far the best. Otherwise, she will have to sign a promissory note that she will die in three months (1000 rubles for each month), or don't accept the deal. For I just cannot imagine you having to look after those lap dogs of hers, Mariya Dmitriyevna, especially with your delicate health. These old women are really impossible! I read your letter aloud to Wrangel (just excerpts, of course). I could not restrain myself and went to see Yelena—she was all alone, the poor thing.

I was so sorry to hear that you didn't feel well during the journey. I can hardly wait for your next letter! I am terribly worried. How did you get there? My very best regards and love to Aleksandr Ivanovich. I hope he will write to me soon. Give him a strong hug for me, and tell him that, as a friend and a brother, I hope he will find better company there. I cannot imagine that in Kuznetsk he will be as little discriminating about people as he was in Semipalatinsk. Were such people really worth having anything to do with, eating and drinking with them, and putting up with all sorts of filth from them? Knowing them is just like deliberately inflicting harm on oneself! They are so revolting and, above all, it is all so sordid! After spending some time with a certain type of person, one feels just as dirtied as after drinking in a low joint. I hope Aleksandr Ivanovich won't be angry with me for my wishes.

Farewell, my unforgettable Mariya Dmitriyevna! Farewell! But I hope we shall meet again, shan't we? Write to me more often and at great length, write about Kuznetsk, about your new acquaintances, and as much as you can about yourself. Kiss Pasha for me. I am sure he was naughty during the journey! Good-bye, good-bye! I cannot believe that we shall not meet again.

Yours,
Dostoyevsky

---

21. Aleksandr Ivanovich was Mariya Dmitriyevna's husband.

Aleksandr Yegorych is Wrangel; Dostoyevsky asked him to send the letter for him because he was avoiding direct contact with relatives and friends living in European Russia.

The governor general of Western Siberia was Gustav Khristianovich Gasfort (1794–1874).

Cossack Gardens was a suburb of Semipalatinsk where some of the inhabitants of the town had summer houses. Dostoyevsky spent the summer of 1855 there with Wrangel.

Pyotr Mikhailovich Peshekhonov was a judge in Semipalatinsk.

Belikhov was the commanding officer of the battalion in which Dostoyevsky served while stationed at Semipalatinsk. It was in his house that Dostoyevsky met the Isayevs. Of humble origin, Belikhov had been promoted from the ranks and was informal with everyone and always slightly drunk, though Wrangel described him as a kind man. He shot himself after having embezzled government funds.

Ordynsky was the battalion paymaster. He had been transferred to Siberia for committing some impropriety, and Wrangel described him as "a repulsive person, almost permanently drunk." However, Dostoyevsky saw him quite often, sometimes spending whole days at his place.

The money for the Isayevs' trip to Kuznetsk (now Novokuznetsk) was "a rather ticklish matter" because it had been borrowed from Wrangel.

22. To M. M. Dostoyevsky
Semipalatinsk, January 13, 1856

I am taking advantage of an opportunity to write to you, my friend. Since last year, when I sent you a letter through M. M. Kh., I have been unable to find another such occasion until now. And now it has presented itself. I must say that last year you repaid me rather poorly for my long letter—you didn't answer much, not even the questions which I expected you to reply to at great length. I don't know what stopped you. Was it laziness? But that would be quite inappropriate under the circumstances. Was it your business? But as I wrote you earlier—I shall never believe that there is any business that leaves a man without a minute to spare. Caution? But if I myself am writing you, there is certainly nothing for you to fear. I hope that this time you will write a bit more, although I probably shall have to wait a very long time for your reply—seven months or so, I should say. On this occasion, I should have liked to tell you in considerable length and detail about my life since I left Omsk and arrived in Semipalatinsk.

But I shall limit myself to this one sheet, because Aleksandr Yegorovich Wrangel, the conveyer of this letter, can give you much more detailed and intimate information about me in many, if not all respects. Do receive him as well as you possibly can and do your utmost to get to know him really well and get close to him. That young man is very much worth it—he is a pure, kind soul. I shall not even go into what he has done for me, the extent of loyalty and devotion he has displayed toward me—a brother couldn't have done more (I don't mean you, in saying that). So do me a favor, try to like him and become as intimately acquainted with him as you possibly can. I have recommended you to him as warmly as can be. Anyway, you with your sociable, kind, and delicate nature, appreciated and loved by all, I don't expect that you will find it very difficult. In any case, I shall describe to you in a few words the character of Al[eksandr] Yeg[orovich] so that it will be easier for you and will spare you all unnecessary effort. He is a very young, extremely gentle man, albeit with a strongly developed point d'honneur; he is incredibly kind, a wee bit haughty (but only on the surface and I rather like that); he has some of the faults of youth; he is cultured, but not brilliantly so and not very deeply; he is studious; he has a very weak character and a woman's impressionability; he is a bit suspicious and something of a hypochondriac; a thing that would anger and enrage another man saddens him— and this is a sign of a great heart. Très comme il faut. In the most disinterested way, he volunteered to intercede for me and do everything in his power to help me. And so we became good friends, and he is very fond of me. I'll tell you more about him later, but, for now, I shall talk about myself.

I suppose you already know, my dear fellow, that some people are working very hard for me in Petersburg and that my prospects are good. Even if I achieve only partial success, i.e., if I am not granted complete freedom, something is still bound to come of it. Al. Yegorovich's brother (who is serving in the Horse Guards) came to see you—I know it from his letter to his brother—and he probably told you about all the efforts that are being made on my behalf in Petersburg. Alek. Yego., I am convinced, remuera ciel et terre himself as soon as he gets to Petersburg in order to help me. He will tell you all about it at greater length and in greater detail than I could possibly do in this letter.

For my part, I shall tell you only that I had made up my mind to do nothing and let things take their course. I shall also tell you, in passing, that I have been promoted to noncommissioned officer's rank, which is quite important because the next favor—if it is granted—will normally be much more important than being made a noncommissioned officer. I have been assured that in a couple of years or perhaps in just one year I could be officially proposed for an officer's commission. I admit, though, that I should prefer to be transferred to the civil service and, even now, I should like that very much, and I may even take steps in that direction. But for the time being at least, I have decided to let things ride, pending the outcome of the present efforts that are being made on my behalf in Petersburg. I repeat that Al. Yegor. will give you a much fuller and more detailed account of all that.

I should like to add a few personal remarks, however: Don't go imagining, my dear friend, that I am thinking of some kind of social advantage or something of that sort, in trying so desperately to improve my lot. That is not so. But believe me, after going through what I have, one acquires in the end a certain philosophy—a word that you may interpret any way you wish. But there are two circumstances that impel me to extricate myself as soon as possible from a difficult situation, and that make me so feverishly preoccupied with myself. And it is of these circumstances that I feel I must inform you.

In the first place, I want to write and to be published. More than ever, I know that I have not chosen that path in vain and that I shall not have burdened the earth with my presence for nothing. I am convinced that I have talent and that I am capable of writing something good. For God's sake, do not take my words as idle boasting. To whom else can I confide my dreams and hopes if not to you? Besides, I absolutely wanted you to know why I need freedom and a certain social position.

Now, I am coming to my second point, which is very important to me and which I've never mentioned to you. You have to know, my good friend, that when I got out of that gloomy prison, I felt happy and hopeful coming here. I was like a patient recovering from a long sickness who, after having been on the brink of death, enjoys with particular relish being alive during his early convalescence. I had great hopes. I wanted to live. How can I explain it to you? The first year of my life here passed unnoticed. I was very happy. God ordained me to meet a family here whom I shall never forget. I am speaking of the Isayevs. I believe I wrote to you about them before and even asked you to do some errand for them. He had quite a good position here, but he didn't make a go of it and, because of some unpleasantness, resigned. At the time I met them, he had already been without work for several months and was still looking for another position. He depended on his salary for a livelihood, not having any private source of income, and so they were gradually slipping into dire poverty. When I first met them, they were still managing to support themselves after a fashion. He contracted debts. He led a rather disorderly life. Actually, he was a rather disorderly man by nature—he was passionate, stubborn, and somewhat coarsened. He had sunk very low, suffered in the public esteem, and he had to bear much unpleasantness; but he was the victim of much persecution on the part of local society that was undeserved. He was as improvident as a gypsy, vain and proud; he could not control his temper; and, as I already mentioned, he had sunk very low. But he was, nevertheless, a highly civilized and infinitely kind person. He was well educated and could keep up whatever the level of conversation. And, despite much that was unsavory in him, he was an exceptionally honorable man.

But it was not he who had attracted me, it was his wife, Mariya Dmitriyevna. She is a lady who is still young, 28 years old, pretty, very cultured, very intelligent, kind, sweet, gracious, with a superb, generous heart. She bore her lot proudly, uncomplainingly. She herself performed the chores of a servant in looking after her irresponsible husband—whom, taking advantage of my position as a friend of the family, I lectured a lot—and her little son. But this caused her to become sick, irritable, and emotional. By nature she was really gay and playful. I was almost constantly at their house. How many happy evenings I spent with her! I had rarely met a woman like her. Most people had broken off with them, partly because of her husband. And, anyway, they were incapable of keeping up acquaintanceships.

At long last, a position as assessor turned up for him in Kuznetsk, Tomsk Province. Since formerly he had been an excise officer on special assignments, the transition from an important and well-paid position to an assessorship was very humiliating. But there was nothing he could do! They were practically without a crust of bread, and it took lots of pleading from me, despite our long and close friendship, before they would allow me to share whatever I had with them. In May of 1855 I saw them off to Kuznetsk, and two months later he died of stones. She was left alone in a strange town, shaken, worn out by long suffering, with a seven-year-old child, and without a crust of bread. She didn't even have any money to pay for her husband's funeral. I didn't have any money either. Right away, I borrowed from Aleks. Yegor. first 25, then 40 silver rubles, and I sent them to her. Thank God, she is now receiving some assistance from her relatives, with whom she had quarreled because of her husband. Her relatives live in Astrakhan. Her father is the son of a French émigré—M. de Constant. He is an old man now, and he occupies the important post of director of quarantine in Astrakhan. He has no private fortune but lives well on his salary, which is quite substantial. He is about to retire, though, and so his income will be reduced. Besides, he still has two daughters on his hands. Then there are the relatives of the husband, quite distant relatives; one of her husband's brothers is a captain in the Finnish Guards Battalion. I know that the husband's side of the family was very respectable, too.

Now, here is the situation, my friend: I have loved this woman for a long time, and I know that she, too, is capable of love. I cannot live without her and so, if my circumstances improved even very slightly and became somewhat more favorable, I would marry her. *I know* that she will not turn me down. But the trouble is that I have neither money nor social position, and meanwhile her relatives are suggesting that she come to them in Astrakhan. If my situation does not change before the spring, she will be forced to leave for European Russia. But this will only postpone affairs while changing nothing. I have made up my mind, and I will carry out my intention even if the earth caves in under me. However, I have no right now to take advantage of this noble woman's sympathy for me and press her to marry me when I have nothing to offer her. Since May, when we parted, my life has been hell. We write one another every week. Al. Yeg. knew the Isayevs, but only during their last weeks in Semipalatinsk. He saw Mariya Dmitriyevna, but knows her only quite superficially. I have been fairly, but not completely open with him on that score. He does not know what I am writing to you in this letter, but I suppose he will speak to you about all these matters.

Until now, I have been thinking all the while of trying to get a transfer to the civil service. The director of the Altai plants, Colonel Gerngross, is a friend of Al. Yegor., and he would very much like me to be transferred to his service and is ready to give me a position in Barnaul at a certain salary. I am considering it, but I feel I should wait until the spring in case something should move ahead in Petersburg. If I am still not allowed to leave Siberia, I intend to settle in Barnaul, where Aleks. Yegor. is also going to be assigned. And then, after a while, I know for certain that I will return to Russia. What I don't know, though, is whether I'd be able to manage on my salary alone. It could not possibly be very large. It goes without saying that I'd look for ways to earn money. It would be wonderful if they would authorize me to have my writings published. Besides, here in Siberia there are good and safe speculative operations to be engaged in, even with very little capital. If I had only 300 silver rubles to spare in Semipalatinsk, those 300 would bring me, for sure, another 300 rubles a year; this is a new and curious land. In any case, my unforgettable friend, I should feel ashamed to ask you to support me. Still, I feel confident that for another year yet you will continue to help me to some extent. But, above all, help me now. If the authorities show any indulgence toward me, I shall ask our uncle for help—let him give me, at least, whatever may be necessary to enable me to make a new start in life.

It goes without saying that I won't write to anyone in the world about my intention of marrying before the event. I am telling you about it only in strictest confidence. And I must admit that I was reluctant to tell even you about it. It is an affair of the heart that shrinks from public view, that shrinks from the gaze and contact of a stranger. That, at least, is how I feel about it. And so, for Christ's sake, divulge it to no one, *absolutely no one*. And, in general, don't mention or show this whole letter to anyone. For heaven's sake, not a word to our sisters; they would start worrying right away and flood me with common-sense advice. But as far as I am concerned, *without what is the most important thing in life for me now,* I don't need life itself. You are the only one I can trust, my kindest and best friend, the only real friend I have.

Now I shall tell you briefly about my life here, just a few words, because the Baron can tell you better than I can about it. My health is quite satisfactory; I haven't had any fits for quite a long time now. I have also succeeded in gaining good standing here. Despite the fact that I am just a simple soldier, all the more important people here are acquainted with me and even consider it an honor. My superiors like me and treat me with respect. The corps commander—the governor general—knows me and is trying to help me. In Barnaul, the mining director—a general—has indicated his readiness to do whatever he can for me, and in his position he can do a lot. But what I should like best would be to return to European Russia, even if it meant serving somewhere for some time. Later, if I could obtain permission to publish, my financial situation would be quite secure. I am sure that all this will come about, although I may have to wait quite a while yet. And until then I may have to go on living in Siberia. If I must wait, I shall. If only the authorities were at all understanding and allowed me to transfer to some civilian post or other with an acceptable salary in the meantime—that is the main thing. I don't know whether any of my hopes will be fulfilled, whether any of my dreams will come true. Perhaps my prospects of marriage will fall through. Then, knowing myself, I can say that I shall be miserable and unhappy. What I must have is money—that's the thing.

As I said, I shall feel ashamed to ask you for money later, but now, at the beginning, you must help me a little bit. Now, I must tell you briefly about my present financial situation. I asked you in my letter to send me 100 silver rubles through Al. Yegor.'s brother. But, my friend, those 100 rubles will hardly be of much help to me, because I am heavily in debt. I actually owe 50 silver rubles, and if I get your money soon, that will leave me with 50 silver rubles; that would tide me over until there was a change in my situation such as, for example, a full pardon. But then, at that moment, I should need a considerable sum of money; I'd have to get some clothes and other things, but there is no point in my listing all I'd need. Those 50 silver rubles that I'll have left I'll have to spend in short order too—my clothes are all worn out, I must get myself some underwear, have my uniform repaired, and order a new greatcoat. There will be very little of the money left; it is quite impossible for me to get by on less than 15 silver rubles a month, provided, that is, that there are no unexpected expenses. Let *Wrangel* tell you about that. Everything here is expensive. But, understand, I am not asking for more. I will somehow manage to pull through with the 100 silver rubles. And perhaps Varinka, the angel, will send me something. (How nicely her letters are written! Where could she have learned to write like that? Her letters are a real delight, not at all like yours, my dear sir—they are much better.) Now if there is a radical change in my official situation, I shall, as I told you, turn to our uncle for help. I cannot believe he will refuse.

Ah, my friend, if only you knew how painful this is for me—I have yet something else to admit to you! I have still another debt, besides the debt I mentioned to you. I owe 125 rubles in silver to Al. Yegor. too, having borrowed from him on various occasions. Don't ask me where the money went—I couldn't tell you myself! I only know that I live very poorly, that I refuse myself everything, but that despite that I get into debt. I am not asking you, my friend, to pay Alek. Yegorovich what I owe him—that would be too much! All I know is that I must pay him back, although he blushes when I mention my debt, and even gets upset when I remind him of it. (He is such a sensitive man!) But enough about money! I know you won't forget me! For my part, my only wish is to get back on my own feet just as soon as possible and not be a burden to all of you.

I'd like to add a few more words about Aleksandr Yegorovich. Listen, if you succeed in becoming his friend, look after him and don't let him slip out of your sight. I'll tell you a great secret about him; I may be wrong to tell you this, but I am doing it for his own good: Il est amoureux fou d'une dame d'ici, d'une dame parfaitement comme il faut, très riche et d'une famille considérée. She is due to arrive in Petersburg at about the same time as he is.

Don't let on to Wrangel that you know about it, but look after him as if you were his own brother, just as I used to look after him; so take my place and watch him because dans cette affaire he is capable of the worst stupidity, i.e., of doing things that may have tragic consequences, which is something I should not like to happen. There is a certain Marquis de Traversay (the son of the Revel one), and although they were boyhood friends, the Baron has good cause to see a rival in the Marquis, which makes it likely that between the two of them they might do something terribly stupid. I won't tell you more. If you do become friends with Aleks. Yegorov. and gain his trust, he will tell you more himself. If not, then there is nothing more for you to know. But, in any case, use the little I have told you and watch over him. His character is weak, sensitive, and even a bit morbid. So stop him from doing things he shouldn't. But whatever else, in the name of Christ the Lord, *not a word to anyone* about this. And never tell Wrangel that I wrote you about it, not even in a moment of confidence, should you become friends. I have done so for his sake, because I love him very much. Now, this secret is known to him, to *me*, and now to *you*—and no one else. Give me your word of honor that you will keep your mouth shut. Although he is not at all open with his brother, I am so much interested in everything that touches Aleks. Yegor. that I am thinking of writing a few words to the brother. Now, in addition to this secret, I can tell you that he does not get along too well with his father, who is a strange, stubborn, distrustful, and suspicious man. His father is terribly fond of him, but even now demands of him, for instance, that he not take one step—not even the most trivial—without his consent (all this out of love). The father, who is rich, in fact very rich, is very stingy with his children; and my Baron dislikes taking money from him anyway because he has a habit of reproaching his children afterward for the money he gives them. I cannot tell you everything in a few lines. But I foresee, I know, that he probably will have considerable unpleasantness with his father. If he confides in you about these unpleasantnesses, console him, and make him see that a father is, after all, a father and that he must try hard to get along with him somehow. He also has a sister who, it seems, is the guardian angel of the whole family. I have read her letters and know her from what the Baron has told me.

January 18

I have written to our sisters, to our uncle (without asking him for anything), to Ivanov, to Maikov, and to Prince Odoyevsky. I asked the Prince to back me up when I solicit authorization to have my work published. Perhaps I shall write a patriotic article about Russia soon.

If they allow me to publish, there will also be money, for I shall ask for it. Have you met Yevg. Nik. Yaku.? If not, make his acquaintance. He is taking a great interest in my situation. Also, please get to know Ivanov better.

For God's sake, don't go imagining things and getting upset about what I have told you about my sentimental attachment. It may work out, and it may not. I am an honorable man, and I am reluctant to use my influence to induce a noble woman to sacrifice herself for me. But whenever it is possible, even if I have to wait five years, I shall carry out my intention.

Please do not be angry with me for asking you for money. Help me out just this time. Soon, perhaps very soon, my fortunes will change.

Farewell, my friend, live happily, and don't forget me. Now that Wrangel has left, I feel completely abandoned. It is very sad.

Kiss all the children, give my regards to Emiliya Fyodorovna. How is she? May God send happiness to all of you. Love me and remember me. I, too, love you very much.

Yours,
D.

---

22. M. M. Kh. was Mikhail Mikhailovich Khomentovsky, the general in command of the brigade that included the Seventh Line Battalion. According to Wrangel, Khomentovsky was a kind and well-educated man who was very sympathetic to Dostoyevsky. In 1861 he wrote to Dostoyevsky, praising his novel *The Insulted and Injured* and his magazine *Time*.

Dostoyevsky was promoted to noncommissioned officer in November 1855 and was commissioned as a second lieutenant in October 1856, remaining in the same battalion.

M. de Constant was Dmitry Stepanovich Constant, father of Mariya Dmitriyevna Isayeva. He was chief of quarantine in Astrakhan, and in addition to Mariya he had not two but three daughters—Varvara, Sofya, and Lidiya. Dostoyevsky and his sister-in-law Varvara became good friends and carried on an active correspondence in 1862 and 1863.

Colonel Andrei Rodionovich Gerngross was the senior officer of the Altai Military District during the 1850s. Wrangel described him as a cultured man who treated

Dostoyevsky with great kindness. Later in the letter, Dostoyevsky mistakenly refers to him as the "general" in Barnaul.

In a letter written less than a month before the present one (not included in this collection), Dostoyevsky had asked Mikhail to send him 100 silver rubles with which to pay back 50 rubles that he had borrowed from Wrangel and to buy some clothes.

The woman with whom Wrangel was in love was apparently Yekaterina Iosifovna Gerngross, the wife of Colonel Gerngross. Wrangel described her as a person of great beauty and exceptional intelligence, and he says she rendered "services and assistance" to Dostoyevsky while the latter was in Siberia (though Dostoyevsky nevertheless did not like her very much). Wrangel eventually broke off with her.

Marquis de Traversay was probably one of the sons of Marquis Jean-François de Traversay (1754–1830), who had emigrated to Russia during the French Revolution and later became a Russian naval minister and a member of the State Council.

Yevgeny Ivanovich (not Nikolayevich, as Dostoyevsky wrote here) Yakushkin (1826–1905) was the son of the Decembrist Ivan Andreyevich Yakushkin. A jurist and ethnographer, he taught law at the Konstantinovsky Surveyors' Institute in Moscow and twice, in connection with his work, traveled to Siberia, where he met Dostoyevsky. He performed a number of services for Dostoyevsky in Moscow and occasionally helped him out with money as well.

23. To A. N. Maikov
Semipalatinsk, January 18, 1856

I have been wanting to answer your kind letter for a long time, my dear Ap[ollon] Nik[olayevi]ch. Something from the past, from bygone times, wafted over me as I read it. I cannot tell you how grateful I am to you for not having forgotten me. I don't know why, but I have always felt that you would not forget me, but perhaps that was simply because, for my part, I could never forget you.

You write that much time has passed, many things have changed, much has been experienced. Yes, I am sure you are right. But one thing is encouraging—we, as people, are still the same. I can vouch for myself. I could write you many curious things about myself. Only don't reproach me for writing this in haste, in snatches, and perhaps not too clearly. But at this minute I am experiencing what you must have experienced when you wrote to me—the impossibility of telling you about myself after so many years, not only in one but even in 50 sheets. We would need to talk face to face, so that each of us could read the other's soul on the other's face, so that the heart could express its feelings in the intonation of the voice. One word said with conviction, with total sincerity, without hesitation, eye to eye, face to face—means much more than dozens of pages of paper covered with words.

I thank you particularly for the news about yourself. I knew beforehand that things would wind up the way they did and that you would get married. You wonder whether I remember Anna Ivanovna. But how could I have forgotten her? I am glad that both you and she are happy, since it was a matter close to my heart before, too; do you remember the year 1847, when it all started? Please remember me to her and assure her of my boundless respect and devotion. And tell your parents that I often recalled—and still recall—with pleasure their friendship and kindness. Did Yevgeniya Petrovna receive the book—the reviews and the essays written by the unforgettable Valerian Nikolayevich for *Notes of the Fath[erland]*? When I was arrested, they took that book away from me, then they returned it, but while I was in custody I simply could find no way of returning it to Yevgeniya Petrovna, although I knew how much she valued it. All this made me very sad. Two hours before leaving for Siberia, I asked Commandant Nabokov to return the book to its rightful owner. Did he do it? Please give my regards to your parents. I sincerely wish them every happiness and a very, very long life.

You may have heard some of the details of my life from my brother. During the hours when I have nothing to do, I write down some of my reminiscences of my stay in the prison camp, the more interesting of them. Actually there is little of a purely personal nature. If I should finish it and if a *very convenient* opportunity ever presents itself, I shall send you a copy written in my own hand as a souvenir from me.

By the way, I forgot to mention—so that now I must make a digression—that this letter will be delivered to you by Baron Aleksandr Yegorovich Wrangel, a very young man with excellent qualities of heart and soul, who came to Siberia straight out of the lyceum with the *magnanimous* dream of getting to know the land, of helping people, etc. He served in Semipalatinsk; we became friends; and I got to like him very much. And since I am going to ask you especially to show him attention and to get to know him as closely as possible, I suppose I'd better tell you a few words about his character. He is exceptionally kind, has no particular convictions, has a generous heart, is intelligent. But he is weakhearted and gentle, although he may seem rather unapproachable at 1st glance. I very much want you to get to know him in general for his sake. He grew up in a milieu that was semi-aristocratic or perhaps 3/4 aristocratic, baronial, which is not much to my liking—nor to his, for that matter—for he does possess some excellent qualities, however much the early influences are still noticeable. Try to use your influence on him if you can—he is worth the effort. He has done a world of good for me. But I love him not just for the kindness he has shown to me. To sum up—he is somewhat suspicious, very sensitive, occasionally secretive and a bit moody. If you get on well with him, talk to him directly, simply, as sincerely as possible, and don't beat around the bush. Please forgive me for my importuning you about the Baron but, I repeat, I am terribly fond of him. All my remarks about him and this whole letter in general are to be kept confidential. But I am sure there is no need for me to tell you that.

You write that you remembered me with warmth and kept on repeating, "Why, why?" I, too, remembered you with warmth, but as to your "whys" I won't say a thing—it would be unnecessary. You say that you have lived through a great deal, that you have changed your mind about many things, and have learned much from life. It couldn't be otherwise, and I am convinced that, even now, our ideas would agree. I have also done some thinking, have gone through a lot and been subjected to conditions and influences that forced me to reconsider and ruminate over too many things, more even than I could cope with. Knowing me as well as you do, you will certainly do me justice and agree that I always followed whatever I believed was the best and straightest path, that I never acted against my conscience, and that whatever I gave myself up to, I did with all my heart. Please don't think that this is in any way an allusion to what may have landed me here. I am now referring to what followed afterward; this is certainly not the place to talk about the past and, in any case, it was nothing but an accident. Ideas change, but the heart remains the same. I read your letter, but failed to understand the main point. I am speaking about patriotism, about the Russian idea, about the feeling of duty, about national honor, about everything that you speak of with such enthusiasm. But, my friend, can it be that you ever felt different about these things? I have always shared the selfsame feelings and convictions. Russia, duty, honor? Yes! I have always been a true Russian—and I tell you this in all sincerity. So what is new in the movement that you have discovered around you and that you consider as some sort of a new tendency? I confess I don't understand you. I read your poems, and I found them splendid—I fully share with you your patriotic feeling about the *moral* emancipation of the Slavs. This is the role Russia must play, our great magnanimous Russia, our holy mother. How beautiful the closing lines of your "Council of Clermont" are. Where did you find the language it takes to express such an immense idea so beautifully? Yes, I share with you the idea that Europe and her destiny will be fulfilled by Russia. To me, this has been obvious for a long time. You write that society seems to have been aroused from its apathy. But you know that our society is not, as a rule, given to manifestations. But who has ever concluded from that that it lacked vitality? Present an idea intelligibly, lay it before society, and society will understand you. This is still true today. The idea has been beautifully presented and in a fully national and chivalrous manner—this is true and must be acknowledged—and our political idea, already bequeathed to us by Peter [the Great], has now been vindicated by all. Until quite recently you may have been taken aback by the influx of French ideas among that part of society which thinks, feels, and studies? It is true that there was something exceptional here. But every exception, by its very nature, provokes a reaction. But you will agree yourself that all healthy-minded people, i.e., those who give the tone to everything, looked upon the French ideas from a scientific point of view, no more than that, and always remained Russian, perhaps even in their devotion to the exceptional. So where do you find anything new in it? I assure you that I, for instance, feel so akin to everything Russian that even the convicts did not intimidate me—they were Russian people, my brothers in misfortune, and I often had the happiness of uncovering magnanimity even in the heart of a robber simply because I could understand him, being a Russian myself. My misfortune gave me an opportunity to find out many things through experience, and perhaps this practical experience has had a considerable influence on me; but what I also learned from that practical experience is that I have always been a Russian at heart. One may err in ideas, but the heart cannot err and cause one to become conscienceless through error, i.e., to act against one's own convictions.

But why, why am I writing you all this, since I realize I can't express what I mean in a few lines, so what good can it do! So I shall rather tell you a lot more about myself. While I was in the prison camp, I read very little; books were just not available. Now and again one turned up. After they let me out and I came here, to Semipalatinsk, I was able to do more reading. Still, I can't get the books I really need, and time is passing. I cannot convey to you how much suffering it cost me not to be able to write in the prison camp. And, by the way, I was seething inside with work. Some of it was coming out well—I could feel that. While I was there, I composed a long story in my head, in definitive form. I was afraid that my initial love for my creation might cool off when the years had passed and the hour of writing came—a love without which it is impossible to write. But I was wrong; the character I had created and that was at the foundation of the entire story required many years to develop and I am certain I should have spoiled everything if I had begun to write in the heat of the moment, before I was properly prepared.

When I left the prison camp, however, even though the whole thing was ready, I did not write it down. I couldn't write. Something, an event that had been long overdue in my life and finally came to pass, carried me away and completely absorbed me. I was happy, I couldn't work. Then sadness and sorrow came down on me. I lost that which had become everything for me. Hundreds of versts came between us. I shan't tell you more about it, although I may some day. But I cannot now. However, I wasn't completely idle. I worked. But I put my main work aside. I had to have greater peace of spirit. As a diversion, I started writing a comedy and, just for the fun of it, I created such a comical setting and so many comical characters and took such a liking to my hero that I discarded the comedy form, despite the fact that I

seemed to be quite successful with it, so that I might, for my personal pleasure, follow for as long as possible the adventures of my new hero and laugh
at him myself. This character resembles me somewhat. In short, I am writing
a comic novel, but up to now I have been writing separate adventures; I now
have a sufficient number and have started *sewing them together* in one
whole. And so now you have a report on my work. I couldn't refrain from
telling you all this because as soon as I address *you* I remember the old days,
my unforgettable friend. Yes, I spent many happy moments with you, so
how could I ever forget you!

You write me a bit about literature. Well, during this past year I have read
hardly anything. But I can give you some of my observations. I like Turgenev
best. It is a shame, however, that with all his immense *talent, he is so uneven.*
I like L. T. very much, too, although I don't think he will write much. (Still, I
may be wrong.) As for Ostrovsky, I don't know him at all, not having read
anything of his from beginning to end, although I have read many excerpts
from his writings in critical reviews. He may know a certain class of Russians well, but I don't believe he is much of an artist. Besides, I have the impression that he is a *poet without an ideal.* Please persuade me that I am
wrong and send me some of his better works, which would enable me to
judge him by something other than the critical reviews. Of Pisemsky, I have
read *Fanfaron* and *The Rich Fiancé*, and nothing else. I like him a great deal.
He is intelligent, good-humored, and even naïve. And he can tell a good
story. But there is one thing that is sad about him: he writes in too great
a hurry. He writes too much and too fast. He needs greater self-respect,
greater esteem for his talent and for art, greater love of art. When one is
young, ideas just pour out of one's head, but that is no reason to catch every
one of them in flight and use it right away, in a hurry. It is better to wait a bit
longer until they crystallize—think more and wait until many small things
expressing one particular thought combine into one great whole, into one
large, three-dimensional image, and it is only then that the thought should
be given expression. The colossal characters created by the colossal writers
were often created tenaciously and over a long period. Surely, there is not
much point in expressing all the intermediary attempts and sketches. I am
not quite sure whether you will understand what I mean. But in the case of
Pisemsky, I feel that he fails to exercise sufficient control over his pen.

As to our lady writers, well, they write as lady writers would—cleverly,
prettily, and in a tremendous hurry to express what is on their minds. Tell
me—why is it that a lady writer is almost never a demanding artist? Even
Georges [*sic*] Sand, indisputably a colossal artist, has often harmed herself
because of this feminine trait.

I have read many of your short poems in the magazines *during all this
time.* I liked them very much. Work hard and mature. And let me tell you in

confidence, in utter confidence: Tyutchev is very remarkable but— etc. And which Tyutchev is it, anyway? Can it be ours, by any chance? But many of his poems are excellent.

Farewell, my dear friend. Forgive me for this disconnected letter. It is quite impossible to say much in a letter, anyway. And that is why I cannot stand Mme de Sévigné. She really wrote letters too well.

Who knows, perhaps some day I shall be able to embrace you! May God grant it! For heaven's sake, tell *no one* (and I mean *no one*) about this letter. I embrace you.

---

23. The reminiscences about prison camp were evidently the raw materials for Dostoyevsky's *Notes from the House of the Dead.* The "comic novel" was *The Village of Stepanchikovo and Its Residents.*

Apollon Maikov had published a collection of poems under the title *1854,* echoing the patriotic mood of the Russian public during the Crimean War. Among them was one called "The Council of Clermont" (Klermontsky sobor), which drew a parallel between Christian Europe, for which the Crusaders had fought the infidels, and Russia, whose soldiers were at that time fighting the equally infidel Polovtsy and Tartars in order to save Europe. The closing lines of the poem were:

> Perhaps our enemies foresee
> That out of icy Russia
> Still unseen there shall come
> A tribe of terrifying giants,
> Giants with an unslaked thirst
> For immortality, glory, and goodness;
> Giants such as the world once
> Saw in Peter's dreaded figure.

The "French ideas" that Dostoyevsky mentions were presumably those of utopian socialism.

The "event that had been long overdue" was his falling in love with Mariya Dmitriyevna Isayeva (Dostoyevsky was then thirty-four years old). The "sadness and sorrow" were her departure from Semipalatinsk for Kuznetsk.

L. T. is Lev Nikolayevich Tolstoy (1828–1910), on whose writings Dostoyevsky frequently commented later in his life. Although they had a number of friends in common, Dostoyevsky and Tolstoy never met.

Aleksandr Nikolayevich Ostrovsky (1823–1886) is principally known today as a playwright. Dostoyevsky later developed a high opinion of him and his work. Two of his plays, *What You Seek You Shall Find* (Za chem poidyosh, to i naidyosh, 1861) and *Who Hasn't Experienced Sin and Sorrow* (Grekh da beda na kogo ne zhivyot, 1863) were published in *Time.*

Aleksei Feofilaktovich Pisemsky (1820–1881) was a novelist, playwright, and educator, as well as a government civil servant. His novels *The Rich Fiancé* (Bogaty zhenikh, 1851–1852) and *Fanfaron* (1854) were published in *Contemporary,* and his article "Letter from an Outside Critic" (Pismo postoronnego kritika, 1861) was published in the Dostoyevsky brothers' journal *Time*. Dostoyevsky later came to hold a much lower opinion of his work.

The "lady writers" is probably a reference to three who were particularly popular at the time. Yelizaveta Vasilevna Salias de Tournemir (1816–1892), who wrote under the pen name of Yevgeniya Tur, published stories in a number of magazines and also published one magazine herself, *Russian Discourse* (Russkaya rech); she was one of the earliest admirers of Dostoyevsky's work. Nadezhda Stepanovna Sokhanskaya (1825–1884) also wrote stories for several magazines, under the pen name of Kokhanovskaya. Nadezhda Dmitriyevna Khvoshchinskaya (1826–1889) published stories in *Notes of the Fatherland* under the pen name of V. Krestovsky.

Fyodor Ivanovich Tyutchev (1803–1873) was a poet whose first collection of poems appeared as a special supplement to the March 1854 issue of *Contemporary*. Dostoyevsky's questions, "Which Tyutchev is it? . . . Can it be ours?," were a joking reference to Nikolai Nikolayevich Tyutchev (1815–1878), a follower of Belinsky and a translator for *Notes of the Fatherland* during the 1840s, who was treated condescendingly, as a dilettante, by figures in the literary world.

Mme de Sevigné (1626–1696) was well known for her beautifully composed letters to her daughter.

24. To A. Ye. Wrangel
Semipalatinsk, Friday, March 23 (1856)

My kindhearted and irreplaceable friend, Aleksandr Yegorovich,

Where are you and what has happened to you? Can you have forgotten me, by any chance? From Monday on, I'll be expecting the letter you promised me with such impatience as if it were the key to my happiness and the realization of all my hopes.

Inside this envelope you will find three unsealed letters: one is for my brother, another for Adj. Gen. Eduard Ivanovich Totleben. Don't be surprised, I'll explain everything! But now I shall proceed in order, beginning with myself. If you had any idea how depressed and disheartened I feel, my almost complete despair at this moment, you would understand why I am waiting for your letter as though my salvation depended on it. It must decide my fate in many, many ways. You promised to write to me as soon as possible upon your arrival in Petersburg to let me know about the things that I am hoping for and that you have been doing your utmost to obtain for me in the most brotherly way for a whole year. You promised to tell me everything frankly, concealing nothing and without adorning the truth or buoying me up with frail hopes. So this is the news I am awaiting from you as if it were life itself. Please don't show my letter to anyone. I am informing you that my affairs are in a stage of emergency.

La dame (la mienne) is sad and despairing, she is continually ailing, she is losing faith in my hopes, in the arrangement of our future, and worst of all, she is surrounded in her small town (she hasn't moved to Barnaul yet) by people who are liable to cook up something sinister; there are marriageable men around there. Obliging old wives are bursting out of their skins trying to persuade her to give her consent to some fellow whose name I don't yet know. In the meantime, they spy on her and are trying to find out who it is who is writing letters to her. As to her, she is still waiting for news from her relatives who, on the other side of the world, must decide her fate here, i.e., whether she is to return to European Russia or to move to Barnaul. Her last letters to me have sounded sadder and sadder. I knew she was in pain and ill when she wrote them. I had the feeling she was hiding something from me. (Alas, this is something I never told you, but while you were still here, par ma jalousie incomparable I used to drive her to despair, and I wonder whether that is not why she is hiding something from me now.) And what do you know? All of a sudden I received news that she had consented to marry someone else in Kuznetsk. It was as if a thunderbolt had struck me. In my despair I didn't know what to do and began writing a letter to her; but on Sunday I received a letter from her, a very nice, friendly letter as usual but even more reserved than the previous ones. It had fewer intimate words and gave the impression that she was being circumspect. Nothing in reference to our hopes for the future, as though the very idea of them had been completely discarded. It seemed she had given up all hope of the possibility of an early change in my status, and finally the shattering piece of news: she had decided to stop concealing things from me and timidly asked me this question: "If there were an elderly, kindly man with a position and material security and if that man had proposed to her—well, what should she reply?" She was asking for my advice. She wrote that her head begins to spin when she thinks that she is on the edge of the world, with a child, that her father is old and may die at any moment, and she asks me, what would become of her then? She asks me to think about her situation with cool detachment as befits a *friend,* and to reply immediately. Yet her earlier letters contained some protestations d'amour. In [several illegible words] she adds that she loves me and that what she is telling me is but one more possibility that must be taken into account. I was struck as if by a bolt of lightning. I swayed, fell, and fainted. I wept throughout the night. Now I am lying in my room [several illegible words]. I have a fixed idea in my head! I barely understand how I go on living and what people say to me. Ah, may God spare all men this terrible, this dreadful feeling. Great is the joy of love, but its sufferings are so intense that it is much better never to love. I swear I reached the bottom of despair. I felt capable of doing something drastic, something I could never have conceived of at another time. That very evening I wrote her—a terrible, desperate letter. Poor thing! My angel! As it is, she is ill, and I was causing her further torment. Perhaps I killed her with that letter of mine. I wrote that I would die if I had to lose her. The letter contained threats and tendernesses and [humiliating?] entreaties and [I don't know what else?]. You will understand me, since you are my guardian angel, my only hope! But think about it—what else could she do, the poor thing, abandoned by everyone, morbidly suspicious of everybody and, finally, having lost all hope that my situation would right itself! Why, she certainly couldn't marry an army private, could she? But this week I read over again all of her last letters. God knows, maybe she hasn't given her consent yet, and that's the way it looks; she was merely vacillating. Mais elle m'aime, elle m'aime, that I know, and I can see—by her sadness, by her gloom, by the repeated outbursts in her letters, and by many other signs that I won't mention to you.

My friend, I have never been completely frank with you on this subject. But what can I do now? I have never lived through such despair— A deadly anguish is tugging at my heart; at night I have horrible dreams; I cry out in my sleep; I am choked by spasms in my throat; and my tears are either stubbornly dammed up or gush out. So try to realize what it feels like and [don't condemn me?]. I am an honorable man. I know she loves me. But what if I am standing in the way of her happiness? Still, I cannot believe in that prospective husband from Kuznetsk! But it would be terrible for a sickly, nervous person like her, for someone with her emotional maturity and education, and intelligence, to give herself to God knows whom, to a man who might even secretly think that wife-beating is a legitimate part of marriage. Good and trusting as she is—and I know her very well—it is easy to convince her of anything, especially when she is driven out of her mind by those old wives (may they be damned!) and by the hopelessness of her situation. I expect to get a definite answer, i.e., I shall find out all the ins and outs by April 2, but in the meantime, my friend, please advise me what to do. Although I really don't know why I am asking for your advice—come what may, I just cannot give her up. At my age, love is no whim; it has been going on for 2 years—yes, 2 years—and during the 10 months of separation, instead of weakening, it has reached [incredible proportions?]. If I lose my angel, I shall perish: either I'll go mad or I'll jump into the Irtysh! *It goes without saying that if my situation cleared up (as a result of the manifesto), she would give me precedence over each and every one,* for she does love me, I am certain of that.

Now let me tell you what in our common language (hers and mine) we understand by the arrangement of my situation. It is my transfer from the army to the civil service with a job paying some sort of a salary (even as low as the 14th civil-service grade) or a good prospect of this happening, together with a possibility of finding some money for us to live on in the meantime, enough to last us at least until my affairs are fully arranged. Obviously she would view my discharge from the army and transfer to the civil service in itself—even if the position carried no rank and was poorly paid—as very hopeful, and it would give her a new lease on life. As to my personal hopes, let me put it this way: what must I *absolutely* have to fend off her prospective husbands and to remain an honorable man in her eyes? And now I would ask you: what, *of the things that I must have,* can I expect; what is likely and what is unlikely? I ask you this because, being in Petersburg, you must know many things that I do not.

As to my hopes, my dear, invaluable and, possibly, my only friend, you have a pure and honest heart—here they are, and please listen to them. The more I think, the more reasonable they seem to me. First of all, is it possible that there will be no amnesty this summer, either with the signing of the peace treaty or with the coronation? (This is precisely the information I am now waiting with such feverish impatience to receive from you.) Secondly, even assuming that this is still in the realm of hope, could I not all the same transfer out of the army to the civil service and go to Barnaul if the manifesto contains *no* other provisions? You know Durov has been transferred to the civil service. As I've told you, that in itself would give her a new lease on life and she would send all those suitors packing, because in her last two letters she writes that she loves me deeply, that she is considering marrying another man only out of *practical considerations,* that she beseeches me not to doubt her love and to trust her when she says that she is considering it only as a possibility; and I believe her when she says this. Maybe she has had an offer of marriage, and people are trying to persuade her, *but she has not yet given her consent.* I have been making inquiries and looking into the rumor [several illegible words], and it turns out that much of it is just plain gossip. Anyway, if she had said yes to them, she would have let me know. Therefore, the matter is still far from being settled. I am expecting a letter from her around April 2. I wrote to her insisting that she be completely frank with me, and so I hope to find out exactly how things stand. Oh, my friend, must I abandon her and let another man take her? Why, I have my *rights* over her, yes, *rights,* do you hear me! And so my transfer to the civil service would be a source of great hope and encouragement.

And, thirdly, how long shall I remain without a rank? What do you think? Is it possible that my career is a dead end? Haven't criminals like me been obtaining everything? I simply refuse to believe it! I trust that even if nothing happens right now, I shall return to European Russia in two years' time. The most important thing now is money. By next September I shall have two things ready, an article and a novel. I intend to make a formal request for permission to publish. If it is granted I'll never go hungry as long as I live. Things are no longer as they used to be. I have so many things finished, so many things that I have thought through, and I'm raring to write! I hope (by

September) to have written a novel that is superior to *Poor Folk*. If I am allowed to publish (and I do not believe—you hear me, I simply do not believe—that permission should be impossible to obtain), why, it will cause a sensation, my book will be sold out, I shall gain fame and fortune and attract the attention of the authorities, and that will hasten my return. Actually, all I need is 2 or 3 thousand paper rubles a year. And so I am acting honorably toward her, am I not? Wouldn't that sum be enough for us to live on? In a couple of years or so we shall return to European Russia, she will live comfortably, and we may even be able to put some money aside. Do you imagine that, after having shown the courage and energy I have over 6 years in struggling against unheard-of sufferings, I shall not be able to earn enough money to provide for my wife and myself? Nonsense! Above all, nobody is aware of my strength and of the extent of my talent, and this is what I am mainly relying on.

Now, one final possibility: Suppose they do bar me from publishing for another year? Well, at the first improvement in my situation, I shall write to my uncle and ask him for 1000 silver rubles to make a new start in life, without mentioning my marriage; I am sure he won't refuse. That should certainly be enough to last us for a year. And after that, things should straighten themselves out. And finally, I could publish incognito and make a little money at the same time. But you should understand that these are the possibilities only in the event that nothing happens this summer (if there is no manifesto). And what if something does happen? No, I am not acting like a scoundrel toward her. And since she herself mentions that [several illegible words] to pack off all her suitors for me if things would only work out for us, this indicates that I could still save her from disaster. But why talk! My mind is made up. I won't give her up! Why, she would go to her perdition without me. Aleks. Yegorovich, my dear friend, if you only knew how anxiously I am waiting for your letter! Perhaps it will bring good tidings! If so, I shall forward the original to her, but if that is impossible, I'll tear off just the lines expressing hopes about my future, and send them to her.

But try to understand what trouble I am in now! I have so many favors to ask of you, and I beseech you for the sake of Christ to do them all. *1st request*. You will find enclosed a letter for *Ed. Iv. Totleben*. Here is what I have in mind. Once upon a time I knew this man very well, and his brother was a boyhood friend of mine. Only a few days before my arrest I ran into him and we greeted each other in an extremely friendly way. And so, who knows, he may still remember me. He is a plain, kindly man, with a generous heart (he's proved it), a real hero of Sevastopol, the equal of Nakhimov and Kornilov. Please take my letter over to him. But first read it thoroughly. You may notice from the tone of the letter that I was hesitant and unsure *how* to write to him. He occupies such an exalted position today, and who am I? Will he want to remember me? Well, anyway, I have written to him the way I have. Now: go to see him in person (I hope he is in Petersburg) and give him my letter in private. You will immediately see from his expression how he reacts. If it is negative, then there is nothing to be done; just explain to him briefly my situation, putting in a good word for me, and, as you leave, ask him to keep the entire matter a secret. He is a very courteous man (of a rather chivalrous nature) and I know that he will receive you and part with you graciously, even if he has nothing *encouraging* to say. If, however, you do see from his expression that he will do something to help me, and if he manifests great interest and concern for me, then you may be completely open with him, tell him whatever you have on your mind, go straight to the point and tell him that *a word* from him now would make a tremendous difference, that he could perhaps intercede for me with the Monarch and guarantee (as a man knowing me personally) that in the future I will be a good citizen. I am sure he wouldn't be turned down. On several occasions, at Paskiewicz's request, the Sovereign granted pardons to Polish criminals. And Totleben is now in such favor and in such high esteem that his intercession would surely be worth as much as Paskiewicz's. But, in general, I am relying heavily on you. I feel certain you will come up with a word from the heart. For God's sake, don't refuse me this.

Concentrate mainly on obtaining a discharge from the army for me (but if something beyond that seems possible, i.e., a full pardon, please don't discount it). For instance, is there no chance of my being discharged with the right to join the civil service, at the level of grade 14, with a possibility of being allowed to return to European Russia and, above all, with permission to publish? In general, I should like you to read my letter to Totleben carefully. Wouldn't it be possible to get things started with a poem? I read in the papers that at a dinner Maikov recited his poems to him. Does he know him, by any chance? If they are acquainted, tell Maikov everything in confidence, and ask him to intercede with Totleben on my behalf and to accompany you when you go to see him. Couldn't you somehow arrange to meet Totleben's younger brother, Adolf? He is a friend of mine, so if you tell him about me, he will throw himself at his brother's neck and beseech him to intercede for me. I need not tell you that before you hand Totleben my letter you must seal it in an envelope. And as soon as you can, send me a report about whether things have turned out right or not. I am just keeping my fingers crossed that *Lamotte* won't have left on a tour of his district by that time! He will be gone for a month. But I don't expect he'll have gone by then. I feel almost certain that he won't. So hurry with your answer. Something else worries me: I wonder whether *Prince Odoyevsky* reacted favorably to my letter. You are not discouraged, are you? Maybe you are going to see Totle. *against your will*. You are my guardian angel! Don't abandon me, don't drive me to despair!

2nd request. Write me in great detail and right away: how did you find my brother? How does he feel about me? Formerly, he was a man who loved me ardently. He wept when we parted. I wonder whether he hasn't cooled toward me. I hope he hasn't changed! How terribly sad I would be! Perhaps he has become interested only in making money and has forgotten everything of the past? But I somehow cannot believe anything of the sort. But how, then, can I account for his sometimes not writing me for as much as 7 or 8 months on end, and then writing God knows what; even in the uncensored letter he sent through Khomentovsky he didn't answer any of my questions, and in it I could find so little of his old warmth! I shall never forget what he told Khomentovsky, who had conveyed to him my request that he intercede on my behalf. He said that *the best thing for me would be to stay in Siberia*. In December I wrote (through your brother, remember?), and I asked him to send me some money at Lamotte's address. You know how badly I needed it then! Well, so far, not so much as a peep out of him! I realize that he may not have the money, because he is in business, but in an emergency one does try to rescue a human being. Furthermore, I won't be sitting on their backs for a long time and will pay them back everything. Besides, if I asked him for money, it was because I remembered his very own words when he was saying good-bye to me. In my letter to him enclosed herewith, I am asking him to send me whatever he possibly can on top of those other 100 rubles. I must have it to face all eventualities (if, for instance, I were pardoned, I'd immediately fly off to Kuznetsk, which is something that I couldn't manage to do without money. Furthermore, if she leaves for Barnaul, I shall persuade her to accept something from me.) I can't write you everything, but I need money. I need it desperately. A man needs money that desperately only once in a lifetime, and 300 silver rubles would save me now. But even 200 rubles would do, even if that included the 100 rubles I asked him for back in December. You must understand that I am telling you all this just because you are my friend; and put out of your mind any thoughts you may have of helping me yourself. As it is, I must seem a *worthless creature* to you; I am infinitely indebted to you! At any rate, read my letter to my brother. Don't show him what I have written to you here; but I have suggested to him to get all the information he needs from you, so tell him all. And what if, like the relatives and old uncles in novels, he is displeased with *my love for her* and tries to dissuade you from helping me? Why, I am 35 years old already. Does he imagine that I love him only for the money he sends me? What nonsense! I have my pride, too! I'd rather that *she and I* ate nothing but bread and perished than take his money if he were to give it in such a spirit! I don't want any handouts! What I need is a brother, and not money! We have had our disagreements in the past, but we ardently loved one another, and I swear I would give my life for him if it were necessary. I have a bad character, but when it comes to standing up for my friends, I will stand up for them to the end. When they arrested us, well, it would have been quite natural and excusable in the first moment of horror for a man to think of himself first. But whom did I actually think of? Only of him, only of how his arrest would stun his poor wife and family; I pleaded with my third brother, who had been arrested by mistake, not to explain the error to the authorities for as long as possible and to send him money, since I assumed he had none. Is it possible that he can have forgotten all that and be angry with me for asking him for so much money now, at the most critical moment of my life?

Please write me how he received you, what impression he made upon you (write me frankly what he thinks *of all this business*), and listen only to the advice of your own golden heart, you, my kindest friend! Yes, and be completely frank about me with Maikov; he is a very good man and is fond of me. And, of course, ask him to keep everything secret.

3rd request. For God's sake, understand me, help me, and don't imagine that my love for her can in any way harm my career. And, second, don't think that I have acted dishonorably toward her, or that for purely selfish reasons I dissuaded her from marrying a man who would be *a good match*. There is no advantage for her in marrying another man, nor any *petty* selfishness in me, and so you have no right to think any such thing. If it were otherwise, I would be prepared to sacrifice my life for her, I swear to you, and I would renounce all my hopes for her sake. Judge for yourself: In every one of her letters, including the very last, she writes that she loves me more than anything else in the world and that her suitor means nothing to her *but a practical way out* [several illegible words], and she implores me to believe that it is still all very nebulous. But you must also understand her position. She is craving for a change in my situation, but nothing seems to be happening, nothing and still nothing! So she becomes panicky and, conscious of being a mother with a small child, she is contemplating marriage in the event that my affairs don't straighten themselves out. In her letter before the last one, she tried to allay my jealousy by telling me that there was not one man in Kuznetsk worth my little finger, that she wanted to tell me something but was afraid to, that all sorts of horrible people were hatching intrigues around her, that it was all being done so very crudely without any regard for the amenities. And in the very same letter she assures me that she needs me more than ever and that she feels that I need her, and she tells me to come as quickly as possible and that we shall have a good laugh about it, the two of us. We would laugh, indeed, over the schemings of the old wives who have pledged themselves to marry her off. Yes, but the poor weak thing is afraid of everything. So they may eventually succeed in driving her out of her wits and, what's worse, they would devour her alive if she didn't succumb to their intrigues, and she would be condemned to live alone surrounded by enemies. And, all the same, you have to understand that for her to get married there is just like death and perdition to her! I know that if there were the faintest glimmer of a hope in my situation, she would come to life, take heart and, after writing to her father (for his permission), she would leave either for Barnaul or for Astrakhan.

As to me (read along the margins, following my numbers) (1) there is no doubt in my mind that we should be happy together. If she married me she would be surrounded all her life by good people and with greater respect than with that man. For, after all, I shall myself be a civil servant, and perhaps very soon.

(2) I feel certain that I shall be able to provide for a family, working and writing. And even if there are to be no pardons for the time being, I still think that it will be possible for me to get transferred to the civil service, to be quickly accepted in the 14th grade, start receiving a salary and, above all, to be published, even if only incognito. So I shall have money. And, after all, there is no need for all this to come about right away—the whole thing will straighten itself out at the proper moment. Shall I tell you what I answered her and what I am asking of her? Here is what: (3) that since she cannot marry before the end of her mourning period, i.e., before September, she should wait before giving *that other man* a definite answer; if, however, there should be no change in my situation by September, then *perhaps* she might give her consent to marry him. You must agree that even if I were being selfish and dishonest in my dealings with her, I still could do her no harm in asking her to wait until September. (4) Besides, she loves me. Ah, the poor thing! She is in a terrible turmoil. How could a woman with her heart and her intelligence spend her entire life in Kuznetsk in God knows whose company! She is in the situation of my heroine in *Poor Folk,* who gets married to Bykov (I must have had a premonition!). I write you all this, my dear friend, so that you will put your whole heart and soul into the effort to help me. I am relying on you as if you were my own brother. If it fails I shall be driven to despair. What use will life be to me in that case? I swear I'll do something drastic then. I beseech you, my guardian angel! And if ever you need a man who (5) will have to go through fire and water for you, you have such a man—*it is I.* Because I never desert those whom I love, whether in happiness or in misfortune, and I have proved it.

And thus, my guardian angel, the *4th request.* In the name of God, waste no time and (6) write to her in Kuznetsk informing her as clearly and precisely as possible of all my hopes. Particularly if there is some *positive* development in my situation, give her *every possible detail* about that, and she will rapidly pass from despair to confidence and be rekindled by hope. Write her *the whole truth and nothing but the truth.* And, above all, write as *specifically* as possible. But if you are somewhat at a loss how to go about it, (7) it is really very easy. Write something like this: "F.M. has conveyed to me your regards" (she did ask me to send you her regards and her best wishes), "and since I know that you take a great interest in F.M.'s fate, I hasten to announce some news that will make you happy: there are such and such hopeful developments concerning him, etc." And finally: "I have been thinking about you a great deal. If I were you I would go to Barnaul. You will be warmly welcomed there, etc." So this is how you can write to her. Ah, something else: (8) She wrote me that, as you were leaving, you sent her a letter. She was very pleased and grateful that you hadn't forgotten her, but she also says that there was nothing in your letter to indicate that she would be happy in Barnaul or, for that matter, that Barnaul would be willing to accept me. For that reason she is not sure that Barnaul society would not receive her with disdain as a pauper when she arrived there. I suppose you were (9) very busy and unsettled yourself when you wrote that vague and hurried letter. I appreciate that, and I am not finding fault with you but, for heaven's sake, please put matters straight now. Do it please, for my sake, my friend, my brother, my guardian angel! Save me from despair, for you—more than anyone else—*would be capable of understanding me!* And finally, in the name of Christ, let me know about all the latest developments in my situation as soon as possible, and with full particulars; I am relying entirely on you for that information. Persuade my brother to help me too, act as my advocate when you plead with him, make him understand that in marrying her I shall find happiness, that we do not need much to live on, and that I shall find within myself enough strength and energy to provide for my family. Tell him that if I get permission to write and to be published, then I am saved; that *I won't be a burden to anyone,* I won't ask anyone for help; and *above all* that I am not about to marry right away anyhow, but shall wait until my future is more or less secure. She will be glad to wait as long as there is a hope that I shall be able to secure my future. You should also remind my brother that I am 35 already and that I have enough common sense for 10 men.

Good-bye then, my dear friend! Oh, I forgot! For Christ's sake, talk to my brother about my money problems. Try to persuade him to help me for the last time. *Understand* the situation I find myself in. Don't forsake me! Why, I am going through something that happens only once in a lifetime. And when else should one rescue one's friends if not at times like these? I take you in my arms and embrace you. How are *your affairs?* Why, I know nothing about them here! I am waiting impatiently for a letter from you. I end this letter with reluctance, for I shall be once more left alone with my tears, my doubts, and my despair.

(13) [*sic*] In the name of God, tell me whether Katerina Osipovna is in Petersburg or not. Plead with the Gerngros[s]es to do something about my

and her affairs. Farewell, I kiss and embrace you once again. You are my hope! You are my savior!

Yours,

D.

---

24. Eduard Ivanovich Totleben (1818–1884) was a graduate of the same military engineering school as Dostoyevsky; his younger brother Adolf Ivanovich was Dostoyevsky's classmate there, though they were hardly close friends, despite what Dostoyevsky says in this letter and the next. Eduard was in charge of the fortifications during the siege of Sevastopol (1854–1855) and, as a defender of the city, had just become a national hero comparable to Admiral Pavel Stepanovich Nakhimov (1800–1855) and Vice Admiral Vladimir Alekseyevich Kornilov (1806–1854), both of whom had held command positions in that battle and had been killed in it.

"La dame" is Mariya Dmitriyevna Isayeva. Her relatives lived in Astrakhan, which to Dostoyevsky seemed like "the other side of the world."

Dostoyevsky was hoping that an amnesty would be declared in a manifesto issued either on the occasion of the signing of the peace treaty ending the Crimean War (which took place in Paris on March 18, 1856) or on that of the coronation of Alexander II in the summer of 1856. A manifesto was indeed issued on the latter occasion, and it commuted the sentences of many of the Petrashevtsy, but not Dostoyevsky's.

The novel that Dostoyevsky says he has ready must be, as in the preceding letter, *The Village of Stepanchikovo*. The "article" was probably a patriotic pamphlet in the same vein as Maikov's collection *1854*, but Dostoyevsky eventually abandoned his efforts to have it published.

Count Ivan Fyodorovich Paskiewicz, Prince of Warsaw (1782–1856), was a general who took part in the campaign against Napoleon and in the wars against the Caucasian tribes and the Turks. He quelled the Polish uprising in 1830 and was the vice regent of the Kingdom of Poland.

Maikov had read a poem at a dinner organized in honor of Totleben by the Society of Amateurs of Chess and the Military Arts on December 5, 1856. According to the *Petersburg Gazette*, the poem "aroused general enthusiasm and brought tears to the eyes of many. Totleben rose and kissed the poet. . . ."

Stanislav Avgustovich Lamotte, a graduate of the University of Vilna, was an army medical officer, exiled to Semipalatinsk for his political activities. It was at Lamotte's address that Dostoyevsky received much of his mail.

On the circumstances of Andrei's arrest, see the note to Letter 14. In his own account of the events in his memoirs, Andrei does not say anything about a request from Dostoyevsky "not to explain the error to the authorities for as long as possible."

The heroine of *Poor Folk*, Varvara Dobroselova, is forced into an unwanted marriage and leaves to spend the rest of her life in a remote village.

"Katerina Osipovna" is probably Yekaterina Iosifovna Gerngross.

There is a poignant sequel to this letter. As Dostoyevsky says, he sent Wrangel a letter to be delivered to his brother Mikhail. But by mistake Wrangel left with

Mikhail not that letter but the one that Dostoyevsky had written to Wrangel, with its expressions of suspicion aroused by the fact that Mikhail had written to him so infrequently. Mikhail read the letter and was deeply wounded; in reply, he wrote a long and moving letter to Dostoyevsky, asserting his loyalty and defending his behavior. In a later letter to Wrangel, Dostoyevsky wrote: "Tell my brother that I send him my love and that I beg him on my knees to forgive me for all the pain I caused him."

25. To E. I. Totleben
[Semipalatinsk, March 24, 1856]

Your Excellency, Eduard Ivanovich.

Forgive me for taking the liberty of imposing this letter on you. I am afraid that if you glance at the signature, a name you have probably forgotten—although once (very long ago) I did have the honor of knowing you personally—I am afraid that you may resent my presumption and throw the letter away without reading it. I beg you to be more forbearing. Do not offend me by assuming that I don't realize very well the immense distance that lies between your position and mine. I have been through too many sad experiences in my life not to understand that distance. I am likewise only too well aware that I have no right at all to remind you now that you knew me once upon a time, in order to establish the flimsiest claim to your attention. But I am so unhappy that I cannot resist the hope that you will open your heart to the misfortunes of a wretched exile and that you will give him even if only one minute of your attention.

I have asked Baron Aleksandr Yegorovich Wrangel to hand you this letter. While here in Semipalatinsk, he did more for me than a brother could have done. His friendship gave me much happiness. He is fully aware of my situation. I have asked him to give you my letter personally and he will do so, although I was not even able to assure him that you would accept it with indulgence. You will understand this hesitation in a man who is a former convict. I have a tremendous favor to ask you, but only a very slim hope that you will respond to it.

You may have heard about my arrest and trial, and the royal prescript that followed the affair of 1849 in which I was involved. You may have noted what my further fate was. I am basing this assumption on the fact that, almost from childhood on, I was a very close friend of your brother, Adolf Ivanovich, to whom I felt a deep attachment. And although I have not seen him in recent years, I feel certain that he must have felt sorry for me and may have told you my sad story. I shall not venture to burden you with an account of this affair. I was guilty and I fully acknowledge it. I was convicted of intent to act against the regime (but no more than that). I was sentenced justly and in conformity with the law. My long, arduous, and painful experience has sobered me and, in many respects, changed my ideas. But then, then I was blind and I believed in various theories and utopias. When I left for Siberia, I at least had the consolation of having conducted myself honorably during the trial; I did not try to blame others for my crime and was even ready to sacrifice my own interests if I saw that a confession from me could shield others from misfortune. But I took it upon myself not to confess everything, and for that reason my punishment was of greater severity. For two years running prior to that I had been suffering from strange mental ills. I lapsed into hypochondria. There were even moments when I would lose my sanity. I was terribly irritable, hypersensitive, and prone to distort the most ordinary facts, investing them with a different appearance and dimension. But I felt that, although this disease did have a strong and pernicious effect upon my life, it would have been a poor and even shameful justification. Moreover, I didn't understand that too clearly then. Forgive me for giving you all these details. But be magnanimous and hear me out to the end.

Then came the period of penal servitude—4 years of a bleak, horrible existence. I lived with brigands, men devoid of human feeling, men with perverted values; and during all those four joyless years I did not see, nor could I possibly have seen, anything except the darkest and the ugliest aspects of life. I did not have by my side a single living creature with whom I could have exchanged a heartfelt word; I endured hunger, cold, sickness, work that was beyond my strength, and the hatred of my fellow convicts, who revenged themselves on me for my being a nobleman and an officer. But I swear to you, what caused me the greatest suffering was the fact that I came to understand my delusions, and the realization that I had been cut off from society by exile and that I could no longer be useful to it and serve it to the best of my abilities, aspirations, and talents. I know that I was condemned for my dreams, for my ideas. Thoughts and even convictions change, even the whole person changes, and imagine what it means to me today to suffer for something that is no longer there, and about which I've completely changed my mind; to suffer for my discarded errors, the fallacy of which I already clearly perceive; to feel within me the energy and the ability to do at least something to make up for the futility of my former life, but to languish in inactivity. At the present time I am a soldier serving in Semipalatinsk and was promoted to noncommissioned officer last summer. I know that many have taken and are taking a serious interest in me, that they have interceded on my behalf. I have been and am being given hope. The Monarch is kind and compassionate. And, finally, I know that anyone who takes it upon himself to prove that an unfortunate man wants to do something good will ultimately succeed. I, too, can do something. Why, I am not totally devoid of ability, of feelings, and of principles.

Eduard Ivanovich, I have a great, a tremendous favor to ask of you. There is one thing, though, that makes me hesitant; I have absolutely no right to bother you with my personal affairs. But you have a noble and generous heart—that is something that can be said—as you so gloriously proved just recently to the entire world. It was my good fortune, quite some time ago, long before others, to have had this opinion of you, and to have learned to respect you a long, long time ago. Today your word can mean a great deal to our merciful Monarch, who loves you and is grateful to you. Remember a wretched exile and help him. I want to be useful. It is very hard for a man with strength in his soul and a head on his shoulders not to suffer from inactivity. I am not suited to a military career. I am prepared to give my all, but I am a sick man and, besides, I feel more inclined to another career more in line with my aptitudes. I have my heart set on being discharged from the army and transferred to the civil service somewhere in European Russia, or even here, and on having some say in where I shall live.

But it is not the civil service that I consider as the main aim of my life. Once upon a time, I was encouraged by the favorable public reaction to my literary efforts. I should like to obtain permission to be published. There have been precedents; political criminals before me have benefited from acts of clemency and benevolence and have obtained permission to write and be published. I have always considered the calling of a writer as an eminently noble and useful one. It is my conviction that only in this capacity could I be truly useful and, perhaps, attract some attention to myself, recover my good name, and earn myself some sort of a livelihood, because all I have is a certain literary talent, and it may be a very limited one at that.

I shall not hide from you the fact that, besides the sincere desire to change my present life for one more suited to my abilities, the one circumstance that my future happiness may depend on (a purely personal circumstance) has prompted me to take the liberty of reminding you of my existence. I am not asking for everything right away, but only for permission to leave the army and enter the civil service.

Please do not accuse me of weakness when you read these requests. I have been through such suffering that I feel I have proved my patience and even a certain amount of courage by my very ability to bear it. But now I have lost courage, and I realize it myself. I have always felt that it was a sign of weakness to bother other people, whoever they might be, and so it is particularly embarrassing for me to bother you with my affairs. But please take pity on me, I beg you. Up to now I have borne my misfortune bravely. But now circumstances have broken me, and I made up my mind to have a try, yes, only to have a try. The idea of writing you and of asking for your help did not occur to me earlier, I swear to you. Somehow, I should have felt uneasy and distressed to remind you of myself. Lately I have followed your heroic deeds with the most disinterested admiration. If you knew what delight it gave me to tell others about you, you would believe me. If you knew how proud I was to recall that I had the honor of knowing you personally. When they found it out here, they bombarded me with questions about you, and I very much enjoyed telling them of you. I am not afraid to write you all this. Your feat is so glorious that even such words as these cannot sound like flattery. The man who will hand you this letter can bear witness to the sincerity and the disinterestedness of my sentiments. The gratitude of a Russian to the man who, in an epoch of misfortune, turned the grim defense of Sevastopol into a source of everlasting glory is understandable. But I repeat again, it never even crossed my mind then to bother you with my personal troubles. It is only now, in this moment of despair, and not knowing where to turn, that I remembered how gracious, natural, and warm you have always been with me. I remembered the bold, noble impulses of your heart, and hope burgeoned in me. I wondered whether you would spurn me now that you have attained such a glorious and exalted position while I have fallen low, so low. So forgive my presumption and especially this long (much too long—I realize it) letter and, if you can do something for me, I beseech you, please do it. And I have another great favor to ask of you, which I implore you not to refuse me: Remember me, when you have a chance, to your brother, Adolf Ivanovich, and tell him that I love him as before and that, during my four years of penal servitude, reliving in my mind my whole past life day after day, hour after hour, he frequently crossed my thoughts. But he knows himself how fond of him I am. I hear that recently he has been very ill. Has he recovered? Is he alive? Forgive me for this further request, but I know of no one else who could help me to fulfill this long-standing wish, and so I turned to you. I know that in writing this letter I have committed a new breach of service regulations: an army private writing directly to an adjutant general. But you are magnanimous, and I commend myself to your magnanimity.

With the deepest respect and with the sincere feeling of gratitude of a Russian, I dare to remain,

The most obedient servant of Your Excellency,

Fyodor Dostoyevsky

---

25. There is evidence that Totleben did intercede on Dostoyevsky's behalf. Whether or not because of this intercession (others were also making efforts for him at the same time), Dostoyevsky was commissioned as a second lieutenant in October 1856 and was granted the right to publish the following year.

26.   To A. Ye. Wrangel
Semipalatinsk, November 9, 1856

I had already received your letter on October 30, my invaluable friend, Aleksandr Yegorovich, but special circumstances prevented me from answering you by the first mail. I was planning at that time to make a trip to B[ar-naul], and I wanted to write you from there after having seen X, which, of course, would have made my letter more interesting. Up to now, however, my trip has not yet materialized, but I'm practically sure that I'll be going next week if the money I've been promised is sent. Then I'll write you from Barnaul, and you can expect that letter in the very near future. As to this letter I'm writing now, don't consider it as a letter, but merely as a few lines by way of a hurried answer of sorts. If you were here, a whole week wouldn't be enough, my unforgettable friend, to tell you all the things I have to tell you.

You write that I owe a debt of gratitude to Totleben and to His Highness, Prince Oldenburgsky, as well as to our infinitely merciful Monarch. I am grateful to them from the bottom of my heart and, if you see Totleben, tell him that I have no words with which to express my gratitude to him. I shall remember his noble act on my behalf as long as I live— But my heart is just: I realize that had it not been for you, my dear friend, and your efforts to help me, it would have been impossible to make such rapid headway in my situation. You have been sent to me by God. I thank you and I hug you very, very hard. You know that I love you.

Now, I shall tell you briefly (not that I shouldn't have liked to dwell on this at great length, but there's just so much you can say in a letter)—you'll never understand, my inestimable friend, the sadness and sorrow into which your long silence plunged me! My friend, I am familiar with the state of mind which inhibits people from taking pen in hand to write even to a person capable of comprehending them, in a word—to me, from whom you had virtually no secrets. X's arrival in Barnaul, at a time when it was being rumored that she would be in P[etersbur]g for the whole winter, troubled me. I knew only too well the effect that her arrival and departure could not fail to have on you; I had as much as predicted everything that you wrote me of in your letter. But such strange thoughts, such suspicions and suppositions kept crossing my mind concerning you and X that I felt greatly depressed and worried about you. It was already known here that you had been named as a member of the expedition, but I was certain that you were still in P—g. I kept wondering every day: Why doesn't he write to me? But I swear that, despite everything, I never once doubted your friendship nor imagined that you might have forgotten me. That you proved by sending me your portrait (which I still haven't received). But, my friend, I understand the misgivings a person might have about aggravating his heartache by talking about it to someone else. Still, couldn't you really have sent me a couple of lines at least? The other reason you give for your silence (namely, that you *hadn't fulfilled a single one of my requests*) makes no sense to me at all. I asked you for money as one asks a brother or a friend when the only choice left is between a noose and resolute action. And so I made up my mind to ask you, knowing that my request might inconvenience you; but then, if you had found yourself in a predicament similar to my own and had asked me to take a terrible risk to help you, I would have taken it. Consequently, I had no qualms about troubling you. (I should have been lost if I hadn't borrowed money here and gone into debt—I needed money not in order to exist but in order to carry out my *intentions*. You know from my preceding letters the mental state I was in. It's a wonder that I still haven't gone out of my mind!) But tell me, most kind Aleksandr Yegorovich, if you yourself didn't have the wherewithal to help me (which was certainly the case, because you never left me in the lurch before), tell me, for God's sake, why couldn't you simply have written *no* or I *cannot* (if your inability to satisfy my request was one of the reasons for your silence)? Did you really think I was incapable of understanding that it was only *the impossibility* rather than lack of friendship that compelled you to refuse me? And what right would I have had to be angry with you for not sending me the money? (As it is, I am completely indebted to you—you who have been and are like a dear and beloved brother to me, for, after all you have done for me, you must allow me to call you that.) Furthermore, I just can't tell you how much I've missed you in recent days (and, besides, of late I have frequently been sick). And so I fancied that something tragic might have happened to you, something of the sort we once spoke of. And there was no one around who could give me any news of you at all.

Finally your letter came and dispelled many of my misgivings; but not all of them. My friend, I am even pleased—although it hurts me to touch the sore spot in your heart—I am pleased that God has prompted you to break off definitely with X. Your relations with her had become thoroughly disquieting for you. The chances are that you would have ended up in disaster. My God, I am so curious at the prospect of meeting X at last! (This should happen soon, and you can rely upon me, my invaluable friend, to report to you, down to the most delicate nuance, the impressions she makes upon me when we meet.) What can I say to you? Can I possibly console you with words? Oh, my friend, no one can understand your despair better than I *who suffer just as you do*. And who are you to be consoled? As though your heart were such that consolation could make it feel better. Time and time alone will heal everything (I say that, but I don't really believe it, judging from my own experience).

Since you are staying in European Russia throughout the winter, do something, plunge into diversions but, in the name of Christ and in the name of God, write me more and more often, and even if it is only a few lines, write anyway. I should like to see you so much, but when? when! You inquire about my feelings for M[ariya] D[mitriyevna]. Well, if you wanted to know anything at all about me, you had to ask me that question, because she is still *all that matters* in my life. I have given up everything, I think of nothing except of her. If I was thrilled about getting my officer's commission, it was precisely because it might enable me to see her sooner. I haven't received the money so I haven't gone yet. My brother has given me some hope. I am expecting it sometime next week and I shall set out just as soon as it arrives. *Father* has promised to let me off for 15 days or so. I am crazy about him [a whole line illegible] her would have led me to my grave or literally driven me to suicide, if [I had not seen her?] [several more illegible words].

Do not shake your head and do not condemn me. I realize that in many respects my behavior toward her is irrational, since there is so little hope for me; but hope or no hope, it's all the same to me. I think of nothing else. All I want is to see her and to hear her voice! I am a miserable madman! This kind of love is a disease. I feel it. I went into debt to make the trip (I tried to get to her on another occasion, but I made it only as far as Zmiyev—it didn't work out). Now I'm planning another trip; it will ruin me, but what do I care! For Christ's sake, don't show this letter to my brother. I am terribly guilty toward him. The poor fellow is making desperate efforts to help me, and here I am wasting money in this way! I asked you for money, too, because I must either satisfy my longing or drown myself. My relationship with her is still the same. Every week I get long letters full of the deepest and most sincere attachment. But she often calls me her brother in those letters. Still she loves me. My merely appearing in Kuznetsk was almost enough for her to come back again to me. Oh, don't ask me to leave that woman and this love! She was the light of my life. She came to me at the saddest moment of my existence, and she brought my soul back to life. Meeting her gave a new meaning to my entire existence. If you only knew what an angel she is, what a soul she has, what a heart! Poor thing, what misery she is going through now! It is terrible to live in Kuznetsk. She is making desperate efforts to get her son into the officer cadet school (I wrote to ask Slutsky to help in that matter and he promised to do whatever he could); is struggling to get her pension; and is living on the crumbs her father sends her, modestly and with a quiet dignity that has gained her the respect of the whole town. Hers is a firm, strong nature. Her marrying that (other) fellow is apparently quite out of the question, impossible for financial reasons (he makes only 300 rubles), and she doesn't want to be a burden on him. I shall write you about everything from Barnaul.

You ask me what I want, my friend, and what you should ask for, and you say, too, that they may transfer me to Russia. But, my friend, the mercy of our angelic Tsar is infinite and I know that, anyway, even if I were not in the service, they would allow me once and for all to return to European Russia in a year or 2. And even if I am assigned to the army, this is still no solution, for in any case I should make a poor officer, if only because of my health. But I shall have to serve. The only reason I want to go back to Russia is to embrace my family and consult competent doctors to find out what this disease I am suffering from is (epilepsy)—what these fits are, which are still continuing and which deaden my memory and all of my faculties each time and which, I fear, will some day drive me into insanity. What kind of an officer am I? If only they would allow me to resign, even if I had to remain here *temporarily*—that is all I wish. I could manage to get enough money to live on. I shouldn't starve here. And then it is a question of *her* (*she* is what matters most), and so let me know *definitely* (as far as possible) (1) *whether I could,* at the earliest possible moment, because of the poor state of my health, submit my resignation (asking, in any case, for permission to return to Russia *to consult doctors*) and (2) whether I should be able *to publish,* which to me is of *the utmost importance* and which you don't *even mention* in your letter. But don't you see—this is my way of earning a living and *making a career* for myself, because I have *confidence* in myself and hope to become well known and achieve a reputation, consideration, and eventually draw attention to my plight. Therefore, I ask you to give me a firm answer to this question: If I submitted something for publication in the near future under my name (or under a pen name)—*could it be published?* In the name of God, my friend, my invaluable brother, don't forsake me, don't forget me, and write me about this as soon as you can and as concretely as possible. Anyway, after I get back from my forthcoming trip I shall be much more definite about my intentions, because so much depends on this trip. And, in the meantime, I want your answer to these two questions.

So you met Goncharov? How did you like him? A gentleman who is a member of the "United Society," who has the soul of a petty official, not an idea in his head, and the eyes of a steamed fish, whom God, as if for a joke, has endowed with brilliant talent.

It is such a shame that you didn't come to know my brother more closely. He is a prince of a man, and I am sure you wouldn't find anyone who would be more devoted to you than he is. I enclose a letter for him. For God's sake, give it to him as soon as possible; don't linger over it. I am writing to you slapdash because there are many things I cannot tell you for certain as yet. I repeat: *my next letter* will be more precise and thorough.

I can't tell you anything about your books and belongings. Stepanov hasn't *a thing*—he told me himself (neither the samovar nor the pots and pans). In the summer, I saw four crates that Demchinsky sent to Ostermeier. Stepanov says you didn't leave anything with him. Demchinsky says he doesn't know what is in the crates. I shall find out about everything in Barnaul, including the books, and shall try to attend to everything you asked me to. If they let me have the suitcase (that you are giving me as a present), I shall take it. Thank you, my friend, for always thinking of me.

I thank you tremendously for your promise to fit me out, but I got outfitted here as best I could (on credit and in one way or another). It is a terrible pity I couldn't have let you know about it sooner, because you may already have sent me everything. It makes me feel so guilty to think that you have spent so much on me. However, I shan't refuse a helmet, a short sword and a sash—in fact, I'll ask you for them—because they are things that cannot be found here (especially the helmet).

I shan't write about the local news. Everything and everyone here is just the same (I shall write about it some other time). I am on quite close terms with Demchinsky (he is very helpful in connection with my *trips* because he himself often accompanies me, since he is having some love affairs in Zmiyev). For God's sake, don't get the idea that he has taken your place with me, because you know very well what kind of a person he is. But he is awfully devoted to me (I wonder why), and I cannot help being grateful to him. Why is it that he isn't overly fond of you? But then, with him it's all a question of *inspiration*. Obukh is in Vernoye.

Farewell, my precious friend, write me as soon as possible, and you can expect a letter from me very soon. I hug you very tight,

Yours,

D.

M. D. has inquired about you 1000 times. She is very worried about you as a result of my letters to her. She likes you immensely and speaks about you almost with veneration. She has infinite respect for you.

---

26. Dostoyevsky was planning a trip to Barnaul because Mariya Dmitriyevna was there at the time. So, too, was Yekaterina Iosifovna Gerngross, with whom Wrangel was in love and whom Dostoyevsky refers to here as "X."

Prince Pyotr Georgiyevich Oldenburgsky (1812–1881) was a prominent figure in education and philanthropy. He founded a law school, a technical institute, and several hospitals and orphanages.

Wrangel had been named a participant in a scientific and archaeological expedition that was to take a round-the-world route to China's east coast, Japan, and the mouth of the Amur River. However, the naval squadron that was to conduct the expedition did not leave until the fall of 1857, and Wrangel was in Petersburg until that time.

"Father" is Dostoyevsky's battalion commander, Belikhov.

The "other" man was Nikolai Borisovich Vergunov, a schoolteacher from Tomsk. Mariya Dmitriyevna had hinted to Dostoyevsky that she might marry him.

The United Society was a charitable organization.

Stepanov was the man from whom Wrangel rented an apartment while he lived in Semipalatinsk. Demchinsky was the adjutant to the military governor of the region. Obukh was an artillery officer with whom both Wrangel and Dostoyevsky were on friendly terms.

27. TO A. YE. WRANGEL

Semipalatinsk, December 21, 1856

My kind, my invaluable Aleksandr Yegorovich,

I don't know how long I have been waiting for your letter now, and in vain. Did you get mine in which I wrote you that I intended to leave Semipalatinsk for a couple of weeks? But even if you did get it, your answer couldn't possibly have reached me yet; but what I have in mind is that letter you promised me without waiting for a reply from me. You promised you would send me the officer's gear. But when I wrote that you shouldn't ruin yourself for me unnecessarily, that I didn't need the complete set of equipment (because, in any case, it would reach me too late), and that if it was true that I was in great need of some of the items such as a shako, dress uniform epaulets, buttons with the number on them, etc., the only reason was that they are unobtainable here and must be ordered by mail. And that is why I wrote that I would accept these minor items from you with gratitude. But if it is the procuring and buying of those articles that is the cause of the delay—if you are waiting till you have completed the purchases before writing to me—then, this is quite absurd. Ah, my dear, unforgettable friend, to whom I owe so much as it is, how can such trifles stop you from writing to me? But perhaps I've got it all wrong, perhaps time has already succeeded in eradicating the memory of me from your heart and you no longer love me as you used to. Who knows? But no, it is sinful for me to talk that way. You have done too much for me to allow doubt to creep into my heart. That would be sheer ingratitude on my part. I want none of these doubts, I chase them from me, I embrace you from the bottom of my heart, and I want to talk to you just as we used to in Semipalatinsk when you were everything to me—a friend and a brother, when we shared all the concerns of our hearts.

In the first place, has it been long since you last saw Totleben? Is he in Petersburg? And if he is, did you convey my thanks to him? Tell him, my friend, that I have no words to express my gratitude, that I shall venerate him for the rest of my life, and that I shall never forget all he has done for me. For God's sake, my good friend, write me about this as soon as possible.

I promised to write you a long letter, but here I am writing only on a single sheet. The reason is that I am not certain that my letter will find you in Petersburg. You wrote that you were thinking of gong to Irbit and, who knows, you may take it into your head to come all the way to Barnaul. In

109

that case, I don't know whether my letter will lie waiting for you in Petersburg or whether it will be forwarded to you wherever you may be at the time. And this is why I am writing briefly about things I could have dwelt on at much greater length. There is yet another reason, which you will understand from the following words: "God alone knows how much I should like to talk to you directly rather than through a letter!"

If I could see you, I would tell you something that I cannot tell you now. Let me say only that I went to Barnaul and to Kuznetsk with Demchinsky and Semyonov (the member of the Geographic Society). We got to Barnaul on December 24 [*sic*], on X's name day, and before he had even seen us, Gerngross asked Semyonov to invite us to the ball he was giving. I liked him very much. But—I don't know why—*he has now suddenly become somewhat prejudiced against you.* He said so directly.

I found her very appealing *in every respect,* but, for no good reason at all, she seemed to be rather avoiding me. She was polite and nice, everything seemed fine, but she clearly did not trust me. But even if she did suspect that I know* I do not see why she should not consider me an honorable man. I must point out that she apparently tried to speak of you as coldly as she could, even with a touch of mockery. I don't know why, but I liked that very much—I don't mean her bantering but rather her *tactics.* She is very intelligent, and I am sure that, if she wants to, she can be a charmer. I wished from the depths of my soul that the qualities of her heart matched the rest. But her heart was well hidden from the curious. Four or five times we got together during the ball and talked. I deliberately abstained from dancing in order to talk to her.

I shan't write about the inhabitants of Barnaul. I got acquainted with a number of them. It is a bustling town, full of gossip and half-baked Talleyrands! I stayed in Barnaul for twenty-four hours and then proceeded to Kuznetsk all by myself. I stayed there for five days, then returned to Barnaul for another twenty-four hours. I had dinner at Gerngross's and remained there till evening. He treated me wonderfully. During dinner I made a gaffe. They have a son, a small boy of about eight, whom I liked very much and who is the spitting image of his mother. I said so. She replied that there was no resemblance at all. I proceeded to analyze the resemblance feature by feature. And just imagine—in the family, as I learned later, they consider the boy to be quite ugly! So that was a fine compliment!

My friend, apparently you were very open with X in Petersburg and showed her my letters. Is that so? At any rate, when I left for Kuznetsk she told Semyonov (with whom I've become very friendly) that I had gone to Kuznetsk to get married, that there was a woman there with whom I was in love, and that she knew it from you.

---

*Several words heavily crossed out, apparently not by Dostoyevsky—Eds.

I received your portrait and I thank you for it, my dear friend. But I did not get the suitcase that you made me a present of. *Gerngross* never said one word about it, and I felt it would be embarrassing to bring the subject up myself. He must surely have forgotten all about it, but it doesn't matter, because possibly it is Ostermeier who has the suitcase. If he does, I'll get it later. In all probability your books and minerals are at Ostermeier's in Zmiyev, in the four crates that were sent to him last summer. On the way back we arrived in Zmiyev at night. I couldn't go to Ostermeier's. *But you may rest assured* that everything will be retrieved and delivered to you. I hope to get back to Zmiyev again.

And now, my friend, I wish to inform you of a matter that is of great importance to me. I must be freely open with you as a friend. Here's the story in a nutshell: *if one particular circumstance does not prevent it,* I shall be married—you know to whom—before Shrovetide. No one except this woman could make me happy. As to her, she still loves me, and I have always carried out her wishes. It was she herself who said *yes. What I wrote you last summer about her* affected her attachment to me very little. She loves me. That I know for certain. I also knew it in the summer when I wrote you that letter. Soon after that she became disenchanted with her new affection. I had already gathered it from her letters last summer. Everything was clear to me. She never had any secrets from me. Ah, if you only knew what sort of a woman she is! I am *certain* I shall marry her, although there is a circumstance that would take too long to explain and that could delay our marriage for an indefinite time. It is a circumstance that is quite beyond our control. But from the way things look now, I do not think *it will intervene.* And if it doesn't, by the time you get this letter, *the whole thing will already be settled.*

I have no money, not a single kopek. By the most conservative, austere estimates I shall need 600 silver rubles *for everything.* I intend to *borrow* them from Kovrigin (he is in Omsk just now, but is coming back very soon). Lately we have been on excellent terms. I expect he will lend me the money. If he doesn't—nothing will come off, for an indefinite time, at any rate. I shall ask Kovrigin to lend me that sum as a long-term loan, for at least a year. But with the next mail I shall write to a rich uncle of mine in Moscow, who has helped our family on more than one occasion, and ask him for 600 silver rubles. If he lets me have them, I'll pay Kovrigin back right away. If not, I shall have to find the money *myself,* because it would be a debt of *honor* and it will have to be paid as soon as possible.

I cannot rely upon my brother. If he had the money, he would give it to me. But he writes that things are not going well, at least for the time being. Hence, the only hope I have, both of repaying the debt and of providing for our life in the future, is to obtain permission to publish. And do not be surprised, my dear friend, at my going around talking of borrowing such a large sum as 600 silver rubles when I haven't a kopek. It is because I have *more than* 1000 rubles' worth of stuff ready for publication. Therefore, even if my uncle disappointed me, I should have enough to repay my debt, as long as they allowed me to publish. But if I don't get permission for another year— I'm done for. Then it would be better for me not to be alive! Never in my life have I been through such a critical moment! And so I want you to realize, my incomparable friend, how important any piece of *news concerning permission to publish* would be to me. And I pray you, as I would pray God, if ever you hear anything about it, please let me know *at once* (as I already asked you in my last letter). I beg you to do so, and if you still feel toward me as you used to, you will do it. Am I right, my friend, or am I deceiving myself? (Why hasn't my *A Child's Fairy Tale*, which you wrote me about, been published? *Have they refused?* This is very important for me to know. It goes without saying that I am willing to publish, *even forever, anonymously* or under a pen name.) If Kovrigin gives me the money, I shall try to start out between January 20 and 25 and shall return to Semipalatinsk about twenty days later, accompanied by my wife. In Barnaul, people somehow *hope* that you will be there. So could we meet there, I wonder?

Are you seeing my brother? For God's sake, see him and put in a good word for me. I am not asking for money—he has none. What I should like him to do, though, is to send me a few things if he can. I should like to have them very much. And ask my brother to write me everything he knows about the *backstage secrets* of today's literary scene. It is very important to me.

But before I take leave of you in this letter, I have one further favor to ask of you, and for this one I go down on my knees and beg you. Do you remember my writing about Vergunov last summer? I asked you to say a word about him to Gasford [*sic*]. Now, he is dearer to me than my own brother. It would be too long to explain our relations to you, but here is what it is all about: His last remaining hope to arrange his life is to take an exam in Tomsk that would qualify him for a higher category and a position with a salary of 1000 paper rubles. He would get all that if he passed the exam. But he can't do it without pull [several words heavily crossed out]. It is all in the hands of the principal of the Tomsk high school, State Councilor Fyodor Semyonovich Meshcherin. Now, if some *influential person* were to write to Meshcherin about Vergunov, telling him that this man will be taking the examination and *calling Meshcherin's attention to him,* there is no doubt that Meshcherin [several words covered with ink]. It is no sin to ask that something be done for Vergunov—*he is worth it.* And so, I beg you, if you have any friend or relative connected with the Ministry of Education in some important capacity, could he not write a letter to Meshcherin about Vergunov? Do you ever see Apollon Maikov? He knows Vyazemsky. Couldn't he write to Vyazemsky, for instance? In the name of God, do whatever you can, think about it, and be a true brother to me. Farewell, my dear friend, I embrace you. For Christ's sake, write as soon as possible and let me know about everything. Farewell.

All yours,
D.

N.B. Don't write and tell X what I have written you about her. Don't give me away. Who knows, she may not like it—

---

27. For an identification of Semyonov, see note to Letter 28.

Dostoyevsky writes that his party reached Barnaul "on December 24," but he obviously means November 24, because even the letter before this one, dated December 14, was written after the trip he mentions here.

Kovrigin occupied an important position in a factory near Semipalatinsk. Dostoyevsky later wrote that Kovrigin did indeed lend him 600 silver rubles "without the slightest hesitation. . . . He is a prince of a man!"

Prince Pyotr Andreyevich Vyazemsky (1792–1878) was a poet and literary critic and, at the time of this letter, deputy minister of education.

28.   To M. M. DOSTOYEVSKY

Semipalatinsk, March 9, 1857

It is two weeks already, my dear, invaluable brother, since I returned from Kuznetsk with my wife, but it is only now that I have found a free moment to write you. My dearly beloved, for God's sake, don't be angry with me for not having written you immediately upon my arrival, with the first mail. You are always in my mind and heart. I love you as much as it is possible to. But, of course, a man of your experience will believe me when I tell you that my new life has brought me so many worries and responsibilities, has made things so hectic for me, that I don't know myself why my head does not split. Nevertheless I have managed to write to Uncle and to our sister (she had specifically asked me to write *immediately*). Uncle has helped me, and I have enough to live on for the time being, and for later, I trust in God's grace, and I myself won't fail to go on working with even greater zeal.

But undoubtedly you would like to know in some detail how my affairs have been settled. Without going into it at great length, I can tell you that, on the whole, everything has turned out fine. A good friend of mine, on whom I was relying while I was waiting for Uncle's help, came to my aid by lending me 600 silver rubles for a year (and even longer). As a matter of fact, my dear fellow, I must tell you that he was by no means the only person who showed a sincere interest in me—there were many others. Two others, for instance, insisted on lending me money (for an unlimited time) and threatened to quarrel with me if I didn't accept their friendly services. So, on top

113

of the 600 rubles, I had no other choice but to borrow another 200—altogether 800 silver rubles, almost all of which had been spent by the time I returned to Semipalatinsk. Actually, to be precise, I spent a total of exactly 700 silver rubles. Now, perhaps you may wonder, brother, how I could have spent such a large sum? Indeed, I never expected to spend so much myself, but I found that there was just no way for me to spend less. The preparations for the journey; the clothes for myself and for her (because she lacked many of the things that were absolutely essential—but they really are the most indispensable things and were even of the lowest quality); then there was the 1500-verst trip in a closed carriage (there was no choice because her health is not too strong, it was freezing cold, and the roads were bad) so that, with one thing and another, I had to pay for four horses; the wedding in Kuznetsk, although it couldn't have been simpler; the rental of an apartment; fitting it out with some sort of furniture, plates, pots, and pans—all that took so much money, you wouldn't believe it.

I knew hardly anyone in Kuznetsk, but there she introduced me to the nicer people, who had treated her with respect. The local police chief and his wife acted as the bride's parents for me, my groomsmen were also quite respectable, kind and simple people, and they, together with the priest and two families she knew, made up the guests at the wedding.

On the way back (we came through Barnaul), I stopped in Barnaul at a good friend's. And there I had a stroke of misfortune. I quite unexpectedly had an epileptic fit that scared my wife to death and filled me with sadness and depression. The doctor (a learned and competent one) told me that, notwithstanding what other doctors had previously told me, I had *real epilepsy* and that I could expect to suffocate during one of the fits as a result of a throat spasm, and that this is sure to be the cause of my death. I myself had begged the doctor to tell me the whole truth on his honor. In general, he advised me to beware of the new moon. (Now the new moon is approaching and I expect a fit.) So I want you to understand, my dear friend, what desperate thoughts are roving around in my head. But why talk about it! It still may not be sure that what I have is real epilepsy. In deciding to get married, I completely took the word of the doctors who assured me that mine were just nervous fits that could disappear with a change in my way of life. Had I known that I had true epilepsy, I wouldn't have married. Now, for my peace of mind, and in order to consult *real* doctors and *to take the necessary steps, I must* resign from the army as soon as possible and move to Russia. But how can I do it? There is only one hope! If they give me permission to publish, I shall earn enough money and then I shall be able to move. Besides, what frightens me is the thought that a fit could occur while I am performing my service duties, for instance, while I am in charge of the guard detail, wearing my tight uniform. Judging from what I have been told by those who

114

have witnessed my fits and seen what happens to my chest and my breathing, I should be certain to suffocate. But God is merciful, so I will only repeat for the tenth time how important permission to publish is to me.

I brought a sick wife back to Semipalatinsk. Although I did my best to prepare everything when I left, more than half remained undone because of my lack of experience, and so we had two hectic weeks after getting here. And, on top of all that, the brigade commander arrived and we had extra duties and inspections; in short, I was completely overwhelmed, and that's why you must forgive me for not having written you immediately after I got back here.

Now my wife feels better. She tells me to ask you to excuse her for not writing you now. She will do so soon. She insists that she hasn't yet *prepared herself* for it. She loves all of you infinitely. She has loved you all before, when I (starting in 1854) began reading her the letters I received from you and she got to know all about you. From what I have told her about you, she has great respect for you and keeps setting you up as an example to me. She is a kind and tender creature, a bit rash and impulsive, and highly emotional; her past life has left painful scars on her psyche. Transitions in her feelings are incredibly quick, but she always remains kind and generous. I love her very much, and she loves me and, thus far, everything is fine.

When I received the money from Uncle (whom I thank from the bottom of my heart), I repaid a part of my debt. At the moment, I have 250 silver rubles in my drawer, but then I need them to live on at least until I get permission to publish, and so I am glad that, for some time at any rate, I don't have to worry. And, somehow, I have a blind confidence in the future, provided God grants me good health. A strange thing: from a terrible experience and misfortune I have emerged with a feeling of extraordinary verve and self-confidence. I'm not sure, though, that that is a good thing. I hope God will send me enough sense not to be overconfident. But don't be concerned and don't fret over me. Everything will turn out all right. But, believe me, I miss you badly, my invaluable friend, my dear, kind, and generous brother! I got your letter, I thank you for the packages (that haven't arrived yet), but when I read of your difficulties, I was distressed that you had spent money on us. I thank you a thousand times, and my wife can't find words to express her gratitude to you. But, I see, my dear fellow, that your business has not been getting any better all this time! It really has me worried! You are relying so heavily on the cigars—what if they don't sell? And that could so easily happen, after all. It seems to me that the greatest drawback is the high price of your cigars. But I am no expert in the matter. May God send you all the luck in the world! Weather this crisis and, for Christ's sake, don't take any more risks, don't get in too deep, but rather go forward little by little—it is safer that way.

But what do you say of our sister Sasha? Why should she make us all blush? Yes, just as I said—blush! Because all the members of our family are generous and dignified. Whom can she take after, to be so vulgar? It has always surprised me that she, my youngest sister, never would write me a line. Can it be because she is a *lieutenant colonel's wife?* But that's silly and stupid. Please write me more about her, in greater detail. It is a pity that I am in such a hurry, otherwise I would have written you more and in greater detail.

Now, let me ask you a question. I asked you before, my dear fellow— what has become of my *Child's Fairy Tale.* Please, my friend, tell me *definitely* (I implore you) whether they really intend to publish it. If they did intend to, did they try, and if they didn't try, why not? For God's sake, write me all about it. This request of mine will be my answer to your assumption that I haven't been barred from publishing. You must agree that the fate of that little piece is important to me in many respects.

My friend, I am so sorry about Butkov! And to die the way he did! But what were you all thinking of to allow him to die in a hospital! It is so sad!

Farewell, my guardian angel, give my regards to all those who remember me. As to me, I remember everyone, and I still love those whom I loved. I feel guilty toward Verochka and her husband because I haven't written them for so long, but I'll write everyone soon. Kiss all the children in turn and remember me especially to Emiliya Fyodorovna. And may God send her every happiness!

My wife is not even adding a line to this letter. When I suggested that she do so, she replied that she would write you a letter of her own, as well as one to Varinka. However, she asked me to convey her sincere regards and very best wishes to you and Emiliya Fyodorovna. And I can witness that she means it most sincerely. Farewell,

Your brother,
Dost[oyevsky]

---

28. Dostoyevsky and Mariya Dmitriyevna Isayeva were married in Kuznetsk on February 6, 1857. Kuznetsk was about 400 miles from Semipalatinsk (1 verst = about two-thirds of a mile). According to the records of the church in which the marriage took place, one of the witnesses was Nikolai Vergunov.

The "good friend" at whose house Dostoyevsky and his bride stopped in Barnaul was Pyotr Petrovich Semyonov-Tyan-Shansky (1827–1914), a geographer, traveler, entomologist, and political figure. He had had some slight contact with the Petrashevsky group and had met Dostoyevsky in that connection. At the time of this letter, he was head of a Russian Geographical Society expedition studying Central Asia.

Dostoyevsky was granted leave for treatment of his epilepsy in June and July 1857. He spent the time at the Ozernoye army post.

29. To Ye. I. Yakushkin
Semipalatinsk, June 1, 1857

Dear Sir, Yevgeny Ivanovich,

Aleksandr Pavlovich has conveyed to me everything you asked him to tell me. I don't really know what I have done to earn your friendship or how I can ever repay your kindness to me. I should like so much to see you and to have the honor of knowing you better. In an effort to be brief, I shan't write you anything about my situation and my hopes. Aleksandr Pavlovich will be kind enough to tell you what I am hoping to achieve in the near future, as well as of my hopes of getting to Moscow. But now I shall come directly to the point that interests me more than almost anything else and that is the key to all my future hopes in my life—the resumption of my literary career.

Aleksandr Pavlovich has sent me 100 silver rubles in your name.

Please, most kind Yevgeny Ivanovich, let me know urgently what this money is and where it comes from and whose it is. I suppose it is yours, i.e., in your brotherly concern, you have sent me this sum to encourage my literary efforts and thus are trying to help me doubly. Aleksandr Pavlovich writes that you have taken upon yourself the task of trying to make arrangements for the publication of my works and that you hope to get me a substantial sum for them when you succeed in selling them. It goes without saying that I won't fail to respond to your encouragement, although I simply have no idea how to thank you for your interest in me.

Thus far, although I have been very anxious to publish, I have restrained myself from trying. I had been under the impression that I had no right to. Now it would seem, however, that my fears were unfounded. Many people have been asking me to submit my writings for publication. So I made up my mind some time ago to do something about it, but I didn't know how to go about it. In the first place, I didn't know where I should send things. I am no longer familiar with the editorial setups of most of the magazines. The last thing I wanted to do (and this is still the case) was to publish under my real name. Lately I have been thinking of *Russian Messenger*. My friend Pleshche-yev (who is now in Orenburg) has informed me that he has written to Katkov about me. And so I should prefer to start with *Russian Messenger*. But here is the snag: What should I offer to the *Messenger*? Let me tell you quite frankly: I decided long ago what I wanted to start with, and I won't start with anything else. Although I do have a few other things, I shall only consider starting publication with a novel or a story.

Recently, i.e., during the past 1½ years or so, I have been mulling over and working on a novel which, unfortunately, is too voluminous. I say unfortunately because it is questionable whether the *Messenger* would be willing to publish a novel of the length of one of Dickens's novels. This is the most important point. In the second place, I should like to know whether you already have some particular publisher or magazine in view that would be willing to publish something written by me. And, thirdly, what is the best and most advantageous place to publish, i.e., which magazine would now be preferable in that sense?

Now I shall tell you exactly what I am working on, without, of course, telling you the plot. It is a long novel, with a character whose adventures have an overall connection between them but which, at the same time, consists of episodes that are quite independent of one another and complete in themselves. Each episode forms a part. So that I could, for instance, have the episodes published one by one, as separate adventures or stories. Of course, it would be desirable to have them published in order. Let me tell you also that the novel will consist of three books, each of approximately 20 printer's sheets and divided into several parts. Thus far, I have written only Book 1, which consists of five parts. I shall not write the remaining two books right away but a bit later, because, in the first place, although they are the continuation of the adventures of the same character, they are of a different nature and form and take place some years later. Anyway, Book 1, as it is, forms a complete and independent novel in five parts. It is already written but has to be polished still further, and so I shall start polishing it part by part and shall send you the parts one by one. As soon as I get your answer, I'll send you Part 1 of Book 1, which forms a wholly independent and complete story.

I should be extremely grateful if you, for your part, would answer the questions I have asked you in this letter. Talk to publishers if you know any personally, and offer it to them. Let me know what they have to say and how much they will offer per printer's sheet. Except for this novel I am engaged in no other work (literary, that is), because it absorbs me completely.

Forgive me, Yevgeny Ivanovich, for bothering you with such details, but I should like to take full advantage of your obliging offer. I thank you for everything once again. Allow me to shake your hand—you are helping me to step back onto the path and assisting me in obtaining what is the most important thing to me. Good-bye, and I do hope that we shall meet soon! Yours always,

F. Dostoyevsky

---

29. Yakushkin and Dostoyevsky's brother-in-law Aleksandr Pavlovich Ivanov taught at the same institution.

The novel that Dostoyevsky was "mulling over and working on" at this time was either *Uncle's Dream* or *The Village of Stepanchikovo*. Neither of them, however, was published in *Russian Messenger*, a magazine founded by M. N. Katkov in 1856; the former appeared in *Russian Word*, the latter in *Notes of the Fatherland*, both in 1859.

30.   To M. M. Dostoyevsky
Semipalatinsk, November 3, 1857

Kind brother and friend,

After receiving your brief note, in which you inform me of your trip abroad—or perhaps it would be more appropriate to call it your assault on Europe—I refrained from answering you right away, as I was waiting for the cigars you promised to send me (for you wrote that you would send them by the next mail), so that I could acknowledge both the letter and the package at the same time. But neither the cigars nor a proper letter from you came. And so I am writing you without waiting for them; above all, because I want to talk to you and, also, to explain a few things to you about my present situation.

In the first place, concerning my private life. We are scraping along, neither too well nor too badly. I am still in the army, although it is my intention soon to put in for my discharge, because I feel it is a crime to neglect my sickness and go without treatment. And my conscience itself asks me: Is this the way to perform one's service duties, when I realize myself that, because of my sickness, I am hardly able to acquit myself of the lightest of my duties? It would be much better to step aside and let someone else take over. As to me, when I am retired from the service, even sick as I am, I shall always manage to be useful through my literary work. Everything abnormal, everything that is not natural, ultimately takes its toll and, I repeat, it is in my opinion a crime to go on stubbornly living in Semipalatinsk, neglecting my affliction, allowing it to worsen.

I am relying on the magnanimity of our exalted Monarch, to whose generosity I already owe so much. He will succor me, a poor, sick wretch, and will perhaps allow me to return to Moscow in order to consult doctors and to treat my affliction. Moreover, where could I make a living for myself if not in Moscow, where there are so many magazines nowadays that would, in all likelihood, accept me as a contributor?

You cannot imagine, brother, how difficult it is to handle literary business while one is away from the scene, to write without even having the indispensable books and magazines at hand. At one point I wanted to write a series of pieces on contemporary literature under the title of "Letters from the Provinces." I have developed a number of ideas on that subject, I have many notes, and I know that it would have attracted attention to me. But in the final analysis, because of the lack of materials, i.e., of magazines covering the past decade, I abandoned the undertaking. And so I am losing everything—literary ideas and my literary career.

You write about my novel, my dear fellow, and ask me to send it to you directly. But let me tell you this: I long ago received an offer from *Russian Messenger*, which is unquestionably the leading Russian magazine today, and I have established contact with it in Moscow through some excellent friends I have there, and also through Pleshcheyev, who is now in Orenburg and has been working for *Russian Messenger* for a year already.

As to my novel, something quite unpleasant happened both to it and to me and here is why: I have resolved and sworn to myself from now on to write nothing that has not been thoroughly thought through, nothing that is not ripe, nothing for the sake of money that must be handed in by a deadline (the way I used to work before). I think that a work of art cannot be taken lightly, that it requires conscientious work, and that if I write something that isn't any good—which is likely to happen often—the reason will be insufficient talent, not negligence and irresponsibility. And that is why, seeing that my novel was taking on gigantic proportions, that it was coming along beautifully, and that I needed absolutely (for money considerations) to finish it in a hurry—I stopped and thought. Nothing can be sadder than this kind of musing while one is working. Eagerness, will, energy—all vanish. I visualized myself being forced to debase the idea that I had been nurturing in my head for three years, and around which I had gathered a huge amount of material (of which there is even more than I can really cope with), an idea that I had already partly realized by jotting down a great number of individual scenes and chapters. More than half the novel existed in rough draft.

But then I realized that I shouldn't be through with even half the work by the time I'd be needing the money in the worst possible way. I used to believe (and managed to convince myself) that I could write and publish in installments, because each part had a semblance of being complete in itself. Doubts, however, began to torment me more and more. It has been my rule for a very long time to abandon whatever I was working on if doubts slipped into my mind, because work done in doubt is good for nothing. But it was a pity to abandon it. It was your letter in which you wrote that nobody would be willing to accept the novel in installments that persuaded me definitely to give it up. In doing so, I was moved by two considerations. What were the alternatives? I thought, either write well, but then I shan't get any money for a year and so my labor is all in vain, or finish it somehow and botch it all up, that is, behave dishonestly; anyhow, I feel incapable of doing that. And so the whole novel, with all the materials connected with it, is now lying in a drawer.

I then set about writing a short novella (although it will run to 6 printer's sheets). When I am through with it I shall write a novel with a Petersburg setting in the vein of *Poor Folk* (but the idea is even better than that of *Poor Folk*). I began working on both of these things long ago, and have written parts of each. Neither of them presents any special difficulties, the work is progressing beautifully, and on December 15 I shall send my first story to the *Messenger*. They will give an advance, a rather substantial one. I shall have

120

some funds. But here is the trouble: the money will have run out completely by January 1. And since, when I sat down to write this letter, it was with the intention of fully explaining my situation to you and of asking a favor of you, I'll come to the point.

Last February, when I got married, I borrowed 650 silver rubles here. I borrowed it from a very decent gentleman, who, however, is somewhat of a crank. I used to be on friendly terms with him. This man, who is fifty or so, told me when he lent me the money (he is rich): "You can pay it back in a year, even two, whenever it is convenient for you; I have everything I need and am delighted to help you." He didn't even want to accept my IOU.

Later, on my return from Kuznetsk, I received 600 silver rubles from Uncle and afterward even another 100 rubles. All I owned, besides my uniform, was a pillow and a mattress. Everything, down to the smallest item, had to be newly acquired. Moreover, during the year, I made about four round trips to Kuznetsk and spent a lot of money in settling the affairs of my wife, who was then my fiancée; I paid three-year-old debts to Khomentovsky and someone else which amounted to some 300 silver rubles (for I *needed* the money at the time her husband died), etc., etc. And then Semipalatinsk is the most expensive town in the world. It's like a desert island here, where Robinson [Crusoe] was finding nuggets of gold but was unable to buy anything he needed. Ever since they formed the province here, prices have been going up. For instance, I pay eight silver rubles a month for my apartment, and that doesn't include either water or firewood. I tried to find a smaller and cheaper apartment, but there are none available—all are occupied—because 3 years ago about 100 civil servants poured into the place and not one of them has yet built himself a house here.

There is a provincial custom here that whoever arrives must be offered a drink and something to eat. You will appreciate what that means when I tell you that one pound of the lowest quality Russian cheese costs up to one silver ruble. There are 150 merchants in town, but trading is done in Asiatic fashion. Only three or four of the merchants handle European goods (i.e., for the gentry). They bring the rejects from Moscow factories here and sell them at incredible prices, prices such as only a man in the throes of delirium or out of his mind would ask. Just try to order a tunic or a pair of breeches. For cloth that costs a couple of silver rubles in Moscow, they ask up to five here. In short, this is the most expensive, miserable little town in the world. And so it is no wonder that the trips, the wedding, the repayment of debts, the purchase of the bare necessities for getting set up, and everyday expenses should have eaten up all our money. And by December 1 I shan't have a single ruble left.

And now, only three months after my marriage, the gentleman who lent me the money has started reminding me of it. This surprised me a good deal, because I had explicitly told him: "If you can wait for a year, lend it to me, if you can't, then forget about it." His reply was unequivocal: "Make it two years if you wish." I quickly gave him an IOU, falling due this coming January 1. I was hoping to receive money for the novel. But now all my hopes have collapsed, or at least any hope of getting money by January 1.

That gentleman, by the way, got married and is sore at me for some unknown reason; and such a tangle has been created that I am very sorry I got myself involved. Everything has been very civilized up to now, but I know that he is preparing to press his claim around January 1— I have not told you everything, but I assure you that I am in a terrible predicament. To make a long story short, I absolutely must pay up by January 1.

By the way, I have received assistance from an unexpected quarter that will also affect my future. It comes from Pleshcheyev. I have been corresponding with him for quite a long time. He is the same sympathetic, noble, gentle soul he always was. He is in the civil service in Orenburg, and if he is not going back to Russia it is because he has fallen in love and is about to marry a *16-year-old* girl, poor but well brought up (for all I know he may already be married; I am expecting a letter from him, since we write each other very often). A couple of months ago he informed me that he was going to receive an inheritance. Some relative whom he never even thought about had died in Moscow. There are many heirs but, according to the will, Pleshcheyev is due to receive exactly 50,000 silver rubles. He wrote me at once that if I needed money he would give me *as much as I wished*, even as much as *5000* silver rubles. However, he won't get his part of the inheritance until April of next year (1858). He writes that if we succeed in getting together in Moscow we won't part again, and that he is prepared to invest his capital in some literary venture, specifying that the key person in it will be me (i.e., *me*).

I replied that I would take 1000 silver rubles from him. That thousand, together with the money I'll get for my 2 stories, will help me to pay my debts, to resign from the army, and to get to Russia in June 1858. The first story (figuring 75 rubles per printer's sheet) will bring me 500 silver rubles around February. However, I shall ask for an advance of 300 and so I shall get up to 800 silver rubles. The two novellas together will bring me up to 1000. And so I am *certain* to get money in February. And in April I shall probably also get the money from Pleshcheyev. But what am I to do on January 1, 1858? Besides, how shall I manage to make ends meet in December of this year? By December 1, I shall have spent my last ruble, and I wonder what I shall live on then? There is nobody I can borrow from now! The only people I would possibly ask are not around. Nor do I have anything I could sell. Nor can I request an advance on my pay (we have a new commanding officer here and, in any case, asking for an advance entails a lot of fuss). And, finally, there is that debt, which torments and haunts me.

And this is why, my dear friend, I am turning to you just once more: Help me for the last time—send me 650 silver rubles now if it is at all possible; it will only be for some three months. You have two guarantees that I shall pay you back for sure and without fail: If you don't believe that I am *sure* to get the money for my work in February, then I am certain to get it in April from Pleshcheyev. But I will send you the sum straightway in February, and you will get it in March, I swear! And so, if you can spare 650 rubles for three months, save me this one last time as you have saved me 1000 times before. Be my benefactor once more, my dear friend, and believe me that I would never stoop to abusing your trust—you will get it back in March, I swear by everything that is sacred! Help me, my brother and friend! I am suffering so much moral torment over this debt that never before in my life have I found myself in such an equivocal, unseemly position. I have not told you everything, but my experience would make a magnificent episode for a novel.

Farewell, my dear brother, I want you to know that you are all my hope. I should have asked Pleshcheyev if it had been possible, but he has *nothing* now, and besides he is getting married. There is one thing I beseech of you: don't delay with your answer, reply *immediately* upon receiving my letter, because I shall be waiting with the utmost anxiety and impatience.

My wife sends you her regards. She has written to Varinka and Verochka, but neither of them has answered her. She feels very bitter about it, and says that it shows you all resent her and are refusing to recognize her as a member of the family. I try to reassure her, but it is in vain. She doesn't know you personally, and she feels very sad about it all.

My stepson, Pasha, has been admitted to the Omsk Cadet Corps School upon his mother's request, made eighteen months ago. We have sent him off. It is an excellent corps school, and the inspector is a man with a noble heart. I know him personally. Still, I was sad for the little lad—he is only ten years old and I had become so attached to him. But since they admitted him, we couldn't possibly decline and, anyway, it would have been ridiculous to do so.

N.B. For God's sake, brother, answer me right away, don't delay! Try to appreciate how important it is to me!

---

30. Two months before this letter, Dostoyevsky had written to his sister Varvara: "My sickness hasn't let up at all. On the contrary, the fits are becoming more frequent. Since last April I have had three fits while on guard duty and, on top of that, three or four others while I was asleep. They are always followed by weakness and sluggishness. It is very hard for me to bear . . . the local doctors are powerless to help me."

The novel he had put aside was probably *The Village of Stepanchikovo*, and the novella on which he had just begun was probably *Uncle's Dream*. The novel he was going to start after that may have been *The Insulted and Injured*, which is set in Petersburg and is somewhat along the lines of *Poor Folk*.

The creditor who had evidently changed his mind about Dostoyevsky's debt to him was Kovrigin.

Dostoyevsky's new commanding officer was a Major Denisov.

The inspector at the Omsk Cadet Corps School was Ivan Vikentevich Zhdan-Pushkin. Dostoyevsky and Durov had stayed at his house for some time after their release from the Omsk prison. On July 29, 1857, Dostoyevsky had written to him, telling him that Pasha had been admitted to the school and asking him to keep an eye on the boy.

31. To M. N. KATKOV
Semipalatinsk, January 11, 1858

Dear Sir:

Back in August, I was informed by your collaborator, A. N. Pleshcheyev, that you would not refuse to publish some work of mine in *Russian Messenger*. For quite some time already, I have been wanting to offer you the novel I am working on for publication. But since it was not finished I really had nothing to offer. What I actually had in mind was for you to read the novel first and then work out the arrangements at some future date. The fact of the matter is that, some nine years ago, I published so much that was mediocre that I just didn't want to do things through correspondence. Now, however, my circumstances have changed, and I am compelled to take another course of action than that which I originally contemplated. Please allow me to explain.

I started thinking of this novel in my spare time during my stay in Omsk. After leaving Omsk about three years ago, I was again able to procure pen and paper, and I got down to work at once. However, I did not hurry the writing. I found more pleasure in thinking everything through, down to the tiniest detail, composing and balancing the parts, writing down individual episodes in full and, most important, collecting material. After working three years like that, I did not lose interest in the work; quite the contrary, I grew more enthusiastic about it. The circumstances were such that I just could not work on it steadily and systematically. However, last May I got down to work on the final draft. I already had the rough drafts of almost all of Book 1 and of part of Book 2. Nevertheless, I still have not managed to completely finish even Book 1, although I am working on it continuously. My novel is divided into three books (and, although each book could in turn be divided into parts, I have broken them up only into chapters), but each book is a thing complete in itself. And so I thought of offering you only one book to start with, since I am unable and, moreover, unwilling to publish Book 2 within one and the same year, and the same is true for Book 3. But all three books could be published within three years. Once you have read Book 1, you will see for yourself that such a division is quite feasible.

This year, circumstances are such that, with the change in my way of life, I am in dire need of money. I thought, in submitting the manuscript of my novel to you (Book 1), of asking you for an advance before publication, hoping you might accede to my request. That is why I hurried to finish it. However, working for the sake of money and working for the love of art are two things I find incompatible. Throughout the entire three years of my previous literary activity in Petersburg, my work suffered because of this. I did not want to profane my best ideas, my best plans for novels and stories by working hurriedly to meet deadlines. I liked them so much, I wanted so badly to nurture them with love and care that I believe I would sooner have died than treated my best ideas dishonestly. I was, however, constantly in debt to A. A. Krayevsky (who, it must be said, never wrung work out of me or pressed me for time), and tied hand and foot. When, for instance, I knew that he had no material for a forthcoming issue, there were times when, on the 26th of the month, i.e., 4 days before publication, I forced myself to invent some story or other; and it was not unusual for me to think up and write a story in 4 days. At times, the result was sad; at others, it did not come off too badly, judging, at least, from the reviews that appeared in other journals. Of course, I often had several months at my disposal in which to prepare something a bit better, but the trouble was that I myself never knew that I had so many *months* ahead of me, because I always imposed on myself a limit of one month, since I knew I would have to come to Mr. Krayevsky's rescue at the end of the month. But whether it was a month that went by or whether it was five, I would go through agonies trying to invent as good a story as possible, because I was loath to have poor stuff published, and it would also have been dishonest toward Mr. Krayevsky to do so.

And, on top of everything else, I was suffering at that time from hypochondria and often in the most acute form. It was only because of my youth that I did not wear myself out completely or lose altogether my ardent love for literature and, together with youth, my devotion to ideas for novels that I held so deeply while biding my time and waiting for the moment when I could start work on them and give them final form. Those years have left a painful impression on me, so painful in fact that the thought of finishing Book 1 of my novel as quickly as possible in order to get money was almost unbearable. And that is why I did not hurry. Besides, I was held back to some extent by one thing or another and by my sickness. Despite everything, though, I wanted to send you half of Book 1 in January (i.e., now) and the second half the following month, so that by March the whole novel (i.e., Book 1) would have been in your hands. But something unforeseen happened and interfered with my plans. (By the way—you may be wondering and perhaps smiling and asking yourself as you read this letter: "Why on earth does he go into all this?" But please bear with me and hear me out to the end. The thing is, I want to ask a tremendous favor of you and all these details are to the point.)

The circumstance that has now stopped me from working on my novel is the following: Last year I was terribly pressed for money and was forced to contract debts. To pay these debts and to take care of my expenses I absolutely had to have 1000 silver rubles by January 1. I wrote to my brother in Petersburg about that sum, and a fortnight ago I received his reply. He writes that he obtained only 500 silver rubles for me, by assuming, in my name, certain literary obligations. One Count Kushelyov has decided to publish, starting next year, a magazine called *Russian Word*. His factotum, one G. Moller [*sic*], went to see my brother and told him that they would like me to become a contributor to that magazine. Knowing that I needed money and that I was now working on a novel, my brother, unaware of my plans for it, took it into his head to sell it to the future *Russian Word*. They gave him an advance of 500 rubles, and the two parties drew up and signed an agreement. So what am I to do now? The money should reach here with the next mail, and I feel obliged to honor the agreement my brother has signed. I had a novel that I had planned a very long time ago, which I liked very much, and which I had even got started on. I've now taken it out of the drawer and made up my mind to resume work on it, finish it, and lose no time in getting it off to my brother. It isn't a very long novel, and I hope to finish it in two or two and a half months at the most, send it off, and then immediately take up where I left off on my old work.

Now, since I shall have received only 500 rubles and not the 1000 that I needed, and since this sum is not enough either to enable me to pay back my debt in full or even to defray my living expenses, I have decided to take the extreme step of humbly appealing to you: If it be your intention to publish my novel this year, would it not be possible for you to send me right now, in the form of an advance, the 500 silver rubles that I need so desperately? I know that my proposal sounds quite eccentric, but it all depends on how you take it. There is one thing, however, that I should hate: your getting the impression that I have such a high opinion of my own talents that it is an easy thing for me to make such a proposal. Believe me, it is dictated only by dire necessity. In exchange for these 500 silver rubles (that is, if you send them to me), I engage myself to send you *the whole* of Book 1 of my novel during the course of the summer so that, if you wished, you could start running it in September. It will be 14 or 15 printer's sheets long, so that it will, in any case, be worth more than 500 silver rubles, which means that the moment you receive my manuscript, you will have recovered then and there the advance you are sending me. I promise to send you the novel *without fail* within the specified time limit (that is why I have set it as far off as possible). Moreover, since you will have sent me the money (if you actually do send it) without even having seen the manuscript, I take it upon myself, in case you do not like my work, to take it back and to write you another as soon as possible. Why, after all, I did occasionally turn out a decent piece among the poor stuff I wrote. So who knows, perhaps it will work out this time.

As to the rate of pay per printer's sheet, we shall discuss it once you have read my manuscript. But actually I shall leave that up to you, as I feel I can fully rely on your fairness. For my part, the only guarantee that I can give you—at least for the present—is *my word of honor*, although, if you were to demand some other guarantee, I should be happy to comply. Finally, by way of further consolation, I might add that the novel I am promising you is the most heartfelt work I have written in a long time. I realize, however, that this is not a strong guarantee either, as it often happens that an author's most cherished work turns out to be very bad, for a great variety of reasons. All I can promise is that I shall try to write it as well as I can.

I hope you will be so kind as to let me know your decision, whatever it may be. I am now putting in a request to resign from the army and hope that, at the end of the summer, I shall be able to obtain permission to move to Moscow for permanent residence. In that case, I shall have the pleasure of coming to see you personally. For the time being, though, my address is: *Semipalatinsk, Western Siberia, Fyodor Mikhailovich Dostoyevsky.*

Please forgive me for the outward appearance of this letter, for the corrections, etc., and do not take them as a sign of disrespect. I can't, for the life of me, write any more neatly. To be on the safe side, I am addressing this letter both to the editorial offices of *Russian Messenger* and to your printing shop.

Please accept, my dear sir, the assurance of my profound esteem with which I remain,

Your most obedient servant,
F. Dostoyevsky

P. S. You may wonder why I am not giving the novel I have been writing for *Russian Messenger* to *Russian Word*. In the first place, I have no idea what *Russian Word* will turn out to be like, I know nothing about its editorial board or its policies. In the second place, in return for the money (500 rubles) they have sent me, I have to send them a piece as soon as possible, and the short novel that I intend to give them can certainly be finished much more quickly than the big novel I am writing for *Russian Messenger*. I seem to have been fated to work for money in the most restricting sense of the term.

---

31. Count Grigory Aleksandrovich Kushelyov-Bezborodko (1832–1870) was a writer of limited talent but, more important, a publisher and patron of the arts.

Yegor Aleksandrovich Moller (1812–1879) was a writer and journalist who published stories in several magazines, including the Dostoyevsky brothers' *Time*. Although Dostoyevsky here calls him the "factotum" for *Russian Word*, in other letters he calls him the "business manager."

Katkov did send Dostoyevsky the 500 rubles he asks for here.

The story that Dostoyevsky sent to *Russian Word* was *Uncle's Dream*, which appeared in that magazine in March 1859. The other novels that he refers to in this letter are probably *The Insulted and Injured* and *Notes from the House of the Dead*, though it is difficult to say which one he is referring to in each instance. However, *The Insulted and Injured* has echoes of his relations with Mariya Dmitriyevna, whom he did not meet until 1855, whereas he has written that he conceived of *House of the Dead* shortly after his release from prison in Omsk, early in 1854.

32.   To M. M. Dostoyevsky
Semipalatinsk, January 18, 1858

I have received three of your letters, my dear friend, the one of November 25, and the other two of December 17 and 19. I was about to answer your first letter right away, but that proved impossible. You wrote that you were sending money, and about your contacts with *Russian Word*. Not knowing whether you would send it, I couldn't write you anything positive. That is why I waited until the money arrived. And now I shall answer you fully. First of all, however, let me thank you with all my heart for sending me the money. You have saved me, and I feel quite secure now, at least for some time. Without your help I should have been lost—I couldn't see any way out of it for me otherwise.

I hasten to answer your letters in the proper order—in the order in which you wrote them.

I got the cigars (I am not sure whether I already wrote you about that). However, the gentleman for whom I had ordered them refused them for a very respectable reason: they were too mild for him. He passed them on to me. Ten-Cate [*sic*] is swindling him, but sends him very strong cigars, just the sort he wants. So I smoked your cigars myself and owe you for them. I'll even things up with you. Let me tell you, too, that your cigars are excellent, but that they got badly frayed on the way here. In any case, I cannot understand why you haven't been successful with them.

Then—you wrote about *Russian Word*. Let us assume that the grand idea is a good one, and that capital to back it will be found. But do you really imagine that money is all that is needed to create an editorial board? And without a proper editorial staff and without original ideas, a magazine is just nothing! I don't know whom he will hire as editors, but I remain quite doubtful, somehow, that *Russian Word* will be a success. For a time, though, the magazine may be quite good as a literary miscellany.

But, after all, what business is it of mine? Best of luck to them. I am very grateful to you, my dear Misha, my constant friend, for having established contact with *Russian Word* and for having carried everything out in so masterful a fashion.

Now let me tell you about my situation: For the time being, I am going to put aside my novel (the long one)—I cannot finish it under the pressure of a deadline! That would just kill me; indeed as it is, it has just about killed me. I shall put it aside until a time comes when I have found some peace and stability in my life. That novel is so important to me, it has become so much a part of me that there is nothing in the world that could make me give it up for good. On the contrary, I am determined that it shall be my chef-d'oeuvre. The idea is too good, and it has cost me too much for me to abandon it completely.

Now something else: as far back as eight years ago I conceived the idea for a short novel—about the length of *Poor Folk*. Recently, I saw it all again; it sort of all came back to me, and I thought through the plan of it anew. And it comes in very handy under the present circumstances. I am about to sit down and write it. I hope to finish it in two months or so. Besides this, my longer novel contains a quite independent episode that is successful in itself but that damages the work as a whole. I want to cut it out of the novel. It also is about as long as *Poor Folk*, but it is in a comic vein. It has fresh characters. *Russian Word* is giving me a year. And so here is what I should like you to do: Write me at once to tell me what would happen if, for instance, I sent you a novel for *Russian Word* in April that would have—as it will—more than five printer's sheets (which is more than the number of printer's sheets for other magazines)—would they pay me for the balance of the sheets in April or would they wait until the beginning of the following year, i.e., until publication? If they will send me the money in April, I shall send you the novel for *Russian Word* as soon as I get your answer. If not, I think I would do it this way: let *Russian Word* wait until the fall, and I shall send them the finished piece (I am talking about that episode from the big novel, presented as a complete thing), and the novel that will be ready at the end of March will be sent to Katkov for *Russian Messenger*. My considerations in this are quite obvious: I shan't miss *Russian Word* in any case—I shall have a piece ready for the publication time even if I deliver it in the fall. But right now I must get myself out of trouble. Katkov has made me a proposal through Pleshcheyev. Now, since I got only 500 rubles from you instead of 1000, I still don't know what to do, because I have given out almost the entire 500 you sent to my creditors. That has left me with next to nothing, and I still owe exactly 350 silver rubles. And for this reason I came up with a rather clever strategem: by the last mail I wrote Katkov a long and businesslike letter, telling him that I wanted to contribute to his magazine and offering him the big novel (the one I have decided to put away for the time being). I informed him that I would deliver it to him in August (not before) and requested an advance of 500 silver rubles because of my precarious situation; and I asked him to send it to me immediately upon receipt of my letter. In writing this, I reasoned as follows: "Since *Russian Word* pays out advances without having seen a thing, why shouldn't *Russian Messenger*?"

This way, in March (in the first half of it), they could send me another 500 silver rubles (and, in general, I feel I have nothing to lose because, since I haven't published anything for eight years, I shall have the appeal of newness with the public. The editors must be aware of this, and that may persuade them to give me an advance; as to me, what have I to lose, being in such a difficult situation anyhow?). If Katkov sent me the money, I should send him *not the big novel* (that I have put aside) but the *shorter one* I am working on now, even though it was *the big novel* I wrote him about (at that time, I did not realize I'd be putting it aside). But what difference can it make to Katkov, as long as I send him something that is good? If I send it to Katkov, I suppose I could ask him for yet another 500 rubles right away, because the novel will be about eight printer's sheets long. Therefore, if I get that second 500 too, I shan't be owing much after that. Katkov will appreciate my punctuality as well as the good quality of the novel (anticipating that it will be good), and will probably send me yet another 500. And that would be really wonderful. It goes without saying that *Russian Word* will then get the episode (the superfluous one from the big novel) from me by September. I am playing fair with *Russian Word;* I shall be delivering on time and, furthermore, I shall take pains with the piece, because I myself very much like the idea of the episode and, in any case, it will be perfectly complete in itself. And so this is how I have arranged everything. I want you to write me what you think of it all.

Now, something else. In your first letter you write that you must have my story by next year. Then, in the other letters, you mention that you have a proposition for me (it is probably the same one). I am very annoyed with you for not being explicit, i.e., what do you intend to publish, with whom, and how? As for the story, you have my word for it—you will get it. Disengaging myself from the big novel seems to have given me wings; I shall finish writing for *Russian Messenger* and then for *Russian Word,* and I shall still have plenty of time. All I ask of you is to write me about everything in greater detail.

I also want to tell you that I applied for a discharge (a few days ago) for health reasons. You know what my plans are. If they do not give me permission to live in Moscow (I requested this in my application for discharge), I shall write a letter to the Sovereign. He is magnanimous, he may grant permission to a sick man, for I shall give as a reason for my plea "the need to consult the doctors of the capital." If permission is still refused me (but why are Toll and Palm in Petersburg, while others are refused? Perhaps they, in fact, found it necessary to forbid some but not all to return to European Russia), I shall go to Odessa, where life is both pleasant and cheap, and then I don't imagine that it would be forever. The Sovereign is kind, and would eventually allow me to return to the capitals. So that is what I am planning to do. Therefore, if all is well, I shall leave here no later than the summer. I definitely intend to take 1000 rubles from Pleshcheyev—he and I shall settle up later, and I have a very good idea how to settle it. Unless I get this money from him, I shan't be able to stir from here. And that is why I have an enormous and most urgent favor to ask you, and why I am addressing myself to your kindness which [part of the letter is missing here].

A sincere explanation: Although I did write you about the clothes, I felt suddenly ashamed of myself somehow. No, brother, I am imposing on you too shamelessly, so let me tell you this: write me frankly—if you have to lay out money for them, don't send them to me, I shall manage without them. But if, being a businessman, you can buy readymade clothes on *credit,* then buy them, but, mind you, only on credit. Also write me how much they cost. I believe there are cheaper ones; if I didn't, my conscience would keep tormenting me. But if it is on credit, I shall be able to send you the money. In the summer I shall have a lot.

Pleshcheyev got married. He often mentions you and sends you his regards.

N.B.B. Don't worry about their not fitting well. Get them in your own size. As you know, I can wear your clothes. You could perhaps take them a *tiny bit* wider and *longer* than you would for yourself.

N.B.B. If you have to pay even a single kopek down *in cash,* I don't want you to send me anything.

You write about the pictures of the entire family. I am delighted over the prospect, and my wife talks of nothing else. Send them quickly, for God's sake. My wife sends her regards to you and Emiliya Fyodorovna. I, too, kiss Emiliya Fyodorovna's hand and give you a very, very hard hug.

Give my regards to you know whom and kiss our brother Kolya if he happens to be in Petersburg.

All yours,
F. Dostoyevs.

Kiss all your children in turn, every one of them. I wonder whether they remember me? When you send me the pictures, add a *description,* so that I shall be able to identify every one of them.

---

32. The first editors of *Russian Word* were its founder, Count Kushelyov-Bezborodko, the poet Yakov Polonsky, and the critic Apollon Grigorev.

It is again difficult to say exactly which novels Dostoyevsky is referring to. However, he did eventually send *The Village of Stepanchikovo* to *Russian Messenger* (which he may have preferred because of its prestige as well as its financial reliability)—but that magazine rejected it, and it appeared in *Notes of the Fatherland* late in 1859.

Dostoyevsky was not given a discharge from the army until March 1859, and then he was barred from entering the provinces of Moscow and Petersburg (the two "capitals"). Instead, he was assigned to live—at his request—in Tver (now Kalinin) until November 1859, when the restrictions were lifted. Tver was about 80 miles northwest of Moscow and 290 miles southeast of Petersburg.

33. To M. M. Dostoyevsky
Semipalatinsk, May 31, 1858

I hasten to answer you by the very first mail, my dear fellow. I am surprised that it should take so long for my letters to reach you. Nevertheless, I do write you often. And if you worry about me, I worry about you, too, particularly of late. I decided that something must have happened to you, in fact, that you must be sick.

I was very sorry to learn about your loss (3,000 rubles). You write that it is not losing the money that grieves you most, but the critical situation in which you find yourself, etc. I don't agree with you, brother; there is nothing wrong with being sad about a loss of money. You have growing children, and 3,000 rubles is not a sum that you will be able to make up very quickly. Is there definitely no hope of recovering the money? I feel very bad, my dear friend, about having bothered you at such an unsuitable time with my errands and requests. But I couldn't help it! You write that you'll be sending the packet shortly. I thank you, my brother, and I hope that this is the last time I shall cause you such trouble. I wanted to wait for the things to come before answering you. But it may still be some time until they arrive. You tell me that you will send me a frock coat and a pair of trousers. I think a plain jacket would have been preferable, because it can be worn on just about any occasion. I'll see what I can do to scrape together some money and order one here, although my financial situation is extremely critical.

You ask me to send you whatever I have written, my friend. Well, I don't remember (in general, my memory has become very bad), I don't remember whether I wrote you that I got in touch with Katkov (of *Russian Messenger*) and sent him a letter offering to contribute to his magazine and promising to send him a story before the end of the year if he sent me an advance of 500 silver rubles immediately. I received those 500 rubles about a month or five weeks ago, along with a very thoughtful and considerate letter. He writes that he is delighted with my participation, complies at once with my demand (500 rubles), and asks me not to push myself too hard, to work unhurriedly, i.e., to forget about a deadline. That's wonderful. And so I am now working on my piece for *Russian Messenger* (a long story). The only trouble is that I didn't make any agreement with Katkov about what rates he is to pay me per printer's sheet, merely saying that I'd rely on his fairness in that matter. I shall also send something to *Russian Word* this year; I am determined to. But it would be a story, not my novel. The novel I have put aside until my return to Russia. I could not do otherwise. It contains a rather felicitous idea, and it has a new character in it such as has never been seen before. But since that type of character is, I expect, very common in real life in Russia, and especially so nowadays, to judge by the movements and ideas that are absorbing everybody, I feel certain that I would enrich my novel with new observations when I return to Russia. There is no need for me to hurry with it, my dear friend, but rather to try to do it well.

You write, my dear fellow, that I probably am ambitious and anxious now to make my reappearance with something exceptionally good and that is why I keep sitting and sitting on my eggs to make sure they hatch. Even assuming that is so, the fact is I have already put aside my novel and am working instead on two stories which may, at best, be passable (and that with the help of God), so I am not really going in for any hatching. But what is this theory of yours, my friend, that a painting must be done all at once, etc., etc.? When did you come to that conclusion? Believe me, everything requires a tremendous effort. Believe me, a light, graceful poem of Pushkin's sounds as if it had been written all at once precisely because Pushkin spent so much time crossing out, correcting, and sticking together those few lines. These are facts. It took Gogol eight years to write *Dead Souls*. A thing that has been written all at once cannot be ripe. They say that there was not a blot on Shakespeare's manuscripts. That is why there are so many enormities and so much bad taste in him; he would have done much better if he had worked harder. You are obviously confusing inspiration, i.e., the first, instantaneous creation of a scene or a movement in the soul (this is what always takes place), with work. I, for example, set down at once a scene as it first comes to me, and I am happy over it, but then I work over it for months on end, for years; I am inspired by it *several times,* not just once (because I love that scene), and several times I add to it or remove something that I had in it. And believe me, it comes out much better that way, as long as there is inspiration. Without inspiration, of course, nothing would come of it.

It is true that in Petersburg they pay very generously nowadays. I understand that Pisemsky received 200 or even 250 rubles per printer's sheet for his *Thousand Souls*. That way one can earn one's living and work without hurrying. But do you really find that Pisemsky novel so wonderful? It is only a mediocrity and, *gilded* though it may be, nevertheless only a mediocrity. Does it have even a single new character, an *original creation,* one that hasn't appeared anywhere before? All he has to offer was made available to us long ago by our pioneering writers, particularly by Gogol. They are old themes presented in a new guise. It is an excellent collage using other writers' patterns, a work by Sazikov based on Benvenuto Cellini's sketches. It is true that, so far, I have read only two installments of it—the magazines get here late. The ending of Part II is utterly implausible and completely ruined. For Kalinovich to go in for deliberate deception is quite impossible. The way his author had previously portrayed him, Kalinovich would sacrifice himself, offer marriage, show off, enjoy the nobility of his behavior in his heart, and be sincere in his conviction that he is not going to deceive her. Kalinovich is so vain that he cannot consider himself a scoundrel, even secretly. Of course, he would enjoy it all, spend the night with Nastenka and, *later*, of course, when he is forced to by real circumstances, he would deceive her, but even then he would soothe his conscience by telling himself that he had acted honorably. But a Kalinovich knowingly deceiving and *spending the night* with Nastenka is repulsive and *impossible*; i.e., such a character is conceivable, but he just couldn't be Kalinovich. But enough said about this nonsense.

I simply can't wait for my release to come through, my friend. I did not ask directly for permission to live in Moscow, but my application for discharge carries the standard formula stipulating that *I shall be domiciled in the city of Moscow*. If they don't object, I shall just go there. Although, what money shall I travel on? I shan't have any money until I finish the story. I don't even know what I am going to live on two months from now. For in two months I shan't have any money at all. Of the 500 silver rubles I received from Katkov, 400 was spent immediately to pay off my debts. I am spending 40 silver rubles a month, but *emergency expenses* never fail to crop up. For eighteen months now there has been one unforeseen expense after another.

My only hope is in Pleshcheyev. He promised me 1000 rubles, but he may not get any money himself or he may only get it in two years. What shall I do then until the end of the year, when I get paid for my work? (They won't pay me before for that.) I don't know. My head is splitting. There is no one left for me to borrow money from now. But you needn't worry too much about me; everything will somehow turn out all right in the end.

Pleshcheyev is going to Moscow and Petersburg. He is leaving in May. Receive him well, and get acquainted with his wife. I have just received a package from Milyukov (his book). It was delivered by some officer whom I did not see. Perhaps he will drop in on me later. Give my best to Milyukov and the others.

What has happened to our family? How are Varinka and Verochka? Not a word from them all this time. Where is brother Andrei? Where is Kolya?

Farewell! I give you a big hug. Give my regards to Emiliya Fyodorovna and kiss the children. My wife sends all of you her regards.

Farewell, Yours,

F. Dostoyevsky

I shall write you again before I get the package and before my release comes through. I shall let you know how I am getting along. But, *in the name of God*, don't procrastinate, and write yourself, in the name of God!

---

33. Mikhail's losses arose from the operation of his cigarette factory.

The "long story" that Dostoyevsky was working on was probably *The Insulted and Injured*, which was published in 1861–1862—not, however, in *Russian Messenger* but in his own magazine, *Time*.

Aleksandr Petrovich Milyukov (1817–1897) was an educator, literary historian, and traveler. He was the author of *Sketches of Finland* (Ocherki Finlyandii, 1856—probably the book that Dostoyevsky mentions here), *Literary Encounters and Acquaintances* (Literaturnye vstrechi i znakomstva, 1890), and other works. He and Dostoyevsky had met in the 1840s, and they resumed contact after Dostoyevsky's return from exile; it was partly through him that Dostoyevsky met his second wife.

34. To M. M. Dostoyevsky

Semipalatinsk, September 13, 1858

Misha, my invaluable friend,

So I see that nothing bad has happened to you, and you just didn't write me. But you cannot imagine how worried I was about you! The things that went through my head! For God's sake, write more often from now on! What does it cost you to answer me at once when you get a letter from me? Why, no more than a few words and ten minutes of your time. Do me a favor and stop torturing me.

What is this constant to-do with your business affairs, my priceless Misha! You seem to be perennially engaged in *plowing back everything*. My dear friend, although, of course, I know nothing about your business, I should like to ask yourself: isn't it time at last to *realize* something? Tell me honestly, for what have you been laboring so hard for all these years? In your field there are people who make millions, but if you could make yourself a hundred thousand, that wouldn't be so bad, either. Please God, you will, my invaluable brother. For you do have a family. At least you would be able to live on that money and bring up your children. And that would be itself an achievement.

I take it pretty much for granted that I shan't make any money during my lifetime. It is true I have no children, but still it is hellishly hard to keep alive.

My only salvation is to be able to move to Moscow as soon as possible. I realize full well that in Moscow and Petersburg everything is very expensive, more expensive even than it used to be. But, aside from the fact that Semipalatinsk is not so cheap either, I am certain that I'd be able to make twice as much in Moscow as I do here. Here, I am working in the dark, I am completely ignorant of everything that is going on. I could have found myself a good job on a magazine, I could have become a partner—in brief, I know I could have done lots of things. Besides, I could have met many kind people who would have been able to help me. I am waiting impatiently for my discharge to come through, but even when it does, I shan't have any money.

Pleshcheyev has written me an encouraging letter saying that he will help me, but adding that perhaps he won't be able to send me the entire sum I had requested (1000 rubles) but only half (500 rubles), and the remainder sometime later. But unless he sends me the whole sum, I shall be stuck here until the spring, which means that I should be wasting my money and going further without treatment. In any case, however, I couldn't leave here before January, because I haven't yet discharged my literary commitments to *Russian Messenger* and to Kushelyov; in fact, I still have a far way to go! All this is preying unbearably on my mind. Ah, my dear friend, if only I could tell you all this face to face and at length; you can't convey anything in a letter.

You write about the offer from the *Contemporary* group. But I couldn't consider their offer unless it were a case of extreme emergency. I swear I feel no resentment against those people, even though they treated me despicably and indecently. Now they are sorry for me, and for that I am sincerely grateful. But I don't want them to think badly of me now or get the impression that I threw myself at them the moment they flashed some money before my eyes. Perhaps this is false pride, but that is how I am. And so I prefer to wait now and to talk business with them only as a last resort. Obviously, you should be careful not to let them know my feelings in the matter—for it would be indelicate to repay their kind feelings with something that may possibly offend them, even if it is not really malicious. This is strictly between you and me.

As to Pleshcheyev, I have no qualms about accepting money from him because if it were I who had money, and he had none, I would give him everything. Besides I shall be making money for him. But even if I had no hope of earning anything, I should still accept it from him. He is a man à parti, and then we are brothers in misfortune. I also take money from you, but my heart bleeds when I do so. But I go on taking it from you. I know that you need every single kopek, but it is my firm intention someday to make everything up to you.

The newspaper you wrote me about is a lovely thing. I have been toying with the idea of something of that sort for a long time, but what I have in mind is a purely literary newspaper. It would be distinguished by a literary feuilleton, reviews of periodicals, analyses of what is good in them and what is bad, opposition to the *cliquishness* that has become so widespread, a greater forcefulness, ardor, wit, and fortitude—that is what is needed today! I say all this with vehemence because I have noted down and outlined a few articles in that spirit on literature, for instance on the *contemporary poets,* on the *statistical* movement *in literature,* on the uselessness of *movements* in art—articles that are written provokingly and even sharply, but above all with a light touch.

But, tell me, do you really intend to publish a newspaper? Why, it is not an easy thing to combine with the running of a factory. You'd better watch out, brother. And also bear in mind that I shall never live in Petersburg, and so it will be difficult for me to help you. But, of course, I shall do my best to help if you really want me to.

My sickness is getting worse rather than better. Last month I had four fits, a thing that has never happened before, and I could hardly do any work. The fits are followed by a state of gloom and melancholy and I feel a completely broken man. I cannot finish my work soon now, either for Kushelyov or for Katkov. I very much dislike the long novella, the one I am writing for Katkov; I have grown quite sick of it! But I have written too much of it to abandon it and start on something else and anyway I owe it to him. And so I shall go on writing this way, for money, to the end of my life! Even supposing I had the greatest talent, it would be wasted on that drudgery. My friend, I kiss you a thousand times, and your children, and I kiss Emiliya Fyodorovna's hands.

I enclose my letter to Pleshcheyev. He wrote me that he would rather I addressed his letter to you, so take it or send it to him right away.

N.B.B. I also enclose a letter, my friend, to Count Kushelyov. About a month ago he wrote me a quite amiable letter and, although he said he did not wish to hurry me, it was quite obvious that he needed my piece. And so I should like you to give him the letter enclosed here. I answer him in his own tone. Would you fill in his first name and patronymic after the word "Count," for I don't know it. It won't matter that it is in your hand, not in the slightest; and you can transmit the letter through Moller, if you wish. Seal it. And tell Moller that I shall do my utmost to finish my piece as quickly as I can. Please be so kind as to do everything exactly as I ask you to do.

My story for Kushelyov will be full of certain comic and even extravagant effects that are, however, for the most part implausible. I should have liked to do something better, but all the ideas I have in my head are more suitable for full-length novels, and I have no other theme in mind but this one, for a story-length piece. And I just don't have the time now to produce a larger work. Farewell then, my dear fellow, and if you write to Varinka, give her my regards.

Give my love to Kolya. I intend to write to Varinka, Verochka and, without fail, to Andryusha. My wife sends all of you her regards. I am very happy to hear that Pleshcheyev's wife is so pretty, very happy. Beauty can do no harm.

---

34. Two months previously, Dostoyevsky had written to Mikhail that, because he had heard nothing from him in so long, he was "worried to death. . . . Are you all right? Are you still alive? . . . I don't want you to die, I want to see you and to hug you at least once again. . . . So, for heaven's sake . . . write me at once. . . ."

The *Contemporary*, which had been founded by Pushkin in 1836, was published from 1847 to 1866 by Nekrasov, who made it a leading literary magazine, with contributions from all the important Russian writers of the day, including Dostoyevsky (*Novel in Nine Letters*). However, it had also published Belinsky's contemptuous evaluation of Dostoyevsky's work since *Poor Folk* and a taunting poem composed by Nekrasov and Turgenev, entitled "Belinsky's Message to Dostoyevsky." Thus, Dostoyevsky considered publication of his work in the *Contemporary* to be a last resort—and it became just that when *The Village of Stepanchikovo* was rejected by *Russian Messenger*.

The "newspaper" that Mikhail had proposed became the monthly magazine *Time*, which the two brothers published and edited from 1861 to 1863. On June 19, 1858, Mikhail had requested authorization from the censor to publish it. The authorization was granted, but publication did not begin until after Dostoyevsky returned from Siberia.

35. To M. M. DOSTOYEVSKY
Semipalatinsk, March 14, 1859

My dear friend Misha,

I hasten to answer you. I have only one hour left in which to write to you and Pleshcheyev, if I am not to miss the mail. First of all, let me thank you, my dear fellow, for all the trouble you gave yourself with Kushelyov for me. That is all very nice, but I am afraid you didn't insist enough and make it clear that I needed the money right now and not sometime later. This way, he may dilly-dally for God knows how long. On Mondays the mail arrives from Russia (it's Saturday today), and if I don't get it on Monday I shall be in an awful fix. Right now I'm in very bad straits financially. Ah, my friend, maybe my discharge will come through shortly, and I am terribly busy with all sorts of things. Now, of course, I am not worried about the money—they will send it to me. However, I wonder whether 1000 rubles will be enough to pay for the moving and travel expenses and all the rest. I have been making calculations and find that it won't be. Out of that thousand, as soon as I get it, I shall have to pay out 350 silver rubles within the next two hours to settle old debts, and the remaining 650 will have to cover everything else, mainly our living expenses here, which will be considerable, because I may have to wait around here until August instead of leaving in April as I originally planned. What's more, you have no idea of all the expenses I have! But what's the use of talking about it! If only they send me that money! Again, my thanks to you.

You write that Kushelyov intends to publish "Uncle's Dream" in March. That's very good. The sooner the better. But, for God's sake, find out more about it and be more precise, if you can. Did Kushelyov and the rest of the editorial staff like it? This, my dear man, is very important to me. And then, is it possible that they won't send me *Russian Word*? I am having a piece published in it, and I cannot read my own work in print! I wrote to you before asking you to see to it that they sent that issue. Maybe you forgot about it, but take care of it now. There's still time to send it. I suggest that they apply it to my account, and charge it against the 1000 rubles advance. I shall even things up with them eventually. Otherwise, just imagine how it would feel not to have any concept of the magazine that is publishing my story! It's impermissible! So, for God's sake, have them send me the magazine right away. I am very curious to know whether the censors have thrown anything out or not. You write about *Poor Folk,* my dear fellow. How is it, my dear friend, that you never wrote and told me before that the novel is selling at 15 rubles a copy? Why, it is very flattering to my self-respect and might have been a source of great satisfaction some time ago. Well, that is forgivable, brother! But if the book is worth such a high price now, then this certainly is the time to sell it, when it is commanding a good price. How good it would be if Kushelyov would publish an illustrated edition. That would be tremendous.

Pleshcheyev is partly dissatisfied with my story, and he may have a point.

Now I am in a great hustle and bustle and have to see to a lot of things. Here's what's up: You write that there will be trouble if Katkov reads "Uncle's Dream" before he gets the novella for *Russian Messenger*. But that will certainly be the case, my friend! They cannot publish my novella before the fall. It is long (12, and possibly more, printer's sheets). I am putting on the finishing touches, and I refuse to be hurried. It will have a lot of faults, I am aware of that, and I am not overly fond of it, but certain things in it will be really good, and that is why I don't want to rush with it. When I sent off the story to Kushelyov I immediately informed Katkov of it, explaining to him with complete candor that, because I was hard up, I could not refuse the 500 rubles paid me as an advance and had obligated myself to Kushelyov, overestimating my capabilities, i.e., believing I could deliver both pieces on time. But my sickness and my desire to do a good job compelled me to slow up. If

Katkov is angry, let him be (and I believe he is, because he didn't answer me). But, on the other hand, I am doing my work for him conscientiously, and there is a chance that what I give him will be good. That is better than hurrying and falling on one's face. I sent off "Uncle's Dream" posthaste. But goodbye for now, my dear friend. There are many other things I ought to write to you about, but I shall leave these for the next mail, after I have received the money from Kushelyov. Farewell; I hug you and your entire family. My wife sends you her regards.

Yours,
F. Dostoyevsky

I, too, dream, my dear brother, about the moment when we shall meet again, and I do so often. Ah, we shall talk and talk, with all the things we have to say to each other. It makes me catch my breath when I think of it.

N.B. I am writing day and night for Katkov. Farewell.

If Pleshcheyev is in Moscow, send him my letter without delay.

---

35. Dostoyevsky received the 1,000 rubles from Kushelyov late in March. *Uncle's Dream* was published in the March 1859 issue of *Russian Word*. It was ignored by the critics.

The piece on which Dostoyevsky says he is working for Katkov "day and night" is *The Village of Stepanchikovo*.

36. To M. M. Dostoyevsky
Semipalatinsk, May 9, 1859

My dear friend Misha,

Your letter of April 8 finally arrived by the last mail, and I was extremely depressed and alarmed by the news of your illness. And my fears still have not passed. I realize very well that fits such as these can have the most dangerous consequences, and until I get letters from you telling me of your complete recovery, I shall not be myself again.

God willing, I shall leave here on June 15, not earlier, and possibly much later. As I have already written you, my discharge was granted by imperial rescript in Petersburg on March 18, but it has just been received here, and I shall have to wait at least until the beginning of June before all the formalities with the local military authorities have been completed and my complete release obtained. But if I do leave on June 15, it is unlikely that I shall receive your answer to *this* letter in time, since the mail moves much more slowly during the spring floods. Still, if you have any affection for me, answer me immediately (giving me all the details about the state of your health) and address it directly to Semipalatinsk. I shall have to spend two or three weeks in Omsk, where I shall have to take the necessary steps to have

Pasha released from the corps school, and your letter will be forwarded to me there from Semipalatinsk (N.B.—but don't address it to Omsk, use the Semipalatinsk address).

My dear friend Misha, I just now visualized so graphically that you might suddenly die and that I should never see you again, that fear still weighs on my heart. Ah, if only I could get from you even four lines soon!

I thank you very much, my dear friend, for sending me the waistcoats, shirts, etc., although I haven't received anything as yet. I gather from your letter that you must have sent all those things in the middle of March. Your letter of April 9 arrived a week ago, but your parcel, sent in the middle of March, is still sitting somewhere along the way. I cannot make any sense of it at all.

I told you before that I had received money from Kushelyov. But I didn't get the magazine from him. Perhaps I'll still get it—he wrote me that he would send me the bill, and he may send the magazine along with it.

Do me a great favor, my dear Misha, and write me all you hear about my novel without hiding anything from me—what they are saying about it, if indeed anyone is saying anything at all. You must realize how interested I am in hearing about it.

I wrote to Kushelyov by the last mail. I had to acknowledge receipt of the money he had sent. I asked him myself to send the magazine. As to my *contributing* to his magazine (he wrote in his last letter that he would wait for my next story with great impatience), I told him that, before anything else, I should like to see him personally and talk it over with him. I said I was thinking of a big novel of about 25 printer's sheets, that I was eager to start working on it right away (and on it alone), but that, because of certain circumstances, I could not sit down to that work, and *that what I should like to talk to him about personally was precisely those circumstances.* That is how I ended my letter to Kushelyov, without giving him any further explanation about the circumstances in question, but I shall tell you what they are.

(1) In order to sit down and write a novel, I must have a year and a half at my disposal.

(2) In order for me to have a year and a half to write, I have to be provided for during that time, and I don't have a kopek to my name.

(3) You keep on writing me such things as that Goncharov got 7000 for his novel, which I find disgusting, and that Turgenev was paid 4000 rubles, which amounts to 400 rubles a printer's sheet, for his *Nest of Gentlefolk* (I have read it at last, and it is extremely good), by the same Katkov who pays me 100 rubles a printer's sheet. Ah, my friend, I am quite well aware that I write worse than Turgenev, but, after all, not that much worse, and I hope to be able to write equally well. So why should I, with all my needs, charge only 100 rubles when Turgenev, who owns 2000 serfs, charges 400? My

poverty *forces* me to hurry and to write for money, *which unfailingly leads to my spoiling* my work.

So, when I do meet Kushelyov I intend to put it to him directly that he should give me eighteen months, pay me 300 rubles per printer's sheet and, on top of that, to enable me to live during that time, give me an advance of 3000 silver rubles. If he accepts, I would guarantee to give him, in addition, a short story by the beginning of the next year—about one and a half printer's sheets long. I have a number of subjects for long stories, but none for short ones. But I hope that, before the New Year, I may somehow stumble upon some inspiration and be able to concoct a brief story for Kushelyov.

You may get the impression that, all of a sudden, I have turned from humility to excessive arrogance in my demands. But then it is connected with a certain circumstance of which you are not aware. And since that circumstance is in turn closely connected with the question you ask me about *Poor Folk,* a question that you want answered immediately, I shall now turn directly to *Poor Folk.*

You want, my friend, to sell it to Kushelyov. That would be fine, but I would rather you didn't do it, because I have another thought in mind. Here it is: I am now finishing my novel for Katkov (it turned out long—14 or 15 printer's sheets). I have already sent him 3/4 of it, and shall send the balance at the beginning of June. Now listen to me, Misha! This novel of course has great defects, among which the worst, perhaps, is its verbosity; but at the same time I am thoroughly convinced that it has tremendous merits and that it is my *best work.* I have been working on it for two years (interrupting myself in the middle to write *Uncle's Dream*). The beginning and the middle are in final form, but the ending is still in the state of a rough draft. But it is into this that I have put my soul, my flesh and blood. I don't mean by that that I have expressed everything I have in me in it—that would be nonsense—I still have many, many things to say. Besides, this novel contains very little that comes from the heart (i.e., of the emotional element such as, for instance, abounds in *A Nest of Gentlefolk*), but it contains two tremendous character types which it has taken me five years to *create and set down,* and which are (in my opinion) perfectly fashioned—characters which are genuinely Russian, but which thus far have been poorly rendered in Russian literature. I don't know whether Katkov will appreciate it, but if the public receives my novel coldly, I probably shall, I confess, sink into despair. On that novel my fondest hopes are based and, above all, my hopes for the consolidation of my literary reputation. Now this is something to think about: the novel will come out this year, possibly in September. I suppose if it excites comment and receives some acclaim, I should then be in a position to ask Kushelyov for 300 rubles a printer's sheet, etc. He would no longer be dealing with an author who had nothing but "Uncle's Dream" to his credit.

Of course, I may be quite mistaken about my novel and its qualities, but all my hopes are hinged on it. Now, if my novel for *Russian Messenger* is a success and, let us assume, a substantial success, then it occurred to me that, instead of publishing *Poor Folk* separately, the following could be done. When I get to Tver and, of course, with your help, my dear friend and my constant helper, I should like next January or February to publish 2 volumes of my collected works, in the following order: volume 1—*Poor Folk*, the first 6 chapters of *Netochka Nezvanova*, polished up (which everyone liked), *White Nights, A Child's Fairy Tale*, and *A Christmas Tree and a Wedding*— altogether 18 printer's sheets; volume 2—*The Village of Stepanchikovo* (the novel for Katkov) and *Uncle's Dream*—altogether 24 printer's sheets. (N.B. Later we could publish a revised or, let's say, completely rewritten version of *The Double*, etc. This will be a third volume, but, for now, just two volumes would do.)

A printing of 2000 copies would cost 1500 rubles at the outside. It could be sold for three rubles apiece. Hence, if I am busy for 1½ years writing the long novel, the gradual sale of the copies will provide me with an income and keep me in funds. Or, as an alternative, we could sell the whole edition to Kushelyov for around three or even 2½ thousand, although *obviously it is absolutely impossible* to approach him about that deal now—we must wait for the successful reception of the novel sold to Katkov. Everything depends on that and this success will facilitate all our negotiations.

N.B. Altogether, I shall send Katkov 15 printer's sheets at 100 rubles per sheet, i.e., 1500 rubles' worth. I have taken 500 from him and, furthermore, when I sent him the ¾ of the novel, I asked him for 200 rubles for my journey, which means that I have taken a total of 700 from him. I'll arrive in Tver without a kopek in my pocket, but very soon after that I shall be receiving 700 or 800 rubles from Katkov. That's not too bad, and it will enable me to manage for a while.

I have been frightened by some people who claim that if Pasha is withdrawn from the corps, I will have to refund them 200 rubles for his upkeep for every year he spent there, i.e., 400 rubles; and where am I going to get them? That would be the final blow to me. All the money I have now is 600 rubles, and with what I expect to receive from Katkov, it would be 800. But then I shall have to buy a carriage, etc., and travel 4000 versts in summertime, when the going is the most expensive (they will harness four and sometimes five horses), which means that I have just enough money for the trip itself. And so how am I going to pay for Pasha?

Farewell, my good friend, my dear, dear Misha, be happy and *well* and give me a chance to hug you very soon. My regards to your wife and kiss all your children. Probably there are many things I haven't written to you about, but I am in a frightful hurry. I've got plenty to keep me busy. Farewell, friend, give my best to Pleshcheyev and ask him why he doesn't write me. Perhaps he is angry with me for pestering him for money? I can't believe it! My wife sends her best regards. Give my regards to all those who remember me.

Good-bye, my friend.

---

36. Dostoyevsky actually left Semipalatinsk on July 2. Tver was about 1,800 miles away by direct route (but see Letter 39), and he arrived there around the middle of August.

In June, Dostoyevsky wrote Mikhail that he had received the clothes he had asked for, as well as some pictures, presumably of Mikhail's family.

The "big novel" for Kushelyov is probably what turned out to be *The Insulted and Injured* (see note to Letter 33).

Goncharov's novel *Oblomov* appeared in installments in *Notes of the Fatherland* in 1859. Dostoyevsky's opinion of this work changed radically later, for he speaks of it quite favorably in *Diary of a Writer.*

Turgenev's *A Nest of Gentlefolk* (Dvoryanskoye gnezdo) came out in the January 1859 issue of *Contemporary* and later that year as a separate book. Dostoyevsky continued to think highly of it, even after he quarreled with Turgenev.

37.   To M. M. Dostoyevsky

Tver, October 1, 1859

My dear Misha,

Your letter came yesterday, but only after I had sent you off mine full of reproaches. You see, my friend, I had become altogether dispirited at receiving nothing from you. And so I beg you in advance to write to me even if you have nothing to say, just write that nothing's happened and don't leave me to worry, for that makes me feel the precariousness and the hopelessness of my situation even more acutely. I hope my behavior and my letter have not infuriated you. Don't be angry, my dear fellow, and write me more often.

I must say your letter surprised me. What's this about Nekrasov? Aren't they being a bit pretentious? Or perhaps he simply hasn't read it yet? I hear Nekrasov is an inveterate card player. Panayev hasn't much time to spare for the magazine either, and the whole thing would have gone to pieces if it hadn't been for Chernyshevsky and Dobrolyubov. You say that we ought to wait a bit, even that it would be more discreet to do so. But, my friend, we have waited long enough as it is. So please go to see Nekrasov yourself (I urge you to do this), try to catch him at home (this is the most important), and talk to him privately about what they intend to do with the novel. Above all, find out whether they are going to run it in two or three issues, what is their real feeling about the novel—and, after discussing all these things, you could mention the matter of money. Do that, for Christ's sake, and elicit from them a final decision. If you don't go to see him yourself, you could wait indefinitely for him to come to you, especially with his card playing. I am relying on you.

And now, my dear friend, I want to tell you about the decision I have reached after due deliberation: I shall start working on a novel (a big one— that is decided) and shall devote a year to it. I refuse to be hurried. The novel is already so well formed in my mind that I wouldn't think of spoiling it by trying to make some deadline. I want to write it in freedom. It is a novel with an *idea,* and it will open doors for me. But in order to write it I must have security. Selling it in advance and living on the money is suicide—it means taking 100 or 120 [rubles per printer's sheet], whereas later I could manage to get perhaps 150 or even 200. I myself shall be the judge, and if the novel turns out well, I shall be the one to name the price. And that is why I object to selling it in advance and why I insist on writing it free of financial concern.

But the question is: Where can I get enough money to tide me over for at least a year? I have given it serious thought, and I have come to the *incontrovertible conclusion* that I should publish my old works myself rather than sell them to some publisher—unless, of course, I were to be offered a very substantial sum, which is, however, very unlikely. Listen now—let us assume that my works will sell very slowly. That doesn't worry me in the least. All I need to live on is 120 to 150 rubles a month. So long as there is that much coming in, it will keep me in groceries.

The next thing you may ask is: Where is the money for publication to come from? I've thought about this. In the first place, I suggest not publishing everything at once, but rather one volume at a time. Altogether, there will be three volumes. The first one will contain *Poor Folk, Netochka Nezvanova* (the two parts), *White Nights, A Child's Fairy Tale, A Christmas Tree and a Wedding, An Honest Thief* (I must rewrite it), and *The Jealous Husband.* Altogether, around 23 printer's sheets of close print. The second volume will contain *The Double* (completely rewritten) and *Uncle's Dream.* The third volume is to contain *The Village of Stepanchikovo.*

I think that the first volume will sell out quite quickly. However, it needs some revising. *Poor Folk* can go just as it is in the second edition, but everything else in the first volume needs some touching up. Now, here is what I would ask you to do for me in this connection: get hold of all the other stories for the first volume. Some of them, like *Netochka Nezvanova,* you may have yourself and, for the rest, try asking Maikov, Milyukov, and others. Do it right away, without losing any time. Give them my regards, and persuade them to allow you to rip my stories out of the magazines containing them. If they let you do so, send them here at once. I'll correct the texts and send them back to you right away. If we can do all that by the end of October, and you have all the corrected texts back by November 1, you could then send them directly to the censorship office. Assuming that the censorship office keeps them until December 1, then, on December 1 we could start printing the first volume.

Now, where shall we get the money for publication? Here we go—it's once again your turn to play. Get the paper needed for volume 1 on credit from some merchant, and promise to settle in six months or less. All we need is 300 rubles or a bit more. I swear, Misha, that I will make good the promissory note you give (on my behalf). If the book doesn't sell and even fails to cover the cost of the paper, I swear, I will get the money—even if I have to dig it out of the bowels of the earth—and redeem the note. You will not be inconvenienced in any way whatsoever. As to the printing, if we can't arrange that on credit, too, then I would take care of one-half of the printing costs and borrow the other half from someone (I wonder whether it wouldn't be possible to ask Sashenka for it?).

This way, the book could be off the presses by mid-January and could go on sale immediately! I am convinced that the first volume will cause some stir. In the first place, it will contain my best things; second, it will bring me into the public eye; third, the *name* is an interesting one; and fourth, if the novel for *Contemporary* succeeds, the book will do well, too. In the meantime, by the middle of December, I shall send you (or bring over myself) a revised version of *The Double*. Believe me, brother, this new version, accompanied by an introduction, will be as good as a *new novel*. People will finally understand how good *The Double* really is! Indeed, I expect, if anything, to attract too much attention to myself—I am issuing a challenge to every one of them! (After all, if I did not revise *The Double* now, when would I do it? Why should I waste an excellent idea and a character of tremendous social significance, which I discovered and created?)

So *The Double* and *Uncle's Dream* must be sent to the censorship office in December. In January it will be printed, and toward the end of February the second volume will come out, and right afterward, almost simultaneously, we could produce the third volume, the one with *The Village of Stepanchikovo*. As to money, either we could borrow some, or we could pay for it out of the proceeds from the first volume. Finally, we could, if absolutely necessary, sell the publication rights to the last two volumes (assuming the first is a success). That would allow me to recover the publication costs, and until then I could live on the money from *Contemporary;* later, once the edition has paid for itself, even if the book moves slowly, it's all the same to me, because even if sales are slow there will be enough to keep us fed. Meanwhile, right from the beginning of December, I would start working seriously on my big novel (which, if it meets with success in a year, could help stimulate the sales of the remaining copies of my *Collected Works*).

And so the first thing you must do now is to let me know right away what you think of all this and, if possible, send me copies of the pieces that are to go into the first volume so that I may emend them.

If you procrastinate, my friend, you should realize that you will be causing me to lose precious time. I shall not do anything (I shall be incapable of doing anything) until you let me know definitely whether you approve and whether you are willing to help me. For God's sake, answer me quickly.

Maikov hasn't showed up. Got a letter from Wrangel. Golovinsky is here now, and introduced me at once to the whole of local society. I have no intention of seeing much of these people, but some of them I shan't be able to avoid; in a provincial town like this one, there is nowhere to hide. This is rather irksome. But there are two or three nice people. I have come to know Baranov and his countess quite well. Several times she invited me "most insistently" to drop in on them sort of casually, in the evenings; I couldn't refuse. It turned out that she wasn't a complete stranger. About twelve years ago I was introduced to her by Sollogub (she is a cousin of his) when she was still single—her maiden name was Vasilchikova.

Mariya Dmitriyevna sends you her regards. I hug you from the bottom of my heart, and I'd give everything in the world to get the hell out of here. In Tver, now, the people will prevent me from writing.

For God's sake, answer me, my dear friend. Good-bye, and hugs and kisses. Give my regards to everybody. Take care of your health as if it were a jewel. Give my love to Emiliya Fyodorovna, Kolya, and Sasha. Write more often.

And that Nekrasov money would have come in handy right now—first of all for you, and secondly, for me.

---

37. The letter "full of reproaches" has been lost, but judging from Mikhail's reply of October 2, Dostoyevsky had written that his brother took too little interest in his (Dostoyevsky's) affairs and that he was too lazy to write to him (Dostoyevsky had not received a letter from him for a week). Mikhail had gone to Tver to visit Dostoyevsky at the end of August and the beginning of September.

Nikolai Gavrilovich Chernyshevsky (1828–1889) was a leading critic and writer. He was arrested in 1862 and exiled to Siberia for twenty-four years; while in prison, he wrote *What Is To Be Done?* (Chto delat?, 1863), which became a classic of the Russian revolutionary movement. Nikolai Aleksandrovich Dobrolyubov (1836–1861) was a journalist and critic and one of the early leaders of the revolutionary movement.

Two volumes of Dostoyevsky's collected works were published in 1860, with the first volume as suggested here and the second volume as suggested in the previous letter. However, Dostoyevsky did not bring them out himself, nor were they published by Kushelyov; instead, they were published by Osnovsky. The revised version of *The Double* did not appear until 1866, when it was published in a separate volume by Stellovsky.

Dostoyevsky thought his name would be "an interesting one" because of his status as a returning exile.

Count Pavel Trofimovich Baranov (1815–1864) was the governor of the Tver region. He was well disposed toward Dostoyevsky and tried to help him obtain permission to live in Petersburg.

Dostoyevsky complained about Tver in other letters as well; for example, on September 22, he had written to Wrangel that it was "a thousand times worse" than Semipalatinsk—"bleak, cold, houses of stone, no activity, nothing of interest, not even a decent library. A real prison!"

38.   To M. M. Dostoyevsky
Tver, October 18, 1859

Got your two letters—one with the money (50 rubles) and the other one with the news that you had been to Krayevsky. Thanks a lot for the money, my dear Misha; it came at just the right moment. But the thing is, my dear friend, I must have it all—I mean everything I can get as an advance on my novel, minus the 750 silver rubles that I owe you. I need it badly. And you'd better not ask me why I need it. But this business with my novel drags on and on with no end in sight. I don't blame you for it, my dear Misha, but why such arrogance on their part? I find it quite ridiculous. Do you mean to tell me that Maikov's recommendation is not enough for Krayevsky or, for that matter, for Dudyshkin? All right, let us assume that Dudyshkin must read it—but why should it take him so long? In a word, it is my impression that they are getting on their high horse and pretending to do us a favor by taking a novel that has previously been rejected. I think, my friend, that it ought to be possible for us to hurry them up a bit.

As to your visit there on Thursday (I suppose with the intention of finding out about the novel) and your apparent timidity about bringing up the subject of the novel, all I can say is that they probably sensed that very well themselves. But I have nothing to reproach you with, my dear boy. You write that Krayevsky was very warm and considerate, and point out that that is a very good sign. In my opinion, it is a very bad sign. It means that they are about to start bargaining. And we don't have to stand for that. In short, if we proceeded with greater determination and independence, I am sure we should command greater respect. We ought to make them feel that we can pretty well get along without them. I think we should definitely hurry them up. It's very likely that if they need the novel, they won't send it back. And when do they intend to publish it? I should have very much liked it to come out this year.

I saw the published lists of the forthcoming contributors to *Notes of the Fath[erland]* and did not find my name among them. Look here, my dear friend, we must strike while the iron is hot, while there is still time. We must make the most of every advantage we have in the situation and use every trick in the books. So take my advice and think it over carefully. Here it is.

You see, as long as Krayevsky has the novel *and has not said the final word,* that is, as long as there is still time, wouldn't it be a good idea to let them know that we have other prospects? They consider (and will certainly maintain as much during the negotiations) that the novel is a sort of reject. Well, we shall have to prove to them conclusively that it is not a reject at all. Then, instead of bargaining, they will start bidding higher for it. The first means to that end is *Nekrasov.* After all, it was he who came to see you and, not finding you in, said he would come back another time, which means that he had something on his mind. So why not go and see him yourself (instead of losing time by writing him a letter and then waiting for a reply)? As things stand already, *Contemporary* looks like an extremely doubtful prospect, so there's nothing to lose; it is not only desirable that you go and see him, it is absolutely essential. There's just a chance that we may stumble on something of interest. If you dropped in on Nekrasov and *found him home,* you could say this to him: "When you came to see me the other day, Nikolai Alekseyevich, it was a shame I wasn't at home. I wrote to my brother about it, and he, too, is very sorry that I missed you. I suppose the object of your visit was that novel, and possibly you had some new proposition in mind. But, you see, the novel is at Krayevsky's, and I'm about to settle the final terms with him, *although there is nothing that binds us to him as yet* (I mean to Krayevsky). So, if you have an offer to make, make it now. I have been authorized by my brother to conclude the deal whenever I see fit and, besides, I have quite precise instructions on the subject. Moreover, let me tell you frankly, my brother will always give priority to *Contemporary*. He told me so himself. And so, what was it you wished to tell me?" Possibly Nekrasov will reply right away, possibly he may ask for time to think it over.

In that case, allow him just one day to make up his mind and tell him that there can be *no more waiting* after that. You understand what we can get out of it: if Nekrasov is in the least bit interested, we can immediately play Nekrasov off against Krayevsky, and they will both start bidding. The novel will go to the highest bidder. And then remember, my dear boy, that I particularly asked you to see Nekrasov to find out all his *motives* and what he thinks of the novel, i.e., whether he likes it. That is very important. What he

149

says will become the opinion of *Contemporary,* their pronouncement on the novel, if they are to acknowledge it in print at all. All that is of tremendous interest to me. Listen to me, my dear boy, and do this. You won't be humiliating either me or yourself in the least before Nekrasov. Dignified sincerity is strength. And, after all, you are not hiding anything from them. We are acting quite openly. And, again, we have nothing to lose as far as *Contemporary* is concerned, and the least we can gain by this maneuver is to put pressure on Krayevsky. Please understand, Misha, that time is of the essence, because the moment *Notes of the Fath.* reveals its terms it will be too late. Then Nekrasov will realize that we don't seem to be getting anyplace with *Notes of the Fatherland* either, whereas now you are approaching him before having begun any serious negotiations with Krayevsky. That makes all the difference in the world.

You should also tell Nekrasov that Maikov likes the novel. Since Maikov is on friendly terms with Dudyshkin, that would carry weight with Nekrasov because he would get the impression that *Notes of the Fath.* seriously intends to take the novel and will hold onto it because they consider it a good thing. It would be wonderful if Maikov praised the novel directly in Nekrasov's presence. But, in general, we must get moving.

Now, the *second means* is to scare Krayevsky.

I wrote you before that Minayev had come to see me and that I had promised him my collaboration on the *Lamp.* So go to Kalinovsky, who is the publisher and the principal backer of the *Lamp,* and, for God's sake, do it right away. You can get his address from Milyukov, who is on his editorial board. As you step into Kalinovsky's office, just tell him simply and frankly something like this: "We have a novel. Nekrasov's terms don't quite satisfy us. Krayevsky has asked for it, and we are about to conclude the final contract. However, we are still uncommitted. In the meantime, Nekrasov came to see me and said he would drop by again, which would indicate that he is considering offering us different conditions. In short, *Contemporary* and *Notes of the Fath.* are bidding for it. Nekrasov is offering 100 rubles per sheet, and it looks as if Krayevsky is going to offer 120. However, my brother needs money; a few days ago he wrote me that Mr. Minayev had been to see him and had asked him to collaborate on the *Lamp.* My brother asked me to have a talk with you. Being a new publication, you are still without influence or subscribers. It is obviously more advantageous for a well-known writer, one whose name *attracts attention,* to be published by a magazine with influence and an established reputation. Consequently, he would consider collaborating with you only if you offered better terms than the others. So what would your offer be?"

(To that, you must not fail to add that I am now writing these most intriguing *Notes from the House of the Dead,* that it will appear in one of the leading magazines, probably *Contemporary,* and that the work ought to add to the author's popularity. And point out to him also that *Notes of the Fa.* is absolutely determined to publish my novel *this year,* which would enable me to publish it as a separate volume next year; but if I published it in the *Lamp,* I should have to wait one more year before bringing it out in book form, which would be a loss for me.)

Now if Kalinovsky asks you for time to think it over, tell him that he should decide very soon. But if he does decide right away and names his price, that would be very much to our advantage. When you negotiate with Krayevsky you could tell him flatly that the *Lamp* is offering more money and pays in advance. Explain to him that your brother is too hard-pressed to bother about glory, that what he is after is money; that your brother is not seeking either the patronage or the prestige of famous magazines, but wishes honestly for the reading public to judge him on his own merits. If the novel is good, it will be good even in Kalinovsky's magazine, and the public will recognize it sooner or later; and if it is bad, then it will be just as bad in *Notes of the Fath.* Therefore, the name of the magazine is of no importance to your brother and *he sees no reason to pay a premium for the privilege of seeing his name in Notes of the Fath.* But if Kalinovsky gives you 150 rubles a sheet, give it to him with joy without a moment's hesitation and may God bless him! I cannot think of anything better that could happen. 2000 plus— why, that's a treasure-trove! I don't give a damn whether the *Lamp* has subscribers or not! If the novel is good—it won't get lost. And I am not in the least afraid of *Contemporary's* and *Notes of the Fath.'s* ire and scorn. In the first place, I am simply not afraid of it, and, in the second, they already know that I have *House of the Dead,* so it's quite unlikely that they'll roast *Stepanchikovo.*

Hence, my dear Misha, here are my terms for Kalinovsky: 150 rubles per sheet; one-half of the money to be paid right away, the other half upon publication. It must come out in January and February.

Do this for me, my dear boy, for God's sake, do; be my friend and prove to me thereby that you are my friend! Try to understand that this is to be my daily bread for the future, and that one must strike while the iron is hot. If you are my friend, you'll do that for me. Please forgive me for giving you all this trouble. I shall make it up to you some day.

Ah, I am already so sick and tired of that novel! No matter what, *answer* me quickly.

Tomorrow I am sending off my letter to the Sovereign in Petersburg, through Adlerberg. I made up my mind to do it a while ago. But, Misha, you mustn't talk too much about it, at least for the time being. I don't know what will come of it. The Sovereign is merciful. However, there can be delays, inquiries made of Dolgorukov, etc. In any case, my dear fellow, I hope to see you very soon. I expect to.

With regard to the letter from Zhdan-Pushkin and the package for Mariya Dmitriyevna—send them here without fail.

Farewell, my invaluable friend; I hug you, and I beg you not to be angry with me. Because my life here is painful, very very painful.

Yours,
Dostoyevsky

Be very polite, amiable, and meek with Nekrasov. Pretend that you have just dropped in on him for a minute and are in a great hurry.

---

38. Semyon Stepanovich Dudyshkin (1820–1866) was the successor to Belinsky and Valerian Maikov as the person in charge of literary criticism for *Notes of the Fatherland;* later he became the the de facto editor in chief of the magazine. *The Village of Stepanchikovo and Its Inhabitants* was published in *Notes of the Fatherland* in the last two issues of 1859.

The *Lamp* was a magazine of Slavophile tendencies that was published by D. I. Kalinovsky between 1860 and 1862. Dmitry Dmitriyevich Minayev (1835–1889), a poet, translator, and satirist, was a member of the editorial staff.

Notes from the House of the Dead first appeared, in incomplete installments, in the newspaper *Russian World* (Russky mir) in 1860; the complete text appeared for the first time in Dostoyevsky's own magazine, *Time,* in 1861 and 1862.

Dostoyevsky's letter to Tsar Alexander II was a plea to be permitted to reside in Petersburg. Count Vladimir Fyodorovich Adlerberg (1790–1884) was at this time minister of the imperial court. Prince Vasily Andreyevich Dolgorukov (1803–1868) (the surname is also spelled "Dolgoruky") was head of the Third Section; he had been a member of the commission that investigated the Petrashevsky affair. Unknown to Dostoyevsky, he had already granted the permission to live in Petersburg; but since Dostoyevsky had meanwhile written to the tsar, he was advised that it would be unwise to move before the tsar had made his decision, which did not happen until the end of November. Thus, ironically, the letter actually delayed Dostoyevsky's return by a few weeks.

39.   To A. I. Geibovich
Tver, October 23, 1859

Our ever so kind and unforgettable friend, highly esteemed Artemy Ivanovich:

I shan't try to justify my long silence to you, but if I am indeed guilty before you, I swear it is without guilt! My wife and I not only have not forgotten you and your nice family, but I dare say that not one day goes by without our remembering you all with great warmth. When I received your letter here, which began so coldly, addressing me as "Dear Sir," I felt deep pangs of conscience and reproached myself for my long silence. It is true that I could have written before, but my affairs were in such a muddle that no sooner did I sit down to write you a letter than some brain-racking problem came up, and I would have to go rushing around, asking for advice, submitting requests, and filling in forms—I cannot tell you the half of it.

I'd do much better to describe to you our wanderings, starting right from July 2, which will give you a very clear idea of what kept me terribly busy and caused me anxiety. I shall never forget the day we parted, when (let it be said in passing) I had an appreciable number of drinks with one and all. On the following day, when we were on our way, we kept talking about you. The weather was wonderful and the road very pleasant all the way to Omsk. I remained for three or four days in Omsk, took Pasha out of the cadet corps school, visited old friends and superiors, including de Gravé and others. Velikhanov [sic] told me that they were asking for him in Petersburg and that he was going there in a month. Through him I got to know a very nice family—the Kapustins (do you know them?), who have since moved to Tomsk—simple, good, and kindhearted people. If you happen to be in Tomsk (for any reason) you absolutely must meet them and remember me to them. I got to know them very well—they are people without any pretensions whatsoever.

Otherwise, however, I disliked Omsk very much, and the town brought back unpleasant thoughts and memories. And it was when we drove out of Omsk that I really said good-bye to Siberia. Now the road was very bad, but when we got to Tyumen we found a magnificent town—a populous center for trade and industry, comfortable—everything you could wish. We stayed there for two days (I don't quite remember for what reason). During the journey—the first half of it—I had two fits, but none since then. Our courier, Nikolayev, turned out to be a wonderful fellow—kind and helpful, although rather inefficient. As a character, as a type—a remarkable man: the kindest and most generous heart, and at the same time somewhat of a show-off. We grew accustomed to him and became very attached to him during the trip, and he was so appreciative that he cried like a child when we parted. If he comes to Ayaguz with the mail, get hold of him—he will have a lot to tell you.

I shall skip many observations and impressions of the journey. We had marvelous weather throughout practically the entire journey, the carriage didn't break down (not once!), we never had to wait for horses, but the prices, my God, the prices at the stations were staggering! You ask for the littlest thing, inquire about the price, and then you look into the fellow's eyes aghast, wondering whether you haven't stumbled on a madman or something! Nowhere else in the world would you find such prices! But nature made it up to use—the magnificent forests of Perm and later of Vyatka are perfection itself. Otherwise, in Perm there is little unutilized land along the road—everything is plowed, cultivated, exploited. Or such at least was my impression.

We spent twenty-four hours in Yekaterinburg, and there we succumbed to temptation. We spent about 40 rubles, buying all sorts of handicraft wares—beads, cuff links, buttons, etc.—and also 38 rock specimens. We bought it all to bring with us as presents, and I must say they were dirt cheap; here those things would cost almost twice as much. Then, one beautiful evening at around five o'clock, on a road that meandered through the foothills of the Urals, in the middle of a forest, we at last stumbled upon the boundary between Asia and Europe. A wonderful pole covered with inscriptions has been set up there, standing alongside a hut, in which we found an old army pensioner. We stepped out of the carriage and I crossed myself, because the Lord had granted that I see the promised land once again. Then we took out your plaited-straw-covered flask filled with bitter orange-blossom brandy (from the Shtriter distilleries), and I drank with the old pensioner to take my farewell of Asia, and Nikolayev drank too, and so did the coachman (and you should have seen how he drove us after that). We talked for a while and then we scattered in the forest to pick wild strawberries, and we picked lots of them.

But if I go on like this, I shall never get to the essentials. In Kazan we got stuck. We had only 120 silver rubles left and that, obviously, was not enough to reach Tver. While still in Semipalatinsk, I had written my brother, asking him to send me 200 rubles addressed to the Kazan post office, general delivery, so we decided to wait for the money and got ourselves a decent hotel room. The prices are outrageous. We waited for ten days, and it cost us 50 rubles. I had already taken out a library card for the Kazan Public Library, not knowing what else I could do. But it so happened that my letter had only reached my brother after a shocking delay. He did, however, finally send me the 200 rubles, and we at once resumed our journey.

We arrived at Nizhny just at the height of the fair; we arrived at night and for a couple of hours wandered all over town, stopping at every hotel and finding every one of them full. Finally we found one that looked rather like a kennel, but we were pleased to get even that. The next day I went out to see Annenkov (he had been deported to Tobolsk and is now a counselor in Nizhny), but he was on leave, and the whole family was away in the country. So I immediately went over to take a look at the fair. Well, Artemy Ivanovich, I must say it is quite an affair! I roamed around for two or three hours, and still managed to see only a tiny corner of it—it would take a whole month to see everything. In any case, it is impressive, I might even say too much so. It fully merits its reputation.

That same day we left Nizhny for Vladimir. In Vladimir I saw Khomentovsky, who is the head of the food supply commission there. He is an excellent and most generous man, who is, however, spelling his own doom. You know what I mean—his drinking. And he is surrounded by God knows whom, people who are certainly unworthy of him. He came to see us, told us about his adventures abroad, and told it all very well. We had quite a lot to drink that evening, the two of us. We had a very long talk, and I learned many interesting things from him. We eventually pushed on from Vladimir. It would have been shorter to go through Moscow, but, in the first place, I was officially barred from entering Moscow. In the second place, to pass through Moscow and to see my sisters without being able to spend at least a week with them was unthinkable. All that could have caused me lots of trouble, so I decided to go to Tver Province not via Yaroslavl, as I had planned back in Semipalatinsk, but via Serpukhovskaya Lavra (60 versts from Moscow), and to go straight to the city of Tver, cutting across Moscow Province. I made that decision only to regret it. This is off the main route, and I had to use independent drivers, who charged three times more, over the 150-verst detour, than the state stagecoach drivers. However, a visit to the St. Sergius Monastery—which I hadn't seen in twenty-three years—amply compensated us for all our troubles. What architecture, what statues, what impressive Byzantine rooms, what chapels! The sacristy left us breathless—it contains pearls (of incomparable beauty) weighing many carats, emeralds over a half-inch long, diamonds worth half a million rubles apiece! I saw costumes there from several centuries, the handiwork of Russian tsarinas and tsarevnas, the domestic clothing of Ivan the Terrible, coins, ancient books, all sorts of rare objects—I would never have left the place.

At last, after long peregrinations, we reached Tver and put up at a hotel. The price was outrageous. We had to find ourselves an apartment. There were plenty of apartments available but not a single furnished one. It was, of course, very inconvenient for me to buy furniture for just a few months. Finally, after several days of searching, I found an apartment that was not quite an apartment really but something in between a hotel room and an apartment, consisting of three small furnished rooms for 11 silver rubles a month. Well, thank God even for that!

And so I settled down to wait for my brother to come. Just before this, my brother had been sick and had almost died. Finally he got better and came. What a joyful occasion that was! The train arrived at around three o'clock in the morning, and the railway station is three versts or so from the town. So I went to meet him in the middle of the night. We had so much to tell one another. But it is really quite impossible to convey such moments. My brother stayed with me for five days, then went to Moscow and, on his way back, spent another two days here. We made up our minds together concerning my affairs. In the first place, we decided to wait until September 8 (everyone was talking about the manifesto, everyone was waiting for it), but there was no manifesto, although there were many pardons. So I went to the local colonel of the security police and asked for his advice. He told me that the surest procedure would be for me to write to Prince Dolgorukov (the chief of the security police). And that is what I decided to do. By the way, I also wrote to Totleben through Wrangel, who happened to be in Petersburg.

In the meantime, a man I used to know and who knows everyone in Tver came through here and introduced me to two or three of the local families and, most important of all, to the governor of the province, Adjutant General Count Baranov, who turned out to be a man of rare qualities and exceptional kindness. I told him, among other things, that I intended to write to Dolgorukov. He showed great interest, but advised me to wait before doing so, because the emperor was traveling at that time and Prince Dolgorukov was accompanying him (N.B.—the emperor returned to Petersburg five days ago). So I waited and, while waiting, I composed a whole series of letters— to Dolgorukov, to Totleben, and also to Rostovtsev. And suddenly I had a brilliant idea—to write directly to the emperor himself. I went to Baranov and asked him what he thought of it, and he fully approved. Moreover, he offered to have the letter transmitted, with his recommendation, by his cousin Count Adlerberg. So I wrote the letter and, while I was at it, I asked to have Pasha admitted to a secondary school or a cadet corps school. It is now five days since I sent the letter. I am waiting for the answer, and you can imagine, my dear Artemy Ivanovich, what a state I am in. It may be that my future has already been decided as I am writing this. There are two possibilities. Either the emperor will simply write at the top of my letter, "granted," in which case I shall leave for Petersburg in a few days, and all my worries will be over; or the emperor will turn my letter over to Dolgoruky to ascertain whether or not there are any *special obstacles in my dossier*. There cannot be any special obstacles, but that will considerably delay the whole procedure, and probably nothing definite would happen before Christmas at the earliest. In one word, I am not myself with all this waiting and uncertainty. The only unshakable hope I have is in the emperor's magnanimity. What a great man he is for Russia, Artemy Ivanovich! From here it is more evident, and I have heard so many things to confirm this opinion. And he has so many difficulties to contend with! There are despicable people who do not approve of his measures of redemption, all those backward men who refuse to get out of the rut they are in. May God help him!

At the same time that I was making all those efforts, I also had money problems. Finally they, too, have been settled. I broke off negotiations with *Russian Messenger,* and *Notes of the Fatherland* gave me 120 rubles per printer's sheet, which means I shall have 1800 or 2,000 silver rubles. On top of that, I am planning to sell a collection of my earlier writings, which should bring me one and a half or two thousand silver rubles, too. And it is on the proceeds of these two transactions that I expect to live for a while. All this has cost me a lot of effort and worry. Indeed, as I write this, my principal troubles are still not over. And that is why, since I was constantly fussing around and doing things, I haven't been able to write to you all this time, Artemy Ivanovich, invaluable friend of ours. But things are changing now, and soon all this turmoil will be over. Of course, I shall still have the day-to-day problems to face, but things will not be as hectic. I shall write you more often, and I hope you will write me too, our dear friend. But don't imagine for a moment that I could ever forget you! I don't believe there is anyone in the world who is more devoted to you and who respects you more than I do. But now that I have told you all about myself, let's talk about you and your unforgettable family.

To start with, I have such vivid memories of the time we spent together in Semipalatinsk, and the hospitality with which you received us, and how close we became toward the end of our stay there. We remember so well and will never forget the kind Praskovya Mikhailovna and the pretty little faces of your young ladies, Zinaida Artemevna and Lizaveta Nikitishna. And this is why I should like you to write to us and to tell us about everything at great length. But more about that at the end of my letter, because there is *one small matter* I should like to discuss with you. You may remember, Artemy Ivanovich, that I have always wished, for the sake of your dear children's education, that you would move to Russia and obtain a better position. Being deeply devoted to you, I used to tell you sadly that the position you were occupying was not worthy of you, that you were contenting yourself with an insignificant salary, were wasting your life, and besides being drowned in work, had to face all the trials and tribulations of the service, all its inconveniences, etc. You must remember all that, and I don't want you to think that I have forgotten it either. When I was in Vladimir, I picked a suitable moment to speak to Khomentovsky. (One thing you can be absolutely sure of, most noble Artemy Ivanovich, is that I shall never speak lightly and frivolously about your affairs, nor shall I speak with just anyone. Besides, all those who know you respect you. Thus, when I speak *with people* about you, I do so in such a way that, even without seeing you, they have to look upon you with esteem. What's more, in speaking about you, I never so much as intimate that you are some sort of petitioner, but rather I speak simply in my own name and in a tone which suggests that you would be an asset in any position.) Khomentovsky is a most honorable man and a man I could talk to; the others I won't bother with. He heard me out attentively and said, very reasonably, that of course, there were some positions open in Russia, that there were even some good and comfortable openings in his own department, but that the salaries were not so very high and, even though they were considerably higher than in the Siberian battalions, life in Russia was much more expensive than in Siberia and, therefore, you would have to have a position that paid *at least* 600 or 700 rubles; otherwise, it wouldn't be worth your while. But he said that there were very few positions at such a salary available, and that there were very many candidates for them. However, Khomentovsky added, he felt that an honest man willing to work could always make his way, but that his chances would be better with a private company. There has been such a mushrooming of private companies, administrations, and societies that *honest* and conscientious people are in great demand and are being offered colossal salaries. The main drawback is that you happen to be in Siberia. If you were living in Russia and were well recommended, things could be arranged very quickly; and these private positions do not require any special technical qualifications, nor does getting them involve any particular difficulties or complicated procedures—the main qualifications are honesty and a willingness to work.

When we were through with this subject, Khomentovsky and I talked about Vasilchikov. I wanted to find out what he thought of him. It turned out that they were on excellent terms (and Khomentovsky wouldn't lie). So I asked him whether you, for example, if you found yourself in a difficult situation, say through unfair treatment in the service, or wished to be transferred somewhere else, etc.—in brief, if you needed help from a person in Vasilchikov's position—could you, in that case, count on Khomentovsky's cooperation? (He and Vasilchikov are still on their old friendly footing.) Khomentovsky thereupon replied that if there were a need for you to make a request connected with service matters, or if you had to write a letter of petition or anything of that sort, he could promise me on his honor that he would personally transmit your request to Vasilchikov, and he feels that, in most cases, we could count on certain success. I am telling you all this, my dear Artemy Ivanovich, so that you should bear it in mind *in case* the need arises. If things come to that, an influential person like Vasilchikov could be very useful.

Something else now. During a conversation with Countess Baranova, after I had gotten settled here in Tver, I said to her on one occasion: "Do you think the count has any need for a perfectly *honest man* for any position whatever?" She replied: "Ah, if only you knew how much he needs such a man!" Then I said a few words about you, described your family to her, etc. But I spoke *in general,* not even mentioning your name or where exactly you were living at the moment. (I thought I would broach the subject later to the count himself.) But as it turned out, she spoke to him about it the very same day, and when I met her again in the house of some common acquaintances, she said to me: "I have spoken to my husband about the officer you told me about. Who is he and where is he stationed?" I told her. When she heard you were in Siberia, she was quite surprised. How could he possibly afford to come to Russia from such a distance? I conceded that it would be quite a problem but suggested that, *assuming* that difficulty were somehow to be resolved, what would happen then? She answered: "Anyone would take an honest man and, first of all, my husband, on your recommendation. But you tell me he has a family, and do you have any idea of the living costs here? It would be quite impossible to give him a post *with a large salary* right off, although it would always be possible to get him a modest position to start with. Unless he were willing to try to find something with a private company. . . ." And that is where matters stand for the time being. I am very glad that, so far, I have broached the matter only vaguely, because later I intend to speak to the count himself and this time seriously. And what I shall speak to him about will not be a position in Tver or in Tver Province—I have other things in mind. I have two courses of action: the first is through the count—in Petersburg I shall meet his relatives (I hope so, at least) and, among them, Adlerberg. The second is through other persons: through Rostovtsev, whom I shall definitely go to see in person and who is a close friend of Pyotr Petrovich Semyonov, a traveler who was with us in Semipalatinsk. I have also great hopes of meeting many other people in Moscow through another man of my acquaintance. I will meet these people because I shall need them later. They are all influential people, and if anything at all can be done to find you a position with the government, it can be done through them. And once again let me repeat, Artemy Ivanovich, that I won't talk lightly or frivolously, that I won't even mention your name when it is not absolutely necessary, and that, in general, I will be very careful in what I say. And if it is impossible to find you a position through these people, then it is really impossible by any other means. Then there is the other *alternative*—finding a position with a private company that would pay a large salary, because I hope to get acquainted with the gentlemen of industry. Or, at least, I do not intend to avoid them.

Now, to conclude. I realize very well, Artemy Ivanovich, that you consider all this quite unfeasible, and I remember the smile with which you used to look at me in Semipalatinsk. But hear me out. In the first place, I have never regarded myself as a distributor of positions and will never accept such an *unbearably* idiotic role. I am a little man and I know my proper place. However, I have a pretty good idea of the milieu I'm dealing with, and I do know how to take advantage of circumstances both for myself and for my friends. I am acting for you as your friend, sincerely, as one who wishes you well with all his heart. And you yourself, even though you looked at me skeptically when I spoke to you about these things in Semipalatinsk, you nevertheless did not forbid me to try. Lastly, I am acting with your interests fully in mind; I emphasize that I speak for you on my own initiative and not on yours, at no time putting you in the position of a petitioner. I always maintain this discretion and never so much as mention your name unless it is really indispensable. Moreover, I study the people I approach and what they have to offer well beforehand. I realize very well myself that nothing much may come of it in the end, i.e., it may not work. But if we have any luck, I won't make a move without first offering you the clearest proof that we have a sure and dependable thing. Then it will be up to you to make the final decision. You and no one else are the master of your own life, and if the proposition seems to be in the least bit vague or risky, you will be able to reject it out of hand.

As to moving from Siberia, that is a purely external matter; it is quite feasible and depends only on money. But, after all, there are many ways of resolving financial difficulties. Finally, I am saying all this to you without the slightest apprehension, since I know to whom I am speaking. You are a sensible man who has his feet firmly planted on the ground and are not one to be lured by unfounded hopes or to chase a stork when you have a titmouse in hand and risk the certain for the uncertain.

So here is my advice to you: Go on considering my dreams and hopes as delirium, but nevertheless allow me to try to find you a suitable position. If God wills it—so much the better, what is there to lose? Anyway, I know you won't laugh at my ardor. You are a generous-hearted man and will understand that I am acting completely disinterestedly—just out of friendship for you, because I am deeply and sincerely attached to you and all of yours. If my hopes turn out to be ridiculous, I shall be the first to laugh at them. But my conscience will remain clear because I know I shall never cause you worry or anxiety—you have too much good sense for that and will never count your chickens before they hatch. In any case, whatever I do can do no harm. And, besides, it is still far off and will not happen soon even in the case of success. But enough about that. We shall speak more of it later, for there are still so many things we have to discuss. I shall be writing you soon again, without even waiting for your answer—just as soon as my affairs are settled. When they are settled, I shall let you know right away; perhaps I shall even write you before that. And I ask you as a friend, as a brother, to write back. And here are my friendly instructions to you: In your very first letter, I want you to inform us first about *Ayaguz*, about your acquaintances and, in general, about your day-to-day life *in great detail*—what sort of people you see, what sort of faces there are around you. Secondly, how are things at your job, speaking generally? Thirdly, write at length about your entire family and especially about Zinaida Artemevna and Lizaveta Nikitishna. What are they doing? How do they keep busy? Do they still remember us? Tell them I kiss their hands and beg them not to be angry with me for not having written them and for still not writing them now. I shall write them a separate letter shortly, because I do remember my promise. Write me how Praskovya Maksimovna's health is and whether she remembers us. Mariya Dmitriyevna sometimes even cries when she remembers you, I swear she does. I believe she has prepared a letter to you. Lastly, write about all our acquaintances in Semipalatinsk and Ayaguz, if there is still anyone left whom we used to know, and give me the news of that dear man Mikhail Ivanovich Protasov. If he is already in Russia, I can't imagine that some day we shan't stumble across him. What are you reading now? Do you have books?

Waiting around here, our life, too, is rather dull. We are not buying even the most indispensable things until such time as we move to Petersburg. I am the only one to make acquaintances and see people, because Mariya Dmitriyevna is reluctant, since we don't have the room to receive them at home. And, anyway, I have gotten to know only three or four families. I know many people but visit only a few of them—those whose company I enjoy. As towns go, Tver is incredibly boring. It has few comforts. Prices are terribly high. The architecture is solid but dull. The theater is nothing much to talk of.

I still haven't been able to sell my carriage. I was offered 30 silver rubles, although people praised it and told me that anywhere else I could get twice as much for it; here, however, there is not much use for it, because of the railroad. And although the railway station is three versts from the town, the whistling of the locomotives of various trains can be heard day and night. We have been to the station several times. It's an interesting place. Well, so we have come to the end of this letter. Farewell, my dear Artemy Ivanovich, good-bye, and don't be too lazy to write and to remember us. As to us, you can count on our not forgetting you. I hug you. Give my sincere regards to Praskovya Maksimovna. I kiss the hands of your young ladies. I shall write again soon. And, in the meantime, I remain yours as ever,

F. Dostoyevsky

P.S. Thank Vasily for his letter. Give him my regards. What has happened to the Novoveiskys? I shall write to Mikhail Aleksandrovich one of these days.

---

39. Artemy Ivanovich Geibovich (d. 1865) had been Dostoyevsky's company commander in the Seventh Line Battalion and had been extremely kind to him. Later, he became mayor of the town of Ayaguz. Dostoyevsky's efforts on his behalf were evidently futile, for he died in Ayaguz. Praskovya Maksimovna (d. 1871), whom Dostoyevsky first refers to as Praskovya Mikhailovna, was his wife; Zinaida Artemevna, his daughter; and Lizaveta Nikitishna, either a niece or an adopted daughter.

Of the cities that Dostoyevsky mentions along his route from Semipalatinsk to Tver, Yekaterinburg is now Sverdlovsk, Vyatka is Kirov, and Nizhny (i.e., Nizhny Novgorod) is Gorky.

Chekan (or Chokan) Chingisovich Valikhanov (1835–1866) was a Kirghiz who had been educated at the officer cadet school in Omsk, where he met Dostoyevsky and they became warm friends. Dostoyevsky had urged him to take up a career in writing, so that he could be "the first native [Kirghiz] to explain in European Russia what the steppe is really like . . . while at the same time serving as an *enlightened* emissary of your native land among the Russians." Some of his work was subsequently published in *Notes of the Russian Geographical Society* (Zapiski russkogo geograficheskogo obshchestva).

Semyon Yakovlevich Kapustin (1828–1891) was a jurist and journalist.

The monastery (*lavra*) in Serpukhov dates from the sixteenth century. That in Sergiyev (now Zagorsk), generally known as the Troitsko-Sergiyevskaya, is one of the most famous in Russia; it was founded in 1340 and contains, among other buildings, the Uspensky Cathedral, with the tomb of Boris Godunov. Dostoyevsky had last visited it shortly before entering the engineering school in 1837.

The manifesto being awaited was the one in which Tsar Alexander II was expected to end serfdom in Russia (which is what Dostoyevsky means by the "measures of redemption"); the "difficulties" the tsar was facing is a reference to the opposition of the aristocracy to this step. The Edict of Emancipation was not issued until February 20, 1861 (Old Style).

The man whom he "used to know" and whom he met again in Tver was Golovinsky.

Yakov Ivanovich Rostovtsev (1803–1860) was a prominent figure in the movement for agrarian reform. A few days before the Decembrist uprising was planned to take place, he informed Tsar Nicholas I of the plot, though without divulging the names of the participants. He was a member of the committee that investigated the Petrashevsky affair (though he was himself related to Durov).

The payment from *Notes of the Fatherland* was for *The Village of Stepanchikovo*.

"Vasilchikov" presumably refers to Prince Viktor Illarionovich Vasilchikov (1820–1878), who at this time held a high position in the Ministry of War.

Vasily had been Dostoyevsky's orderly in Siberia and had then entered the service of the Geibovich family.

Novoveisky was a deportee of Polish origin whom Dostoyevsky had helped when they were both in Semipalatinsk.

40. To M. M. Dostoyevsky
Tver, November 12, 1859

Yesterday I received your letter (of the 9th), my dear Misha, and I want to write you, even if it is only a couple of lines. It would be hard for you to imagine how sickening I find it to be sitting in Tver without having even the faintest idea of how matters stand for me. If only there were some way of gauging the situation I could plan accordingly, but as it is, I am completely in the dark about what is going on in Petersburg. I wrote to everyone, I pleaded with one and all, but I haven't heard a thing. I agree with you that, in this instance, I have chosen the hardest possible way. I berate myself for it every day and keep waiting. If only somebody would remind Adlerberg of me!

What if my letter was not even presented? I wonder whether you couldn't spare a free moment (if you can find one) to go to see Wrangel and ask him to drop a gentle hint to Totleben to speak to Adlerberg or Dolgorukov—that Dolgorukov should remind Adlerberg or hand my plea to His Imperial Majesty himself. Ah, if only matters could be speeded up! We all know how merciful the tsar is, but there are all these formalities and delays!

My prime consideration is that, in order to sell my works, I *must* be in Petersburg. Incidentally, I've come up with a plan: Rather than actually sell them for money, I'd prefer, if possible, to have them published in Moscow in 2000 copies by Shchepkin and Soldatenkov. They won't pay me anything, but they will print the books, and, as they sell, they will refund themselves the capital invested plus a reasonable percentage. It would take too long to explain the various reasons why I prefer this arrangement, but it is what I would do right away if, on my arrival in Petersburg, I could immediately obtain money to live on (in addition to what I shall receive from Krayevsky). You can understand why I am so concerned with all this, since my life and my future are at stake. But don't really take my words à la lettre and, if an opportunity presents itself, sell my works for cash and, indeed, seek out such an opportunity without waiting for me to return to Petersburg. Don't forget, the days are passing, and it's high time we began publishing. Not only is time slipping by, but financial opportunities as well. . .

But to hell with money! What I am most impatient for is to give you a big hug and to be already living near you and yours. It is terribly painful for me to live here. I cannot start working on anything because of all sorts of nervous disturbances; time is going by. You cannot imagine, dear Misha, what waiting can do to one! A month! And will it be over in a month? It may take another three or four. You write about an idea that would require 15 to 20 thousand for a start. All that torments me no end, brother; it seems that we are cursed or something. I look at others—I see no talent in them, no special abilities, but they break through and manage to accumulate capital for themselves. But we keep banging our heads against a wall. I am quite convinced, for example, that the two of us have much more skill, ability, and knowledge of affairs than the Krayevskys and the Nekrasovs. Why, they are nothing but literary peasants! But, nevertheless, they thrive and we are stuck on the rocks. You, for instance, went into business and put a lot of work into it. But what do you have to show for it? How much have you made? You can even consider yourself lucky that it paid your living expenses and that you managed to bring up your children. Your business reached a certain point and then stopped. This is a sad state of affairs for a man with your abilities. No, brother, we must stop and think, think seriously and risk investing in some literary venture, such as a magazine, for instance. But we shall give it more thought and talk it over when we get together. There is still time.

It is true that my novel came out to very little—13 to 14 printer's sheets, and I shall get much less for it than I have anticipated. But what does it matter! Please send me a separate copy even before the book goes on sale—try to understand how concerned I am about it all. For 8¾ sheets I should get 1050 rubles, which means that when the book comes out, my share, minus what I owe you (375 rubles), will be 175 and not 125 rubles [*sic*]. Please make every effort to get the money as soon as possible, and send my share to me right away in case I need it urgently—who knows, the decision concerning my whole future may have been made by then. I shall need the money at that time to move out of here. And so let me have it as soon as possible.

Farewell, I hug you; write me something quickly,

Yours,

Dostoyevsky

As soon as my novel comes out, write me immediately and in great detail everything you hear about it—what people say about it, if they say anything at all.

---

40. Nikolai Mikhailovich Shchepkin (1820–1886) was the son of the well-known artist M. S. Shchepkin and a member of the legislatures of the city and the province of Moscow. Kozma Terentevich Soldatenkov (b. 1818) was a patron of the arts. Together, they published a number of distinguished works of literature, history, and art, including translations of Shakespeare and Aleksandr Afanasev's collections of Russian legends and folk tales.

On November 9, Mikhail had written to Dostoyevsky that Pleshcheyev was thinking of opening a printing shop in Moscow. Mikhail had warned him that it would not be successful, and he suggested to Dostoyevsky that it would be better if Pleshcheyev joined him, Mikhail, in a business that could quickly make them both rich. The fifteen or twenty thousand rubles would be needed for an initial investment.

In the same letter, Mikhail informed his brother that he had finished proofreading the first part of *The Village of Stepanchikovo* and that it came to only eight and three-quarters printer's sheets. He estimated the whole novel would amount to only thirteen or fourteen sheets—far shorter than Dostoyevsky had anticipated.

PART
II
1860–
1866

returned to Petersburg at the beginning of an extremely agitated period of Russian life. Alexander II had made clear that he intended to liberate the serfs, and this was effectively done in 1861; other major reforms of the army, the censorship, the law courts, and the local administrations were also announced and initiated. Relaxation of the censorship encouraged the birth of a spate of new publications—among them, Fyodor and Mikhail Dostoyevsky's monthly journal *Time,* launched at the beginning of 1861. Fyodor was the effective editor-in-chief, even though, as an ex-convict, his name could not appear on the masthead; Mikhail, who had previously run a factory, took charge of the finances. It was in this journal that Dostoyevsky published two major works: his first post-Siberian novel, *The Insulted and Injured,* and his memorable *Notes from the House of the Dead,* an account of his years in prison camp. Both works were quite successful; but the second—an unprecedented, relatively unvarnished portrayal of the harsh realities of life among the Siberian convicts—created a furor. Its publication brought Dostoyevsky much greater fame and adulation than he had ever known in the 1840s.

Dostoyevsky's marriage with Mariya Dmitriyevna was not a happy one, and the strains of his home life with his constantly ailing, tubercular wife led him to seek consolation elsewhere. He was strongly attracted to the actress Aleksandra Shubert, the wife of his old friend Dr. Stepan Yanovsky, though whether they had an affair remains obscure. The success of *Time* allowed him to make his first trip to Europe in the summer of 1862, stopping first in Paris to consult specialists about his epilepsy and then going on to London for a visit with Aleksandr Herzen. Dostoyevsky greatly admired Herzen's writings during the 1850s and felt no hesitation about visiting the great exile, whose weekly the *Bell,* published in London, had become the voice of the progressive (though not revolutionary) opposition in Russia. The impressions gathered during this first European voyage were later used in Dostoyevsky's scintillating series of travel sketches, *Winter Notes on Summer Impressions.*

By 1863 Dostoyevsky seemed to have achieved his goal of obtaining financial security and reaffirming his place in the forefront of the Russian literary scene; but catastrophe lurked just around the corner. A Polish revolt against the Russian Empire broke out at the beginning of that year, and an ambiguous article in *Time,* meant to defend the Russian cause, led to the accusation of pro-Polonism. The magazine was ordered closed in the spring of 1863, and the result for the two Dostoyevsky brothers was economic disaster. But Dostoyevsky nonetheless decided to travel in Europe during the summer; he believed that his health improved there, and, in addition, he wished to enjoy unhindered the company of a new young mistress. During the winter of 1862–1863, he had met an attractive young contributor to *Time*, Apollinariya Suslova, and the two began a secret affair. They did travel together in Europe for several months, but Suslova by this time was no longer willing to continue on the old terms; despite Dostoyevsky's ardor, relations between them remained platonic during the trip.

Permission for the Dostoyevsky brothers to publish a new journal, under the name of *Epoch,* was finally granted; but this enterprise began under great handicaps and never succeeded in recapturing *Time*'s subscribers. Dostoyevsky published the first part of *Notes from Underground* in the first issue, but his contribution attracted little attention; the second installment was written during the death agonies of Mariya Dmitriyevna, who died in April 1864. Two months later Mikhail Dostoyevsky unexpectedly died, and Fyodor took the fateful decision to obtain in advance the money that would have been left him in the will of his wealthy Aunt Kumanina and invest it in the magazine, which he attempted to carry on single-handedly. He personally assumed all of his brother's debts and thereby saddled himself with a burden that would weigh him down for most of the remainder of his life.

The death of both his wife and older brother left a gaping hole in Dostoyevsky's existence, and he tried to compensate for their loss by unsuccessfully proposing marriage to Anna Korvin-Krukovskaya, a young and high-spirited contributor to *Epoch* of very good family. To make matters worse, the collapse of *Epoch* for lack of funds in the late spring of 1865 exposed Dostoyevsky to the pursuit of creditors threatening to place him in debtors' prison. Determined to raise funds for a trip to Europe, he signed a murderous contract with a publisher named Stellovsky requiring him to provide a new novel within six months' time at the risk of losing the rights to his own work for a number of years. With the money thus obtained, most of which went to cover his debts, he traveled to Wiesbaden with the hope of raising more funds by gambling; but he was wiped out at the roulette tables and remained stranded there for several months while sinking deeper and deeper into distress and appealing to both Turgenev and Herzen for loans.

It was at this time that a plan for a novel called *The Drunkards,* for which he had failed to obtain any advance, was set aside for a story about a student dropout who decided to commit a murder for "humanitarian" reasons. This was the origin of *Crime and Punishment,* into which the previous project was later absorbed as a subplot. Pinned to the wall by his need for financial succor, Dostoyevsky reluctantly decided to appeal for an advance on this story to M. N. Katkov, the editor of *Russian Messenger,* even though the two had engaged earlier in sharp polemics and Katkov had been largely responsible for the campaign leading to the closure of *Time.* With the help of his erstwhile Siberian friend Baron Wrangel, now secretary of the Russian embassy at Copenhagen, Dostoyevsky finally extricated himself from Wiesbaden and returned to Petersburg in October 1865.

Katkov's letter of acceptance containing the advance was forwarded to Dostoyevsky from Wiesbaden, and this marked the beginning of Dostoyevsky's long association with *Russian Messenger*. A month later Dostoyevsky discarded the original manuscript version of *Crime and Punishment* because he had worked out a new plan, and the novel began publication in January 1866. It continued to appear throughout the year, though the work was interrupted by the need to honor the contract with Stellovsky (fulfilled by the composition of *The Gambler* in a month). In April 1866 the first attempt was made on the life of Alexander II, and Dostoyevsky's reaction to this event, which shook him profoundly, is recorded in a letter to Katkov, who was carrying on a violent press campaign against the radicals while the final chapters of Dostoyevsky's novel were being published.

The year ended in a whirlwind of activity for Dostoyevsky. He completed *Crime and Punishment* and wrote *The Gambler* at the same time. In order to accomplish this feat, he employed a stenographer, Anna Grigorevna Snitkina. He and the young woman, twenty years his junior, worked together very successfully for a month. Dostoyevsky found her very attractive, proposed marriage, and was accepted.

41. To A. I. Shubert
[Petersburg] March 14 [1860]

Most kind and unforgettable Aleksandra Ivanovna,

Yesterday I saw Stepan Dmitriyevich (I went to see him). He showed me your two letters and told me that you remember us all. For that I send you my greetings and kiss your little hand. I am so very happy that they received you well in Moscow. I wrote to Pleshcheyev and reminded him to be sure to announce your forthcoming debut in the *Moscow Messenger*. I even wrote and told him how I felt your talent ought to be described. I did so in just a few words, because he knows himself. I cannot tell you how much I should have liked to be present at your first appearance. I believe that my brother intends to go to Moscow on business after Holy Week, and I will certainly accompany him, so there's a chance that I'll be able to make one of your opening performances. You have left behind with all of us such a well of sympathy and admiration that you will understand that my desire is an expression of the utmost sincerity.

Stepan Dmitriyevich is staying at the Kulikovs', with whom I have become acquainted. I went to see him twice, the first time the day after you left, when I did not find him at home; I did yesterday. We spoke a great deal about you. I looked at your portrait. I also saw the other picture of you, the small one, where you still have short hair and are much plumper. But I liked the big portrait of you better—it is more like you, more what you look like now.

Suddenly Stepan Dmitriyevich asked me, "Did you tell Maikov that Aleksandra Ivanovna had lost some money? How is it they know about it? I have not even seen the Maikovs." Then he went on to ask me, "And do you know how much she lost?"

I looked at him and did not know very well what to say. I saw he knew that I knew about the loss. So I said, "I heard it was 2 rubles."

"What are you talking about!" he said. "It's 320 rubles. Why, didn't she tell you?"

Whereupon I replied that you had told me and my brother, but that I could have sworn it was a joke, because you did not seem in the least perturbed and were only concerned about packing and leaving.

Stepan Dmitriyevich then asked me whether I contemplated going to Moscow. I told him that I might be going after Holy Week with my brother, and he said that he might go there himself. He told me then that I ought to drop you a line (as a matter of fact, I had been thinking of writing you before that). I told him that I would enclose a letter for you in my letter to Pleshcheyev and would ask him to deliver it to you. He said, "Or in my letter, and I shall see that she gets it." I shall see him tomorrow at Milyukov's and tell him that I have already sent you a note.

I can imagine how busy you must be, what a hectic time you must be having, and how absorbed you are in all your affairs! A new life! May God grant that you enjoy this little upheaval and crisis in your life. People here remember you a lot and often talk about you, and I more than anyone else. Do you remember, Aleksandra Ivanovna, the time when, during that dinner at my brother's, you told me that I had such a sad and lenten face? You had such a good laugh at my face then. I think of all that and realize how much I should like to see you, to talk to you, to kiss your little hand. Do you know that the final picture I have of our last meeting is of Storozhenko? In general, when one thinks of a person, the setting in which one saw him for the last time always comes to mind.

If I had the least scrap of talent for writing even a one-act comedy, I should have written one for you. I want to try. If I succeed (others will be the judge of that), I shall present it to you as a sign of my deepest respect.

It's boring here, in fact very boring indeed. The weather is miserable. I have many petty chores to do, when I just want to write. In general, you can't imagine how dull and sordid it all is, at least as far as I am concerned. I wonder whether spring won't bring a bit of life. If only I could get away from this foul Petersburg for a week or so! But who knows, perhaps our escapade to Moscow will materialize after all.

Farewell, ever so kind and esteemed Aleksandra Ivanovna. Please do not be irritated by my erasures and my catlike scratchings. For one thing, my handwriting is the only thing I have in common with Napoleon, and, then, I am quite incapable of writing two lines without corrections. Farewell. I kiss your little hand again and wish most sincerely, from the very bottom of my heart, that everything may be bright, carefree, limpid, and successful in your life.

All yours and with infinite respect,

F. Dostoyevsky

---

41. Aleksandra Ivanovna Shubert (1827–1909), née Kulikova, was a well-known actress who had made her debut in Petersburg in 1843. She married an actor, M. Shubert, and a year after his death in 1854 she married Stepan Dmitriyevich Yanovsky, a physician who had been a friend of Dostoyevsky (see note to Letter 18). He was opposed to her stage career, and she left it for a while after her marriage to him but returned later.

Moscow Messenger (Moskovsky vestnik) was a weekly political and literary publication which appeared from 1859 to 1861. Pleshcheyev was a member of the editorial board.

The Kulikovs referred to were probably the family of Aleksandra Ivanovna's brother, Nikolai Ivanovich Kulikov (1815–1891), who was a playwright, actor, and stage director.

In her memoirs, Aleksandra Ivanovna tells of an incident in which, "in secret from my husband," she borrowed 300 rubles from the theater administration and then "lost the money even before I got home—I must have dropped it while driving in the sleigh."

Aleksei Petrovich Storozhenko (1805–1874) was a novelist, a contributor to *Notes of the Fatherland* and *Northern Bee,* and a member of a circle of writers and actors.

42. TO N. V. MEDEM
St. Petersburg, September 20, 1860

The editorial board has the honor to submit most respectfully to Your Excellency a supplement to the piece *Notes from the House of the Dead* in an effort to ascertain whether Your Excellency would consider it possible to authorize publication of the piece if accompanied by this additional material. The supplement nullifies the impression produced by the piece in its original form without, however, distorting in the slightest the truth of the matter it treats, which Your Excellency has been pleased to recognize and which is of the utmost concern to the author and the editorial board.

If the reason for withholding permission to publish the piece could be the fear that it might produce in the minds of the people a false impression of life in prison camp, the piece as it now stands aims at creating the impression that, no matter what the government has done to improve the conditions of prison life, penal servitude still continues to be a moral torture which automatically and inescapably punishes the crime.

As to the opinion expressed by Your Excellency that this piece would have a better chance of being passed for publication in some other magazine (a monthly one), the editorial board begs Your Excellency to take into account the following considerations:

(1) The editorial board of *Russian World* intends to confer on that magazine as serious a character as possible. Therefore, the magazine is essentially designed for the more or less well-educated classes, and not for the masses, as is to some extent evidenced by the two issues that have already been published.

(2) If the editorial board is deprived of the possibility of continuing publication of this piece and it appears later in some other magazine, the editorial board of *Rus. World* will have no excuse *in the eyes of the public* for having published only the beginning without the promised continuation; and it is possible that the press will attack and publicly ridicule the editorial board at a moment that is very critical for it—when its first issues are coming out—while the true reason for discontinuing publication of the piece in *Rus. World* will remain unknown both to the public and to the journals.

---

42. Baron Nikolai Vasilevich Medem (1796–1870) was an infantry general and a professor at the military academy. At the time this letter was written, he was the chairman of the Petersburg Censorship Committee.

The first four chapters of *Notes from the House of the Dead* had appeared in the September 1860 issue of *Russian World*. The editorial board had learned that the censors had some misgivings about chapter 2, which, in describing the life of the convicts, mentioned, for example, that they managed to get wine and that the bread was "very good." It was thought that this might give wrong ideas to "people who are morally unstable and uneducated, who may mistake the humane ways of the government for weakness and consider the punishments for heinous crimes too lenient." Dostoyevsky therefore prepared a supplement and was asking for permission to publish the remaining chapters together with this "corrective."

43.   To N. N. Strakhov
Paris, June 26/July 8, 1862

So you are going abroad in the first days of July, my dear Nikolai Nikolayevich? God speed you. At least by that time you should have beautiful weather; now the weather all over Europe is quite foul. But when I think that you are leaving Mikhail Mikhailovich behind all alone, it gives me the shivers. As you say yourself in your letter, my dear Nikolai Nikolayevich, we are going through a bad period, a period of painful and anguished waiting. But a magazine is a noble venture, an undertaking not to be exposed to danger, because magazines—as a medium for independent, up-to-date ideas—must be preserved at all costs. As to the task, i.e., what actually to do, what to talk and write about—there will always be something to keep you busy. My God, when I sit here and think of all that has not yet been said or done, I am burning to get out of this vaunted faraway land and join you in spirit, if not in body, back in Russia. Each and every man must be active now and, most important, must act as common sense dictates. There are too many confused ideas in our society. A sort of bewilderment has come over us.

You write, dear Nikolai Nikolayevich, that you want first to make a trip to Moscow. Well, I only hope that the senators of journalism won't catch you in their nets there! What if Katkov were to tempt you with some theory neatly drawn up in the limitless fields of the abstract—No, no, I am only joking. Ah, my dear fellow, how I should like to see you now! And do you know what—I believe it is quite possible and that we ought to try it. The trick is not to lose sight of each other's whereabouts, and the most important thing is to remember the dates. Thus, I am leaving Paris for Cologne on July 15 (our style) at the earliest. I shall spend one day in Düsseldorf and then take the river steamer up the Rhine to Mainz and, after that, on to the Oberland, i.e., perhaps to Basel and the rest. And so I shall be in Basel on the 18th or 19th, our style, and in Geneva on the 20th, 21st, or 22nd. Therefore, any letter you may write me from wherever you are will reach me in Paris as long as it gets there no later than July 15, and I shall then know where to find you. We could even do it this way, for instance: Say you write me from Berlin or from Dresden that on such and such a date you will be in such a place (and that you can always figure out ten days or so in advance), and I shall look for you there. Moreover, if you do still another thing: Buy yourself the Reichard *Guide* so that in each city you will know what hotels there are (and what the rates are). Then if, for example, you are in Berlin you could drop me a line and let me know you'll be stopping over in Geneva in such and such a hotel on such and such a date. Then I in turn would ask for you in that hotel. It may happen, however, that once in Geneva, you won't like the hotel, and instead of stopping there will go on to some other hotel, but there is nothing to prevent you from leaving your address with the first hotel (the one agreed upon) for those who may inquire about you (i.e. for me), and you could give the hotel portier a tip of a franc or so to take care of this, and that way I am quite certain to find you. Besides, I am very curious to know your itinerary.

Ah, Nikolai Nikolayevich, Paris is a most tiresome town, and if it were not for the many really remarkable things it possesses, one could die of boredom here. Upon my word, the French are a nauseating people. You wrote me about the smugly arrogant, shitty characters who are infesting our spas, but I swear to you that it's as bad here as back home. Our own are simply a debauched lot who, for the most part, recognize themselves for what they are, but here people are quite convinced that things are just as they should be. The Frenchman is quiet, honest, and polite, but he is a hypocrite, and money is everything to him. He has no ideals whatever. Not only is he without convictions—you mustn't even ask him to think. The level of general culture is incredibly low (I am not talking of authentic scholars, since there are not many of them; besides, I don't believe that learnedness is culture in the sense in which we have become accustomed to understand that word). You may laugh to hear me make such judgments after having spent only ten days in Paris. I agree, but (1) what I have seen in these ten days does, for the time being, confirm my opinion; and (2) there are certain facts that can be noted and interpreted in half an hour, but that clearly indicate whole aspects of a social condition just by the sheer fact that they can and do exist.

Will you stop over in Paris? Let me tell you that it is not worthwhile going to Paris just for three days, but then it would be quite boring to spend a whole two weeks *merely as a tourist*. You may come to Paris if you have something special in view. There are many things that are worth seeing and studying. I still have some time to spend in Paris, and therefore I want to take advantage of every minute to view and study it as much as is possible for a simple tourist such as I am. I am not sure whether I shall write something about it, but if I do feel very much like it, I don't see why I shouldn't write about Paris among other things. The trouble is, however, that again I don't have the time—to write a decent "letter from abroad" would take me at least three days, but where can I find those three days here? But I'll see about that when I get back.

One more thing, dear Nikolai Nikolayevich—you cannot imagine the feeling of solitude that envelops the soul here. It is a painful, depressing sensation! Let us assume you are an unattached man and there is no one in particular for you to miss. Still, you would feel that you had lost contact with your native soil, with your familiar daily routine, with your current family concerns. It is true that, so far, my stay abroad has been very disappointing: The weather has been nasty and I am still knocking around in northern Europe and the only one of the wonders of nature I have seen is the Rhine with its banks (which, Nikolai Nikolayevich, is really a wonder!). What will it be like when I descend from the Alps onto the plains of Italy? Ah, if only we could do it together! We would see Naples, walk around Rome, and, who knows, we might fondle some young Venetian lass in a gondola (what would you say to that, Nikolai Nikolayevich, eh?) But . . . "nothing, nothing, silence!," as Poprishchin would say in such a case.

Good-bye, Nikolai Nikolayevich. I shan't tell you in detail my impressions of my foreign travels. It is impossible to describe everything in a letter, and I am incapable of doing it in bits. And what impressions can I have at this juncture! I have been abroad for only nineteen days, after all. I embrace you from the bottom of my heart. Give my regards to the very dear and sweet man Tiblen (of whom, for some reason or other, I have become very fond lately) and to the charming, infinitely respected Yevgeniya Karlovna. How is she? By the way, if you do go to Moscow, this letter may not reach Petersburg in time to catch you. In any case, I am addressing it to the editorial offices of *Time*.

Farewell, or, rather, until we meet again. I cannot imagine that we shall fail to meet during our travels! I would never forgive myself if that were to happen. I shake your hand warmly. Give my regards to all our common acquaintances. How is your badly mannered cat behaving? Addio [*sic*].

Yours, Dostoyevsky

---

43. Dostoyevsky and his brother Mikhail had founded a magazine, *Time*, in 1861. Strakhov was their principal editorial collaborator. With both him and Dostoyevsky abroad, Mikhail was left with all of the work of putting out the magazine.

Dostoyevsky did not actually stay in Paris until July 15 but went to London for eight or ten days to see Herzen. He later did write his impressions of Europe, under the title of *Winter Notes on Summer Impressions* (Zimniye zametki o letnikh vpechatleniyakh), which appeared in *Time* in 1863.

Poprishchin is the main character in Gogol's *Diary of a Madman* (Zapiski sumasshedshego, 1835). Dostoyevsky quotes from the entry for November 13.

Nikolai Lvovich Tiblen (1825–1870?) was a successful publisher in the 1860s. Yevgeniya Karlovna was his wife.

44. To I. S. TURGENEV
Petersburg, June 17, 1863

My dear and much respected Ivan Sergeyevich,

For God's sake, forgive me for not having answered your last letter from Baden. Moreover, I feel terribly guilty—so much so that I have considerable and grave pangs of conscience—for not having replied to your two earlier letters, either. The fact of the matter is that your last letter reached me when I was going through a most hectic and difficult time, i.e., at the moment when we were ordered to suspend publication of our magazine. This caused such a to-do, such distress, and all sorts of other unpleasantnesses that for a whole month I was incapable of raising my hand to take up my pen. Can you believe me? As to the earlier letters, my wife's sickness (consumption), my parting with her (because, having lived through the spring, i.e., not having died in Petersburg, she has left the city for the summer or perhaps for even longer; and it was I who accompanied her on the journey from Petersburg, which she could no longer bear because of the climate), and finally there was my own serious and rather prolonged illness on my return from [should be "to"] Petersburg—all this interfered with my writing to you until now. If it had been merely a question of observing the proprieties, I could have found the time for it. But I remember I felt like having a talk with you or, rather, discussing with you at some length what was happening on our literary scene. And for that, well, I just didn't have the time, and I kept putting it off until it was too late.

And so our magazine has been closed down, as you may have heard, assuming one can get Russian newspapers in Baden. The closing took us rather by surprise. In our April issue we carried an article entitled "The Fateful Question." You know the orientation of our magazine: it is a predominantly Russian orientation, even anti-Western. So it doesn't seem very likely that we would take the Poles' side, does it? Nevertheless, we were accused of taking an unpatriotic stand, of sympathizing with the Poles, and our magazine was closed down for an article that we thought highly patriotic. It is true that the article contained some clumsily worded passages, some statements that were not explicit enough, all of which led to its being misinterpreted. This failure to make the thought completely clear was, as we realize now, really very serious, and we have only ourselves to blame. But then, we were counting on the fact that the general political position of our magazine was well known in the literary world, and so we thought that the article would be understood and the ideas that were not explicitly expressed would not be misconstrued. And that was our mistake.

The idea of the article (it was written by Strakhov) was the following: The Poles despise us so much, consider us such barbarians, and are so anxious to show off their European civilization to us, that a spiritual (i.e., the only really firm) reconciliation between them and us is not in sight for a long time to come. But the meaning of the article was missed, and it was interpreted thus: that *we ourselves* were, in effect, asserting that since Polish civilization was so much superior to ours, and ours so inferior to theirs, they are naturally right and we are wrong. And then, some magazines (*Day,* among others) set out to prove seriously that Polish civilization is really skin-deep, that it is aristocratic and Jesuitic and, therefore, is not really superior to ours. Just imagine—they are trying to prove this to us when we were trying to say just that in our own article; and they go to the trouble of convincing us of it when it is *specifically* stated in our own magazine that the vaunted Polish civilization has always carried death in its heart. This was spelled out directly in our article. The remarkable thing about this business is that a great many honorable individuals who pounced violently upon us admitted themselves that they *had not read* the article in question. But enough about that—what's done cannot be undone.

You write that you intend to spend the entire summer in Baden-Baden.

You know, maybe we'll see each other there. I have asked for permission to go abroad, and I have hopes that I'll go. I am very ill with epilepsy, which is getting worse and worse and driving me to despair. If only you knew how dejected I feel after my fits, sometimes for whole weeks on end! Actually, I am going to Berlin and to Paris—but for the shortest possible time—for no other reason than to consult specialists on epilepsy (Trousseau in Paris, Ramberg in Berlin). There are just no specialists in Russia, and I receive such a variety of contradictory advice from the local doctors that I have lost all faith in them. If I find myself in your parts, I shall make a point of coming to Baden to see you.

As to your request, much respected Ivan Sergeyevich, concerning that sum of money, my brother under present circumstances could not accede to it. In the first place, our magazine no longer exists; in the second place (to be quite honest), he has been completely ruined by the closing down of the magazine and his family almost reduced to beggary. So please do not hold it against us.

Good-bye then, my dear Ivan Sergeyevich. Perhaps we shall meet quite soon. I shan't write to you about anything else now. I don't know whether there is going to be a war, but all Russia—the army, society, and even the people as a whole—is in a patriotic mood, just as in 1812! I say this without *exaggeration*. Something enormous is being set in motion. Come what may, Europe does not know us well. It is an immense national movement. Good-bye for now.

Yours sincerely,
F. Dostoyevsky

---

44. In 1862, Mariya Dmitriyevna had moved to Vladimir for the summer; and in the fall, when Dostoyevsky returned from abroad, they settled in Moscow.

Armand Trousseau (1801–1867) was a French doctor who lectured at the Hôtel Dieu hospital in Paris.

Turgenev had asked Dostoyevsky for an advance of 109 rubles and 50 kopeks, "against the account of our future business relations." Turgenev owed that sum to P. V. Annenkov (see note to Letter 85).

The "patriotic mood" that Dostoyevsky refers to and the rumors of war, as well as the closing down of *Time*, were all outgrowths of the efforts of the Russian government to suppress rebellions in Poland.

45.   To V. D. Constant
Paris, September 1 (New Style) [1863]

My dear and much respected Varvara Dmitriyevna,

You may already know from my letter to Pasha that I have reached the city of Paris safely and in good spirits and have now settled in here, although I don't think it will be for very long. I don't care for Paris, although it is absolutely magnificent. There are many things to see here but, once you have seen them, a terrible boredom seizes you. It would be very different if I had come here as a student, to study something or other. Then, of course, I should have a great deal to keep me busy, and many things to see and hear. But for a tourist like me, who has come simply to observe the local mores, the French are loathsome, and I already know just about what there is know about the city. Really, the best thing about this place is its fruit and its wine—of that, at least, one doesn't get tired.

I won't write you about my private affairs—"letters are senseless; apothecaries write letters." Instead I shall write you about a few little business matters. As a matter of fact, my dear Varvara Dmitriyevna, I am about to ask you for a small favor. You see, on my way here, I stopped over in Wiesbaden for about four days and, well, as you may imagine, I did some gambling there—roulette. And, believe it or not, I did not lose but won, although I did not win as much as I wanted to—not 100,000—but still I did win a tiny sum. (N.B.—By the way, dear Varvara Dmitriyevna, don't mention this to a soul. I say this although I realize there's no chance of this happening because you see so few people, but I have in mind Pasha, above all. He is still stupid, and he may take it into his head that it is possible to make a career out of gambling and will put his faith in it. Why, recently he got the notion that he would become a salesman in a shop in order to make money and that therefore there was no need for him to go on with his studies, and he informed me of his decision. And anyway, it is not proper for him to know that his Papa frequents gaming rooms. And so, not a word about it.)

During those four days, Varvara Dmitriyevna, I had a good look at gamblers. There were several hundred of them placing their stakes there and, I give you my word, there weren't more than two of them who knew how to play. They all were losing their shirts, because they didn't know how to play. But there was a Frenchwoman and an English lord—those two knew how to play and they were not losing; on the contrary, they almost broke the bank. Please do not think that, in my joy over not having lost, I am showing off by saying that I possess the secret of how to win instead of losing. I really do know the secret—it is terribly silly and simple, merely a matter of keeping oneself under constant control and never getting excited, no matter how the game shifts. That's all there is to it—you just can't lose that way and are sure to win. But the difficulty is not in finding this out, but in being able to put it into practice once you do. You may be as wise as a serpent and have a will of iron, but you will still succumb. Even Philosopher Strakhov would have succumbed. And so, blessed are those who do not gamble and look upon roulette with disgust, as the most idiotic thing there is.

But let us get back to the point. I won 5000 francs, my dear Varvara Dmitriyevna, that is, I won 10,400 francs at first and took them home with me and locked them in my suitcase, and I made up my mind to leave Wiesbaden the next day without returning to the gaming room. But I succumbed to temptation and lost half of my winnings. And that is how I wound up with only 5000 francs. I have decided to keep part of these winnings, but part I am sending to Petersburg: part to my brother, to keep for me till I get back, and part to you to be turned over or sent on to Mariya Dmitriyevna. Please forgive me, my dear, for counting on you for help without knowing for sure whether it will be all right with you. But remembering your friendship, I took this for granted. Altogether, I am sending you *30* doubloons, i.e., double Prussian gold friedrichs. Each doubloon is worth 41 francs, 50 centimes, here in Paris. But that is not its real worth. It is thievery on the part of the local money-changers; it is worth more. One gold friedrich sells for *20 francs, 75 centimes*, here, and our imperial is worth *20 francs, 55 centimes*, which shows that a gold friedrich is rated higher here than our imperial. The exchange rate must be the same in Petersburg. Hence, we may reckon that a gold friedrich is at the very least equal—if not superior—to our imperial. The *30* doubloons I am sending you are the equivalent of *60* gold friedrichs, and so, counting a friedrich on a par with an imperial, they will bring you somewhat more than 300 rubles when exchanged for paper money. I suppose you might do a bit better than that on the exchange, because the price of gold is high in Russia. Now, the favor I am asking you is the following. Of these 30 doubloons, I want you to take five and put them away somewhere for the time being. This will be for Rodevich, to cover Pasha's needs (in order not to give the money directly to Pasha), in case I come back later than planned. The remaining 25 doubloons can be changed for bills at a money-changer's. I am sure the money-changers won't cheat you too much. Please don't be unduly concerned—whatever they give will be good enough. If you prefer, you could even ask my brother Mikhail Mikhailovich to have the doubloons changed for you and to hand over the money to you. Once the money is changed, please notify Mariya Dmitriyevna that I have sent her 25 doubloons, which were exchanged for such and such a sum, asking her, at the same time, how she wishes to have the money sent to her—by mail or in some other fashion. In my opinion, the best way is by mail, especially since there is no other way. But it is possible that Mariya Dmitriyevna would prefer you to hold on to the money for the time being, perhaps until my return. Well, that is a different matter then and, in that case, please do as she wishes, if that is what she wants. In general, let it be just as she desires. You will oblige me very much indeed, my dear, if you will take care of all of this for me. Don't turn me down, in the name of God. I have already written to Mariya Dmitriyevna and told her that you will let her know as soon as you get the money and will ask her how she wishes it to be sent to her. I wrote her that she should then immediately get in touch with you. You may even hear from her earlier. I am sending the money only today. Up to now I have been beating my brains out trying to find out what is the best way to send money. The post office categorically refuses to accept it, because it is established custom here to send money through the banks, and no other way. But I was reluctant to go through the banks, because a bank would charge me more for the transfer and, besides, I should lose on the exchange, since gold is worth less here than back home. So I finally managed to locate a sort of private but reliable firm here that transfers money, and I am transmitting the sum through it. How they will deliver it to you I don't know, except that it will take time, eight days or so. So you will receive this letter long before the money reaches you. But at least this way you have advance notice. If any difficulty should arise, get in touch with my brother Mikhail Mikhailovich, i.e., send him word asking him to come to see you *on a matter concerning me,* and that will do it. But I mention this just to be on the safe side, for I am sure no difficulties will arise. In any case, forgive me, my good and much respected friend, for so imposing on you. But I am relying on your kindness, you know.

My health is so-so. I don't expect to stay in Paris for long. I may go to Italy. It all depends on the circumstances. Write me, my dear, whatever you know about Pasha or have heard about Mariya Dmitriyevna (if you have heard anything). I am terribly and deeply concerned about her health. May God grant her better days! And write me all you hear (if anything) about my brother Kolya. How is he feeling? Please keep your eye on Pasha. Let me know what Rodevich says about him, if you hear something. Pasha has me terribly worried.

Finally, write me, if only a few words, just about yourself, i.e., how things are going, how your spirits are, how your health is, and all that. I love you and respect you immensely, my dear, and so you must not feel that I am asking this out of mere curiosity. And do write me as soon as possible, so that your letter will reach me here, because I may not stay in Paris very long. And don't wait until the money arrives; write even before it comes. I am sure it will get there, there is no need to worry about it.

Farewell, I shake your hand hard.

Yours,
F. Dostoyevsky

---

45. A few days earlier, Dostoyevsky had written to his stepson Pasha, asking how he had fared in his examinations and admonishing him to "avoid stupid acquaintances and the Yusupov Gardens" (an amusement park in Petersburg frequented by the lower classes).

"Letters are senseless; apothecaries write letters" are words spoken by Poprishchin in Gogol's *Diary of a Madman.*

This letter is the first sign of Dostoyevsky's passion for gambling. A week later, he wrote to Varvara Dmitriyevna that he had lost most of the rest of his winnings at roulette, and he asked her to send back some of the money he had sent to her, which she did. He then expressed to her his fears that Mariya Dmitriyevna might now not have enough for her needs and that she would blame this all on Mikhail, because "she cannot stand my brother." Consequently, he pleaded with her to send Mariya Dmitriyevna "75 rubles or so, telling her that my brother has started paying back and not letting her know that it is really from you."

When Dostoyevsky was preparing to go abroad, he placed his stepson in the care of a tutor, Mikhail Vasilevich Rodevich, who had been an occasional contributor to *Time*.

46. To M. M. Dostoyevsky
Turin, September 8/20, 1863

You write me, my good Misha, how utterly distressing it was for you to read my letter and how difficult it is to satisfy my request for money. But if you knew, my friend, how oppressed I was by the thought that my letter would undoubtedly place you in an extremely difficult situation, you would have agreed that I had already been sufficiently punished for my losses. In general, I spent a miserable time waiting for your letter here in Turin, which is the most boring town, particularly because I was lonesome for you and everyone else. The trouble is that I had been without any news at all from home ever since I left Petersburg for abroad. I was imagining God knows what things about you, some of them so horrible that I almost died of anxiety. There is nothing to say about our physical sufferings. There were none, but we lived in constant dread that they would bring us the hotel bill, and we didn't have a kopek to our name—that would have meant a scandal, the police (that's the way things are done here—there's no getting around it, unless there is someone to stand surety for you and you have luggage; there have been such cases, etc., etc., and I am not alone), a real mess! I pawned my watch in Geneva to a really princely man. He even refused to take any interest, in his desire to help out a foreigner, although he gave me only a pittance. I won't redeem it now—I need the money. She has pawned her ring, but we have a signed agreement giving us until the end of October (New Style) to redeem it. But all that is of no importance.

What concerns me most is: what is happening to you? That is what interests me. I repeat, God alone knows the things I have been imagining here. I hoped that you would write me something about the magazine, but your letter is so brief, not a whisper about it. Is that conceivable? For God's sake, enlighten me. But the main thing is to work and to persevere. If it isn't *Time*, then we can put out something else. Otherwise we are lost. I have a feeling that I shall need lots of money to tide me over for at least three months while I'm writing a novel. Otherwise there won't be any novel. But where shall I get the money? Well, I suppose I could manage somehow or other, but what about you and your family? In short, I want to get back as soon as possible.

You ask why I left Paris so quickly. In the first place, I found it nauseating; in the second place, I did so out of consideration for the person I am traveling with.

It was sad to read about Kolya. I don't trust Besser at all—he is a quack, not a doctor. That's my opinion. If only Botkin were treating him. Give my regards to Kolya. Go and see him. Send someone of your family to see him. It is so hard for the poor, dying soul. Tell him that I send my love and think of him often, indeed every day.

I shall give you the details about my trip as a whole when I see you. I have had a lot of different adventures, but I feel terribly bored, despite the presence of A.P. Over here, even happiness is hard to bear, because one is isolated from those whom one loves and those for whom one has often suffered. To seek happiness after abandoning everything, even that in which I could be useful, is sheer selfishness, and that thought poisons my happiness today (if, indeed, there is such a thing as happiness).

You ask in your letter how a man can gamble away his last kopek, especially when he is traveling with someone he loves. Let me tell you, my dear Misha, that in Wiesbaden I devised a system of play which I put to the test and won myself 10,000 francs. But the next morning in my excitement I failed to stick to my system, and lost right away. In the evening I went back to my system, stuck strictly to it, and quickly and effortlessly won 3,000 francs again. Now, tell me yourself, after this happened how could I help getting carried away, how could I fail to believe that as long as I held hard and fast to my system, happiness was in my grasp? And I need money—for myself, for you, for my wife, to enable me to write my novel. Here people win tens of thousands just like that. Yes, I came here hoping to save you all and to stave off misfortune. And then, too, I had faith in my system. And what's more, when I got to Baden, I walked up to the roulette table and won 600 francs *within a quarter of an hour.* That whetted my appetite. Suddenly I started losing; I could no longer restrain myself and lost everything I had with me. After I sent you the letter from Baden, I took the *last* money I had and went back to play. I started with four napoleons and won 35 napoleons within half an hour. This extraordinary piece of luck went to my head, and I risked those 35 napoleons and lost the whole 35. After paying the landlady, we had six gold napoleons left for our journey. In Geneva, I pawned my watch.

In Baden I saw Turgenev. I went to see him twice, and he came to see me. Turgenev didn't see A.P. I didn't want him to know. He is down in the dumps, although his stay in Baden has restored his good health. He lives with his daughter. He told me all about his moral anxieties and doubts—philosophical doubts that have acquired *a real existence.* He is somewhat of a prig. I did not conceal from him the fact that I was gambling. He had lent me his

"Ghosts" to read but, because of my gambling, I had no time for it, so I returned it to him unread. He says he wrote "Ghosts" for our magazine and that, if I write him from Rome, he will send it to me there. But what do I know about the magazine?

I must write an article. That I know, because I can't do a thing with the 1,450 francs you sent me; I mean I could do plenty with that sum, but it won't get me home. But it is awfully difficult for me to write. I have torn up everything I have written in Turin. I am fed up with writing on order. However, I have not lost hope of sending something from Rome. Because it just has to be done. May God grant eternal peace to Uncle. I am thinking of Aunt—she will have her hands full and a nasty time ahead. I shouldn't count on our inheriting anything. Still, if there is something, let me know right away.

In the name of God, keep me informed about everything. I hug you, thank you, and kiss you.

Yours,
F. Dostoyevsky

Don't tell anyone about my predicament. It is a secret. I mean about my losing.

Good-bye. Write, for God's sake. But now address your letters directly to Naples.

Write at once, and please write about your situation. In Rome I shall find all your old letters, from all of you. And maybe I'll send you some little piece from Rome.

I shall be back on time. Anyway, I am short of money.

Kiss all your children, especially Fedya. Give my special regards to Strakhov and to everyone to whom you think I should send regards. Tell Strakhov that I am reading the Slavophiles assiduously, and that I have discovered a few things that are new in them. And how is Ap. Grigorev? How is everybody? Write about all of them.

Have you heard anything about Rodevich and about Pasha?

I am writing as briefly as I can. I can't wait to get out of this nasty Turin, but I still have a number of letters to write—to Mariya Dmitriyevna and Varvara Dmitriyevna.

. Thank Varvara Dmitriyevna if you see her. What a wonderful person she is! You know what I am afraid of? That Mariya Dmitriyevna will write you something unpleasant. But I don't think she will, really. Of course, she may not need money until the middle of October. But I cannot be sure. Perhaps I have put her in an embarrassing situation. She had an obligation to lay out 100 rubles, but was reluctant to do so. However, when I wrote her that I was sending her money, she made payment. And so now she may be out of money. That sends shivers down my back. I wish some one of you had sent me news about her health.

---

46. This letter was a response to one from Mikhail, in which he had written that his brother's announcement of his gambling loss and his request for money "killed me, killed me on the spot."

The "A.P." that Dostoyevsky was "traveling with" was Apollinariya Prokofevna Suslova (1840–1917). She and Dostoyevsky were on intimate terms from 1861 or 1862 until 1866.

Dostoyevsky had learned from Mikhail that their brother Nikolai (Kolya) was in the hospital under the care of Viktor Vilibaldovich Besser (1825–1890), professor of general pathology, diagnostics, and clinical therapy at the Army Medical Academy. (Despite what Dostoyevsky says here, he himself later went to Besser for treatment.) Sergei Petrovich Botkin (1832–1889) was a well-known clinician. Nikolai recovered and lived another twenty years.

Mikhail had also written to Dostoyevsky of the death of their uncle, Aleksandr Alekseyevich Kumanin. After much dispute, each of the Dostoyevsky brothers and sisters later received a modest sum from the estate.

Apollon Aleksandrovich Grigorev (1822–1864) was a major literary critic, a poet, and the head of the group of young men who constituted the editorial board of *Muscovite* (Moskvityanin). He was also a regular contributor to Dostoyevsky's publications, and he was one of the founders of the current of thought that became known as *pochvennichestvo* ("attachment to the soil"), which numbered Dostoyevsky among its adherents.

47. To N. N. STRAKHOV
Rome, September 18/30 [1863]

Kind, dear Nikolai Nikolayevich,

In his last letter, which I received in Turin nine days or so ago, my brother wrote that you intended to write me a letter. But for two days now I have been in Rome, and still no letter from you. I shall be waiting impatiently for it. So now I am writing you myself, but it is not my intention to expatiate on my travel impressions or to acquaint you with ideas that have come to me in the course of my journey. I'll leave all that for my return, when we get together for a good chat, as we've often done in the past. No, this time I must ask you for an immense favor, and I must warn you beforehand that I am in need of all the sympathy and affection (if I may so express myself) that, I feel, you have shown me on more than one occasion.

The fact is that if you are willing to do me this favor you will literally save me from much that is unpleasant beyond words.

Here is what it is all about:

From Rome I shall go to Naples. From Naples (in 12 days or so from today) I shall go back to Turin, i.e., I shall be back there in about fifteen days. By the time I reach *Turin* I shall have run out of money entirely and shall arrive there *literally penniless.*

I don't suppose that the ban on *Time* can have been lifted yet and, in any case, I have reason to believe that my brother, at the present time, is in no position to help me.

I just cannot do without money, and when I get to Turin it is absolutely essential that there should be some waiting for me at the post office. Without it, as I said, I am lost. Besides the fact that I shan't have any money to pay for my return journey, there are still other circumstances. I mean I have other expenses here that I cannot possibly avoid.

And so I beseech you, in the name of God and of Christ, do for me once again what you did for me once before, just before my departure.

At that time, you went to see Boborykin (of *A Library for Reading*). When *Time* was suspended, Boborykin wrote me personally, inviting me to join his staff as a collaborator. Therefore it is possible to approach him. However, when you asked him for 1,500 rubles in July he didn't give it to you, because July is a difficult month for publishers. But, as I remember it, he said something about the fall to you then. Well, it's the end of September now, the time when subscriptions come in, so money must be available. And what I am asking for is not 1,500 rubles, but a mere 300 (three hundred rubles).

N.B. Let Boborykin know, as *Contemporary* and *Notes of the Fath[er-land]* already know, that (except for *Poor Folk*) I have never in my whole life sold any of my writings without receiving an advance. I am a man of letters—a proletarian—and if a person wants to have my work it's up to him to see that my needs are taken care of beforehand. I abhor this practice. But that is the way things are done and they are not likely to change. But I continue.

Now, I have nothing finished on hand. However, I have put together a rather successful (in my own judgment) plan for a story. For the most part I have jotted it down on odd scraps of paper. I was even on the verge of getting down to writing it, but it is impossible here. It is too hot and in the second place I have come to a place like Rome for just a *week;* how can I spend that week writing, *with Rome* beckoning to me? Furthermore, walking makes me very tired.

The subject of the story is as follows. A certain type of Russian expatriate. Mind you, there was a great deal of talk in the press this summer about Russians abroad. All that will be reflected in my story. And, in general, my story will reflect (as far as possible, of course) our national life at the present moment. I have in mind a man who is straightforward, highly cultured, and yet in every respect unfinished, a man who has lost his faith but *who does not dare not to believe,* who rebels against the established order and yet fears it.

He reassures himself with the thought that there is *nothing for him to do* in Russia, and therefore he bitterly criticizes those in Russia who call on Russian expatriates to return home. But it is impossible to tell you everything. This character is alive (I see him as if he were standing right before me) and you will have to read about him when I have written him up. The main thing, though, is that all his vital sap, all his energies, rebellion, daring, have been channeled into *roulette*. He is a gambler, and not merely an ordinary gambler, just as Pushkin's Covetous Knight is not an ordinary miser. (This does not mean that I compare myself with Pushkin—I say this only for clarity's sake.) He is a poet in his own way, but the fact is that he himself is ashamed of the poetic element in him, because deep down he feels that it is despicable, although the need to take *risks* ennobles him in his own eyes. The whole story is the tale of his playing roulette in various gambling houses for over two years.

Just as *House of the Dead* attracted the attention of the public because it was a portrayal of convicts, who had never been portrayed *graphically* by anyone before, so this story is bound to attract attention as a *graphic* and very detailed representation of gambling at roulette. Besides the fact that materials of this type are read with considerable curiosity in our country, gambling at spas, especially where Russian expatriates are concerned, has some (perhaps not unimportant) significance.

Lastly, I hope I shall be able to give expression to all these very interesting themes with feeling, with understanding, and without digressing too much.

The story will be a minimum of one and a half printer's sheets, but probably two, very likely more.

I can deliver it to the magazine, at the very latest, by November 10, *and possibly earlier*. But, in any case, certainly no later than the tenth, so that the magazine could publish it in its November issue. On that I pledge *my word of honor*, and I am sure that no one has ever had any grounds for doubting my word of honor.

My fee is 200 rubles per sheet (in case of absolute necessity, 150). But I am extremely reluctant to reduce my price. And so the best thing is to insist on 200. The story may turn out to be not at all bad. Why, after all, my *House of the Dead* did arouse some curiosity, didn't it? And this one will be a description of a hell of its own kind, in a way like the "bathhouse" in the prison compound. I intend and I shall do my best to paint a picture [four heavily crossed-out words].

And now, here is what I have mind:

Forgive me, dear and much respected Nikolai Nikolayevich, for imposing on you in such an offhand and unceremonious fashion. I realize that this is an imposition on you. But how can I help it? If, on my return to Turin in 15 or (maximum) 17 days, money isn't waiting for me there, I shall literally

186

be lost. You don't know the situation I am in, and it would take me too long to tell you all about it now. Moreover, on one occasion you showed me considerable kindness, so please come to my rescue once more.

Here is what I want. As soon as you get this letter, I beg you (and you are my last hope) go at once to see Boborykin. Tell him that I have given you authority to speak for me. If you have to, you may show him the relevant passages of this letter. Make him the offer. (Of course, do it in a way that will not be too humiliating for me, even though I have got myself into a very difficult situation abroad. Anyway, I am confident that you can*not* but handle the matter in a dignified way.) Get the money and send it to me at once, i.e., give it to my brother, who knows how to get it to me.

And if it turns out to be impossible to come to terms with Boborykin, perhaps you could make arrangements with some newspaper, even *Anchor* (give my love to Ap[ollon] Grigorev) or *any* other magazine. Of course, not with *Russian Messenger* and, if possible, avoid *Notes of the Fath*. Yes, for God's sake, avoid it. Indeed, I'd rather do without the money. I suppose even *Contemporary* would be all right, although Saltykov and Yeliseyev are likely to play some dirty trick there (although, who can tell, perhaps I am being unfair). I don't suppose my piece would disgrace *Contemporary*. In any case, you could approach Nekrasov directly. That is *sine qua non*. And settle the matter directly with him. That would not be at all bad—in fact, I think it would be even better than a deal with the *Library*. It is quite possible that Nekrasov is not all that angry with me. Besides, he is above all a *businessman*. It goes without saying, my dear Nikolai Nikolayevich, that the whole business would have to be settled in two days, or three at the most. It will literally be the end of me—yes, the end of me—if I don't find money waiting for me in Turin. Don't write me in Naples, but directly to Turin, and I beseech you to write *no matter what*.

So as soon as you get the money, take it to my brother. I personally need 200 rubles, but under no circumstances less than that; the remaining *one hundred* rubles my brother will send to Mariya Dmitriyevna. And so you must get hold of three hundred. Now there's nothing more to write. I am placing myself and almost my entire future in your hands. That is how important this is to me. Perhaps I shall tell you all some day. But, for the time being, I just beseech you to do what I ask, hug you from the bottom of my heart, and remain all yours.

Dostoyevsky

Strange: here I am writing you from *Rome* and not one word about Rome! But what could I have written you? Good God, could it possibly be described in a letter? I got here at night, the day before yesterday. I visited Saint Peter's yesterday morning. It made a strong impression, Nikolai

Nikolayevich; it sent shivers down my spine. Today I made the tour of the *Forum* and all its ruins. Then the *Coliseum*! Well, what can I tell you? . . .

Give my regards to all: Grigorev and everybody else, particularly your brother. I would also ask you to be sure to convey my respects and heart-felt regards to Yuliya Petrovna. Do so the first opportunity you have of seeing her.

The Slavophiles, of course, have uttered a *new word,* in fact, such a word that even the chosen few have not quite digested it yet. But what an astonishing *aristocratic satiety* is displayed at a time when social problems are being solved.

Couldn't Tiblen be of help to you in some way or other? I mean, of course, only in a dire emergency. Give my regards to him and to *Yevgeniya Karlovna.* Convey them to her the moment you see her.

---

47. Pyotr Dmitriyevich Boborykin (1836–1921) was the chief editor of *A Library for Reading* from 1863 to 1865 and a prolific author. He had had a European education and spent most of his life in Europe.

The story that Dostoyevsky refers to here is *The Gambler.* It was published in 1866 and was ten printer's sheets in length rather than two.

Anchor (Yakor) was a weekly newspaper published by Stellovsky and edited by Grigorev. It first appeared in 1863 and lasted a year and a half.

Dostoyevsky did not want his story published in the *Russian Messenger* because he believed that its editor, Katkov, had been primarily responsible for the closing down of *Time.*

Mikhail Yevgrafovich Saltykov-Shchedrin (1826–1889) was a prominent writer. He had attended meetings of the Petrashevsky circle and had been exiled to Vyatka, returning to European Russia four years before Dostoyevsky. Some of his writings were published in *Time,* but Saltykov was principally identified with the liberal camp represented by *Contemporary,* which carried on a polemic with *Time.*

Grigory Zakharovich Yeliseyev (1821–1891) was a church historian who later turned to journalism. In 1861 he originated the "Domestic Review" (Vnutrenneye obozreniye) section of *Contemporary,* a feature that became a fixture of Russian magazines.

48.   To I. S. TURGENEV
Petersburg, December 23, 1863

Most kind and much respected Ivan Sergeyevich,

P. V. Anenkov [*sic*] has told my brother that you apparently do not wish to have "Ghosts" published because there is too much of the fantastic in it. We are terribly concerned about this. First of all, let me tell you frankly that we—that is, my brother and I—are counting on your story. It would be a great help to the first issue, as we *resume* publication of our magazine, which will have to make a name for itself again. I am telling you this from the outset so that you will not suspect me of having only personal gain in mind when I mention other reasons to you in the course of this letter. Let me add one more fact, for the accuracy of which I give you my word: We are in much greater need of your story than of displaying your name on the cover of our magazine.

Now, I should like to say a few words about the impression your story left on me. Why do you think, Ivan Sergeyevich (that is, if you actually do think so), that your "Ghosts" is unsuitable for these times and that it will not be understood? On the contrary, the hacks who for six years have imitated the masters have driven realism to such a point of triviality that people would welcome a work that is purely poetical (the more poetical the better). Many will receive it with some bewilderment, but it will be a pleasant bewilderment. This will be the case for all those who understand anything at all, whether they belong to the old or the new generation. As to those who don't understand a thing—why do we have to bother with them? You would not believe what their own attitude toward literature is. All they demand of it is a narrow utilitarianism. You may write the most poetic work for them; they will put it aside and pick up something in which there is a description of someone being flogged. *Poetic truth* is viewed as wild raving. They want nothing but the reproduction of actual events. Our prose is terrible. *Quakerism!* That being so, there is no need to pay any attention to them. The healthy part of the public is waking up and craves a bold departure in art. And your "Ghosts" is quite a bold departure, and it would set an excellent example (for all of us) if you were the first to dare to set out on such a course. The form of "Ghosts" will bewilder everyone. But its realistic aspect will dispel all bewilderment (except the bewilderment of imbeciles and of those who *are unwilling* to understand anything except their own quakerism). However, I know a case of one utilitarian (a nihilist) who, although dissatisfied with your story, declared that it was impossible to tear himself away from it and that it had made a strong impression on him. The fact is that we have a very large number of people who like to pose as Nihilists. But here, the main thing is to understand the realistic side. In my opinion, there is too much that is real in "Ghosts." The real element is the *sadness of the intelligent and perceptive person living in our times,* a sadness you have detected and conveyed. "Ghosts" is filled with this sadness. It is "a string sounding through the mist," and it is a good thing that it is sounding. "Ghosts" resembles music. And, by the way, what do you feel about music? Do you consider it a pleasure or an absolute necessity? In my opinion, it is the same as language but expresses something that consciousness has not *yet* mastered (not reason, but the whole of consciousness) and, for this reason, it has an absolute utility. Our utilitarians would not understand that, although those among them who love music have not *given it up* and indulge their taste for it just as before.

The form of your "Ghosts" is excellent. Yet, if there were one thing about which one might have some misgivings, it would certainly be its form. And so the whole matter boils down to the question: Is there a place for the fantastic in art? But who is there to answer such a question! If "Ghosts" can be reproached for anything, it is that the story *is not sufficiently* fantastic. It could be more so. That would have given it greater *audacity*. In your story it is explained that the apparition is a vampire. I, for my part, feel that this explanation is unnecessary. Anenkov does not agree with me and argued that this was an allusion to a loss of blood, i.e., a loss of positive strength, etc. But then, I disagree with him, too. It is enough for me that I have only too acutely understood the sadness and the beautiful form in which it has been molded, i.e., its *unmitigated* discontent with all reality. And your *tone* is right, too—a tender, sad sort of tone, and not overbearing. As to your descriptions, such as the one of the crag, etc., they are intimations of some elemental, still unresolved idea (the very same idea that is present throughout). We do not know whether this idea will ever bring an answer to the questions asked by men, but at present it only further saddens and terrifies the heart, and yet we do not want to tear ourselves away from it. No, sir, as a matter of fact, this idea is very timely indeed, and such fantastic things are *very positive*. [The end of this letter is missing.]

---

48. Turgenev had promised his story "Ghosts" (Prizraki) to the Dostoyevsky brothers for publication in *Time*. When publication of the magazine was suspended, Dostoyevsky freed him of his promise but pleaded with Turgenev not to publish the story elsewhere, in the hope that the magazine would soon be permitted to appear again, though perhaps under another name. Turgenev complied, and the story was finally published in *Epoch*, the successor to *Time*, in 1864. Turgenev apparently did make some changes in response to the criticisms expressed by Dostoyevsky in this letter; for example, he no longer described the apparition as a "vampire." Some years later, he wrote to a friend, "It is strange that he [Dostoyevsky] should choose for his parody [in *The Devils*] the only one of my stories that was published in the magazine he once edited, *Epoch*, and for which he lavished expressions of gratitude and praise upon me in his letters!"

The Quakers were well known among Russian intellectuals. Dostoyevsky uses the term "Quakerism" as an expression of anti-artistic moralism.

49. To M. M. Dostoyevsky
Moscow, March 26, 1864

Dear brother,

The day before yesterday I got a copy of *Epoch* at Cherenin's—I don't know how he received it so quickly—and I've been reading and looking it over for a day and a half. Here is my impression: The number could have been more elegantly presented; there are innumerable misprints, suggesting *extreme* carelessness; not a single editorial introductory article giving some insight into our general orientation, except Kositsa's piece (a good piece, in fact a very good one, but quite insufficient for the first issue of a new magazine). I am well aware that this is the result of the rejection of several articles by the censors. But to me that makes it even worse, because our first two issues now look like some sort of a miscellany. There is also some trash, although it is quite excusable when one has to put out two issues in great haste. I am referring to Spielhagen's novel, to "The Trial," and to "Notes of a Landowner": these three pieces take up half the space of the two issues. Unfortunately, I haven't read Yerzhinsky yet—if he's good, everything is saved; if he isn't, then we're in a real mess.

Now for the good points. All the pieces I have read are very interesting. (I haven't read Spielhagen's and maybe it's good; I was only objecting to the enormous amount of space it takes up.) The cover is colorful, and the titles of the articles are enticing. Some of the articles are quite decent, such as "Ghosts" (in my opinion it contains a lot of rubbish; there's something sordid, morbid, and senile about it; it evidences a *lack of faith* due to impotence—in a word, the whole of Turgenev and his convictions. However, the poetical element will go a long way in making up for it. I reread it a second time); the articles of Strakhov; Ap[ollon] Grigorev; Averkiyev; "An Analysis of the Polish Uprisings"; the selections from Smidt; "Perch"; "The Poor Lodgers"; and even Milyukov. I liked Gorsky's piece very much. In Gorsky's defense, I would like to say that it is not literature, and it is stupid to judge it by literary standards; it should be viewed as a collection of *facts*, very useful facts. I haven't read "Savonarola" yet, and I should like very much to know what kind of a piece it is. But the luster of all that is diminished because of the many articles banned by the censors.

Fod God's sake, ask Strakhov to edit his piece for our next issue with one eye on the censors, or to write a new series of articles. And there must be a lead editorial as soon as possible!

I also have complaints concerning my own piece. There are terrible misprints in it, and it really would have been better not to publish the next-to-last chapter at all (the most important chapter, in which the main idea is expressed) than to publish it as is, i.e., with sentences chopped out, which distorts the meaning. But what can be done! The censors are a bunch of pigs—those places where I mocked everything and occasionally employed blasphemy *for the sake of form* they allowed to stand; but when, from all that, I deduced the need for faith and for Christ, they took it out. What are the censors doing? Are they part of a conspiracy against the government, or what?

If the number fails to impress people, it is sure to arouse curiosity. And that's to the good. On the whole, then, the number is very acceptable, considering the exigencies of time. As for variety, I never expected there would be so much. It is a pity, though, that it is quite impossible to make out what our orientation is and what exactly it is that we are trying to say.

Please answer me as soon as possible, my dear Misha, and tell me all you can about what people have said about the magazine. Here the public has not received it so far, and so I haven't heard anyone's opinion yet.

Mariya Dmitriyevna is so weak now that Aleks[andr] Pav[lovich] won't guarantee a single day. She *certainly* won't live more than two weeks. I shall try to finish my story as quickly as possible, but you can judge for yourself what a favorable time it is for writing.

Have you heard anything from Pasha? He hasn't written me anything, except for one single letter, although I ordered him to write every week. What is happening to him, and how is he getting on? For God's sake, tear yourself away for a moment some time and either have a talk with him or send someone to his place to see what is going on there. He is a real good-for-nothing!

Something else, brother: He may later reproach me for not having let him come to Moscow to say a last farewell to his mother. But it is Mariya Dmitriyevna who categorically refuses to see him and who chased him away from Moscow the last time he was here. And she still feels the same way: she does not wish to see him. And one cannot hold it against a consumptive for being so moody. She has told me that she will ask for him herself, to give him her blessing, when she feels she is about to die. But, although she may die this evening, this morning she was making plans for spending the summer in a summer house and for moving to Taganrog or Astrakhan in three years. But it is impossible to mention Pasha to her. She is terribly suspicious, at once becomes apprehensive and says, "You mean then that I am very weak and am about to die?" Why should I torment her in what may be her last hours? And that is why I cannot remind her of Pasha. I should like him to understand this and, if you can, explain it to him somehow or other, but, at the same time, don't frighten him unduly (although I don't think he is easily frightened).

And one more very important favor. As soon as Mariya Dmitriyevna dies, I shall send a telegram immediately asking you to send Pasha to Moscow right away, on the very same day. It is inconceivable for him not to be present when she is buried. All his suits are light, and so it is indispensable that, *before he leaves,* you should manage to buy him, in a ready-made clothing store [the top corner of the page is torn here, and a few words are missing] a black jacket, trousers, and waistcoat [words torn out] *the cheapest you can find.* All that I shall [words torn out] to you. I beg and beseech you, the only friend I have, to do this and render me this immense service, at a moment particularly difficult for me, just as soon as you receive my telegram, and it could be very soon.

N.B. And when you send *Pasha* on his way, push him hard to make sure that he goes, because otherwise he may invent some excuse for himself and postpone his departure until the next day. Get someone to keep an eye on him on that day. Do it, for the love of God.

You write that you sent the money on Monday; I haven't received it as yet.

I am still not completely well, i.e., it is not my former sickness, but rather the aftermath—primarily weakness. I get terribly tired, although I don't know from what.

Good-bye, dear fellow. This is not a cheerful letter. Look after your health. I embrace you and the entire family.

All yours,
F. Dostoyevsky

---

49. Cherenin's was a Petersburg bookstore. Dostoyevsky is here writing about the first issue of *Epoch*, a double issue for January and February 1864. The magazine was being edited and published in Petersburg by Mikhail.

Kositsa was Strakhov's pen name. His article, "A Letter to the Editors of *Epoch*" (Pismo v redaktsiyu *Epokhi*), was a satirical piece directed against the nihilists.

Friedrich von Spielhagen (1829–1911) was a German writer whose novel, *Problematische Naturen* (1860–1861), began to appear in translation in this issue under the title of *Mysterious Natures* (Zagadachnye natury). It occupied 200 of the 900 pages of the issue. Dostoyevsky later wrote Mikhail that he had read half of the translated segment and had not found "anything extraordinary in it . . . the natures are *anything but* mysterious, they're all too common. . . . There is much genuine poetry, but, withal, what a lot of tripe."

"The Trial" was an account of the murder some twenty years previously of the Duchess of Praslin by her husband and a governess, written in the form of a detective story.

"Notes of a Landowner—The Old and New Ways" (Zapiski pomeshchika—starye i novye poryadki), by O. Yerzhinsky, was a study of relations between landowners and peasants before and after the emancipation of the serfs in 1861.

The article by Apollon Grigorev was entitled "The Russian Theater" (Russky teatr).

Turgenev's story "Ghosts" was the lead item in the issue.

Dmitry Vasilevich Averkiyev (1836–1905) was a playwright, a Slavophile, and a conservative. The article that Dostoyevsky refers to was "Fathers and Sons at the University" (Universitetskye otsy i deti), and it dealt with the situation at the universities in the early 1850s.

"An Analysis of the Polish Uprisings" (Chto takoye polskiye vostaniya) was an unsigned article that interpreted the Polish uprisings as the death pangs of a degenerating state.

The "selections from Smidt" presumably refers to an article by Ivan G. Dolgomostev, based on Friedrich von Smidt's *Geschichte des polischen Aufstandes und Krieges in den Jahren 1830 und 1831* (History of the Polish uprisings and battles in 1830 and 1831). A Russian translation of that work had been published in Petersburg in 1863.

"Perch" (Yershi) was an excerpt from the novel *The Petersburg Slums* (Peterburgskiye trushchoby), which was later published in full in *Notes of the Fatherland*. Its author was Vsevolod Vladimirovich Krestovsky (1840–1895), a frequent contributor to *Time* and *Epoch* as well as the author of novels attacking the nihilists, Polish revolutionaries, and Jews.

"The Poor Lodgers" was one of the "ultra-naturalistic" exposés popular at the time; its full title was "The Poor Lodgers. In the Hospital and in the Freezing Weather" (Bednye zhiltsy. V bolnitse i na moroze). The author was Pyotr Gorsky, who also published a collection of satirical essays and stories in 1864.

The article on Savonarola was by Nikolai Alekseyevich Osokin (1843–1895), a professor of history at Kazan University.

Dostoyevsky's own contribution to this issue was Part 1 of *Notes from Underground*.

Aleksandr Pavlovich Ivanov, Dostoyevsky's brother-in-law, was a physician.

Mariya Dmitriyevna came from Astrakhan and her parents had a house in Taganrog.

50. To M. M. Dostoyevsky
Moscow, April 13, 1864

My dear friend Misha,

I received your two letters today, one of them containing the 100 rubles and a postscript of two lines for which I thank you (I mean for the letter and the postscript) from the bottom of my heart; and another, dated April 10, which I hasten to answer. I have already written you about my story in two of my letters.

I told you it was not ready and that I had let you down at a most critical moment (during the publication of the first issues of the magazine), by leaving you without my stories and articles when I myself know only too painfully [several words heavily crossed out], my dear friend. But what is to be done? It was all due to outside circumstances entirely independent of my will. I would gladly have given a year of my life for each issue of the magazine, to have averted that. I am a bundle of nerves, and in a state of mental distress, and all I do is extract money from you because my expenses, instead of decreasing, keep growing. All this causes me endless torture, and I don't know how it will all end.

But let me come to the point. About the story, I repeat again what I wrote you before: It is stretching out and it looks as though it will come off well; I am working as hard as I can at it, but progress is slow, because I am forced to spend most of my time on other things. The story is broken up into three chapters, each of which is at least one and a half printer's sheets long. The second chapter is in a chaotic state, I haven't even started on the third, but the first is being polished. The first chapter will probably contain one and a half printer's sheets, and I think it could be polished up in five days or so. But does it really have to be published separately? People will laugh at it, especially since without the other two chapters (and they are the most important) all of its flavor is lost. You know what *transition* is in music, don't you? Well, in this case, it is just the same thing. The first chapter sounds like mere verbiage, but then suddenly that verbiage develops in the two following chapters into unexpected catastrophe. If you write asking me to send you the first chapter by itself, I shall send it to you. So write, without fail. I am still capable of making such a minor sacrifice and sending you that chapter. But then you wrote me yourself that you wanted the issue to come out by the holidays. So when do you want me to send it to you? You don't really want it to come out after the holidays, do you? That will slow down the subscriptions.

Now, speaking of subscriptions. Listen, brother, I am certain—and your own experience should have taught you—that the subscriptions will just about come to a halt now, and that even if we were able to offer a Turgenev with each issue, that would not bring up the number of our subscribers *by very much.* You have that long piece of Zarubin's. So run it. It's not bad. Take Milyukov's story, etc. Concentrate your efforts on criticism, criticism above all. There is no doubt that our orientation is obvious enough to the reading public, but there are not enough articles *specifically* spelling out our orientation. Oh, of course it is desirable, indeed absolutely indispensable, that March should be better than the first two issues. But what can we do? And, anyway, there's little chance now of getting new subscribers this year. But we shall make up for that with the next issues, by what we have to show for the whole year, and by the end of this year we shall have earned ourselves a magnificent number of subscribers for next year. That I can guarantee. But for this year, get the money here, from Aunt. I suppose you have already received my letter answering you on that subject. It would be crazy not to try (with all the chances you have of success) getting that loan! So hurry up, get the issue ready to be published before Easter, and come over here during Holy Week.

By the way, if it is at all possible, get a piece from Gorsky with a provocative title for the March issue. That is the sort of article the public reads. I watched everyone here in Moscow—young and old—reading that article and talking about it. It is clear, it is understandable. And alluring. On the other hand, Turgenev's piece made no impression on the so-called "masses," who are as legion as the grains of sand on a beach. Print as much of *Mysterious Natures* as possible, too. And promise that the next issue will *certainly* contain the continuation of *Underground.* Announce that I have been sick.

I saw the announcement of the publication of the March issue of *Notes of the Fath[erland]* in the papers. That announcement by itself is as bad as a dose of medicine.

I have already written you about Chayev and have been waiting for your reply. I devoted about half a page to him, and I am as certain of having done so as I am of being alive at this moment. You must have skipped that passage somehow, or my letter may have got lost on the way. Personally, I have no idea about that play. He read it here at every literary reading there was. Aksakov praised his verses in the newspaper *Day*. Chayev is a cultured man and has a good grasp of Russian history. Ostrovsky said that the play lacked dramatic quality, that it is just a *chronicle,* but that the versification is excellent and that it has some very successful scenes. The play was sent to Boborykin a long time ago. His friend Dmitriyev (the story "The Forest," etc.) wrote him a few days ago that he would pick up the play from Boborykin and bring it to *Epoch*. Boborykin could not make up his mind to publish it in its entirety, but wanted to print just some isolated scenes. Chayev wouldn't agree. He was asking Boborykin for 100 rubles per printer's sheet. I told him that there was no chance at all that you would pay him that much, in any case (and you cannot pay it, anyway). And so if Dmitriyev brings you the play, *don't run it without having agreed on the price.* Chayev wanted to write you himself. He is a very good man. But read his play carefully. It is quite possible, after all, that it is rather heavy in its entirety. And that kind of writing doesn't bring in any new subscribers. Well, that is all I have to tell you about Chayev.

Now, about Strakhov. What a splendid thing it would have been had he scribbled me a few lines about that business earlier. As I was leaving, I told him that you had the money ready for Boborykin whenever he asked for it. And so now they've decided to. I would give anything to know what is behind it. It is not mere curiosity but a matter of honor. I shouldn't like Boborykin to imagine that I *hoodwinked* him. As God is my witness, I would have given my story to him first no matter what the circumstances. But if I did not give it to him, still I have no intention of allowing them to laugh at me for 300 rubles. If I had not taken 300 rubles from them, I wouldn't have given a damn about their sneers and if the circumstances had been appropriate, I would have given them my story. But when the editors of *Library* had bound me, if not by a promise, then by my word of honor and by the money paid to me, the least they could have done was to refrain from ridiculing me *in the pages of their magazine,* as if to say, "We have bought you and you won't dare to wriggle out of it or take offense. You will have to give us your story whatever happens." Oh no, gentlemen, I am not one to sell myself or my freedom of action for 300 rubles!

And that is why I am dying to know in detail how Boborykin went about it and *what he actually said* when he demanded the money. I am terribly reluctant to return the 300 rubles to Boborykin before I have had a chance to thrash matters out with him. At the present time, I cannot even write Boborykin a letter from here, because God only knows what happened there and what I should say exactly. That is what I should like to find out first. But something must have happened there, because otherwise Nik[olai] Nikolayevich would not have suddenly started *demanding* money from you. During my stay in Petersburg I was writhing in agony from my sickness, and I had other things to think about than the *Library*. I remember that Nikolai Nikolayevich kept urging me to go to see Boborykin, but I had neither the time nor the strength, and then there was something else that prevented me from going there. It was this: if by then Boborykin already had *some* inkling of my being offended, it seemed to me that the most elementary courtesy demanded that *he should take* the first step—not to apologize, but simply to explain. But he didn't even do that much. And so please ask Nikolai Nikolayevich on my behalf whether he couldn't do the following *for me*, who am so deeply attached to him: Delay the repayment of the money to Boborykin, if only for a little while. I understand only too well the very unpleasant and ambiguous position in which I have placed him (not I, really, but Boborykin and circumstances). He was the intermediary between Boborykin and myself at the very beginning of the loan. He gave him my word of honor and, in acting as intermediary, it was as if he *himself* had guaranteed the loan to Boborykin. Thus, if Boborykin is angry and offended and demands his money, it is obvious that Nikolai Nikolayevich will find himself in a painfully unpleasant situation. *And so if he does, in fact, feel* that his position is extremely ambiguous, let him pay the money back; and you may let him have the money—it's all right with me, even though it may cast doubt on my honor. For if I do return the money without a word *the implication is* that I really had deceived Boborykin. *But if it is at all possible to gain a bit of time,* beg Nikolai Nikolayevich to do so. And in the meantime, find out from him for me what actually happened. I hope he won't refuse to give you all the details, because I am sure he would not have kept them secret from me (I have no right to insist that he be completely open with me and tell me everything that went on between him and Boborykin *in private*). Once I knew whether *something* had happened and what it actually was, I would prepare for Boborykin a short letter, a model of refinement and cordiality, that would justify me without a hint of resentment, and I would send that letter to you to be handed over to Nikolai Nikolayevich. Nik. Nikolayevich could examine it himself, i.e., he would ascertain whether it contained anything of possible embarrassment to himself insofar as he was, after all, the intermediary in that affair; following which, the letter together with the money would be forwarded to Boborykin by the editorial office of *Epoch* or, if it were feasible, delivered by Nik. Nikolayevich.

To sum up, I beg you urgently: (1) to inform me (in case it is still possible to defer repayment of the money) how Boborykin feels about the whole business, and (2) whether he is accusing me *publicly*. Has anything insulting been said either about me *or* about Nikolai Nikolayevich? And therefore I want you to communicate this part of my letter to Nikolai Nikolayevich. The final decision is up to him. I repeat—if deferring repayment of the money causes him the *slightest* inconvenience, let him have the money at once so that he can pay it back. But if it is at all possible to gain time, I should first like to find out more about the whole business and then act accordingly.

I could have written to Boborykin without delay, had it not been (as I mentioned earlier) for the fact that, in the first place, I am in the dark about the present situation, which, for all I know, may be extremely ticklish and, in the second place, I don't know how Nikolai Nikolayevich, who has acted as a go-between in this business, looks upon it all. In a word, the story is quite a tangled one.

And also, by the way, don't let Nikolai Nikolayevich hold it against me that I have not written to him directly. If he were fully aware of the conditions of my life here, he would understand why I have been unable to find time to write him about this business. And even at this moment I am up to my neck in so many things that I can hardly concentrate on this business with Boborykin. In fact, I wanted to write to Nikolai Nikolayevich after reading his article in *Epoch,* and if I had got down to writing that letter I should probably still have forgotten to mention Boborykin to him in it.

Farewell, brother, I embrace you. Keep well and in good spirits.

Your devoted

F. Dostoyevsky

I do not have a kopek left of the 100 rubles I received from you on the second day of the holidays. That is the kind of life I live.

I hope, my dear friend, that you approve of what I have written about Boborykin. Perhaps when he reads it, Nik. Nikolayevich will be willing to wait. Actually, what I have written is the truth. Otherwise, I should have been incapable of settling the matter. But for me, for me to keep asking you for money at such a time as this—I have never before gone through a more painful period.

I am sending you Apollinariya's story under separate cover. I commend it to your attention. It is highly publishable.

Tuesday, April 14. I finished this letter last night at 2 A.M. At that moment Mariya Dmitriyevna took a turn for the worse. She asked for a priest. I went over to Aleksandr Pavlovich's and sent for the priest. We stayed by her side all night. At 4 A.M. she received the last rites. I went to bed at 8 in the morning, and they woke me up at 10. At the present time Mariya Dmitriyevna is feeling better.

---

50. The story of his that Dostoyevsky writes about here is Part 2 of *Notes from Underground,* which carries the title "Concerning the Wet Snow." Although he

speaks of a three-chapter structure, the final version was divided into ten chapters. Part 2 was published in the April issue of *Epoch*. The March issue contained a notice that, "because of the illness of the author, the continuation of F. M. Dostoyevsky's story *Notes from Underground* has been postponed until the next issue."

Pavel Alekseyevich Zarubin (1816–1886) was a self-taught man who had already published several pieces in *A Library for Reading*. The story referred to here is "Events of the Forties" (Proisshestviya sorokovykh godov), which began running in the March issue of *Epoch*.

The April issue of *Epoch* contained two pieces by Milyukov: "On Ukrainian Literature" (O malorossiskoi literature) and "Leaves from a Memo Book" (Listki iz pamyatnoi knizhki).

"Get the money . . . from Aunt" is a reference to previous letters between Dostoyevsky and Mikhail concerning the latter's proposal to ask for a loan of 10,000 rubles from their Aunt Kumanina in order to keep *Epoch* afloat.

The article by Gorsky that Dostoyevsky refers to is presumably the one that appeared in the first issue of *Epoch*. Neither the March nor the April issue carried anything by him.

Nikolai Aleksandrovich Chayev (1824–1914) was a playwright who succeeded Ostrovsky as director of the repertory programs of the Moscow theaters. The play referred to here is *Prince Aleksandr Tverskoi* (Knyaz Aleksandr Tverskoi), published in *A Library for Reading* in 1864.

Ivan Sergeyevich Aksakov (1823–1886) was a Slavophile and one of the most important writers of Dostoyevsky's time. Among the newspapers and journals he edited were *Day* (Den, 1861–1865) and *Moscow* (Moskva, 1867–1868). In the early 1860s, Dostoyevsky, then taking a relatively "Westernizing" position, engaged in polemics with the Slavophile views being presented in *Day*.

The writer Nikolai Dmitriyevich Dmitriyev (1824–1874) was little known even during his lifetime. His story "The Forest" (Les) had been reviewed by Apollon Grigorev in *Time* in 1861.

The story by Apollinariya Suslova was "In One's Own Way" (Svoyei dorogi), which was published in the June issue of *Epoch*.

51. To M. M. DOSTOYEVSKY
Moscow, April 15, 1864

Dear Misha,

I have just sent you a telegram through Aleks[andr] Pavlovich—I asked you to send Pasha here. He may have a black frock coat of some sort, but I suppose the trousers will have to be bought. I am afraid that he may have occasioned you some expense. It would be good if he could get away at least by tomorrow, April 16, on the 12 o'clock noon train.

Yesterday Mariya Dmitriyevna suffered the decisive crisis: blood gushed from her throat, flooded her chest, and began to suffocate her. We all expected the end. We were all near her. She said good-bye to everyone, made peace with all, and made her final dispositions. She sent her regards to your whole family and wished you all a long life. Especially Emiliya Fyodorovna. She expressed her wish to make peace with you. (You know, my friend, that she was always convinced that you were her secret enemy.) She had a bad night. Today, just now, Aleksandr Pavlovich said *definitely* that she will die during the day. And there is no doubt about it.

I shall go over to Aunt to ask her for money. She cannot refuse, because it is impossible that she should have no money on hand.

I don't know what will happen to me. I only beg you not to abandon me. I shall have very large expenses. Send me *as much as you can spare* for everything. Do it in the name of God. I will make it up to you.

Two days ago I received a letter from Boborykin. But, under the present circumstances, I cannot answer him *right away*. I cannot think of literature at this time. But I shan't wait too long to answer him, and he will get my reply in a week at the latest.

He demands the money from me directly. One of his sentences is insolent to the point of rudeness. I want to answer him; I shall answer him politely and write him that *I am asking you to give him back the money for me; that I hope that you will do so, and that Boborykin should not hold it against you if, taken by surprise by my request, you need a little time to pay him back; that in any event (I assure him), you will pay him without fail and that the delay will be quite insignificant.*

That is the gist of what I am writing to Boborykin about the money. I have no other alternative, Misha, as you must agree yourself. We must pay him back without fail, and soon. In any case, I shall present you to Boborykin and Nik[olai] Nikolayevich as being in no way involved in the business and actually under no obligation to pay my debts for me. And so, if you do pay him, it will only be in response to my insistent plea and, of course, only if you wish to do so.

I shall then probably write to Strakhov as well. And I shall send you a copy of my letter to Boborykin.

Inform Strakhov of the contents of the telegram. He will appreciate that, at such a time, I cannot be too precise in answering such a person as Boborykin. In fact, it would be a good thing if he conveyed this to Boborykin.

But I think it would be better if you didn't mention to Strakhov anything about the letter I am now writing you.

Farewell, my dear friend, I hug you hard.

Yours,
F. Dostoyevsky

P.S. Now, at any rate, I cannot send you the story (*not even the beginning*). That cannot be helped. But it will be ready for the April issue.

Come to Moscow during Holy Week. Get out the next issue as soon as you can. However it turns out, it will certainly be better than *Notes of the Fath[erland]*. And perhaps better than *Contemporary*, too. The organization of the material is of great importance, and you know how to handle that.

Mariya Dmitriyevna is dying quietly, in full consciousness. She has blessed Pasha in his absence.

52. To M. M. DOSTOYEVSKY

Moscow, April 15, 1864

My dear brother Misha,

Mariya Dmitriyevna passed away just a few moments ago, at 7 P.M., wishing all of you a long and happy life (those are her words). Remember her by a kind word. She went through so much suffering of late that I find it inconceivable that anyone would refuse to make his peace with her.

Farewell, dear brother, I hug you hard.

Yours,

F. Dostoyevsky

P.S. Aleksandr Pavlovich transmitted your letter to me this very minute. Do as you think best, but my feeling is that you are going about it the wrong way. After all, I am your friend and wish you well. Nothing will come of it. I shall show your letter to Varinka.

Farewell, friend,

Yours,

D.

---

52. In the letter to which Dostoyevsky refers in the postscript, Mikhail had told him that he preferred to approach their aunt concerning the 10,000-ruble loan through their sister Varvara (Varinka), rather than directly as Dostoyevsky had advised him. Subsequently, Dostoyevsky—contrary to Mikhail's specific request— asked the advice of Aleksandr Pavlovich Ivanov, who "stated categorically," as Dostoyevsky wrote to Mikhail, "that Aunt wouldn't let you have the money under any circumstances." Instead, Aleksandr Pavlovich offered to lend Mikhail forty shares he owned of the Moscow-Yaroslavl railway to use as collateral for a loan. Mikhail apparently did take advantage of this offer, obtaining a loan of 5,000 rubles.

53. To A. M. DOSTOYEVSKY

Petersburg, July 29, 1864

My very dear brother Andrei Mikhailovich,

I hasten to satisfy your request, although I don't have a minute to spare. All the affairs of our brother have become, as is natural, my responsibility and, for almost three weeks now, I have been in a continuous whirl.

Our brother Mikhail died of an infection of the liver and of the effusions of bile into the blood that it caused. That was his sickness. He had been suffering from it for a long time—according to the doctors, two years or so. But with liver trouble you can carry on for a long time and not pay any attention to it, especially if you are very busy. And he always was. Last year the magazine was banned. For him, it came like bolt of lightning, and it wrought such swift havoc in his affairs and threatened him with such frightful disaster that, during the whole of last year, he was constantly in a state of alarm, agitation, and apprehension.

It would be difficult for me to explain it all to you in detail, but I can tell you briefly this: His affairs had been going badly for a long time, but became even worse after the war and the ensuing monetary crisis and the drop in general credit. He accumulated great debts. When we started putting out the magazine, we spent a lot of money and could not avoid going into debt. On the other hand, we had as many as 4000 subscribers in our second year of publication, which represented a turnover of 60,000 rubles, and this situation held true and is the case with *Epoch* to this day. However, it was still not possible to pay off all the debts. The total indebtedness, including old and new at the moment when *Time* was closed down, amounted to around 20,000. By that time, our brother had already spent the money from subscribers to pay off the debts. But then, thanks to his punctual payments, he still had credit and sufficient turnover (it would take too long to explain all this to you) to make it possible for him to fulfill his publication commitments to the end of the year without too much difficulty.

But all of a sudden everything collapsed—the magazine was closed down and, with that, the credit collapsed, too. It had been a difficult year, and Mikhail's health had suffered from the strain. But, at long last, he obtained permission to publish *Epoch*. However, he had to start by taking a loss, since he had to let all of the 4000 subscribers have the magazine for 6 rubles instead of at the full subscription rate (15 rubles). But our brother coped very well with that difficulty: *he borrowed, reckoning on* a quite safe thing for one whole year (he had already started operating his own printing press—two-thirds of it on credit) and in that way he could have kept the magazine going very nicely until the next subscription. And he calculated that in a year and a half not a kopek of debt would be left.

However, God decided differently. A little over three weeks before he died, he felt slightly sick—vomiting, diarrhea, and then, all of a sudden, the spread of bile through his system. It must be said that he was negligent, and although he did consult doctors and take the medicines they prescribed for him, he refused to stop working and stay at home. They were in their Pavlovsk summer house, but he kept coming into town to attend to the business of the magazine and of the printing press, and to other matters.

I was hoping to go abroad for health reasons. I got my passport and went to Moscow for a week. On my return from Moscow at the end of June, I realized to my horror that the sickness, which he had dismissed as a very minor matter when he saw me off for Moscow, had taken a turn for the worse. Finally, Besser (a famous doctor) frightened him by telling him that it was very grave and that he needed serious treatment. So Mikhail stayed at their summer house, and I did not go abroad. Instead I went out to Pavlovsk every day, and he kept wanting to rush into town all the time, expecting to recover from his illness any minute.

In the end he grew weaker. But on Sunday, July 5, he suddenly felt better. Besser had not lost hope, although he had informed us that Mikhail was suffering from an infection of the liver. However, none of us expected a tragic end, absolutely no one, not even the doctors. Then, heartened by the fact that he felt better, he at once began busying himself with affairs that evening. On Monday evening, he learned that the censors had banned one of the articles in the issue. The next day he told me that he felt very bad and that he hadn't slept all night. In the state he was in, he should have left off business altogether. Anything that went wrong, the smallest piece of unpleasant news, was real poison for a man as sick as he was. He could turn a fly into an elephant and spend a sleepless night worrying ceaselessly.

We called in Besser. He called me aside and told me directly that there was no hope left now, because during the night *the bile had flowed over into the blood* and his blood was already poisoned. Besser said that Mikhail was already feeling somnolent, that he would fall asleep toward the evening and never awake again. And that is exactly what happened: he fell asleep and slept almost peacefully. And on Friday, the tenth, at seven in the morning, he passed away without waking. Consulting doctors were brought in on three occasions. Every possible remedy was tried. The doctors were summoned from Petersburg, but it was all in vain.

I shall not try to tell you how much I have lost with him. That man loved me more than anyone in the world, more even than his wife and children, whom he adored. Probably you have already heard from someone or other that in April I buried my wife, who died of consumption in Moscow. Within a single year it is as though my life has been shattered. For a long time these two individuals were everything in my life. Where shall I find people like them now? And I do not even feel like looking for them. Anyway, it would be futile. A cold, lonely old age and epilepsy are all that lie ahead for me.

All the affairs of our brother's family are in great disorder. I am taking upon myself all matters connected with the magazine (it's a tremendously complicated business). There are lots of debts. The family is penniless, and the children are all minors. They are all crying and grieving, especially Emiliya Fyodorovna, who on top of everything else is worried about the future. It goes without saying that, from now on, my services are at their disposal. I would have given my health and my life for a brother such as he was to me.

Here is the situation his affairs are in: The magazine has 4000 subscribers and will probably have even more next year. Consequently, there will be an annual turnover of at least 60,000 [rubles]. In two years the family could pay back *all* the debts and, besides, live quite well during that period without suffering any privations. I shall remain, in reality, the editor of the magazine, although someone else has been appointed by the authorities. By the third year, the family will be able to put aside about ten thousand rubles every year, which was the goal our brother was trying to achieve, a realistic estimate, but which the closing down of the magazine last year made unattainable. However, all this year I shall have to publish the magazine at a loss, because most of the subscribers will be paying 6 rubles instead of 14.50 rubles for it to compensate them for the 8 issues of *Time* that they did not receive last year, because of the ban.

It was a very hard year for Mikhail. At the beginning of the year he borrowed 9000 rubles from our aunt (payable in two years) and 6000 rubles from Aleksandr Pavlovich (in stocks that he put up as collateral here for 5000 rubles). With that money he began operating his own printing press, which he also thought of putting up as collateral for another 5 thousand or so (it is worth 10). Thus, he hoped to see his way through to the end (that is, until the next subscriptions, which still would have brought in a minimum of 60,000). And that was all he needed. On top of the rest, he had another 8000 rubles of debts here.

But he is dead, and although Emiliya Fyodorovna has already been appointed executor and the magazine declared the property of the family, the credit our brother enjoyed has, for the most part, disappeared with him. The upshot is that all that we have at our disposal are the 5000 rubles that we should get for the mortgaged stocks, about 3000 that are coming to us before the end of the year, and the printing press that has been only partly paid for. The situation is quite difficult as far as money is concerned, but with God's help we'll manage. Now, dear brother, listen to what I have to say. Never before has the family been in such straits. I hope we'll pull through. If, though, you could lend the family just 3000 rubles (the 3000 rubles that you inherited from Uncle and that you probably haven't spent yet) for the magazine until March 1 at 10 percent interest, you would be doing a good and noble deed and would be of considerable help and comfort to poor Emiliya Fyodorovna. Reimbursement by March 1 is guaranteed, and I am prepared to secure her loan, too. Now, I leave it up to you. Judge for yourself. It will be very hard for us, but I am firmly convinced that I can sustain the publication until January. The extra 3000 would fully cover any eventuality. But do as you wish. Aleksandr Pavlovich was not afraid to give our brother money last spring. I am writing you this on my own initiative. Emiliya Fyodorovna sends you her regards. She is still in no condition to write anyone. Farewell. Think over what I have told you. It would be a good and noble action and is absolutely without risk.

My warmest and fraternal regards to your wife, and kisses to your children.

Good-bye, my dear boy.

Your brother,
F. Dostoyevsky

By the way, you have repeatedly accused us all of not writing to you. Brother was in a constant state of anxiety these past two years. As for me, I spent the last year at the side of my poor sick Masha, who was ill with consumption. This summer I was counting on going abroad, to Italy and to Constantinople and then, on my way back through Odessa, I thought I would spend three days with you in Yekaterinoslav, even if it meant making a detour.

---

53. Dostoyevsky is writing from Petersburg because he had gone to Pavlovsk, fifteen miles south of the capital, to be with Mikhail during his illness, and he then remained in Petersburg because that is where the editorial work for *Epoch* was being performed.

The war that Dostoyevsky mentions was the Crimean War (1853–1856), whose effects were damaging to Mikhail's cigarette-manufacturing business.

As an ex-convict, Dostoyevsky was not permitted to serve officially as editor of *Epoch*. The man appointed to that post—at Dostoyevsky's recommendation—was Aleksandr Yustinovich Poretsky (1819–1879), who had been in charge of the "Domestic Review" section for *Notes of the Fatherland* and subsequently for *Time*. Poretsky was the composer of a children's song, "Ah, We Have Caught You, Birdie, Stay!" (Akh, popalas ptichka, stoi!), which has been known to every Russian child ever since.

At the time of this letter, Andrei was working as an architect in Yekaterinoslav (now Dnepropetrovsk).

54. TO A. YE. WRANGEL
Petersburg, March 31, 1865

My dear and good friend, Aleksandr Yegorovich,

I can understand that you must have been quite surprised and, knowing your feelings toward me, undoubtedly offended by my silence after your two intimate and affectionate letters. But do not be either surprised or offended. I meant, at the time, to answer you right away, but *I could not do it*. Why? You will find the answer below. But could I possibly have forgotten you who were my friend when I had no other friends, you who were witness to my infinite happiness and to my bitterest despair (do you remember that night in the forest near Semipalatinsk when we were seeing them off?), you who were still my friend later, here in Petersburg, and who used your influence on my behalf? On the contrary, during all these years I have often thought of you and remembered you.

But what sort of life have I had in the interim? I owe you an explanation and even an account to make you understand why I left your recent letters unanswered. So listen to what I have to say, and I shall tell the whole story of my life during all this time—well, not really everything, for that would be impossible, because the most important things cannot be told in a letter. There are other things I am simply incapable of telling. And so let me rather give you a brief account of my life in the past year.

I suppose you know that four years ago my brother started a magazine. I helped him. Everything went fine. My *House of the Dead* literally caused a sensation and reestablished my literary reputation. My brother went heavily into debt with the launching of the magazine, and he had started paying off the debt when, all of a sudden, in May 1863, the magazine was closed down for having published an impassioned patriotic article that was misinterpreted as an outrageous attack on government policies and prevailing public sentiment. It is true that the author (one of our closest collaborators) was also partly to blame because he forced the tone of his article to such a point that it was completely misconstrued. By the time they understood the real intent of the article it was too late, and the magazine had been banned. From that moment on, my brother's affairs became hopelessly entangled, he lost his credit, debts came to light and he could not meet them. After much trouble my brother obtained permission to publish the magazine under a new name, *Epoch*. Permission was not granted until the end of February 1864, and the first number could not come out until March 20. This meant that the magazine got off to a late start, and subscriptions everywhere were now at a standstill, since the public traditionally subscribes to magazines only during the three months of December, January, and February. *Time*'s old subscribers, who had not received all the numbers to which they were entitled when the magazine closed down, had to be taken care of. They were informed that they would have to pay an additional six rubles to receive *Epoch* in 1864. Since there were hardly any new subscribers but only old ones paying a supplement of six rubles for *Epoch*, my brother was forced to publish the magazine at a loss. That unnerved him completely and finished him. He went into debt again, and his health began to deteriorate. I was not at his side at that time. I was in Moscow at the side of my dying wife. Yes, Aleksandr Yegorovich, my invaluable friend.

You write that you sympathize with me in my terrible loss, the death of my guardian angel, my brother Misha, but you still have no idea how I have been crushed by life. Yet another being, one who loved me and whom I loved beyond measure—my wife—died of consumption in Moscow, where she

206

had moved a year before her death. I had followed her there and remained by her bedside throughout the winter of 1864. She died on April 16 of last year, in full possession of her senses, remembering all those to whom she wished to bid a fond farewell, and she remembered you, too. I pass on her regards to you, my good and old friend. Think well of her when you remember her. Oh, my friend, her love for me was limitless, and I also loved her beyond measure, but we were not happy together. I shall tell you all about it when I see you, but for the time being I shall only say that, in spite of the fact that we were decidedly unhappy together (because of her strange, suspicious character and morbid imagination), we could not stop loving one another; the unhappier we were, the more attached we became to each other. Strange as it may seem, this is how it was. She was the most honest, the most noble and generous of all the women I have known during my lifetime. When she died, although I had suffered (a whole year) watching her die, although I appreciated and poignantly felt what I should be burying together with her—I never realized the degree of pain and the sense of emptiness I should feel when they covered her grave over with earth. Now, already a year has passed, but that feeling persists, undiminished . . . After I had buried her, I rushed off to Petersburg to my brother's. He was all I had left then. But within three months he also was dead, after ailing for only a month, so that the crisis that resulted in his death came almost unexpectedly and lasted only three days.

And now I have been suddenly left all alone and I am simply afraid. My whole life has suddenly been snapped in two. In the half that I have left behind me was everything that made my life worth living; in the other half, as yet unknown, everything is strange and new, and there is not a single being who could take the place of the two I have lost. There was literally nothing left for me to live for. Establish new connections, plan a new life for myself—the very idea repelled me. It was then that for *the first time* I realized that there was no one who could take *their* place, that *they* were the only creatures in the world I really loved, that a new attachment not only could not be developed, but indeed ought not to be developed. Everything around me grew cold and empty. And so, when three months ago I received your warm, kind letter full of old memories, I felt sadder than I can convey to you. But listen further.

April 9, 1865

Nine days have passed since I began writing this letter to you, and during these nine days I *literally* haven't had one moment to spare to finish it. Can you believe it, Aleksandr Yegorovich, in the three months since I received your two letters, and especially since the second one, when I began to be troubled by the thought of what you must think of me—can you believe me when I say that I literally have not had *one single minute* to spare in which to answer your letter—that that is why I have been silent until now. Whether you believe it or not, I am nevertheless telling you the truth. And why was that so? You will learn why right now. Let me take up where I left off.

When he died, my brother left only three hundred rubles, and that money was used to pay for his funeral. Moreover, there were debts amounting to twenty-five thousand rubles. Ten thousand rubles were long-term debts that presented no inconvenience to the family, but the remaining fifteen thousand were notes that had to be met. You may ask: How could he have hoped, in that case, to pay for the six issues of the magazine during the second half of the year (he died in July 1864)? The fact is that he had extraordinarily good credit and, besides, he could fully borrow on the strength of a loan already in operation. But he died, and the entire credit of the magazine collapsed. There was not a kopek with which to publish it, and we still had to put out six numbers, which would cost 18,000 rubles at the minimum and, on top of that, satisfy the claims of creditors amounting to 15,000, which meant that a total of 33,000 was needed to get through the year and keep the magazine going until new subscriptions came in. His family was left literally without any means of support—they were reduced to beggary. I was the only hope they had left and they all, the widow and the children, gathered close around me, expecting me to save them. I had loved my brother infinitely— how could I possibly have abandoned them?

There were two courses open to me: (1) To stop publishing the magazine and leave it to the creditors (for a magazine is, after all, an asset and is worth something), together with the furniture and other household junk; take the family to live with me, go on with my literary work, write novels, and keep my brother's widow and orphans. (2) To find money and continue publishing the magazine at all costs. How sorry I am that I did not choose the first course! In that case, of course, the creditors would not have received 20 rubles on a hundred. But then, the family could have refused the legacy and would not have been legally responsible for the debts at all. As for me, in all the five years that I worked for my brother's magazine, I earned between eight and ten thousand a year. So I could have provided for them and myself but, it goes without saying, only by working all my life from morning until night. However, I preferred the second course, i.e., to continue publishing the magazine. Indeed, I was not the only one to prefer it. All my friends and former coworkers shared my opinion.

April 14.

"There has been another interruption. . ." If you only knew, Aleksandr Yegorovich, in what terrible and oppressive occupations I pass my time! I take up where I left off:

Besides, I had to pay back my brother's debts—I did not want his mem-

208

ory to be tarnished. There was a way: hold out until the yearly subscriptions came in, pay back a part of the debts, try to improve the magazine from one year to another, and in three or four years, when all the debts had been paid, turn the magazine over to someone else, after making sure that my brother's family was adequately provided for. And then I could have relaxed and set about writing again the things that I have been wanting to express for a long time.

So my decision was made. I went to Moscow, succeeded in persuading my old and rich aunt to let me have right away the 10,000 rubles that she was to leave me in her will, returned to Petersburg, and resumed publication of the magazine. But the situation had already seriously deteriorated: Permission to publish the magazine had to be obtained from the censor's office, and that took some time, with the result that the June issue could not come out until the end of August. The subscribers, who are not concerned with all these matters, began to protest violently. The censor's office would not allow me to have my name on the magazine either as publisher or as editor. I had to do something drastic. I began publishing in three printing shops at the same time, sparing neither money nor effort nor health. I alone was the editor, I read the proofs, dealt with the authors and the censors, edited the articles, raised the money, sat up until 6 A.M., slept only 5 hours a day and yet, although I finally did put the magazine in order, it was already too late. Would you believe it—the September issue came out on November 28 and the January 1865 issue on February 13. That comes down to 16 days per issue, and each issue comprised 35 printer's sheets. What an effort it was! But the worst thing is that, while working like a galley slave, I had no time to write and publish a single line of my own in the magazine. With my name nowhere to be found, the public, not only in the provinces but even in Petersburg, had no idea that I was the editor of the magazine.

And then, all of a sudden, there was a crisis among magazines in general. Subscriptions fell off to all magazines at the same time. *Contemporary,* which had always had 5,000 subscribers, wound up with 2,300. All the other magazines suffered losses. We were left with only 1,300 subscribers.

There are many reasons for this countrywide crisis in the Russian press. They are quite obvious, albeit complex. But we shall come to that later. Just imagine our situation, and my own particularly! To prevent my brother's old debts from interfering with the progress of the business, I personally assumed about ten thousand rubles of them myself. I reckoned that if the magazine had a bad year and only 2,500 subscribers instead of 4,000 as formerly, even then we could have managed. We should at least have been able to pay back our debts. My calculations were sound: never, since the beginning of Russian journalism in the thirties, had the number of subscribers dropped by more than 25 percent in a single year. And then, all of a sudden, all the magazines lost about one-half of their subscribers, and we dropped a whole 75 percent. It cannot be ascribed to poor management. It was, after all, *I* and not my brother who had launched *Time*, too; *I* who had given it its orientation; and *I* who had edited it. In short, we found ourselves in the situation of a landlord or a merchant whose house or factory has burned down and who, from being a well-off man, has become a bankrupt.

When the subscriptions started coming in, demands were made for the payment of the debts, most of them incurred by my late brother. We paid with the money from subscriptions, reckoning that after paying these debts there would still be something left over to continue publishing the magazine with. But subscriptions stopped coming in and, after issuing two numbers of the magazine, our money had run out.

It was just at that time that your letters reached me. I had gone to Moscow to look for money and for a partner who would come in with me on the magazine on most advantageous conditions. But, besides the magazine crisis, Russia is also going through a monetary crisis. Now, for lack of funds, we cannot go on publishing the magazine and are compelled to declare ourselves temporarily bankrupt, and I owe 10,000 rubles in promissory notes and 5,000 borrowed on my word of honor.

Of these sums, three thousand must be paid, come what may. Moreover, I need 2,000 to redeem my right to publish my works—that right has been mortgaged—and start publishing them myself. There are booksellers offering me 5,000 rubles for that right, but it would not be in my interest. I stand to gain more by publishing them myself. Now, to pay my debts, I want to publish my new novel in installments, as is done in England. Furthermore, I also want to publish *House of the Dead* in installments and in a deluxe illustrated edition. And finally, next year, I want to publish my complete works. All that will, I hope, bring me 15,000 or so, but it will be backbreaking work.

Oh, my friend, believe me, I would be more than willing to go back into penal servitude for as many years as I spent there before, just to pay my debts and feel a free man again. But now I shall again have to start writing a novel under the threat of a stick, i.e., prompted by dire need and working in a hurry. The novel will be effective, but is that what I need? Being forced to work for money's sake has crushed and devoured me.

Nevertheless, for a start, I need at least three thousand. I am searching for that money in every corner—if I don't find it I am lost. I have the feeling that only a lucky break can save me. All the reserve of strength and energy that I had has been replaced by a sort of vague anxiety, something that is close to despair. Anxiety, bitterness, intensely cold agitation—this is not at all my normal state; and, besides, I am all alone. Nobody, nothing from the past forty years is with me any longer. And yet I feel as though I were just about to start living. Funny, isn't it? The vitality of a cat.

Now that I have told you everything, I realize that I have given you not so much as an inkling of the most important thing—my intimate, my spiritual life. And this is bound to be, so long as we can communicate only by letter. I don't know how to write letters, nor do I know how to write *about myself* in *moderation*. But then it is quite a difficult thing to do, anyway—there are many years between us now, and what years!

And how opportune it was that you should have written me at this time. You brought the past back to me. I love you as you were then—young and kind—and I shall remember you that way as long as I live. By the way, though, I have no idea of what you are like *as a family man*. I suppose (remembering the past) that you must be happy now. But I am curious to learn what fresh and unknown shading family life has given to your character.

Thank you for the photographs of your family. I spent a long time looking at the pictures, examining them closely, trying to guess.

I went abroad twice, in the summers of 1862 and 1863. Each time, I was away for three months. I traveled in Germany (covering most of it), in Switzerland, in France, and in Italy (also extensively). On both occasions, while I was abroad my health recovered with startling rapidity. So I had made up my mind to spend three months abroad every year, especially since it involved no financial burden, in view of the high prices of our life at home. My reason for going on these trips was my health—to rest and recuperate there, to be in condition to work better during the remaining 9 months of the year in Russia. But last year the death of my brother forced me to stay at home, and now my debts and my work are completely ruining my health. But oh, how much I should like to go away, if only for a month, to refresh my spirits, to get some fresh air, and to come back to life. I would certainly pay you a visit. And, who can tell, perhaps that is just what will happen. There is no need for me to be here during the publication of *House of the Dead,* and when I am abroad I write constantly, because I have more time and tranquility than at home, and this is especially true when I settle down in one place. Yes, I would pay you a visit without fail.

I promise to send you a photograph if you answer this letter quickly, if you have not been angered by my long silence. And, anyway, why should you be angry, good gracious, as if I were to blame!

I live alone with Pasha, my stepson. He is already going on seventeen, and is studying. He remembers you very well and sends you his regards.

Oh, there are so many things I could tell you if we were to see each other again.

Farewell, my good friend, I embrace you warmly from the bottom of my heart. May you be happy. From now on, I shall answer your letters promptly. Write soon.

I am afraid this letter may not find you in Copenhagen any longer.

All yours, as ever and always,

Fyodor Dostoyevsky

---

54. At the time of this letter, Wrangel was serving as secretary at the Russian embassy in Copenhagen.

The "night in the forest" was the occasion on which Dostoyevsky and Wrangel were seeing off Mariya Dmitriyevna and her first husband, who were leaving Semipalatinsk for Kuznetsk.

Epoch was approved for publication at the end not of February but of January 1864, and Mariya Dmitriyevna moved to Moscow not "a year before her death" but in November 1863.

The "long-term debts that presented no inconvenience to the family" must be a reference to the money borrowed from Dostoyevsky's aunt and brother-in-law.

55.   To N. P. Suslova
Petersburg, April 19, 1865

My ever so dear and esteemed Nadezhda Prokofevna,

I am enclosing herewith my letter to Apollinariya or, to be more precise, a copy of the letter I am sending to Apollinariya in Montpellier by this same mail. Since you write that she is about to come and join you in Zurich, my letter to her may miss her in Montpellier. And as it is absolutely essential to me that she get my letter, I beg you to hand her this copy as soon as you see her. I would also ask you to read the letter yourself. You will find in it clear answers to all the questions you ask me in your letter, i.e., whether I like "to savor other people's sufferings, tears," etc. And also an explanation concerning cynicism and filth.

Let me add here for you personally that, after all, this is not the first year you have known me, that whenever I was crestfallen I turned to you to find solace and, of late, it was you alone I sought out when my spirit was heavily oppressed. You have seen me in my sincerest moments and so can testify whether I thrive on other people's suffering, whether I am coarse (inwardly), whether I am cruel.

Apollinariya is a great egotist. Her egotism and vanity are colossal. She demands *the utmost* of people, all the perfections; she will not excuse a single failing out of respect for other good features, but she herself refuses to acknowledge even the slightest obligation toward others. She chides me, to this day, for having been unworthy of her love, she constantly complains and rebukes me. But it was she who, in 1863, met me in Paris with the words: "You have come a bit late," meaning that she had fallen in love with someone else, although two weeks earlier she had written me an ardent letter telling me she loved me. It is not for having fallen in love with someone else that I reproach her, but for the four lines she sent me at my hotel containing the brutal words: "You have come a bit late."

There are many things I could write you about Rome, about our life together in Turin, in Naples, but what would be the point? what good would it do? Besides, I have already told you so much during our talks together.

I am still in love with her, very much in love, but now I do not want to love her any more. She is *unworthy* of that sort of love.

I am sorry for her, because I can foresee that she will always be unhappy. Nowhere will she find a friend and happiness. Anyone who demands everything of others while eschewing all obligations will never find happiness.

It is possible that my letter about which she complains was written in an irritated tone. But it is not rude. She took it for rudeness because I dared to contradict her, dared to say how hurt I was. She has always treated me haughtily. She was offended because I, too, wanted at long last to speak up, complain, disagree with her. She will not countenance equality in our relations. All human feeling is absent in her relations with me. Why, she knows very well that, to this day, I am still in love with her. So why does she have to torture me? She does not have to love me, but then she doesn't have to torment me. Besides, many things I wrote in that letter were not meant seriously. But, in her irritation, she takes seriously what was intended as a joke, and so it seems rude.

But enough of that. You, at least, should not blame me. I have a high regard for you; you are a person such as I have rarely met in my life, and I do not want to lose your sympathy. I value highly your opinion and the image you have of me. And I am writing to you *in such a straightforward manner* because, I don't have to tell you, I am seeking no favors nor am I hoping to get anything out of you. And so you cannot possibly dismiss my words as flattery or as an effort to please, but will accept them as the sincere expression of my innermost feelings.

Your sister wrote me that you were in Zurich and would be for some time to come. Listen to me (if you are able and care to): Wherever you may be, dash off occasionally a few words about yourself to let me know how you are. I am not asking you to take the trouble of writing me often. All I want is for you to remember me now and then. And I shall always be most interested to hear from you.

I want to repeat to you once more my customary advice and wish: Do not insulate yourself from the world, give yourself to nature, to the outside world and outside things, if only a little bit. The outward *life* is real and contributes to the powerful development of our human nature, it gives us substance. But please don't laugh at me too much.

I am in a ghastly situation. I don't know how I shall extricate myself. You will understand certain things from my letter to Apollinariya.

For the time being, my address is still the same. If you write me soon, I shall answer you and give you a more *permanent address,* which you can use all the time.

I hope to see you again, but when will it be? Farewell. May you be happy as long as you live. I press your hand hard, and hope that some day, at least, we'll be seeing each other. How will we both feel then? Anyway, I shall always remember you.

All yours,
F. Dostoyevsky

P.S. You have youth now, the springtide of life—that is such a happy time! Do not waste your life, preserve your soul, and believe in truth. But *do not go searching for it too fixedly* through your life, because if you do you may easily lose your way. But you have a heart, and you won't lose your way. As for me, I am reaching the end of my life—I feel it. It makes no difference, though—you are dear to me for your youth and freshness, and besides, I love you as the most cherished of sisters.

---

55. Nadezhda Prokofevna Suslova (1843–1918) was the first Russian woman physician. In the early 1860s she audited courses at Petersburg University and then at the Military Academy of Surgery. When she was expelled from the academy in 1865, she entered the University of Zurich, from which she received her medical degree in 1867. She was Apollinariya Suslova's sister.

56.   To Ye. P. Kovalevsky
[Petersburg] June 6, 1865

Your Excellency, Yegor Petrovich:

Difficulties force me once more to have recourse to the assistance of the Literary Fund. In the summer of last year, I was planning to go abroad to try to get at least temporary relief from fits of epilepsy. But then my brother's death obliged me not only to remain in Petersburg, but also to take upon myself the difficult task of continuing the publication of the magazine in order to honor our obligations to subscribers, to pay off my late brother's debts, and to provide his family with some sort of livelihood. This work, over a period of a year, has shattered my health; I have had to cope with all the managerial and editorial duties, as a result of which, moreover, I have had practically no time to write a single line of my own. Thus, now, when I have been forced to give up the magazine, which does not even belong to me and which has cost me ten thousand rubles of my own money, I find myself in debt, with my name signed to thirteen thousand rubles' worth of promissory notes and, on top of all that, temporarily without any means of support. I am now working on a piece for which I can ask to be paid only in the fall. I must complete it as soon as possible, so that, once I get the money, I can begin paying off my debts.

Although many of my creditors are willing to wait until next year and have agreed to payment in installments because they understand that the only way I can pay them back is by my works, others, though a small minority, refuse to wait and have already proceeded against me.

In view of these special circumstances, I am moved to ask you, much respected Yegor Petrovich, to petition the committee of the Literary Fund to grant me a loan of *six hundred* rubles, payable on February 1, 1866. This time I cannot offer any collateral, because my works, which I offered as collateral on the two previous occasions when I requested help from the fund, have already been pledged for a long time now and the money used up to cover the expenses of the magazine. If, however, there is no possibility of obtaining for me these 600 rubles *in the form of a loan,* I ask that you present to the committee my request that I be given the entire sum as an outright grant, since, if I received aid in that form, nothing would prevent me from returning the 600 rubles to the treasury of the Literary Fund at the first opportunity. I consider it my duty to add that I am making this remark for the simple reason that I would greatly regret it if the already modest resources of the fund were further depleted for my personal benefit.

The reason for my requesting 600 rubles is that I have been sued for 700, and only by promising to pay 600 (by June 9) have I managed to dissuade my creditors from *seizing my belongings* and having me locked up in debtors' prison. Considering the present state of my health, it would be very difficult, if not altogether impossible, for me to get down to work in confinement. Let me add that, once I have paid the 600 rubles, my creditors will, by and large, leave me in peace for the rest of the year and, consequently, I shall be able to set about my work with greater equanimity.

Please accept my assurances of the profoundest respect.

I have the honor of remaining,

Your most obedient servant,
Fyodor Dostoyevsky

---

56. Yegor Petrovich Kovalevsky (1811–1868) was a writer and statesman, and the first chairman of the Society for Assistance to Needy Writers and Scholars (Obshchestvo dlya posobiya nuzhdayushchimsya literatoram i uchonym), informally known as the Literary Fund. Dostoyevsky had been a member of the committee of the fund (its governing body) and had received loans from it in 1863 enabling him to go abroad for his health. As collateral, he had pledged to the society "ownership and publication rights in perpetuity to the totality of my works or any part thereof." The

request made in this letter was reported to the committee on June 7 and was immediately approved in the form of a grant. Later, Dostoyevsky frequently gave readings of his works for the fund's benefit.

Epoch was forced into bankruptcy early in 1865. The last issue to be published was that for February, which appeared on March 22.

The "piece" (*rabota*) that Dostoyevsky had started to work on turned out to be *Crime and Punishment*.

57. To A. A. KRAYEVSKY
[Petersburg] June 8, 1865

Dear Sir, Andrei Aleksandrovich,

Having thought over our very brief conversation of some time ago, I think it would be worthwhile—for the sake of precision and to avoid all possible misunderstanding—to set forth my request to you in writing.

My request has two forms:

(1) I ask for 3000 rubles immediately, as an advance on my novel, which I *formally* engage myself to deliver to the editorial offices of *Notes of the Fa[therland]* no later than the first days of *October of this year*.

(2) In the event of my death or in the event of my failure to deliver the manuscript of the novel to the editors of *Notes of the Fa.* on time, I offer as a guarantee the full and perpetual right to the publication of *all* my writings and, equally, the right to sell or convey them—in brief, the right to dispose of them as of their own property.

N.B. My novel is called *The Drunkards* and will deal with the current problem of drunkenness. Not only will the problem be analyzed, but it will be shown in all of its ramifications, primarily in scenes of family life, in the rearing of children under such circumstances, etc., etc. It will comprise at least 20 printer's sheets and possibly more. I am asking 150 rubles per sheet (for *House of the Dead* I received 250 rubles per sheet from *Russian World* and *Time*).

(3) In case the editors of *Notes of the Fa.* do not like my work (or if they consider my price too high), they will have the option of returning the manuscript to me and holding on to my guarantee until I have refunded the 3000 rubles (plus 10 percent). The anticipated deadline for the repayment of the sum in that eventuality will be some time before January 1, 1866. Moreover, the publisher of *Notes of the Fa.* will be entitled to receive the royalties for all articles wherever and whenever published by me until repayment of the 3000 rubles plus the interest due.

(4) I have no right to take back the work at my own discretion or not to deliver it to the editors of *Notes of the Fa.*, even if I refunded the 3000 rubles with interest, i.e., the editors of *Notes of the Fa.* have the right to claim my work, while also having the complete right to return the manuscript to me without my consent and to reclaim their money.

The other form of my request is:

I ask for 1500 rubles and assume the formal obligation to deliver my novel by the date specified above. But I ask that I be freed from the requirement of putting up collateral. As for all the other conditions, they would remain the same as stipulated above.

Allow me to make one more observation:

If it were at all feasible to make available to me at one time such a considerable sum as 3000, I would earnestly call your attention to the fact that this would be the most desirable way for me and, I should think, the most satisfactory for both parties. Two booksellers, Stellovsky and Voganov (*knowing that I was in difficulty*), have at this very moment already been offering me 2000 in cash for the right to publish all my writings *just once*. Therefore, it would seem to me, my works do offer a sufficient guarantee. Now, taking into consideration the fact that my proposals on other points give almost every sort of guarantee to the editors of *Notes of the Fa.*, I hope that in the event that you are interested in publishing my novel in *Notes of the Fa.*, you will not refuse to give me the 3000 if you are able to do so. Such an agreement would solve all my problems for the current year.

Accept my assurances of sincere respect,

Your obedient servant,

Fyodor Dostoyevsky

---

57. Dostoyevsky may have put his request in two forms either because his writings had already been pledged or because he was planning to offer them elsewhere as security for 1,500 rubles. Krayevsky did not accept either form, explaining that he lacked ready cash and had a large backlog of fiction for his magazine. This led Dostoyevsky to make a deal with Stellovsky.

The "Voganov" whom Dostoyevsky mentions may have been the Petersburg banker and industrialist Otto Maksimovich Vogau, who was also known as Vogan.

58.   To I. S. TURGENEV
Wiesbaden, August 3/15 [1865]

Most kind and much respected Ivan Sergeyevich,

When I say you in Petersburg a month ago, I was selling my writings for whatever I could get, because I was about to be packed off to debtors' prison for the magazine's debts, which I had been stupid enough to take upon myself. My writings were bought by Stellovsky (the rights to a double-column edition) for three thousand, part of it in promissory notes. With some of the three thousand I appeased the creditors momentarily, and the rest I distributed to those to whom I was obligated, after which I went abroad to regain my health, at least to some small extent, and to do some writing. Out of the three thousand, I left myself a mere 175 silver rubles for my trip abroad, which was the most I could afford.

But two years ago in Wiesbaden I won around 12000 francs within a single hour. Although this time I did not expect gambling to be a panacea, it would have been very pleasant indeed to win 1000 francs or so to tide me over for at least three months. I arrived in Wiesbaden only five days ago, and I have lost everything already, just everything, including my watch, and I even owe money to the hotel.

I feel loathsome, and ashamed to be bothering you with my affairs. But I really have no one else right now to whom I can turn and, in the second place, you are much more intelligent than the others, and so it is morally easier for me to turn to you. Here is what I have in mind: I am asking you, as one human being to another, for 100 (one hundred) thalers. I am expecting a bit of money from Russia, from a magazine (*Libr[ary] for Reading*), which they promised to send me when I left, and also from one gentleman who *must* help me. It is quite unlikely that I can pay you back before *three weeks;* then again, it might be earlier. In any case, a month at the latest. I feel horrible inside (I thought it would be worse) and, above all, I'm ashamed to bother you, but what can you do when you are drowning?

My address is: Viesbaden [*sic*], Hotel Victoria, à M. Théodor Dostoiewsky. But what if you are not in Baden-Baden?

Yours truly,
F. Dostoyevsky

---

58. Shortly before leaving Russia to go abroad, Dostoyevsky had made an arrangement with Boborykin and N. N. Voskoboinikov, copublishers of *A Library for Reading*, under which he promised to send the magazine a story and possibly some "letters from abroad" in return for an advance.

The "gentleman who *must* help me" may have been Herzen. He and Dostoyevsky had become friends in 1862, when the latter visited him in London.

In response to this letter, Turgenev sent Dostoyevsky fifty thalers. Dostoyevsky wrote him a brief thank-you note, saying, "They were a great help, although they did not basically improve my situation." Nearly ten years later, he still had not repaid the loan. Turgenev thought the amount had been one hundred thalers and demanded that sum from Dostoyevsky, who paid him fifty thalers, insisting that that was the correct amount. This was one of the factors precipitating a quarrel between the two writers. Subsequently, Turgenev discovered among his papers Dostoyevsky's thank-you note, in which the amount of fifty thalers was mentioned.

59. To A. P. Suslova

[Wiesbaden] Thursday, August 12/24 [1865]

I keep bombarding you with letters (and always unfranked). Did you get my letter of the day before yesterday (Tuesday)? I am still hoping to hear from you today.

My affairs are in a lamentable state, nec [*sic*] plus ultra; it is not possible to sink any further. Down deeper there must be another zone of misery and filth of which I have no inkling yet. I have still had nothing from Herzen, no answer or reaction. Today it is exactly one week since I wrote him. Today is also the date on which I had promised my landlord on Monday I would pay him. I don't know what will happen. It is still only one o'clock in the morning.

I just cannot believe that Herz[en] would be reluctant to answer me! Could he really have decided not to reply? That is out of the question. For what reason? We are on excellent terms, as even you have seen for yourself. Could someone have turned him against me? But in that case it is inconceivable (even more inconceivable) that he would leave my letter without *some* answer. So, for the time being, I am still convinced either that my letter to him went astray (which is rather unlikely) or, to my misfortune, that he is not in Geneva at the present time. The latter is more likely the case. If that is so, I probably can anticipate that either (1) He left town for a short while, in which case I can still hope to get his answer any day now (as soon as he gets back); or (2) He has left for a long time, in which case it is extremely likely that my letter will be sent on to him to wherever he is now, because he surely must have left instructions for the mail that arrived in his absence to be forwarded. Hence, I may still hope to hear from him.

I shall continue to hope for an answer all this week until Sunday—but, of course, it will be no more than a hope. And I am now in such a predicament that hope alone is not much to live by.

But I could stand all this if I weren't so depressed. I am tormented by my inactivity, by the uncertainty of waiting around without any firm perspective in view, by the waste of time, and by this accursed Wiesbaden, which has so sickened me that it makes me disgusted with life! And in the meantime you are in Paris, and I shan't be seeing you. Herz. is also preying on my mind. If he did get my letter and *does not desire* to answer me, think how humiliating that would be for me, and what a thing for him to do! What could I possibly have done to deserve it? Is it my disorderly ways? I agree I have led quite a disorderly life, but what is all this bourgeois morality! If nothing else, he could answer me, or maybe he feels that I do not "deserve" his help (as the hotel owner feels that I do not "deserve" to be served my dinner). But it is inconceivable that he won't answer me—he must simply be away from Geneva.

I have asked you to help me out if you can borrow from someone or other. I am not very optimistic, Polya, but if you can, do it for me! You must agree that it would be quite difficult to find anyone in a more troublesome and painful predicament than I am in at this moment.

This is the last letter I shall be writing until I have at least some news from you. I am all the time under the impression that my letters may be lying around and getting lost in the Hotel Fleurus if you do not happen to be there yourself when they arrive. I am not putting postage on them because I don't have a single kopek. I am still going without dinner, and this is the third day already that I have been living on just my morning and evening tea. And a strange thing—I don't feel at all like eating. The bad part is that they are trying to make things unpleasant for me and sometimes refuse to give me a new candle in the evening, especially if there is the tiniest stump of the previous night's candle remaining. But, actually, I step out of the hotel between three and six in the afternoon every day so as not to let on that I am going without any dinner. Some bluff, Khlestakov style!

To be sure, I have the vague hope that in a week or ten days at the latest, I shall get something from Russia (via Zurich). But I can hardly last out until then unless I have some help.

And yet I refuse to believe that I shan't get to Paris and see you before you leave. That is just not possible. But then, my inactivity may be causing my imagination to play tricks with me—and I have been reduced to sheer inactivity.

Farewell, my dear, and unless something quite out of the ordinary occurs, I shan't be writing any more. *See you again.*

All yours,
Dos.

P.S. I embrace you once more, very hard. Did Nad[ezhda] Prok[ofevna] arrive and when? Give her my regards.

4 o'clock

My dear friend Polya, I just this minute received an answer from Herz. He was in the mountains, and that is why his letter was delayed. He did not send any money. He says my letter reached him at a quite hopeless moment and that he cannot spare 400 florins, but that 100 or 150 guldens is quite a different matter, and that if that would be of any help to me, he would send me that sum. And he begs me not to be angry with him, etc.

Isn't it rather strange, though—why didn't he send me the 150 guldens, since he said himself he could spare them? He could have sent me the 150, saying that it was the best he could do. That is how things are done. But there's no mystery here: either he is very short himself or else he is just stingy. But then, he could not have doubted that I would pay him back, since he has my letter. After all, I'm not a man beyond redemption. No, I'm sure he is in a tight spot himself.

To ask him for help again—that is quite impossible! But then what am I to do now? Polya, my friend, help me, save me! Find 150 guldens somewhere, that is all I need, really. In 10 days (or maybe before that) something will *surely* arrive from Voskoboinikov for your sister in Zurich. And although it may not be much, it will certainly be not less than 150 guldens, and I shall pay you back then. For you may be sure that I shouldn't want to put *you* into an unpleasant situation. That, certainly, is out of the question. Ask your sister for advice. But, in any case, let me hear from you soon.

All yours,

F. Dostoyevsky

Now again, I have no idea what will happen to me.

---

59. In *The Inspector General*, Khlestakov, the main character, also tries to hide from a hotelkeeper and others the fact that he has no money.

Nikolai Nikolayevich Voskoboinikov (1838–1882) was an engineer by profession (he built the stone bridge across the Moscow River) but later became a journalist. He was copublisher of *A Library for Reading* at the time of this letter, but in the 1870s he joined the staff of the *Moscow Gazette* (Moskovskiye vedomosti), eventually becoming assistant to the chief editor.

A couple of weeks after writing this letter, Dostoyevsky wrote to Wrangel in Copenhagen, confessing his gambling losses and asking him for a loan of 100 Danish rigsdalers, which Wrangel eventually sent to him.

60.   To M. N. Katkov

[Wiesbaden, first half of September 1865]

K[ind] S[ir], M[ikhail] N[ikiforovich],

May I hope to have my story published in your magazine, R[*ussian*] M[*essenger*]?

I have been working on it for 2 months now here in Wiesbaden, and it is nearing completion. It will contain between five and six printer's sheets. I still have a couple of weeks' work left on it, or perhaps a bit more. In any case, I can promise definitely that in a month at the very latest I could deliver it to the editorial offices of *R.M.*

The idea of my story, as far as I can see, in no wise runs counter to your magazine. Indeed, quite the contrary. It is a psychological account of a crime. The action is topical, set in the current year. A young student of lower-middle-class origin, who has been expelled from the university, and who lives in dire poverty, succumbs—through thoughtlessness and lack of strong convictions—to certain strange, "incomplete" ideas that are floating in the air, and decides to get out of his misery once and for all. He resolves to kill an old woman, the widow of a titular councilor, who lends out money for interest. The old crone is stupid, deaf, sick, and greedy, and she charges Jew rates; she is wicked and makes the life of her younger sister, whom she treats as a servant, wretched. "She is good for nothing," "what does she live

221

for?" "Is she of any use to anyone at all?" and so on. These questions disorient the young man. He decides to kill and rob her in order to bring happiness to his mother, who is living in the provinces, and to wrest his sister, who is living as a companion in the house of some landowners, from the lewd demands of the head of the household, demands that may lead to her perdition. He also wants to finish his studies and to go abroad and, afterward, for the rest of his life, to be honest, firm, and steadfast in the performance of his "humanitarian duties toward mankind," which certainly would "expiate his crime," if one can actually call a crime his act against a stupid, deaf, vicious, sick old crone who herself does not know why she is living and who may die anyway in a month or so.

Despite the fact that such crimes are very difficult to carry out, i.e., criminals practically always leave glaring clues, evidence, etc., behind them, and leave too much to chance, which almost always leads to their discovery, he, by sheer accident, carries off the execution of his enterprise quickly and successfully.

Afterward, almost a month goes by before the final catastrophe. He is not and cannot possibly be suspected. And it is just at this point that the entire psychological process of crime unfolds itself. Insoluble problems arise before the murderer; unsuspected and unforeseen feelings torment his mind. Divine truth and human law take their toll, and he ends up by being *driven* to give himself up. He is driven to this because, even though doomed to perish in penal servitude, it will make him one with the people again, and the feeling of being cut off and isolated from humanity that he had experienced from the moment he committed the crime had been torturing him. The law of truth and human nature won out [illegible words]. The criminal himself decides to accept suffering to expiate his deed. However, it is rather difficult for me to make my idea completely clear.

Besides this, my story contains the suggestion that the legal penalty imposed for the commission of a crime frightens the offender less than the lawmakers think, partly because *it is he himself who demands* it *morally.*

I have seen that myself in even the most backward individuals in the crudest circumstances. I would like to show that this feeling is present in an educated man of the new generation, so that the idea would be more striking and more tangible. Several recent occurrences have convinced me that there is nothing terribly unusual about my *subject,* namely, the fact that my murderer is well educated and is even a young man with praiseworthy inclinations. Last year in Moscow I heard of a student who, expelled from the university after the Moscow student disorders, decided to break into a post office and kill a postal employee. There is also considerable evidence in our newspapers that the extreme inconstancy of our principles has resulted in horrible acts. (The seminary student who made a pact with a young girl to kill her, killed her in a barn, and was picked up one hour later while he was eating his lunch, and other such things.) In brief, I am convinced that my subject will in a way explain what is happening today.

It goes without saying that this outline of the idea of my story entirely leaves out the plot. But it will be engrossing—that I will vouch for—although I cannot take it upon myself to judge its artistic merits. I have been too often forced to write very, very poor pieces because I have had to hurry to meet deadlines, etc. But this particular story has been written unhurriedly and with ardor. And I shall try, *if only for my own sake,* to make the ending as good as I can.

About six years ago I sent a story of mine to *R.M.,* for which I received an advance from you. But there was a misunderstanding, the deal was not consummated, and I took my story back and returned the money to you. It is possible that I was partly wrong, but it is also possible that I was partly right on that occasion. Most likely it was a combination of both. But as I see it now, I am rather prepared to blame myself for having acted upon a whim and having been too touchy. I do not remember the details. Is it, therefore, too much to hope, my esteemed Mikh. Nik., that you, too, are prepared to forget them?

During the past six years I have been paid between 250 rubles (for *House of the Dead,* the beginning of which was published in the old *Russian World*) and 125 rubles per printer's sheet, a price offered me only recently by a publisher. I leave the price entirely to your discretion—you may determine it after you have read my story. I understand that many writers working with you proceed in this way. But in any case, I should like to get per printer's sheet no less than the minimum I have been receiving up to now, i.e., 125 rubles. But again, I leave this entirely up to you, and I firmly believe that that will be to my best advantage.

Forgive me if I pass on now to my private affairs. I find myself in a very bad situation at this moment. I went abroad at the beginning of July with hardly any money, to gain back my health. I was hoping to wind up a work I had started, but then I got involved in another story (the one I am writing now) and I do not regret it. However, this forces me to ask you for an advance of three hundred rubles now, in the event, of course, that you are interested in my work. I beg you, much esteemed Mikhail Nikifor., not to view my request for 300 rubles as in any way a condition for offering my piece to you. That is not the case at all. It is simply a favor I am asking of you to help me out at a particularly difficult moment and, of course, a favor which is worthy of consideration only if—I repeat again—you manifest your willingness to take my work.

My address here is— Whatever your decision, I should greatly appreciate it if you did not leave me for a long time without an answer from the editors of your magazine. In my present straits, every minute is precious. I imagine that, although I myself hope to be back in Russia in a month, I shall be able to send you my work in three weeks.

---

60. In this draft, Dostoyevsky is outlining, of course, the story of Raskolnikov in *Crime and Punishment*. The work that he had been "hoping to wind up" may have been the story of the Marmeladov family, about which he had written to Krayevsky some three months previously (see Letter 57). Evidently the two stories had been conceived independently of each other and then merged into one in the process of development. In a letter of September 28, 1865, to Wrangel, Dostoyevsky wrote that "the piece I am writing now may turn out to be the best thing I have ever written, if only I am allowed time enough to finish it."

The incident that had occurred six years earlier concerned *The Village of Stepanchikovo* (see Letter 38 and the note to it).

Katkov did send Dostoyevsky the advance of 300 rubles that he asks for. About two months later, Dostoyevsky wrote Katkov asking for another 700 rubles, which he also sent (see Letter 62).

61. To A. Ye. Wrangel
Petersburg, February 18, 1866

My excellent and old friend, Aleksandr Yegorovich,

I am to blame for my long silence, but my guilt is guiltless. It would be difficult for me to describe my present life and all the attendant circumstances so that you might clearly understand all the reasons for my long silence. The reasons are too complicated and too numerous for me to go into them, but there are a few things that I shall mention.

In the first place, I am working like a prisoner. It is that novel for *Russian Messenger*. It is a big novel—in *6 parts*. At the end of November much of it was complete and ready; but I burned it—and now I feel I can admit it—because I just did not like it. I became fascinated by a new form, a new plan, and I started all over again. I am working night and day, and still it is not enough. According to my calculations, I shall have to deliver up to 6 printer's sheets to *Russian Messenger* each month. That is dreadful, but I would deliver that much if my mind were free. A novel is a poetic affair, and it requires a peaceful mind and imagination. But I am being molested by creditors, i.e., they are threatening to have me thrown into prison. Up to now, I have not succeeded in reaching an agreement with them, and I am not at all sure that I ever shall. Although many of them are sensible people and have accepted my proposal to extend payment over 5 years, there are some with whom I have been unable to reach any understanding whatever. You can imagine how disconcerted I am. It is shattering my spirit and my heart, and it leaves me depressed for days on end, when I am supposed to sit down and work. And that is why it has also been so difficult for me to find a peaceful moment in which to communicate with an old friend. That's the truth, by God!

Then there is my bad health. When I first came back I was terribly bothered by my epileptic fits—it looked as if they were trying to make up for the three months I had spent abroad, when I didn't have any at all. And, on top of that, for a whole month now I have been suffering from hemorrhoids. You probably know nothing about that affliction and how painful its attacks are. This is the third year in a row that I have been suffering from this disorder for two months of the year, in February and March. Imagine, I had to spend *fifteen days* (!) stretched out on a sofa, 15 days during which I could not take my pen in hand. And now, during the 15 days remaining, I have to write 5 printer's sheets! And to think I had to remain stretched out when otherwise I was quite healthy, just because I could neither sit nor stand, since the moment I tried to get up from the sofa I was seized by spasms! But these past three days or so I have been feeling much better. Besser took care of me. I clutch at every free moment to communicate with friends. How terrible I felt about not answering you! But it was not only you—there were others whom I did not answer who also have claims upon my heart.

So much for these vexatious incommodities, but I haven't yet said a word about troublesome family matters, about the innumerable difficulties connected with the affairs of my late brother and his family and of our defunct magazine. I have become nervous and irritable, and my character has deteriorated badly. I don't know where it will all lead to. During the entire winter I made no visits to anyone, didn't see anybody or anything. I went only once to the theater—to see the premiere of *Rogneda*. And things will go on like this until the novel is finished, that is, unless they send me away to debtors' prison.

Now—in reply to your letter. You write that I would be better off in government service. I doubt it. I am better off where I can get more money. My literary reputation is already such that I shall always be able to earn my bread (if it weren't for the debts). There will always be bread in my house, gingerbread, in fact, and of the sweetest kind, as was the case right up to last year.

And while we are on the subject, let me tell you about my present literary work, which will give you a good idea of how things stand. Finding myself in a most difficult situation while abroad, I wrote to Katkov offering him my work at my lowest rate—125 rubles per their printer's sheet, which corresponds to a rate of 150 rubles per sheet of *Contemporary*. They accepted. Later I found out that they had been only too happy to accept, because they had nothing in the way of fiction for this year: Turgenev is not writing at all, and they have quarreled with Lev Tolstoy. So I had come to their rescue. (I know all this from reliable sources.) But they were very cagey and crafty with me. The truth is that they are terrible skinflints. They felt the novel was rather bulky, and they were taken aback at the thought of having to pay for 25 (or maybe even 30) printer's sheets at 125 rubles a sheet. In brief, their whole policy is to lower the rate per sheet (and they have already approached me about it), while mine is to raise it. And so now we are engaged in a silent struggle. They obviously want me to come to Moscow. But I am biding my time, and here is what I am aiming at: With God's help, this novel may turn out to be something extraordinary. Before I go to Moscow, I want to see that at least three parts of it (i.e., one-half of the total) are published in order to make an impact on the public; then we'll see whether they will still want to reduce my fee. On the contrary, they may decide to increase it. By then it will be Holy Week. Besides, I am trying not to ask them for money in advance—I am being very austere and living like a pauper. I shall get what is coming to me in good time, and if I were to take money from them in advance, I should no longer feel morally free when the day for the final money settlement arrived. The first part of my novel was published around two weeks ago in the January issue of *Russian Messenger*. It is called *Crime and Punishment*. I have already heard many enthusiastic reactions. It contains new and daring ideas. What a shame I cannot send you a copy! Is it possible that no one where you are receives *Russian Messenger*?

Now listen: Suppose I manage to wind it up successfully, just as I should like to. You see, what I am hoping for is to sell the second edition to a book merchant and make another *two* or even *three* thousand. Why, I certainly wouldn't get that much in the government service, would I? And I'm sure that I can sell a second edition, because this has been the case for every one of my writings up to now. The trouble, however, is that I still may spoil my novel, and I have a foreboding that I shall. And if I'm sent away to debtors' prison, then I am sure I shall spoil it and I might not even finish it, and then the whole thing will blow up in my face.

But I have been gabbing too much about myself. Don't regard this as egotism. It is characteristic of anybody who spends too long sitting in silence in his corner. You write that you and all your family were sick in turns. That is distressing, for life abroad ought at least to have brought you the compensation of good health! Imagine the plight of you and your family if you had been spending this winter in Petersburg! It has been horrible here, and summer may meant the arrival of cholera, too. Please convey my sincere respects and my wishes for all possible happiness, starting wth good health, to your wife!

My good friend, you, at least, are happy in your family life, whereas destiny has refused me this great and *unique* human happiness. Yes, you have many obligations to your family. You wrote me of your father's offer and of your refusal to accept it. I have no right to give you advice on this subject, for the simple reason that I am unaware of *all* the facts. But you can take this advice that comes from a friend: Do not make a hasty decision, don't say your last word, and leave the final decision until the summer, when you come here in person. Such decisions affect one's whole life and may be the turning point in one's existence. Even if you decide this summer to remain in government service, still don't give your final answer and let things take care of themselves.

I expect to be in Petersburg in the summer, so we shall see each other. Then we shall be able to talk over many things. I am delighted, by the way, that you are so much interested in the Russian scene and in our intellectual and civic life. As a friend of yours, I am very pleased that you are, although I do not agree with you on everything. Your views on many things are rather unusual. I am wondering whether you get your information from foreign newspapers? They systematically distort everything that concerns Russia. But that is a vast problem. In my opinion, when one lives abroad one invariably comes under the influence of the foreign press. I have even experienced it myself. However, I have a feeling that we shall see eye to eye on many things, on very many, in fact.

The *News* is put out by two publisher-editors, *Skaryatin and Yumatov*. Farewell, my good friend, until we meet again. I hope that I shall have happier news to tell you in my next letter. Please God. For now,

All yours,

F. Dostoyevsky

Kiss your lovely children for me.

All those things of yours that I still have are safely stored in my dresser. My dear friend, I am in debt to you. Wait a little while, and I shall pay you back. For the time being, I am trying to save like a miser, but if you knew how much money I have been obliged to spend here!

I still don't know what I am going to do when I have finished my novel. The most important thing is that it will revive my literary reputation and may enable me to undertake something by the fall. I have a plan, but I must be sensible about it. Here is another piece of news: Subscriptions to all magazines and the sales of books are increasing sharply. I have this information from the booksellers and besides, I have my own facts.

---

61. *Rogneda* was an opera by Aleksandr Nikolayevich Serov (1820–1871). Judging from a letter written to Dostoyevsky by Strakhov in 1863, Dostoyevsky was on friendly terms with the composer.

Tolstoy's *War and Peace* had started running in the first two issues of *Russian Mes-*

senger in 1865. No more of it appeared for a year, and when the *Messenger* did resume publishing it, only relatively brief installments were printed. These events gave rise to a rumor that there had been a quarrel between the author and the magazine's editors.

Dostoyevsky eventually received 4,000 rubles from the *Messenger* for *Crime and Punishment.*

The *News* (Vest) was an ultrareactionary newspaper; it even disapproved of the emancipation of the serfs. It appeared from 1863 to 1870, except for an eight-month suspension resulting from its publication in January 1866 of the text of the Address of the Moscow Gentry to the Tsar.

62.   To M. N. KATKOV

Petersburg, April 25, 1866

Dear Sir, Mikhail Nikiforovich:

Thank you most kindly for your help in sending me the 1000 rubles. I am genuinely sorry for being so late in thanking you. I sent off *three chapters* to the editorial office of *R. Messenger* about a week ago. And I shall try not to be late with the next installment. It is very difficult for me to work here, because of my poor health and because of domestic circumstances. I shall, however, finish it in time. My trip abroad has been delayed because of the present situation, for I have been under police surveillance ever since my return from exile. On top of this, there is war in Europe. So I have no idea at all where I shall spend the summer.

You cannot imagine with what delight I am now reading the *Moscow Gazette*. Now everyone can see and understand that it has always been an independent newspaper, accepting no subsidies and subject to no pressure. It was most important that this should at last become general knowledge. That is fundamental. Please forgive this frankness on my part, but it is a fact that until now the public, or at least most of it, was convinced of the opposite. It is a good thing that everybody has now learned the truth. And what a contemptible role our subsidiers have taken upon themselves! Look at what they are defending! (Subsidiers * —that is a word I would like to put into circulation; it conveys, above all, the *permanence* of a trade, just as engraver and dancer indicate the permanence of a craft, a trade. Subsidier would imply the permanence of receiving subsidies, from anywhere and anyone.)

I shall say in all honesty that I always have been, and I believe always shall remain by conviction a true Slavophile, except for some very minor points of disagreement, and for that reason I could never fully subscribe to the *Moscow Gazette*'s position on various questions. I fully appreciate, much esteemed Mikhail Nikiforovich, that this will not frighten you unduly. But

---

*A word coined by Dostoyevsky; in Russian, *subsidery*—Eds.

the reason I am telling you this is that I wanted to convey to you firmly my sincere gratitude and utmost esteem for your honesty and for the excellent work you are doing, particularly at the present time. And in order to tell you that, I don't quite know why, but I felt that I first had to tell you about my own actual convictions. Perhaps this is all too naive, but why shouldn't we be naive at least once in our lives?

The reports from Petersburg in the *Moscow Gazette* are all true. But there are very many people here who believe that the whole business is the doing of the Nihilists alone, and that the root of the evil will not be found until it is flung up in the course of history, years later. I have heard people say that the *Moscow Gazette* tends to play down the role of nihilism; that the center and the root of the evil are of course not here but elsewhere; and that the nihilists, by themselves, are capable *of anything*. The doctrine that "everything should be shaken up par les quatre coins de la nappe, so that at least there may be a tabula rasa for action"—such a doctrine needs no roots. All nihilists are socialists. Socialism (especially in its Russian variety) specifically requires that all links should be cut. Why, they are absolutely convinced that, given a tabula rasa, they could at once build a paradise on it. Just as Fourier was sure that if he succeeded in building one phalanstery the whole world would soon be covered with phalansteries—those are his own words. And our own Chernyshevsky liked to say that if he were given a chance to speak to people for a quarter of an hour, he was sure he could persuade them, then and there, to turn to socialism. Our poor, defenseless Russian boys and girls have their own ever-present *fundamental* attitude, which will support socialism for some time to come, namely, their enthusiastic longing for the right and the purity of their hearts. There are plenty of crooks and scoundrels among them, but all these high school and university students, so many of whom I have seen, have given themselves over heart and soul to nihilism in the name of honor, truth, and true usefulness! The trouble is that they are helpless against these inanities and they accept them as an ideal. A healthy knowledge will, of course, eradicate all that, but when will that come about? How many victims will socialism devour before then? And finally, although this healthy knowledge will take root one day, it will be some time before it clears away the weeds, because such knowledge is still only knowledge and not a direct form of civic and social action. Meanwhile, the poor dear children are convinced that nihilism provides them with the most complete manifestation of civic and social duty and freedom.

Your information about the *reaction* is also very accurate. Everyone is apprehensive, and it is already clear that at the root of their fears lies intrigue. But do you know what some people say? They say that April 4 proved mathematically the mighty, extraordinary, sacred union of the Tsar with the people. Given such a union, there could be much greater trust in the people and in society on the part of certain high government officials. Nevertheless, it is now anticipated that there will be limitations on speech and thought, bureaucratic supervision. But how can we combat nihilism without freedom of speech? It might even be advantageous if even the nihilists were allowed to speak up freely: they would make all Russia laugh with the *explicit* presentation of their doctrine. As things stand now, however, they look like wise, mysterious, and enigmatic sphinxes, and that fascinates the innocents.

Some people even wonder whether the investigations should not be made public. After all, it is possible that not a single one of the bureaucrats is capable of talking to the nihilists. So if the investigations were public, our whole society would help and the people's enthusiasm would not be dampened, as it is now, by bureaucratic secrecy. In this clumsiness and timidity of the government, many see the attachment to old practices. And, as a result, they are mistrustful, and they begin to fear the reaction.

Please accept my assurances of complete respect.

Fyod. Dostoyevsky

Please forgive me for the blots in this letter. Do not take it as a lack of respect. I am unable to avoid them, even if I recopy.

---

62. The "domestic circumstances" probably refer to Dostoyevsky's efforts to pay his debts, about which he had written in several previous letters. The "situation" delaying his trip abroad was probably Dmitry Karakozov's attempt to assassinate Tsar Alexander II on April 4, 1866. War between Austria and Prussia did not break out until June 1866, but in April it already appeared to be unavoidable.

Dostoyevsky's words of praise for the *Moscow Gazette* probably relate to the position that the newspaper took at the beginning of 1866 toward the court party of Grand Duke Konstantin Nikolayevich, who was then chairman of the State Council and had a reputation as a "liberal." In an article on the recent uprising in Poland, the paper had written: "The real roots of the rebellion are not in Paris, Warsaw, or Vilno, but rather in Petersburg, in the action of those people who do not protest against those who are promoting the evil." In the eyes of the supporters of this view, the first among those who were "promoting the evil" was Konstantin Nikolayevich, who had been governor general of Poland and had advocated a conciliatory policy and, in the Committee on Peasant Reforms, had come out in favor of the abolition of serfdom as well as the introduction of public trials and limitations on corporal punishment. Following publication of several articles that were sharply critical of the government, the Minister of Internal Affairs ordered the *Gazette* closed for two months; however, the order was lifted earlier, after Katkov had been given an audience with Alexander II during a visit of the tsar to Moscow.

63.   To A. V. Korvin-Krukovskaya
Moscow, June 17, 1866

Much respected Anna Vasilevna,

Do not be angry with me for not having answered you all this time—I was in a quandary and did not know myself what I should be doing this summer. So if I did not answer your letter immediately, it was because I imagined I should be seeing you soon in person, on my way abroad. But now, although I have received permission to go, things have taken such a turn that it is no longer possible for me, at least now, to leave. There is one matter I must absolutely attend to in Moscow. In short, since I was unable to tell you anything definite and precise, I did not answer your letter.

I have been in Moscow for only four days or so, and I have no idea at all when I shall be free. The main trouble is that, besides finishing a novel (which I am thoroughly fed up with), I have so much work to do that I don't see how I can possibly wind up my affairs. And the things I have to attend to are important, because my whole future depends on them.

Imagine, by the way, what happened to me (a very amusing and typical incident). Last year I was in such dire straits that I was forced to sell the publication rights for an edition of all my previous writings—on a one-time basis—to a speculator named Stellovsky, a rather nasty man and a thoroughly incompetent publisher. Our contract has a clause in it which obliges me to deliver to him, by November 1, 1866 (at the latest), a novel of at least 12 printer's sheets, failing which, Stellovsky is entitled to publish, over a nine-year period, at no cost and at his discretion, anything I may write, without paying me any remuneration whatsoever. In brief, that clause is exactly like the clauses in Petersburg leases by which the landlord always demands, when leasing an apartment, that in case of fire in the tenant's apartment, the tenant must compensate him for all damage occasioned by the fire and, if necessary, build him a new house. People sign such contracts without taking them seriously, and that is exactly what I did. The 1st of November is only 4 months away. I tried to buy off Stellovsky with money, by paying a forfeit, but he refused. I pleaded with him for a three-month postponement, but he refused again and told me *to my face* that, since he is convinced that I no longer *have the time* to write a novel of 12 printer's sheets, the more so as I have thus far written only half, if that much, of the novel I owe to *Russian Messenger,* he feels that it would not be in his interest either to agree to be paid off or to extend the deadline because, the way things stand, whatever I write in the future will be his.

So I have decided to perform an unprecedented and eccentric feat: to write 30 printer's sheets of two different novels within 4 months. I shall work on one in the mornings, on the other in the evenings, and finish everything in time. And, would you believe it, my dear Anna Vasilevna, I have always been rather fond of eccentric and extraordinary things of this sort. I do not fit into the category of solid and [one word heavily crossed out] mortals. Forgive me—I have been bragging! But what else is there left for me besides bragging; the rest is really not much fun, after all. But how do you like that for literary enterprise? I am sure none of our writers, living or dead, has ever written under the conditions under which I write *constantly*. The very thought of it would kill Turgenev. But if you only knew how painful it is to spoil an idea that you have given birth to, that has aroused your enthusiasm, which you know to be good—and to be forced to spoil it, and to do so in full awareness!

You want to come to Pavlovsk. Let me know exactly when that will be. I should like very, very much to stay for a while at your place in Polibin. But do you think I could work there in the way I have to? That is the question. And then, would it be very considerate on my part to come to your place and work there day in and day out? Write me about everything. Please do not abandon me. My regards to your family. Good-bye.

> Your sincerely devoted,
> Fyodor Dostoyevsky

If you are going to answer me *right away*, here is my address: *Moscow*, Fyodor Mikh. Dostoyevsky, care of Aleksandr Pavlovich Ivanov, the Konstantinovsky Surveyors' Institute, Staraya Basmannaya Street, near the Church of Nikita the Martyr.

Please forgive my untidy corrections in this letter and do not take them as a lack of consideration.

---

63. Anna Vasilevna Korvin-Krukovskaya (1847–1887) was a writer and a political and social activist. Two of her stories had been published in *Epoch*; after accepting the first one, Dostoyevsky wrote her a letter lavishly praising the qualities of her writing. Her younger sister, the eminent mathematician Sonya Kovalevsky, has asserted that Dostoyevsky was in love with Anna for a while.

The two novels that Dostoyevsky was to work on simultaneously were *The Gambler* and (the continuation of) *Crime and Punishment*.

64. To N. A. LYUBIMOV
[Lyublino] Friday, [July] 8 [1866]

I am one day late, much respected Nikolai Alekseyevich, but as compensation I have reworked it and I hope that this time it will be *satisfactory*.

Good and *Evil* are clearly delimited, and it will be quite impossible to confuse them now or to misinterpret the meaning. I have also made the corrections you suggested—all of them—and a few others for good measure. I shall go even further and thank you for having given me the opportunity of revising my manuscript before sending it to the printers. I can tell you unreservedly that I myself would not have allowed it to go without making some revisions.

And now I have a *tremendous* favor to ask of you: *For the sake of Christ,* leave all the rest just as it is. I have done everything you suggested—everything is separated, delimited, and clear. The *Reading of the Gospel* has been presented in a different light. In a word, allow me to place implicit trust in your solicitude for my poor little novel, my kind Nikolai Alekseyevich!

The 4th chapter I shall send you in the very near future, but not before *Wednesday*. Perhaps I shall be able to let you have it on Tuesday. In general, I'll try not to lose any time.

Your fully devoted,
F. Dostoyevsky

---

64. Lyublino was a small village about five miles from Moscow. The Ivanov family had rented a house there for the summer, and Dostoyevsky had decided to do the same.

Nikolai Alekseyevich Lyubimov (1830–1897) was a physicist who became managing editor of *Russian Messenger* in 1863, when Katkov had begun devoting much of his time to the editing of the *Moscow Gazette*. He was the author of *M. N. Katkov and His Historical Merit* (M. N. Katkov i yego istoricheskaya zasluga, 1889).

The "Reading of the Gospel" is the scene in *Crime and Punishment* in which Raskolnikov and Sonya read about the resurrection of Lazarus (Part IV, Chapter 4, in the book form). Despite Dostoyevsky's plea, Katkov made a number of changes in this and other chapters after Dostoyevsky had made his revisions. Subsequently, though, Dostoyevsky wrote to Katkov: "I do not regret *all* the deletions. . . . Some of them actually improve the passage. I have been painfully aware for twenty years now of a fault in my writing—long-windedness—but I am quite unable to rid myself of it."

65.   To N. A. Lyubimov
Petersburg, November 2, 1866

Dear Sir, Nikolai Alekseyevich,

On October 31 I finished, and yesterday handed over, the 10-sheet novel I had contracted to deliver to Stellovsky (I told you about it and also Mikhail Nikiforovich [Katkov] when I asked him for a month's grace). I started and finished work on these 10 printer's sheets in one month. I am now getting down to work on the ending of *Crime and Punishment*. I shall work unwearyingly, with the *firm* determination to finish it by the 20th of December and to make it at least as good as what has already been published.

I could, of course, start—although no earlier than November 15—sending you my novel piecemeal, chapter by chapter, so that the forthcoming issue, no. 10, of R[ussian] M[essenger] could come out with several of them; and that I am able to guarantee. But I wonder, much respected Nikolai Alekseyevich, whether it would not be better if the entire 3rd part of the novel were to come out in 2 issues, nos. 11 and 12—that is, only in the event it is feasible not to run any of it in no. 10 (informing your readers at the same time that in the next 2 issues, i.e., in the current year, they will definitely be given the concluding chapters of *Crime and Punishment*).

If this could be done, I feel that the ending of the novel would produce a much stronger effect. And that is the way I would very much like it to be handled myself.

However, *I shall abide entirely by the decision of the editors,* and so I beg you most earnestly, much esteemed Nikolai Alekseyevich, to inform me of the decision of the editors. As for me, I won't waste a single moment and shall be ready for whatever decision is made.

And one more most urgent request. At the present time I have completely run out of money. ¾ of the money I received from the editors had to be turned over to my creditors, who, by the way, continue to badger me nevertheless. So I have nothing to live on. Please explain my situation to Mikhail Nikiforovich and convey to him my special and urgent request for him to help me out once again if possible. I require 500 (five hundred) rubles now. According to my calculations, I now owe the editors 600 (six hundred). You may be sure—and please tell this to Mikhail Nikiforovich—that only after having failed to arrive at any other solution and finding myself down to my last ruble did I make up my mind to bother him once again. As God is my witness, this was not an easy decision for me to take, particularly in view of the fact that, on several occasions already, I have taken advantage of the generosity of the editors.

Aleksandr Fyodorovich Bazunov, to whom I happened to reveal my intention of writing to you, [said] that he would be happy to lay out one-half of that sum (i.e., up to 250 rubles), upon receipt of a money order from the editors.

Please accept my assurances of sincere respect.

Your humble servant,
Fyodor Dostoyevsky

P.S. I have hired a stenographer now and, even though I read over and revise whatever I dictate three times, stenography practically doubles the speed of my work. This was the only way I could finish writing the 10 printer's sheets for Stellovsky in *one* month—I could not have written even five otherwise.

D.

---

65. The novel of ten sheets was *The Gambler,* which was published as a separate volume by Stellovsky in 1866.

Lyubimov did send Dostoyevsky the 500 rubles he asks for (see next letter).

Aleksandr Fyodorovich Bazunov was a prominent publisher and book dealer; he served as publishing agent for the Academy of Sciences, the Ministry of Justice, and the Ministry of Finance.

The stenographer whom Dostoyevsky had hired was Anna Grigorevna Snitkina, a student at a stenography school in Petersburg who had been recommended by Milyukov when he learned of Dostoyevsky's plight in trying to meet the terms of the contract with Stellovsky. She began working for him early in October 1866. One month later, he declared his love to her, and they were married on February 15, 1867. For further information, see the biographical sketch.

66. To N. A. Lyubimov
Petersburg, November 8, 1866

Kind Sir, Nikolai Alekseyevich,

I have received two money orders for a total of 500 rubles from the editors of *Russian Messenger,* for which I wish to express my special appreciation.

About four days ago I received a query from the editors as to when I would send in the novel. But the answer to this query, much esteemed Nikolai Alekseyevich, was already contained in my letter to you. It is rather I who am waiting with great interest for your answer, because it is of great importance to me as the author of the novel.

I wrote you that I could start sending you the 3rd part of Cr[ime] *and* Pun[ishment] even this month, although not before the 15th, if the editors felt that it was absolutely necessary. But in that case I could give you only a few chapters, not exceeding 2½ or 3 printer's sheets. *If you tell me to send it, I shall send it.*

But I inquired whether it would not be possible to do as follows: to announce in the October number that the publication of *Cr. and Pun.* would be completed this year without fail, and then print the final installments in the November and December issues. My *only* reason for asking you this is that, if this were done, the impression produced on the public by the novel would be much stronger and more complete, incomparably so. Please forgive an author's vanity and don't laugh at it, because it is quite an excusable feeling. Possibly it will produce no effect whatever, but still, as I labor over the novel now, it is quite forgivable (I even feel that it is essential) for me to count on a success. Otherwise, in my opinion, an author should not even have the temerity to take pen in hand. In short, I should like to finish the novel in order to revive the impact, so that people will talk as much of the novel as a whole as they did when it first came out.

On the other hand, however, I have no wish to place the editors under any constraint. And consequently I await your decision, and I shall comply with whatever you say. In the meantime, I am working nonstop. In order to save myself from disaster, I wrote, in less than a month's time, a 10-sheet novel for the publisher Stellovsky (with the assistance of stenography). But there is work and work.

In anticipation of your reply, I remain, with sincere respect and devotion,
Your humble servant,
Fyodor Dostoyevsky

---

66. *Crime and Punishment* did indeed make the impact that Dostoyevsky had hoped for. Strakhov later recalled: "They were reading nothing else but it; it's the only thing that lovers of reading were talking about, and in talking about it they usually complained of the oppressive strength of the novel, of the painful impression it made, rendering even those with strong nerves almost ill and forcing those whose nerves were weak to give up reading it." Moreover, as soon as it had finished running in *Russian Messenger,* both Bazunov and Stellovsky bought the rights to it, the former publishing it as a separate volume in 1867 and the latter doing the same in 1870.

67.   To A. G. Snitkina
Petersburg, December 9, 1866

My dear Anya, my lovely name-day celebrant,

In the name of God, do not be angry with me for being so stupidly over-cautious. I have decided not to come to see you today, as I still do not feel quite well. It is nothing at all—just a certain weakness and a slightly coated tongue. You see, my angel, I absolutely had to be at Bazunov's. But then Bazunov is only one verst away from me, whereas you are four times farther. Isn't it better to be a bit too careful, perhaps, and be sure to be completely recovered tomorrow, than to go on being sick for yet another week? Actually, I shouldn't have gone to Bazunov's, either. Yesterday I sat up until two in the morning revising chapter 5 (and couldn't sleep at all after dinner—they kept bothering me and gave me no peace). That finished me. I didn't get to sleep until four in the morning. And today I feel sort of sluggish and my face is not fit for a name-day celebration, so that I suppose I'd better sit it out at home. I shall have just soup for dinner, the same as yesterday.

Please don't be angry with me, my winsome one, for writing you about such inanities, for I myself am rather inane today. But, for God's sake, don't worry. The most important thing for me today is to be able to sleep. I feel that sleep will strengthen me. And you, do come by in the morning as you promised. Good-bye, then, dear friend, I embrace you and congratulate you.

Infinitely loving and infinitely believing in you,
All yours,
F. Dostoyevsky

You are my whole future—hope and faith and joy and bliss—everything.

---

67. This is Dostoyevsky's first known letter to Anna Grigorevna; 163 more came later, most of them strewn with extravagant expressions of adoration. Concerning this letter, Anna Grigorevna later wrote that Dostoyevsky had sent his stepson Pavel

to the name-day celebration in his place, to give her both the letter and a gold bracelet.

68.   To A. G. Snitkina
Moscow, December 29, 1866

Don't be angry with me, my priceless and everlasting friend, Anya, for writing just a few lines this time just to say hello to you, to kiss you, and simply to let you know that I have arrived in Moscow and have not done a thing since my arrival here, for I haven't poked my nose outside yet. The trip was all right. The sleeping cars are a monstrosity—outrageously damp, cold, and stuffy. The whole day and all night until dawn I suffered from a toothache (a very bad one); I either sat very still or lay down, constantly calling to mind the memories of the past 1½ months. I went soundly to sleep toward morning, and when I woke up the pain had subsided. I came into Moscow at 12, and at half-past twelve I was already with the family. They were all very pleased and surprised to see me. Yelena Pavlovna was there. She has grown very thin and even her looks have deteriorated. She seemed very sad; she paid only casual attention to me. After dinner my toothache came back. Sonya and I were left alone for half an hour. I told Sonya everything. She was terribly pleased. She approves fully, and denies that the kinds of obstacles suggested by Yunge exist. Of course, I didn't go into any great detail. There are still many things that we shall have to talk over together. She shakes her head and is somewhat doubtful about my succeeding with Katkov. What really troubles her is that such a thing should hang so precariously on such a thin thread. I asked her whether, during my absence, Yelena Pavlovna had spoken of me, and she said, "My goodness, yes, all the time." But I don't think that it could really be described as love. In the evening I learned from my sister and from Yelena Pavlovna herself that she had been miserable all the time. Her husband is a horrible man; she is better to him. He won't allow her out of his sight. He is irascible, torments her day and night, and is jealous. From everything I have heard I conclude that she never had time to think of love. (This is absolutely true.) I am very pleased, and as far as I'm concerned the matter is closed. As for our marriage, I shall announce it to my relatives the moment I have some encouraging news from Katkov.

Throughout my first day here, i.e., yesterday, my teeth ached continuously. During the night my cheek swelled up and, because of that, they don't hurt today. I shall go to see Lyubimov today, but I don't intend to see Katkov. And, in general, I still have no set plan of action as yet—I shall see how things turn out. I shall try as hard as I can to wind things up quickly so that I can be back with you as soon as possible. I won't stay here a moment longer than I can help. I often feel very depressed. It is a sort of abstract depression, as if I had committed a crime against someone. I keep thinking of you, and every minute I see you in my mind's eye. No, Anya, I love you intensely, and

Sonya also loves you; she would so much have liked to see you. She is very touched and concerned.

And now I embrace you hard and kiss you until my next letter and our reunion. I shall write you a fuller and better letter in two or three days, as soon as I get something accomplished. But now I am in a great hurry—I have a feeling that I am going to miss everyone (what a disaster that would be!). What can I do—everyone is on holiday and off his regular time schedule.

How did you spend the day yesterday? I hoped I would see you in my dreams—but I didn't. I opened a book to read your fortune, i.e., I opened it and read the first line on the right-hand page—it came out quite amusingly and rather to the point. Farewell, darling, see you soon. I kiss your sweet little hand and your lips (of which I keep thinking a great deal) a thousand times. I feel sad and preoccupied; all my impressions seem to be fragmented. Masenka is adorable—she is still a child. Fedya also appeared. All the other children were terribly nice and pleased to see me. Yulya did not deign to come out. But in the evening she sent from her room to ask me whether she might tell my fortune. Several of her friends were assembled there and were telling fortunes by the mirror. I replied that I should be delighted. Mine came out as a brunette wearing a white dress. I sent to tell them that it was rubbish, that they had not guessed right.

Will you not be seeing Pasha, darling? Give him my regards and tell him that Sashenka and Khmyrov asked me a great many things about him and that they were awfully sorry he had not come and would not be coming; they were very much hoping to see him and even consulted the cards to see whether he was coming or not.

I kiss you countless times. I wish you a happy New Year and *new happiness*. Pray for our venture, my angel. Now that matters are coming to a head, I find I am scared. But I shall work at it with all my strength. I'll write you in two or three days. I haven't lost heart, however.

I am completely, unalterably, totally yours. I have faith in you, and you are my whole hope for the future. You know, one appreciates one's happiness more at a distance. And now I feel the need to hold you in my arms incomparably more strongly than I ever have before. Give my deepest respects to Mama and give my regards to your brother, too.

With boundless love, yours,

F. Dostoyevsky

P. S. Sonechka is urging me and insists on my going to the post office in person, because if this letter is mailed from there, it may still leave today.

---

68. Dostoyevsky had gone to Moscow to see the editors of *Russian Messenger* to ask them for an advance on his next novel; he needed the money for his wedding and

for a trip abroad that he and his bride were planning to take, both for the sake of escaping his creditors and in the hope of finding relief from his epileptic attacks. Katkov did give him 1,000 rubles immediately and promised another 1,000 in two months.

While in Moscow, Dostoyevsky visited the Ivanovs. Yelena Pavlovna was the sister-in-law of Vera Mikhailovna (Dostoyevskaya) Ivanova. Anna Grigorevna gave the following explanation of Dostoyevsky's remarks about her in this letter:

> It had been an old wish of Vera Mikhailovna's that Dostoyevsky should marry Yelena Pavlovna as soon as her husband, who had been sick and on the verge of death for many years, had died. F.M. seemed to be receptive to his sister's suggestions. During the summer of 1866, when he was living in Lyublino . . . near the Ivanovs' summer house, where he frequently saw Yelena Pavlovna, he once asked her whether she would marry him if she were free. As she gave no definite reply, F.M. did not consider himself bound by any promise. However, he was oppressed by the thought that he might have given her some hope that could now never be realized.

A few days later, however, Dostoyevsky wrote Anna Grigorevna that Yelena Pavlovna had taken the news of his forthcoming marriage "rather well," and Anna Grigorevna has written that she "remained on the most friendly terms with F.M., me, and my children until the end of her life."

The other family members mentioned in this letter are:

Sonya (Sonechka)—Sofya Aleksandrovna, Vera's oldest daughter.

Masenka—Mariya Aleksandrovna, Vera's second daughter, whom Anna Grigorevna described as "an excellent musician, a pupil of Nikolai Rubinstein. When [Dostoyevsky] stayed with the Ivanovs . . . he always asked M.A. to play his favorite pieces for him, especially Mendelssohn-Bartholdi's 'Wedding March.' . . ."

Fedya—Fyodor Mikhailovich, a son of Mikhail Dostoyevsky.

Yulya—Vera's third daughter.

Sashenka—Aleksandr Aleksandrovich, Vera's oldest son.

Concerning "Yunge," Anna Grigorevna described him as "a famous oculist with whom F.M. was on very friendly terms. When F.M. told him about his forthcoming marriage, and he heard that the difference in age between him and his future wife was twenty-five years (I had just celebrated my twentieth birthday and F.M. was forty-five), Yunge tried to dissuade him from marrying me, arguing that, with such a difference in age, there could be no happiness in married life."

The brother whom Dostoyevsky mentions was Ivan Grigorevich Snitkin (1849–1887).

PART III

1867–1871

DOSTOYEVSKY'S

life took a new turn with his marriage to Anna Grigorevna Snitkina in February 1867. Two months after the wedding, Dostoyevsky and his new wife left for western Europe, primarily to escape harassment by his creditors.

The following years, which saw the composition of two of his great novels—*The Idiot* and *The Devils*—were also among the most disorderly and frustrating of his entire life. Dostoyevsky's second marriage was a happy one; his wife admired her husband and, though sorely tried, she did her best to adapt to his idiosyncrasies. But life abroad increased his moodiness and irritability, his epilepsy worsened, and he was haunted by the fear that absence from Russia would deprive him of the atmosphere needed for his work. Obsessed by the desire to return, he repeatedly left his young wife behind in one European city or another while he visited gambling casinos in an effort to win enough money to pay off his debts; but he always failed and was then forced to write abject, pleading, and remorseful letters to his wife for aid. Whenever some funds did become available, however, he shared them, despite his acute poverty, with the family of his older brother and his scapegrace stepson Pasha.

Dostoyevsky's exasperation at being forced to live in Europe spilled over into venomous rancor against Western influences and their advocates in Russian culture, who, he had now come to believe, had exercised so harmful an effect on Russian society. He began to compose an article on Belinsky, which has since been lost; but his letters contain scurrilous remarks about the critic he had once so fervently praised. Turgenev's most recent novel, *Smoke* (1867), which contained some withering criticisms of Russia as compared with Europe, led to a bitter quarrel between the two men when Dostoyevsky, who had not yet returned a loan obtained from Turgenev two years earlier, paid him a courtesy call in Baden. Later in the same year, while living in Geneva, Dostoyevsky attended a session of the congress organized by the left-wing League of Peace and Freedom and heard Bakunin as one of the keynote speakers. During this time Dostoyevsky was working on the first drafts of *The Idiot*, in which he wished to depict a moral ideal more sublime than the one proffered by the Russian radicals.

In February 1868 Anna Grigorevna gave birth to a daughter, whom they named Sonya, but the baby died three months later and was buried in Geneva. Dostoyevsky was then living on advances from the *Russian Messenger*, to whose publisher he had promised a novel; and despite his prostration he was obliged to continue sending installments of *The Idiot* to the journal. In September of that year, the Dostoyevskys left Switzerland and moved to Florence, where they remained for eight months and where *The*

243

Idiot was finally completed. This work did not have the same sensational success as *Crime and Punishment;* and Dostoyevsky, who had hoped to obtain enough money from the sale of the book rights to allow him to return to Russia, received no immediate offers for its republication. Meanwhile, he had sketched in a letter to Apollon Maikov the plan for a novel called *Atheism,* which would involve the central character's quest for faith among all shades of Russian opinion and culminate in the discovery of "Christ and the Russian soil, the Russian Christ and the Russian God."

In July 1869 the Dostoyevskys left Florence for Dresden, and in September Anna Grigorevna gave birth to another daughter, Lyubov. Several months later Dostoyevsky read about the murder of a student in the Petrovsky Academy in Moscow by a radical group called the Society for People's Justice, whose leader and organizer was Sergei Nechayev. This incident became the nucleus for his next novel, *The Devils,* originally conceived as a "pamphlet" that would be written very quickly and allow him to express all his revulsion against radicalism. He intended to reserve his major energies for another book, which had grown out of the idea for *Atheism* and which was to consist of five long stories to be entitled *The Life of a Great Sinner.* This projected work was never written as such, but elements of its plan, preserved in Dostoyevsky's notebooks, entered into his last three major novels—*The Devils, A Raw Youth,* and *The Brothers Karamazov.* A novella, *The Eternal Husband,* was published at the beginning of 1870. Dostoyevsky continued to work on *The Devils,* and material from *The Life of a Great Sinner* soon appeared in the drafts; the character of the work accordingly changed from that of a tendentious pamphlet to that of a novel incorporating some of Dostoyevsky's deepest themes.

When the Franco-Prussian War broke out in July 1870, the Dostoyevskys, living in Dresden, could observe the patriotic fervor of the German populace. The first chapters of *The Devils* were sent to the *Russian Messenger* in October 1870, though the novel did not begin to appear until more than a year later. The establishment of the Paris Commune in the spring of 1871, and the burning of the city that ensued, horrified and fascinated Dostoyevsky, who saw in such destruction the ultimate consequences of revolutionary radicalism. In July the Nechayev conspirators were unprecedentedly placed on public trial (political crimes in Russia were usually tried in secret), and Dostoyevsky used the full newspaper accounts for the second and third parts of his novel.

By the summer of 1871, Dostoyevsky had made up his mind that, whatever the legal risks involved in returning home, it was impossible for him any longer to remain abroad. At the beginning of July, he burned the manuscripts of *The Idiot, The Eternal Husband,* and early versions of *The Devils* in preparation for crossing the border. Fortunately, Anna Grigorevna succeeded in saving his working notebooks from the flames. On July 8, 1871, Dostoyevsky returned to Petersburg after his four-year expatriation.

69.   To A. G. Dostoyevskaya

Hombourg, * Wednesday, May 22, 1867

10 A.M.

Hello, my sweet angel!

I got your letter yesterday and it made me madly happy, although it horrified me at the same time. What is the matter with you, Anya, what is this state you are in? You keep crying, you cannot sleep, and you feel miserable. How do you think I felt when I read that? And that was after only five days, so what must it be like now? My darling, my irreplaceable angel, my treasure, understand that I am not reproaching you—on the contrary, you are all the more dear to me and the more precious to feel that way. I realize that there is nothing to be done if you are really unable to bear being without me and are so worried about me (I repeat that I am not reproaching you, that I love you—if such were possible—twice as much for it, and I know how to value it); but at the same time, my darling girl, you will agree that it was sheer folly on my part and inconsiderate of me to leave you to come here. Judge for yourself, my dear: First of all, my own misery at being away from you itself played a great part in preventing me from finishing successfully with this cursed gambling and leaving this town to come and join you, because my mind was not free; and, in the second place, how painful it was for me, knowing the state you were in, to stay on here!

Forgive me, my angel, but I must go into some of the intricacies of my venture, of the game, so that you will see more clearly what it is all about. Already on twenty or so occasions I have observed as I approached the gaming table that if one plays coolly, calmly and with calculation, *it is quite impossible to lose!* I swear—it is an absolute impossibility! It is blind chance pitted against my calculation; hence, I have an advantage over it. But what usually happened? As a rule, I would start with *forty gulden,* I would take them out of my pocket, sit down, and stake one or two gulden at a time. Within a quarter of an hour, I would usually (*always*) double my money. This was the moment to have stopped and left, at least until the evening, so as to calm one's excited nerves (furthermore I have made the observation— and thoroughly substantiated it—that I can never maintain my coolness and detachment in gambling *for longer than half an hour at a time*). But if I left the table it was only to go out for a smoke and then rush back to the game.

---

*Here in the heading, Dostoyevsky writes "Hombourg" in Latin letters, using the French spelling, but in the body of the letter he transliterates the city's name into Cyrillic letters (Gomburg).—Eds.

Why did I do it, knowing almost for sure that I wouldn't be able to restrain myself, i.e., that I would lose? It was because I told myself, on getting up in the morning, that this would be my last day in Homburg, that I would be leaving on the morrow, and that therefore I couldn't waste any time in getting to the roulette table. I pressed myself hard to win as much as I could in a single day (since I was to leave the next day), and I lost my composure, became tense, started to take chances, became exasperated, laid my bets haphazardly because my system had broken down then—and lost (because anyone who plays without a system, relying upon sheer chance, is a madman). The whole mistake was for us to have parted and that I didn't bring you along with me. Yes, yes, that's what it is. So here I am, missing you badly, while you are almost dying without me. My angel, I repeat—I am not reproaching you for anything and you are even dearer to me for being so miserable without me. But judge for yourself, my sweet, by what happened to me yesterday, for instance.

After mailing my letter in which I asked you to send me money, I went to the casino. I had only *twenty* gulden left in my pocket (that I had kept for an emergency), and I risked *ten* gulden. I made an almost superhuman effort to stay calm for *a whole hour* and to play systematically, and ended up winning *thirty* gold fredericks, i.e., 300 gulden. I was so elated and felt such a terrible and *maddening* urge to finish with it all *that very day,* to win at least as much again, and leave this town right away that, without giving myself a chance to draw breath and recover my senses, I rushed back to the roulette table, started laying stakes in gold—and I lost *everything, the whole lot,* down to the last kopek; or to be more exact, I was left with *two* gulden for tobacco.

Anya, my darling, my joy! Try to understand that I have debts that I must pay and that people will say that I am a scoundrel. Try to understand that I shall have to write to Katkov and then sit around in Dresden and wait. I simply had to win. It was *essential!* I am not gambling for my amusement. Why, that was my only way out—and now everything is lost because of a miscalculation. I am not blaming you, but I'm cursing myself for not having brought you along with me. If you gamble in small doses every day, it is *impossible* not to win. That is true, absolutely true, and experience has proved it to me twenty times over. And it is with this knowledge that I am leaving Homburg as a loser; and I also know that if I could give myself just four more days, in those four days I surely could win everything back. But I most certainly won't go and gamble now!

My sweet Anya, please understand (I implore you once more) that it is not you, not you, whom I'm blaming. On the contrary, I blame myself for not having brought you along.

N.B. N.B. In case yesterday's letter should somehow get lost I shall sum up here what it contained. I asked you to send me *forthwith* twenty imperials through a banker, i.e., to go to a banker and tell him that you wish to send 20 pieces of gold to such and such an address in Homburg (be precise about the address), poste restante, to so and so, and the banker would take care of the rest. I asked you to be as quick about it as possible so that the money would go off that same day. (The money order they gave you at the banker's would have to be enclosed in a letter and sent to me registered.) If you hurried, all this would not take you more than a hour, so that the letter could leave the same day.

If you manage to send it off the same day, i.e., *today* (Wednesday) I shall get it tomorrow, Thursday. If you send it off Thursday I shall get it Friday. If I get it Thursday I shall be in Dresden *Saturday,* and if I get it Friday, I shall be there on *Sunday.* That is certain. Yes, *certain.* And if I succeed in winding up all my business, I may even return home the next day instead of *the day after next.* But it is unlikely that I can settle everything on the same day and be ready to leave (I must get the draft cashed, get ready, pack, and get to Frankfurt in time to catch the Schnell-Zug). And although I shall try as hard as I can to be there the following day, it is more likely that I shall be back only the day after.

Good-bye, Anya, good-bye, my precious angel, I am terribly worried about you, but you have absolutely no need to worry about me. My health is *excellent.* That nervous disorder that you fear in me is only physical and mechanical! It is not a mental perturbation, that is for sure. It is something that my nature demands, it is how I am made. I am nervous and I could never be calm even without all this! Besides, the air is wonderful here. I *couldn't be* healthier, but I am really suffering for you. I love you and that is why I am suffering.

I hug you hard and kiss you countless times,

Yours,
F. D.

---

69. Two months after they were married, Dostoyevsky and Anna Grigorevna left Russia. They arrived in Dresden about the middle of April, and a month after that Dostoyevsky left his new wife there and traveled to Bad Homburg to try his luck in the gambling casino. From there, he wrote to Anna Grigorevna daily, each letter, like this one (the sixth), filled with expressions of love and yearning for her and recriminations toward himself for having left her alone and for having lost his money at roulette, and yet repeating the hope that, somehow, he would eventually end up winning. Through it all, his wife showed considerable forbearance. She wrote in her diary during this period: "What can I do? Apparently he just has to [gamble]. The best thing will be if that unhappy notion about winning gets knocked out of his head."

70. To A. N. Maikov
Geneva, August 16/28, 1867

What a long time I have kept silent and left unanswered your kind letter, my dear and unforgettable friend, Apollon Nikolayevich. I call you *unforgettable friend,* and I feel in my heart that I am right to call you that: you and I are such *old* friends, we are so *used to* each other, that life, which has separated us and even sometimes *led us into different ways,* has not only not parted us, but may, in fact, have even finally bound us closer together. If you write that you have felt my absence a bit, then how much more have I felt yours. Besides my conviction, which is confirmed daily, that our thoughts and feelings are similar and closely allied, you must also bear in mind that I, besides having lost you, also find myself in a foreign land where there are not only no Russian faces, Russian books, Russian thoughts and concerns, but even no friendly faces at all! Really, I cannot understand how an expatriate Russian with any feelings and sense can fail to notice this and be hurt by it. Perhaps these faces are congenial to one another, but we feel they are not congenial to us. *That's the truth!* And how can anyone live his life abroad? Without a homeland there is suffering, believe me! It may be all right to go away for half a year or even a year. But to leave the way I did, with no idea of when I would be back—that is very bad and hard. The mere thought is painful. And I need Russia. I need her for my *writing,* for my work (not to mention the rest of my life), oh, how badly I need her! I am like a fish out of water, stripped of strength and resources. In general, we shall talk about that. I must talk to you about many things and ask for your advice and your help. You are *the only one* I have whom I can talk to from here. NB: By the way, you must read this letter on the quiet and not talk about me to anyone to whom it is no concern. You'll see for yourself. One more thing: why haven't I written you all this time? I do not have the strength to give you a full answer to that. I felt my situation was too unstable and had been waiting to get a little bit settled down, at least, before beginning to correspond with you. You are my one and only hope. Write more often, don't let me down, my dear friend! And from now on, I shall write you very often and very regularly. Let us be in constant touch with one another, for God's sake! That will take the place of Russia for me and give me strength.

Now let me tell you, tant bien que mal, about these four months, withholding nothing from you.

You know how I left and for what reasons. There were two main reasons: 1) to save not only my health, but my very life. My fits had already begun to recur every week, and to feel and to be so acutely *aware* of this nervous and *brain* disorder was unbearable. My mind was actually beginning to be affected—that is the truth. I was conscious of it, and my nervous disorder drove me sometimes to moments of madness. The 2nd reason was the circumstances in which I found myself: My creditors wouldn't wait any longer and, by the time I was leaving, Latkin and then Pechatkin had already started proceeding against me, and I just escaped arrest. I must say, though (and this is not just a pretty phrase or empty words), that to be in *debtors' prison* would have been very useful to me from one point of view: Reality, material, a second *House of the Dead*, in brief, there could have been at least 4 or 5 thousand rubles' worth of material there. Only I had just gotten married and, besides, would I have pulled through a stifling summer in the Tarasov establishment? This posed an insoluble problem. If I were unable to write at Tarasov's, as my fits grew worse and worse, how would I manage to pay off my debts? And the burden had grown to awful proportions. So I left, but I left with death in my heart. I did not believe in living abroad, i.e., I believed that the moral effect of living abroad would be very bad: alone, *away from my material,* with a young creature who with naive joy eagerly looked forward to sharing my nomadic life; but I could see that in this naive joy there was much inexperience and youthful impulsiveness, and that worried and tormented me a great deal. I was afraid that Anna Grigorevna would find it wearisome if we were left alone to ourselves, and as a matter of fact we have been *alone,* the two of us, until now. I felt unsure of myself—I am morbid by nature, and I anticipated that she would tire of me. (N.B. It is true that Anna Grigorevna has proven to be a stronger and deeper person than I had known and thought her to be, and in many instances she has simply been my guardian angel; but at the same time there is much of the child and the twenty-year-old in her and that is good and natural and *inevitable,* but I hardly possess the strength or ability to respond to it. All this flashed through my mind as I was leaving, and although, let me repeat, Anna Grigorevna has turned out to be better and stronger than I had expected, nevertheless I am still worried.) Finally, I was worried about our meager financial means: we left with very limited funds, although I had taken *an advance* of *three* (!) thousand from Katkov. To be sure, I had reckoned on beginning work just as soon as I got abroad. But how did things actually turn out? To this day I have done nothing or next to nothing and am only just beginning to get down to working really seriously. It is true that when I say that I have done *nothing* as yet I am not quite sure about that, because I have felt many things deeply and have *plotted some of it out;* but I have still set little of it down in *black and white,* and the *black and white* is what matters in the end, because that is the only thing they pay you for.

As soon as I could get out of boring Berlin (where I spent one day, during which those boring Germans succeeded in setting my nerves on edge to the breaking point, and where I went to the Russian baths), we went on to Dresden, where we rented an apartment and settled down for a while.

I experienced a very strange impression—I at once began wondering what I was doing in Dresden, why it *had to be* Dresden and not some other place, and why I had had to throw up everything in one place and move to another. The answer was obvious (health, debts, etc.). But the bad thing about it was that I realized only too clearly that now it made no difference to me where I was, in Dresden or anywhere else in a foreign country, where I would still be a slice lopped off the whole. I wanted to get down to work right away, but I felt positively that I could not work, my heart was just not up to it. And so what did I do? I vegetated. I read, I wrote a little something. I was overcome by nostalgia and then later by the heat. The days passed monotonously by. Anya and I went out regularly for a walk after dinner in the Great Garden, listened to the vulgar music, then read, and went to bed. There turns out to be a definite streak of the antiquarian in Anna Grigorevna (and I find this very sweet and amusing). Thus, for her it is a whole business to go and visit some stupid town hall, involving taking notes and describing it (she does this in her shorthand squiggles and has filled 7 books); but most of all she is interested and impressed by the picture gallery, and I am very pleased about this because it means she has been stirred by too many impressions to be bored. She would go to a gallery every day. She and I talked and gossiped a great deal about all our friends in Petersburg and in Moscow, about you and about Anna Ivanovna, and this made us feel somewhat sad.

I won't describe my thoughts. Many impressions had accumulated. I read the Russian newspapers, and they were balm to my soul. In the end I felt that I had accumulated enough material for a whole article on Russia's attitude toward Europe and on the upper stratum of Russian society. But why talk about it! The Germans got on my nerves and so did the way of life of our Russian upper class, with its faith in Europe *and civilization*. I was terribly shaken by what happened in Paris. A fine lot, too, those Paris lawyers shouting vive la Pologne! Bah, how disgusting it all is, but, above all, how stupid and unimaginative! I have become still more confirmed in my old belief that it is even, in a way, to our advantage that Europe does not really know us and views us with such contempt. And the details of the trial of that little shitter Berezowski! So much nauseating red tape but, worst of all, how they still blabber away and still revolve round and round the very same spot!

Russia, too, as seen from here by us, stands out in deeper relief. There is, on the one hand, the extraordinary fact of the solidity and unexpected maturity of the Russian people in welcoming all our reforms (to mention only judiciary reforms) and, on the other, the news about the flogging by the district police inspector in Orenburg Province of a merchant of the 1st guild. One can be certain of one thing—the Russian people, thanks to their benefactor and his reforms, have at last, bit by bit, reached a position where, willy-nilly, they will have to learn to be efficient and look out for themselves, which is the whole point. I swear I feel that, when it comes to deep-seated change and reforms, our time is almost more important than that of Peter. And how about the railroads? To get south quickly, as quickly as possible; that is the whole trick. When that time comes, *true justice* will be everywhere, and what a great renewal that will be! (One thinks and dreams about all these things here; it all makes one's heart beat faster.)

Although I have been seeing hardly anybody, one does unavoidably stumble on people here. In Germany I came across a Russian who resides abroad permanently and who makes a trip to Russia every year for about three weeks to collect his income and then returns to Germany, where he has a wife and children, who have all become Germanized. I once asked him, by the way, what prompted him to become an expatriate. This is what he replied, literally (and with irritable insolence):

"Here there is civilization, there—barbarism. Besides, there are no differences of nationality here: Yesterday I was traveling in a train and I couldn't tell a Frenchman from an Englishman or from a German."

"And that, *in your view,* is progress?"

"Of course it is; there's no question about it."

"But let me tell you that that is not so at all. A Frenchman is above all else a Frenchman and an Englishman an Englishman, and their highest ambition is to be themselves. More than that—that is their great strength."

"That's not true at all. Civilization must level everything and we shan't be happy until we forget that we are Russians and until everyone is just like everyone else. Don't listen to Katkov!"

"You don't like Katkov, then?"

"He's a scoundrel."

"Why?"

"Because he dislikes the Poles."

"Do you read his magazine?"

"No, I never read it."

I report the conversation verbatim. The man in question is one of those young progressives, although it would appear that he keeps very much to himself. Abroad, these people turn into growling, squeamish Pomeranian dogs.

Finally, our loneliness in Dresden wore down both Anna Grigorevna and myself. Above all, there were the following facts: (1) From the letters forwarded to me by Pasha (he has only written to me once), it turns out that the creditors have started proceedings against me (therefore, *I cannot return to Russia before paying the debts*[)]. (2) My wife has realized she is pregnant. (*Please keep this* between us. It will be nine months in February, which is one more reason why we cannot go back.) (3) The question arises—what will happen to my Petersburg relatives, to Emiliya Fyodorovna, to Pasha, and to a few others? Money, money, but there is no money! (4) If we must hibernate, let it be in the south. Anyway, I want to show Anna Grigorevna some things, to distract her, to take her around a bit. So we have decided to spend the winter somewhere in Switzerland or Italy. But there is no money— whatever we have borrowed has already been spent. I wrote to Katkov, described the whole situation, and asked him for another 500-ruble *advance*. And what do you think—he sent it to me! What a wonderful man he is! There is a man with a heart for you! We left for Switzerland. But now I shall tell you the despicable and disgraceful things I did.

My dear Apollon Nikolayevich, I feel that I can trust myself to your verdict as my judge. You are a man and a citizen, you are a man with a heart, a fact of which I became convinced a long time ago. You are an exemplary husband and father, and, finally, I have always valued your judgment. I don't mind confessing to you. But I am writing this for *you alone*. Do not subject me to the judgment of other men!

Since Baden was not too far out of my way, I took it into my head to stop over there. A tempting idea plagued me: to risk 10 louis d'or in the hope that I might wind up with an extra 2,000 francs, which, after all, would take care of us for 4 months, everything included, and would also cover my expenses in Petersburg. The most disgusting thing about it is that I had won on some previous occasions. And the worst part of it is that I have a vile and overly passionate nature. Everywhere and in everything I drive myself to the ultimate limit, all my life I have been overstepping the line.

And right away the devil played a trick on me: In three days or so, I won *4000* francs with incredible ease. Now let me tell you how I visualized the whole situation: On the one hand, there was that easy win—in three days I had turned a *hundred* francs into four thousand. On the other hand, debts, lawsuits, anxiety, the impossibility of going back to Russia. And, finally, the third and the most important point—the gambling itself. You know how it ensnares you. No, I swear, it is not just avarice, although I did need money for money's sake above all. Anna Grigorevna pleaded with me to content myself with the 4000 thousand [*sic*] francs and to leave at once. But then it was such an easy and opportune occasion to set everything aright! And one sees such examples. Besides your own gains, you witness daily others picking up 20,000, 30,000 francs. (You don't see those who lose.) What's so saintly about them? I need money more than they do. I took the risk, went on playing, and lost. I went on to lose every *last* thing I had; in my feverish exasperation, I lost. I started pawning clothes. Anna Grigorevna pawned *everything* she had, down to the last knickknack. (What an angel she is, the way she tried to cheer me up! How lonely she felt in that accursed Baden, in the two small rooms over a blacksmith's to which we had moved.) In the end—that was that—everything was lost. (Oh, how loathsome the Germans turned out to be when that happened, what a bunch of usurers, scoundrels, and crooks, every one of them! Our landlady, realizing that we couldn't move out until we had received money, raised the rent in the meantime!) But we had to save ourselves, to get out of Baden. I wrote to Katkov again, asking him for another 500 rubles (without explaining to him what had happened, but with the letter coming from Baden, he probably more or less understood). Well, sir, he sent it! He did! And so now I have taken 4000 *in advance* from *Russian Messenger*. But here is the snag: of those 500, more than half went toward paying interest and redeeming our furniture in Petersburg, which Anna Grigorevna's mother had done for us. Upon my request, R[ussian] *Messenger* sent the money to her. Then 100 rubles went to pay our debts in Baden; we are still expecting to receive another 50 rubles from Anna Grigorevna's mother (part of these same 500 rubles that we still have coming to us). And we had about 200 francs left to take care of our trip to Geneva. (Why Geneva? Do you think I know myself? But what's the difference?) So we did move to Geneva and rented a chambre garnie from two old women and now, i.e., on our fourth day here, our *total capital* amounts to 18 francs. Except for the 50 rubles we are expecting any day from Anna Nikolayevna, there's no other money on the horizon for the next two months or so.

But to finish with Baden: we had the most awful 7 weeks in that hell. Almost as soon as I arrived in Baden, in fact on the very next day, I met Goncharov at the casino. Ivan Aleksandrovich was so embarrassed at seeing me at first! The state councilor, or acting state councilor, was also losing. But when he saw he couldn't hide from me and, anyway, that I was gambling myself only too unabashedly, he stopped trying to do so. He played with feverish ardor (for small stakes, in silver), played throughout the whole 2 weeks he spent in Baden, and apparently lost a considerable sum of money. But he is a good man, and may God send him health; when I lost everything (and he had seen a lot of gold in my hands), he lent me 60 francs at my request. He must have strongly disapproved of me for having lost everything, instead of losing half as he had.

Goncharov talked continually of Turgenev so that, although I had kept putting off going to see him, I at last made up my mind to pay Turgenev a visit. I went over one morning, around 12, and found him having his lunch. Let me tell you frankly—I never liked the man personally, not even before. Worst of all is the fact that I have owed him 50 thalers ever since 1867 [*sic*], ever since Wisbaden [*sic*] (and to this day I haven't paid him back!). I also dislike his aristocratically farcical embrace—he hurries up to you as if intending to kiss you, but instead offers you his own cheek. He lords it terribly; but above all else, I am irritated by his book *Smoke*. He told me himself that the main idea, the basic point of his book, was expressed in the sentence: "If

Russia should be swallowed up by the earth, it would not be a loss to mankind nor would it cause great concern." He declared that this was his fundamental conviction about Russia.

I found him tremendously upset by the failure of *Smoke*. But I must admit I was not familiar with all the details of that failure. You had written me about Strakhov's piece in *Notes of the Fa[therland]*, but I was unaware that he had received a whipping from all quarters or that in the Moscow Club they had apparently collected signatures to sign a protest against *Smoke*. He told me about it himself. I must confess that I could not have imagined anyone displaying his wounded pride with such naiveté and clumsiness as Turgenev did. And these people, by the way, boast about their being *atheists!* He told me that he was an out-and-out atheist. But, my God, deism gave us Christ, i.e., a concept of man so lofty that it cannot be understood without reverence, and it is impossible not to believe that this is the eternal ideal of mankind! And what have these Turgenevs, Herzens, Utins, and Chernyshevskys to offer us? Instead of the loftiest divine beauty, on which they spit, all these people are so disgustingly vain, so shamelessly petulant, so shallowly proud, that one simply can't make out what they are hoping for or how anyone could follow them. He reviled Russia and the Russians in a horrible and disgusting way. But the one thing I've noticed is that all these stupid little liberals and progressives—especially those who are still of Belinsky's school—derive their principal pleasure and satisfaction from abusing Russia. The difference is that Chernyshevsky's followers simply abuse Russia and frankly wish it would collapse (especially collapse!), while these offspring of Belinsky's add to that that they *love Russia*. But not only do they hate everything that is in any way peculiar to Russia so that they disavow it and delight in turning it at once into a caricature, but if they were finally confronted with a fact that could not be refuted or distorted into a caricature and with which they could not fail to agree, I believe they would be painfully, *excruciatingly,* desperately unhappy.

I noticed, for instance, that Turgenev (like all those who have been out of Russia for a long time) is totally ignorant of what's going on there (although they do read the papers here) and had lost all feel for Russia to such a shameful extent that he is incapable of grasping ordinary facts that are no longer disputed even by our Russian nihilist who only tries to caricature them in his own way. Among other things, Turgenev said that we ought to crawl before the Germans, that there is one common, inescapable road for everyone—civilization—and that all attempts at Russianism and independence are piggishness and stupidity. He told me that he was writing a long article against all the Russophiles and the Slavophiles. I advised him, for the sake of convenience, to order a telescope from Paris.

"What for?" he inquired.

"It's a long way from here," I said. "You'll train the telescope on Russia and you'll be able to watch us. Otherwise it is difficult to make us out from here."

This made him very angry. Seeing him so irritated, I said with feigned innocence that, I must say, I put on very successfully: "Why, I never suspected that all those criticisms of you and the failure of *Smoke* would anger you to such an extent. I assure you *it's not worth it*. To hell with it all."

"But I am not at all angry, I assure you," and he blushed.

I changed the subject and began talking of private and personal matters. Then, as I picked up my hat, I told him, without in the least intending to—it just slipped out—everything about the Germans that had accumulated in my heart during the past three months.

"Do you have any idea what cheats and crooks one comes across here? I assure you that the common people here are much worse and more dishonest than ours are and that they are more stupid—there can be no doubt about it. So, you see, when you talk about civilization—well, what has civilization done for them, and what do they have to be so proud about?"

He went white (literally, I am not exaggerating, not in the slightest!) and said: "When you say that, you offend me *personally*. You know that I have settled here for good and that I consider myself a German now rather than a Russian, and I am proud of it." I replied: "Although I have read *Smoke* and have been talking to you for a whole hour now, I should never have expected you to say that, so please forgive me if I have offended you."

Then we said good-bye, very politely, and I promised myself that I would never again set foot in Turgenev's house. The next morning at *10* sharp, Turgenev drove over to my place and left his calling card with my landladies. But since I myself had told him on the previous day that I couldn't receive him before *twelve* and that we didn't get up until *eleven*, I interpreted his coming *at 10 o'clock in the morning* as a clear hint that he did not wish to meet me and that he had paid me a visit at 10 o'clock precisely to make me understand as much. Throughout the entire 7 weeks I met him only once, at the casino. We exchanged glances, but neither of us was willing to acknowledge the other.

Perhaps, my dear Apollon Nikolayevich, you will find in poor taste the malicious joy with which I have described Turgenev and the way we insulted each other. But believe me, it's more than I can stand—his views offend me too deeply. Personally, I don't really care one way or the other, although his cavalier manner does not make him particularly attractive; but to stand by and listen to Russia being so abused by a Russian renegade, by a man who could have been useful, is plainly unacceptable. I had noticed his kowtowing to the Germans and his hatred for Russia for a long time—as much as four years ago. But his present irritation and frenzy, which has him foaming at the mouth against Russia, stems solely from the fiasco of *Smoke* and from the fact that Russia has had the audacity to refuse him recognition as a genius. It is sheer vanity and that makes it even more repulsive.

But the hell with the lot of them!

Now let me tell you, my dear friend, about my plans. Of course, I acted shamefully in losing that money. But, relatively speaking, I didn't lose much of my own money. Still, I could have lived on that money for two or perhaps even four months, given the way we live. I've told you already—I was unable to stop while I was winning. Had I lost 10 louis d'or to start with, I would have quit immediately and left town, as I planned to. But it was winning those 4000 francs that was my undoing! I couldn't resist the temptation of trying to win more (when it seemed so easy) and in one stroke wipe out my insolvency and for a time provide the wherewithal for myself and all those who depend on me—Emiliya Fyodorovna, Pasha, and the others. But that does not excuse me in the least, because I was not alone, but with a kind and beautiful young creature who has complete faith in me, whom I must defend and protect and whom, therefore, I had no right to ruin by risking everything, no matter how small the sum. My future looks very bleak to me—primarily because I cannot go back to Russia, for the reasons I have explained to you. But above all there is the problem of what will become of those who depend on me for support. All these thoughts are worrying me to death. One way or another I must get out of this predicament sooner or later. But I have only myself to rely on, because there is nothing else in sight.

In 1865, when I got back from Wiesbaden in October, I managed to persuade the creditors to wait a tiny bit longer, made a concentrated effort, and got down to work. I succeeded, and my creditors received substantial sums. Now I have arrived in Geneva, and the ideas are there in my head. There is the stuff for a novel, and with God's help it will turn out to be something big, and perhaps won't be too bad. I love it terribly and I'll write it in joy and anxiety.

Katkov told me himself in April that he would like and would prefer to start printing my novel in January 1868. That is how it will be, then, although I shall be sending installments before that.

Although there are no creditors around here, my situation is worse than it was in 1865. Then, at least, Pasha and Emiliya Fyodorovna were there, before my eyes. Moreover, I was on my own. But Anna Grigorevna is an angel, and you cannot imagine how much she means to me! I love her and she tells me that she is happy, completely happy, that she does not need either entertainment or people, and that she is perfectly content to be together with me alone in a room.

256

Fine. So now I face six months or so of uninterrupted work. But by then my wife will be expecting the baby. Geneva is a good town: there are doctors here and people who speak French. But the climate is very poor. It is gloomy, and the autumn and winter are terribly unpleasant. Perhaps, if we get the money, we'll be in a position to move to Italy in two and a half months or so. In general, it would be better to spend the winter either in Italy or Paris. I don't know, though, which would be more convenient and cheaper. But then we may very well stay on in Geneva until the spring.

My financial calculations are as follows: If the novel is published, Katkov won't refuse to let me have another three thousand or so in advance next year. So it looks as if there will be enough for us, for Pasha and Em[iliya] Fyod[orovna], and even a little something for the creditors (to cheer them up). As for the novel, it could be sold or midway through the year resold for a second edition.

You are the only person I have, my dear friend, you are my Providence. Don't deprive me of your help in the future. Because I shall be calling on you to take part in all my affairs, big and small.

I think you understand clearly what all these hopes of mine are based on: obviously the whole outcome depends on *one single* condition—namely, *that the novel is good.* Consequently, I now have to give it my undivided attention.

(Ah, my dear friend, it is burdensome, too burdensome and presumptuous of me to have accepted the challenge three years ago to pay off all those debts and, in a thoughtless moment, to have signed all those IOU's! Where was I to get the health and energy needed for that! And if experience had already shown that success was possible, still under what conditions? The condition was that every single piece of writing I would produce should be so thoroughly successful as to arouse sufficient interest among the public. Otherwise, everything would collapse. If only that were possible, if only it could be calculated with mathematical certainty!)

Now, one final word. Hear me out, consider carefully, and help me!

We now have 18 francs. Tomorrow or the day after we expect from Anna Grigorevna's mother the 50 rubles still coming to us from the Katkov money. And this is *all*, absolutely all we'll have until Katkov sends more. (Anna Grigorevna's mother is just now, at this moment, in such a situation that she cannot spare a single kopek for us.)

But I cannot possibly ask Katkov for anything *now*. In 2 months it will be different: By then I shall have sent him fifteen hundred rubles' worth of my novel and explained my situation to him. He could retain 1000 rubles in payment of my debt and send me 500. I am relying fully on him: he is a kind and generous man.

But how can I subsist during these 2 months while I'll be writing? Don't judge me, but be my guardian angel instead! I am well aware, Apollon Nikolayevich, that you have no money *to spare.* I should never have asked you to help, except that I am drowning, indeed, I have gone under completely. In two or three weeks I shan't have a single kopek left, and a drowning man stretches out his hand, quite oblivious of everything else. And this is what I am doing now. I know that you are well disposed toward me, but I also know that you are scarcely in a position to help me out financially. And, notwithstanding, I am asking you for your help because I have *no one else* to turn to, and if you don't help me, then I shall perish, utterly perish!

Here's my request:

I am asking you for *150* rubles. Send them to me in Geneva, poste restante. In 2 months, the editors of *Russian Messenger* will send you 500 rubles in my name. I shall ask them to do so myself. (And *there is not the slightest doubt* they will send the money, provided I send them my novel. And *I will*—that is also beyond any doubt.[)]

And so I am asking you to let me have this sum *for two months.* Save me, my dear friend! I shall reward you for as long as I live with friendship and affection. If you don't have the money, borrow it from someone for me. Excuse me for writing *in this way* but, remember, I am drowning!

From September on, Pasha will be without money (I do not even speak of Emiliya Fyodorovna!) and so, of the 150 rubles, give him 25 for the time being, and tell him to stint and hold himself in for a couple of months. Later I'll let you know how much of Katkov's 500 rubles you should let him have. (This is why I intend to ask the editors of *Russian Messenger* to remit the money to you in your name, in the future, because I'll be asking you to help me in the coming months with some of my Petersburg transactions, i.e., certain payments and remittances will be made through you. Please don't worry, there will be nothing that will place you in an *ambiguous* position. All I am asking for is your friendly participation. I am pleading with you because, besides you, I have *no one, no one* in Petersburg except you whom I can rely on!)[)]

I also ask you to write me as soon as possible. Don't leave me to my fate. God will reward you.

Tell Pasha to write me here, in Geneva, and tell me about everything that has happened to him, and if he has any letters for me, to send them on as he did last time. I have received just one letter from him in all this time; I don't think he has any love for me at all. And that pains me deeply, you know.

My address is: M-r. Theodore Dostoiewsky, Suisse, Genève, poste restante.

Let me know your address, too, when you write. Since I don't know the number of your house I am sending this letter through Anna Nikolayevna Snitkina (Anna Grigorevna's mother) and she will see that you get it.

In any case, I beg you most earnestly to write me as soon as possible, my dear friend, and tell me as much as you can about all our friends, about what is going on, what is in the making, and what you are doing yourself. In brief, moisten with a drop of water a soul that has become parched in the desert. In the name of God!

My regards to all *yours,* your parents, and especially Anna Ivanovna. Anna Grigorevna also sends her her special regards. We have thought and talked of you so often.

When shall we meet again?

Give me some advice, too, about what I should do. Tell me how you view my situation. Have you heard anything about my Petersburg affairs, at least from Pasha?

In my next letter I'll write about something else as well.

In Geneva I live in complete isolation and haven't met any of the Russians here.

Neither the sound of Russian nor a Russian face!

Good-bye, I hug you hard and kiss you.

All yours,

Fyodor Dostoyevsky

---

70. Latkin and (Yevgeny) Pechatkin were Dostoyevsky's principal creditors after the closing down of *Epoch.*

The "Tarasov establishment" was the debtors' prison.

Anna Ivanovna was Maikov's wife.

The event in Paris that had "terribly shaken" Dostoyevsky was the second attempt on the life of Tsar Alexander II, this time by the Polish refugee Anton Berezowski on May 25/June 6, 1867. Public opinion in Paris strongly supported the would-be assassin, portraying him as an idealist seeking to avenge his homeland, and a group of Parisian lawyers staged a demonstration in which they shouted "Vive la Pologne!"

The reforms to which Dostoyevsky refers were the establishment of local governing bodies (*zemstva*) and measures to separate the judiciary from the executive and to institute trial by jury and the organization of a legal bar.

The flogging incident that Dostoyevsky mentions was probably one reported in the newspaper *Voice* (Golos) on July 14/26, 1867. (It took place in Ufa rather than Orenburg Province.) A police constable had demanded money of a merchant; when the latter refused, his clothes were torn off, he was stretched out on the floor, and several policemen gave him "more than 300 strokes of the birch, twice changing the birch in the process."

Turgenev's *Smoke* (Dym, 1867) had indeed gotten harsh treatment from the critics. Turgenev, on the other hand, considered *Smoke* "the only competent and useful book I have ever written," so it is quite likely that he was upset.

This letter probably contributed to the hostility between the two authors. By a route that is not entirely clear, an unsigned copy of the passage describing their encounter found its way into the hands of the publisher of *Russian Archives* (Russky arkhiv), P. I. Bartenev, with the request that it not be published before 1890 but be preserved "for posterity." Turgenev learned about this and early in 1868 dispatched a letter to Bartenev, denying that he had expressed to Dostoyevsky the "shocking and absurd opinions about Russia and Russians which he ascribes to me," going on to say that "I consider him, because of his morbid fits and for other reasons, as a person not fully in possession of his mental faculties. . . ," and concluding: "There is no doubt that by 1890 neither Mr. Dostoyevsky nor I shall be attracting much attention from our fellow countrymen, but even if we are not completely forgotten by then, we shall be judged not by one-sided denunciations but rather by the overall results of our work."

Nikolai Isaakovich Utin (1840?–1883) was a revolutionary prominent among Russian émigrés in Europe. He had fled Russia in 1863 (and was sentenced to death in absentia for his activities as a member of the Land and Freedom Society), served on the editorial board of various magazines, and was a member of the First International. He was granted permission to return to Russia in 1880.

The 1865 success that Dostoyevsky refers to was the publication of *Crime and Punishment.* The novel he started writing in Geneva was *The Idiot,* which ran in installments in *Russian Messenger* in 1868 and 1869. Contrary to Dostoyevsky's hopes, it was not especially successful and was not published in a separate edition until 1874.

71. To A. N. Maikov

Geneva, December 31, 1867/January 12, 1868

My dear and good friend Apollon Nikolayevich,

At last the time has come when I can write you a letter several pages long! You didn't think I had forgotten you, did you? I know you wouldn't think that of me. Don't hold it against me—you, if anyone, will understand. Believe me, *I haven't had a single hour of leisure,* and I mean that literally. I have neglected everybody. What is my poor Pasha doing? I haven't sent him any money for two months now. (I literally do not have a kopek that I could have sent to him!) I shall tell you about everything in this letter, and I shall await your answer with morbid impatience. Being in the dark is killing me.

And here is how things have been with me: *I have been working and suffering.* Do you know what it means to *compose?* No, thank God, you do not! I don't think you have ever written on order, by the yard, and experienced that hellish agony. After I had taken so much money from *Russian Messenger* (4500 rubles—it's awful!) I fully hoped at the beginning of the year that poetic inspiration would not abandon me, that the poetic idea would flare up and develop artistically by the end of the year, and that I should manage to satisfy everybody. And this seemed even more probable to me in that there are always many embryonic artistic ideas flashing and pulsating through my head and my heart. But then, they just flash, and what I have to do is to give them full substance, a thing that invariably happens suddenly and unexpectedly, but there's no telling when it will occur; and it is only after the full image has been communicated to the heart that I can go on to the artistic execution. And at this point one can count on its not failing. Well, sir, throughout the summer and autumn I put together various ideas (some were quite ingenious); but experience warned me every time that this or that idea was either false or unmanageable or not viable enough. Finally, though, I fixed on one of these ideas, began working on it, and wrote a great deal. But then, on December 4, foreign [sic] style, I threw it all out. I assure you that I could have made a tolerable novel out of it, but I grew terribly sick of it precisely because it would have just been tolerable instead of *positively good*. I had no use for that. Well, what was I to do now? It was already December 4! And meanwhile my living conditions were presenting the following appearance:

I do not remember (since I don't remember anything) whether I wrote and told you that when my every means of existence was finally exhausted, I wrote to Katkov asking him to send me 100 rubles a month. I believe I did write to you about it. He agreed, and they began sending me the money regularly. But in my letter (of thanks) to Katkov, I *emphatically* confirmed, giving him my word of honor, that he would have a novel and that I would send the editors a substantial part of it in December. (I promised the more readily since the writing was going strong and so much was already on paper!) Then later I wrote him that my expenses were considerable and asked him whether he couldn't send me 200 instead of 100 rubles from the allotted sum (500 rubles) for that one time (for December). His consent and the money came in December, at the very moment when I had destroyed the novel. What was I to do? All my hopes had crumbled. (I finally understood that my work, my novel, was my one and only hope, that if I wrote a satisfactory novel, I should be able to pay off my debt to my publisher, send you a substantial sum for Pasha and Em[iliya] Fyodorovna, and have something to live on for a while; but that if I wrote a *good* novel, I would be able to sell it for a second edition, too, and perhaps make some money that would enable me to pay off a half or ⅔ of the promissory notes I had signed and return to Petersburg.) But all has come to nought. When I received the 200 rubles from Katkov, I confirmed in my letter to him that the novel would *definitely* be ready for the January issue, and though I apologized for the fact that *the first part* would be *late* in reaching the editors, I promised it *without fail* by January 1 (our style), and I implored them not to bring out the January issue of *Russian Messenger* without my novel (the magazine never comes out before the middle of the month, anyway).

Then (since my entire future depended on it), I set about the painful task of inventing a *new novel*. Nothing in the world could have made me continue with the first one. I simply could not. I turned things over in my mind from December 4 through December 18, new style. I would say that on the average I came up with six plans a day (at least that). My head was in a spin. It's a wonder I didn't go out of my mind. At last, on December 18, I sat down and started writing a new novel, and on January 5 (New Style) I sent off 5 chapters of the first part to the magazine (about 5 printer's sheets) with a promise that the remaining *two chapters* of the first part would be there by Jan. 10 (New Style). Yesterday, the 11th, I sent them those 2 chapters, so they now have the *whole first part*—6 or 6½ printer's sheets.

They must have received the first batch on December 30 (our style) and should get the second on January 4; hence, if they wish to do so, they can still publish the first part in the January issue. I have given the editors my word of honor to send them the second part (of which, of course, not a single line has yet been written) by February 1 (our style), punctually and unfailingly.

So do you understand, my friend, that I could not possibly have thought of writing letters to anyone and, besides, what was there for me to write? And so, try, in your humanity, to *understand* me and, as a friend, forgive me for my forced silence. Furthermore, this has been a very painful period for me.

Now, to finish with this subject, let me tell you about the novel. As a matter of fact, I have no idea of what the thing I have sent them is like myself. But as far as I can form an opinion, it is not terribly catching and not at all impressive. For a long time already, there was one idea that had been troubling me, but I was afraid to make a novel out of it because it was a very difficult idea, and I was not ready to tackle it, although it is a fascinating idea and one I am in love with. That idea is—*to portray a perfectly good man*. I believe there can be nothing more difficult than this, especially in our time. I am sure you will agree entirely with this. The idea used to flash through my head in a somewhat artistic form, but only *somewhat*, not in the full-blown form that was needed. It was only the desperate situation in which I found myself that made me embark upon an idea that had not yet reached full maturity. I took a chance, like at roulette: "Maybe it will develop as I write it!" That is a quite unforgivable thing to do.

On the whole, a plan has taken shape. As I go along, various details crop up that I find fascinating and stimulating. But the whole? But the hero? Somehow the whole thing seems to turn on the figure of *the hero*. That is the way it has evolved. I must establish the character of the hero. Will it develop under my pen? And imagine what uncontrollable horrors emerged: It turned out that, besides the hero, there was a heroine, which means that there were TWO HEROES!! And apart from the two heroes there are two other characters of absolutely major importance, that is, *semi-heroes*. (And there is a multitude of supporting characters for whom I feel very responsible, and the novel will be in eight parts.) Of the four heroes, two are already clearly outlined *in my mind*, one is not yet outlined at all, and the fourth, the main hero, is still extremely pale. Perhaps he is not so vague in my heart, but he is terribly difficult. In any case, I need twice as much time as I have (at a minimum) to write it.

The first part, in my opinion, is weak. But I think there's still a way of saving it, since what I have done thus far *compromises* nothing and can be developed satisfactorily in later parts (may that be so!). The first part is, essentially, just an introduction, calculated only to arouse some sort of curiosity about what is to come later. But I am absolutely unable to judge myself. The only reader I have is Anna Grigorevna; she does like it very much, but, after all, she is no judge *in my profession*.

In the *second* part everything will have to be definitely set (but still nowhere near fully explained). It will contain a scene (one of the capital ones), but how well it will come off remains to be seen, although the rough draft is *ready* and looks fine.

In general, everything is still in the future, but I am looking to you for a severe critique. Everything hinges on Part 2; it is the most difficult. But you must also let me know what you think of the first as well (although I know, in my heart, it is no good). Still, write me. Of course, *I implore you*, let me know, as soon as *Russian Messenger* appears, whether it contains my novel. I am still very worried that it may have arrived too late. And it is absolutely essential to me that it should come out in January. So be so good as to let me know right away, if only a few lines.

When I sent Part 1 to Katkov, I wrote him just about exactly the same thing as I am writing to you now. The novel is called *The Idiot*. And yet, no man can be a competent judge of his own work, especially on the spur of the moment. Maybe the first part isn't really that bad. If I have not amply developed the main character, this is surely in accordance with the demands of the overall composition. That is why I am awaiting your verdict with such eager impatience. But enough about the novel. All the work I have done since December 18 has got me so keyed up that I cannot think or talk about anything else. But now I shall say a few words about our life here, since I last wrote to you.

Obviously, my work is my life. But it is a good thing that now, thanks to the *one hundred rubles* I receive regularly every month, our needs are fully taken care of. Anna Grigorevna and I live modestly but quite comfortably. But there are expenses lying ahead, and we must always have something in reserve, if only a small sum. In about a month and a half, Anna Grigorevna (who is bearing her delicate state superbly) will make me a father. I don't have to tell you what expenses this will involve. But then I shall ask the editors for 200 rubles a month during that period, and they will send them to me. Why, I have already sent them nearly 1000 rubles' worth, and by February 5 will send them another 1000 (and perhaps that batch will be good—more solid and more impressive), and so I am entitled to ask them for a larger sum. By the way, dear fellow, had I not torn up the novel, I could certainly have paid you back before New Year's the money you lent me. But now I beg you to wait another two months or so because, until I send in Part 2, I shan't be able to ask the editors for any substantial sum. But by then I shall settle with you without fail. But what torments me most and causes me the greatest sorrow is the thought of what may be happening to Pasha. My heart bleeds, and the thought of him, added to all my *literary torments* in December, was simply driving me to despair! What is he doing? I did not send him any money either in November or in December, but then he hasn't written to me since before November. When I last sent him money through you (60 rubles from Katkov), I wrote him a long letter and also asked him to make a small inquiry that was of *tremendous* importance to me and very easy for him to make. I begged him to answer me. But he never wrote back so much as a single line. For the love of God, do give me some news of him. Does he hate me or what? But why, why? Is it because I sent him practically all the money I had and am waiting with burning impatience for the time when I'll be able to send him more? I cannot believe that he hates me. I put it all down not to his heart but to his irresponsibility and his inability to make himself do anything, even write a letter, just as he has still not been able to make himself learn the multiplication table yet, at the age of twenty.

He stayed with Emiliya Fyodorovna and still got into debt, even though up to November I was sending him enough money. At that time I paid Emiliya Fyodorovna back through you. But what happened in November and December? She and her family are in a difficult position themselves. Fedya is working, but he cannot provide for all of them, and I shan't be in a position to send them any money for another month. (And then it will have to be through you, please, my dear fellow. *Katkov will send the money to you.* Don't turn me down and don't get too annoyed with them. They are very poor. And I shall remain your servant for as long as I live and shall prove to you how much I appreciate everything you have done for me.) I shall write to Fedya tomorrow. Are they still living in Alonkin's house? As a matter of fact, what I asked Pasha to do was to let me know Alonkin's first name and patronymic (I have forgotten them) so that I could write to him. Alonkin trusts *me* all right, but he will lock them out of the apartment if he does not hear from me, because it was I who had promised to see to it that the rent would be paid. But neither Pasha nor Emiliya Fyodorovna ever informed me of Alonkin's *first name and patronymic.* And how can I write a letter to Alonkin without them? He is a merchant and would be offended.

But now I think I may, after all, send them money sooner, even though we are in very tight circumstances pending the confinement. And although we are getting along without denying ourselves the prime necessities, we are constantly pawning things. We redeem them whenever we get money and then pawn them again toward the end of the month. Anna Grigorevna is a true help and consolation to me. Her love for me is boundless, although of course our characters are quite different. (She sends her special regards to you and Anna Ivanovna. She is terribly fond of you for thinking so highly of her mother, whom she adores. She, for her part, thinks extremely highly of you and of Anna Ivanovna in every respect, and has a most sincere, ardent, and profound esteem for you.)

As far as physical discomfort in Geneva goes, the worst has been the cold. Oh, if you only had some idea of how stupid, dimwitted, petty, and savage this tribe is! It is not enough to travel through this country as a tourist—you must live here to appreciate it fully! But I have accumulated too many impressions to be able to describe them to you, even briefly, now. In this despicable republic, bourgeois ways are developed to the nec [*sic*] plus-ultra. In the government and throughout Switzerland, there are factions and continuous squabbling, there is terrible misery, an oppressive mediocrity in everything; a Swiss worker is not worth a Russian worker's little finger—the sight and sound of him are ridiculous. They have barbaric customs, and if only you could see what they consider good and what they consider bad! The level of development is low: the drunkenness, the thievery, the petty larceny that has become the rule in their commerce. They have a few redeeming features, however, that still make them infinitely superior to the Germans. (In Germany I was above all struck by the stupidity of the people—they are incredibly stupid, they are immeasurably stupid!) And yet, back home, even a highly intelligent man like Nik[olai] Nik[olayevich] Strakhov refuses to see the truth. "The Germans," he says, "invented gunpowder." Sure, but it just worked out that way for them! And we, at that time, were building a great nation. We arrested the advance of Asia for all times. We endured untold sufferings, we *knew how* to endure them not only without losing the Russian idea that will renew the world, but strengthening it; finally, we endured the Germans, and withal, our people are infinitely superior, more noble, more honest, more ingenuous, more gifted, and are imbued with a different idea, the loftiest Christian idea, which Europe, with its moribund Catholicism and stupidly self-contradictory Lutheranism, doesn't even understand. But never mind about that! What does matter is that I am so depressed being away from Russia, so homesick for my country, that I feel thoroughly miserable! I read the newspapers *Mos[cow] Gaz[ette]* and the *Voice*, every issue without missing a word. Congratulations to the *Voice* on its new orientation. There are so many things I would like to talk over with you, my friend, so much has accumulated during this time! But maybe this year I shall embrace you. Still, I count on your writing to me. For the love of God, do write me, my dear fellow. Why, it is the only consolation I have in my grim and humdrum isolation. Anna Grigorevna finds happiness in being with me. But I need you, and my country, too.

There are still abundant woodlands in Switzerland, and in the mountains still incomparably more here than elsewhere in Europe, although they are dwindling every year at a frightening rate. And imagine this: 5 months a year it is terribly cold here and they have the bises* (blustery winds that come across the mountain ranges). And for 3 months it's almost the same sort of winter as back home. People shiver with the cold and never take off their flannel and quilted clothes (and since they have no bathhouses of any sort, I leave it to you to imagine the filth to which they have become accustomed); they do not provide themselves with special winter clothing, but go around dressed almost the same way summer and winter (and flannel alone is quite inadequate for this sort of winter). And with all this, they don't have enough common sense to improve their houses even the least bit! Tell me, what use is a fireplace, even if you keep stoking it with coal or wood *all day long*? And to keep it stoked all day long costs 2 francs a day. And the quantity of wood that is squandered, with no warmth in return! Why, if they just had double windows, even with their open fireplaces, it would be quite possible to get along! I won't even mention the fact that if they installed stoves, they could save all these woodlands. As it is, in 25 years there will be nothing left of them. They live like real savages. But then, what endurance they possess! In my room, even when heated intensely, the temperature would never rise above +5° Reaumur (five degrees above freezing!)[.] I would sit in that cold in my overcoat, waiting for money, pawning my things, and working out a plan for my novel—what do you say to that? They say that this winter the temperature dropped to −10 degrees in Florence and to −15° in *Monpele* (Monpellier). Here in Geneva, the thermometer never went lower than 8 degrees below zero, but what difference can it possibly make when the water ices over in your room, anyway? We moved recently to another apartment; we have 2 nice rooms, one perpetually cold, the other warm; in the warm room the temperature is constantly around +10 or +11, so that it is reasonably comfortable.

I see I have written a great deal and have managed to say very little! And that is just what makes me dislike letters. The main thing is that I am waiting for a letter from you. For God's sake, write me quickly. In my present state of dejection a letter written to me can almost be rated as a *good deed*. Oh, yes—I forgot to ask you not to repeat to anyone for the time being what I have written you about the novel. I wouldn't like *Russian Messenger* to somehow catch wind of it, because I lied when I told them that I had a great

---

*Dostoyesvsky transliterates the French word *bise* into Cyrillic letters.

deal written in *draft* and that I was now simply revising and recopying it. I shall have it ready in time anyhow and—who knows, maybe on the whole it will turn out to be quite an acceptable novel. But here I go talking about the novel again—it has become an obsession with me, I tell you.

My health is very satisfactory. Attacks have become very rare, and this has been the case for the last 2½ or 3 months now. Please give my sincere regards to your parents. Give my regards to Strakhov, too, if you see him. And ask him in turn to give my regards to Averkiyev and Dolgomostev. Especially Dolgomostev. Have you seen him at all?

I hug you and send you my love,

Your faithful and affectionate,

Fyodor Dostoyevsky

Give my special regards to Anna Ivanovna.

I have had a letter from Yanovsky. He is a very kind man, but sometimes rather strange. I am very fond of him.

My best wishes for the New Year! I wish you every, every happiness—you, at least, be happy!

When and where is *The Song of Igor's Campaign* being published? Please, please, as soon as it comes out, send it to me, wherever I may be at that time.

---

71. The characters of *The Idiot* to whom Dostoyevsky refers are the main figure, Prince Myshkin (the "perfectly good man"); Rogozhin, the merchant; and the two women, Nastasya Filippovna and Aglaya.

Ivan Maksimovich Alonkin (d. 1875) was a member of the gentry and the owner of the house at the corner of Meshchanskaya Street and Stolyarny Lane in Petersburg where Dostoyevsky had lived before going abroad. Emiliya Fyodorovna was living there under an arrangement that Dostoyevsky had made with Alonkin before leaving.

The *Moscow Gazette* was a conservative newspaper, published by Katkov. The *Voice,* published by Krayevsky, had been a liberal newspaper but was becoming more conservative at this time.

On the Reaumur temperature scale, the freezing point of water is 0° and the boiling point 80°. Thus, +5° Reaumur corresponds to about +6° Celsius and about +43° Fahrenheit.

Ivan Grigorevich Dolgomostev (d. 1867) had been a contributor to *Time* and *Epoch.* He was apparently one of the most fanatical adherents of the doctrine of *pochvennichestvo;* according to Strakhov, the vagueness and internal inconsistencies of the doctrine contributed to the fact that he died insane.

The Song of Igor's Campaign is a traditional Russian epic. Maikov had written to Dostoyevsky that he was making an intense study of the epic in connection with a verse version that he was writing. It was not published until 1870, in the magazine *Dawn* (Zarya).

72. TO S. A. IVANOVA
Geneva, January 1/13, 1868

My dear, invaluable Sonechka,

Although you expressly asked me to write to you, I remained silent. And yet, apart from the fact that I felt a strong special need to communicate *with you*, I *had to* answer you if only on one particular point you made in your letter and to do it right away, as quickly as possible. Tell me, how could you, a friend of old standing and a person very dear to me, imagine that I left Moscow feeling angry with you and without even offering you my hand! How could that be possible? Although my memory is, indeed, quite poor, and I don't remember the details, I am positive that *nothing* of this kind can have happened and that you simply got a false impression. In the first place, I am as sure as two times two is four that there couldn't have been any reason for it, and in the second place, and more important: Am I one to break off so easily with my friends? You really don't know me very well, my dear girl! I was very hurt when I read that. You *must* have understood, Sonya, how much I appreciate and respect you and how much I value your affection. I haven't met many people like you in my life, Sonya. You may ask exactly what it was that caused me to become so much attached to you. (You can ask others if you don't believe me.) But it is so terribly difficult, my dear, to answer such a question. I remember you almost since the time you were just a little girl, but I began to watch you closely and to recognize a rare and exceptional person in you, with a rare and beautiful heart (just four years ago), and I really came to know you that winter when Mariya Dmitriyevna died. Do you remember when I came to see you after having been sick for a whole month, after having been a very long time without seeing all of you?

I am very fond of all of you, but particularly of you. I am extremely fond, for instance, of Mashenka, for her gracefulness, for her ingenuous and enchanting manners; I discovered only quite recently her serious-mindedness (oh, you are all so talented and favored by God!), but it is you to whom I am especially attached, and my attachment is based on a particular impression that is very difficult to dissect and analyze. I like your restraint and the natural and noble feeling you have of your own worth, and I like the awareness you have of it. (Oh, you must never betray it in any way—just go straight ahead in life, shunning all compromise. Strengthen within you your good inclinations, because everything must be strengthened, and it is enough to compromise just once with one's honor and conscience to leave for a long time a vulnerable place in one's soul, so that the moment you are faced in life with a choice between something that is difficult and something that is advantageous, you will immediately retreat before the difficulty and settle for what is advantageous. I am not just talking generalities—what I am saying now is a sore point with me myself, and what I have said about vulnerability is perhaps based on personal experience. And it is quite possible that what I like in you is precisely what I find lacking in myself.[)]

I love, above all, your uncompromising attitude toward honor, the staunchness of your views and convictions, an attitude which is, of course, so ingrained in you that you are scarcely aware of it yourself, because you could not be aware of everything, being as young as you are. I also admire your intelligence, so calm and capable of making clear distinctions and producing clear insights. My friend, I agree with everything you write in your letters, but to agree with your accusation that there has been even the slightest wavering in my friendship for you—that I never shall! Perhaps the whole thing is simply due to some petty incident, some ugly temperamental outburst of mine. But even so, that could *never* have been directed toward you personally, but rather toward someone else. So please don't ever offend me again with accusations of that sort.

As to my long silence, despite your request that I write to you soon, I give you my *word of honor* that from now on I shall send you a letter regularly every month. In a letter to Aleksandr Pavlovich and Verochka, I explained, as well as I could, the reason for my silence. All this time I have been in such a miserable moral mood and under such strain that I felt a great need to withdraw into myself and to be left alone with my sadness. It was painful for me to sit down and write a letter and, besides, what could I have written about? About my sadness? (It would certainly have been detectable in my letter); but it is poor material for a letter.

And then, things have been rather hectic around here. My entire future depends on my work. Besides, I had taken about 4500 rubles in advance from the editors of *Russian Messenger,* giving them my word of honor, and repeating it again and again throughout the year in every letter I wrote them that I would have a novel for them. But then, just when I was about to send the novel to the editors, I was forced to discard it, because I didn't like it anymore (and since I no longer liked it I couldn't write it well). I destroyed much of what I had written, although my ability to pay back my debts and my livelihood and my entire future depended on it. So about three weeks ago (December 18 New Style), I got started on a new novel and began working day and night. The idea for the novel is an old favorite of mine, but it was so difficult that for a long time I did not dare to tackle it, and if I have done so now it is only because I was in a state verging on despair. The main idea of the novel is to portray a positively good man. There is nothing more difficult in the world, and this is especially true today. All writers—not only ours but Europeans as well—who have ever attempted to portray the *positively* good have always given up. Because the problem is a boundless one. The perfect is an ideal, and this ideal, whether it is ours or that of civilized Europe, is still far from having been worked out. There is only one positively good figure in the world—Christ—so that the phenomenon of that boundlessly, infinitely good figure is already in itself an infinite miracle. (The whole of the Gospel of Saint John is a statement to that effect; he finds the whole miracle in the Incarnation alone, in the manifestation of the good alone.)

But I am anticipating too much. I shall mention only that, of the good figures in Christian literature, the most complete is that of Don Quixote. But he is good only because at the same time he is ridiculous. The figure of Dickens's Pickwick (a conception infinitely weaker than that of Don Quixote, but still a tremendous one) is also ridiculous, and that's the only reason it succeeds. Compassion for the good man who is ridiculed and who is unaware of his own worth generates sympathy in the reader. And this ability to arouse compassion is the very secret of humor. Jean Valjean is another powerful attempt, but he engenders sympathy because of his terrible misfortune and society's injustice toward him. But there is nothing of this sort in my novel, absolutely nothing, and that is why I am terribly afraid that it will be a positive failure. It is possible that some particular details may not come off too badly. I am afraid it will be boring. It's a long novel. I wrote the whole *first part* in 23 days and sent it off a few days ago. It will definitely be quite unimpressive. Of course, it is just the introduction and so, happily, nothing, for the moment, is compromised; but then, hardly anything is explained or expounded. My only desire is that it arouse a degree of curiosity in the reader, so that he will want to read the second part. I shall start working on the second part today and shall finish it in a month (why, this is just how I have worked all my life). I have the impression that it will be more solid and more important than the first. Wish me at least some success, dear friend! The novel is called *The Idiot* and is dedicated to you, i.e., to Sofya Aleksandrovna Ivanova. Ah, my dear friend, if only the novel turns out to be, even to some small extent, worthy of the dedication! In any case, I am in no position to judge myself, especially as engrossed in it as I am now.

My health is eminently satisfactory, and I can stand the hard work, although a difficult time lies ahead of me because of the delicate condition of Anna Grigorevna. I'll spend another four months or so working here, and then I hope to move to Italy. I must have isolation. I am very worried about Fedya and Pasha. I am also getting off a letter to Fedya by this same mail. Actually, living abroad is very painful to me, and I am longing to return to Russia. Anna Grigorevna and I are completely alone here. As for my life here: I get up late, light the fire in the fireplace (it's awfully cold here), and we drink our coffee; then I get down to my work. At four o'clock I go out for dinner in a restaurant, where I eat for 2 francs, wine included. Anna Grigorevna prefers to eat at home. After that I go to a café, where I drink coffee and read the *Moscow Gazette* and the *Voice* from beginning to end. When I am through I take a walk for half an hour or so to get some exercise and then return home and go back to work. Later I stoke the fire again, we drink tea, then I get back to work again. Anna Grigorevna says that she is frightfully happy.

Geneva is dull and gloomy, a stupid Protestant city with an awful climate; but so much the better for my work. Alas, my dear friend, it may be quite impossible for me to return to Russia before September! But as soon as I do I shall hurry over to see you and give you a big hug. I am thinking about starting a new publication when I get back home. But this, of course, is contingent on the success of the novel I am working on now. And just imagine— working as hard as I am, I am still not sure that what I have sent reached my publishers in time to come out in the January issue. There will be some unpleasantness there yet!

Somehow we'll find each other, somehow we'll see each other, somehow we'll get together! I often think about you, all of you. A few nights ago I dreamed of you and Masenka—I saw a whole story in my dreams: Masenka was the heroine. Please give her a big kiss for me. But what is this about your health? You gave me a big scare. Don't be sad, my dear, that is the main thing. Moreover, don't be in too much of a hurry, don't worry too much; let nature take its course, and things will work out for the best by themselves. There are an infinite number of opportunities in life, and worrying too much is a waste of time.

My wish for you is that you be vigorous and firm of character, although I am sure you are, anyway. So, my dear girl, attend to your education and bear in mind the importance of acquiring a specialty, but, above all, do not be in too much of a hurry; you are still very young, everything will take its course, but I want you to know that the question of women's rights, and especially where it concerns the Russian woman, is certain to take a few great and beautiful steps forward even during your lifetime. Of course, I am not speaking here of our precocious lady-wonders—you know yourself what I think of them. But a few days ago I read in the newspaper that a former friend of mine, Nadezhda Suslova (Apollinariya Suslova's sister), had passed the exams for the degree of doctor of medicine at the University of Zurich and had defended her doctoral dissertation brilliantly. She is still only a very young girl; actually she is 23 now, a rare person, generous, honorable, and noble!

There was much, so much I wanted to tell you and now, writing you all this, I still haven't said 1/10 of what I had to tell you. So it will have to wait until the next letter, my dear friend!

There is one very interesting matter that concerns you particularly that I should like to talk to you about. Don't forget me and keep writing. And, above all, take care of your health. Give one more hug to Masenka. I heard that [a name has been heavily crossed out, apparently by the addressee] has been promoted to the rank of lieutenant general of the papal army and that he will pipe a polka of his own composition during the ceremonies celebrating the rout of Garibaldi, while Cardinal Antonelli dances with the chancellor general (for a lady) in the presence of the pope, and Yulinka will watch in a fury. Kiss her too, if she is willing to allow you to kiss her (on my behalf!). Kiss Vitya also for me, as well as the *much-vaunted* Lyolya and then all the rest. And, finally, give a big hello from me to your brother Aleksandr Aleksandrovich.

I embrace you and kiss you,

Your friend *always*
Fyodor Dostoyevsky

I will keep my word of honor—to write you every month. But, in the name of God, write me, too!

---

72. In later years, *Don Quixote* was the book that Dostoyevsky most admired. In *Diary of a Writer*, he wrote: "If life on earth comes to an end and human beings in some other world were asked whether they understood their life on earth and what conclusion they had come to about it, a man could just present the volume of Don Quixote and say: 'Here is my conclusion on life. Can you condemn me for it?'"

"The rout of Garibaldi" is a reference to his defeat by French and papal troops near Mentana, on November 3, 1867.

Giacomo Cardinal Antonelli (1806–1876) was the principal adviser to Pope Pius IX. He headed the State Council of the Papal States, a position that gave him great power, and he was one of the most vigorous opponents of the unification of Italy.

Yulinka (Yuliya), Vitya (Viktor), Lyolya (Yelena), and Aleksandr Aleksandrovich were Sonya's brothers and sisters (she had nine altogether).

73.   To A. N. Maikov
Geneva, February 18/March 1, 1868

My good, my only, my invaluable friend—(all these epithets apply in your case, and I am happy to apply them)—do not be angry with me for my unconscionable silence. Judge me with the same understanding and the same heart as you have before. Although my silence was *unconscionable*, it was almost literally impossible for me to answer your letter, though I tried to on several occasions. I got bogged down, my mind and all my faculties alike, in my Part 2, trying to get it ready by the deadline. I did not want to bungle it completely—too much depends on its success. But now I am not even hoping for a success, but only to avoid a total disaster; I'll still be able to save the situation in the later parts, since the novel will be a long one. I finally sent off Part 2 (it was terribly late, but I think it may get there in time). What can I tell you about it? Well, I cannot say anything about it myself, so much so that I am not even capable of the slightest opinion. I rather like the closing scene of Part 2, but the fact that I like it doesn't mean much; what will the readers say? The rest of it is just about the same as the first part, i.e., it seems rather dull. If only the reader can get through it without too great boredom—I don't pretend that it's any more successful than that.

You know, my dear fellow, you promised me that the minute you finished Part 1 you would write and tell me what you thought of it. And so I go and hang around the post office every day, but there is nothing from you, and yet surely by now you must have seen the *Russian Messenger*. I have drawn the quite obvious conclusion that my novel is weak and that out of consideration for my feelings, out of feelings of pity and conscience, you are putting your reply off rather than confront me with the truth. But that is precisely *the kind* of truth I need to know! I am longing for any opinion. Without one, it is sheer torture.

It is true, of course, that you did write me two letters before the magazine came out, but I cannot believe that you would keep count of letters in such a situation! But enough of this.

I wish you knew, my dear friend, with what joy I read and reread, again and again, every letter I get from you! If you could only imagine what my life here is like and what it means to me to receive letters from you! I see no one here, I have no news of anything, and even the Russian newspapers (*Moscow Gazette* and *Voice*) have not been arriving since the beginning of the year. Anna Grigorevna and I live here with just each other for company, and although we get along pretty well together and love each other and, besides, are both very busy, our life is all the same dull—for me, in any case. Anna Grigorevna assures me in all sincerity (and I have become convinced she is telling the truth) that she is very happy. Imagine, so far nothing has happened and the gentleman expected has not yet come to join us in this world. I am expecting him any day, because all the signs are there. I expected him yesterday, on my nameday, but he did not come. I shall wait for him again today and if not, it will be tomorrow for sure. Anna Grigorevna is waiting in awe and loves the impending little visitor boundlessly. She has been bearing up cheerfully and heartily, although of late her nerves have given way a bit, she is occasionally assailed by somber thoughts, worries that she may die, etc. This makes things rather depressing and wearisome. We have very, very little money, but at least we are not in utter poverty, though there are expenses lying ahead. But despite her condition, Anna Grigorevna has been taking shorthand for me and has done some copying, besides managing to do all the sewing and preparing everything a baby needs.

Worst of all is the fact that Geneva is such a dreadful town—a dismal place. Today is Sunday and there is nothing more dismal and unattractive than their Sundays. But to move out of here now is out of the question—we shall have to stick it out here for another five weeks or so during her convalescence, and even after that it is not clear what our financial situation will be. This month will be a difficult one for me—my wife's health and Part 3; even though I may be late with it, I still have to send it out regularly. And then, when I have also sent off Part 4, I hope we shall be able to leave Geneva. That should be somewhere around May. It is a good thing, at least, that the winter has suddenly turned milder here. The whole month of February the weather here was clear and warm, exactly like the clear April days we have in Petersburg.

I am always intensely interested in everything you write me about. I am always looking for something in the newspapers as one might search for a lost needle, and I make conjectures and guesses. Even from here I can sense the base and disgusting trends in our literature and journalism. How naive all that rubbish is! The people on the *Contemporary*, e.g., are scrambling for the last profits with the same old Saltykovs and Yeliseyevs, and it is always the same stale hatred for Russia, the same old refrain about the workers' associations in France, and nothing else. As for Saltykov's attacks on the zemstvo—that is just as it should be. Our liberal cannot help being at the same time an archenemy of Russia, and he is aware of it. Just let anything succeed in Russia, or let anything at all be to her advantage—and there he is spouting venom. And this I have noticed a thousand times over. Now our extreme liberal party has clashed with the *News*, but that was bound to happen. And as for the cynicism and villainy of all that riffraff, I occasionally see evidence of it in newspapers.

The editorial office of the *Russian Messenger* sent me the first issue. I read it from cover to cover. I did not find your piece—you must have been too late, or else they are saving you to embellish the February number. In the January issue I found Polonsky (a lovely poem) and Turgenev with a very weak story. I read the review of *War and Peace*. I should so much like to read the whole thing. I have read half. It seems to be quite a major work, although, unfortunately, it has too many petty psychological details. I wish there were rather fewer of them. On the other hand, though, it is perhaps just because of these details that it has so many good things.

For God's sake, write me more often of what's new in literature. You mentioned *Messenger of Europe* (is that Stasyulevich?)—I believe this particular trend has become quite prevalent at home.

Would you believe it—I have no idea what *Moscow* and the *Muscovite* are.

Your "Sofya Alekseyevna" is a delight. But here is something that occurred to me: Wouldn't it be great if "Sofya Alekseyevna" became one episode in a *whole poem* about that period, i.e., a *Raskolnik poem*, or part of a novel in verse about that period? Haven't such thoughts ever occurred to you? I feel that such a poem would make a tremendous impression. But what finally has been decided about *The Song of Igor's Campaign*? You don't say where it is to appear. I suppose it will be in *Russian Messenger*. In that case I shall be able to read it! Just imagine how impatient I am to see it! Have you given any other public reading of it besides the one you mentioned? Write me all about it. What did you read at the Krylov celebration besides what you sent me? I read about it in the newspapers, but it wasn't clear.

Things seem to have quieted down a bit of late back home, but I've been reading about the subscription for the famine victims. The Slavs and their aspirations seem to provoke the hostility of so many of our Russian liberals. I wonder when those damned dregs of obsolescence and retrogression will finally be skimmed off? For it really is quite impossible to consider a Russian liberal as anything but obsolete and retrogressive. What once used to be described as "educated society" is a collection of elements that have fully repudiated Russia, do not understand her, and have become Frenchified—that is what a Russian liberal is and what makes him a retrograde. Just remember the best of the liberals—think of Belinsky, for instance—isn't he a conscious enemy of the fatherland, isn't he a retrograde?

But to hell with them all! Here, I encounter only lousy little Poles who come to the coffeehouses in throngs—but I don't have anything to do with them. I have not met the priest here yet, but I shall have to when the child is born. But you must realize, my friend, that our priests, i.e., those living abroad, cannot be like the one from Wiesbaden about whom I spoke to you when I was leaving Petersburg. (By the way, have you gotten to know him? He is a rare human being—virtuous, humble, dignified, with an angelically pure heart and *passionate* faith. I believe he has been appointed inspector at the academy now.) But I hope that the priest here will turn out to be good, too, although he is bound to have been spoiled by the aristocracy. Here in Geneva (according to the Journal des Etrangers) there are an awful lot of Russian aristocrats and, as a matter of fact, it strikes me as very strange that, instead of spending their winter in a place like Montreux, for instance, these people should stay in Geneva, where the climate is so bad.

If I ever manage to move from here one day, it will be to Italy. But that day is still quite far away, and in any case when it comes I shall let you know my new address immediately, so there won't have to be any delay in your writing me. And so, for God's sake, do write.

I cannot say that my health is too good. As the spring draws closer, my attacks are becoming more frequent.

I read your account in which you describe your service on the jury and it made my heart pound with excitement. I have formed this picture (from what I've read) of our courts of justice: The moral fiber of our judges and, above all, of our juries is infinitely above the European. They have a Christian approach to crime. Even Russian expatriate traitors agree with this. But it seems to me that one thing has not been well established yet: I have the impression that, in this *humanitarian* approach to the criminal, there is too much that is bookish, liberal, and borrowed. Sometimes this seems to be the case. However, I may be terribly wrong, because I see it from so far away. But, at any rate, in essence we are infinitely superior to the Europeans in this respect. And in general all Russian moral concepts and goals are loftier than those of the European world. We have a more spontaneous and noble faith in goodness and in Christianity than in any bourgeois solution of the problem of comfort.

A great renewal through Russian thought is being prepared for the world as a whole (that thought, as you correctly point out, is closely tied up with Russian Orthodoxy), and this will come about in a century or so—this is my impassioned belief. But if that great mission is to be fulfilled, the *political power* and leadership of the Great Russian tribe over all Slavdom must be achieved definitively and indisputably. (And to think that our little liberals preach the splitting up of Russia to make a confederation of states! Ah, the turds!)

I have a tremendous favor to ask you or, to be more precise, 2 favors, and I am placing my hopes in your kind heart and your brotherly interest in me. Here is what it is all about. When I sent Part 2 to Katkov I asked him to send me 500 rubles. It is horrible, but what else could I do? I simply had to ask him. At first I had great hopes: (1) of writing 4 parts (i.e., 23–24 printer's sheets) and (2) of writing them all *well*—and then I would have asked him for this big favor. But I repeat—I had no choice. Now, with the submission of Part 2 to the editors, I have delivered a total of 11½ printer's sheets—that is, about 1700 rubles' worth. Altogether I owe them 4560 rubles (ouch!), which means that now I am still 2860 rubles in arrears. And at such a moment, I come asking them for yet another 500 rubles, i.e., I am again increasing my debt, making it 2860 + 500 = 3360 rubles. But, in view of the fact that by May 1 I shall have delivered another 1700 rubles' worth of work, I shall once again reduce my indebtedness to the original figure of 1700 rubles at the most. It was torture for me to ask them for the 500 rubles. If only the novel turns out to be good! Then I would feel less compunction for having asked them for the money. I don't know whether he will send it to me or not. But, in any case, I thought I would let you know all about it and, at the same time, ask you for these 2 great favors:

1st favor: I have asked Katkov, in case he agrees to the 500 rubles, to send 300 rubles to me here in Geneva and 200 to you personally at your Petersburg address. But although you may get those 200 rubles, I shall still have to go on behaving like a scoundrel toward you because I won't be able to let you have one single kopek of that money for yourself in payment of what I owe to you (although, I'm sure, you need it badly)! This worries me and Anna Grigorevna so much that sometimes we talk about it at night. But, notwithstanding this, I am asking you to please wait a little longer, and in so doing, you will save me from some terrible anxiety. This anxiety—and this is the *2nd favor* I have to ask you—stems from the fact that I cannot even imagine without trepidation what can be happening to poor Emiliya Fyodorovna now. She does have Fedya, but isn't it callous and inconsiderate on my part to rely upon that poor young man and to burden him with the entire responsibility for the family? Isn't he too young, doesn't he have to struggle too hard to provide for them all? And, of course, he might eventually *lose patience,* and that may lead him astray in the end. That could really very well happen. I feel that I must do something, that it is my obligation to help. Even if it is only a tiny crumb. And besides them, there is Pasha. And there it is the same thing again: a young boy, not even of age, cannot possibly provide for himself. To leave him to his own resources would be callous and stupid of me. It would be cruel. It is tantamount to sending him to his perdition, for he won't be able to cope with it. And he was bequeathed to me by Mariya Dmitriyevna, it was her last request to me. And so, *I implore you,* if you do receive the 200 rubles, to dispose of them as follows: give *100* to Emiliya Fyodorovna right away, and 100 to Pasha. But give Pasha only 50 rubles for the time being (without telling him that you have the other 50), and 2 months hence, let him have all of the remaining 50. (In addition to regular living expenses, there are always clothes and linen to be mended and other *unavoidable* minor expenses—in short, he cannot do with less than 50 rubles at a time.) If Katkov agrees, you ought to receive the 200 rubles 2 weeks from now, although it could possibly be a month. I shall inform Pasha about this, so that he doesn't drop in on you too soon. You wrote to me that the other time they bothered you a lot—please forgive them, dear fellow! As for Emiliya Fyodorovna, you could perhaps either deliver it yourself or let her know through Pasha that she can come and pick it up. All that depends, of course, on whether you get the money, and this I shall explain to them. Well, there you have my 2nd request. I realize that I am imposing upon you quite shamelessly but, my dear friend, you can save me so much torment. The thought of the situation they are in causes me such distress that I would rather be in their place myself. And to think that everything, my whole future depends on whether this novel succeeds or fails! Ah, it is so difficult to be poetic under such conditions! How different is the life of, say, Turgenev, and how dare he, under his circumstances, come up with a Yergunov! And when I tell you that he himself told me that he is a German and not a Russian and that he feels it is to his honor to consider himself German rather than Russian—that is the *literal* truth!

Good-bye, my friend. What makes me most happy for you is that you do not allow yourself to fall into spiritual idleness. There are aspirations, ideals, and goals to be achieved seething in you. That is a great deal. In our time, if a man is caught by apathy, he is lost, dead and buried.

Good-bye, I hug you hard and wish you all the best. Write me and tell me at least something of what you think of my novel. Anything at all.

I read the political news quite regularly. Much of it is, of course, lies. However, I am terribly worried by a certain weakening and servility in our foreign policy of late. And on top of that, there are many internal opponents of the sovereign's reforms. He is the only hope there is. He has already demonstrated his firmness. May God grant him a long reign.

Anna Grigorevna sends her regards to you, Anna Ivanovna, and Yevgeniya Petrovna. So do I—please remind them of me. I believe someone will arrive today. It will be either Misha or Sonya—that has already been settled.

Farewell, my dear friend,
All yours,
F. Dostoyevsky

---

73. Maikov did report on the reception of the first installments of *The Idiot* (though without giving his own opinion) in a letter written toward the end of February: "I have a piece of very pleasant news for you: success, and curiosity and interest aroused by the personally experienced moments of terror [presumably referring to the account of the death sentence in chapters 3 and 4], the original problem of the hero . . . the general's wife, the promise of a powerful character in Nastasya Filippovna, and much, much else—all this has attracted the attention of everyone I have spoken with. . . ." Dostoyevsky wrote back, on March 14 (New Style): "Until your letter arrived, I was in complete despair because I felt that the novel was a failure. . . . So you can imagine how much your letter cheered me up. . . . That gave me back all my courage."

Saltykov and Yeliseyev were among the former contributors to the *Contemporary* who, in 1868, took over publication of *Notes of the Fatherland*. In the January issue, there appeared a scathing satire by Saltykov of the proceedings of the newly established zemstvo organizations, in which he intimated that they were little more than façades for the self-enrichment of the gentry.

Yakov Petrovich Polonsky (1819–1898) had been the editor of the *Russian Word* at the time that Dostoyevsky's story "Uncle's Dream" was published in that magazine. Subsequently, the two became good friends, and Polonsky was a frequent contributor to *Time* and *Epoch*. The poem of his that appeared in the January issue of the *Russian Messenger* was "The Bacchante and the Satyr" (Yakhanka i satir).

Turgenev's "weak story" was "The Story of Lieutenant Yergunov" (Istoriya leitenanta Yergunova).

The "review" of *War and Peace* (actually, more a summary of its contents) was by the historian Pyotr Karlovich Shchebalsky (1810–1876).

Maikov, in his letter of January 7 (to which this letter is a reply), had described *Messenger of Europe* (Vestnik Yevropy) as "a venomous sheet of the Westernizers," which had recently suggested that "our western territories be left to take care of themselves, and that the Poles be allowed to take advantage of all our reforms, and [it] assures us that this will appease them and bind them to us." The journal's founder was Mikhail Matveyevich Stasyulevich (1826–1911), a historian, journalist, and public figure.

Moscow was a journal edited by Aksakov. When it was closed down by the censors, a successor journal, *Muscovite* (Moskvich), was put out by essentially the same people.

The full title of Maikov's poem was "The Musketeer's Legend about Tsarevna Sofya Alekseyevna" (Streletskoye skazaniye o tsarevne Sofii Alekseyevne). It was published in the February 1868 issue of *Russian Messenger,* but Maikov had evidently sent it to Dostoyevsky in manuscript or in proof.

The celebration of the hundredth anniversary of the birth of the fabulist Ivan Andreyevich Krylov (1768–1844) was held in Petersburg on February 2 and 3. On the latter date, Maikov read his poem "At the Monument to Krylov" (U pamyatnika Krylovu) and another reported by the newspapers as "Musketeers" (Streltsy— probably the "Musketeer's Legend" mentioned above).

Poor harvests had caused a famine in Central Russia in 1867–1868. A committee had been formed, headed by the future Alexander III, to raise money to help the victims.

"The Slavs and their aspirations" is probably a reference to events in Serbia and Bulgaria, where nationalist movements were struggling for independence from Turkey.

The Russian Orthodox priest in Geneva whom Dostoyevsky had not yet met was Afanasy Konstantinovich Petrov. Later (Letter 76), Dostoyevsky expressed his conviction that the priest was working for the secret police. The priest whom Dostoyevsky had met (and borrowed money from) in Wiesbaden was Ioann Leontevich Yanyshev (b. 1826), formerly a professor of theology and philosophy at Petersburg University and a tutor to the wife of the future Alexander III; at the time this letter was written, he was rector of the Petersburg Ecclesiastical Academy.

On March 5 (New Style), Anna Grigorevna gave birth to the Dostoyevskys' first child, a girl, whom they named Sonya, after Dostoyevsky's favorite niece, the daughter of his sister Vera.

74.   To A. N. Maikov

Geneva, March 20/April 2 [1868]

My dear and good friend Apollon Nikolayevich,

First of all, I can't thank you enough, my dear fellow, for having done all the things I asked you to, which proved troublesome and caused you to do so much running around for me. Forgive me for putting you to such bother, but you are, after all, the only person on whom I can count (which, I confess, is no warrant for making life unpleasant for you). Secondly, I thank you for your regards, congratulations and best wishes to the three of us. You are right, my dear friend, you depicted the sensation of being a father as it is in nature and you took your beautiful words from nature—it is all perfectly true. For nearly a month, now, I have been experiencing a gamut of utterly fresh sensations that I never knew until the first time I set eyes on my Sonya, and which I felt again just now, when, by our joint efforts, we washed her in a basin. Yes, an angelic soul has indeed flown into our house. However, I shan't describe my sensations to you. They are growing and developing with each day. Listen to this, my dear boy: The last time I wrote you I was in such a panic that I *forgot* (!) to tell you that Anya and I agreed last year, when *we still were in Dresden* (and she just now bitterly reproached me for having forgotten to mention it), that *you would have to be Sonya's godfather.* Don't let me down, my dear fellow! The matter was settled nearly 10 months ago, as far as we are concerned. If you refuse, you will make Sonya unhappy. The first godfather, and he turns her down! But you won't refuse, my friend. I hasten to add that it will cause you not the least bit of inconvenience, and if it draws us still closer, I'm all for it. The godmother is Anna Nikolavna—did she tell you? For God's sake, let me know what you've decided as soon as possible, because I have to know for the christening. A month has gone by and she still has not been christened! (Is that the way things are done in Russia?) And let me tell you that your godchild (and I am sure that she is your godchild) is extremely pretty, despite the fact that she so incredibly and ridiculously resembles me. It's even uncanny. I wouldn't believe it if I hadn't seen it for myself. The baby is just a month old but she even has exactly my facial expression, my whole physiognomy, up to the wrinkles on the forehead, and she lies there just as if she were composing a novel! I am not even talking about her features. Her forehead is startlingly like mine. From all this, you might conclude that she cannot really be all that beautiful (because I am no *beauty* in any but Anna Grigorevna's eyes—and I say that in all seriousness!). But you, being an artist, know very well that one can be pretty and yet resemble someone who is not at all good-looking. Anna Grigorevna sends you a special plea to be the godfather. She is terribly fond of you and of Anna Ivanovna and holds you in boundless esteem.

You are too much of a prophet: You prophesy that with the new responsibilities I have now, I shall become an *egotist*—and this has unfortunately come true, and it could not be otherwise: just imagine—during this entire month I haven't written *one single line!* My God, what am I doing to Katkov, with all my promises, words of honor, and obligations! I was overjoyed when, after I had written to Katkov that I would be late with the installment of my novel because of my wife's confinement, *Russian Messenger* announced, at the end of Part One, that the novel would be continued in the April issue instead of the March one. But now, alas, I have 20 days at the most to have it ready for the April issue (I am frightfully behind), and I still have not written a single line! So tomorrow I shall write to Katkov and apologize to him, but he cannot make himself a fur coat out of my apologies. Nevertheless, I must try to get my stuff ready for the April number, however late it may be. And meanwhile, apart from everything else, my very livelihood (where money is concerned) depends on these people. Indeed, the situation is desperate. But what can I do—the whole month has been exceptionally hectic, fraught with anxiety and concern. There were nights on end when I couldn't get to sleep, not only because of mental strain, but because I actually had no other choice. That is a horrible thing for a man suffering from epilepsy. My nerves are now unstrung in the extreme. We had a particularly miserable month of March here, with snow and freezing temperatures, almost as bad as in Petersburg. Anna Grigorevna was in a terrible physical state [(]don't tell this to Anna Nikolavna FOR ANYTHING, as she is liable to imagine God knows what; it's just that Anya is slow in recovering and, on top of that, she is breastfeeding the baby[)]. She clearly does not have much milk, and so we are using a bottle, too. With all that, the baby is very healthy (touch wood!). And Anya is beginning to get out of the house for some fresh air. Today, the weather is sunny and beautiful for the third day in a row and things are already starting to turn green. I can't quite get over all this.

I am also terribly worried about money. We were sent 300 rubles. That was 1025 *francs* at the going rate of exchange. There's hardly any of it left now. Our expenses have grown, we had to pay old bills, redeem our pawned belongings, and then, exactly three weeks from today, we shall be faced with considerable expenses since we are moving to another apartment (we are being turned out of this one because of the baby's crying), and, besides, other bills will be coming up. It's a nightmare! And, of course, we'll have to get along somehow for at least another two months, counting from today, until I can hope to receive anything further from the *R. Messenger*. But in any case, I can't get anything from the *R. Messenger* until I have delivered Part 2. But when shall I write it, unless I can once again do it in *18* days, as I did for the installment that appeared in the January issue?

Your disposition of the money was very good. But now, unpleasant as it is for me to bother you, I must ask you to send to me, in Geneva, the 25 rubles that you still have, *immediately if possible*. That is how badly I need money! (N.B.—Simply put a 25-ruble note in the letter, register it to make sure it does not go astray, and send it here, to my address. They change even our Russian bank note here. The only thing that worries me, though, is that I gather there are new 25-ruble bills in circulation now, and they may not be familiar with them here, so would you please send an old one.) I am very glad that you gave Pasha 50 rubles instead of only 25. It's just as well. I am very pleased to hear that he is working. Please, dear fellow, would you, just once in a while, check up on him for me! If I write to him, I shall tell him that I have learned from you that you have given him 25 rubles as a loan and that I have paid you back. But what concerns me is the possibility that Pasha may not write me and congratulate me on Sonya's birth. Others have—you;

Strakhov, who wrote me from Moscow; Anna Grigorevna's friends from Petersburg—but not a word from Pasha at this time, nor even an answer to the letter I sent to him through you around a month and a half ago (did you get it, by the way? Somehow you made *no* mention of it). And I really feel that he could have answered that particular letter.

And while I'm about it, there's something else *extremely important:* I still don't know whether he went to Moscow or not, whether he went to see Katkov. This is something I absolutely must know. Bear in mind that I sent Katkov a long apologetic letter, solely on that account. It is essential for me to know. Please, my dear friend, if you can possibly find out what happened, do it for me!

(I have solemnly and officially announced to Emiliya Fyodorovna the birth of my daughter, but not a word, no acknowledgment whatever! And even before that, when I asked her for a very important piece of information concerning the apartment and the landlord, Alonkin, she didn't answer me either. I am positively bewildered. Why, it is even rude, simply preposterous!)

On the subject of wills and your other advice, I have always felt exactly as you do. But, my friend, my sincere and loyal friend (perhaps my only friend!)—why do you consider that I am such a kind and generous man? No, my friend, no, I am not as kind as all that, and this saddens me. In Pasha's case, he was entrusted to my care by poor Mariya Dmitriyevna on her deathbed! And so how can I abandon him altogether? (Actually, you never suggest that I should.) No, no, I still feel I must help him, the more so as I am genuinely fond of him. Why, I had him in my house for more than 10 years when he was growing up! He is like a son to me. We lived together. And, anyway, to abandon him to himself, young as he is—it is quite unthinkable! And, poor as I may be, I feel I must help him now and then. He certainly is frivolous, no doubt about that, but wasn't I, perhaps, even worse at his age (I remember it). And this is just the time when he needs the most support. If I leave an impression of goodness and kindness on his heart now, it will stand him in good stead, as he matures. As to his working now and fending for himself, I am positively delighted—let him do some work. And you, I give you a big brotherly hug and embrace you for having gone to see Razin and for speaking to him about Pasha.

Now when it comes to my attitude toward Em[iliya] Fyodorovna, there again, my late brother Misha is involved. Surely I don't have to tell you what that man was to me from my first moment of consciousness! No, you really have no idea! Fedya, my godson, is another young man, and he has been earning his bread by hard work. And in his case, too, I must occasionally help him, *if it is at all possible* (because he is young, after all, and there is no reason why he should carry the entire load; it's too much for him). And I must tell you that, except for paying for their apartment, I have contributed only 250 rubles to their upkeep during the whole of the last year. And why are you trying to pass yourself off, my dear boy, as such a practical, selfish person? Didn't you lend me 200 rubles? And didn't you lose almost 2000 rubles when Misha died and our magazine collapsed! For, although I have sworn to make good all my brother's debts, as a matter of honor, *for reasons of the heart,* so to speak, yet it is hardly likely that I shall be able to pay (all the debts!) but only those that are due on promissory notes that I countersigned or settled or had transferred to my name. But I need not have brought all this up in any case, since I consider your advice absolutely correct. As for myself, there is a proverb: Never brag when you're going into action. I keep writing that I ought to help such and such and so and so, etc., when I have no idea of what is going to happen to me, myself.

Horrible and disgusting though living abroad has become to me, there are times, you know, when I think with terror of what will happen to my health when God bids me to return to Petersburg. It's bad enough having these attacks here, but what will it be like back there? My mental faculties are drained—I can't remember things, for example.

Everything you write about Russia and, above all, your mood (rose-colored) makes me very happy. It is perfectly true that there's no point in bothering oneself with the various particular cases—as long as the whole is all right and that whole has impetus and a goal. All the rest is bound to come as part of the tremendous regeneration that is taking place under our present great Sovereign. My dear friend, you look at it just the way I do, and you have at last expressed what I was saying even publicly as far back as three years ago, when I was still publishing the magazine, but no one understood me—namely, that our constitution is the mutual love of the Monarch for the people and of the people for the Monarch. Yes, love, not conquest, is the fundament of our state (something, I believe, the Slavophiles were the first to discover) and it is a sublime idea on which many things will be built. This is the idea that we shall proclaim to Europe, which understands nothing whatsoever about it. Our wretched, uprooted fraternity of clever gentlemen, alas, was bound to end up like that. They will die as they are, because there's no changing them. (Just look at Turgenev!) But the newer generation—that is where we should look. (A classical education could be of great help—what is this about Katkov's lyceum?)

Living here abroad, I have definitely become an uncompromising monarchist when it comes to Russia. If anyone has accomplished anything in Russia, it has certainly been he alone (and this is not the only reason, but simply because he is the tsar, who is beloved by the Russian people both for himself and because he is the tsar. In our country, people have given and continue to give their love to every one of our tsars, and it is only in him that they finally believe. For the people this is a mystery, a sacrament, an anointment)[.] The

Westerners understand nothing of this and they, who pride themselves on basing their theories on facts, have overlooked the primary, the greatest fact of our history.

I like your idea about the importance of Peter [the Great] for Pan-Slavism. This is the first time in my life that I have heard that thought expressed and it is absolutely true. But you know what—I read the *Voice* here, and I often come across terribly distressing things in it. For instance, reports about the disorganization of our railroads (the newly built lines), about zemstvo affairs, about the sad state of the colonies of settlers. What makes it so terribly hard for us is that we have so few men capable of getting things done. Talkers we have, but men of action you can count on your fingers. Of course I am not speaking here of men in high positions, but simply of lower-rank officials who are so badly needed but who are so lacking. Granted there have been enough judges and jurors. But what about men for the railroads? And in certain other places. There is a terrible clash between the new people and new demands, on the one hand, and the old order, on the other. And I am not even speaking of the vitality of their ideas: there is no dearth of free-thinkers, but there are no true Russians. What counts is the awareness of being Russian. Oh, God, how helpful publicity is to the tsar and all Russians—even the hostile publicity of the Westernizers.

How I wish our strategic railroads (the Smolensk and the Kiev lines) could be completed as rapidly as possible and also that we could have those new model rifles quickly. Why did Napoleon have to increase his army and risk taking such an unpopular step at a moment so critical for him? I'll be damned if I understand. But it won't end well for Europe. (I am somehow absolutely convinced of it.) It would be bad if we got involved in it. If only they could have held off for a couple of years. And it is not only Napoleon. Apart from Napoleon the future looks menacing and we must prepare for it. Turkey is dangling by a hair, the Austrian situation is very unhealthy (I am only analyzing the factors, without making judgments), in the West the damned proletarian problem has become acute (but it is hardly even mentioned in the reports on current political developments!), and lastly and most important—Napoleon is an old man and in poor health. He won't live long. While he lasts, though, he will make more blunders and France will become even sicker of the Bonapartes. So then what? Well, that is the contingency that Russia must, without fail, start preparing for and rapidly, for it may all come very soon.

I am so pleased that the Crown Prince has revealed himself in all his goodness and grandeur to the country and that Russia has affirmed her trust in and love for him. If she could have but half as much love for him as she feels for his father, it would be good enough. As for our Alexander, may God grant him another good forty years of happy life. He has done almost as much for Russia as all his predecessors put together. But the most important thing is that he is so beloved. This is the *mainstay* of the entire Russian movement now, and our whole rebirth depends on it and on it alone. Oh, my friend, how much I long to come back, how sickening my life is here! It is a miserable life. And the worst of it is that I cannot work properly here. If only I could finish the novel to my satisfaction, how good that would be! It would be the dawn of my entire future.

Anna Grigorevna is not depressed and honestly says that she is happy. But I am fed up. I go nowhere, see no one. But even if we had friends, I doubt that I would go to see them. I have let myself go completely, and I am not working well. I get out of the house for only a couple of hours each day, at five o'clock, when I go to the café to read the Russian newspapers there. I don't know a soul here, and I am glad I don't. It makes me sick when I run into our *know-it-alls*. Oh, the poor wretches, oh, the nonentities, oh, the garbage swollen with vanity, oh, the turds! Disgusting! I met H[erzen] by chance in the street, and for ten minutes we spoke to each other in politely hostile tones, made a few digs at each other, and parted. No, I can't take them any more! They have fallen so far behind the times! The extent to which they understand nothing! And you should see how puffed up they have become, so very puffed up!

I scan the papers hungrily for announcements of the publication of issues of our magazines and of their tables of contents. I find strange names and surprising combinations of articles. Take, for instance, *Notes of the Fath[er-land]*—yes, it's rags instead of banners, that is a fact! Don't give them anything, my dear friend; better wait for a while. But I can see that the problem of where to publish apparently bothers you. I shouldn't worry, my friend. If I weren't in a hurry now, I would write more about it. I have an idea for you, but it would take a whole letter to set it forth, and I don't have the time just now. I shall write you about it soon. The idea occurred to me in connection with your "Sofya Alekseyevna." Don't laugh, I am really serious about it. You will see for yourself what sort of an idea it is! Let me explain. It is neither a novel nor a poem. But that is just as it should be, just what is needed, and it will be so original and new and so essentially Russian that it will stagger you! I shall explain the plan to you myself. Pity it will have to be done by letter instead of face to face. It could bring you glory and, most important, it will *have* to be published as a separate book after some excerpts have first been published, and the book will *certainly* be a bestseller.

So you did finish "The Apocalypse"? And I had imagined you had given it up. Of course, there is no way of escaping ecclesiastic censorship—and that is as it should be—but if you have translated it faithfully they will certainly authorize it. I received a letter from Strakhov. It pleased me enormously. I intend to answer him very soon, but since he failed to give me his address (I have forgotten it!), I'll write to him at your address, and I will ask you to transmit it.

My dear boy, write me more often. You cannot imagine how much your letters mean to me! Here it is already April 3 their style, and April 25 is the very latest (minimum!) for me to send an installment of the novel, but *I don't have a single line,* not a single line has been written! My God, what will become of me! Well, good-bye, then. I kiss and embrace you, Anya sends you her regards, and both of us send our regards to Anna Ivanovna.

All yours,
Fyodor Dostoyevsky

P.S. For the love of God, write me everything you hear about *The Idiot* (if you do hear anything at all). I need to know, I have to know, I absolutely must know, for God's sake! The closing scene of Part 2, about which I wrote you, is the same as that which was published at the end of the first part. And I was counting on it so much! However, I still believe that the character of Nastasya Filippovna is completely right. By the way, there are many little things at the end of Part 1 that are taken directly from life, and some of the characters are straight portraits, e.g., General Ivolgin and Kolya. But your judgment may be quite right.

---

74. Maikov did agree to be Sonya's godfather, and the baby was baptized on May 19. But eight days later, she died of pneumonia. A few days afterward, Dostoyevsky wrote to Maikov:

Perhaps my love for my firstborn was quite ridiculous, perhaps I sounded ridiculous when I wrote about her. . . . This little, three-month-old creature, so pathetic, so tiny, was already a person and an individual to me. She had begun to recognize me, to love me, and she smiled when I approached her. When I sang her songs in my funny voice, she liked to listen to them. She did not screw up her face or cry when I kissed her; indeed, she stopped crying when I came near her. . . . I am not afraid to say it—I would willingly be crucified if it could bring her back to life.

Anna Grigorevna was of course also crushed. On July 5, Dostoyevsky wrote to his niece Sonya that his wife "still cries all night long. . . . She is growing thin, her nerves are on edge."

Anna Nikola(ye)vna, Anna Grigorevna's mother, joined the couple in Switzerland shortly after Sonya's death and lived with them, except for a few brief intervals, until their return to Russia in July 1871.

Dostoyevsky is worried about whether Pasha went to see Katkov because Anna Nikolayevna had written him that Pasha intended to demand some money from Katkov; in fear of this, Dostoyevsky had written an anticipatory letter of apology. However, the whole affair turned out to have been a fabrication by his mother-in-law.

Pasha had recently gotten a job in the archives of the Polish chancellery, and Aleksei

Yegorovich Razin (d. 1875) was an official there. Razin, a popular writer of children's books, had been in charge of the "Domestic Review" section of *Time* and a contributor to *Epoch,* and he spoke to Pasha's superior on the boy's behalf. Nevertheless, Pasha lost the job within a few months—the second time this had happened in a year.

Katkov and two other men had founded a lyceum in 1868 with the aim of making it a model for classical secondary education. Dostoyevsky may have read about it in the *Moscow Gazette,* which was published by Katkov and devoted considerable space to secondary education.

In his letter of March 7, to which this letter is a reply, Maikov had referred to "the Pan-Slavic significance of Peter" in connection with a plan he was drawing up for a history textbook. He added: "Just wait a while and keep cool—we shall one day all be proud of Peter . . . when we have forgiven him certain things."

Dostoyevsky had probably read about the "disorganization of the railroads" in the *Voice,* which carried letters in almost every issue from people complaining about the lack of organization, the graft and corruption, and the negligence of the railroad administration and engineers. The *Moscow Gazette* and *Petersburg Gazette,* which Dostoyevsky was also reading, carried many stories about the shortcomings of the zemstvo organizations. All of these issues, as well as the scandals about mismanagement among the colonies of settlers in Siberia, Central Asia, and Turkestan, were being reported in the liberal press; hence Dostoyevsky's statement that "even the hostile publicity of the Westernizers" was helpful.

Maikov had written that construction of two new railroad lines had begun and that "in a year, our army will receive modern weapons, and, mark my words, the conversation will be different then."

"From the Apocalypse" (Iz Apokalipsisa) was a translation that Maikov had done of that book of the New Testament. It was published in the April 1868 issue of *Russian Messenger.*

In the letter that pleased Dostoyevsky so much, Strakhov had written: "Well done! . . . Your *Idiot* interests me . . . almost more than anything else you have ever written. . . . Your fears that it might be dull are quite unfounded. . . ."

Maikov's own appraisal of the parts of the novel that had been published so far was that it had "flashes of genius" but "more *plausibility and verisimilitude* than truth," and that most of the characters "seem to live in some fantastic world," illuminated by "a sort of unreal gleam"—which may have led Dostoyevsky to make the defensive remarks about the things "taken directly from life" and the "straight portraits."

75. To S. A. IVANOVA

Geneva, March 30/April 10, 1868

My dear, invaluable friend Sonechka,

Forgive me for not having answered your good letter right away. And even now I must write in great haste. I am terribly busy, exhausted by worries, and, above all, preoccupied by the thought that I may not manage to deliver the installment of my novel to the editors in time. And I don't even speak of the particularly hectic time I've had these past five weeks. Believe it or not, I have spent whole nights on my feet. And we've had the most awful, cold and rainy month of March here in Geneva, so that Anna Grig[orevna] has been recovering only very slowly. I have written next to nothing of my novel. In the 2nd issue of *Russian Messenger* it was announced that "the continuation of the novel will appear in the April issue." They gave me thus a one-month respite, but now it looks as if I may be late for the April issue, too! How can I bear that thought? I have now exactly 10 days left before the installment must be in the mail. I shall be working day and night. Ah, Sonechka, this business is twice, three times more laborious and, above all, more crucially important, more capable of affecting my *entire future career* (without the least exaggeration) than may appear at first glance. To start with, I am afraid that my good relations with R[ussian] *Messenger* may be spoiled. You cannot imagine how considerate Katkov has been toward me up till now and how far he has trusted me! During the whole year he sent me money whenever I asked for it, which meant that by the New Year my debt to *Russian Messenger* had swollen to 5060 rubles. That is a terrifying amount! Because, after all, I could get sick, die, and send in nothing at all or something that was very poor. Their trust in me is extraordinary. Up to now I have published 1800 rubles worth of my novel (in two issues), but I have been obliged to ask for another 400 rubles (as I find myself in a terrible situation). And though I have made this request, my work is still not ready and *that is why* I must work day and night now. Thank God, Anna Grigorevna is feeling better and is now able to help me (she takes down shorthand and recopies), because by myself I would never be able to manage. My second and most important concern is that the novel should come off well. If it doesn't, all is lost. It absolutely must run through a second edition, that is, the sales from a second edition would bring me an additional three, or at least two, thousand rubles, failing which I won't be able to return to Russia (where debts and all sorts of difficulties in reestablishing ourselves will have to be met). Besides, if the novel doesn't succeed, my earning power will drop in a flash—they will offer me half of what they are paying me now per sheet, and they will be reluctant to pay me even that much. As it is, I always need money in advance.

I am terribly worried about the novel, and there are moments when I feel almost certain it won't come off well. The idea is too beautiful and perhaps I won't be able to do justice to it, especially working under such pressure and living abroad. (You wouldn't believe, my angel, what it means to live abroad for a long time and to lose contact with Russia: you don't have the same ideas, the same enthusiasm, the same energy as in Russia. Strange though it may seem, it is so.) By the way, I have received some heartening reports. I received some letters and critiques from Petersburg just after the publication of the first part, and they came from very authoritative people. Over there, my novel has been acclaimed as a *perfection,* the best thing I have ever written—in a word, an enthusiastic reception. But I don't trust that: the idea of the novel is one whose strength lies not in its immediate effect, but in its very essence. That essence is beautiful in the original concept, but how will it come off when written down? But even if I am ultimately successful in its realization, still, a novel that is effective is more profitable. It sells at a better price. And money is everything to me, I need it so badly, the filthy lucre!

My darling Sonya, the novel is dedicated to you and that is spelled out en toutes lettres at the beginning. But I am sure that you haven't read or seen it yet because, in the first place, you have other things to worry about and, in the second place, because you probably do not get the magazine (in the very next letter I write to the editors, I shall ask them to send you *Russian Messenger* for the whole of this year *postage paid,* and the only thing I ask of you is to make sure they send it to the correct address).

It is going to be a huge novel—40 printer's sheets—and I shall be busy writing it all summer. But, as Geneva is such a terrible place for me and for us all and affects our health so badly, I wouldn't be able to write anything if I stayed here. I am asking Katkov for 400 rubles which will enable us to move to *Vevey,* which is very close by (it is a 4-hour journey across the lake by steamboat), and it can all be done within the day. Vevey lies in the same bend of the lake as Montreux, Chillon, and Villeneuve, i.e., places known the world over for the extraordinary mildness and excellence of their climate. The locality is protected on all sides by the mountains. Renowned throughout the world, it is one of the most picturesque sites on earth. Besides, life is cheaper there. And finally, I am so sick of Geneva that I feel as if I had an abcess on my heart. I have spent many depressing moments here, and so has An. Grigorevna. Our daughter, Sonya (our angel), is in fine health, but she will be a *hundred* times better there. And I shall work on my novel there for four months or so, until I've finished it. I shall notify you of my address, but for the time being, until I let you know definitely, keep writing to me in Geneva—your letters will reach me wherever I am. (And you must not forget to give me your address either, because we must write to each other more often now. I love all of you deeply, and Anna Grigorevna and I think of you constantly. Only in the family of the dear departed—only in your family—have I found real relatives and a heartwarming corner for myself. We must never *part,* though thousands of versts may separate us.)

But enough said about myself, let us talk about you, you who, ever since your last letter, have been constantly in the minds of myself and Anna Grigorevna (who loves you, loves and *esteems* you, as much as I do). An idea occurred to both of us, a plan that concerns you, and I hasten to share it with you. Actually it requires spelling out in some detail and at far greater length, but for the time being I shall say only a few words. Here it is: *Wouldn't you like to study stenography?* Now listen carefully, Sonechka: Stenography is a highly valued skill, it is not a humiliating trade at all (although actually there is no such thing anyway, in my opinion), it brings honor and ample rewards to the person who has mastered it. It is a skill which leaves you free and consequently women find it very suitable (Anna Grigorevna, for instance, who, by the way, *did not have time* to become fully proficient at it, is determined to pursue it further as soon as we get back to Petersburg). This skill requires for its best practitioners an extensive and, to some extent, a specialized education. You can readily understand this: In order to make summaries of serious meetings for the newspapers, a person must be extremely well educated. It is not enough just to reproduce a verbatim report, it must afterwards be polished; it must convey the spirit, the meaning, *rendering precisely* what has been said and written. Thus, in the case of a political account, a rather solid historical background is needed and especially a grasp of more recent history. You will understand this, even though I have put it briefly. (N.B. If you are receptive to my idea, the next time you go to the country, get yourself somehow the whole of Thiers's *Le Consulat et l'Empire*. It contains a great deal of contemporary history, and you should read it, not as one reads a novel, but, so to speak, as if you were studying it. That would just be a start, but of course you will have to read something like 50 books of this sort before you acquire the firm and serious knowledge which is the solid foundation for this discipline.)

Now, in case of success (of my novel), we hope to be back in Petersburg either by the fall or by the winter. I'll make a trip to Moscow, and we can discuss it seriously and arrive at a definite decision. And if we are all agreed, you could come and stay with us in Petersburg while you are studying. That should take a year and a half or two years, at the most. You won't really be separated from your family since you'll be able to go to Moscow three times or so a year (I, for instance, will have to go there quite often, too, because I do not want to sever my literary ties with *Russian Messenger*). You will live with us and that won't inconvenience us in the least. Anna Grigorevna and I are enthusiastic about the idea, and it always comes up whenever we speak of you, which is every day. Besides, Sasha will be in Petersburg too.

Oh, my dear friend, if you only knew how worthwhile it would be for you. It would do you good to get away from your family for a while, because I can see what an awful state you're in. You write that you wonder whether you are not an encumbrance on your family and are harmful to it! Why, you don't realize your own worth, and never have. You—harmful! You have always undervalued yourself, you don't know your own value. Your spirit, your general attitude, your personality make you a great asset to the family.

Oh, do not break up this harmony, this unity! Just try leaving your family for a while, and you will see how mutually interdependent you are. And then you will understand your true value.

You may object that in saying this I am contradicting myself by suggesting that you should move to Petersburg. That is not so, because there is another factor involved here: You must part from them temporarily, precisely to enable you all to know how valuable you are to each other; and then you will realize how great are your obligations toward them and toward yourself. And do you realize that, in acquiring that skill, you will be a support to your family and, at the same time, your own livelihood will be assured for the rest of your life. You are only at the beginning of life: In 10 years drastic changes will have taken place in our country. Perhaps there will be a demand for stenographers in every Russian province for the zemstvo councils and the courts. You must seize the moment and acquire this skill while it is still in its infancy in our country.

You also write in your letter about *self-sacrifices* that horrify you: "It is horrible to live all one's life against one's convictions"—those are your words. God forbid that you do anything of the sort! Oh, do not throw away your life, do not humiliate yourself morally, do not spell the doom of your family, for your unhappiness will not make any of them happy. Or do you think that you are like [two crossed-out words] my niece? That you can give yourself to a worthless husband such as her husband? That would be disgusting! But then, too, you must know, my friend (you are as close to my heart, Sonya, as my dear daughter!), you must understand that you *cannot* remain unmarried. You must find happiness (you absolutely must!) and the sooner God wills it, the better! And you are free to choose according to your heart and your convictions. And that, too, my dear, would be as easy for you to do while living with us as in your parents' house in Moscow. I don't claim that it would be *easy*, but only that it would be *just as* easy. Do not be angry with me, my friend, for telling you, a young girl, all this so bluntly and openly. I am talking like a friend, like a brother, I am not holding back anything.

But I have now come to the end of my letter. I am in a hurry. You will realize that I must still write you many pages on this subject and discuss many things with you. Anna Grigorevna, who was the first to think of this plan, will write to you at the very first opportunity (she is breastfeeding the baby and doesn't sleep nights; the baby is not even 6 weeks old yet). But when you answer me (and I am not, of course, expecting you to give me your *final decision*, your full and *immediate* agreement in your next letter), I shall write you so much about it, it will be enough to fill an issue of a magazine, and I shall have a few free days. Then I shall give you many more details. For the time being, I hug you hard and so does Anna Grigorevna, and I love you with all my heart. Give Verochka a big hug for me and tell her how much I love her and how strongly I sympathize with her; Masenka, too, and all the others. My regards to everybody. Let us be loyal to one another, all of us, and *let us not drift apart*. Let us be one large family. Anna Grigorevna sends her love to all of you. She is painfully grieved about the death of your father. She understands how you feel, for she herself lost her father, whom she loved very dearly, 2 years ago.

My dear Sonya, do you really not believe in the continuation of life and, above all, in the progressive and infinite, in the consciousness and universal fusion of all? But, you know: "le mieux n'est trouvé que par le meilleur." That is a great thought! So let us become worthy of the best worlds, of resurrection rather than death in the lower worlds! Have faith! Oh, how much I would like to be with you and to have long talks with you! But it is already *exactly* a year since we last saw each other, or even more. That is a lot.

Good-bye, my dear, my golden one,

I am yours, all, all yours,

your friend, father, brother, pupil, everything—everything!

F. Dostoyevsky

Hug Verochka as hard as you can. For heaven's sake, see to it that Masenka does not give up her music! You must all understand finally that the matter is too serious for her. Why, she is so obviously talented. A musical education is indispensable for her, she will need it all her life.

---

75. Ten days after this letter, Dostoyevsky wrote to Maikov that he was still "making no progress" on the novel: "Whatever I write, I tear up. . . . Two days ago I had a most violent attack, but yesterday, nevertheless, I worked in a state verging on madness. . . ." On June 23/July 5, he wrote in another letter to Sonya: "Despite my bereavement [for his infant daughter], I have sat up day and night working on the novel (ah, how I cursed my work, how unpleasant and horrible it was to write!) . . ."

Dostoyevsky had the dedication to Sonya removed from subsequent editions of *The Idiot.*

The "dear departed" here is Sonya Aleksandrovna's father. He had died early in February, at the age of 55, and Sonya had written Dostoyevsky about it.

L'Histoire du Consulat et de l'Empire (History of the Consulate and the Empire), by the French statesman and historian (later first president of the Third Republic) Louis Adolphe Thiers (1797–1877), was a work of nineteen volumes (1845–1862).

Sonya did not take her uncle's advice about studying stenography. However, possibly as a consequence of his intercession, she did get a job with *Russian Messenger* as a translator.

76. To A. N. Maikov
Vevey, July 19/August 2, 1868

My most kind, beloved and unforgettable friend, Apollon Nikolayevich,

I take my pen in hand just to jot down three lines to you.

Back in *June,* I sent you a long letter in reply to yours of the month of May. That (May) letter of yours showed me not only that you were in no wise angry with me (as I, like a fool, might have imagined owing to my morbid nature), but also that you were still fond of me just as before. I didn't answer immediately because for 20 days I had been working night and day and the results were very disappointing. But now, *I have not yet had* any reply from you to my June letter, which was long and of the utmost importance to me. There are two possible explanations: (1) either you are angry with me for some reason or (2) your letter or mine got lost on the way.

I simply refuse to accept the first assumption. Your letter (the last one, in May) was so friendly that I cannot comprehend that, after expressing such kind feelings toward me, you could again suddenly become angry with me, and so I *implicitly assume* that my letter got lost. And I assume this to be the case for other reasons as well: I have heard that there is an order to keep me under surveillance. The Petersburg police open and read *all* my letters, and since the Russian priest in Geneva is by all evidence a secret police agent (this is not a guess but a fact), some of the letters that I have received have been held up at the local (Geneva) post office, where he has—I know this on good authority—secret connections. Finally, I have received an anonymous letter warning me that I am under suspicion (God knows of what), that orders have been received to open all my correspondence, and that as soon as I present myself at the Russian frontier, I shall be detained and most thoroughly searched on the spot.

That is why I am firmly convinced that either my letter did not reach you or your letter got lost on the way to me. NB (But how intolerable this is for an honorable man, a patriot who is loyal to his adored Sovereign to the point of betraying his former convictions—how can I stand being suspected of having some sort of connections with some sort of miserable Polacks or with *The Bell.* Ah, the fools, the fools! I am trying to serve them, and they tie my hands. When I think of how many guilty people they have overlooked, but Dostoyevsky remains suspect!)

But that is not what I wanted to tell you. This letter will be handed to you directly by my wife's sister.

Still, as I said, this is not a letter but just three lines, because I just don't know what to write to you, not having received your letter. Apollon Nikolayevich, my friend (you yourself called me your friend!), how miserable I felt during this time whenever I thought that you were angry with me!

Write to me, write to me, in either case: if you are angry—tell me why; if you are not, write and tell me that you still love me.

I have been very unhappy all this time. Sonya's death has been torture to my wife and to me. My health is nothing to brag about—attacks, the climate of Vevey sets my nerves on edge.

As soon as I get enough money, I intend to leave Vevey. But, notwithstanding, if you answer me right away, use the same address: (Vevey, Lac de Genève) poste restante.

I am dissatisfied with my novel to the point of disgust. I have desperately tried to work but I haven't been able to—my soul is sick. Now I shall put the finishing touches on Part 3. If I straighten out the novel, I will straighten out myself, if not—I am finished.

My wife's nerves are unstrung, she is losing weight, and her health keeps getting worse and worse.

Before writing to you, I wrote a letter to Pasha. He had asked me if he could borrow some money in my name from a certain person who lends money (a former agent of a printing shop whom I know). Since your letter confirmed that he was very hard up, I authorized him to ask the man for a loan and wrote out an IOU for 200 rubles, just as I was asked to do. And since then, *not a word* from Pasha.

And I am behaving criminally toward you. I still owe you your 200 rubles! I shall pay them back to you—don't condemn me! If you knew how much I have had to endure—but I'll pay you back! We'll see how Part 3 comes off.

If I do move away from here, it will be mainly to save my wife.

She sends you her regards and shakes your hand. Convey her and my sincere regards to the much esteemed Anna Ivanovna.

All yours,
F. Dostoyevsky

I have serious reasons for suspecting that Pasha has not received either my letter or the IOU. The IOU is for 200 rubles. If it was intercepted in the mail, where do you think it can be? It is, after all, an important document.

Should I not address myself to a certain *person* and ask him to see to it that an end be put to suspecting me of having betrayed my country and of dealing with the Polacks, and to intercepting my letters? It is disgusting! They should know, after all, that the nihilists and the liberals of *Contemporary* have been slinging mud at me for over two years now, for having broken with them, for hating the Polacks, and for loving my country. Oh, the scoundrels!

---

76. A directive dated November 28, 1867, from the Third Section, the tsarist secret police, instructed the chief of the Odessa security police "to intercept Lieutenant

Fyodor Dostoyevsky, retired, on his return to Russia from abroad, to subject him to the most thorough search and, in the event that anything prejudicial is found on him, to surrender same forthwith to the Third Section of His Imperial Majesty's Chancellery, in which case Dostoyevsky himself is to be placed under arrest and remanded to the Third Section." There is also documentary evidence that Dostoyevsky was being kept under surveillance by the Third Section.

The Bell was the critical magazine being published in London by Herzen and other Westernizers.

The man to whom Dostoyevsky had addressed an IOU was Mikhail Mikhailovich Gavrilov, who was connected with the firm that had printed *Epoch* and who had loaned money to Dostoyevsky before.

The "mud" that Dostoyevsky says was being slung at him may have been a reference to the severe criticism of *Crime and Punishment* that had appeared in several periodicals. For example, *Contemporary* had said that Raskolnikov was a slur on "a whole body of young men whom he accuses of indiscriminate attempts at murder for the purpose of robbery," and it protested against Dostoyevsky's "making Raskolnikov's scientific convictions the motivating force behind the murder," thus "playing into the hands of obscurantists who contend that enlightenment is the cause of universal evil."

77.   To A. N. Maikov
Milan, October 26/November 7, 1868

My dear Apollon Nikolayevich,

It's been quite a while back—around three weeks ago—since I received your letter. I didn't answer right away because I was caught up body and soul in my work, and although I could have found an hour or so to answer your letter, the work takes so much out of me that I swear I have no strength left for writing letters, the more so when I would like to speak from the heart. And so I decided to wait for your second letter, which at last arrived yesterday and for which I thank you very much, my invaluable friend. But let me say, first of all, that I have never been in any way annoyed with you and I say this in all honesty and sincerity. As a matter of fact, I thought it was you who might have resented something I had done. In the first place, you stopped writing to me, you from whom a letter is a great event in my life here—a breath of Russia, a holiday in the true sense of the word! But how could you possibly imagine that I could have taken offense at some idea or something you said! No, that is not the kind of heart I have. Listen: I was 22 when I met you (at Belinsky's, the first time, do you remember?), and since then life has tossed me about a number of times, now here, now there and has occasionally surprised me with its variations. And yet after all this, now, at this moment—well, you are the only one, i.e., the only man in whose heart and soul I have faith, whom I love, and whose ideas and convictions are identical to my own. Is there any wonder then that you are almost as dear to me as my late brother was?

Your letters have gladdened and encouraged me when my morale was so low. In the first place, my work has been a torture to me and a drain on my strength. For almost a year now, I have been writing three and a half sheets a month. That's hard. Besides, there is no Russian life here, no Russian sensations—and I have always needed them to write. Finally, even if you admire the idea of the novel, its execution has not been too brilliant up till now. What distresses me deeply is the thought that, if I had started writing this novel a year earlier and then could have spent two or three months correcting and rewriting, I would have produced something altogether different, believe me. Now, as things have turned out, I see this clearly.

I have started in directly telling you about myself and my novel. But I want to explain my situation from the beginning, so that you will see more clearly what follows. And so here is how things stand:

It is impossible to write more than 3½ sheets a month for a whole year running. That is a fact. And because of that fact, I won't be able to finish the novel this year, and only one-half of the final and fourth part will be published. Even a month ago I still hoped to be able to finish it, but now I see that it is out of the question. And then, Part 4 (it is long—12 sheets) is the crucial one, and all my hopes are set on it! Now that everything has become crystal clear, I have come to the bitter conviction that never before in my literary career have I had a better and richer poetical idea than the one that has taken shape in the detailed plan that I have worked out for Part 4. But so what? I must rush ahead at full speed, write without rereading, hurry like mad and, in the end, still miss the deadline! And without even thinking of myself, what kind of position am I putting *Russian Messenger* in and what will Katkov think of me? He has always behaved so honorably in his dealings with me. But now they will be forced to give the end of the novel in a special supplement next year and that will represent a loss to the magazine! I have even decided to write to them and to decline payment for whatever comes out next year, to compensate the magazine for the loss incurred in printing a special supplement. And that will badly undermine my financial situation.

My life here is becoming really too painful for me. There is nothing Russian around—I haven't read a single Russian book or newspaper for 6 months now. And then there is the complete isolation. In the spring, after we lost Sonya, we moved to Vevey. Anna Grigorevna's mother joined us there. But Vevey has an exasperating effect on the nerves (a fact well known to all the local doctors, who, however, did not warn me of it when I asked their advice). Toward the end of our stay in Vevey, both my wife and I became ill. And so, two months ago, we crossed the Simplon Pass and came to Milan. Here, the climate is better, but life is more expensive, it rains a lot, and it is deadly boring to boot. Anna Grigorevna is patient, but she is homesick for Russia and we both cry when we think of Sonya. Our life is gloomy and monastic. Anna Grigorevna, who is a very active and enterprising person, has nothing to do here. I can see that she is bored and, although we love each other if anything even more than 1½ years ago, it still oppresses me to think that she must share my sad, monastic life. It is very hard on her. And God knows what lies ahead of us. If, at least, the novel were finished, I would be free.

As for returning to Russia, that is something not readily conceivable. I do not have a thing to my name. That means I would be locked up in debtors' prison as soon as I arrived. And it is quite clear that I would be unable to work there. With my epilepsy, I couldn't stand the prison regimen, and so I wouldn't be able to do my work in prison. So, how would I be able to pay my debts then, and what would I live on? If only my creditors would allow me one year of peace (but they haven't allowed me one month of peace in three years), I would take it upon myself to pay them off during that year with my work. However large my debts may still be, they amount to only ⅕ of what I have already paid back through my work. Indeed, it was in order to work that I left the country. And now, the whole idea of *The Idiot* has practically come to naught. And even if the novel has or will have some merit, it won't be much of a sensation and it has to be that, if it is to sell for a second edition. Only a few months ago, I was blindly counting on it, and it would have brought me a certain amount of money if it had come off. But now, with the novel not even finished, all hope of a second edition must be ruled out.

If I could move back to Russia, I would know what to do and how to make money—after all, I used to manage it once upon a time. But here my mind is becoming dull and narrow. I am losing touch with Russia. There is no Russian air here, no Russian people. I cannot understand the Russian émigrés for the life of me—they must be mad!

So that is the state of our affairs. But we cannot stay in Milan either—life here is too uncomfortable, too gloomy. In a month, we would like to move to Florence, and I shall finish the novel there. I am still receiving money from Katkov. It is terrible how much we spend en tout, even though we stint on everything. Soon, when the novel is finished, Katkov will obviously stop sending me money. That will mean new trials and tribulations. Nevertheless, my debt to Katkov has been drastically reduced, even considering everything I have received from him from the beginning.

I have completely lost touch with your life, although I am entirely with you in spirit. And that is why your letters are like manna from heaven to me. I was awfully pleased to hear about the new magazine. I have never heard anything about Kashpirev, but I am delighted that Nikolai Nikolayevich [Strakhov] has at last found an occupation worthy of him—he must be the editor-in-chief and not limit himself to running some section or other of the new magazine; he must become the soul of the new periodical. If he does, it will be a serious magazine. I was very glad to get a letter from him six months or so ago. I didn't answer him because I didn't know his address, and he didn't give it to me in his letter. He included an excerpt from his letter to Katkov, in which he offered to run the literary criticism section for *Russian Messenger.*

I don't know what Katkov answered Nikolai Nikolayevich, but I do not know that all the editorial posts in both his magazine and his newspaper are occupied and occupied very firmly; as Gogol put it, once a man gets himself settled into a job, the spot will crack under him before he vacates it. And between you and me, even if Katkov did want to make changes in his editorial staff, I doubt that he would be able to carry them out.

But as things stand now, this is the best thing that could have happened to Nikolai Nikolayevich; but the most important thing is that he be in full control. It would be a very good thing if the magazine were distinctly in the true *Russian spirit,* as you and I understand it, although not necessarily purely Slavophile. (In my opinion, my friend, we shouldn't run *too much* after the Slavs—I emphasize the too much. They must come to us of their own accord. After the Moscow Slavic Congress, some of those very Slavs went home and made some supercilious jibes at the Russians, saying something about the Russians having taken it upon themselves to guide others and putting on airs toward other Slavs, when they themselves have so little self-awareness, etc., etc. And believe me, many Slavs, those in Prague, for instance, judge us by completely Western standards, from the German or French point of view, and they are perhaps even surprised to find that in our country the Slavophiles set small store by generally accepted forms of Western civilization. So we should be in no hurry about running after the Slavs. To study them—that is a different matter; to help them—that's fine, too, but to bend over backwards to win their brotherhood—there is no need for that; by all means let us consider them and treat them as brothers, but that is no reason to act overzealously.

I also very much hope that Nikolai Nikolayevich will give a political coloration to the magazine and, it goes without saying, awaken people to an awareness of themselves. Self-knowledge is our weakest spot, it is something we badly need. In any case, under Nikolai Nikolayevich, it will be a brilliant undertaking and I am looking forward with inexhaustible pleasure to reading his articles, a thing I haven't had a chance to do for a very long time, indeed, not since the time of *Epoch.*

It would be a good thing if the magazine put itself in an independent position in the literary world proper from the start. It should not, for instance, pay two thousand rubles for an awful stew like "Minin" or any other of Ostrovsky's historical dramas, just in order to have Ostrovsky's name; but if he were to offer that comedy about the merchants—well, for that, he could be given the money. Or *The Swarm* by Kokhanovskaya, whose name I read with horror, after the disgust and shame *The Swarm* aroused in me when I read it two years ago—that oily hallelujah that made even Aksakov screw up his nose. But if she were to offer something like *The Bolt,* it would be something to be proud of. Or take that pompous Yergunov, who has written himself out. In short, I believe that writers should be taken in hand once and for all and that they shouldn't be paid just for their names alone, but for what they have to offer, which is something that until now no magazine has dared to do, and that goes for both *Time* and *Epoch,* too.

A magazine cannot start publication without a first-class literary work in its 1st two issues; it would mean losing out on 1000 subscribers from the outset. Don't think I just like to give advice, it is out of love that I am saying this. I hope Nikolai Nikolayevich will send me the magazine. And there is no need to tell you that I accept from the bottom of my heart your offer for me to become a contributor to the magazine. The only thing is that I am very busy right now. But as soon as I finish my novel, I shall be able to think of something. I would so much like this magazine to be really good. Write me in greater detail about it, my dear friend. Are you giving some of your things to the magazine yourself? Let them have something substantial and complete for the first issue, your *Song of Prince Igor's Campaign,* for instance. What is the name of the magazine? Have they already put out subscription notices? If they intend to start publishing at the beginning of the New Year, it is high time they did so.

It so happens I read that "book" you wrote about just a short time before I got your letter, and I must say that I was outraged. Such insolence is inconceivable. Of course, I should just ignore it, and that was my first impulse. But what worries me is that if I fail to protest, it will be taken as an endorsement of that contemptible libel. But where should I send my protest? To Le Nord? But I write French poorly, and besides, I would like to proceed with tact. I am planning to move to Florence and to seek the advice of the Russian consulate there and ask them how best to go about it. Of course, that is not the only reason why I am moving to Florence.

You have suggested that I should move to Venice (which is vaunted in all the travelers' guides and by all the doctors as a healthy place in the winter). I would like to go there very much if only to provide some distraction to Anna Grigorevna and, who knows, maybe I shall, for it is not really far from here. But on the other hand, I have very little time to spare, and moreover, for the two of us, it would cost at least 100 francs, even if we traveled third class and stayed for only three days, and 100 francs is an awful lot for us at the present time, although it is not unusual for us to receive 1000 francs from Katkov occasionally. But whenever I get such a sum, I have to set aside immediately enough to last us for a month or a month and a half, and then pay off the debts that always manage to accumulate; and then there are also the moving expenses and the clothes. And inasmuch as the future is so insecure, we must tighten our belts. And first and foremost, I have to work day and night and finish the novel or else there will be nothing at all.

I would like to meet Lamansky very much. I'd be terribly pleased to read Samarin's book, especially since all these matters are always on my own mind, but where shall I be able to get it? The situation here is utterly hopeless. But then, even in Geneva, the only Russian books one finds lying around in the bookstores are such things as *What Is To Be Done?* and all sorts of other rubbish by our émigrés. If one does come across Russian books of another sort, say, some little work of Gogol or Pushkin, it is only by accident. In the selling of Russian books, there is no order, no rhyme, no reason anywhere. It is rare even to find a place that sells them. Here, in Italy, there is nothing at all. I wish I could find Samarin's book, but it is unobtainable.

I am also worried and concerned about my relatives. I was unable to send Pasha anything all summer long, but he's no angel, that one. But I'm not angry at him—there is no reason why he should love me particularly, and I have no right to judge him too severely for the mistakes he makes at work. A poor, uneducated boy, alone and unaided—how could he help making mistakes? But I am afraid of worse things to come, and I am terribly anxious to help him out as soon as possible. And then, in November Emiliya Fyodorovna will have to vacate my apartment at Alonkin's because I cannot pay him the rent. All this is worrisome, but, notwithstanding, the most important thing for me is to finish my work!

As for the money I owe you, my dear friend, I am too ashamed even to think of it! What distresses me most is that you have acted like a true brother toward me, and I dare say there are brothers who would not have done what you have done. After all, you do have your own family to think of. But since I am, after all, earning money, I shall pay you back. Things are bound to clear up for me someday, but what I desire above all else is to return to Russia. I'm sure I'd be able to manage much better there. And when I think that, if we had been in Russia, Sonya would probably still be alive!

Anna Grigorevna is fond of you, she thinks and speaks of you with pleasure. Give my regards and hers as well (very eager regards in her case—she has asked me three times today to be sure not to forget) to your wife and your parents. And my regards also to all who still remember me. I am sorry about Kovalevsky—he was a kind and *useful* man—so useful, indeed, that perhaps only now, after his death, will we fully realize it.

All yours,
F. Dostoyevsky

For God's sake write me. *In any case*, here's my address:
Italie, Milan, a M-r Dostoyevsky poste restante.

---

77. Though Dostoyevsky says he was twenty-two years old when he met Maikov, he must have meant to say it was twenty-two *years ago*. At the age of twenty-two, he was still at the army engineering school and had not yet become acquainted with Belinsky.

The new magazine that Dostoyevsky refers to is *Dawn*, which was published from 1869 to 1871 by Vasily Vladimirovich Kashpirev (1836–1875), who was also the publisher of an important reference book, *Landmarks of the New Russian History* (Pamyatniki novoi russkoi istorii, 1871–1873). The magazine had Slavophile leanings, and Strakhov later wrote Dostoyevsky that Kashpirev "was a student of *Time* and *Epoch*."

The expression of Gogol's that Dostoyevsky quotes is from *Dead Souls*, where it is applied to "fat officials."

The "Moscow Slavic Congress" is a reference to the gathering of a large number of scientists, scholars, and political figures from the southern and western Slavic nations on the occasion of an ethnographic exhibition in May 1867. The visitors were the object of special solicitude on the part of the Slavic Philanthropic Committee, which was trying to show them that the idea of Pan-Slavism had a deep hold on Russian society.

Kokhanovskaya's novel *The Swarm—Feodosy Savvich at Peace* (Roi—Feodosy Savvich na spokoye) was published in Aksakov's magazine *Day* during the first half of 1864. Going beyond even the Slavophile position, it was an idealization of Muscovy and of the patriarchal order and serfdom. An earlier novel of hers, *The Bolt* (Gaika), had been published in part in *Pantheon* (Panteon) in 1856 and in full in *Russian Word* in 1860.

"That pompous Yergunov" is a sarcastic reference to Turgenev (see Letter 73 and the note to it).

The book that outraged Dostoyevsky was *Les mystères du palais des czars* (The mysteries of the palace of the tsars), supposedly written by one Paul Grimm and published in Wurzburg in 1868. (A man named August Theodor Grimm had been a tutor to children of the imperial family, and in some Russian circles it was believed that Paul Grimm was actually his transparent pen name.) Maikov had written to Dostoyevsky that "the plot is built around a group of conspirators and, would you believe it, you and your wife are the principal conspirators. . . . While I was reading it, it occurred to me that it might not be a bad thing if you wrote a piece in some periodical, say *Le Nord*, and tore the author apart." Dostoyevsky did begin a letter in which he condemned "the European's extraordinary ignorance of everything connected with Russia" and the proclivity of European publishers to "provoke hostility toward Russia," but the letter was evidently never completed.

Vladimir Ivanovich Lamansky (1833–1914) was a historian and a professor at Petersburg University. An influential member of the Slavic Philanthropic Committee and editor-in-chief of *News* (Izvestiya), the journal of the Slavic Society, he was living at this time in Venice.

Yury Fyodorovich Samarin (1819–1876) was a writer and political figure, one of the most important Slavophile thinkers. The book mentioned in this letter is *The*

Outlying Regions of Russia (Okraini Rossii, 1868, with other sections published in later years), which Maikov had called "a ripe product of Russian national self-awareness."

What Is To Be Done? (Chto delat?, 1863) was the classic novel by Chernyshevsky.

78.   To N. N. Strakhov
Florence, March 18/30, 1869

Much esteemed Nikolai Nikolayevich,

First of all, let me thank you for having been so prompt in answering me. In my situation that in itself is half the battle, because it enables me to organize my work and my plans accordingly. In the second place, I thank you for having arranged for *Dawn* to be sent to me, and, in the third place, for the good news about Apollon Nikolayevich. I'll write him directly one of these days in reply to his letter. And if he praised me to you, you can be certain that I, too, have nothing but praise for him. Even during our recent *misunderstanding*, which was due to distrustfulness on my part, I never lost one drop of my sincere, friendly affection for him. As to his being a good and honorable man, I haven't had any doubt about that for a very long time and I am delighted that you two have hit it off so well together.

Even if *Dawn* is not yet the success we hoped it would be, it is still quite an achievement, and that is nothing to laugh at. And though you may not be able to muster the third thousand subscribers, if you manage to maintain present standards until the end of the year—and I am emphatic about this—you will be on firm ground. There is no other monthly magazine with an orientation as concrete and well defined as yours. The second issue made an extremely agreeable impression on me. I shall say nothing about your article except that it is *real* criticism, precisely the *word* that needed to be said and that will help to explain the cause better than anything. As for Danilevsky's article, I feel it is becoming more and more important and developing into a major contribution. Why, I have no doubt that it will be the future bedside book of every Russian for a long time to come. And how much the language it is written in contributes to that—its clarity, its accessibility, despite a strictly scholarly presentation. How much I would like to talk about that work with you, Nikolai Nikolayevich—yes, particularly with you—but then, there would be too many things we would have to say! It coincides with my own conclusions and convictions to such an extent that there are pages over which I stop in amazement at the resemblance of our conclusions, because for a long time now, for two years already, I have been jotting down some of my thoughts with a view to writing an essay that was to have almost the same title, would have followed exactly the same line of thought, and would have reached the same conclusions. And you can imagine my happy surprise when I found almost exactly what I had been aspiring to realize in

302

the future already realized so elegantly and harmoniously, with an extraordinary force of logic and scholarship that I would certainly never have been able to achieve, try as I might. I am so anxious to read the continuation of that work that I rush to the post office every day and keep calculating how much longer I shall have to wait for the arrival of *Dawn*. (I wish the editors would publish three chapters instead of only two! As it is, when I finish reading the two chapters I keep thinking that now I'll have to wait a whole month or maybe even 40 days!—since *Dawn* is not too renowned for its punctuality, isn't that so?)

My other reason for being so impatient to see the rest of Danilevsky's work is that I am somewhat apprehensive about his final conclusion—I am still uncertain whether Danilevsky will point out with *full force* the quintessence of Russia's mission, which is to reveal to the world the Russian Christ, whom the world does not know and whose principle is embodied in our native Orthodoxy. I believe that in this lies the very essence of our future civilizing mission and of the resurrection, perhaps, of all Europe, and the whole core of our mighty future. But I cannot express myself in a few words, and I am even sorry I got started on this subject. Still, I would like to say one more thing to you: it is impossible that a magazine with such a strict, salutary, firmly based, genuinely Russian orientation should fail to succeed and to leave a happy impression upon its readers, coming in the wake of the pitiful, affected, shrill, lopsided, and sterile negation of everything which is so common among us.

Furthermore, *Dawn*'s second issue is rich in material. It has some very good articles. The number is agreeable to look at.

But I was quite puzzled *for a while,* my dear Nikolai Nikolayevich, by a few lines in your letter. What is this you write, so ruefully and with such perceptible sadness, about your article having had no success, about people's *failing to understand* it, about their not finding it interesting? Did you really expect, then, that everyone would understand it right away? If they had, it would have been, in my opinion, a rather poor recommendation for your article. Anything that is understood too quickly and readily is not quite solid. It was only toward the end of his career that Belinsky achieved the recognition that he sought, and Grigorev died without having achieved *anything* to speak of in his lifetime. I have been accustomed to look upon you with such respect that I thought your *wisdom* would also extend to a case like this. The core of the matter is so subtle that it always eludes the majority. They understand it only when it has been completely chewed up for them, and until then they show little interest in any new idea. And the more simply, the more clearly it is presented to them (i.e., with the more talent), the more *common* and *ordinary* it will seem to them. Why, that is just a law of nature! You will excuse me, but I couldn't suppress a smile as I read your naive remark that "even *very clever* people do not understand." But it is just people of that sort who are always the least likely to understand, and, indeed, they even prevent others from understanding. And the reasons for that are only too obvious, and it is, of course, also in the nature of things. But you yourself tell me that Gradovsky and Danilevsky are enthusiastically backing you, that Aksakov came to see you, etc. Isn't that enough to reassure you? And I remain firmly convinced that you understand your own ability well enough and have enough impetus to go ahead, that *you* will never lose your sense of the importance of your contribution and never abandon the cause! So please, stop frightening me so, for the moment you leave, *Dawn* will fall apart.

And now, to *business*. My own financial situation has slightly improved as I have received some money from Katkov, who apparently appreciates me as a contributor, for which I'm very grateful to him. But I was in such dire need before that the money I have received will only do for a very short while. And very soon I shall be penniless again. But you must believe, my dear Nikolai Nikolayevich, that it is not the money alone but also a genuine sympathy with *Dawn* that makes me anxious to contribute to it (and I don't think you will question my sincerity). But despite that, it is quite impossible for me to accept Kashpirev's proposition as set forth by you in your letter. The reason for this is that it is *physically* impossible for me. One thousand rubles, and even that to be deferred (when what counts for me is that the first payment should be made not sometime soon, but *right now*)—that is simply not enough for me at the present time. You will agree yourself that if I undertake what is, relatively speaking, a long piece of ten to twelve printer's sheets, it should take me almost until September to finish, and if all I can expect to get out of it is a thousand rubles, in my situation, that is very inadequate. Of course, even when I made you the offer previously, I was in the very same circumstances. But *a month ago, owing to the silence of* Russian Messenger, my *need* was so pressing that getting a thousand rubles *in full and right away* had a special value for me. Now, however, it would be more to my advantage to get down to work—and to do so as soon as possible— on next year's novel for *Russian Messenger,* which will assure me of a livelihood until then. And, anyway, I never had any intention of severing my connection with Katkov. Nevertheless, here is what I can now suggest to *Dawn instead of the former* proposal, in the event that they are still sufficiently interested in my collaboration and that what I propose is congenial to the interests of the magazine:

I have a story, not very long, roughly two printer's sheets or possibly a bit more (though it may come to three or even three and a half of *Dawn*'s sheets). I had considered writing this story four years ago, the year my brother died, in reaction to something Ap[ollon] Grigorev had said at the time in praise of my *Notes from Underground.* He said: "Keep on writing in that vein." But this is nothing like *Notes from Underground,* it is completely different from it in form, although in essence it is the same, the essence of all my work, that is, Nikolai Nikolayevich, if you will grant that, as a writer, I have a special individual essence. This is one story that I could write very quickly because there is not a single line, a single word in it that isn't clear in my mind. Besides, much of it is already sketched out (although nothing is yet *written*). I could finish this story and send it to *Dawn* long before September 1st (although I don't suppose you'd even want it earlier, for I don't see you publishing me during the summer months!). In short—I could even send it to you in *two* months. And that is all I am capable of contributing to *Dawn* this year, despite my eagerness to write for a publication that people like you, Danilevsky, Gradovsky, and Maikov are writing for. Here, then, are my conditions, which I would appreciate your transmitting to Kashpirev in answer to his first reply:

First of all, I ask for an advance of 300 rubles *right away*. Of that sum (in the event my conditions are accepted) I would very much like you, Nikolai Nikolayevich, to give 125 rubles to Mariya Grigorevna Svatkovskaya (I gave you her address in my last letter) and to send me the remaining 175 rubles here in Florence *no later than one month from today*, i.e., from March 18/30. I mean that I would like the 175 rubles to be here and in my hands by April 18 *our style*. If that is done, I shall send off my story two months later and shall try not to disgrace myself, i.e., I will do my utmost to deliver a first-rate piece of work. (I am not one to cook up themes for money—if I didn't have a story worked out in my mind already, I wouldn't have laid down conditions.)

And now, Nikolai Nikolayevich (I beg you, as a friend), do not be angry with me for these stipulations, this haggling, etc. It is not really haggling at all, but an accurate and clear explanation of the situation I am in, and the more precision and clarity I bring to this point, the easier it will be for us to do business together. But I know you too well personally not to feel confident of your opinion of me. You wouldn't have written such kind letters if you didn't respect me to some extent, both as a man and as a writer. And I have always (and in all our relations with one another) highly valued your opinion.

And now I have a *tremendous* favor to ask of you, Nikolai Nikolayevich: please notify me *immediately* on receipt of this letter of Kashpirev's decision. I *must* know absolutely so that I can make my calculations and, above all, arrange my work accordingly. If you happen to be too busy, send just a few lines to let me know.

Mariya Grigorevna Svatkovskaya's address is:

Peski, opposite the First Army Hospital, Yaroslavskaya Street, No. 1, (to the Mistress of the House), i.e., she is the proprietor.

Good-bye, dear and much esteemed Nikolai Nikolayevich, your letters mean so much to me! Anna Grigorevna sends you her best regards and I remain your totally devoted,

Fyodor Dostoyevsky.

P.S. My rates are, as I have already said, 150 rubles per printer's sheet of the size of *Russian Messenger*'s. Needless to say, if the story exceeds two sheets in length, *Dawn* will have to pay the remainder.

P.S. Who was it who told you my health was not good: it is actually very good indeed, and my attacks, although they continue, are *literally* only half as frequent as they were in Petersburg, at least that has been so since we moved to Italy.

---

78. The "good news" about Maikov was that he remained on friendly terms with Dostoyevsky, who had feared that he resented the fact that Dostoyevsky had still not repaid a 200-ruble loan.

Strakhov's article in the second issue of *Dawn* was a continuation of his appraisal of Tolstoy's *War and Peace*. He lauded it for its "Russian" approach and presented it as a work that symbolized the struggle between Russian and Western principles.

Nikolai Yakovlevich Danilevsky (1822–1885) was a naturalist and philosopher. He had been a member of the Petrashevsky circle, where he was regarded as the principle authority on Fourierism; he was arrested and imprisoned, but, on the strength of his assurance that his interest in Fourier was purely theoretical, the case against him was dismissed. His major work, *Russia and Europe* (Rossiya i Yevropa), was published in installments in *Dawn* during 1869; it was an important work in the Slavophile tradition, though Danilevsky rejected some of the Slavophile tenets.

Aleksandr Dmitriyevich Gradovsky (1841–1889) was a professor of law at Petersburg University. He was a moderate liberal who supported the reforms started in the 1860s, but he also idealized the Russian regime and insisted on the compatibility of absolutism with local self-government.

"Kashpirev's proposition" was that Dostoyevsky be paid in installments for his contribution to *Dawn*.

The story that Dostoyevsky alludes to is what became *The Eternal Husband*, and it turned out to be not two but ten (of *Dawn*'s) printer's sheets in length. In connection with this length, Dostoyevsky later wrote to Maikov: "It is not because it got out of hand under my pen, but rather because the subject grew as I was writing it, and new episodes came in." The story was published in the January and February 1870 issues of *Dawn*.

Mariya Grigorevna Svatkovskaya was Anna Grigorevna's sister.

79.   To A. N. Maikov
Florence, May 15/27, 1869

What a long, long time it has taken me, my good and only friend, to respond to your kind and sincere remarks. But you are right, because I consider you and you alone, of all those whom I have happened to meet and with whom I have had to go through life during what will soon be forty-eight years, as a man after my own heart. I doubt that there has been (nor is there now, for that matter) a single man in all these 48 years that has meant as much to me as you do (I am not including my late brother). And although you and I come from quite different social backgrounds, in our hearts and in the meeting of our hearts, in our minds and in the views that we hold dear, we are almost like birds of a feather. Even the conclusions we have reached in our thinking and as a result of our experiences in life have of late shown a surprising similarity in the two of us, and I believe, too, that the same flame is burning in our hearts. Just take the following fact, my dear friend, as an example. Do you recall that last year, in the summer I believe and, I think, exactly a year ago (just before the summer holidays, to the best of my recollection), I wrote you a letter. (Then, for three or four months, I didn't get an answer from you; that interrupted our correspondence, and when we took it up again in the fall, we wrote about quite different things and forgot where we had left off in the summer.) Well, in that letter, at the end of it, I wrote to you in a spirit of serious and profound enthusiasm about a *new idea* that had occurred to me, especially for you, for your work. (I.e., if you please, this idea came to me all by itself, as something independent and, I felt, full blown; but since I could not possibly conceive of myself as the person to carry that idea out, I naturally set it aside for you, in my mind's eye. So perhaps, even, it sprang up within me precisely *for you,* as I said before, or, to put it better, inseparably bound up with my view of you as a poet.) If you had answered me right away that summer, I would have sent you a tremendously long explanation of my idea, going into every conceivable detail, for I had already thought out what to write to you down to the last line.

But the way things have turned out I think it was better that you did not answer me. Judge for yourself. The idea I had at that time (and now I'll tell you only a few words about it) was that one might bring out—in the vein of fascinating and enchanting verse that is memorized effortlessly and by itself, as always happens with profound and beautiful poetry—a series of epic legends (ballads, songs, short poems, romances, whatever you want to call them—here the essence and even the scansion of the verse depend on the poet's soul and appears suddenly, ready-made in his heart, quite independently of himself. . . . I'll make a considerable digression here: in my opinion, a poem is like a natural precious stone, a diamond in the poet's soul, complete in all its essence, and so this is the first act of the poet, as a *maker and creator,* the first part of his creation. We can even say that it is not he who is the actual creator but rather life itself, the mighty essence of life, God, living and real, manifesting his power in the diversity of creation here and there, and most often, in great hearts and in powerful poets, so that, if the poet himself is not the creator—(and this is a point with which you must agree particularly, as a connoisseur and a poet yourself, because the creation suddenly appears in the poet's soul too completely, with too much finality and readiness)—and so even if he himself is not the creator, the poet's soul is the mine in which the diamonds are formed and outside of which they cannot be found. Then comes the poet's *second* act, no longer so profound and mysterious, but only his artistic performance: once he has received the diamond, he must polish and mount it. At this point the poet is not much more than a jeweler.)

So what I had in mind concerning that series of epic legends in verse (in thinking of those epics, I sometimes had your "Council of Constance" in mind) was to present them with love and in the light of *our idea* from the very beginning, to show the whole of Russian history from a Russian perspective, distinguishing places, those moments and points at which Russia, at various times and at various places, seems to have focused and expressed herself all at once in her entirety. In the thousand years of the country's history, there are as many as ten, or possibly even more, such all-expressive moments. And it is these moments that must be seized and related in the epic, to be conveyed *to one and all*, not, however, as an ordinary chronicle, no, but rather as a stirring poem which, even without strict adherence to the facts (as long as it is completely clear), will lay hold of the main point and convey it in a way that shows the idea from which it emerged as well as the love and the suffering that brought forth that idea. But there must be no egoism in it, *no personal note*, it must be ingenuous, as ingenuous as possible, with just the love of Russia gushing from it like a hot spring—and nothing else.

Thus, in the third, or was it the fourth, epic (I was composing them in my head then and a long time thereafter), I came up with the capture of Constantinople by Mohammed II. (And it occurred to me directly and by itself as an epic of *Russian history*, spontaneously and unintentionally; afterwards I was surprised myself that, without a moment's hesitation or even reflection or conscious thought on my part, I simply placed the fall of Constantinople in the context of the *history of Russia*, without giving it a second thought.) The entire catastrophe was contained in the terse and simple narrative—the Turks forming a tight ring around Tsargrad; the last night before the assault, which was to take place at dawn; the last Emperor walking through the palace—"The King walked in long strides"—as he goes to pray before the icon of Our Lady of Vlakhern; the prayer; the assault; the battle; the Sultan entering Constantinople on horseback, blood dripping from his sword. At the Sultan's command, a search is made for the last Emperor's body and it is found in a pile of corpses and recognized by the eagles embroidered on his boots; Hagia Sophia; a trembling Patriarch, the last Mass, the Sultan, still on horseback, galloping up the steps and entering the cathedral (historique); reaching the middle of the cathedral, he pulls up his horse in perplexity, looking around musingly and confusedly, he utters the words: "This is the house of prayer for Allah!"

Then the icons are thrown out, and the communion table, the altar is destroyed, the temple is turned into a mosque, the corpse of the Emperor is buried, and in the Russian tsardom, the last of the Paleologues arrives with a two-headed eagle instead of a dowry; a Russian wedding; Prince Ivan III in his wooden hut instead of a palace, and there enters into that wooden hut the great idea of the pan-Orthodox significance of Russia and the cornerstone is laid for her future supremacy in the East; the sphere of Russia's future is extended, she is to be not simply a mighty country, but a whole new world whose destiny it is to know Christianity through the Pan-Slav Orthodox idea and offer mankind a *new* message when the West has decayed, and it will decay when the pope has completely distorted the image of Christ and thus engendered atheism among the defiled peoples of the West.

And this was not the only idea I had about this epoch. It was my intention, along with the tableau of the wise Prince, inspired by a grand and profound idea, sitting next to the humbly dressed Metropolitan and the Russified "Fominishna" in that wooden shack, to make a sudden transition, in another ballad, to the end of the fifteenth and the beginning of the sixteenth centuries in Europe, to Italy, to the papacy, to church art, to Raphael, to the cult of Apollo Belvedere, to the first rumors about the Reformation, about Luther, America, gold, Spain and England. It would be a vast, vivid tableau *parallel* to the foregoing Russian tableaux, but with intimations of what that tableau portends, of the future of science, atheism, *human rights* in the Western sense, not in ours—everything that has contributed to bringing about what is and what will be. In my ardent musings, I even felt that the Russian epics should not end, for example, with Peter, who definitely requires a particularly good legend and a good epic ballad giving a bold and *frank* appraisal of him, *as we see him*. I would have liked to go on to Biron, to Catherine, and further on to the emancipation of the serfs, and to our boyars scattered all over Europe with the last paper rubles, and to the Russian ladies whoring around with the Borghese, to our seminarists preaching atheism, to the Russian counts, the super-humanitarian citizens of the world, who write criticism, stories, etc. etc. The Poles would have been given a lot of space in it. And I would have ended with fantastic pictures of the future: Russia in two hundred years alongside torn and darkened Europe with all its civilization reduced to a brutish state. I wouldn't have stopped short of *any flight of the imagination . . .*

I'm sure you must think I'm mad right now, specifically and chiefly because I have let my pen run on and on, when these are things that must be discussed face to face, not written about, for it is quite impossible to explain anything properly in a letter. But I got carried away. You see, when I read in your letter that you were writing those ballads, I was terribly struck by one thing: how could it happen that the two of us, who had not seen each other for years, could have had the same idea for the very same poem? First it caused me great joy, but then I began to wonder—is this the way we both see it, i.e., are our ideas really identical?

My idea is, you see, that these ballads could become a great national book and make a solid contribution to a resurgence of self-awareness in the Russian man. Just think, Apollon Nikolayevich, every Russian schoolchild will learn these poems and know them by heart! But along with the poem, he will assimilate the thought and the viewpoint contained in it, and since that viewpoint is a true one, it will remain engraved *in his heart* for the rest of his life. And since these verses and poems will be relatively short, everyone in the world who can read Russian will read them, just as they have read "The Council of Constance" and know it by heart to this day. And so, these are not just poems and literature—they are knowledge, a sermon, a heroic deed. When I was on the point of writing you about it last year to persuade you to take up that idea, I was wondering: How shall I be able to convey it to him so that he can fully understand what I have in mind? And then, all of a sudden, a year later, you become *inspired by the same idea* all by yourself and *feel that you must* give it literary form! Therefore the idea is right! But one thing, one thing is absolutely indispensable—the poems must have an exceptional poetic charm, they must take hold of people, take hold of them completely, take hold of them to such an extent that they memorize them automatically. Ah, my friend, bear in mind that your entire career as a poet until now may have been just an *introduction*, a *foreword* and that only now have you reached the point where you can confidently give expression to a *new word, your new word!* And so, regard the matter more seriously, more profoundly and with greater enthusiasm. And, above all, with more simplicity and ingenuousness. And also, use rhyme and not the old Russian meter. Don't laugh, this is important—*today, rhyme is the popular form, while the old Russian meter is pure academism.* No blank-verse poem is learned by heart. Folk songs are no longer composed in the old meter, they are rhymed. If there is no rhyme (nor more frequent use of trochee)—I think you may spoil the whole thing. You may laugh at me, but what I am telling you is the truth, the unvarnished truth!

I can tell you nothing about Yermak—I'm sure you know best. I believe that at first there should be the derring-do of the Cossack—his vagabondage and his looting. Then, a man of genius is shown under his sheepskin jacket;

he senses the magnitude of the enterprise and its potential significance, but only after the whole thing has got off to a good start and is running smoothly. At this point there is born in him a *feeling* of Russianness, an Orthodox feeling of oneness with the Russian root (it may even be a spontaneous feeling, something akin to nostalgia), and this results in his sending emissaries with a petition to the great Sovereign, who, in the eyes of the people, fully embodies the Russian nation. (N.B. Do you know when, in my opinion, the fullest and the most important expression of this concept reached its complete and final development? It did so in our century. Of course, I am speaking of the people and not of the boyars and the seminarists who are rotten through and through.)

But that's enough about that. There is only one thing I am sure of—it is that our ideas coincide, and I am overjoyed by it. Please send me something of what you have already written, as much of it as you can. I won't make bad use of it. You can see for yourself that it interests me *to the point of distraction!*

You may ask now why I haven't written you all this time. But I haven't written you for such a long time that I find it difficult even to answer that question. The main reason was despondency, but if I were to say anything more about it and explain it, there would be too many things I'd have to tell you. And my despondency was so great that if I had been alone, I might have fallen sick from it. It is a good thing for me that I have Anna Grigorevna with me, who, as you know, is once again expecting. Her state worries us both (Anna Grigorevna's mother is staying with us now, which, in view of her present condition, is essential).

A little while ago we had a major misfortune, which has kept us in Florence, although a month ago we had decided to move to Dresden. It all came about because of money. I ended up promising a story (it will be a very short one) to *Dawn*. The very kind Nikolai Nikolayevich [Strakhov] (who perhaps is angry with me now) arranged the deal. He transmitted 125 rubles to Mariya Grigorevna Svatkovskaya—60 rubles for the payment of interest and the remaining 65 to be divided between Pasha and Emiliya Fyodorovna (25 rubles to Pasha and 40 to Em[iliya] F[yodorov]na)—and in addition he promised to send me here, in Florence, 175 rubles by a *definite* time. It was that time and money that I was counting on to enable us to leave Dresden. But then a little blunder occurred: Instead of sending me the money by registered mail, *Dawn* sent it through some exchange office—and I received it 10 or 12 days later (and since I didn't receive it through the mail, there was even a chance that I wouldn't receive it at all, because the exchange office might not have found me in Florence). Thus, for about two weeks, while we were waiting for the money, we lived beyond our means and spent all the money we had, so that then, the money wasn't enough for the move. I sent a plea to *Russian Messenger* to help us out. I will be sending a novel to *Russian Messenger* in January. In Dresden, I'll work without letup.

But in general, there are plenty of troubles and annoyances. Florence is getting terribly hot, the city is stifling and sweltering, our nerves are on edge, and what is particularly bad for my wife is that at the present time we are squeezed (and all the while en attendant) into a small, cramped room overlooking the marketplace. I was sick of Florence anyway, and now, with the heat and overcrowding, I cannot even sit down to work. I feel terribly depressed in general, but most of all by Europe; I look on everything here like a wild animal. *Whatever happens,* I have decided to return to Petersburg by next spring (as soon as I have finished the novel), even if they throw me into debtors' prison. And without even speaking of my spiritual interests, my material interests are also hurt by my staying abroad. Consider this element, for instance: regardless of anything else, the fact of the matter is that the third and fourth and fifth editions of my works (the lot of them) have been sold out. *The Idiot*—and I don't care to discuss at this point what its real worth is—is still *good merchandise.* I know for sure that a second edition would sell out in one year. So why shouldn't it be published? It is just the right moment now and, moreover, I have a special reason for wanting to have it republished. So what I did was to ask Mariya Grigorevna Svatkovskaya, six weeks or so ago, to do the following errand for me: to drop in on A. F. Bazunov at his bookstore (with a letter of recommendation from me) and simply ask him whether he wouldn't be interested in publishing a 2nd edition of *The Idiot* (it could be ready by next winter if he started working on it now); that I was asking 2000 rubles (but would come down to 1500 if he paid me a lump sum; otherwise I'd agree to his paying me in installments); the legal aspects and the formalities of the contract need not delay matters, because I could send a valid, certified power of attorney from here. I told Mariya Grigorevna not to insist, but just to get a *yes* or *no* answer from Bazunov and to inform me here of the outcome. If he says *no* (although he is well placed to know that my books have always sold out thus far and the kind of merchandise they represent), that's his affair, it doesn't matter to me. I shall publish it at my own expense as soon as I get back and I won't lose any money on it. It didn't seem like a burdensome mission, don't you agree? It should have taken her no time to exchange a few words with Bazunov. But what happened? Six weeks have passed and I haven't heard a thing from Mariya Grigorevna. And the only reason I called upon her (the first time ever) was that when she was in Switzerland last summer she herself very warmly offered her services to me to take care of any details in Petersburg.

Thus, I am obviously losing out simply because I am not on the scene. And that's not the only thing! There are a tremendous number of things that

I cannot get along without that I left behind in Russia! I am not sure whether I wrote you or not about a literary idea I have (a novel—*a parable about Atheism*) compared to which everything else I have written previously during my literary career is sheer rubbish and a mere prelude and to which I am going to dedicate myself the rest of my life. But I cannot conceivably write it while I'm living here; to do so I absolutely must be in Russia. Without Russia, it cannot be done.

And then all the torments, all the petty troubles I am plagued with! At least they could have spared me that! In the name of God, Apollon Nikolaye-vich, write me about Pasha, and about his squabbles with Emiliya Fyodo-rovna! It may be all nonsense, but to me it is important. And although Emi-liya Fyodorovna doesn't mention Pasha in it, the letter I received from her a few days ago is full of reproaches. These people have a strange way of look-ing at things, indeed. I recognize that they are poor, but, after all, I can help them only to the extent of my own capabilities.

Look here, Apollon Nikolayevich, I have another favor to ask of you—if you can do it, fine; if you can't, forget about it. But, for God's sake, don't put yourself out. There's not much work involved, but the matter is delicate. It concerns Bazunov again. Would you please go to his bookstore and find out whether or not he is interested in paying 2000 rubles for the rights to *The Idiot*? (I don't want to let him have it for 1500.) As you perhaps know your-self, you can be very straightforward with Aleksandr Fyodorovich Bazunov. I don't want you to make any special effort and, above all, don't force the issue, but if the conversation really gets under way (Bazunov loves to seek people's advice), you could perhaps (for friendship's sake) slip in a good word about *The Idiot*. But remember, I don't want you to go overboard. Once you have the answer, please write to me. Well, that's all I have in mind.

Of course you won't, I know you won't refuse to do this for me (this is a very important matter for me even though I don't want to come down on the price, but if he says *no*, that's up to him. I won't lose anything, I'll publish it myself or wait). But what makes the matter ticklish is that I did ask her to handle it for me, and what's more, confidentially, although I told her at the time that I would inform you of the result. So don't you think she might be offended that I am bypassing her now by asking that favor of you instead? But really, why should she feel offended, knowing as she does that you were supposed to hear about it all from me? Besides, she still has not answered me, despite the fact that precious time is running out, while the matter is for me one of great importance. The least she could have done was to have let me know that she did not want to do that errand for me and thereby, at least, have untied my hands instead of just leaving me completely in the dark. Any-way, I don't think it could cause any embarrassment if you just went to see Bazunov and asked him, on my behalf, whether he had received any kind of an offer from me for publishing *The Idiot*. Then, on the basis of his reaction, you could also discuss terms with him. So that in a nutshell is the favor I am asking of you, Apollon Nikolayevich! If you can possibly do it, I shall greatly appreciate it. It goes without saying that I am not asking you to close the deal (that cannot be done without a power of attorney and a contract), but only to make overtures, i.e., to find out whether Bazunov is interested and whether his word is good, and then write me just a couple of lines to let me know.

But, above all, don't be angry with me or reproach me for bothering and troubling you. Furthermore, I think you should know that I am going to write to Mariya Grigorevna shortly and ask her to forget about the Bazunov business and to consider my request to her as if it had never been made. I would have done so in any case, i.e., even if I had not thought of asking you to contact Bazunov. But best of all, the best thing by far, would be if you would take it upon yourself to go and see Mariya Grigorevna and simply ask her whether she has made any headway or just forgotten about it! I'm afraid, though, that this may be asking too much of you; as it is, you already have more than your share of scurrying about.

I still hope to leave this place soon and go on to Dresden again. Letters addressed to me in Dresden will be forwarded to me in Florence if I do stay on here, because I have arranged this by letter with the Dresden post office. But that is only a precaution, since I still look forward to leaving for Dresden soon, and so, if you do feel like writing me (which I ardently hope you will), from now on, address your letters, in any case, as follows: Allemagne, Saxe, Dresden, a Mr Theodor Dost-y, poste restante.

Actually, there are a number of important reasons for our moving to Dresden, not the least being the fact that we are familiar with the city, it is comparatively cheap, we even know some people there, and it is the place where Anna Grigorevna would like to realize her expectations (that should be toward the beginning of September—I mean the expectations). Anna Grigorevna thanks you very, very much for your kind words; she often remembers you and she misses Russia badly. I'm very glad that her present "occupation" will take her mind off her homesickness somewhat.

Good-bye, my friend! Here I have covered three sheets but what have I told you? Nothing much. We have been separated for too long and after a long separation there is an enormous accumulation of things that are inscrutable. I have some idea of all that is going on in Petersburg from the *Russian Messenger* and *Dawn,* and I read the *Voice,* which is available in the public library here. What do you think of Danilevsky's *Europe and Russia* [*sic*]? In my opinion, it is an extremely important work, although I am afraid that it is not given enough prominence in their magazine. I consider Averkiyev's comedy about Frol Skabeyev [*sic*] the best piece of writing I've seen this year. I was even ecstatic about it when I read it for the first time, but now, after having taken a second look at it, I have a somewhat more guarded view. I shake your hand heartily and hug you.

All yours as ever,
Fyodor Dostoyevsky

---

79. This letter is an answer to one from Maikov, in which he told Dostoyevsky of his plan for writing a series of tales from Russian history for the elementary schools. Some of them, dealing with the Mamayev massacre, the fall of Constantinople, Ivan the Terrible, and the conquest of Siberia, among other subjects, were published in *Dawn* in 1869.

The "Russified 'Fominishna'" is a reference to Sofya, niece of the last emperor of Byzantium, who married Ivan III.

Ernst Johann Biron (1690–1772) was a minister and favorite of Tsarina Anna Ivanovna, who reigned from 1730 to 1740.

Yermak Timofeyev (d. 1584) was a Cossack leader and the conqueror of Siberia during the reign of Ivan the Terrible. He became a legendary hero of Russian folk poetry.

Frol Skobeyev, a comedy in five acts by Averkiyev that was published in the March 1869 issue of *Dawn,* is based on a seventeenth-century adventure story in which the title character, a poor member of the gentry, abducts an aristocrat's daughter, marries her in secret, and later obtains the forgiveness of her parents and becomes wealthy and famous.

80.   To A. N. Maikov
Dresden, October 27/November 8, 1869

My invaluable friend,

I received your letter with the 100 rubles and Hirsch's bank note, yesterday, *on Sunday.* Since Hirsch's is closed on Sundays, I couldn't answer you straightway; but I want you to know that today I got the note cashed there and received everything coming to me.

The conclusion I draw from all this is that, if I hadn't written to you and if you hadn't been the sort of man you are, I would still not have received anything at all, and perhaps nothing in the future either, neither money nor even an explanation. You write that I shouldn't be furious with Kashpirev; I suppose I won't be furious with him, especially since you affirm that he is himself in straitened circumstances and that that was the cause of the whole thing. But I want you to put yourself in my position and judge for yourself whether I could help being furious. My answer to that is that, even viewing the situation with utmost Christian charity, as you write, one still can't help being outraged. *The least he could do was to have answered me.* But it is past now, and I consider the matter closed, especially since he himself is having such a hard time of it. And I can assure you, in all sincerity, that there was no real malice in my heart even at the time I wrote you that letter.

As to what you yourself have done for me, there is nothing I can say. I'll never forget it. Thank you.

You did just the right thing in not showing him my letter. I was solely interested in your conveying to him its *substance*. So I am extremely grateful to you for not having let him see the letter itself.

As for the interest charges and expenses I incurred, which he wishes *to reimburse* me for—I feel that is quite unnecessary. When you see him, please tell him that I won't allow it under any circumstances. I am no usurer! And then, all sorts of things happen in life. Indirectly, I could always blame someone every time I fail in something: you, Yanovsky, Krayevsky, Aksakov, Saltykov, everybody in fact. Suppose I go to buy a winter coat, and I meet a passer-by who tells me that in such and such a shop there are beautiful and inexpensive coats. I go to the shop and it turns out later that they overcharged me 20 rubles. Can you imagine my claiming that sum from the chance acquaintance? Everything that happens to us in life is due to a combination of an infinite number of circumstances that cannot be imputed just to its primary cause. And in what happened to me now, Kashpirev was not only not the primary cause, but was even only indirectly involved. So, I want no compensation of any kind from him, just thank him for his offer and tell him that that offer is enough for me but that I can't accept it.

And you, I thank you again. You really came to my rescue just in time— another moment and I'd have done something stupid.

Nevertheless, there are many favors I must ask of you. I realize that it is indecent of me to pester you like this, but as I see no possibility whatever of managing without your assistance and mediation, I take the liberty of bothering you again. In the name of God, do not be angry with me.

The first thing I would like to ask you is to act as a sort of intermediary between me and Kashpirev with respect to my story. I'll write him myself about it, too, but a word from you, a man whom he probably values highly and who, what's more, is a well-wisher of *Dawn,* would carry a lot of weight. Here is what it is about:

(1) The story (which cannot possibly be sent to *Dawn* before 2 weeks from today) will not contain just three and a half printer's sheets, as I told Kashpirev originally (though actually that was just the *minimum* number of sheets, not the *maximum*), and may finally have six or even seven sheets, in terms of the *Russian Messenger*'s sheets. Two-thirds of the story has been completed and is already in final form. I did everything in my power to cut it down, but I was unable to do so. But what is important is not the length but the quality. And on that score I cannot say anything myself—for I am plainly incapable—but must leave it to others to judge. But what worries me is that

Kashpirev wants (and he wrote me about it) to announce my story in advance. I wouldn't like that in the least, I mean, not for anything in the world! Try to persuade him not to advertise it when you talk to him privately! I realize that I have no say, that he can act just as he pleases in this matter, that I have no way of preventing him, but I just wonder whether he wouldn't accede to my request.

(2) In our original agreement, I myself wrote him that he was free to publish my story either this year or next, although I indicated my preference for this year. Now, when I send him the manuscript, I shall ask him to run it in December (or even in the November issue, if I manage to send it off in time). It would make things extremely difficult for me if he deferred publication until next year. I have my special reason for this, arising out of a convergence of circumstances. It is not prompted by pecuniary considerations, but rather by something *quite different.* I would like to appear in the December issue. This is of the utmost importance to me. When my brother was publishing *Time,* we both arrived at the conclusion, at the end of the first year, that for a new magazine, in its *first year* of publication, the last issues of that first year were *more important for attracting subscribers* than the January and February issues of the following year. The increase in subscriptions fully bore out that line of reasoning. If Kashpirev wants to announce my story beforehand, it would suggest that he values me as a writer, and if he really does, it would be more to his advantage to run my story in December. Please discuss the matter with him, and when my story arrives at the editorial office, do whatever you can to bring him around to my point of view. It is very important to me, although, of course, it is entirely up to him.

(3) My story will be seven printer's sheets long in terms of *Russian Messenger*'s sheets, which is about the equivalent of eight and a half sheets in *Dawn.* I would be delighted if it were printed in a single issue rather than broken up into two installments. I shall particularly insist on this point. Please inform him of that.

(4) Up until now, I have received 500 rubles in advance from him. If the story is seven printer's sheets long (*Russian Messenger* sheets), I'll have another 500 rubles coming to me. (If it turns out to be, say, only six instead of seven sheets, he'll owe me only an additional 400.) So couldn't he settle our accounts before the number comes out, let's say, during the first half of December, by which time he will have a clear indication as to how the subscriptions are coming in? I shall ask him about that when I send the story, and I beseech you (for God's sake, don't turn me down!) to collect the money from him (no matter when he pays it). If you are agreeable, I'll write him to that effect. Out of that money, I want first of all to pay you back, with warm and boundless gratitude, the 200 rubles I owe you. Reimburse yourself directly

out of Kashpirev's money; I'll write and let him know. The remaining 200 or 300 rubles are to be used to redeem some things we pawned in Petersburg before leaving the country, most of them belonging to my wife. We would like to spend at least 200 on redeeming things of which the actual value may be as high as 600 and which may be lost to us if we don't redeem them soon enough. Anna Grigorevna's younger brother, Ivan Grigorevich, will come to see you about this (after you have received the money). You need not hesitate to give him the money and he'll do the redeeming (he'll come only after you have received the money and won't bother you before). This is a special favor we are asking of you and the reason for my troubling you is that I cannot deal directly with *Dawn* because they are so uncooperative when it comes to questions of money. Of course, if he cannot give me the money in December, all this will have to be postponed until January. And no one will come to ask you for the money before you have received it. They will come to see you only after you have it available. All I am asking you now is to be good enough to pick up the money from Kashpirev, obviously when he is in a position to pay it, and I don't suppose that this will cause you any particular inconvenience. As it is, I have already imposed upon you much too much. I am not asking you *to obtain* the money from Kashpirev, but only *to pick it up* when it becomes available.

And finally, my last and most important request—concerning Emiliya Fyodorovna. Since I have received your 100 rubles and the draft on Hirsch, that means that I have now received 175 rubles altogether from *Dawn*, instead of the 200 that Kashpirev promised me. So, I wonder if it wouldn't be possible for the remaining 25 rubles to be turned over to Emiliya Fyodorovna *without delay*?! I beseech you in the name of *Christ* not to fail to ask Kashpirev to do it! My heart is heavy for not having helped them for such a long time! And she and Katya are having such a bad time now that it is impossible to imagine anything worse. After I have sent Kashpirev the story, I shall do my utmost to convince him to pay to her at least another 25 rubles at the earliest opportunity (that should not upset the above calculations), and to do it through you. Your assistance in that matter, my friend, will be a service to God more than to me. You can always get her address from Pasha. But what is most important is for you to get those remaining 25 rubles from Kashpirev to her right away. I daresay he will have 25 rubles readily available! Please be good enough to take the trouble for me. Reassure me, for I am *very* anxious. As for Pasha, he will just have to be patient; I'll help him later, too.

I wasn't planning to say anything at this time about your stories from Russian history because there are so many things I have to say on that subject, but I can't restrain myself and so I shall write a few lines. I have read them and there's no need to tell you that I do like them. But what is terribly disappointing is the likelihood that after you write another story or two you'll toss the whole thing aside. I am almost certain of it—you will simply let the matter slide. What a pity, because think of the good you could have done! Let us suppose that you decide to devote a whole year of continuous work to these stories, that you work unhurriedly and turn out at least twenty-five stories (because I am convinced that the stories of the post-Petrine period, presented from a sound Russian point of view, will turn out to be even more interesting and, *what's more, more useful*). If you proceeded that way, you would come up with a book that could be published as a separate volume (which you should do without undue delay, *avoiding at all costs* (!) selling the rights to a bookseller but publishing it on your own). The book would be extraordinarily useful in all the elementary and secondary schools, etc., and it would become *compulsory*. Neither Karamzin nor Solovyov are read in the schools in their entirety, but your book could be read from beginning to end and would serve to strengthen for all times the clear, sound ideas in the mind of the schoolboy and the student. If, as you tell me, even old men say that they can learn many things from your stories, then surely they will buy the book for their children. For twenty years or so, the book will be an indispensable element in the education of the young. The prior publication in magazines of half of the stories would help recommend the book and popularize it.

Now let us examine it purely from the economic standpoint. Why, it is *capital* you have there, and perhaps important capital at that. In twenty years it may go through a number of editions. So why throw it all over and fail to take advantage of a good opportunity? After all, it's your idea, your own, personal idea! If you procrastinate, some talented man like Razin (of *God's World*) will beat you to it, steal your idea, write the stories himself, publish them, pick up a nice profit, and pull the rug out from under you. So don't throw it all away—that's the thing that counts.

By the way, isn't there any way of convincing Kashpirev to send me *Dawn* once and for all! The September issue came out on October 8, and today it is already the 27th, and I still haven't got it! Why, I consider myself a subscriber, I asked to be one and I am going to pay for it. I can just imagine what their out-of-town subscribers have to put up with! No, sir, you can't run a magazine that way! Even if all their contributors were as great as Pushkin and Gogol, their magazine would still burst like a bubble because of their inefficiency. They're ruining themselves. Krayevsky succeeded thanks to the punctuality and efficiency he demonstrated in the conduct of the commercial side of his enterprise. And it's the same sad story for every number I get! The sheer torment of it all!

The more a subscriber enjoys a magazine, the more exasperated he feels when it is run so inefficiently. Even the most loyal of subscribers becomes disenchanted!

The way I look at it is that if I am a contributor to a magazine, I simply must be intimately acquainted with it.

Now, on the subject of Stellovsky. I enclose herewith a *copy* of the copy of my 1865 contract with him, accurately recorded, even down to the grammatical mistakes. I was forced into signing this contract by Stellovsky, who confronted me (through Bocharov) with the IOU's held by Demis and Gavrilov, and threatened to have me locked up in prison. Things went so far that I had a visit from the deputy police chief of the precinct, who came to take me in. But then I became good friends with that police officer, and I learned many things from him that came in handy later for *Crime and Punishment*. It is a shocking contract. Please show it to Pasha right away. Let him examine it carefully and show it to his notary. That Stellovsky is such a crook, he'll hook you where you least expect it. *For the time being,* this is how I view matters: let Stellovsky buy *The Idiot* for 1000 rubles, 500 down and 500 in short-term IOU's. With regard to the advance for *Crime and Punishment,* in order to avoid all possible confusion, I would be willing to wait until next year, i.e., until it is published; the negotiations, therefore, will be concerned solely with *The Idiot*. However, if he insists, we can settle the other matter too, but then, we must take every precaution to avoid any pitfall. But better take *The Idiot* separately. Anyway, there can be no question now of his publishing *Crime and Punishment;* he cannot do so until my contract with Bazunov runs out, i.e., until January 1, 1870 (that should be checked with Bazunov, although I'm quite sure that I sold him the rights up to the year 1870). Pasha should draw up a draft contract with his notary, show it to you, send it to me here, and thereafter submit it for Stellovsky's final approval. But it is essential that Pasha and his notary examine attentively the copy of the old contract I am enclosing here, because it is very possible that Stellovsky will try to hook me, in this way, *for example:* in the copy of the contract, it says in one place that in the event that Stellovsky wanted to publish *Crime and Punishment,* I would get such and such per printer's sheet . . . etc., etc. Now, since he won't be allowed to publish it until 1870, I also won't be paid until *after publication.* So, if he gave me, for instance, an advance on *Crime and Punishment* now, before 1870, he might later contend that thereby the contract had been voided, since he doesn't have the right to publish the novel until 1870 and so only had to pay me for it then. So, at every point in the contract for *The Idiot* which might in any way be misconstrued, it must be explicitly stated that this or that disposition in the present agreement does not in any sense invalidate our old contract, which remains in full force, etc.

320

But we shall have a clearer picture of things when we get down to business. The matter, however, ought to be attended to rapidly. It is inconceivable that Stellovsky would not publish *Crime and Punishment,* i.e., relinquish his rights to it, and consequently it may be to his advantage to publish *The Idiot,* too. The chances are, therefore, that he may be seriously interested. And I certainly could use 1000 rubles.

It is a shame, though, that Stellovsky is such a crook and a trickster. He would, *for instance,* very much like to wheedle an extra year on his copyright to *The Idiot,* that is, that his copyright should run for *two* years from the end of next year. And if that is so, isn't he trying to pull a fast one on me somehow? He may include in the contract, for instance, a clause saying that he will publish *The Idiot* in the same format as his edition of "Works of Russian Literature" and then he will tack on *Crime and Punishment* and claim that, by selling him the rights to *The Idiot,* I have implicitly extended his right to reprint *all* my other works for yet another year (and perhaps even indefinitely); that since he bought it in order to publish it in the same format as the works of mine that he had published previously, and since it is to be published along with *Crime and Punishment,* it would no longer be feasible for him to sell *The Idiot* separately, but only with the rest of my works and therefore his rights to publish my other works must be extended by one year, etc., and hence the old contract is invalidated, and so on and so forth.

By far the best thing would be if his rights to *The Idiot* expired at the same time as his rights to publish my other works. In short, show this sheet of my letter to Pasha and thank him, my dear fellow, for his efforts. I'll write him soon. (To judge from his letter, he has become so much more intelligent!) As for the transaction, I feel that if we are to go through with it, we should do so as soon as possible. We should never lose sight of the fact, though, that Stellovsky is an unscrupulous schemer, and conduct ourselves accordingly. Provided all goes well, I shall be able to help both Pasha and Emiliya Fyodorovna out of Stellovsky's 1000 rubles.

I don't know for certain, but I think that my story will be called *The Eternal Husband.*

Good-bye, my dear friend. Anna Grigorevna sends you her regards and thanks you. Lyuba is well and is beginning to be aware of all around her. Lyuba sends her regards to you and Pasha.

All yours,
F. Dostoyevsky.

---

80. Sergei Mikhailovich Solovyov (1820–1879) was a professor at Moscow University (1845–1875) and one of the most eminent Russian historians. His *History of Russia from Ancient Times* (Istoriya Rossii s drevneishikh vremyon, 1851–1879) covered the period up to 1774 in twenty-nine volumes.

Ivan Petrovich Bocharov was Stellovsky's lawyer.

"Lyuba" was the Dostoyevskys' second child, Lyubov, who was born in Dresden on September 14/26, 1869.

81. To S. A. Ivanova
Dresden, December 14/26, 1869

My dear and sweet friend Sonechka,

At last I can write you something. I read your letter, which I received I'm not sure when (especially, since like every woman, you never date your letters), three months or so ago, and I didn't answer you simply because I *could not* answer you. I was busy writing that damned story for *Dawn*. I got started late and finished it only a week ago. I think I worked on it for exactly three months and turned out at least eleven printer's sheets. You can imagine what hard labor it was!—especially since I got to hate that horrid story from the very start. I set out to write three printer's sheets at the most, but all sorts of details crept in, and it wound up eleven sheets long. That work wore me out completely and, to make matters worse, I didn't answer anyone's letters, even if they were on the most important business, and was constantly in such a gloomy mood that I couldn't even answer you.

Don't be angry with me, my invaluable friend. I want you to know that I have always loved you deeply and that a day has seldom gone by without my thinking of you. You may, of course, consider my words exaggerated and think that I am being sentimental. I assure you, however, that this is the truth. Every single day my thoughts go back to Russia until my head swims. I am madly longing to return, and as I think of Russia, you all come to my mind, Verochka's entire family, and particularly you. While here abroad, I have come to realize that, of all the people in my native land, of all the places there, all of you and your household are dearest to my heart. So that's why, as I recall and think of Russia, I also think of you every day. And it all seems to me like so long ago—as though it were in the days of my *blossoming youth* (I can imagine Mashenka bursting out laughing at that flight of fancy). From this you can gauge that I unwittingly see myself as old now—an old old man. And perhaps I'll die soon.

In the meantime, my daughter Lyubochka came into this world on September 26, which makes her *exactly* three months old today. I cannot convey to you how much I love her. Anya is feeding her herself and, poor soul, it is very hard on her—I am afraid that breast-feeding may be bad for her health. Luckily for us, Anya's mother is living with us and looking after the child. The girl is strong, cheerful, and very intelligent for her years (i.e., for her months), she sings along with me when I sing to her and laughs all the time—a rather quiet and easy baby. She looks ridiculously like me, down to the minutest traits. We shall christen her in a few days, a thing we had also postponed until I finished my work! I want your mother to be the god-mother and will write her about that. Apollon Nikolayevich Maikov will be the godfather and her partner in this. I am quite certain that Verochka will agree—she couldn't possibly disappoint me and turn me down.

Now I'll tell you a few words about our life here. It is a dull life. In the bedroom, there is Lyuba to be looked after and the daily chores, and, as for me, up to now it has been nothing but work. Dresden is a very dull town in its own right. I cannot stand these Germans. It's a good thing that I have hardly had any fits (I haven't had a single one in exactly three months despite the strenuous work). But, on the other hand, I have rushes of blood to the head and the heart (God knows what it is—I can't explain it to you).

I get up at one in the afternoon—because I work at night, and even if I didn't I couldn't sleep anyway. From three to five in the afternoon, I work. Then I go out for a half-hour's walk—straight to the post office and back through the Royal Gardens, always taking the same route. We eat our dinner at home. At seven, I go out for another walk and again return through the Royal Gardens. When I get back I have some tea and at 10:30 I sit down to work. I work until 5 in the morning. Then I lie down and as soon as it strikes six, I fall asleep. That's my whole life. During my evening walk, I stop by the reading room where they have the Russian newspapers and I read the *Petersburg Gazette,* the *Voice,* and the *Moscow Gazette.* Anya's life is even duller than mine—feeding and looking after Lyuba prevent her even from going out for a good walk, which is something she badly needs. No distrac-tions—there just aren't any here. It's pointless to go to the stupid German theater. One can, though, go and listen to the music, which is not bad at all, and, as a matter of fact, the tickets to the concert hall are very cheap. I have been there above five times, but Anya cannot do that either, because she can-not leave the baby.

We have no acquaintances here at all. For reading matter, we are receiving *Dawn* and *Russian Messenger.* Anya's brother, Ivan Grigorevich, is here in Dresden and lives practically next door to us. He has been here for two months now and sends you his regards. Anya is writing to you on her own. It is all decided now—I'm coming back next year. I cannot bear living away from home any longer, and because of our limited means and the lack of spare time, we cannot even take advantage of our trip abroad. I should defi-nitely visit Mount Athos and Jerusalem—it is essential—but I cannot do so at the present time, and in five days I shall have to start on my new work, and God knows when I shall finish it.

I expect that as soon as I get back to Russia (which will possibly be around the end of the summer next year) I'll go directly to Moscow (I'll have to go there for business reasons anyhow) and we shall be reunited. What will it be like to meet after three and a half years? It's hard for me to realize that so much time has passed. The only thing I am sure of is that I shall find your heart unchanged. Otherwise, I have no inkling of how my new life there will shape up (that is, if I am to go on living at all) and how it will all be (I mean, even in general). Of course, I intend to go on working and maybe I shall settle in Moscow altogether. I must do something for Anya and Lyuba. And there's also something else I'm thinking of—I am afraid that we, I mean I and all of you, may have grown apart from each other in all this time I have been abroad.

But all this is still in the future, and for now, I'll answer one point you raise in your letter, my darling girl, my sweet, precious, kind, and noble Sonya: Please don't write me things like "the end doesn't justify the means." It wasn't really that it offended me, but it did pain me. I was saddened by the thought that perhaps, after all, time has gradually been leading to our estrangement. The business about Aunt's death and her will happened, as I may have told you already, like this:

Maikov wrote to me what might be described as an *ardent* plea "to save the family." His letter was brief but *extremely precise* and eloquent in the information it contained: it was to the effect that Veselovsky, the executor of our late aunt, was infuriated by the fact that 40,000 rubles had been bequeathed to a monastery. That piece of information came from Kashpirev, a *friend* of Veselovsky, and Veselovsky apparently told him that if he had known my address he would have written to me immediately asking me to defend the interests of those who had been deprived of their rightful share. Maikov ended his letter by advising me to write to Veselovsky.

Which of them was not telling the truth, I still don't know, because I never received any further answers to my inquiries. I suppose every one of them lied, but *out of friendship* and half unwittingly. Only Maikov cannot possibly have lied—he just is not that sort of man. So it must have been Kashpirev—and I want you to note that Maikov, who is on friendly terms with Kashpirev, informed me that Kashpirev is a *friend* of Veselovsky's. The most likely explanation, then, would seem to be that Kashpirev, giving credence to some half-rumor, added the other half in his excitement and the result was the mess that ensued.

As to Aunt's will, I am quite familiar with it, the more so since I received *everything* that I was entitled to; and, as you well know, I sank my whole share, 10,000 rubles, then and there into my brother's magazine, of which I was never *the owner*, and, in so doing, I sank *my* 10,000 rubles to help my brother's family. After having sunk those 10,000 rubles in someone else's business, I went on paying out money for that same business—that is, paying the debts that were in part owed by the magazine and in part by my brother personally—I can't exactly say how much, but here are a few figures that might give you some idea.

The whole of the 7000 rubles I received for the second edition of *Crime and Punishment*, following its extraordinary success, was spent on paying back the debts incurred by the magazine to Prats, the owner of the printing shop and the paper manufacturer, and I mean the whole 7000 rubles down to the last kopek. After that, I spent 2000 rubles in cash, which I had realized from the sale of my works to Stellovsky, to meet the debts incurred by my brother as well as by the magazine. Besides that, I paid out another fifteen hundred rubles or so on various minor expenses. And after all that (and there are things I've left out), there are still another four thousand rubles or so of outstanding debts left by the magazine, i.e., by a business that was not mine, and because of them, for almost three years, I have been roaming about abroad to avoid being thrown into prison. Nevertheless, in the end, I will pay *everyone*, every, every one.

And so my dear friend, my invaluable and unforgettable Sonya, I would be the last one to try to appropriate what doesn't belong to him or to engage in lawsuits in order to deprive others, as my brother Andrei Mikhailovich, my aunt's other executor, has accused me of doing in a most tactful letter he sent me. But he does not know me very well as a man, and I forgive him from the bottom of my heart, especially since I have always truly considered him as a brother despite certain things that may have happened.

Having received that announcement from Maikov, along with his advice as to what I should do, and being surprised that I had heard nothing of Aunt's death (may she live in good health for many years yet), I wrote a letter to Veselovsky who, instead of answering me, forwarded my letter to Andrei Mikhailovich so that he could answer me himself. But my letter was much too clear and precise to be miscontrued. I am confident that Andrei Mikhailovich, being the orderly and methodical man he is, will see to it that it never gets lost.

The point of the matter is that five years ago already I had a very good idea of what was in our aunt's will (through my unforgettable late brother Misha), and I knew positively that it contained no clause about the monastery. In the light of that fact (please follow my reasoning), it was evident that such a bequest could only have been made very recently, subsequent to the death of your father (who certainly would not have advised her to make that bequest to a monastery, if for no other reason than that it would have been damaging to your own interests and thus have been the height of folly!), in which case it was traceable to the influence of some clever priests on my aunt. Living abroad for so long and not knowing what was going on over there, I could very easily infer that from the explicitness of Maikov's letter. (Because when I am told, for example, the *very* words that Aunt's executor, Veselovsky, had spoken to Kashpirev, can there be anything more *explicit* than that? I certainly could not imagine that these very words had never been uttered. It is quite amazing that someone should have lied, I don't understand a thing, but I have all the documents in my hands—all their letters.) On the other hand, I likewise knew very well that Aunt was not of sound mind, so that if there had been any truth in that story about the monastery (which I was assured there was by *a firsthand witness,* i.e., by her executor, Kashpirev's *friend*), then it was patently clear that the most flagrant injustice and legal subterfuge had been perpetrated. I wrote to Veselovsky immediately and sent what follows to the address that had been given to me:

"This one and that one have written me, among them a friend of yours, your own such-and-such words to me on the subject of the will. In addition, I have been informed that you regret that you cannot contact *me* with a view to starting proceeding against the will, and so I ask you now (1) to explain to me everything connected with the death of my aunt and with her will. (2) If the bequest to the monastery was not the result of criminal inspiration of a woman who was weak in the head during the last moments of her life, but was made by her before, while she was still in full possession of her mental faculties, I would, of course, then *consider it my duty* to respect her last will and I would not be a party to any legal action against anyone. Now if you—a lawyer—consider that there is something irregular here, i.e., something done while she was not in full possession of her mental faculties, then I am prepared to start a legal action, as you suggested. But please furnish me with greater detail about the entire situation and explain to me the manner in which I could be of some utility to you." That is the *sense* of my letter to Veselovsky.

I assure you, my dear friend, that in writing him that letter, I was not seeking my own advantage. And if Aunt had bequeathed everything to a monastery of her own free doing, I would never have dared to initiate anything, out of respect for her personal wishes. But tell me, how could I have acted otherwise given the circumstances? And don't you think that the least I could do was to ask for an explanation?

Now, Veselovsky forwarded that letter *of inquiry* to my brother Andrei Mikhailovich, asking him to answer me. Andrei Mikhailovich sent me a whole notebook in reply. And in his reply, Andrei Mikhailovich ignored the point I had made in my letter to Veselovsky in which I made it quite clear that I would not dream of going against my aunt's wishes if she had been of sound mind at the time, and he accused me of wanting to go against our aunt's will in any case, on the grounds that she had drawn it up while she was not in full possession of her senses and, of course, on the grounds that we, her nephews the Dostoyevskys, were the most rightful heirs. He urges me to desist from any further involvement as well (this can be seen from the tone of his really most tactful letter), emphasizing strongly the fact that there is practically nothing left of the estate already, that the securities in which our aunt's capital was invested are of such doubtful value that it is highly unlikely that even one-half of the money will ever be recovered. I plan to answer my brother Andrei in a few days (I haven't thus far). Moreover, I want you to know that I consider him a perfectly scrupulous man.

So that is the whole story, which, I'm sure, will be used as horrendous evidence of what a greedy money-grubber I am! Believe me, my dear friend, if I stay alive for another eight years or so, I shall pay all my debts, I shall spend the last of my earnings to take care of certain people in Petersburg, even if it means depriving Lyuba; and I shall surely refund to you, in the fullness of my heart, all the money my brother, three months before his death, received as a loan from Aleksandr Pavlovich at *my behest* and secured, as far as possible, by *my* verbal guarantee. That money, which came from your kind and wonderful father, who, at my request, came to my brother's rescue at a difficult moment, has always weighed on my conscience—for no other reason than because I love you all so much. And so you, at least, my precious one, must not think of me as a money-grubber!

By the way, to finish with this subject, the part of my brother Andrei Mikhailovich's letter dealing with *the present state of our aunt's holdings* is very curious. If you wish, I'll tell you something about it, but just you and in the utmost confidence, because I don't wish to quarrel with Andrei Mikhailovich. It doesn't look as though all you people will get much out of it. It's a pity. I'm also sorry for my sister Sasha and for my brother Kolya, and for Katya (Misha's daughter). As for myself, I received *all that was coming to me*—the full 10,000 rubles—back in 1864, and my position is—as it has been—that I am entitled to nothing further. Quite honestly, I even feel that I owe Aunt interest, although I haven't been able to pay her a single kopek thus far. In general, whenever I think of all I owe, I get frightened. It seems the more you pay, the more you still owe.

Keep in mind what I've said here and hold on to this letter for future reference, i.e., as a reminder that I not only disclaim any further share in the estate, *but that I also feel obligated to pay Aunt the interest that has accrued over the past five years.*

I wanted to write only one page about this business, but instead I have filled a whole letter with it. And now, I come to another matter of importance to me. Last spring, I promised *Dawn* a story. I went so long without getting any money from *Russian Messenger* in Florence that I didn't get to Dresden until August. Then most recently there was Anya's confinement. Finally, I got down to work on the story for *Dawn* but, instead of *one* month, as I had planned, I spent *three* months writing it. In the meantime, I had made a firm commitment to *Russian Messenger* to give them a novel by January, in view of the fact that I still owed them money. I told them frankly what had happened and promised to send them the first installment of the novel in time for their February number. *Dawn,* however, will be running my story in its January number. I imagine the publishers of *Russian Messenger* will be upset with me for this, and I can't entirely blame them. But how could I help it? I had no idea that things would take such a turn, nor could I turn over to *Russian Messenger* the story I had written for *Dawn;* I have something much more important in store for it. It is a novel, of which only the first section will be published in *Russian Messenger.* I expect it will take five years to complete, and it will be divided into three sections—three stories, each one of them complete in itself. That novel is my fondest dream, my life's ambition—and I don't mean just from a monetary standpoint. It contains my main idea, which has crystallized only in these past two years. But to do justice to it, I must not write it in a hurry. I don't want to spoil it. This idea is everything I have lived for. On the other hand, to write that novel, I have to be in Russia. The second half of my first story, you see, takes place in a monastery. It is important for me not only to see a monastery (I've seen many as it is) but to live for some time in one. That's why it's hard for me to stay abroad and essential to return to Russia. I am happy with Anya, but she, too, is longing to get back home, and have I the right to deprive her of her country for the sake of personal considerations?

Write me . . . Perhaps our correspondence will become livelier now. Please love me a little bit. My address is still the same:

Allemagne, Saxe, Dresden à M-r Th. Dostoiewsky poste restante.

Don't forget the poste restante. I hug and kiss you.

Your very loving
F. Dostoyevsky

---

81. Anna Grigorevna's brother Ivan was a student at the Petrovskaya Agricultural Academy, where he knew of the Nechayev circle and was acquainted with the student Ivanov, who was killed by members of the circle on November 21, 1869. According to Anna, her brother, while visiting them in Dresden, told Dostoyevsky about student life "eagerly and at great length," and she believed that Dostoyevsky's description, in *The Devils,* of the park of the Petrovskaya Academy and of the grotto where Ivanov was murdered was based on her brother's account. However, *The Devils* was not the work that Dostoyevsky was planning at the time to write for *Russian Messenger;* that, rather, was a work first called *Atheism* and later *The Life of a Great Sinner,* which was never to be realized. (As will become evident in the next letter, Dostoyevsky conceived of it as consisting of five separate novellas, which could be published separately.)

The whole affair of the Dostoyevskys' Aunt Kumanina's will was based on a false premise. The aunt had not died.

82. To A. N. MAIKOV
Dresden, March 25/April 6, 1870

Much esteemed and most kind Apollon Nikolayevich,

Excuse me for not having replied sooner, although I have been dying to write to you all the while. But first of all, it was my work and then my health and the anxiety that grew out of my isolation—anxiety about my health— and I have been very depressed. My heart has begun to beat irregularly, and I am unable to sleep. So I went to a doctor, a prominent professor; he examined me thoroughly: "It's absolutely nothing at all, just nerves. But your nerves are in a really bad state." We ought to get out of Dresden for the summer. It would be nice to go to the seaside and do some bathing. It would be good for my wife, too. There is no doubt that the air of our homeland would be best of all, and *everything* you wrote about it in your letter is the absolute truth, the truth of truths. But, Apollon Nikolayevich, can you be ignorant of why I do not come home and why I cannot put an end to this accursed life abroad? Does it make any sense to return just to be marched off to debtors' prison? It is quite impossible for me to return for some time yet. But don't you realize how homesick I feel myself and how I long with every fiber in my body to return to Russia? And my wife, who is so depressed—do you think I enjoy seeing her in that state? Furthermore, I know for a fact, *positively,* that back home I would be three times better off financially than I am here. Let me tell you, once and for all, all there is to tell on that score, my dear friend: I swear that, even if I knew for *certain* that they would lock me up in debtors' prison, it wouldn't stop me, for I have experienced things much worse than that in my life. I would sit it out there for a year and then buy myself out. But whereas that would have been feasible before (only five years ago), now it is definitely out of the question, and I know it for sure. In my present state of health, I wouldn't last even six months in a public prison, and what's more I wouldn't be able to work at all. And I have a slew of themes to write about. What you say about my writing while living here is absolutely right; it is evident that I shall lose touch—not with recent developments, not with what is going on in Russia (I probably know that better than you since *every day!* I read *three Russian newspapers from cover to cover* and I receive two magazines), but I shall lose contact with the *living stream of life*—not with ideas but with the flesh-and-blood substance, and God knows how that affects artistic work! All that is true, but how can I help it? Make a deal with the creditors, beg them to give me an extension for a year and then pay them in full? But would they accept? If I could pay them half of what I owe, perhaps they'd give me one year's extension. I keep thinking of it day and night. Even if I paid them only 30%, they might accept! But it is difficult even to get in touch with them now; God knows whether all of them are still in Petersburg. But it has to be done because there is no other way out. The sum total of *dangerous* debts, i.e., the ones covered by IOUs, amounts to 4000 rubles now, I believe, which means that I must have two thousand to make the down payment and another thousand to pull out of here and to get settled in Petersburg. So you see I must have three thousand. And where am I to get them? But, believe me, if I hadn't left Petersburg then, I would have repaid absolutely *everything* in two years. Actually, I only left because Pechatkin had started a legal action against me, a fact about which I had prior knowledge. How do you think I would have felt to be locked up in a prison then, just after getting married? I couldn't bear the thought of it and I left. And that was that.

But I shall give some hard thought to the matter in the summer when something turns up. Now I am working on something for *Russian Messenger.* I owe some money there, and I put myself in a rather awkward position with regard to them by giving *The Eternal Husband* to *Dawn.* And so I must at all cost finish the thing I'm writing for them. Besides, I have a firm commitment to them and, when it comes to literature, I am an honest man. What I am writing now is a tendentious thing, I want to give full vent to my feelings. (I can imagine how the nihilists and the Westernizers will howl at me and label me a *reactionary!*) But the hell with them, I shall get off my chest everything I have on it. And, you know, I am completely in the dark—I have absolutely no idea whether it will be a success or not. One moment I have the impression that it will be a tremendous success and that I shall rake in the money on a second edition, the next moment I feel that it will fall flat. But I'd rather fail completely than have a moderate success. You whacked me on the head with a club with your remark about the "strained imagination" which you noticed in *The Eternal Husband*—it depressed me no end! However, I'll just have to leave it to God. Only if you are confident that the result will be successful can you work with enthusiasm. And I am working with enthusiasm. So I am confident.

But I haven't thanked you yet for your good offices and for having gone to see that scoundrel Stellovsky, and all the rest. You cannot even begin to *imagine* how much you have done for me by that. You have restored my peace of mind and healed my wound. I shall admit everything to you now (and to you alone): I believed that Pasha had deceived me! I was so miserable, I kept praying for him. And then, at last, your letter swept away my doubts: he is just a scatterbrain, but otherwise he is a good and honest boy! I repeat—you have healed the wound in my soul. As for Stellovsky, he can go to hell! And, believe it or not, I am even pleased in a sense at the way things turned out. It is so painful to have dealings with that crook!

In the meantime, however, I am in a ghastly situation (Mister Micawber). I don't have a kopek to my name, and I have to hold out until the fall, when I shall have money. It is almost impossible for me to ask *Russian M[essenger]* for money; in the first place, suppose they refuse? And in the second, it would be taking too much money in advance from them. I am certain to get money from them, although it will only be in the fall; but then it will be a large sum. I am quite sure of what I am telling you here. Still I shall have absolutely nothing to live on until autumn. Perhaps you think I am spending a lot here, wallowing in luxury? Would you believe then that for 8 months, since we moved to Dresden, I have lived on *The Eternal Husband* alone, roughly 100 thalers a month, and that despite the confinement, the most necessary upkeep, and living costs that aren't so cheap. So in the end I got into debt and am still in debt to this day.

A month ago, N. N. Strakhov made me a firm offer to continue contributing to *Dawn*. I suggested he should offer Kashpirev my novel for next year but on condition that he pay 500 rubles now and after that one hundred rubles a month for five months, that is, 1,000 rubles in all. I didn't think it was asking too much: Kashpirev had been giving Stebnitsky as much as fifteen hundred rubles a year in advance. (Moreover, a magazine can't operate unless it pays out advances; otherwise it would fail to attract any writers.) Nikolai Nikolayevich replied that Kashpirev was agreeable, that they would send me the money in April, but that he wanted my work to be delivered some time this autumn. I told them that I definitely could not do it this year. Kashpirev, by the way, has not written me himself yet. I am waiting for their final decision.

You will have to agree that if I take anything further from *Russian Messenger,* then my future work, too, will belong to *Russian Messenger* for a long time to come. I shall certainly finish what I am writing for them now in three months or so. Then, after taking a month off, I would get down to work on something for *Dawn*. I have been idle for a year and a half running (I don't count *The Eternal Husband*), and I am impatient to begin writing again. What I am writing for *R. M—r* now won't tire me too much. But for *Dawn*, I promise something good, and I want to do it well. This thing for *Dawn* has been ripening in my head for two years. It is the very idea about which I wrote to you earlier. It will be my last novel. It will be about the size of *War and Peace* and you would approve of the idea for it, as far at least as I can judge from our previous conversations. This novel will consist of five large novellas (each of 15 sheets; in these 2 years my entire plan has taken shape). The novellas are completely independent of one another, to such an extent that it will even be possible to sell them separately. And it is the first of these novellas that I intend for Kashpirev. It is set back in the forties. The overall title of the novel is *The Life of a Great Sinner*, but each novella will have its own title. The main question which will run through all the parts of the novel is the question that has tormented me either consciously or unconsciously all my life—the existence of God. In the course of his life, the hero turns from atheism to faith, to fanaticism and sectarianism, and then back to atheism. The 2nd novella will be set entirely in a monastery. It is in this 2nd novella that I place all my hopes. Perhaps, at long last, people will no longer say that I have written nothing but trifles. (I confess this to you alone, Apollon Nikolayevich: I intend to make the main figure of my 2nd novella Tikhon Zadonsky, of course under another name, but also a bishop who has retired to a monastery.[)] A 13-year-old boy who has participated in the perpetration of a criminal offense, intelligent and perverted (I know that type) (comes from our educated circles), the future hero of the entire novel, is placed by his parents in the monastery to be educated. The young wolf-cub and boy-nihilist comes into contact with Tikhon (you know, of course, Tikhon's character and his entire personality). I shall also put Chaadayev into the monastery (of course, likewise under another name). Why couldn't Chaadeyev spend a year in a monastery? Assume that after his first article, because of which he had to be certified by doctors every week, Chaadayev was unable to restrain himself and published abroad, let's say, a pamphlet in French— Well, it's quite plausible that they would have sent him to spend a year in a monastery for it. Chaadayev could have visitors there, Belinsky, for instance, Granovsky, even Pushkin. (You understand, of course, that it won't really be Chaadayev in my book, that I'm simply using the type.) In the monastery there is also Pavel the Prussian, and Golubov and the monk Parfeny (I know a great deal about that world and have been familiar with Russian monasteries since my childhood). But most important are Tikhon and the boy. For God's sake, don't tell anyone about the contents of this second novella. (I never tell anyone about my themes in advance—I feel embarrassed, somehow, in doing so, but to you I confess.) It may not be worth one kopek to others, but to me it is a treasure. So, please, don't say a word about Tikhon. I wrote to Strakhov about the monastery, but I didn't tell him about Tikhon. Who knows, perhaps I will succeed in drawing a majestic, *positive,* holy figure. It won't be a Kostanzhoglo or that German fellow in *Oblomov* (I forget his name). How do we know: Perhaps it is Tikhon who is the *positive* Russian type our literature has been looking for, rather than Lavrovsky or Chichikov or Rakhmetov or the others, and not the Lopukhovs or the Rakhmetovs. It is true that I won't be creating anything, I'll only show the true Tikhon whom I accepted in my heart enthusiastically a long time ago. But, if I succeeded simply in doing that, I would consider it an important achievement for myself. So don't tell anyone about it.

But for the 2nd novel, for the monastery, I must be back in Russia. Ah, if only it can be arranged! But the first novella is the childhood of the hero. Of course, there are no children on a stage; this is a novel. And, luckily, I can write this while I am out of the country, and I am offering it to *Dawn.* Can they turn it down? But 1000 rubles is not such a lot of money, after all. It's up to them, but in acting that way they will miss out on everything and everyone. Anyhow, it's their business. Yesterday I wrote to Strakhov, asking him for a prompt and definite answer; otherwise, I'll have to find an alternative and lose no time about it. If I approached *R—n M—r*, it would also take time, so I hope *Dawn* won't tarry too long. (I expect it will take me six years to write the whole novel.) If you can put in a good word for me at *Dawn*, please do so, my dear fellow, because it would be extremely unpleasant for me to have to address myself to *R.M.* at this moment. Three months from now, it would be quite a different matter. Moreover, I personally would very much like to work for *Dawn*. Its orientation is the one I agree with the most, except, of course, for a few things here and there. But it's just as they wish. Were it not for my poverty I wouldn't be running after them and offering them my services. And note this: no sooner do I involve myself with a magazine than they begin pressuring me and saddling me with the tightest deadline. But I'd sooner die now than coerce myself. *Russian M—r* alone has never put pressure on me. They are real gentlemen there!

By the way, dear Apollon Nikolayevich, where did you ever get that idea about Yanovsky from? It had never occurred to me, even for a second! I was quite astonished to read what you had written. Anyway, I know absolutely nothing about Yanovsky's history in that respect. Why, did he really have some such experience?

Nihilism isn't even worth talking about. Wait until the upper layer, which has cut itself loose from the Russian soil, rots through and through. And you know, it seems to me sometimes that many of those young scoundrels, those decaying youths, eventually will become real, solid *pochvenniki*, true Russians deeply attached to their native soil. As to the rest, let them rot away. They will be struck dumb by paralysis. Ah, but what a lot of scoundrels they still are!

Anna Grigorevna is terribly flattered by Anna Ivanovna's opinion. She is, you know, full of pride for me. But if you only knew how happy I am with her. The only blight on our happiness is that we still cannot return home. But then, we may return, after all! Lyuba is teething and is suffering. You'd be surprised to see what a healthy child she is. But were it not for Anna Nikola[ye]vna, Anna Grigorevna's mother, Lyuba would have died. We would have been lost without her.

Ah, there are so many things I'd like to ask you about, but I must say good-bye for now. Don't forget me altogether and don't abandon me, because I remain, you know,

Your ever unchanging,
Fyodor Dostoyevsky

Anya sends her regards to you and Anna Ivanovna. I also would like to express my profound respects to Anna Ivanovna, and my sincere gratitude for her cordial words about Anya.

By the way: When he sent me 400 rubles a month ago, Kashpirev wrote that there are still another 50 to 100 rubles to come, but he hasn't sent them so far. If this is really the case, please, my dear Apollon Nikolayevich, hint to him somehow to send them on, *in the name of Christ,* because 50 rubles would make a great difference to me.

Do you like Strakhov's critiques? I think very highly of them.

---

82. In the letter to which this is a reply, Maikov had written of an unsatisfying "duality of emphasis" in *The Eternal Husband* and had gone on to say, "I feel that you have strained your imagination," a condition which he suggested could be eased only by Dostoyevsky's return to Russia.

Tikhon Zadonsky (1724–1783), born Timofei Savelevich Kirillov, had been rector of the Tver Seminary and bishop of Voronezh before entering the Zadonsky Monastery in 1769. In 1861, his remains were discovered, and a number of descriptions of his life were published during the next few years, emphasizing his humility and forgivingness.

Pyotr Yakovlevich Chaadayev (1794–1856) was a philosopher and writer who had great influence on both the Slavophiles and the Westernizers. Following publication of his "first philosophical letter" in 1836, in which he criticized Russia for having cut itself off from Europe, he was declared insane, and for several months doctors examined him periodically to verify the state of his mental health.

Timofei Nikolayevich Granovsky (1816–1855) was a professor of history at Moscow University whose lectures were extremely popular. Several of them had been published in *Time*.

Pavel the Prussian (1821–1895) was a Russian-born religious figure, a leader of the Schismatics, who went to Prussia in 1848 to escape repression. There, he founded a monastery near Gumbinnen (now Gusev, in the Soviet Union). In 1868, he rejoined the Orthodox church and returned to Russia, where he became renowned for his Orthodox writings. Konstantin Yefimovich Golubov was one of his pupils, who was also at first a Schismatic but later returned to Orthodoxy.

The monk Parfeny (d. 1868) was a recluse at the monastery at Mount Athos, who wrote a great deal against the Schism. Dostoyevsky mentioned him in connection with *The Brothers Karamazov* (see Letter 138).

"Stebnitsky" was a pen name used by Nikolai Semyonovich Leskov (1831–1895), author of the novel *Blind Alley* (Nekuda, 1864) and other works written from a conservative point of view. He had also been a contributor to *Epoch.*

Kostanzhoglo is a character in Gogol's *Dead Souls,* in which Chichikov is the main character. The "German fellow" in Goncharov's *Oblomov* is Stoltz. "Lavrovsky" is probably meant to be Lavretsky, the central character in Turgenev's *A Nest of Gentlefolk.* Lopukhov and Rakhmetov are characters in Chernyshevsky's *What Is To Be Done?*

83. To S. A. Ivanova
Dresden, August 17/29, 1870

My dear Sonechka,

Forgive me for not having answered you right away (on receiving your letter of August 3; I also received your short note of July 28). At times I have been beset with such a slew of problems, troubles, and burdens that I am incapable of doing anything, least of all writing a letter. There is only my work, which has to be done whatever my state of mind, and there are even moments when I cannot stand it and cast everything aside. My life is no bed of roses. This time, I would like to explain a few things about my situation, but only the main things, because I don't like letters, in which it is difficult, after so many years of separation, to speak about things that matter to one and be understood. The only letters that can be written are business letters to people with whom one is not linked by affection.

The main problem is that I need to return to Russia. This is a simple enough statement, but then I cannot describe to you in detail the torments and the *disadvantages* I suffer from living abroad. I shall skip all the moral considerations (homesickness, the need I have, as a writer, for the Russian ambience, and such). But take, for instance, the anxieties about my family alone. After all, I can see how nostalgic Anya is for Russia and how utterly tired she is of living here. Moreover, if I were back home, I would have many more ways of earning a livelihood; here we have become quite impoverished. Granted we do have enough to live on, but we cannot afford to hire a nanny. A local nanny demands a room to herself, linen, fantastic wages, three meals a day, and a beer ration (taken for granted of foreigners). So, Anya is not only feeding the child herself, but also has to stay awake at night to look after her. She has no distractions nor, for that matter, any time for them. And, above all, her health is poor. But what is the point of my telling you all this when it cannot possibly be described since there are a hundred or two hundred such *trifles,* and they all add up to a horrible strain.

What a pleasure it would be, for instance, if I could take my wife and child home to Petersburg this fall (as I dreamed of doing last spring). But in order to leave and to reach our destination, I need at least 2000 rubles, i.e., not counting the debts I'll have to pay and all that, but simply *to leave* here and *to get* there.

At this very moment I can see you shrugging your shoulders and saying: "Why such a large sum? What exaggeration!" But for heaven's sake, my kind friend, get out of the habit you have of judging people's affairs without knowing enough about them—these 2000 rubles are indispensable, and even then will provide for just the barest essentials. You can take my word for that. And where am I to get that sort of money? Now, Lyuba has to be weaned, and she also has to be vaccinated. There are so many things Anya has to tend to in her weakened and visibly enfeebled condition. I observe all that, and it just about drives me out of my mind. And even if I did get hold of the money for the journey in three months or so from now, by then it would be winter already and it would be quite out of the question to transport an infant a thousand versts in the bitter cold. And so we'll have to wait for the spring. But will there be money in the spring? Bear in mind that, at the present time, I am just about managing to scrape along here and, even so, we depend on borrowed money for half of our subsistence.

But enough of that. Let me turn to another subject, although everything is closely connected with the main problem.

Did I write to you in detail about my difficulties with *Russian Messenger,* owing to the fact that I had given my story to *Dawn* at the end of the last year while I still owed money to *Russian Messenger* and after I had given them my word a year earlier that my next work belonged to them? Did I tell you how it all happened, how my story just dragged itself out until I suddenly realized that I wouldn't be able to deliver anything to *Russian Messenger* by the beginning of the year? They never said a thing to me about *it,* they simply stopped sending me money. At the beginning of this year, I wrote Katkov saying that I would start sending him the novel from the middle of the year, i.e., from June on, so that, if they wished, they could publish it late this year. Now, listen to me: I worked myself to exhaustion, because I realized that, being away from Russia, if I severed my literary connections with R[*ussian*] *Messenger,* I would have nothing to live on (because it is difficult to establish connections with other magazines by correspondence) and, besides, the idea that the publishers of *R. Messenger,* who had *always* treated me so wonderfully, should consider me a rogue caused me genuine suffering and *torment.* The novel I had been writing was long and very original, but the concept was of a type rather unfamiliar to me and I needed a lot of self-confidence to come to grips with it. Well, it was too much for me, and it collapsed. The work limped along, I felt there was a major flaw in it but I couldn't put my finger on it. In July, after my last letter to you, I suffered a whole series of epileptic fits (every week). They had such a devastating effect on me that I couldn't even think of working for a whole month; besides, it would have been risky.

But then, about two weeks ago, when I resumed work on my novel, I all of a sudden realized where the hitch was, where I had gone wrong. And, at the same time, in a moment of inspiration, I perceived a new, fully structured plan for the novel. Everything had to be radically changed. Without the slightest hesitation, I crossed out everything I had written (roughly speaking, 15 sheets) and restarted the whole thing from the 1st page. A whole year's work was thus destroyed. Ah, Sonechka, if you only knew how difficult it is to be a writer, I mean, to endure this way of life. Believe me, I can tell you that if I had two or three years of an assured livelihood in which to write this novel, as is the case with Turgenev, Goncharov, and Tolstoy, it would be something that people would still be talking about 100 years from now! I am not bragging, probe your conscience and your memories of me—am I a braggart? The idea is so beautiful and so meaningful that I myself bow low before it. But what will come of it? I know in advance: I shall be writing the novel for 8 or 9 months, trying to squeeze it all in, and I shall mess it up. You'd need two or three years to do it properly. (Besides, it's a voluminous work: it will run to 35 sheets.) The details might not be too bad, the characters will be well drawn though a bit rough. There will be much that is superfluous and unnecessarily long-winded. Myriad beauties (I mean that literally) won't ever get in at all, for inspiration depends to a large degree on time. Well, I'm still going to tackle it! Imagine the agony of deliberately doing violence to yourself!

But, for the moment, that's not the issue—what does matter is that all my plans have fallen apart. I was confident that, after *R. Messenger* had received a substantial part of the novel by August 1 together with my request for an advance to tide me over, I would receive the money at the beginning of the year and get back on my feet. But now, what am I going to do? Even if I can manage to send them something by September 1, it won't be much (and my whole purpose was to send them a large amount at once to justify asking for an advance), and I would be too ashamed to ask for an advance. The 1st part (there will be 5 in all) will be only 7 sheets long, so how can I possibly ask them? And yet, inasmuch as all my plans have now gone awry, I honestly don't know at this moment what I am going to live on. Well, just think what it means to work in such a state of mind.

Finally, there are many uncertainties. Let us assume that I drive myself and send the 1st part by September (since some of the original material is still usable, and I shall be able to deliver about 7 sheets in September). In that case, (1) it won't appear, of course, until sometime next year, which means that, once again, I haven't kept my promise, and (2) will they want to renew our old relationship? Are they not being truculent? Are they not looking for a reason to be offended? Since I owe them money, they will take my novel all right, but will they let me have an advance? And that isn't all there is to it—I want to preserve our former friendly relations. Have you, by any chance, heard anything, Sonechka? I mean, are they still interested in my working for them and what exactly are they saying about me? If you know anything at all, write me. But for heaven's sake don't bring me into the conversation yourself, and don't ask them any questions. However, if you are on very friendly terms with someone there, you can say that I am working for them but that I am redoing the entire novel, and that, in any case, I shall shortly begin sending it to them in installments. But I leave it to your discretion. The best thing, though, would be to say nothing: matters like this can be mentioned only in the course of a free, spontaneous conversation, but I definitely don't want you to try to wheedle it out of them. Wheedling information out of them may be harmful to you and make them wary of me. And it is not fitting for you to do so, either. Therefore, it would be best if you said nothing to them. Two months from now I'll know how things stand. I'm positive that *Dawn* will accept my novel on bended knee. But I would like very much to resume my old relations with *R. Messenger.*

Well, all these things worry me a great deal and prevent me from living and working in peace; and there are many other things which I won't mention. Since the war broke out, credit has become generally unavailable, and life has become more difficult. But I'll pull through somehow. The main thing is good health, but I don't even have that, I mean, it's not as good as it used to be. On the subject of the war—well, I don't agree with you at all. Without war, man becomes sclerotic from living in comfort and wealth and completely loses his capacity for generous ideas and feelings, and imperceptibly becomes brutal and lapses into barbarism. I am speaking here of whole nations. Without suffering, happiness cannot be understood. The ideal passes through suffering like gold through fire. The heavenly kingdom is attained through effort. France was becoming too callous and was in decline. Temporary pain means nothing; she will bear it and awaken to a new life and a new idea. If not for the war, there would be a continuation of the old sententiousness, on the one hand, and cowardice and carnal pleasures, on the other.

The name of Napoleon will become insufferable once and for all. This new future life and transformation are so important that even great suffering is nothing in comparison. Don't you really see the hand of God in it? Our seventy-year-old Russian policy toward Europe and Germany will now also have to change. The Germans themselves will reveal to us, once and for all, the sort of people they are in reality. In general—there will be a great change throughout Europe. What an impact! How much new life will surge forth everywhere as a result! Why, even science was degenerating in the narrow materialistic atmosphere, in the absence of any noble idea. What does temporary suffering matter? You write: "They wound, they kill, and then they bandage the wounds and look after the wounded." Remember, the greatest words ever uttered in this world: "I want charity, not sacrifice."

It looks, at this moment or in the days ahead, as if much will be decided: Who deceived whom? Who made the strategic blunder, the Germans or the French? In my opinion, the Germans. This was my feeling 10 days ago already. But still it looks as if the Germans will temporarily come out on top. The French are on the verge of an abyss into which they will *temporarily* fall—it is the dynastic interest to which the country is being sacrificed. And there are many things I could write you as a result of my private observations of German behavior in the present situation, but there is no time for that.

I totally disagree with your philosophizing about the choice of a life and about marriage. My dear, how much I love you and want you to be happy! Ah, if only I could see you again soon! You know, I have the feeling that your life now must be lonely, laborious, extremely monotonous and secluded. Beware, my dear. Perhaps you do not notice the monotony and the seclusion. That's bad! But what can I say in a letter? I can only go on discoursing, while what is needed is action. If only I could see you soon! Anya says of you that one could fall in love with your style alone (i.e., reading your translations). With my next letter, I shall send you Lyuba's picture. Always put down your address. Andrei Mikhailovich wrote me only about Varvara Mikhailovna and nothing about Verochka. You write about another trustee in Moscow. What is he up to? Do you remember my writing you about the *note* Andrei Mikhailovich sent me in the winter about the state of Aunt's affairs when he took over after your father's death? It is very curious indeed. It is a fact, though, that he never cast any doubt on the scrupulous honesty of your late father. But he did point out his mistakes. But when and by whom could it ever be ascertained whether mistakes were or were not made? But you know something—it is quite unlikely that the heirs will get even as much as *30 percent* of Aunt's legacy.

Do not say a word about my frank remarks. I have no wish to quarrel with anyone in my absence, I have enough ill-wishers as it is. And in general, do not let anyone else read my letter. I am telling this in confidence to you alone.

Give my regards to everyone. Remember me to everybody. I give you a big kiss, and I want you to know that you have no greater well-wisher and friend than I. Just saying this to you makes me happy. Write, and don't forget me as I sit down to my hard labor.

Yours, with all my heart and soul,
F. Dostoyevsky.

My heart aches for my Petersburg relatives. I haven't been sending them anything. And I won't be able to send them anything until the beginning of next year, and they are living in poverty. That weighs on my conscience. I promised to support them. I am especially sorry for Pasha.

P.S. It is because you are not familiar with my relations with the creditors that you assume that it would not be in their interests to have me locked up. On the contrary, they will have me locked up precisely because, for certain reasons, *that* would be more to their advantage. Did I write you before or not that I do have one hope of obtaining about five thousand rubles, for three years or so, immediately upon my arrival in Petersburg? In that case I could avoid prison. This hope is not altogether without foundation. But I must handle it in person—it cannot be done in my absence without jeopardizing the whole business. This has nothing to do with my work as a writer. If, however, the novel I am working on now were a success, I'd have a better chance of getting hold of those 5000 rubles. But I would like all this to remain strictly between us.

Good-bye, my friend, your
D.

---

83. The novel that Dostoyevsky is writing about here is *The Devils.* The war that had broken out was the Franco-Prussian War.

84. To M. N. Katkov
Dresden, October 8/20, 1870

Dear Sir,

Much esteemed Mikhail Nikiforovich:

I sent off today only the first half of the first part of my novel *The Devils* to the office of *Russian Messenger,* but I shall send the second half of the first part in the very near future. Altogether there will be *three* parts, each 10 to 12 sheets long. Henceforth, there will be no further delays.

If you decide to start publishing my novel next year, I think it important for you to know, if only in a few words, what my novel will actually be all about.

One of the major episodes in my story will be the murder of Ivanov by Nechayev, which caused such a stir in Moscow. Let me make it clear from the outset that I never knew either Nechayev or Ivanov and that I know nothing about the murder except what I have read in the newspapers. And even if I had known the circumstances, I wouldn't have made use of them. I only take the accomplished fact. My invention may depart radically from the reality, and my Pyotr Verkhovensky may not bear the slightest resemblance to Nechayev; but it seems to me that in my startled mind, I have conjured up the character, the type, that really corresponds to this crime. To be sure, there is some value in depicting such a man, but not enough to have intrigued me. In my opinion, these pitiful freaks are not worthy of literature. To my own surprise, this character comes off in my story as a partly comical figure. And therefore, although the whole incident forms one of the main plots of the novel, it is, notwithstanding, only an accessory and a setting for the activities of another character who could actually be called the main character of the novel.

This other figure (Nikolai Stavrogin) is also a sinister character, also a villain. I see him, nevertheless, as a tragic figure, although I am sure that

340

many will say when they read my story, "What on earth is this?" I embarked on this epic because for a long time now, I have been wanting to portray such a character. In my opinion, he is Russian and broadly representative at one and the same time. It would sadden me grievously if I failed to carry off his portrayal. And I would feel even sadder if my character were adjudged to be stilted. He comes straight from my heart. Of course, this character is seldom met as a full-fledged type, but it is a Russian character (from a certain stratum of society). But before you judge me, wait for the end of the novel, much respected Mikhail Nikiforovich! There is something that tells me that I shall cope successfully with this character. I won't explain it in detail now, because I am afraid I might not put it the right way. Let me say one thing, though: this character is revealed through the action, through happenings, rather than by my description of him, so that there is a hope that he'll come out alive.

For a very long time, I had trouble with the beginning of the novel. I rewrote it several times. To tell the truth, something happened with this novel that had never happened to me before: week after week, I would keep putting the beginning aside and work instead on the end. But, besides this, I am afraid that the beginning is not as lively as it might be. In the 5½ sheets (which I sent you), I have barely managed to set up the plot. But then the plot, the action, will expand and develop suddenly. What I can guarantee is that, as the novel progresses, it will hold the reader's interest. It seemed to me that the way I have it now is for the best.

But not all the characters will be somber, there will be radiant ones, too. In general, I am afraid that much of it may prove to be beyond my capacities. For instance, I intend here, for the first time, to touch upon a category of people that heretofore has been little treated in literature. I have modeled my character after Tikhon Zadonsky. Like him, he is a Holy Man who lives in retirement in a monastery. I put him in contrast with the hero of the novel and, for a time, bring them face to face with each other. I am very nervous about it; I have never tried it before; but then, I do know something about that world.

Now, on another subject.

Think what you want of me, Mikhail Nikiforovich, but I have become so impoverished that, embarrassing though it is to me, I cannot avoid asking a favor of you! I have absolutely nothing to live on, and I have a wife and a child. Although in delicate health, until a month ago she was nursing the baby, when she should be getting some rest, the child prevents her from sleeping nights. And not only do we have no nanny, we don't even have a servant. This breaks my heart. Now, there are times when my work takes my mind off all this; but there are others when this situation weighs heavily on me.

I am well aware that I owe you a lot as it is. But with this novel, I shall be even with your magazine. But now, I am asking you for 500 rubles. I know that that is a great deal, but then I owe almost that much here. Please allow me to reckon on the kindness of your heart. I beg you to answer me very quickly; I am afraid that these days, in Germany, letters often get lost. Just the thought that this letter may go astray is enough to drive me out of my mind. My address remains unchanged:

Saxe, Dresden. A m-r Theodore Dostoevsky, poste restante.

Please accept the assurance of my utmost esteem.

Your sincerely devoted,
Fyodor Dostoyevsky

I have reread this letter and feel ashamed of myself. Please don't judge me too severely, Mikhail Nikiforovich!

---

84. Sergei Gennadiyevich Nechayev (1847–1882) had been a teacher in Petersburg. In 1869, he went to Geneva and met Bakunin, who gave him a document certifying him as a member of "The Russian Section of the Worldwide Revolutionary Alliance." On returning to Russia, he organized several revolutionary groups, one of which eventually murdered one of its own members, Ivan Ivanovich Ivanov, because he was believed to have been "distrustful" of Nechayev. Nechayev was convicted of the murder and sentenced to twenty years at hard labor, to be followed by permanent exile in Siberia, but he died while still in prison. Nechayev became a symbol of the utterly single-minded, unscrupulous revolutionary, as a result of his "General Rules of the Organization," which were read in court during his trial in 1871. (See also the note to Letter 81.)

85. To A. N. Maikov
Dresden, October 9/21, 1870

My dear and much esteemed Apollon Nikolayevich,

I've left your letter—a letter which delighted and surprised me—unanswered until today because I was occupied with a troublesome piece of work that I wanted to finish at all costs. And for that reason, I not only haven't answered two or three letters that have accumulated here, I haven't even read anything during all this time (except, of course, for the newspapers). The work I am involved in is just the beginning of a novel I'm doing for *Russian Messenger*. I shall be working on it day and night for at least another six months, so I am already sick of it in advance. There is, of course, something in it that impels me to write it, but, in general, there is nothing in the world that is more distasteful to me than literary work, I mean the actual writing of novels and stories. That is what I've come to. As for the idea of this novel, it's not worth explaining. It is impossible to tell you about it properly in a letter, for one thing, and, secondly, you'll be punished enough if you take it in your head to read the novel when it gets published. So why inflict it upon you twice?

You write me a good deal about Nikolai the Miracle Worker. He will not abandon us because Nikolai the Miracle Worker is the Russian spirit and her unifying force. You and I are no longer children, much esteemed Apollon Nikolayevich, we know, for instance, this fact: Whenever Russia is threatened, not even by a national disaster, but just by serious trouble, then the most un-Russian part of Russia, i.e., some liberal, a Petersburg official or a student, even they become Russians, begin to feel themselves Russians, although they may be ashamed to admit it. Last winter I happened to read in a *Voice* editorial a serious admission to the effect that "during the Crimean campaign, we rejoiced over the Allies' successes and over our setbacks." No, my liberalism never went that far; I was still in penal servitude at that time and *did not* rejoice at the success of the Allies, but, together with my comrades, the poor wretches and common soldiers, I felt I was a Russian and wished success to Russian arms, even though there was still a good dose of that mangy Russian liberalism in me, preached by turds like that dung beetle Belinsky and such like. And I didn't consider that I was being inconsistent in feeling myself a Russian. It is true that the facts have also proved to us that the disease that afflicted cultured Russians was much more virulent than we ourselves had imagined and that it did not end with the Belinskys and the Krayevskys and their ilk. But at that moment that thing happened which is attested to by Saint Luke: The devils had entered into a man and their name was legion, and they asked Him: suffer us to enter into the swine, and He suffered them. The devils entered into the swine, and the whole herd ran violently down a steep place into the sea and was drowned. When the people came out to see what was done, they found the man who had been possessed now sitting at the feet of Jesus, clothed and in his right mind, and those who saw it told them by what means he that was possessed of the devils was healed. Exactly the same thing happened in our country: the devils went out of the Russian man and entered into a herd of swine, i.e., into the Nechayevs, the Serno-Solovyoviches, et al. These are drowned or will be drowned, and the healed man, from whom the devils have departed, sits at the feet of Jesus. It could not have been otherwise. Russia has spewed out all the filth she has been fed and obviously there is nothing Russian left in those spewed-out wretches. And bear this in mind, my dear friend, that a man who loses his people and his national roots also loses the faith of his fathers and his God.

Well, if you really want to know—this is in essence the theme of my novel. It is called *The Devils*, and it describes how the devils entered into the herd of swine. There is no doubt that I shall write it badly; being more a poet than an artist, I have always tackled themes beyond my powers. And so I'll make a mess of it, that's sure. The theme is too powerful. But, inasmuch as none of the critics who have thus far passed judgment on me has failed to accord me some talent, the chances are that this long novel won't be too bad in spots. And that's all I can say.

I understand that you still have many *intelligent* people in Petersburg who, although they were horrified by the scum who entered the pigs, still remember nostalgically the good old liberal and humanitarian times of Belinsky and think that those days of enlightenment must be brought back. And that notion still lingers on today in the most recent converts to nationalism and their ilk. The old men do not give up: the Pleshcheyevs, the Pavel Annenkovs, the Turgenevs, and whole magazines, such as the *Messenger of Europe,* cling to that orientation. I wonder whether they still give out to girls graduating from secondary schools books like the complete works of Belinsky, in which he bewails the fact that Tatyana remained faithful to her husband? No, all this is not going to be eradicated soon and that is why we have nothing to fear, even from outside political perturbations, such as, say, a European war over the Slavs, although it is a terrifying prospect: we are on our own against *the lot of them.* Present circumstances seem to assure us of two or three years of peace—shall we understand our situation? Shall we be prepared? Shall we have built enough roads and fortresses? Shall we procure at least another million rifles? Shall we stand firmly on our frontiers and will action be taken on the reform of per capita taxation and of recruiting? These are the things we need, while the rest, i.e., the Russian spirit, unity—all that exists and will impose itself with such strength, with such integrity and holiness, that even we are incapable of fathoming the full depth of that strength, let alone the foreigners, and to my mind nine-tenths of our strength lies precisely in the fact that foreigners do not and never will understand the full depth and strength of our unity. Oh, how clever they are! For the past three years I have been reading assiduously all the political newspapers, i.e., the major ones. How remarkably well they know their own affairs! What prescience! What a knack they sometimes have for hitting the nail on the head! (What a difference from our political papers, with their imitative rubbish, except perhaps for the *Moscow Gazette.*) But, you know something, whenever it comes to Russia their press sounds exactly like a feverish man in the darkness muttering God knows what! I daresay that, in Europe, they know more about the star Sirius than they know about Russia. And this, for some time yet, is a source of strength for us.

And another potential source of strength is our own faith in our individuality, in the sacredness of our destiny. The whole destiny of Russia lies in Orthodoxy, in *the light from the East* that will spread to the blinded mankind of the West, which has lost its faith in Christ. All of Europe's misfortune, all, all of its ills, without exception, harken back to its loss of Christ with the establishment of the Roman church, after which they decided that they could manage just as well without Christ. Now, just imagine, my dear friend, even among such eminent Russians as the author of *Russia and Europe*, for example, I have not come across this concept of Russia, that is, the idea of her exclusive, Orthodox mission among men. And since this is so, it is still too early to demand self-reliance from us.

But I have gone too far afield, and here I am on my fourth page already. I am getting along somehow, I'm trying to work, everywhere I am behind, everywhere I neglect my promises—and I am suffering because of it. Anna Grigorevna is depressed, too, so I don't know what to do. We really ought to return home in the spring, but I don't have the money even to pay our fares back, let alone to pay my debts. I have very few acquaintances here, yet there are a lot of Russians in Dresden, as many as there are English people. They're all trash, these people, I mean, by and large. And, my God, what trash! What do they have to wander around for?

My daughter is in good health, well fed; she has been weaned and is now beginning to understand what is going on around her and even to talk. But she is a very nervous child, and I'm concerned about this, though she is in good health. What is this you write about Pasha, my much esteemed friend, about his getting married, but without giving me any of the details? If you do know anything, in the name of Christ, let me know! Pasha himself has never written me anything about it. He is, after all, very dear to me. It would, of course, be quite ridiculous on my part to pretend to be able to influence his decisions one way or the other from this distance and after 3 years of separation. Nevertheless, it makes me sad. I have a nephew called Misha who got married at an even earlier age than Pasha. But then, Misha is a very intelligent boy and he has a lot of character. But Pasha—that's quite a different matter, i.e., when it comes to character and some sort of self-control.

If you write me something about it, you will be really rendering me a great service. My wife sends you her regards. Lyuba kisses you. Good-bye, I wish you good health and all the best,

All yours,
Fyodor Dostoyevsky

---

85. Maikov, in his letter to which this is a reply, had alluded to several recent momentous events—the overthrow of Napoleon III, the proclamation of papal infallibility, and the establishment of the German empire—and had then asked, "Where is our Nikolai the Miracle Worker? . . . without faith in [him] a Russian cannot go on living . . ." Nikolai the Miracle Worker, or Saint Nicholas, was regarded as the patron saint of Russia.

The Serno-Solovyoviches were two brothers, Nikolai Aleksandrovich (1834–

1866) and Aleksandr Aleksandrovich (1838–1869), who had been active in the revolutionary movements of the 1860s. Nikolai was sentenced to twelve years at hard labor and permanent exile in Siberia; he died in Irkutsk. Aleksandr fled abroad and was sentenced in absentia to lifelong exile; after showing signs of mental illness, he died by poisoning in Geneva.

Pavel Vasilevich Annenkov (1812–1887) was a literary critic, a prominent Pushkin scholar, and a valued friend of the "old men" of the generation of the 1840s—Belinsky, Gogol, Herzen, Ogaryov, Turgenev, and others. He did not think highly of Dostoyevsky's literary merits, and Dostoyevsky was also offended by his liberal and Westernizing positions.

It is in Pushkin's *Eugene Onegin* that Tatyana declares her faithfulness to her husband despite her continuing love for Onegin. It is not quite accurate, however, to say that Belinsky "bewailed" her attitude.

The author of *Russia and Europe* was Danilevsky.

86. To A. N. Maikov
Dresden, March 2/14, 1871

My dear and much esteemed friend Apollon Nikolayevich,

First of all, a word about our unfinished business.

I have decided to finish with it, i.e., *to start a case* in court. Cases more difficult than this one have been won and, in this instance, my claim as supported by the contract is unassailable. To make a long story short, this is what I want and it is my irrevocable decision. Since I wouldn't think of burdening you with the responsibility of a legal action, besides the fact that you are not a lawyer, I implore you *to delegate* the case (you are empowered to do so by my power of attorney) to some well-known lawyer (Spasovich, Arkhangelsky, or someone like that)—*regardless of the cost*—and let him engage a formal legal action *at once* against Stellovsky to recover the money (the figure, based on the number of printer's sheets, should be indicated; if there is an error, let the court itself decide). But the lawyer will know best how to go about it. The main thing is to give the lawyer a copy of the contract and ask him to study points 8 and 13 closely, particularly 13, because I intend to claim payment of damages. This is what I would like you to bring to the lawyer's attention.

It is essential to establish the fact that Stellovsky was unwilling to pay; otherwise, we won't be able to bring suit under point 13. I suppose, though, that the lawyer will begin by demanding *formally* that Stellovsky pay the full sum in cash (no IOUs). (I believe this is done with the assistance of the police—but the lawyer must know.) If, then, Stellovsky refuses to pay up—within three days, let's say—we could file suit under point 13, i.e., claim both payment and damages. If he pays, however, then to hell with both him and point 13. That would close the case.

And so, all I am asking you is this: (1) to hand over and entrust the whole case to a lawyer immediately, but only to a good one and no matter what it costs.

(2) To do so right away and without the slightest concern for my interests. (N.B. According to the law, a lawyer receives his fee at the end of the trial, isn't that right? So there is nothing to stop you.) But for God's sake, don't lose any time, act as soon as you get this letter. Don't have any second thoughts: this is the way I want it done and if my money goes down the drain, it will be my own doing. And so, for heaven's sake, hand the case over to a lawyer. If you still happen to have the letters I wrote you at the beginning of all this business, when you do see the lawyer read them to him or let him read those passages in the letters that reflect my views on the matter.

Finally (3) You could make one more attempt to do it on your own before bringing in a lawyer. In that event, the following should be done as soon as you receive this letter: You should, my dear friend, immediately write a most laconic note to Stellovsky (without a trace of suspicion or concern for my interests) telling him that I intend to start legal proceedings against him and, accordingly, am asking him, Stellovsky, for the last time to pay me the money he owes me. At the same time, in the note you should designate for him (as drily and as severely and formally as possible) a date, say, *the day after tomorrow,* and an hour when he can find you at home and bring the *full* amount of the money. And add that you will not and do not intend to wait for him beyond that day and hour and that you are acting this way in accordance with *my* instructions.

There are two possibilities: Either Stellovsky won't show up—in which case you should immediately go to see a lawyer and have him take action— or he does come and pays up. In that case, you should obtain either the entire sum or at least one-half of it in cash; and his IOU (in the event that he proposes an IOU for half the amount) should be payable in not more than 3 months.

Or else Stellovsky will show up without the money and begin asking for a delay and making all sorts of propositions. In that case, hear *nothing* of it. If he asks for a postponement (for instance, if he says that he will have the money in 2 weeks and will pay then), don't listen. At the most, you can give him until the following day, i.e., one more day. And not one hour more. For God's sake (to avoid jeopardizing our legal action) don't get involved in any discussions or arguments about the matter.

Finally, if Stellovsky arrives with the money after the legal proceedings have been initiated but before the case reaches the court—and that is certainly what he will do, because he will be anxious to avoid a lawsuit— let the lawyer himself decide what the best course of action is under the circumstances.

And above all, don't allow matters to drag out, do *exactly* as I have asked you to. It is my money, after all, *this is the way* I would like it to be done, and if I lose money in handling things *my way*, it's no skin off your teeth, since that's the way I wanted it. So please do *exactly* as I ask you (and without any qualms whatsoever, without any preliminary inquiries, visits to Stellovsky, dispatches to him, queries, etc.). And don't waste a single day.

Otherwise you will spoil Stellovsky with all sorts of concessions with the result that he would be a fool to come across.

Also, for God's sake, don't check with me and don't ask for my approval, because that just delays matters. Just do exactly as I am asking you now and that is all.

N.B. Don't give him more than two days' grace in the note you send him. Under any pretext! And then, go see the lawyer at once.

I repeat—get yourself a good lawyer. (I want no more gentlemen with bushy eyebrows, but a real lawyer. A prominent lawyer may take the case even though there's not much in it for him, because it is a literary affair and will give him publicity, and so he won't refuse.)

Above all, do exactly as I am asking you, unabashedly, unquestioningly, and *without worrying about my interests.* Do just as I say, in the name of God.

Your flattering comments about the beginning of my novel delighted me no end. My God, I have been worrying about it so much and I am still worrying. By the time you read this letter, you will probably also have read the second half of Part One in R[ussian] *Messenger*'s February issue. What will you say then? I am very, very worried. As to future installments—I am simply in despair and wonder whether I'll be able to cope with them. By the way—there will be 4 parts altogether—forty printer's sheets. St[epan] T[rofimovich] is a secondary character and the novel will not really be about him at all. His story, however, is closely intertwined with other events (the major ones) of the novel and that is why I took him, if you will, as the cornerstone of the whole. However, Stepan Trofimovich's benefit performance will take place in part 4: this man's fate will be settled in a most original way in it. I cannot answer for anything else in advance, but for that passage I can. But I repeat—I am scared as a frightened mouse. It was the *idea* that tempted me and I have become infatuated with it, but will I be able to cope with it? Won't I make a shitty mess of the entire novel? That's what's so terrible!

Would you believe it, I have already received several letters from various quarters congratulating me on the first part. That has encouraged me tremendously. But, without flattering you, I can tell you outright—your opinion is the most precious to me of all. In the first place, I know you wouldn't say things just to please me and, in the second place, there is an expression in your appraisal that is a stroke of genius. "*These are,*" you write, "*Turge-*

nev's heroes grown old." That is brilliant! While I was writing, I was myself thinking of something of the sort, and now you have expressed it in these few words as a formula. I am grateful to you for that phrase—you have made the whole matter clear to me.

This novel is awfully hard going, I don't feel well and I am slipping into a period of very frequent attacks. I am worried about falling behind and not meeting my deadlines. I am loath to spoil it by hurrying. It is true that I have a soundly constructed and well thought out plan, but still, hurrying could spoil everything.

I have definitely decided to return in the spring. Ah, we will have plenty to say to each other then! I have received *Conversation.* I wonder what it holds in store. And you are right—they have no section on aesthetic matters at all. In what way is *Dawn* inferior to any magazine? In my opinion, it is better than any. It is the disorganization and the *incompetence* of the management that—mark my words—will bury it. I don't agree with your opinion of Strakhov: he is the only literary critic we have at this time. And severe criticism is, after all, *Dawn*'s forte. If they could hang on and learn how to publish a magazine, they would make it. I don't think that *Conversation* could really offer serious competition to *Dawn* even if it were to last. But it will harm it.

Good-bye. Thank you for your kind feelings toward me. The buds are opening here, it is the real beginning of spring. But good-bye for now, and see you soon,

All yours,
F. Dostoyevsky.

For God's sake, don't forget me and drop me a few lines now and then.

---

86. Vladimir Danilovich Spasovich (1829–1906) was not only a prominent lawyer but also a brilliant lecturer (at Petersburg University) and a literary critic. Dostoyevsky devoted a chapter to him in the *Diary of a Writer* for February 1876 (see the note to Letter 109).

Conversation was a new magazine (not to be confused with the old *Russian Conversation*) edited by Sergei Andreyevich Yurev (1821–1888), a mathematician who later turned to literary pursuits and in 1878 was elected president of the Society of Friends of Russian Literature. When Dostoyevsky says the magazine has "no section on aesthetic matters," he is presumably referring to the absence of any critical reviews. The first issue contained "A Maritime Legend" (Pomorskoye skazaniye), by Aleksei Tolstoy (under the pen name of "Borivoi"), and Pisemsky's novel *In the Whirlpool* (V vodovorote). The magazine lasted for two years.

87. To N. N. Strakhov
Dresden, March 18/30, 1871

Much esteemed Nikolai Nikolayevich,

First of all, please forgive me for not having answered your letter for so long. It was due to a number of circumstances. I was sick for a while and, above all, I was in a state of depression following an epileptic fit. When a sudden attack occurs after a long lull, a deep moral depression sets in. It drives me to despair. Before, that state of dejection lasted for about three days after an attack, but now it persists for seven or eight days, although the attacks themselves occur much less frequently in Dresden than elsewhere. Then, *I am depressed about my work*—it is torturously difficult for me to write. I just have to be back in Russia, even though I have become completely unaccustomed to the Petersburg climate. Nevertheless, I must return at all costs. But why bother listing all the things that depress me, let me just say that all that distracted me and it is only now that I can sit down and talk things over with you, although you have been very much on my mind since I received your letter.

You cannot imagine, Nikolai Nikolayevich, what sad and painful thoughts occurred to me on reading your letter. What is this all about? Everything that made *Dawn* original, everything that so sharply distinguished it from the other magazines—all that they consider an obstacle to success. And it was the only Russian magazine that still offered pure literary criticism! Why, it is precisely because all the others have discarded literary criticism that it is most needed now. It gave *Dawn* its special character. They have become frightened of gossip and jibes. They should have done just the opposite— have insisted more often, in every issue, on their idea, and the future would have been theirs. I don't know about others, but as for me, every time I received *Dawn,* the first thing I did was always to cut the pages containing your articles and then savor them. Of course, I didn't always fully agree with you (for instance, in your manner and tone, i.e., in your excessive gentleness or in your overestimation of certain phenomena in literature and in life— and I am not speaking of Lev Tolstoy here), but I found it all tremendously interesting. Your article on Karamzin was so penetrating and so bravely outspoken that I felt great joy here that a voice like yours was still to be heard back home. You mentioned it casually in a letter at the time, and later I myself read something about it and, as far as I can judge, they seem to have branded it as reactionary. Can it be that your publishers are now in agreement with the others, by any chance?

In any case, your voice cannot and should not be allowed to fall silent. There is no doubt in my mind, judging from what you tell me of your *new* relations with *Dawn,* that it amounts to semiretirement. Well, what have you decided to do then, Nikolai Nikolayevich? In three or four months, we shall perhaps see each other and then we can talk about all these things to our hearts' content. But in the meantime—what? Undoubtedly it would be best to continue *for the time being* with *Dawn,* to publish a few more of your excellent articles in it, and then, in the fall, give serious thought to your situation. If by then you are not firmly established in *Dawn* on terms that are eminently acceptable to you, I wonder whether you really ought to stay on. (I am not thinking of your pride here at all; what I am concerned with is literary criticism, the continued presence in our midst of a literary magazine with a sane critical outlook.) But what if *Dawn* itself feels that literary criticism is *not so essential?*

I hope, Nikolai Nikolayevich, that, this letter being a confidential one, it will remain strictly between the two of us. By the way, you mentioned very casually in your letter that you would like to start writing your literary reminiscences. What do you have in mind? In fact, will anything come of it at all? You spoke of the time when we published our old magazine, of Ap[ollon] Grigorev, of us. I understand only too well that that period should be deeply, and perhaps pleasantly, engraved in your memory (as a reminiscence of your youth). But isn't it too early to be writing of such things, and, moreover, is it of any interest at the present time? My own feeling is that it is both premature and of no interest to others. And yet, here is an idea that just occurred to me:

Some important, serious work *outside* your usual articles of literary criticism (i.e., mainly in a different form), something new, albeit still in the field of literary history, would really be an excellent thing for you to do. (N.B. I, for one, read with great relish in your article on Karamzin the fervent and remarkable pages in which you reminisce about your student years.) So, if *Dawn* leaves you with so much free time now, you could have something ready by the fall. How do you feel about *Conversation,* for example? They have no literary criticism at all, but it is my impression that they would be only too eager to publish a piece prepared by you in the summer, and that could pave the way for the future. Lest there be any misunderstanding or misconstrual of what I am suggesting, let me say straightway that this cannot be considered a betrayal of *Dawn.* I am not persuading you to abandon your old flag and to desert to the service of another. But you must agree that it all comes down to an answer to this question: does *Dawn itself* wish your collaboration or doesn't it? Does it appreciate your work or doesn't it? But we should certainly know how things stand in the very near future.

As for *Conversation,* I have absolutely no idea what to expect of it, although I have read the first number. They sent it to me and asked me to contribute. It goes without saying that I would be delighted to contribute, provided I have the time. At any rate, I am not bound to anyone anywhere except by my debts. But money is not such a ticklish problem—it merely

takes money to surmount it. (This does not at all mean that I am not thinking about my novella for *Dawn;* I am thinking about it a great deal and will
deliver it come what may.)

I repeat again: I am looking forward with yearning but also apprehension
to the moment when I'll be meeting all my old close friends in Petersburg
again. By the way, I have one more favor to ask of you: if the question arises,
don't say anything *definite* about my impending return. I'd like to avoid
being bothered by my creditors for at least the first week after my arrival. I
anticipate that they'll pounce upon me right away and that frightens me because I have no money, nothing else but expectations.

Drop me a line, Nikolai Nikolayevich, I am devoted to you and respect
you and I say this in all sincerity. My address is still the same (it is essential
to indicate poste restante).

Writing doesn't come to me here, Nikolai Nikolayevich, or if it comes, it
is sheer torture. What this means I cannot say. I can only suppose that it is
vital for me to return to Russia. I must return.

I am extremely grateful to you for not having forgotten to write me about
my novel. You have cheered me up tremendously. I perfectly agree with what
you say about the *tone;* my inability to sustain the tone troubled me for a
long time. When I get back to Russia my work will even have to be interrupted. But anyway, I will finish the novel this year.

I also want to thank you for clearing up some of my misapprehensions. If
I had to do it over again, I wouldn't write you that letter. I was in a state of
terrible nervous tension at the time.

Where will you be spending the summer—in the city or in the country? I
would like to know in advance. I believe I'll be coming back right in the
middle of summer. You can imagine what a hectic time it is preparing for the
journey, my dear Nikolai Nikolayevich! When I left I was on my own with a
young wife and now I am coming back, still with a young wife, *but with
children too!* (This is a secret: one is a year and a half old, the other is still x,
y, or z.) So just imagine the fuss and bother of moving!

Your most devoted,
Fyodor Dostoyevsky.

---

87. In the letter to which this is a reply, Strakhov had written that *Dawn* was not
proving to be a popular magazine and might soon have to close down, and that in
any case the publishers had decided to print fewer of Strakhov's articles. He had also
said that Dostoyevsky's new novel, *The Devils,* was "fascinating" and would probably become a "major success." "Stefan Trofimovich is a delight. I do not think you
sustain the tone of the narrative throughout, but the first pages, in which the tone is
set, are spellbinding."

The Dostoyevskys' first son, Fyodor, was born in Petersburg on July 16, 1871.

88.   To A. G. Dostoyevskaya
Wiesbaden, Friday, [April 16/]28, 1871

Anya, for the sake of Christ, for the sake of Lyuba, for the sake of our whole future, don't start worrying and getting all upset—read this letter carefully to the end. You will see at the end that disaster isn't really a reason for despair, but on the contrary, something may even have been gained by it which will be much more valuable than the price paid for it! And so calm yourself, my angel, hear me out—read this to the end. For Christ's sake, don't fall to pieces.

You, my precious one, my lifelong friend, my heavenly angel, you have, of course, gathered that I have lost everything—the whole of the 30 thalers you sent me. Remember that you are my only salvation and that there is no one else in the world who loves me. Remember, too, Anya, that there are misfortunes that carry their own punishment. As I write this, I am wondering: What will this do to you? How will you take it? I hope nothing terrible will happen to you! And if you feel sorry for me at this moment, don't, that would make it even worse for me.

I didn't dare wire you nor do I dare now, after your latest letter in which you write that you will be worrying about me. I can just imagine how it would have been had you received a telegram tomorrow saying Schreiben sie mier [sic] . . . what would have become of you then!

Ah, Anya, why did I have to go?

Here is how it happened today. First of all, I got your letter at 1 P.M., but not the money. Then I went home and wrote you an answer (a nasty, cruel letter; why, I almost reproach you in it). I suppose you will get it tomorrow, Saturday, if you stop by the post office not earlier than 4 o'clock. I took my letter to the post office and there the man told me again that there was no money for me; it was then two-thirty. But when I came by again, for the third time, at four-thirty, he gave me the money, and when I asked at what time it had arrived, he replied very calmly, "Around 2 o'clock." So why didn't he give it to me when I was there before, well after two? Then, when I saw that I had to wait until half past six for the next train out of here, I headed for the casino.

Now Anya, you may believe me or not, but I swear to you that I had no intention of gambling! To convince you of that, I will confess everything to you: when I wired you asking you to send me 30 thalers instead of 25, I thought I might yet risk another 5 thalers, but I was not sure I would do even that. I figured that if any money were left over, I would bring it back with me. But when I got the 30 thalers today, *I did not want to gamble* for two reasons: (1) I was so struck by your letter and imagined the effect it would have on you (and I am imagining it now!) and (2) I dreamed last night of *my father* and he appeared to me in a terrifying guise, such as he has only

353

appeared to me twice before in my life, both times prophesying a dreadful disaster, and on both occasions the dream came true. (And now, when I think of the dream I had three nights ago, when I saw your hair turn white, my heart stops beating—ah, my God, what will become of you when you get this letter!)

But when I arrived at the casino, I went to a table and stood there placing imaginary bets just to see whether I could guess right. And you know what, Anya? I was right about ten times in a row, and I even guessed right about Zero. I was so amazed by this that I started gambling and in 5 minutes won 18 thalers. And then, Anya, I got all excited and thought to myself that I would leave with the last train, spend the night in Frankfurt, and then at least I would bring some money home with me! I felt so ashamed about the 30 thalers I had *robbed* you of! Believe me, my angel, all year I have been dreaming of buying you a pair of earrings, which I have not yet given back to you. You had pawned all your possessions for me during these past 4 years and followed me in my wanderings with homesickness in your heart! Anya, Anya, bear in mind, too, that I am not a scoundrel but only a man with a passion for gambling.

(But here is *something else* that I want you to remember, Anya: I am through with that fancy forever. I know I have written you before that it was over and done with, but I never felt the way I feel now as I write this. Now I am rid of this delusion and I would bless God that things have turned out as disastrously as they have if I weren't so terribly worried about you at this moment. Anya, if you are angry with me, just think of how much I've had to suffer and *still* have to suffer in the coming three or four days! If, sometime later on in life you find me being ungrateful and unfair toward you—just show me this letter!)

By half past nine I had lost everything and I fled like a madman. I felt so miserable that I rushed to see the priest (don't get upset, I did *not* see him, no, I did *not*, nor do I intend to!). As I was running toward his house in the darkness through unfamiliar streets, I was thinking: "Why, he is the Lord's shepherd and I will speak to him not as to a private person but as one does at confession." But I lost my way in this town and when I reached a church, which I took for a Russian church, they told me in a store that it was not Russian but sheeny. It was as if someone had poured cold water over me. I ran back home. And now it is midnight and I am sitting and writing to you. (And I won't go to see the priest, I won't go, I swear I won't!)

I had one and a half thalers left in small change. That would have been enough for a telegram (15 groschen) but I am afraid to send it. I don't know how you will take it! And so I decided to write you a letter and send it off the next day at 8 A.M., and to make sure that you get it on Sunday without delay, I am sending it directly to our home address rather than poste restante. (For, what if, expecting me to come, you didn't bother to go to the post office?) But I still may send you another letter poste restante tomorrow, though I will be rather late in getting it off. But I will write you for sure the day after tomorrow—on Sunday.

Anya, save me once more and for the last time—send me another 30 (thirty) thalers. I will arrange things in such a way that it will be enough. I will be very economical. If you can manage to send it on Sunday, even late, I will be able to come back on Tuesday or, at the latest, on Wednesday.

Anya, I prostrate myself before you and kiss your feet. I realize that you have every right to despise me and to think: "He will gamble again." By what, then, can I swear to you that *I shall not,* when I have already deceived you before? But, my angel, I know that you would die(!) if I lost again! I am not completely insane, after all! Why, I know that, if that happened, it would be the end of me as well. I won't, I won't, I won't, and *I shall come straight home!* Believe me. Trust me for this *last time* and you won't regret it. Mark my words, from now on, for the rest of my life, I will work for you and Lyubochka without sparing my health, and *I shall reach my goal!* I shall see to it that you two are well provided for.

If you cannot manage to send the money on Sunday, send it on Monday as early as possible. In that case, I will be with you around noon on Wednesday. Don't worry if you cannot send it on Sunday, and don't think too much about me, that would be *too much,* I don't deserve it!

But what can happen to me? I am tough to the point of coarseness. More than that: it seems as if I have been completely morally regenerated (I say this to you and before God), and if it had not been for my worrying about you the past three days, if it had not been for my wondering every minute about what this would do to you—I would even have been happy! You mustn't think I am crazy, Anya, my guardian angel! A great thing has happened to me: I have rid myself of the abominable delusion that has *tormented* me for almost 10 years. For ten years (or, to be more precise, ever since my brother's death, when I suddenly found myself weighted down by debts) I dreamed about winning money. I dreamt of it seriously, passionately. But now it is all over! This was the *very* last time! Do you believe now, Anya, that my hands are untied?—I was tied up by gambling but now I will put my mind to worthwhile things instead of spending whole nights dreaming about gambling, as I used to do. And so my *work* will be better and more profitable, with God's blessing! Let me keep your heart, Anya, do not come to hate me, do not stop loving me. Now that I have become a new man, let us pursue our path together and I shall see to it that you are happy!

And Lyuba, Lyuba, oh, how despicably I have behaved! But I am thinking only of you. I can just imagine how you will feel when you read this! And even before you get this letter, how much you will worry when you find I have not come back, and the things you will imagine! Will they bring you this letter in time? And what if it gets lost! But how could it get lost since my telegram sent to the same address reached you? But to make sure, I will also send a few lines addressed to poste restante tomorrow and will mail it during the day.

I keep wondering: will I get a letter from you tomorrow or won't I? Probably not! You are expecting me back tomorrow so why should you write?

If you *cannot* send me the money on Sunday, write me a letter. I would be so happy to receive even a few lines in your hand, even if you cursed me in them. If you cannot manage to write on Sunday, send me a letter the first thing on Monday together with the money (that is, if you haven't already sent the money on Sunday). In any case, your letter will reach me before the money and it would make me so happy to hear from you!

Anya, when I think about how you will feel when you get this letter, it makes me go all cold inside. That is the only thing that causes me suffering. As for the rest—the boredom, the loneliness, and the uncertainty—I am sure I can put up with all that. I deserve worse! I will try to keep myself busy; in the three days ahead, I'll get off two letters that I have to write—to Katkov and to Maikov! But believe me, Anya, our resurrection has come about and believe, too, that now I shall reach my goal and make you happy!

I kiss you both and hug you, forgive me, Anya!

From now on, all yours,

Fyodor Dostoyevsky

P.S. I *shall not go* and see the priest, in no event, whatever happens. He is a witness of things that took place long ago and that time has vanished. It would be painful to me even to meet him!

P.S.S. Anya, my eternal joy, my only happiness—don't worry, don't torment yourself, preserve yourself for me!

Don't worry about that accursed, insignificant 180 thalers. It is true that this leaves us without money once again, but not for long, though, not for long (possibly Stellovsky will save us). To be sure, we are faced with the appalling necessity of pawning things again, which you find so odious! But this is the last time, the very last time! Back home I'll make money, I know I will! If only we could get back to Russia quickly! I will write Katkov and implore him to *advance* the date of payment, and I am certain that he will be responsive.

In the name of God, don't worry about me (ah, you are an angel, and, even if you cursed me, you would be sorry for me), yet I know that you will worry. But you may be at peace: I shall be regenerated in these three days and start a new life. Oh, how anxious I am to be back together with you! The only thing that frightens me is the thought of how you will take this letter. But of one thing you can be sure—of my infinite love for you. And from now on I will never do anything that will make you miserable.

P.S.S.S. I will remember this as long as I live and each time I think of it I will bless you, my angel! Let there be no mistake, now I am yours, all yours, undividedly yours. Whereas, up till now, *one-half* of me *belonged* to that accursed delusion.

---

88. "Schreiben sie mier" (should be "mir") was a signal that Dostoyevsky and Anna Grigorevna had arranged that meant he had lost at gambling and she was to send money to him.

The priest whom Dostoyevsky refers to may have been Yanyshev (see the note to Letter 73).

Dostoyevsky did keep his word this time: He never gambled again.

89.   To N. N. Strakhov
Dresden, April 23/May 5, 1871

As always, your letter was extremely interesting, much esteemed Nikolai Nikolayevich. But what strange things I learn: I could never have imagined that you would finish with *Dawn altogether*. I gather this from your letter, and you also write that you are delighted to have a rest and that you have taken up translating. Now, you cannot do that, Nikolai Nikolayevich; you cannot abandon your important work like this. We have no critics whatever. You are literally the only one. For two years I was happy to know that there was a magazine whose main characteristic was that it differed from all the others by its emphasis on criticism. And now they themselves have destroyed what was independent, original, their own. I reveled in your articles and was an ardent admirer of yours, and I am firmly convinced that you have a lot of other admirers besides myself and that, in any case, you must continue. It would be cowardly of you to give up like that. You must forgive me for using that word, but, knowing you as well as I do and as long as I have, I feel that you get too easily discouraged after a first setback. But there are bound to be setbacks in every enterprise. And besides, you'll see yourself that you won't be able to stand it: you will "take a break," as you say in your letter, but you won't content yourself with just translations and you'll start putting out brochures on the side. So, instead of that, why shouldn't you provide for yourself and get yourself a position with another magazine (maybe *Conversation*)? I do have the impression that there are people on *Conversation* who would understand you better and appreciate you more than the people at *Dawn* did.

Here is the conclusion I have reached on this subject, Nikolai Nikolaye-vich, something that you probably sense, too, but haven't fully grasped yet, just as was the case with me until most recently. Here's what it is: As a result of the tremendous upheavals that have occurred, starting with civic institutions and reaching all the way up to the strictly literary sphere, the cultural level and understanding of our society have been undermined, temporarily weakened and debased. People believe that they have no time to spend on literature (as if it were a toy—that's how educated they are!) and the level of sensitivity in criticism and of literary taste has suffered a terrible decline. And so, a critic appearing in our midst today, whoever he is, would fail to produce a proper impression. People like Dobrolyubov and Pisarev were acclaimed precisely because, in effect, they rejected literature—a whole sphere of the human spirit. But it is impossible to acquiesce in this state of affairs and I feel that you must continue your activity as a critic. And so, forgive me for advising you, but here is what I would do if I were in your position.

In one of your brochures, I found a brilliant idea and, what's more, one that had never been formulated in literature before, to wit, that any talent that was the least bit genuine and significant always ended up by turning to national feeling and becoming national and Slavophile. Thus, that idler, Pushkin, anticipated all the Kireyevskys and Khomyakovs and created the chronicler in the Chudov Monastery, i.e., expressed the very essence of the Slavophile idea before any of the Slavophiles and, moreover, expressed it incomparably more deeply than any of them has up to this very day. Take another look at Herzen: How much he longs and needs to turn onto that same path, although he cannot do so because of the nasty traits in his personality. But that's not the half of it: This *law* about turning onto the national path can be observed not only among the poets and professional writers; it is manifest in all fields of human endeavor. So that, ultimately, we can deduce another law from it: If a man is really talented, he will try to return to the people from the washed-out layer of society; but if he has no real talent, he will remain in that spent layer and will, moreover, become an expatriate, a convert to Catholicism, and so on and so forth. That stinkbug Belinsky (of whom you still think highly) was impotent and feeble in talent, and that was why he maligned Russia and deliberately caused her such great harm (much more will be said about him in the future, mark my words). But the thing is that this idea of yours is so powerful that it definitely warrants further development in a special study. So write an article on this very subject, develop it as an independent study, and publish it in *Conversation*. I am sure they will be delighted to have it. It will be a continuation of your critical writings, but in another form. Two or three articles like that a year and I predict success for you. And besides, this way the public won't forget you, and people will say that you have now joined a circle in which you are better understood. *Conversation* is no *Dawn*. But the main thing is, why give up your literary career?

Forgive me, though; we could understand each other better if we could talk in person. Alas, if you are going to Kiev, there's no chance of my finding you in Petersburg. I won't be back before June, owing to the situation of my finances. And so our meeting will have to wait until the fall. It would be nice if, before leaving Petersburg, you wrote me another letter. I am always happy to hear from you. But let me tell you this about your latest verdict about my novel: in the 1st place, you overrate me for the things that you find good in the novel and (2) you put your finger on its major defect. Yes, I have suffered from it and am still suffering from it now; I am utterly incapable (something I never learned) of controlling my material. Many separate novels and novellas get squeezed into a single one so that there is no proportion and no harmony. You bring all that out with devastating accuracy. For years it has plagued me because I have been acutely aware of it myself. But even worse than that: Not questioning my own capacity and getting carried away by poetic inspiration, I attempt to express an artistic idea that may be beyond my powers. (N.B. The poetic impulse is always so strong that, for example, it was stronger in Victor Hugo than his capacity for executing it. And traces of such a disparity are to be found even in Pushkin.) And that is what kills me.

I must add that the move to Russia and the numerous problems that will have to be tended to during the summer are bound to do serious harm to the novel. But I do thank you for your sympathy.

What a pity that we won't be able to see each other for such a long time yet. But, in the meantime, I remain,

Your most faithful and devoted,

Fyodor Dostoyevsky.

---

89. Dmitry Ivanovich Pisarev (1840–1868) was a critic who was regarded as one of the most extreme of the nihilists. He argued that literary works should be judged in terms not of aesthetic qualities but of social usefulness; he was renowned for the aphorism, "Boots are better than Shakespeare." He was arrested in 1862 and spent four years in the Peter-and-Paul Fortress. His death, by drowning, may have been a suicide.

The Kireyevsky brothers, Ivan Vasilevich (1806–1856) and Pyotr Vasilevich (1808–1856), were early Slavophile thinkers. Ivan edited the short-lived magazine *European* (Yevropeyets, 1832), and Pyotr compiled a collection of folk songs, but both of them were known more by their personal interactions than by their published writings.

Aleksei Stepanovich Khomyakov (1804–1860) was a poet, historian, philosopher, and journalist, and a prominent Slavophile. His most important work was *Notes on World History* (Zapiski o vsemirnoi istorii, published posthumously), in which he gave central importance to the role of religion.

The "chronicler in the Chudov Monastery" is a reference to the monk Pimen in Pushkin's *Boris Godunov*.

In his letter to Dostoyevsky, Strakhov had made favorable comments on several characters and scenes in *The Devils* and had gone on to say: "When it comes to the content, the richness and variety of ideas, you have no peer in our literature and even Tolstoy himself is monotonous by comparison. . . . But . . . you clutter up your works, make them too complicated. If the material of which your stories are made were simpler, their effect would be stronger."

90.   To N. N. Strakhov
Dresden, May 18/30 [1871]

Much esteemed Nikolai Nikolayevich,

So you led off your letter with Belinsky. I had a feeling you would. But just have a look at Paris, at the Commune. Are you, then, one of those who say that it has failed again because of the lack of the right people, the right circumstances, etc.? During the entire 19th century, that movement either has been dreaming of paradise on earth (starting with the phalanstery) or else, the moment it has come to the real test (in 1848, 1849—and now), has displayed a most degrading impotency to say anything even the least bit positive. It's all the same old Rousseau with his dream of re-creating the world through reason and experience (positivism). Well, it would seem we have enough facts by now to affirm that their inability to say anything new is no accident. So they chop off heads. Why do they do it? Only because it is the easiest thing to do. It would be incomparably more difficult to say something. Wishing something does not mean achieving it. They wish happiness for man and they content themselves with Rousseau's definition of the word "happiness," i.e., with a fantasy that has not even been justified by experience. The burning of Paris is monstrous—"We didn't succeed, so let the world perish, because the Commune is more important than the happiness of France and of the whole world." But then, to them (and to many others as well), this rage does not appear monstrous, on the contrary, they find it *beautiful.* Thus, the esthetic idea has become muddled in the new man. The moral foundation of society (taken from positivism) not only fails to produce results, but even fails to define itself and gets all entangled in wishes and ideals. As if today there were not ample evidence to demonstrate that this is not the way to found a society, that these are not the paths that lead to happiness, and that the origin of society is elsewhere than has been supposed until now. So where does it originate? They write many books but miss out on the essential: They have lost Christ in the West (through the fault of Catholicism) and that is the reason, and the only reason, why the West is declining. The ideal has changed—and this is all so clear! As to the decline of papal power along with the decline of the head of the Roman-Germanic world (France and the others)—what a coincidence!

All this demands long and time-consuming explanations, but what I am actually driving at is this: If Belinsky, Granovsky, and all that riff-raff could have had a glimpse at the present situation, they would have said: "Oh, no, this is not what we dreamed of; this is an aberration; we must wait a while longer and the dawn will appear and progress will reign and mankind will reconstruct itself on sound principles and will be happy!" They would never have agreed that once we had embarked on that path we were bound to wind up with the Commune and Félix Pyat. They were so obtuse that even *now*, after it has all already happened, they would have ignored it and gone on dreaming.

I have berated Belinsky more as a phenomenon of Russian life than as a person—the most putrid, stupid, and shameful phenomenon of Russian life. There is only one extenuating circumstance—the inevitability of such a phenomenon. And I assure you that Belinsky would have consoled himself with the thought: "Why, the reason the Commune did not work out was that it was above all French, i.e., it retained within itself the poison of nationalism. And therefore we must look for a people that is completely free of nationalism, a people who can, like me, give their mother (Russia) a slap on the face." And once again, foaming at the mouth, he would have started writing his rotten articles, disgracing Russia, denigrating her great phenomena (Pushkin) in order to turn Russia once and for all into a *vacuous* nation fit to head the cause of *all mankind*. And he would have accepted enthusiastically the Jesuitic ways and the lies of our leading forces. But here is something else: You never knew him, but I did, and I watched him, and now I have figured him out completely. That man who, in front of me, called Christ foul names was nevertheless incapable of bringing himself or any of the world's leaders forward where they could be compared with Christ. He couldn't fail to notice how much pettiness, malice, impatience, irritability, villainy, and above all vanity there was in them all. And while reviling Christ he never asked himself: "Whom shall we put in his place, since we are all so disgusting?" No, he never stopped to think about the fact that he was himself disgusting. He was extremely pleased with himself and that in itself showed his peculiar, evil-smelling, shameful obtuseness.

You say he was talented. Not in the least. And, my God, what nonsense Grigorev wrote about him in that poetic article of his! I remember my amazement when I was still very young on reading some of his purely esthetic pronouncements (for instance, on *Dead Souls*). He treated Gogol's characters with an almost monstrous scorn and a lack of true understanding, and was only happy when he felt Gogol had *exposed* something. During these past four years that I have spent abroad, I have reread his critical essays. He berated Pushkin when Pushkin discarded his false tone and came up with such works as *The Belkin Tales* and *The Black Man of Peter the Great*. Amazingly enough, he proclaimed that *The Belkin Tales* were worthless. To him, Gogol's *Carriage* was not a consummate artistic creation but merely a comic tale. He rejected the ending of *Eugene Onegin*. He was the first to accuse Pushkin of being a courtier. He declared that Turgenev was no artist, and he said that after reading Turgenev's extremely significant story, "The Three Portraits." I could give you as many more examples as you wished to prove the untruth of the legend about the critical flair and the "receptive vibration" that Grigorev erroneously ascribed to him (because Grigorev himself was a poet). And so, we still continue to judge Belinsky and many other phenomena of our life through the distortions of a multitude of extraordinary prejudices.

Is it possible that I failed to say anything about your article on Turgenev? I read it with admiration—as I read all your articles—but with a tinge of disappointment as well. Since you say that Turgenev has lost his focus and is hedging and *doesn't know what to say* about certain things that are happening in Russian life (in *every instance* treating them sarcastically), you should also have recognized that his great artistic talent has waned (and was bound to wane) in his latest writings. That is a manifest fact: he has declined as an artist. *Voice* accounts for it by his living abroad, but it goes deeper than that. You still find his former artistry in his latest works, too. Isn't that so? However, I may be wrong (not in my judgment of Turgenev but in my interpretation of your article). Possibly, you didn't express yourself very clearly . . . But you know what—all that is landowner's literature. It has said all there was for it to say (beautifully in the case of Lev Tolstoy). But that, the apogee of the landowners' word, was the very last. The *new word* that is to replace that of the landowners has not yet been heard, but then there hasn't been time. (People like Reshetnikov haven't said anything. Nevertheless, the Reshetnikovs express the idea that something new is needed in literature, something that is *not landownerish*, although they express it in a clumsy way.)

I would so much like to get to Petersburg in time to find you there! But I have no idea when I'll get back. (Between us—I hope it will be in a month.) But if I don't get the money in time, I'll miss the opportunity and be compelled to prolong my stay here again. But that would be awful and senseless!

As for my novel, I'll either make a filthy, disgraceful mess of it (I have already started spoiling it) or I will cope with it and maybe something good will come of it. I am aiming *at success with the public*. This is my new motto. (All this must remain between us, in the name of God.)

And I was so hoping that you would be the first person I'd see in Petersburg. I realize that it is of cardinal importance for you to have a change of scenery. But please, don't think of staying in Kiev for good. Your letters have begun to cause me serious anxiety about you. You are one of the people who have had a most telling effect on me in my life and I am sincerely fond of you and feel a great deal of sympathy for you. You are just going through a state of depression (you have even started talking of death!). Ah, it would be so good if we could get to see each other!

So it looks as if *Dawn* won't ever come out again. Is that really so? How sad. I have been waiting for the April issue for 2 months now and have not seen it advertised in the press. I have an idea that may save *Dawn* from going down, in fact a whole plan. But it would take too long to describe here, and, anyway, I know none of the particulars of *Dawn*'s circumstances. I only think it wouldn't be bad if the magazines started to specialize (at least one should start). *Dawn,* for instance, should concentrate *exclusively* on esthetics and criticism and have no other departments. And really, I think this could work out. It is a pity I cannot explain my thoughts to you more fully right now.

I really had a good time reading (in your letter) about Turgenev. That rogue is true to himself artistically. I have experienced his ways on *my own hide.* There are many things I could explain to you but I will leave it until we meet.

Your most sincerely devoted,

F. Dostoyevsky.

If you can send me a line—do so. The address is still the same.
My wife sends you her best regards.

---

90. Félix Pyat (1810–1889) was a French writer, a member of the Constituent Assembly after the revolution of 1848, and a participant in the Paris Commune of 1871, during which, among other things, he sponsored a decree banning the publication of all writings hostile to the Commune and demanded the razing of the Vendôme column and other structures.

Belinsky's published opinions about Pushkin's artistic merits were far more favorable than Dostoyevsky acknowledges here. For example, concerning *The Black Man of Peter the Great,* he wrote: "What simplicity, and at the same time, what depth! What a palette! What colors!" The same is true, though perhaps to a lesser extent, of his comments about the works of Gogol and Turgenev that are mentioned here.

Fyodor Mikhailovich Reshetnikov (1841–1871) came from a background of extreme deprivation and maltreatment and drew on his experiences to write a novel, *The Inhabitants of Podlipnaya* (Podlipovtsy, 1864). It presented a harrowing picture of rural life—people who changed their shirts once a year, ate chaff and bark, could barely count, and indulged in incest. He made no effort to present this grim subject matter in an "esthetic" form. After publication of this book, the descriptions of rural life that were found in Turgenev and Grigorovich seemed delusory.

Concerning Turgenev, Strakhov had written of his "faintheartedness," "shameful cowardice," and "total lack of faith."

PART IV

1872–1881

THE LAST

ten years of Dostoyevsky's life were perhaps the happiest in his erratic and storm-tossed existence. He and his wife returned to Petersburg in July 1871, his son Fyodor was born shortly afterward, and the family was surrounded by old friends and new admirers of his work. P. M. Tretyakov, a wealthy merchant and connoisseur of the arts, asked Dostoyevsky to pose for a portrait by the famous painter V. G. Perov, to be exhibited in Tretyakov's gallery along with the portraits of other illustrious personages; and this invitation, which Dostoyevsky accepted, indicates the new status he had attained. The summer of 1872 was the first of several which he and his family spent in the resort town of Staraya Russa.

The first installments of *The Devils* in 1871 had been widely appreciated by readers hostile to nihilism (and detested by the young generation sympathetic to the radical cause). Dostoyevsky was accordingly taken up by the virulently antiradical novelist and publicist Prince V. P. Meshchersky, who was close to court circles, and through him met K. P. Pobedonostsev, then a member of the Senate and tutor to Crown Prince Alexander. In December 1872, with the permission of the secret police, Dostoyevsky accepted the post of editor of the *Citizen,* a weekly journal owned by Meshchersky.

Dostoyevsky's creditors, of course, were alerted to his return as well, but Anna Grigorevna, who had taken all business matters into her competent hands, managed to beat them off and to persuade them that their only hope of repayment was to leave Dostoyevsky in peace to write. In addition, she realized one of Dostoyevsky's long-cherished dreams: to publish his own works and reap all the profits. This was done beginning with *The Devils,* and the Dostoyevskys soon became the publishers and distributors of his books. Anna Grigorevna's business acumen thus laid the foundation for the relative prosperity and tranquillity of these last years, though Dostoyevsky never ceased to worry about the economic future of his children and family after his death.

Dostoyevsky's relations with the *Citizen* lasted for two years. Prince Meshchersky did not give him a free editorial hand and was much more unqualifiedly a supporter of repression than Dostoyevsky himself, who believed in dialogue with the radicals rather than force. This led to clashes between publisher and editor that Dostoyevsky found more and more difficult to tolerate. In his weekly column, "Diary of a Writer," which became one of the *Citizen*'s most popular features, he presented a noticeably more sympathetic version of radicalism than can be found in his bitter letters of the preceding years in Europe. Indeed, Dostoyevsky soon offered his next novel, *A Raw Youth,* to N. A. Nekrasov for publication in the radical journal

Notes of the Fatherland. This led to a distinct cooling of relations with old friends and allies like N. N. Strakhov and Apollon Maikov, who tended to regard Dostoyevsky's moderation as a betrayal of principle. But Dostoyevsky had not really changed his attitude of opposition to radical aims and ideas; rather, he had observed among them a revival of secularized Christian values, which he thought made it newly possible to find a common ground of debate.

A second son, Aleksei, was born to the Dostoyevskys in August 1875. That same year he requested permission to publish the *Diary of a Writer* as a monthly publication entirely written by himself, and he launched this unique and immensely successful journal of comment and opinion, which also contained such small fictional masterpieces as *A Gentle Creature* and *The Dream of a Ridiculous Man.* Here Dostoyevsky voiced forceful opinions on all the current issues confronting Russian society and very quickly became one of the most influential shapers of Russian public opinion; he also received a huge correspondence and wrote many letters of the greatest interest in reply. Among them are his answer to Arkady Kovner, a young Jewish journalist imprisoned for swindling, who had charged Dostoyevsky with anti-Semitism, and his response to V. A. Alekseyev explaining how Dostoyevsky interpreted the New Testament phrase about "stones turned into bread." Dostoyevsky considered the *Diary of a Writer* to be a notebook for *The Brothers Karamazov,* and there are many connections between themes and motifs in the *Diary* and those he would later use in his final novel.

Dostoyevsky, however, found it impossible to produce the *Diary of a Writer* and do any extended creative work at the same time. In October 1877 he announced that he would temporarily cease publication with the December issue for reasons of health and without further explanation; but in fact he wanted time for his next novel. Seven months later, Dostoyevsky's three-year-old son Aleksei died suddenly and unexpectedly from the effects of a prolonged epileptic attack. The disconsolate father made a trip the next month, in the company of the young philosopher and poet Vladimir Solovyov, to the Optina Hermitage and visited the famous elder (*starets*) Father Amvrosii, who uttered words of consolation to the grief-stricken Dostoyevsky that were later repeated by Father Zosima in the novel. Many details of monastery life gathered on this visit were also included in the book.

The first part of *The Brothers Karamazov* was published in January 1879, and Dostoyevsky wrote many letters concerning it to the editors of *Russian Messenger,* to friends, and to readers who flooded him with their reactions. In June 1880, while *The Brothers Karamazov* was still being published to great acclaim, Dostoyevsky spoke at a celebration in Moscow honoring the memory of Pushkin. His speech created the sensation that he described in a letter to his wife; all accounts of the event confirm Dostoyevsky's triumph, which ended in an unrivaled outburst of enthusiasm and adulation on the part of the public.

The last section of *The Brothers Karamazov* was sent to *Russian Messenger* in November 1880, and on January 28, 1881, Dostoyevsky died from a hemorrhage of the lungs caused by chronic emphysema. He was buried on February 1 at a huge funeral, which turned into a moving manifestation of the esteem in which he was held by the vast variety of his countrymen.

91.   To A. A. Romanov
[Petersburg] February 10, 1873

Your Imperial Highness, All-Gracious Sovereign:

Allow me to have the honor and happiness of presenting my work for your attention. It is almost a historical study, in which I have sought to account for the possibility of such monstrous phenomena as the Nechayev movement occurring in our strange society. In my view, it is not an accidental or isolated phenomenon. It is a direct consequence of the profound estrangement of Russian education from the native, home-grown foundations underlying Russian life. Even the most talented advocates of a pseudo-European development for Russia became convinced long ago that it was absolutely criminal for us Russians to dream of an indigenous culture. And most terrifying of all is the fact that they are completely right; because once we have *proudly* proclaimed ourselves Europeans, we have, by that very act, renounced being Russians. In our embarrassment and fear over lagging so far behind Europe, in intellectual and cultural achievements, we have forgotten that we, as Russians, perhaps carry within ourselves, in the depths and reaches of the Russian spirit, the capacity for bringing a new light to the world, if we will only follow our own path of development. In our enthusiastic self-denigration, we have forgotten the immutable historical law that without *arrogant* confidence in our own worldwide importance as a nation, we will never be a great nation or create anything original for the benefit of mankind. We have forgotten that all the great nations have manifested their might by being so "arrogant" in their opinion of themselves, and that they have each made a contribution to the world, even if it is no more than a single ray of light, precisely because they have remained themselves, proudly, unwaveringly, constantly, and *arrogantly* self-reliant.

To harbor and to express such thoughts is today tantamount to condemning oneself in our country to the role of pariah. And that, despite the fact that the principal opponents of our national self-reliance would be the first to turn away with horror from the Nechayev affair. Our Belinskys and Granovskys would never have believed it if they had been told that they were the direct spiritual fathers of the Nechayev band. And it is this kinship of ideas and their transmission from fathers to sons that I have tried to show in my work. I am far from having succeeded, although I worked conscientiously.

I am flattered and inspired by the hope that Your Majesty, heir to one of the loftiest thrones in the world, the future leader and ruler of the Russian land, may take even slight notice of my avowedly weak but honest attempt to portray in artistic form one of the most dangerous cankers of our present civilization, a civilization which is strange, unnatural, and alien but which thus far has maintained its sway over Russian life.

Allow me, Your All-Gracious Sovereign, to express my feelings of limitless respect and gratitude and to remain your ever so faithful and devoted servant,

Fyodor Dostoyevsky

---

91. Alexander Alexandrovich Romanov (1845–1894) was heir to the Russian throne, the future Tsar Alexander III (1881–1894). The work that Dostoyevsky was sending to him was *The Devils*.

92.   To M. P. Pogodin
[Petersburg] February 26, 1873

Much esteemed Mikhail Petrovich,

You are wrong (I say this in all honesty) when you say "you finally answered me out of sheer necessity." I was telling the *truth* when I wrote that it had been my intention to answer you more warmly. Your opinion and your affection are dear to me, and if I did not answer you it is because I find myself in the following situation:

We have no secretary, although I will now insist that we get one, as I have come to realize that one is indispensable. But even if we had a secretary, I still know from experience that I would have to deal personally with the regular contributors and the authors of new articles; that I would have to reread those articles (which is hell); that I would have to familiarize myself with the tremendous backlog of material left by the editor who preceded me. Rereading articles consumes an enormous amount of time and affects my health because I keep feeling that it is taking me away from my true work. Then, once I decide to print an article, I very often have to edit it from beginning to end. For instance, I almost completely rewrote Gensler's literary vignettes (in the current issue). And then I have to plow through the rubbish in the newspapers. But what riles me most is that there are so many topics on which I would like to write myself. I am a bundle of nerves when I conceive and start putting together an article; then I set about writing it and, oh horror, comes Thursday and I realize that I won't be able to finish it in time. However, I do not want to leave anything out of it. And so I discard it completely and start writing something else in a great hurry (because I may have given Meshchersky my word that I will contribute an article myself and the magazine is counting on it). So I often seize upon some new subject on Thursday night which I can work up into a piece within twenty-four hours to meet the Friday deadline. All this, I repeat, puts a great strain on my health. So where could I find time to write you a letter, if I wanted to say *something* in the letter.

There are many things that worry me, for example, the fact that we have absolutely no contributors for the literary criticism department. I was so pleased when Strakhov came back from the Crimea (now, I thought, we will have some literary criticism), but then he suddenly fell seriously ill.

Finally, there is so much that needs to be said, and that's why I joined this magazine. But now I realize how difficult it is to express myself. Here is my idea and my goal: Socialism—whether consciously or in the most preposterously unconscious form, or used as a disguise for despicable acts—has affected almost an entire generation. The facts are clear and ominous. One reads in the newspapers of even ignorant yokels suddenly coming up with some catchword or other that obviously emanates from the socialist camp. We must combat this, because everything has been contaminated. My idea is that socialism and Christianity are the antitheses of one another. And this is a point that I would like to develop in a series of articles, but I haven't got around to it yet.

At the same time, the outlines of novels and short stories teem in my head and take shape in my heart. I think them through and note them down and every day I add new touches to the outline I have jotted down, but then I realize that my whole time is being taken up by the magazine and that I simply cannot do any more writing—and that fills me with regret and despair.

Well, that will give you some idea of the life I lead. I would love to come to Moscow and have a heart-to-heart talk with you about many things. There is a possibility that I will come for a short while in the spring, but I'm not sure. You ask about my health. Perhaps you have heard that I am an epileptic. On the average, I have suffered one epileptic fit a month for many years, ever since Siberia, the only difference during the past two years being that it takes me five days to return to a normal condition after an attack rather than three, as was the case for almost twenty years. But, strangely enough, it is now five months since I had my last attack! They have stopped. I don't know what to attribute it to, but I am afraid of some impending crisis. However, I do not spend much time thinking of my health.

I do not have a photograph of myself, but I will get one made and send it to you along with my newly published novel, *The Devils*. If you read it, much esteemed Mikhail Petrovich, please let me know what you think of it.

I first met Belinsky in June 1845, just about the same time that I met Nekrasov.

I will tell Maikov about everything. I haven't seen him for some time now, a whole week.

The *Citizen* is doing rather well, although only relatively so. We have 1800 subscribers, i.e., already more than we had last year, and the subscriptions still keep coming in at a steady, regular rate. But the total number will not, I think, be too high this year and, as a matter of fact, I doubt that it will exceed 2500. Ivan Sergeyevich Aksakov was in Petersburg last month and he told me that he did not have more subscribers than that during the first two years either. As for the sales of single issues, the figure is five times (or even better) that of last year. In general, by the end of the year, we should have worked out a regular and orderly routine which, I feel, we are lacking at present. This is a new business for me and I am not confident that I am up to it.

I received the proofs of the *speech* long ago and while I was reading them, as usual, lots of ideas flashed through my mind, but I would like to discuss them first with Maikov, whom I have not seen for a long time. About two weeks ago, I came down with a bad cold.

We all read the speech delivered before the Slav Committee but we could not publish it (it's not a question of its being too late even now—why should it be?) for the sole reason that the *Citizen* had already published Filippov's articles on that subject, i.e., on the disputes between the Greeks and the Bulgars. Did you read it? If you did, you probably noticed that it contains a point that is partly at odds with your own view. And since the *Citizen* has already taken a stand on the issue, publishing your piece would be tantamount to its contradicting itself. From the standpoint of canon law or, rather, from the religious standpoint, I think that the Greeks are in the right. Even for the sake of the noblest aspirations and objectives, we have no right to *distort* Christianity, i.e., to view Orthodoxy as, to say the least, a thing of secondary importance, as the Bulgars do in the present instance. On the whole, however, I find Filippov's views somewhat narrow (as a result of his zeal). Did you read, much esteemed Mikhail Petrovich, in the February issue of *Russian Messenger* for this year the article, "Panslavism and the Greeks," by Konstantinov? (I wonder if it was not actually written by Leontev, who has already published something on Eastern Europe some time ago.) The article actually startled me. If you haven't read it, do so, and let me know what you think of it. I would like to write an article about it. What struck me particularly was the final conclusion about what the Eastern question must mean for Russia from now on (a struggle against the *whole idea* of the West, i.e., against socialism). The strangest thing is that *R[ussian] Messenger* published the article, albeit with reservations.

Concerning Feodosiya and Kiev, I will do everything you say and I will write you.

You refer to Maikov and to me as "young men," much esteemed Mikhail Petrovich, and you have every right to do so, because when Maikov and I reach your present age, we will probably be unable to take on such projects as your work on Peter [the Great], or to write so rapidly, simply, clearly, and convincingly as you did in your replies to Kostomarov and, by and large, to Ilovaisky—you had a magnificent idea and you applied the impact to the right point, as in mechanics, by challenging Ilovaisky in the *Russian Messenger*. For you have, in effect, a whole edifice to back up your arguments, while they have not even piled up enough bricks to build their own edifice and use what they have to toss at the opposition in the heat of the quarrel. Nevertheless, a fight is a good thing and a good fight produces material from which to build the future. But I still cannot read Kostomarov without indignation.

I think that I have answered all your questions now. Where are you planning to go in the country, much esteemed Mikhail Petrovich?

I myself have absolutely no idea at all where I will spend the summer. At times I feel that I was definitely crazy to take on the *Citizen*. For instance, I cannot live without my wife and children, but in the summer, for the sake of their health they have to get away to the country—somewhere as far from Petersburg as possible. But I will have to stay here and work on the *Citizen*. So that means I must be separated from my family. It's quite unbearable.

I firmly shake your hand, and may God preserve you,

All yours,

F. Dostoyevsky

---

92. Mikhail Petrovich Pogodin (1800–1875) was a historian, archaeologist, and journalist of right-wing Slavophile persuasion. He had been the editor of several important journals and a friend of Pushkin and Gogol. The speech referred to was one that he had delivered in January 1873. In 1864, he had engaged in polemics with the historian Nikolai Ivanovich Kostomarov (1817–1885) over the latter's skepticism about the heroism of Dmitry Donskoi at the Battle of Kulikovo, and in January 1873 he had published an article in *Russian Messenger* challenging the contention of the historian Dmitry Ivanovich Ilovaisky (1832–1920) that "the theory of the Norman origin of the Russian princes is unfounded." (Ilovaisky later served as president of the Society of Friends of Russian Literature and compared Dostoyevsky's novels unfavorably with those of Tolstoy; see Letter 103.)

Dostoyevsky had taken the position of editor of the *Citizen* (Grazhdanin) late in 1872 (after overcoming objections from the Third Section), when the previous editor, Gradovsky, had quarreled with the publisher, Prince Vladimir Petrovich Me-shchersky (1839–1914), over editorial autonomy. Meshchersky subsequently became one of Alexander III's most reactionary advisers, arguing even for the abolition of the zemstvo organizations.

Gensler's "Harbor Scenes—A Skit" (Gavanskiye stseny. Sharzh) appeared in the *Citizen* in February 1873. The same issue carried an article by Pogodin on Belinsky.

"Konstantinov," as Dostoyevsky surmises, was a pen name for Konstantin Nikola-yevich Leontev (1831–1891), a former physician and diplomat who subsequently became a magazine writer and editor, a censor, and, a few years before his death, a monk. In the article referred to here, he posited a basic antagonism between the land-rich peoples of Eastern Europe—not only the Slavs, but the Turks, Greeks, Rumanians, and Hungarians as well—and the industrial West, and he anticipated that Eastern Europe would "rise as one single unit to become a bulwark against god-lessness, anarchy, and general depravity."

93.   To A. G. DOSTOYEVSKAYA
[Petersburg] Monday, July 23, 1873

My sweet Anya,

I have only just received your Friday letter—it's terrible the time it takes to get here! The things I imagined in that time and how worried I was! Tell me, my darling Anya, is that any way to write?: "Something terrible has happened to me . . . I am in a great distress . . ." and then no explanation of what actually happened. For God's sake, write *immediately* and tell me what it is all about, for otherwise, I'll be furious and will quarrel with you and won't come to see you until you write. And for Heaven's sake, never do that again—life is painful enough for me even without that. Write me at once, do you hear.

You gave me a lot of pleasure with the things you wrote about the children. Always write me about them—it brings me back to life and makes me feel as if they are by my side.

Besides the awfully depressing thoughts and the almost morbid feeling of despondency that descend upon me whenever it occurs to me that I will have to suffer through at least another six months of the hard labor to which I have condemned myself by accepting this job on the *Citizen*—well, besides all that, I am also seriously afraid of falling sick. Just last night I had bouts of fever, my back ached, and my legs felt weighted down. Today, however, I feel much better. But I sleep poorly, have nightmares and bad dreams, and my stomach is upset. Write me each time as soon as you get my letter, without waiting until the next day, and then I'll answer your letters the same way as well.

I answered Meshchersky's rude letter beautifully—without being unduly provocative, calmly, sternly, very much to the point. He won't dare to make such a display of himself again. Anna Nikolayevna came in on Saturday morning and took a few things from your chest of drawers (some 6 items, the red checkered cloak, I believe, curtains and other things) and, on top of that, she took 10 rubles from me. So now, after paying for the housekeeping expenses, I am suddenly left with just 53 rubles (I had given 10 to Misha the day before). Also on Saturday, Misha went to Klein's bookstore, as I had asked him to, and what do you think—they told him that they'd sold 50 copies but that Klein himself was not in town, that he had left for Moscow and wouldn't be back in Petersburg until early August, and that he didn't leave any money behind. (Very likely, 50 copies is only the number they admit to having sold but they have actually sold more.)

Meanwhile, Monday is payday for the contributors. So I got up at 10 this morning and made the rounds of the moneylenders. None of them would let me have more than 60, not a kopek more, and only at one place, near the Anichkov bridge, in Lopatin's house, did I manage to convince them to let me have 70. But I am worried because they gave me a receipt which says that I have sold my watch and been paid in full the sum of 70 rubles. They tried to reassure me by saying that it was the customary form used by private banks. It is possible, of course, that they are being perfectly straightforward. That way I had enough money: I paid out 106 rubles, which left me with 15 rubles plus some change to live on. But then I have no watch.

Now I am all alone, even Strakhov is not here. I am developing a great fondness for one of my new colleagues, Belov (he writes literary criticism), but he lives so very far away. Otherwise, I think we could have hit it off well together. Iv[an] Gr[igorevi]ch didn't come today either, and the only visits I have had were those of Pasha and poor Misha yesterday. Misha's wife, who almost died, has recovered and it was her name day yesterday, but Misha couldn't scrape up any money other than the 10 rubles.

On the night of Saturday to Sunday, between nightmares, I dreamed that Fedya climbed onto the window ledge and fell from the 4th floor. When he started falling, turning in the air, I put my hands over my eyes and shouted in despair: "Farewell, Fedya!" And then I woke up. Quick, write me about Fedya and whether anything happened to him in the night between Saturday and Sunday. I believe in second sight; it is an established fact, and I won't feel reassured until I get your letter.

During the night, I wake up 10 times or so, sleeping only an hour at a time or less, and I often find myself covered with sweat. Last night, between Sunday and Monday, I dreamt that Lilya was an orphan and had fallen into the hands of some wicked women who enjoyed torturing her and flogged her with birch twigs, large ones, like the ones soldiers used to be flogged with. When I got to her, she was already breathing her last and kept saying "Mommy, Mommy!" That dream is almost driving me mad today.

And in general, I feel that no good will come to me from this summer and this work. As to my coming to you, don't expect me until August 5—there's not the slightest chance of my coming before. I am not worried, though, about our next issue. No. 31, which is to come out on July 30—i.e., Iv. G—ch will at last be receiving some money and he'll help me out. But I am not satisfied with the editorial side. I have to write a very long article myself, but I am very distraught.

Today, Nastya came by (while I was out) and Aleksandra finally gave her the letter from Prokhorovna. (N.B. Aleksandra had been to see her without me but had not found her at home.) Nastya read the letter and, when Aleksandra tried to convince her to write to her mother, she replied: "But there's nothing to write about—I'm alive and well and have not received any letters either from father or from my brother." Nevertheless, she promised she would write. Tell that to Prokhorovna and give her my regards.

I hug you sincerely with all the ardor of my heart. Write right away. Write about the children and tell me what the terrible thing is that happened to you. Don't forget that, do you hear? Don't upset me further, don't exasperate me. I kiss you 1000 times and Lilya and Fedya too. I often think of them and keep worrying—if anything happens, what will become of them!

All yours,
F. Dostoyevsky

In general, don't worry about my health (assuming that you are worried). I have quite a solid constitution. The weather here is bad—it rains about 20 times every day and there has been thunder and lightning for 3 nights in a row now, and that is why I don't sleep well.

---

93. Yevgeny Aleksandrovich Belov (1826–1896) had taught history in Saratov, where he befriended Chernyshevsky. At first a Fourierist, he was interrogated in connection with Chernyshevsky's arrest and evidently changed his views radically afterward, becoming a Slavophile. A number of his articles were published in the *Citizen*.

The "very long article" that Dostoyevsky says he has to write evidently never did get written.

Prokhorovna was the Dostoyevskys' nanny; Aleksandra was their maid.

94. To A. G. Dostoyevskaya
[Petersburg] Sunday, August 19, 1873

I am awfully sorry, my sweet girl, that I scared you so. Here's how it happened: on the 15th—or maybe it was the 14th—I got a letter from you and gathered from it that you were very worried about my health. So I wrote you right away that I had recovered (which was the truth) and put everything down to excesses and fatigue. I mailed the letter and then spent the whole night of the 15th to the 16th working. As I was getting ready to go to bed, at 5 in the morning, indeed, when I was already in bed, I suddenly remembered that in your letter you had also said that the best time for you to leave [Staraya] Russa would be either the 24th or the 16th or 17th, because on the 19th there would be a general rush back to town and everything would be crowded. So I thought: here she is worrying about my health and I don't know when she'll get this letter; she'll get my other letter (the alarming one), and then, on the spur of the moment, she may decide to leave on the 16th or the 17th. But, it would be a shame to deprive the children of fresh air while the weather is so nice there and it is hot and dusty in Petersburg. So I jumped out of the bed, composed a telegram, dressed, and took it to the telegraph office, which is luckily only a few steps away. I handed it in at 10 minutes to six, reckoning that even if you had decided to leave that very day, the 16th, there was still a chance that the telegram might reach you in Russa in time to stop you from leaving. So that is how it all happened. I admit that the thought did occur to me that it might alarm you quite a bit. But I had no idea that it would frighten you that badly. So stay there, darling, as long as you can and come at the end of the month. I am very much concerned about your trip, Anya. The weather is fine now. But according to my calculations, there will be a full moon on the 25th and, along with it, torrential rains. The children must have real winter clothing *in reserve*. And you'll have to argue to get seats in the train, you'll have to insist. You'll be lucky if you manage to get good seats. In that respect, you'll have the greatest difficulty on the Nikolayev line.

I have an awful lot of work, Anya, mostly editing other people's articles, and I am sweating over it like a man sentenced to hard labor. Indeed, I am quite surprised at my own resistance and ability to stand it. There are 1000 little worries which I won't bother you about, Anya, but there are also some big worries, serious ones, that I had foreseen.

The most serious problem right now is our apartment. We simply cannot stay there, Anya, and this is not a rash decision but one I have thought through carefully. I have talked the matter over with Anna Nikolavna, and she agrees that to stay there *is out of the question*. Slivchansky is some sort of a madman (I am seriously convinced of it). He may tell us in December, *for no reason whatsoever,* that he wants us to move out and he'll kick us out into the street. Aleksandra's passport has expired. He has seen her passport himself and knows very well that she is not a vagrant. She sent her expired passport to the mayor's office in Kronstadt and enclosed the money for the new passport to be sent to her, and she has received a postal receipt certifying that they had received her old passport. But now 2 weeks have passed and she hasn't heard a thing from Kronstadt as yet. So now Slivchansky has started to pester her and is threatening to kick her out of his house. Today he ran into her and told her: "I'll write a letter to your master that'll teach him a thing or two!" This is a rather strange way to treat his tenants, trying to chase away their servants for trifles that, in any case, he cannot possibly be held responsible for.

Then, two days ago, Gladkov sent over a letter that had just been received at the editorial office, a very important letter addressed to me from the Prince. Besides the porter in our office, we have a messenger and, in compliance with the Prince's wishes, he deliberately wears a Russian-style coat and a beard but underneath he has a well-cut suit and stylish boots. The messenger arrived in a hurry, carrying a large sealed package, came upstairs and was about to ring the bell when suddenly the landlord called out to him from the top landing: "Hey, you, how dare you use the main entrance! You peasant! I don't want people in peasant clothes using the main entrance! Go round to the back entrance!" And he grabbed the fellow by the sleeve and dragged him downstairs and the fellow had to cross the yard to leave by the back entrance. But I'm sure he must have seen that the man had a letter in his hands. You must agree, Anya, that some people might resent such treatment. What if Meshchersky had been here, for example? And then people whose business may not be particularly urgent might simply not bother to look for the back entrance. The messengers from the bookstores who come to pick up the books may just up and leave. In fact, if the landlord finds out about it, he may not allow them to take copies of my books through the main entrance. He gets up at dawn and spends the whole day walking up and down the flights of stairs and going around the house, he spies on everyone and sees that everything is in order. I thought of going and asking him for an explanation about *the messenger*, but then I figured that he'd tell me then and there to move out of his house. And so I made up my mind to put up with it until your return.

But today again—further persecution. On holidays, Aleksandra sometimes asks me to allow her to go out to visit some friends of hers (very seldom). And since I have to go out, too, I usually lock the apartment and leave the key with the janitor so that whichever of us—*Aleksandra* or I—returns first can always obtain the key from the janitor and get into the apartment. Well, about 4 days ago I had left the key with the janitor. But the landlord found out about it and forbade the janitor ever again to accept the key from me. So now whenever I leave the house and Aleksandra is out, I must leave the key in a certain place on the shelf in the outhouse. But that involves a certain amount of risk, and I have money belonging to the magazine in the apartment! If he sees our children in the courtyard, he is sure to find fault with something or other and call down their nanny; he has done this with others. Well, I'd certainly beat him up then. And so I have decided to move out no matter what. To be constantly intimidated throughout the winter, to live under the continuous threat of an explosion—why, given my susceptibility, I'd be sick in no time! Ah, Anya, I realized the sort of a man he was that time when, remember, we came to see him about the cat, and he just said "Clear out." Also bear in mind that since last winter rents have gone up by 30 percent. Knowing he can get as many tenants as he wants, he can afford to have a good time at our expense.

I have decided that I'd be willing to pay as much as 900 rubles just to move out! I absolutely refuse to stay in this apartment, I can tell you that! And if we have to pay more for rent, we'll be better off in other ways—in the children's health and in my peace of mind. In peaceful conditions I can write more and better. I have told you that many times before, but you have never paid much attention to my words. I tell you, I'll make more money in a peaceful atmosphere. I haven't made an issue of anything or tried to argue with the landlord; rather I am avoiding him, in spite of all his provocations, because I am afraid of a scene. Yesterday I saw an apartment near St. Vladimir's Church—it's very nice but the rent is 900 rubles. I'll look around some more. I'd even rather go and rent something in the Peski district than stay in this house. The problem for me is how to move the books.

Good-bye, darling. And since you write that you love me, try to understand our situation, give it some serious thought. Because afterwards we'll be in real trouble if he decides to kick us out into the street in the winter.

Besides, it really is a lousy apartment, it's constricting and the nursery and your room are stuffy. Our dining room alongside the steps is quite useless—there's nothing that can be done with it. Good-bye, I hug you. If I find an apartment, I'll take an option on it and give them a deposit without even waiting for your return, because apartments go every day. Good-bye then, all yours,

F. Dostoyevsky.

If I do find an apartment even before you leave Russa, I'll wire you the new address, although I don't really expect to move before your return.

Anna Nikolavna and Olga Kiril[l]ov[na] have already moved to a new apartment (900 rubles) near the technological institute. They are still without a nanny and are looking for one. Iv[an] G[rigorevi]ch left around five days ago and has already written them from Moscow. Grisha sits with his handies clamped over his eyes and cries—he misses his papa; he keeps wandering about looking for him, and they're beginning to worry about the child.

Someone came to see me [several lines crossed out] he told me he had already looked there. He looks like a man who will get his money when he sets his mind to it.

Once more, I embrace you and Lyuba and Fedya.

P.S. They just brought me your letter and I had to reopen the envelope, which I had already sealed, although I have no time to spare. On the subject of the cook, I'd say this: I don't know myself what will happen later; Aleksandra is a good worker, very good, in fact, and she cooks well. She is well mannered and well behaved, but the question is whether she'll be able to cope when the family is all together and whether she'll be willing to stay with us when there is more work to do—that I cannot say. So, if you find someone who is not irritable, who is *clean* (that's the first requirement), and who cooks *well* (you hear?), then *hire* her and *bring her* along with you. This is my last word on the subject. In that case, we'll let Aleksandra go. (She has her faults, for instance, she is too sensitive, but *she is not afraid of work*, far from it, in fact.) And so, bring your own girl. As for Prokhorovna, if it were possible I'd keep her forever! Talk it over with An[na] Nikolavna and Olga Kiril[l]ovna! They have changed nannies 6 times and are still looking for one. The children are covered with scratches and bruises. They both say that our Prokhorovna is a treasure.

All yours,
F. Dostoyevsky

P.S. As I am leaving the house and Aleksandra is not at home, I have hidden the money in every corner of the apartment, and I'll leave the key in the prearranged place in the outhouse.

Kiss the children, Lyuba and Fedya. I bless them and hug them! Goodbye. Yesterday Olga Kiril[l]ovna came to see me on her own. We sat and drank tea. She actually came to find out from Aleksandra about the maid whom Aleksandra had promised Anna Nikolavna she would find for them.

---

94. Staraya Russa was a town about 150 miles southeast of Petersburg known for its mineral springs and salt lakes. The Dostoyevskys had rented a summer house there for the first time in 1872 and had returned in 1873, but Dostoyevsky had subsequently gone to Petersburg because that is where the editorial work for the *Citizen* was being performed.

Olga Kirillovna was the wife of Anna Grigorevna's brother Ivan Grigorevich; Grisha was their son.

95.   To D. D. KISHENSKY
[Petersburg] Wednesday, September 5, 1873

Dear Sir, Dmitri Dmitriyevich:

Your rude letter took me completely by surprise and angered me at first. But now that I have looked further into the question, and collected and re-read all of your previous letters to me, I have come to the conclusion that what happened between us was the eternal classical story of Gil Blas and the Archbishop of Grenada. But I will proceed in order, starting first with the question of money. No one writes to me like that about money and everybody knows me as far as that is concerned. On August 22, I gave the editorial secretary (as I always do when paying out-of-town contributors) the sum due to you for the prologue. It was only after I received your letter yesterday that I learned from him that he had sent it out to you not on the 22nd but on the 28th. Mr. Putsykovich, our secretary, is an absolutely honorable man, although he may not always be punctual. He has promised to find the postal receipt tomorrow without fail. *The money has been sent* to you and, if you have not received it, I cannot explain why you have not nor am I under any obligation to do so. Nobody can ever say of me that I *held up* anyone's money. And after rereading all your letters now, as I was forced to do, I find that, in your anger, you just could not find anything better to begin with than with that money! And to do that to me of all people! All sorts of things might have made you angry with me, but I would never have expected that you would start that way.

You write:

"In my last letter, I believe I stated quite clearly that I did not wish to be treated like a schoolboy and to have my play spoiled on the pretext of editing it."

What is this last letter you speak of? The last letter I received from you dates from July 31, and it came along with your article "Blunders." There is nothing of the sort in that letter. And there was nothing said in that tone in your earlier letters either. Besides, I would never have tolerated being addressed in that tone. The tone of our correspondence has been quite different from that. I have no such letter and have never received anything of that description. Quite the contrary—look at this passage I found in your letter:

". . . that's one thing I cannot change! As for the rest—do as you think fit, much esteemed Fyodor Mikhailovich, only please take my observations into account. I trust myself to *your* editing and I won't argue and split hairs over what you rightfully decide!

"But, most seriously, I plead with you to spare all the final monologues!

"I am so reluctant to have them cut."

This is an exact quotation from your letter of July 27. And in none of your letters thereafter do you rescind your permission to edit your material. And if you go so far as to say ". . . I plead with you to spare all the final monologues"—that implies that you have consented to large cuts. So what is this you write me now?

In my letters I told you quite directly and openly what I thought should be changed; I told you that your writing was very uneven and, what's more, that your syntax was quite inadequate. Your characters philosophize too much, and often at the wrong time and without any connection with the plot. I made only a few minor changes in the prologue. I shortened the extraneous bit of philosophizing in the scene where, as soon as he enters, Gordeyev proceeds to hold forth to his fiancée about debauchery (I cut out only a few words there), and I also slightly changed the scene where she sits on his lap to make it a bit more natural and plausible. Moreover, wherever I could, I lightened the dialogue and made it sound more like people talking. You write that I *misrepresented you*. So let us invite four experts—two of your choice, two of mine—to judge the matter and decide: have I or have I not *misrepresented* you?

But all this is quite impossible now. How could I know in advance that you, who had entrusted me with editing your play *after all* I had so clearly and frankly told you about it, would pounce on me for the first minor correction? Had I known that, I would never, of course, have started publishing your play. Your letters had led me to believe that you were a quite different sort of person.

What do you mean by the phrase "on the pretext."— "I do not wish to have my play spoiled *on the pretext* of editing it." Does this imply that I *intentionally* distorted it, concealing the act under some *pretext*? I edited it as my conscience dictated, but you seem to suspect something. Otherwise, how is one to explain the phrase *on the pretext?* Do you believe, then, that I was out to harm you? And all that after what took place before! Who would ever believe anything like it! And you think that it is all right for you to write people such offensive letters? Is it possible that you discard people as soon as they do something that annoys you, like an old pair of boots, and that you can think so nastily of a man whom, the day before, you considered your friend? (I have your letters before me as I write this.)

You ask in the most tactless way why I haven't sent you back your play. Well, and why didn't you answer me yourself? I wrote you quite clearly, suggesting that you correct your play yourself, as follows: "I am not sending you the manuscript, assuming that you have another copy or the rough draft. But if you don't, let me know and I will send it to you." Why didn't you answer that? I waited and waited and seeing that no answer was forthcoming, I decided that you must have a copy. You could have sent me a simple postcard with two lines on it and I would have sent you your manuscript forthwith. And tell me, why would I *hold on* to your play against your wishes? I kept it pending your answer, simply because I was expecting the return to Petersburg of someone whose opinion I greatly value and who liked your first play. I wanted to ask him for his advice.

What do the sentences with words underlined mean, such as this:

["] I *entrusted* to you *the only* copy of the manuscript of *The Fall* and it is your obligation, as an honorable man, to return it to me![")

I don't understand that tone, and it puzzles me even now, coming from you. What do you mean by *entrust?* You just sent us a manuscript like anyone else, not knowing whether we would publish it or not. And why do you have to appeal to my *honor?* Why, I would like to know, would I be interested in holding on to your play? I obviously do not consider it such a precious thing, and I wrote you so in no uncertain terms. But even if it were that precious, I still would never have kept it after all the things I have had to bear because of it!

P.S. I have *every* wish for a full measure of success for your play (for instance, on the stage). This last wish [the letter breaks off here.]

---

95. Dmitry Dmitriyevich Kishensky was a little-known playwright. His drama *Bottoms Up* (Pit do dna) had been published in the *Citizen* earlier in 1873, and thereafter Kishensky sent Dostoyevsky long letters with projects for a series of articles on the nihilists. In July, he submitted his play *The Fall* (Padeniye), a lampoon of the younger generation; Dostoyevsky published the prologue in the *Citizen,* but apparently only after making some changes to soften the image it presented of the nihilists. Kishensky resented the changes; his letter to Dostoyevsky to which this is a reply begins, "I would like to ask you, if I may, to what I should attribute your new offhandedness with me (besides the corrections), which has resulted in my not receiving up to now either my play or the payment for the prologue."

Viktor Feofilovich Putsykovich (1843–1909), the editorial secretary of the *Citizen,* had been a writer. He succeeded Dostoyevsky as editor of the *Citizen* when Dostoyevsky resigned in 1874, and in 1877 he became its proprietor. From 1879 to 1881, he published and edited the journal *Russian Citizen* in Berlin. Dostoyevsky had a more or less friendly relationship with him but did not think very highly of his abilities.

The incident between Gil Blas and the archbishop of Grenada occurs in the novel *L'histoire de Gil Blas de Santillane* (The story of Gil Blas de Santillane, 4 vols., 1715–1735), by Alain René Lesage (1668–1747). The archbishop had demanded of his valet Gil Blas a candid opinion of his sermons, threatening to discharge him if he failed to warn his employer of any weakening of oratorical talent; but when Gil Blas did suggest, very tactfully, that a sermon the archbishop had delivered was a bit weaker than the preceding one, the archbishop promptly had him driven out of the house.

The person whose return to Petersburg Dostoyevsky was awaiting was probably Strakhov.

96. To M. N. Longinov
[Petersburg] November 11, 1873

Your Excellency, Mikhail Nikolayevich:

I assume that I am responsible for having inadvertently allowed *certain expressions* to slip into some article or other in a recent issue of the magazine *Citizen,* which is edited by me, expressions that could have been grounds for forbidding the sale of the magazine at the stalls. I sincerely regret that the employment of such expressions, due to an oversight on my part, was sufficient to cause the attribution to my publication of ideas that *run counter to its entire policy,* and I have the honor to most humbly request Your Excellency to consider the possibility of graciously interceding for us with the Minister of Internal Affairs to persuade him to allow us to resume the sale of our magazine in single issues at the stalls, inasmuch as the measure taken against us has severely affected us financially at the end of the year.

Please receive my assurances of respect and loyalty,

Your faithful servant,
Fyodor Dostoyevsky.

---

96. Mikhail Nikolayevich Longinov (1823–1875) was a literary historian. He had been a columnist for the *Contemporary* and several other magazines and had served as secretary of the Society of Friends of Russian Literature, earning a reputation as a liberal and an opponent of censorship. In the mid-1860s, however, his views underwent a radical change; from 1871 to 1875, he served as head of the Chief Administraton for Affairs of the Press, in which position he issued censorship regulations that were even more stringent than the previous ones.

The items in the *Citizen* that had provoked the censor's wrath were an editorial criticizing the government for not taking sufficiently vigorous action to cope with famines and two articles on education in which "a highly placed figure was shown in an unfavorable light." A couple of months after this letter, Dostoyevsky wrote to Orest Fyodorovich Miller (1833–1889), a professor of literature at Petersburg University and later coauthor, with Strakhov, of the first biography of Dostoyevsky, that he had been summoned to the censor's office and told that "although it is permissible to write and publish facts on the famine that have been released, it must be done without presenting them in any special light and without 'alarming' the public."

97.   To A. F. KONI
[Petersburg, middle of February 1874]

Dear Sir, Anatoly Fyodorovich:

Allow me to thank you from the bottom of my heart, in the first place, for rescinding the order for my detention and, in the second place, for your kind words about me in your letter to the much esteemed and most kind Mrs. Kulikova, which afforded me the opportunity and the great pleasure of becoming more closely acquainted with her.

But it is advisable that you should know more precisely when I will be in a position to fulfill my obligation. Just now, on top of everything else, I go out every day to take my treatment of compressed air. I expect, however, to finish the treatment by March. Thus, if it does not clash with anything you may have in mind, I think I will be perfectly (and no matter what happens) prepared to serve my sentence *at the very beginning of March.*

But if for any reason I must serve it before, I am certainly always *ready* to do so. As it is, I am extremely grateful that, owing to your efforts on my behalf, I have gained this respite of a few days, and I wish to thank you once again for that.

Please accept the assurance of my sincere and profound respect,

Your obedient servant,

Fyodor Dostoyevsky

---

97. Anatoly Fyodorovich Koni (1844–1926) was a jurist, criminologist, writer, orator, and artist. At the time of this letter, he was the prosecutor of the Petersburg Circuit Court, where a complaint had been lodged against Dostoyevsky for a news item published in the *Citizen* in May 1873. The item reported that soon after a Kirghiz deputy began a speech, the tsar interrupted him and said, "Ah, so you speak Russian!" Since Dostoyevsky had not received from the Minister of the Court the authorization required for the publication of any information touching upon "the emperor and all persons of the imperial family," he was sentenced to two days in prison. However, the sentence was repeatedly postponed, on this last occasion by virtue of Koni's intercession; Dostoyevsky finally served it on March 21 and 22, 1874.

When Dostoyevsky met Koni in connection with this affair, the two men were drawn to each other, and Dostoyevsky visited Koni frequently thereafter and learned a great deal from him about legal procedures, which he later used in *The Brothers Karamazov*.

Kulikova was the niece of the actress A. I. Shubert, with whom Dostoyevsky had been on very friendly terms in the 1850s and 1860s (see Letter 41 and the note to it).

98.   To V. P. Meshchersky

[Petersburg] March 1, 1874, 4 P.M.

My dear, most kind and much esteemed Prince,

For heaven's sake do not imagine that I am forever eager to get into a squabble with you and to oppose everything you suggest when it comes to the policy of the magazine. Just try to take into account the reasons that make me feel the way I do and why my personal opinion is what it is, and you will agree that I simply cannot refrain from expressing myself on something that concerns me very directly.

I am speaking of Polonsky's letter. I cannot make you out at all: you told me yourself that it was "so nicely written." And yet, it is a most offensive personal attack on you and the crudest *distortion* of your ideas, a distortion that may even be deliberate and not merely a product of the present-day vulgarity and stupidity with which people currently expound their cheap liberalism because they find personal profit in it (starting with that pig Turgenev and finishing with that thief Palm). Polonsky writes: "If you had written specifically about A, about B, about C, if you had pointed them out to us, named them, then, etc. . . . ." This, in my opinion, is a thoroughly dishonest device. Who could be such an out-and-out *informer* as to point out *every-one* by name? I, for instance, was dying to write about Olga Ivanovna [*sic*], who figured in that trial involving the Tambov stock forgery, to describe her *as a typical unconscious victim of the nihilist scum,* to portray fully and in the most revolting manner that slut who may never even have heard about nihilism and to point her out as a sign of our times. Nevertheless, I could not bring myself to expose her to the public's judgment. So how can he demand that you point out A and B (i.e., that you *inform on them to the government*) when, besides the disgrace they would be exposed to, they might, as a consequence of your exposure, lose their jobs and be subject to further persecution. It would be possible *to point out* A and B directly by name, but *only in the event that,* for instance, the authorities had already found them out, taken them to court, and convicted them, such as was the case with Kolosov in the trial I mentioned above. Such is the Jesuitic thinking inherent in Polonsky's objection. Everything is twisted and distorted in his argument. He makes three errors of logic in every two lines he writes, which, however, does not prevent him from adopting a triumphant tone. Yet you decide that it should be published.

Perhaps you might wish to answer in your "Letter from a Pretty Woman." That would suit me fine! There is nothing I would like better!

But you must agree, my dear Prince, that I could not tolerate publishing such a slanderous lampoon against us and our magazine and in *our own* magazine.

Therefore I find it necessary to remove myself completely from all further argument on the subject and, moreover, to make certain reservations. Please read these reservations, which I have written on the proofs. *I won't insist on every word in it.* I only hope that there is nothing in it that you will find disparaging to you as a writer. If you do, let me know and I will clear the point up. I cannot tell you how exasperated I was by Polonsky's cheap liberal objection.

I firmly shake your hand,

F. Dostoyevsky

P.S. I have just crossed out a part of my reservations. But now I would like you to tell Polonsky yourself that I do not want him to involve me in any way, in my capacity as editor, and that, if he does, I will give him a piece of my mind.

D.

---

98. In the issue of the *Citizen* for January 29, 1874, there appeared the first of a series of "Letters from a Pretty Woman" (Pisma khoroshenkoi zhenshchiny), signed by "Vera N." but actually written by Meshchersky. It purported to be the chatter of a

"pretty woman" who could afford to speak the truth just because she was pretty—and the truth she wanted to convey was that young people were being contaminated by "contemporary ideas" and were playing at being nihilists merely because it was the fashionable thing to do. In a second "letter," published on February 18, the blame was placed on the schools, both higher and lower, because they were staffed with teachers who were godless naysayers; instead of icons, the walls were covered with Darwin's monkeys. The March 4 *Citizen* published a response from Polonsky, who signed himself "Olits" and, in the same playful tone, disputed "Vera's" notions, pointing out, for example, that she had named no specific persons—"It would have been more convincing if you had ridiculed A, B, or C, or if your indignation had been provoked by some particular officer or some stupid *schoolboy* writing diatribes against the government. . . ." Meshchersky answered in a third "Letter from a Pretty Woman," in which he used some of the words of Dostoyevsky in this letter. Polonsky wrote a second reply, and the exchange then ended with a fourth "Letter from a Pretty Woman."

The "reservations" of which Dostoyevsky speaks were printed as a comment on this sentence in the second "letter": "Our generation is *nothing* and there is nothing else to say about it." The comment read: "The editorial board of this magazine cannot approve of the way our lady contributor puts it. . . . Nevertheless, we publish these letters verbatim because they are, after all, a sign of the times. Even if only a tenth of what they contain were true, it would still be quite horrible. And one-tenth *is* true."

Dostoyevsky calls Palm a "thief" because, in the preceding year, while employed as manager of the Poltava branch of the national bank, he had been indicted for embezzlement.

The Tambov stock forgery case involved a rather sordid group of people who were tried in the Petersburg Circuit Court (Koni was the prosecutor) for having printed counterfeit shares of the Tambov Railroad Company. One member of the group was an Olga Ivanova (not Ivanovna, as Dostoyevsky writes), who double-crossed other members of the group in both their sexual and their criminal activities.

99. To A. G. Dostoyevskaya
Petersburg, Thursday, June 6, 1874

My dear Anya,

Since saying good-bye to all of you, I have felt terribly depressed. This is now my second day at the Hotel Dagmar, which (as it turns out) is a real dump, and as I sit in my miserable room, I keep seeing you and the children in my mind's eye. Besides, the journey took a heavy toll on my nerves. But let me tell you everything in proper order.

I arrived in Petersburg yesterday, sleepy and quite broken by the trip and from dozing in a sitting position. I put up at the Dagmar because it was the first hotel that I came across near the station. As soon as I had had some of their horrible tea, I set off on my business. At the editorial office I learned that the Prince was still in Petersburg, and I also picked up 6 rubles from the sale of two copies of *The Idiot* (that's all they've sold). Then I went to the Mutual Credit Society, where Misha was waiting for me, and without my even *asking* him, he paid me back two pieces of gold. But it turned out that Mutual Credit would not secure a note for me because you have to be a member of the society for that. (By the way, Shevyakov glanced at me but didn't give me so much as a nod; I, of course, responded in kind.) But then Misha suggested we go at once to the Volga-Kama Bank and make arrangements there. The transaction was worked out *on the spot*, partly because the bookseller Nadein, who happened to be at the Volga-Kama Bank on his own business, recommended me to a certain bank official who, according to Nadein, "adores your work." I took out the loan in my own name. I have left a copy of the terms they gave me with Misha for safekeeping while I am abroad. I think it is quite safe and don't think you will be angry with me for having done it this way: the obligation is in my name, it was signed in the presence of witnesses, and I'll be able to get the copy back from Misha in time when I return from abroad. The note falls due September 5, i.e., three months from now; after the deduction for interest, I received 117 rubles 50 kopeks altogether. If you prefer, though, I'll write Misha and tell him to send the copy of the terms to you in Staraya Russa. But I personally see no need for it. Misha told me that he had seen the *announcement* placed by Korsh and Polyakov (although not bearing their signatures) in the *Petersburg Gazette* about the Ryazan *estate* being put on sale. Today (Thursday), it is in the *Voice*, too, get a copy and read it. The announcement is brief but pompous: potential buyers are invited to make inquiries either at Liteinaya Street (probably at Korsh's) or in Pavlovsk, Soldatskaya village, Tolmachev house.

Misha heard a strange rumor somewhere that Gubonin (he owns a share of the railway line) wants to buy it and that our relatives were offering him the whole 5000 desyatinas at 80 rubles per desyatina and that he seemed interested. This is probably just an empty rumor, but it would be really wonderful.

Nadein was terribly (beyond belief) ingratiating, almost to the point of adulation, I didn't quite know what to make of it. He made me a firm offer to publish a *complete edition of my works,* assuming the entire cost of publication against only 5% of the sales, and as soon as he has gotten that, the whole edition will belong to me. I didn't commit myself, promising only to give him my answer upon my return from abroad; I believe he was quite pleased that I hadn't rejected his offer outright. It's something really worth thinking about, but I'll leave the decision up to you. It seems to me (for several reasons) that the interest of the booksellers has been stimulated by Orest Miller's three articles about me in the *Week,* extremely favorable on the whole. But I'll come back to that later.

Then, I went to see the banker Viniken and was given a draft on Berlin (and not on Ems, because their bank has no correspondent there). I exchanged 450 rubles for 417 thalers plus a few groschen. I changed some of the remaining money into gold napoleons (15 of them) and kept the rest in Russian bills for traveling expenses. Then I went to Buntig and he replaced the springs. Then I went to Gubin's—he was out but I learned he would be back home in the evening. Then I went to Strakhov's and found Maikov there; he had come to town to attend the Wednesday (Committee) meeting. Maikov somehow seemed rather cool. I learned from Strakhov that Turgenev wants to spend the whole year in Russia to write a novel and that he has been boasting that he will describe "all the reactionaries" (i.e., including me). Good luck to him. However, I will have to pay him back his 50 rubles the first thing in the fall.

Then I had dinner at Wolf's and went back to Gubin's. This time, he was in. Gubin sounded rather hostile when he spoke of Polyakov. He said Polyakov had been to see him and he made him a copy of the court order. But (according to Gubin) Zayenchkovsky wants to appeal, on the advice of his attorney. But that, of course, is sheer nonsense. Gubin added that an IOU guaranteed by Zayenchkovsky would not be reliable. But he also said that Sokovnin was still willing to take the debt upon himself, in the form of an IOU endorsed by his wife. But he wants to see the court order first. According to Gubin, the whole matter should be settled at the notary's on Friday, i.e., tomorrow, although Gubin suspects that Matusevich (the bailiff) will refuse to produce the court order on the pretext that there is a law that says that, if a bailiff returns a court order, the legal claim is estopped. Gubin wants to settle everything somehow and he hopes that it will all be done on Friday. The result of all this is that I am not too clear about the whole thing, though I gather that he is not too happy over the negotiations with Zayenchkovsky. (Matusevich had already presented his claim and the court order to *both* of Stellovsky's trustees, though, and Gubin says that, any appeals notwithstanding, the proceedings for recovery will not be stopped.) I asked him to inform you if anything important happens; he has your address.

From Gubin's I went to Polyakov's. It was around 7 o'clock but I didn't find him in. As a matter of fact, nobody even answered the doorbell. The apartment was empty and a card tacked on the door indicated that Polyakov was in Pavlovsk (and gave his address). So I decided to stay in Petersburg for one more day, i.e., through Thursday, and in the evening I went to a reception at the Prince's, where among the other guests were Maikov and Strakhov. The Prince's leg is ailing and he is going to take a cure in Soden (an hour and a half away from Ems). They all were very pleased to see me. The Prince was extremely friendly. They all told me that I looked much better and someone even said that I had put on weight (although I was terribly sleepy and my clothes were all rumpled). The Prince took me aside and told me he didn't know what to do about the *Citizen*—he didn't have the money to continue publishing it and no one would lend him any. I am terribly afraid that if the magazine were to stop publication I might in some way be held responsible for refunds to subscribers (i.e., I'm not afraid that the Prince wouldn't pay up, but that, initially, there might be some sort of scandal and my name mentioned in that connection in the press). But, quite obviously, he is very eager to go on publishing the magazine. Putsykovich is convinced of it, i.e., that the *Citizen* will continue to come out a whole year yet.

The Prince and some relative of his (a great admirer of mine) upset me terribly by telling me that I should really go to Soden, not Ems, because Ems is in a deep valley in the mountains and is very rainy and damp. And I know that there is nothing worse for me than damp weather. They all urged me to go to see the famous Dr. Fryorikh while I am in Berlin and to ask his opinion. I am not sure I'll follow their advice.

But there's something I forgot to tell you: Before going to Polyakov's, I went to see Bretzel, who gave me a brief note to a Dr. Ort in Ems. And then, without my asking him, Bretzel suddenly declared that if I saw that Ems was not doing me any good, I should move to Soden, which is quite similar. So this Soden, which keeps popping up on all sides, is perplexing, and I suppose I really should stop in and see Fryorikh. But since Koshlakov *firmly* advised me to take the treatment at Ems, I am *definitely* going to Ems now, despite all this talk, and once I'm there, I'll decide, and even then, not before I have spent two or three weeks there.

Bretzel asked me about your health and he *emphasized* that, while you are in Staraya Russa, you should drink the mineral water Schwalbach Weinbrun (there is also Schwalbach Stahlbrun—but it is too strong for you). I don't think I have mixed up the names. According to Bretzel, it can do you no harm *whatever*, while it could do you a lot of good. I asked him *to write you* immediately and prescribe to you the manner in which you should take it. And here is my own advice to you, Anya, which I beg you to heed: consult Schenck immediately, and, if he thinks Schwalbach can be of the slightest use to you, send Bretzel 10 rubles at once and *he will see to it himself* (as we have agreed) that 20 half-bottles of the mineral water are sent to you from Stoll and Schmidt (that will cost 7 rubles, according to their price list, plus 3 rubles for sending it). Now, even assuming that you start the cure after June 20, you will still have ample time to reap the maximum benefits from it. In 20 days (drinking a half-bottle a day), you'll see whether it's worth continuing and, if it is, after you've finished about 15 half-bottles, send Bretzel another 10 rubles and he'll have another 20 half-bottles sent out to you. And when you've drunk 40 half-bottles, you can consider the cure completed. Bretzel swears that it will do you a lot of good. So don't stint yourself a miserable 20 rubles, darling; you'll feel better! If, however,

Schenck advises you against it (I don't expect he will), simply write Bretzel and tell him that you were able to find the mineral water in a pharmacy in Staraya Russa (Bretzel, in fact, said he thought you could) and that you will follow his advice and drink it.

But there is one thing I ask of you: If you do decide to follow the treatment and do, in fact, find the water at the pharmacy, do not buy it there because I am afraid you might make a mistake and get yourself the *wrong* Schwalbach. I'd rather Bretzel had it sent to you. Please, my angel, don't tarry and consult Schenck (it is high time to call him in, anyway, to have a look at Fedya). Don't try to save those 20 rubles. Health is more precious than anything.

I went to see Kashpirev today. His leg is again in a cast. Dr. Cadet has promised him that he will be able to walk by winter, although with a limp. In a week, they are moving to their summer place near Gatchina. He said that he was going there on doctor's orders. I didn't see Sofya Sergeyevna, she was not at home. He thanked me for having come to see him. He looked very miserable. I had dinner with Strakhov at Wolf's, after which I stopped over at Bazunov's (he is likewise going abroad, on Sunday). I *explicitly* asked them to send you the June and July issues of *Russian Messenger*. (I am taking the May issue with me.) They promised they would.

Then (at seven o'clock) I drove over to Polyakov's place and once again no one answered the bell. He may not have received your letter yet. I was very annoyed, because if it hadn't been for that appointment (which had been set for between 6 and 8), I might very well have gone straight to Pavlovsk. But then, I slept until 11 o'clock and then decided that if I went to Pavlovsk only to discover that he had already left for Petersburg, I would not have time to see him in Petersburg, either. Perhaps he'll write you. If he does, write him that I went to see him (on the 5th and 6th). Don't fail to mention it.

Tomorrow morning I'll have to get up at 8 to do all the things I need to do. But now I feel terribly tired after writing you this letter. It is already eleven o'clock. I'll go to bed in an hour. My heart is heavy and I feel sad. I am thinking about all of you, of my sweet little Fedinka who made the sign of the cross over me, about my angel Lyubochka, and about you, Anya, my darling. In the name of God, take good care of them. I know that you love them. And treat Nanny with consideration. You might find another who might seem more efficient, but I doubt that she would love the child as this one does. She is a weak old woman, but she jumps out of bed in an instant every time Fedya so much as stirs in his cot. Don't be angry with me for writing you about these things. Why, you know very well how much I love you all. And I feel so miserable now, all by myself.

I hug you hard and I am expecting that there will be a letter from you when I get to Ems. I kiss Lyuba and Fedya and send them my blessings. Give my best regards to Aleksandr Karlovich, Anna Gavrilovna, Father Ivan, and everyone (and to Nanny and Praskovya too). Ah, my angel, I am so afraid something may happen to you all. So write to me.

Although the weather has been clear in Petersburg (except for today, when it is overcast), it is unseasonably cold. I am afraid that I may have to spend an extra day in Berlin, because I'll get there on Sunday and the bank will surely be closed.

So good-bye then, I kiss you hard, you yourself and all of you, one thousand times and I bless you all again.

Yours forever,
F. Dostoyevsky.

I am afraid the train journey will tire me terribly, unless I am lucky and can get a whole seat to myself and sleep on the way. Don't forget that Schwalbach. Tell the children I'll bring them back sweets and toys.

---

99. The Dostoyevskys had again rented a house in Staraya Russa for the summer. However, Dostoyevsky left for Petersburg on his way to Ems, where he was to receive treatment for his emphysema.

Dostoyevsky had published a new edition of *The Idiot* himself in 1874; the copies were kept at the offices of the *Citizen*.

Misha (Mikhail Mikhailovich), Dostoyevsky's nephew, was an employee of the Mutual Credit Society.

Vladimir Shevyakov was the second husband of Dostoyevsky's sister Aleksandra. Dostoyevsky had quarreled with both of them over the inheritance from their Aunt Kumanina, who had died in 1871, leaving an estate in Ryazan Province; part of the estate was a forest of 5,000 desyatinas (13,500 acres). Fyodor Adamovich Korsh (b. 1852) and Boris Borisovich Polyakov were Petersburg lawyers who were helping Dostoyevsky in connection with the inheritance. (Korsh later became a theatrical agent and playwright and founded the Korsh Theater in Moscow.) P. I. Gubonin was a railroad magnate and cofounder of the Baku Petroleum Society.

Mitrofan Petrovich Nadein (1839–1916) was a populist and the proprietor of the "Bookstore for Out-of-Towners" in Petersburg.

Miller had published not three but two articles about Dostoyevsky; they were part of a series of public lectures he had delivered entitled "Russian Literature after Gogol." They were indeed quite laudatory.

Bunting (not Buntig, as Dostoyevsky writes) was a dentist, and the springs referred to were in the dental plate that Dostoyevsky wore.

Vasily Ivanovich Gubin, a lawyer and a member of the Petersburg Slàv Philanthropic Society, had previously helped Dostoyevsky negotiate with magazine publishers and in other ways had been involved in his financial affairs. Now, together with Polyakov, Zayenchkovsky, and Sokovnin, he was helping Dostoyevsky in the protracted litigation with Stellovsky over the latter's publication in 1870 of *Crime and Punishment*.

Mavriky Osipovich Wolf (1825–1883) was a leading publisher and bookseller.

Dostoyevsky had resigned as editor of the *Citizen* in April 1874, ostensibly because of poor health but actually because he was in constant disagreement with Prince Meshchersky, its publisher. The magazine continued to be published until 1878 and then resumed publication in 1888 with a subsidy from Tsar Alexander III.

The doctor whose name Dostoyevsky transliterates as "Fryorikh" was Theodor Frerichs (1819–1885), a professor at the medical school of the University of Berlin and a specialist in lung diseases. Dr. Dmitry Ivanovich Koshlakov (1836–1891) was a professor of internal medicine at the Military Academy Medical School. Bretzel was the Dostoyevskys' family doctor in Petersburg. Schenck was a Petersburg doctor who spent the summer tending sick soldiers in Staraya Russa.

Sofya Sergeyevna was Kashpirev's wife and the editor of a children's magazine.

Aleksandr Karlovich Gribbe was the owner of the house in Staraya Russa that the Dostoyevskys had rented; Anna Gavrilovna was his wife. Father Ivan (Ioann) Rumyantsev (d. 1904) was the priest of St. George's Church in Staraya Russa and the owner of the house that the Dostoyevskys had rented the previous year.

100. To A. G. Dostoyevskaya
Ems, Wednesday [June 12/24, 1874]

So here I am in Ems now, my sweet darling Anya, I arrived here yesterday around noon but I was so tired from the journey and from rushing around in Ems that I was absolutely in no state to write you last night (as I had intended); my head was spinning and there was a ringing in my ears. I left Petersburg on a cold and rainy Friday morning. I got to Eydtkuhnen feeling quite fresh as I had managed to sleep four hours or so during the night and was even able to stretch myself out. In Eydtkuhnen it was even colder than in Petersburg and it continued that way until Berlin, where it was so cold on the day I arrived that I seriously considered putting on my quilted topcoat. On the 2nd night on the train I hardly slept at all. I had many interesting and amusing adventures on the way, which I'll tell you all about when I see you again.

I arrived in Berlin on Sunday and the office of the Mendelsohn bank on which I had a draft from Viliken [*sic*] was closed. The doctors do not receive on Sundays either, and so I had a day of unbearable boredom ahead of me. However, instead of going to bed (the train arrived at 7 A.M.) I went to the Royal Museum to look at Kaulbach's work. I find nothing in it except cold allegory. But the other paintings, the old masters of various schools, are not bad and it is a shame we didn't visit the museum on our first trip here. But, God, what a dull, horrible town Berlin is! I am bored and I miss you all incredibly. I kept looking at Lyubochka's photograph, glancing at it two or three times and then trying to visualize her.

On Sunday, the Germans were all out in the streets and in their Sunday best, they are a gross and unrefined people. In a pastry shop, a young man advised me to drive out to the Krol Theater behind the Tiergarten, where there is an amusement park and an opera house. They were actually giving *Fidelio* and I would have loved to go, but by the time I got home I felt so tired that I just fell into bed and went to sleep. In the morning, I stopped in at Mendelsohn's and then I went on to Frerichs. This luminary of German science lives in a palace (I mean it literally). While I was waiting in the reception room I asked another patient how much one paid Frerichs, and he told me that there was no fixed fee but that he himself paid 5 thalers. I decided that I would give him three. He spends three minutes with each patient, or at most five. He saw me for literally just 2 minutes and simply touched my chest with his stethoscope. Then he uttered one single word: "Ems," and sat down and, without saying a thing, wrote 2 lines on a scrap of paper: "Here's the address of a doctor in Ems. Tell him Frerichs sent you." I put down three thalers and left: I might just as well not have gone to see him at all.

That day the stores were finally open and I went out to buy a shawl for Anna Gavrilovna. It was no easy matter. I searched and searched from one shop to another. In Berlin there are shops galore, and merchandise galore, but it took me a long time to find anything—either they couldn't understand what I wanted or they deliberately showed me something else. Finally, in one store, they gave me the address of another store and there, although they didn't carry shawls either, they sent someone out to get some and I finally bought one. I think it is very beautiful and the material may be even better than yours, because the color is *blacker*, indeed, it is as black as it is possible to be, whereas yours has a rusty tinge to it. They assured me that the quality of the color is very highly valued. It is the same size as yours, without any embroidery but with a simple fringe (they all come that way). They asked 22 thalers for it. I bargained, made for the door, but finally they agreed to let me have it for 19. They had another shawl that they were offering for 18, but it was not the same black. I made up my mind to take the first one then, despairing of finding anything else. When I told them I had bought an embroidered shawl (yours) for less than that, they asked me how long ago it was, and when I said it was five years ago, they burst out laughing: "Since then," they told me, "the prices of almost all these goods have gone up by some 25 *percent*." Since Anna Gavrilovna gave me 14 silver rubles, which, at the current rate of exchange, represents about 16 thalers, that means I spent an extra 3 or at most 3½ rubles. I think, my sweet Anya, that we can make her a present of the difference (she is so fond of you and the children), and I don't suppose you will be angry with me for this. So from now on I'll be carrying this shawl around in my suitcase wherever I go, because to send it to Russia by mail is simply out of the question—it would cost too much—and so I'll bring it home myself.

After that I bought myself a lot of cigarettes and as there was still plenty of time for me to go to the Krol Theater, I drove out there. The day was clear. The amusement park is an unspeakable horror, but it is teeming with people and the Germans stroll around there with obvious delight. The 10-groschen entrance fee also covered admission to the theater, but only to standing room in the gallery. The theater is a huge, dark auditorium that can hold up to 1000 spectators; the stage is ten yards wide and there is a 12-man orchestra (not bad at all). And you can imagine what they were giving—*Robert*. I stayed through half the 1st act and then fled from those horrible German singers, going directly to my hotel because it was time for me to get ready to go. Finally, we left for Ems at 10 P.M. Here, the nights are dark, like in winter. That night I didn't sleep a wink, for we were packed like herrings in a barrel, but when the sun began to rise—ah, Anya, my sweet, I saw a sight such as I had never seen in my life before! Switzerland, the Wartburg (remember?), is nothing compared to the last half of the journey to Ems. This is like the most enchanting, delicate, fantastic landscape in a fairy-tale world: hills, mountains, castles, cities like Marburg and Limburg with their lovely towers in a wonderful setting of mountains and valleys. I had never seen anything like it, and it lasted all the way to Ems, which we reached on a warm, sunlit morning.

Ems itself is a town completely different from any other. Yesterday the weather was delightful. The little town lies in a deep valley between tall hills about two hundred sazhen or more in height and covered with forest. The town nestles against cliffs (the most picturesque in the world) and is actually nothing more than the two banks of the rather narrow river, there being no room for the town to expand any further, squeezed as it is between the mountains. There are promenades and gardens—it is a lovely place in every way. I love the location, although people tell me that when it rains or there is simply a cloudy day, the whole thing changes so drastically and the atmosphere becomes so gloomy and depressing that it fills a perfectly healthy man with melancholy.

One thing, though, that does not impress me very favorably here is the accommodations. The prices, the prices—it's terrible! All our plans and calculations of how I would take myself a private apartment in Ems turn out to be quite impossible, because *there just aren't any private apartments*. About 5 years ago Ems was just another town, but now that it has suddenly become famous and people have started coming here from all over Europe, every landlord has had enough sense to transform his house into a *hotel*. And so, today, all that is available are two kinds of hotels: the real hotels—there are about 10 of these—and literally all the remaining houses that are now called *Privat-Hotels*. They offer the same type of rooms, the same kind of maid service, and almost all of them even have dining rooms. The smallest house has as many as 20 rooms. I put up at the Hôtel de Flandre, which is near the railway station, and for 25 groschen they gave me a little room that I can't turn around in; it lacks the most indispensable furniture (no clothes closet, not even a chest of drawers), and they pointed to three nails in the wall on which, they said, I could hang my clothes. And the chambermaid is horrible.

I went out at once to look for an apartment and I inquired at 15 houses or so. The prices are the same everywhere, although for 25 groschen (that is the lowest price for a room) or a thaler, I was shown rooms slightly larger and more comfortable than mine, but still very small and, above all, in places packed with lodgers who sing and who bang doors, and I'm figuring on writing a novel! The table d'hôte in all hotels and restaurants is served at one P.M., because everybody gets up at 6 A.M. so as to be at the spa by 7; it closes at 8:30, when they turn off the water and do not serve any after that.

At 4 o'clock, without having eaten lunch, I went to see the doctor to find out, at least, how many weeks he was going to prescribe for my stay in Ems. I went to see Dr. Ort (recommended by Bretzel) and not Gutentag (the one recommended by Frerichs), and I gave Ort the letter from Bretzel. Ort also has a magnificent place and he also has a crowd of patients. He read Bretzel's note, examined me very thoroughly, and declared that I have a catarrh that is *not chronic,* and nothing else, that there is nothing even remotely suggestive of consumption, but that my complaint is quite serious, because without treatment, I would find it increasingly difficult to breathe, that besides the general disorder of my system (stomach upsets, bouts of fever, etc.), the back part of my chest is in bad shape, and when I told him that I didn't feel any-thing particular there, he persisted in his opinion but said that the trip had *certainly* aggravated my condition and that in a few days there might be some improvement there, he guaranteed the success of the treatment, but he prescribed the water, not from the Krenchen springs, as Koshlakov had sug-gested, but from another spring, the Kesselbrunen, because, he explained, I have a predisposition for diarrhea, as Bretzel had written him. And now, I am furious with myself for having forgotten to tell him that I am more prone to constipation than to diarrhea and I am afraid that it may be a mistake for me to take the Kesselbrunen cure. I will go back to see him in 5 days or so and have a talk with him. He prescribed a diet for me—I am to eat more acid things and use vinegar (for instance, with lettuce) and also eat meat with fat. Moreover, he advised me to drink red wine, either French or the local wine from the Ems area. From tomorrow morning on, I'll start getting up at 6 o'clock and going out to drink the water (two glasses a day). The local wine is horribly sour and costs 20 groschen a bottle! As for the French wine, it is quite beyond my means—a thaler for a bottle of Médoc that costs 50 kopeks at Feik's in Petersburg.

Then I started looking around for places to dine and found that in the big hotels (the Roussicher Hof and the Englysch-Hotel), besides the table d'hôte at one o'clock, they serve diners a part for a thaler and 10 groschen, i.e., 40 groschen. I ordered myelf such a dinner and it consisted of perhaps ten courses, well prepared, 5 of which were meat dishes, so that I got tired of eating and sent half the dinner back. For the table d'hôte, they charge only 25 groschen, but you do get less for it. There is no other kind of dinner you can get in Ems. You can buy separate courses anywhere, but then they charge you about 15 groschen per course! I finally decided to rent an apartment in a house. The landlady is an old woman in spectacles, with a husband, polite, but a shrewd old lady. There is a maidservant. She has 26 rooms in her house. They showed me two apartments to choose from—one a beautiful, comfortably furnished, large room with a balcony at 14 thalers a week, the other a 2-room apartment, much smaller, but also very comfortably furnished; one of the rooms is quite light but the other, the bedroom, is considerably darker, because, although it does have two windows, it faces a blank wall about 2 arshins away. She was asking 14 thalers a week for that, too. I bargained strenuously and got her down to 12 thalers a week. On top of that, she agreed to make me coffee, dinner, *a snack* at suppertime—all for one and a half thalers a day. All told, it will come to 22½ thalers *per week*.

I forgot to tell you (the main thing) that Ort has scheduled my treatment not for 6 but only for 4 weeks. Therefore, although the money is going awfully fast, there will be enough. In the evening I moved from the hotel to my landlady's. *In case you may need it,* here is the address of the house—*Haus Blücher,* No. 7 (i.e., I am staying in No. 7—the number refers to the room, not to the house), but I want you always to write me poste restante, because, who knows, I might move out of there.

A concluding word about Ems—there are lots of people here from all over the world, it's all elegance and glamor but, still, one-third of its rooms are not occupied. And the stores are lousy. I wanted to buy a hat, and I found only one shop with merchandise that was even as good as what you'd find in the secondhand shops at home. And it's all displayed with great pride, the prices are unimaginable, and the merchants turn up their snouts at you.

Anya, my angel, write as often as possible to me, your poor husband. I may not get a letter from you until the day after tomorrow, and you have no idea how anxious I am to hear about the children. My nerves are frayed (from the journey) and last night when I found myself alone I almost felt like crying. I think of my little angels Lyuba and Fedya and I worry lest anything should happen to them. So look after them, my sweet, and write me frankly about everything. If only I could be sure that you won't fall sick or something! Last night I kept twitching very violently (I have dreamed about you three nights in a row already). Farewell, I hug you hard and I kiss and bless my little angels. I'll get up tomorrow morning at 6 o'clock and go and drink the water, which means that I'll have to get to bed at 10 in the evening. When will I be able to write my novel—during the day, when the sun is shining brightly and gives everyone the urge to go out walking and the streets are bustling with activity. If only I could so much as start work on the novel and get something down on paper. Getting started is half the battle. I see now that I will have to return home much sooner than I had planned. I'll write more about that in my next letter. I'll write you three or four days after I get your letter. My regards to everyone, including Nanny. I kiss you a thousand times and I love you infinitely. Imagine, the night before last, I dreamed about you in Berlin in the following situation: we had just gotten married and I was taking you abroad; I was terribly in love with you; but it seems that Lyuba and Fedya already existed, but they were away somewhere and we were talking about them.

Good-bye. Your,

Dostoyevsky.

---

100. Ems, or Bad Ems, is a health resort southeast of Koblenz. Eydtkuhnen was a railroad junction on the border between Lithuania and East Prussia. It is now within the Soviet borders and is known as Chernyshevskoye.

Wilhelm von Kaulbach (1805–1874) was a popular German painter of the time. It is likely that Dostoyevsky saw his two best-known paintings, *The Battle of the Huns* and *The Destruction of Jerusalem.*

The two operas that Dostoyevsky mentions are *Fidelio,* by Beethoven, and *Robert le Diable,* by Meyerbeer.

The *sazhen* and *arshin* are old Russian measures, equivalent to about seven feet and twenty-eight inches respectively.

The novel that Dostoyevsky mentions is *A Raw Youth,* which he had contracted with Nekrasov for publication in *Notes of the Fatherland* before leaving for Ems.

101. TO A. G. DOSTOYEVSKAYA
[Ems] Monday, July 8/20, 1874

My dear, sweet friend, Anya.

I got your letter today, and although I won't be able to send this off in today's mail, I'll nevertheless make a start on it. First, let me thank you for writing more often, that's wonderful of you. It used to be so painful waiting for your letters before. When I sent you my last letter (I believe it was on Wednesday), I was very sad to read what you wrote about your health though glad to know that Schenck had taken you off mineral water for the time being. After all, if Schwalbach has such a bad effect on you, it makes sense to give it up. But I gather from your letter that Schenck wants you to give it up only temporarily and then begin it again—so I wonder if he doesn't see signs that the water is having an effect? Possibly your state of depression and irritation is due solely to the action of the waters? Here, Krenchen has exactly the same effect on me and although I am still bored and depressed, as if I were in penal servitude, I am no longer as irritable as I was only a short while ago. And I could tell you about many other effects upon my organism if I wanted to! My fever completely disappeared on the very day after I sent you my last letter, and I no longer sweat at all, even though the heat here is terrible. The fact that my fever vanished without my using any medicines leads me to believe that it was simply due to the effect of the waters rather than to a cold.

You also write me, my darling Anya, my dear wife, about other attacks. I know what you mean, because I have had similar experiences: At first violent desires; then suddenly it all went away and I was turned into a mummy; and then it started again, although weakly, but nevertheless with nocturnal consequences, which is very bad because it does, after all, affect the chest. As for the cure itself, I seem to feel better, touch wood: I breathe more easily, have hardly any hoarseness or shortness of breath, and, for the third morning in a row, I have coughed very little on waking up. The bad thing, however, is that I do catch colds now and then: Whenever there's the slightest draft that blows on my sweaty chest, I catch a cold and keep coughing throughout the evening and the following day (seldom longer than that, these colds seem to pass quickly). Now (according to the doctor's latest decision) I still have another 9 or 10 days of the treatment. I wonder how it will work out? Will it really all heal? But even if I should stay here until August 1 (New Style), then that will make only four weeks on Krenchen altogether (the fifth week I was on Kesselbrunen, which I don't suppose can be taken into account). And Koshlakov said six weeks! The two most important factors now are, first, to complete the cure, and second, not to overdo it.

Besides, I am so fed up with this place that I sometimes feel I would rather leave without completing my cure. I have heard some patients even say that it is quite impossible to be completely cured here with one visit, even if the effect of the waters is very substantial. They say that the main thing is the 2nd time, i.e., if you return the following summer for a 2nd course of treatment—then, they say, the sickness will be completely eradicated. But it's not that easy! No matter what they think, the very prospect of such an ordeal is chilling.

Ah, Anya, how I hate everything here. What a despicable lot, these Germans! But the Russians here are maybe even worse than the Germans. Every two weeks practically the whole population of Ems changes. No more than 1/3 of the old population stays on, while the others leave, and you suddenly become aware of a whole new set of faces. I can't even begin to tell you, Anya, how repulsive are the faces you see around here now: earlier in the season, there were still a number of people who were here from the time of the visit of the emperors, but what you see now is God knows what. I try hard to avoid making people's acquaintance, although there are some people here (mainly Russians) who are doing everything to get themselves introduced to me. And on top of everything else, Ems is a damned expensive little town. I am paying a lot to live here, and the fact of the matter is that every German looks upon you as a source of income and they have no qualms about adding things to your bill that you never ordered, just hoping that you won't bother to check it! But I'll tell you about all these petty details later, although I wonder whether there will be any point in raking over all this filth at another time.

Tuesday July 21

Your stories about the children, Anka, my love, simply give me a new lease on life and make me feel as if I were there with you. I enjoyed Lilya's "kind people" tremendously. I read your letter in the garden as soon as I got it from the post office: I chose a secluded bench where I could read undisturbed and suddenly I burst out laughing, taking even myself by surprise. But you know, there is a great flaw in the way we are bringing up our children—they have no acquaintances of *their own,* i.e., friends and companions, i.e., little children like themselves. I must also admit that, although you do keep me informed, I am nevertheless terribly worried about the children. Why did Schenck find Fedya's fever alarming? Does he think it might be something serious? Anyhow, I'll soon be seeing you all again. It wouldn't be a bad idea for us to write more often now, if for no other reason than to agree beforehand on the time we can stop our correspondence. I expect I'll leave here around August 1, but who knows, Ort may very well decide to keep me here until August 7. Although there is a noticeable improvement in my health, progress is rather slow. It is true that there are still 9 or even 10 days to go until the first of the month, but I'm somehow dubious that the cure will be complete by that time because just today, for example, my cough has been worse since the morning, owing to the dampness in the air and the drop in the barometer, although it hasn't actually rained. I cannot really imagine that suddenly all my troubles are over, although there has been a definite improvement.

And then again, if I have to take a long cure, will my organism be able to withstand it? I have just heard the story here of a patient who took a treatment of 20 baths (I'm not taking any baths) and felt a great alleviation. Encouraged by this result, his doctor then prescribed another 10 baths, which had such a debilitating effect on the man that they nullified all the benefit of the previous treatment and the patient left sicker than when he arrived. Ort has made a special point of asking me (and he asks me every time) whether I have noticed any weakness, loss of strength. The last time I answered that I felt nothing of that sort, but I wonder if I was telling him the truth. For some time already I have been feeling constantly tired, although I eat, drink, sleep, and get around just as before. The waters here are very strong, and my guess is that Ort is careful not to disrupt my organism and thus lose all the previous benefits derived from the cure.

The other day I met Stackenschneider here; he is the prosecutor of the Kharkov Circuit Court. He just got married in Kharkov, in May, and is spending a couple of months abroad with his wife. (Just like us, remember, except that it wasn't just for two months.) He is a very simple and straightforward young man, not at all stupid. He came to see me and told me that they had been to Paris and that *they had spent practically all their money* there, and that they now had to keep a very close watch on what they spent so as to be able to get back home. But about 5 days ago, in Zurich, Switzerland, he felt a slight pain in the chest and went to see a famous medical authority, who examined him and, alarmed by what he saw, expressly ordered him to take immediate advantage of his stay abroad and take at least a two-week cure of Krenchen (they send many people here for only 2 weeks or as little as 10 days). They are now staying in a cramped apartment, although they do go to the best table d'hôte for dinner. She is 18 and is extremely pleasant to look at (*hautes couleurs*), very Russian, and they both curse the Germans terribly. I haven't been to see them and I'll see to it that when I pay them my return visit they will both be out. The thing is that I find it all so boring, every new face, every new acquaintance bores me. Confound it, Anya, I do have the right to consider myself above all these people, not, of course, from the standpoint of moral virtues (let God decide about that) but from that of intellectual development. Things that amuse them bore me, their thoughts are to me dull and puny, their tone is vulgar, their education nonexistent, their independence nil; and to make up for it, they are so pompous and behave so commonly. I am not speaking now about the Stackenschneiders, but about all the scum that has gathered here, both the Russians and the Germans.

Sometimes I am so irritable that, although I promise myself to keep my mouth shut, sometimes I cannot restrain myself. At the Krenchen spring, where they fill the glasses with water (you hand in your glass and they fill it for you behind a grating), the crowding is terrible. The ones who do the worst pushing and shoving are the women and—who would have thought it—the elderly Germans. People thrust out their glasses and strain forward with arm outstretched, shaking all over as they wait. Almost every day, I am unable to restrain myself and I hear myself lecturing one of those Germans: Mein Herr, man muss ruhig sein. Sie werden kriegen. Man wird nicht verzeihen. And (as I have learned) some of the Germans taking the waters now refer to me as "the bilious Russian." And the reason for that—can you imagine—is mainly that I don't permit people to spill water on me (as happened once) and above all that I won't allow the people standing behind me with their glasses to rest their hands on either my shoulder or my back. The Germans are so ill-bred (all of them) that if one of them is standing behind someone else in line, waiting for his turn, and since he's holding a glass in his hand and in his impatience keeps raising it to show that he is waiting, in order to take the weight off his arm, he will frequently rest his hand with the glass in it on the shoulder of the person standing in front of him, even if it happens to be a lady. Once, when a German tried to do that to me, I wouldn't let him and gave him a little lecture on his bad manners. The German flushed and replied that there was no room here for drawing-room manners. I said that if a man was well mannered, he'd always find enough room to behave properly. And that ended our argument. Ah, Anya, believe me, when you return home sometime before 9 o'clock, exhausted from a 1½-hour walk (after taking the waters) and are having a cup of the worst coffee in the world, which you nevertheless gulp down with tremendous appetite, and then remember one of those morning encounters, you just burst out laughing. But there are times when I get seriously upset: after all, you can't blame everything on the effect of the waters—there are some things which are in themselves terribly unsettling regardless of the effect of the waters.

Just the other day, to mention another incident, at a table d'hôte, I noticed that a large Russian family alongside me was trying to strike up an acquaintance with me. Well, so be it. I didn't say a word to them, but suddenly they all began to greet me like an acquaintance of theirs. The father (a frightfully fidgety fellow) tried to engage me in a conversation on literature. So the following day there was nothing else to do but move to the other end of the room, which must have indicated my feelings to them clearly enough, since the other place had been my regular one. But what do you think he did? He came over to talk to me in my new place. However, there are some decent people among the Russians.

I see, however, that I am writing you about a lot of trivialities. The main thing is that it is deadly boring here! I swear that before this I didn't know the true meaning of the word boredom. I will make the sign of the cross when I leave Ems! But, speaking of that, where will I go when I leave Ems? The doctors here, as a rule, like to see their patients spend at least a week in some place where they can get some fresh air after they have completed the treatment, like the Bavarian Tyrol or even Lake Como. But it looks as if my funds will be so depleted by that time that, although I'll have enough to see me through here, I won't be able to stop anywhere on the way home. I just won't have enough on hand for that.

Anka, my darling, my joy, the object of my dreams, I hug you very, very hard. Be healthier, be gayer (why don't you at least play preference, as you used to do last year?), and keep looking after the children. I kiss and bless our little ones. Remind them of me. Tell them that all I do is think of them. Good-bye, then. It has started to rain (when the temperature is 25 degrees) and although the post office is not far from here, I don't know how I'll get there. Once more, I hug you and I kiss you *all over, in a way you cannot even imagine yourself.*

My regards to Nanny and to all.

All yours,
F. Dostoyev.

I have grown very thin here, my whole body—*the effect of the waters.*

---

101. Both Kaiser Wilhelm I and Tsar Alexander II had been in Ems earlier that summer. (It was from here that the kaiser, four years before, had sent the famous "Ems dispatch" that provoked the Franco-Prussian War.)

Adrian Andreyevich Stackenschneider (b. 1843), a lawyer and magistrate, was the brother of Yelena Andreyevna Stackenschneider, a friend of Dostoyevsky's.

102.   To A. G. Dostoyevskaya
Staraya Russa, December 20, 1874

My dear Anya,

I got your sleepy little 10-line letter and was pleased to hear that you had at least reached your destination safely. The most important thing is your health. What sort of a time are you having? I am waiting for your return, not only with impatience, but also with curiosity. I hope you will have quite a few things to tell me when you get back. The children, thank God, are in excellent health, touch wood! They don't disturb me, I sleep late in the mornings. Today the weather is not too cold or windy, but it is rather damp and frosty. Nevertheless, I let them go out for a visit to the priest and gave them money for the sleigh. Lilya is awfully sweet and so is Fedya, although he has got a bit out of hand, he won't listen to Nanny and is mischievous. He sleeps very well at night and so does Lilichka. They are waiting for you to come back and yesterday they both declared that they love you very much. Yesterday at dinner time, the priest (Georgiyevsky) dropped in and sat for an hour, after which we went to the post office together.

Alas, none of the booksellers has given a sign of life yet. It looks as if *House of the Dead* will be a flop, unless eventually sales start gradually coming in from libraries and a few fans. They don't seem to appreciate us too highly, Anya. Yesterday, I read in the *Citizen* (and you may have heard about it yourself) that Lev Tolstoy has sold his 40-sheet novel to the *Russian Mes-*

403

senger, which will start running it in January, and that he is getting *five hundred* rubles per sheet, i.e., 20,000 rubles in all. And to think that they were hesitant when it came to giving me 250 rubles, while they are only too eager to pay 500 to L. Tolstoy! They underrate me a bit too much, I can tell you, and that is because I have to live off my work.

Now Nekrasov might very well put the squeeze on me if he finds something in my work that clashes with the policy of the magazine: He realizes that R[ussian] *Messenger* won't buy my novel now (i.e., for the coming year) because *Russian Messenger* has a surfeit of novels. But even if it meant that we had to go out begging in the street, I wouldn't change one single line to conform to their policy! Doesn't Polyakov have any news about that business of ours? If only we could get some money quickly so that we could weather any *emergency* that might arise! If not, we may find ourselves like crawfish in the shallows.

There is still no information from Nekrasov.

Good-bye, Anya, I embrace you. You won't get this letter before the 22nd and, who knows, you may already have left by that time. So this will be my *last* letter to you—for if I wrote you one tomorrow, there's scarcely any chance that it would reach you in time. So bear that in mind and don't start worrying. There's no need for you to worry about the children, either—I am looking after them and it isn't any special hardship for me. Please don't lose my letters or leave them behind where you are stopping in Petersburg, because I wouldn't want strangers to read them. Give my regards to Mikhail and [*sic*] Nikolayevich and also to your brother, if this letter gets to you in time. How is Anna Nikolavna? Did she leave with Iv[an] Grigorevich? Give her my regards too.

Good-bye. Look after your health in Petersburg. The newspapers are full of reports about the outbreak of typhus. For God's sake be careful.

We are all yours,

I, Lilya and Fedya,
F. Dostoyevsky.

I was just at the post office and there was no letter from you. What can have happened? Now I will be miserable all night!

---

102. Dostoyevsky had returned to Russia early in August. He and his family had stayed on in Staraya Russa, but at the time of this letter Anna Grigorevna had gone to Petersburg in connection with the publication of a new edition of *Notes from the House of the Dead.* In February 1875, after she had returned, Dostoyevsky went to Petersburg for a couple of weeks both to attend to business matters and to take "compressed air" treatments for his lung ailment.

The novel of Tolstoy's that began appearing in 1875 was *Anna Karenina.* In comparison with the 500 rubles per printer's sheet that he was paid, Dostoyevsky received 150 rubles per sheet for *Crime and Punishment*, *The Idiot*, and *The Devils*, 250 for *A Raw Youth*, and 300 for *The Brothers Karamazov*.

Mikhail Nikolayevich Snitkin was Anna Grigorevna's cousin, at whose house she stayed while in Petersburg.

There was a typhus epidemic in Petersburg during the winter of 1874–1875; as many as 2,000 new cases a day were being reported.

103.   To A. G. Dostoyevskaya
Ems, Tuesday, June 10/22, 1875

I got your short letter on Sunday, my dear Anechka, i.e., the one you wrote on Tuesday, June 3, and, as you indicated, at seven A.M. However, it didn't leave Staraya Russa on that day, but only on the next, for it bears the Staraya Russa postmark of June 4, and the reason is that they *deliberately* kept it at your post office for an extra day in order first to send off your previous letter (written on May 28) on June 3rd, after it had been lying around collecting dust at the post office for 5 days. If they had sent both letters at the same time, it would have been tantamount to a clear admission of their negligence. Please, go and give them a good piece of your mind, Anya, and tell them you want no nonsense.

What you write about your nerves and your irritability worries me a great deal. What will it all lead to? I am worrying about everything here, because my own nerves are terribly on edge. For God's sake, my sweet, don't be so pessimistic, it could be a thousand times worse, and, after all, we have lots to be thankful for, if only for our children. It gave me such pleasure to read what you wrote about them. But I keep worrying, and I think about them and all of you night and day: all is well now, but what if something were suddenly to happen? Some totally unforeseen event—that's what I am most afraid of.

In any case, we will soon be together again. I don't plan to stay here very long. And even if I don't manage to do any work on the novel, I still intend to return home as soon as possible. I am not sure that the treatment will do me any good this time. So far I can see no improvement at all, but then, today is only the tenth day of the treatment. I have even more phlegm than I had in Staraya Russa, and I can actually feel that the lesion is not healing. Besides, the climate here is quite harmful to the treatment. Since my last letter to you right up until today, it has not stopped pouring, and I'm not exaggerating. So how can a treatment be effective in such a damp place? I am forever having the sniffles. Dampness and, to add to that, boredom. I sometimes feel this boredom will drive me crazy or to some violent act! I am at the end of my rope. It is torture in the full meaning of that word, it is worse than being locked up in prison. If only I were writing, I would lose myself in my work. But I can't even do that because the plan hasn't crystallized and I foresee tremendous difficulties. I cannot go ahead until I have worked out the ideas, and besides, I have no inspiration in my present state of depression and that's crucial. I'm reading about *Elijah and Enoch* (it is superb) and Bessonov's *Our Century*. The lop-eared comments and explanations of Bessonov, who can't even express himself in Russian, make me furious on every page.

I am reading the Book of Job and it transports me into ecstasy. I put the book down and pace the room for as much as an hour. I almost weep. And if it were not for the vulgarity of the translator's comments, I might be quite happy. It is a strange thing, Anya, this book was one of the first things that impressed me in life, at a time when I was still almost a baby!

Except for that, I have no diversions here whatsoever. There is, of course, music twice a day at the spa, but even that is disappointing—they seldom play anything of real interest, it is usually some potpourri, or some sort of "March to the Glory of Germany," some Strauss, Offenbach, and finally, the Ems-pastillen polka, so that you just don't want to listen anymore. Besides, the crowd gets in the way, a dense crowd of five thousand people in a relatively constricted area, milling around and pushing each other, like chickens in a farmyard. And it is even worse on these rainy days, when all these wet people are squeezed against each other with their wet umbrellas under some shelter, and what makes it so bad is that everybody is there at once, because there are fixed times for taking the waters. And it is just at such moments that the orchestra plays the Ems-pastillen polka. I am subscribing to only two Russian newspapers. I have received the *Russian Messenger*—it is full of rubbish.

There are some Russians around, but not many and, as before, no one I know. From the Visitors' List I learned that Ilovaisky (the professor from Moscow) was here with his daughter. He is the Ilovaisky who presided at the meeting of the Friends of Russian Literature when they read the passage from *Anna Karenina* when she was traveling in the train—after which Ilovaisky loudly proclaimed (to the Friends) that we had no need for gloomy novels, even if they are written with talent (i.e., my novels), but rather we needed novels with a light and playful touch, like those of Count Tolstoy. I haven't met the fellow personally and I doubt that he can be too eager to make my acquaintance, and I, of course, have no intention of taking the first step.

I keep hoping that somebody else will show up, but by that time, God willing, I will be writing my novel and won't have any time to spare. Ah, I wonder what I will manage to write and whether I will manage to write anything at all. I am terribly distressed because I am all alone here. Although, back home in [Staraya] Russa, I was all alone in my room, I knew at least that the children were in the next room and I could, if I wished, go and talk to them, even if it was just to scold them for making too much noise—that was enough to invigorate me. But, above all, I knew that Anya, who is really the other half of me, was close by. And I see now that it is really impossible for me to be separated from her and that as time goes on, the more impossible it becomes.

Well, that is all I can tell you about myself. I changed my mind about moving and stayed at the Hotel Luzern. Here, by the way, is my address, in case you need it: Bad-Ems. Haus Luzern. Logement No. 10, a M-r Dostoewcky [sic]. (Keep writing to Poste restante as before, the address is just in case of an emergency.) I have come to realize more and more that my landlords are, after all, quite considerate people. There is less noise under my windows, and the landlords' children, a little girl and boy, aged 4 and 3, have grown fond of me and bring me flowers. The landlord and landlady (their name is Meuser) own the house and some land, but she does the cooking herself and makes coffee, while he is a schoolteacher and also gives private lessons.

My neighbors are out all day long and only come back to sleep. One of them is a very handsome German merchant from Berlin and the other a nineteen-year-old youth, a Frenchman, Monsieur Calopin, a very courteous young man. On the second floor, just below me, a German family occupies three rooms. The mother of the family, a rather stout German lady, is so absent-minded that occasionally she climbs up three or four flights of stairs instead of two and finds herself right at my door, which she throws open with a flourish and then stands there for three seconds or so, not knowing where she is. Then she screams: "Ah mein Gott!" and dashes off downstairs. That has happened twice so far—once in the morning and once in the evening.

But I must admit that I am just as absent-minded myself: just yesterday, instead of going to my hotel, the Luzern, I walked into the hotel next door, the Genz, took my key from the board, i.e., the key of room No. 10, climbed up to the 3rd floor, and started opening the door of room No. 10 (which is in exactly the same location as my room in the Luzern). At that moment, the landlady and the maid came running toward me and explained that I didn't live there, but next door at the Luzern. It was lucky that they recognized me as someone living next door at the Luzern, for otherwise they might very well have taken me for a thief.

Anya, my sweetie, write me every three days and don't spare the details. I wait for your letters like manna from heaven. Don't hold it against me, my angel, that I sound so blue in my letters: God willing, I'll get down to work and forget all about my depression. And then, I expect, my cure will also become more effective.

Today the sun is shining and it is warm.

I know that I won't be spared one source of gloom, and that is about you: I am constantly afraid that something may happen to you. I have become terribly soft these past 8 years at home, Anya; I cannot bear being separated from all of you for even a short time—that is the point I have reached. Anya, my sweetie, I keep thinking of what lies ahead, in both the near and distant future. Just one thing: if God grants us life, we should be able to make appropriate arrangements for the children.

Cheer up, then, my darling, try to get more fun out of life, get out, go for walks, chase away painful thoughts. Do you have a doctor? You absolutely must arrange for a doctor to come and see you regularly.

The news about Iv[an] Grigorevich is very characteristic. He is *unhappy* in the fullest sense of the word. The only thing I am afraid of is that he won't have enough patience. But he, like you, Anya, has a sense of duty, and, for the sake of the children, he will find the strength to bear it and refrain from doing anything too drastic. But he really should be stricter with her, in fact I feel he should get rid of her altogether.

I hug you and I bless all the children. Anya, if we have a daughter this time, why not call her Anna? Let there be a second Nyuta in the family! What do you say to that? I'm all for it.

Once again, I embrace you and everybody else.

All yours,

F. Dostoyevsky.

My regards to all.

I see you often in my dreams. However, I have started having nightmares, too (the effect of the waters). I am very much afraid that I'm going to have an attack, since I haven't had one for a very long time now. If I do have one, the chances are that I'll have another three or so in the course of a month, as is always the case following a long interruption. What will become of the novel then?

---

103. "Elijah and Enoch" is a reference to the Old Testament prophets. Dostoyevsky had apparently taken the Bible along with him because he needed it for the writing of *A Raw Youth,* on which he was still working.

Pyotr Andreyevich Bessonov (1828–1898) was a professor of Slavic languages and literature at Kharkov University and a specialist in folklore. He edited—with commentary blatantly slanted toward Slavophile views—a collection of folksongs gathered by Kireyevsky, of which volume 10 was published under the title *Our Century through Russian Historical Songs* (Nash vek v russkikh istoricheskikh pesnyakh, 1874).

The Society of the Friends of Russian Literature (Obshchestvo lyubitelei russkoi slovesnosti), founded in 1811, was a learned society affiliated with Moscow University; it published scholarly journals and books and organized ceremonies honoring Russian writers, including the dedication of the monument to Pushkin in 1880.

"The news about Ivan Grigorevich"—Anna Grigorevna's brother—was that he had apparently broken up with his wife in a dispute over an affair she was having with another man.

Anna Grigorevna was seven months pregnant at the time of this letter; "Nyuta" is short for "Anyuta," a diminutive of Anna. However, the child, born on August 10, was a boy, and the parents named him Aleksei (Alyosha). He died when he was less than three years old.

104.   TO A. G. DOSTOYEVSKAYA
Ems, Friday, June 13/25, 1875

My sweet darling Anya,

I received your dear little letter of Saturday (June 7) yesterday, Thursday, and I thank you for it. Above all, for the reassuring news that you have called in a doctor. That was something that had worried me a great deal. It was very painful to me to think that you wanted to keep *it* a secret at any price until the very last moment. I am also grateful to you for the children— for looking after them so well, for being pleased with them and for having shown them to the doctor.

But for all that, I get a letter only once every 4 days from you, whereas I myself write you every 3 days. I sent you my last letter on Tuesday. That day, a thick milky fog suddenly enveloped the whole of Ems; it was so opaque that it was impossible to make out anything 20 or 30 paces away, and it hung low overhead for twenty-four hours with the temperature at 20 degrees and without any breeze, so that it was suffocating and damp, and you had no idea what to wear—if you put on light clothes, you risked catching cold from the dampness; if you put on heavy clothes, you would sweat and catch cold that way, too. The fog had lasted for twenty-four hours, and then suddenly it began to rain. And since then, for the third day in a row, it has been pouring bucketfuls, and when I say *bucketfuls,* I mean just that. A thunderstorm like that, in our climate, would last for only $\frac{1}{4}$ hour. Here, without exaggeration, we've had three full days of torrential rains—and I'm supposed to go and drink the waters. All my clothes have got soaking wet. The ground here is stony and usually it dries almost immediately, as soon as the sun comes out, but after three days of rain everything is so drenched it feels as if you were walking in porridge and your feet and trousers get soaking wet. The umbrella offers no protection. And what good can the treatment be when I am continuously suffering from a cold—a light cold, perhaps, but a cold nevertheless, and I am coughing and sneezing. They predict, though, that the weather will clear up by this evening.

As far as my treatment goes, I still don't know what to say, because, despite the weather, there is some reason to believe that I may be getting some benefit from it. I am now taking the maximum dose—4 glasses in the morning and 2 in the afternoon. But I need not tell you how lonely I feel here and how shattered my nerves are. What torments me most of all is that my work is not progressing. All this time I have been sitting, racked with doubts, and I can't find the strength to begin. No, this is not the way to write works of artistic value, on command, under the threat of a stick; rather, one must have the time and the inclination. But now the time has come, I think, for me to get down to serious work, but what will come of it, I don't know. In the state of depression I am in, I could very well spoil the whole idea.

I am expecting an attack any day now, but it hasn't come yet. I also find it strange that I seem to have started to lose weight, which didn't happen to me last year, although it is obviously due to the effect of the waters. However, my appetite and digestion are good. Well, that's all there is to say about my health.

What I am principally concerned with is you. I am waiting to have your thoughts about the renting of the apartment. I don't expect to continue with the treatment here for very long, so I suppose the apartment should be rented early, i.e., probably during the 1st half of July. I am very anxious to get back to all of you as soon as possible because with you near me at least I won't be worrying so much about you and the children. And I will come back to life when I am with my family again. And above all, Anya, I will be able to keep an eye on you during the critical days; here, I live in constant fear that some accident may occur. At the same time, the thought of my novel and when I will write it drives me to distraction. I cannot afford to be late with it and, besides, we need the money. We'll manage somehow during the coming winter, something will develop, Anya. Everyone in the literary world, however, has positively turned his back on me; I will not run after them. Even the *Journal de St. Petersbourg,* which at first rather approved of *A Raw Youth,* seems to have received instructions from some quarter to roast it and now, in the last issue, they write that the ending of the 2nd part is quite dull and "il n'y a rien de saillant." Well, you may say anything about it you wish, you may even criticize it for being melodramatic, but the one thing you cannot say is that it is lackluster. Anyway, I realize that the novel is dead and that it will be buried with full honors amidst general scorn. But enough about that—time will tell and I am not the least bit discouraged about the future. Just you keep well, my helper, and we'll pull through somehow.

I am still completely alone, I don't know a soul here. Quite a number of Russians have arrived, but they are all aus Revel, aus Livland, with names like Storch or Borch, or with Russian-sounding names like Pashkov and Panchulidzev, etc. They are all completely unknown to me. But I have the strange impression that they know me. Earlier today, for instance, I addressed some gentleman at the spring, asking him the most insignificant question in German, and he straightway answered me in Russian, but I had no idea that he was a Russian. That shows that he knew about me, for, otherwise, God knows how he could have guessed that I was Russian. But in general I try to keep away from people. My life here is sickening and unbearable. The landlords make absolutely miserable coffee and abendbrod; but I order my dinner from another hotel (I have canceled the arrangement I had before) and it is twice as good as what I used to get from the Hotel Goedeke.

They sent me one issue of the *Citizen* but since then they seem to have gone on strike. There's no point in my writing to ask them to go on sending it to me.

I meet Kaiser Wilhelm at the spa quite often. He is a very simple and pleasant, handsome old man of 80, though he doesn't look more than 60. He wears elegant civilian clothes. One day, there was a tall thin woman of 30 or so sitting in the crowd with her glass, wearing a very ordinary black dress and a rumpled black shawl. All of a sudden, the Kaiser walked over to her as if she were an acquaintance and stayed there chatting with her for nearly a quarter of an hour. When he was taking his leave, he tipped his hat to her and gave her his hand, which the woman shook like the hand of any ordinary mortal, without curtsying or anything, as etiquette would demand. She turned out to be some duchess from a once very powerful family, and a very rich woman. However, in the crowd she looked like a plain woman, and our Russian society whores, who had probably been eyeing her in contempt until then, just stood there gaping.

Last night I dreamed about Fedya and Lilya and I am worried: perhaps something has happened to them! Ah, Anya, I think of them day and night. Suppose I should die now, what would I leave them? If only I could finish this accursed work I am stuck with now and get on to something else! But we will talk about all that when we meet again and, in the meantime, I must see to it that I cope with the task at hand. I kiss and I bless Fedya, Lilya and . . . but, Anya, what is this you write about *twins?* Ah, you! But actually, in that case, my kisses to the twins as well and Godspeed to them. As for you, I kiss you thirty-five times, as Fedya says. Write more often about yourself. As for me, I will keep you posted regularly every three days.

A million kisses to you and the children, all yours,

F. Dostoyevsky.

My regards to all who should get them.
Have you heard anything about Ivan Grigorevich?

---

104. When Dostoyevsky says, "Everyone in the literary world . . . has positively turned his back on me," he was probably referring to the fact that part 2 of *A Raw Youth* had gone largely unnoticed. The conservative magazines—*Moscow Gazette*, *Russian Messenger*, and *Citizen*—hadn't even mentioned it.

105. TO A. N. PLESHCHEYEV

Staraya Russa, August 21, 1875

Dear and much esteemed Aleksei Nikolayevich,

Forgive me for bothering you. I have sent off 3 chapters (there will be 5 altogether in the September issue) of part 3 of my novel. I don't know, is Nikolai Alekseyevich [Nekrasov] in Petersburg? I doubt that he is, and so I am writing to ask you, as an old friend, to do me a favor: couldn't you suggest in proper quarters that they send me the proofs here *as quickly as possible?* I expect to be in Petersburg around September 5. But it wouldn't do any harm if the proofs were sent to me now . . . And most important, couldn't you somehow see to it that no cuts are made. In my story, every character speaks his own language and expresses ideas that are peculiar to him. Moreover, the "Pilgrim" who speaks in "biblical" language does so very carefully and I myself have exercised censorship over every one of his words. In the name of God, Aleksei Nikolayevich, do whatever you can to help me out in this.

All yours,

F. Dostoyevsky

---

105. The "'Pilgrim' who speaks in 'biblical' language" is Makar Ivanovich Dolgoruky, the principal character in the opening chapters of part 3 of *A Raw Youth.* Dostoyevsky may have feared that Makar's sermon on meekness and humility would conflict with the viewpoint prevailing in *Notes of the Fatherland* and that the editors might therefore make some changes.

106. TO P. A. ISAYEV

Petersburg, January 7, 1876

Dearest Pavel Aleksandrovich,

I enclose the 30 rubles you asked me for. You give me such a detailed account of your illness that I assume you must have completely recovered by now. The Trishins told me that you were laid up for two weeks once in October as well. I wish you better luck and better health in the new year.

You write that you have written me two letters. I *did not get* either of them and I must admit to you that it seems incredible: why should all my letters reach me except the two from you?

I'll tell you, too, Pavel Aleksandrovich, that the money I am sending you is just about the last I have. I have finished my work and have been paid everything that was coming to me for it, and at the present moment I am almost without a kopek. I am not publishing any magazine; however, I would like to publish my work and, since I have no capital to pay for it, I am planning to put it out on a subscription basis. But I have only just announced the opening of subscriptions and it is quite uncertain whether I will be repaid not only for my own work but for the costs of publication as well.

So, in sending you 30 rubles, I am taking them away from my poor children. I know that I will die soon, and when they are left without me, there will *not be a single hand to offer them a kopek.* As it is, I am still continuing to pay the old debts incurred by the magazine and only a month ago I had to pay 1100 rubles to Yev[geny] Pechatkin for the paper he delivered to the magazine ten years ago under the terms of an agreement by which *I took upon myself what was really other people's responsibility.* For doing so, I have received nothing but kicks. Furthermore, I heard that in Moscow some people were reproaching me for "abandoning you and not helping you." Permit me to ask you whether I haven't helped you out with money and sometimes by going to see people for your sake who are not really worthy of receiving a visit from me, and who, because of you, treated me condescendingly? Haven't I dozens of times either recommended you personally or asked others to recommend you so that you could get a job? Is it my fault if you could never hold on to anything?

When your mother was dying, she said to me: "Don't abandon Pasha." Well, until now, I haven't abandoned you, but now you are almost 30 years old and I am not responsible for the circumstances in which you find yourself now. I feel I can no longer help you, since I have small children of my own who would be the innocent sufferers. That you should know.

I think something rather strange is happening to you: you warn me in advance that even if you receive the money you won't answer me anyway *because you are up to your ears in work.* But really, that's simply outrageous.

If you forgot to send your regards to my wife in your letter, the least you could do was send a kiss to my children. They are sick with scarlet fever at this moment and for a whole week Fedya has been near death.

Good-bye.

Yours sincerely,
F. Dostoyevsky

I knew that Mikh[ail] Mikhailovich intended to go to Moscow but I was not aware that he had already been there and come back. I kiss your children very affectionately.

---

106. The work to which Dostoyevsky had just announced the opening of subscriptions was *Diary of a Writer.*

107.   To V. S. Solovyov
[Petersburg] January 11, 1876

Dear and much respected Vsevolod Sergeyevich,

I am still in quarantine (although my children are getting better) and this is why I haven't been to see you all this time. I of course like your suggestion of placing before the public some information about *Diary of a Writer* (as you can readily understand), but there's nothing much I can tell you for the moment beyond giving you the most general idea. The first number will start with a very brief *preface,* and then there will be something about children—children in general, children with fathers, children without fathers, children and Christmas trees, children without Christmas trees, delinquent children . . . Of course, these won't be rigorous studies or reports, just some heartfelt words and remarks.

Then I'll write about *things I've heard and read*—everything or anything that has struck my imagination during the preceding month. *Diary of a Writer* undoubtedly will be somewhat like a feuilleton, with the difference that a monthly feuilleton naturally cannot be exactly the same as a weekly feuilleton. Its account of an event will not be as a news item so much as an effort to show what more enduring effect it (the event) will leave behind it, more related to a general trend. Finally, I have no intention whatsoever of confining myself to simple reportage. I am not a chronicler. What I have in mind is a *diary,* in the full sense of that word, i.e., an account of what has caught my personal interest, even if it is just a whim. I am uncertain myself, my good Vsevolod Sergeyevich, whether it will amount to much of anything; at times I feel that I shouldn't have gone into this venture. But anyway, it is all in God's hands, though, to tell the truth (and this is between us) I have hardly written a line yet! But I do have more than 4 printer's sheets worth of material and *notes* (for the 1st issue).

Thank you for wishing good health to the *Diary,* and I, for my part, wish the best of health to you and your family, and as far as your own articles are concerned, they are *healthy enough* as it is. I have been pleasantly struck by the penetration of some of them. (N.B. I'm not saying this in the least because you wrote about me, although I do thank you for that, too.)

All yours,
F. Dostoyevsky.

The *Voice* (Sunday, January 11) carried an announcement of the forthcoming publication of *The Historical Studies and Articles of K. P. Pobedonostsev.* This is something you really must mention. It is bound to be extremely significant, a major and original contribution. I am expecting a great deal from that book. His is a tremendous intelligence. It is coming out at the end of January.

Also at the end of January [the next installment of] *Anna Karenina* will appear in R[ussian] *Messenger.* So there you have something to write about—the forthcoming publication of these 3 things. As for *A Raw Youth,* it will come out on January 16th, according to the publisher Kekhribardzhi.

---

107. Vsevolod Sergeyevich Solovyov (1849–1912) was the son of the historian Sergei Mikhailovich Solovyov (see note to Letter 80) and the author of historical

novels. He shared many of Dostoyevsky's views and admired his work, and they had been friends and correspondents since 1872. He wrote a column on literary affairs for *Russian World*, and he did announce in it the forthcoming publication of *Diary of a Writer*.

Dostoyevsky's children were recovering from scarlet fever.

Konstantin Petrovich Pobedonostsev (1827–1907), a historian of law and judicial institutions, was the tutor to the future tsar Alexander III and subsequently became a figure of great influence in the government and the court. He was an opponent of Western rationalism and liberalism and of limitations on the powers of the tsar, and he was responsible for the policy of Russifying Jews and other minorities.

Dostoyevsky had signed a contract late in 1875 with the publisher P. Ye. Kekhribardzhi for a separate edition of *A Raw Youth*.

108.   To A. M. DOSTOYEVSKY
Petersburg, March 10, 1876

My dear and much respected brother, Andrei Mikhailovich,

I am sending you my book, which has been rather sloppily produced by the bookseller Kekhribardzhi. He printed it, announced it in the newspapers, stored the edition somewhere and didn't put it on the market for 2 months—all of which certainly didn't help the book. Of myself, I can tell you that I am working terribly hard and that I took upon myself something quite beyond my strength. I am publishing the *Diary of a Writer;* the subscription is not large, but individual copies are selling quite well (all over Russia). I am printing 6,000 copies altogether and all of them are sold, so that I suppose I can say it is doing well. Anna Grigorevna helps me out, but her health has been so undermined (especially by the nursing of the children) that I have become seriously worried about her.

I see your children from time to time. I would like to tell you, my dear brother, that it gladdens my heart when I look at your family. It would seem that, of us all, you are the only one to whom it has been given to continue our family line honorably: the members of your branch of the family are exemplary in their behavior and well educated, and the sight of your children gives one a feeling of joy. At least your family does not give the usual impression of mediocrity, and all its members have the noble bearing of the *best* people. Bear in mind and treasure the thought, brother Andrei Mikhailovich, that the aspiration to be counted among the *best people* (in the literal, loftiest sense of that word) was the fundamental idea of our father and our mother, despite certain lapses from it. And you, more than any other Dostoyevsky, have realized that idea in the family you have founded. I repeat, that's the impression your whole family has made upon me. The family of our brother Misha has slipped a great deal and is quite lowly and uneducated. And my own family is so young that I cannot yet tell what will come of it. I would so much like to remain alive for, say, another 7 years or so, to give them some security and to put them on their own feet. Yes, it would be pleasant to me to think that my children would remember what I looked like after I am dead.

I wish you all conceivable happiness and I shake and kiss your wife's hand. Remember me to your children, too. Mine are well again. I am taking good care of them. What a nice little girl the Rykachovs have! We paid them a visit and it was a pleasure to look at them. Your daughter came to see me a few days ago. I myself had a bout of fever and this is the 5th day that I've stayed at home, taking quinine, and everything is going well. Anna Grigorevna sends you all her warmest regards,

And, in the meantime, I remain all yours,

F. Dostoyevsky

---

108. Kekhribardzhi's edition of *A Raw Youth* was indeed sloppily printed, with many typographical errors, which in some instances altered the meaning of the text.

Dostoyevsky's critical remarks about Mikhail Mikhailovich's family may reflect his poor relations with Mikhail's widow especially. Actually, one of Mikhail's sons, Fyodor, was a musician and later became director of the Saratov School of Music; a daughter, Mariya, married the philosopher M. I. Vladislavlev; and another daughter, Katerina, married Professor V. A. Manasein, founding editor of the journal *Physician* (Vrach).

109.   To KH. D. ALCHEVSKAYA

Petersburg, April 9, 1876

Highly esteemed Khristina Danilovna!

Please forgive me for not having answered you right away. When I received your letter of March 9, I was already in the midst of work. Although I am usually finished with it by about the 25th of the month, there are still all sorts of chores I have to do in connection with the printing, mailing, and so on. Besides, I was in bed with a cold this month and haven't quite recovered from it even now.

Your letter gave me great pleasure, especially the chapters from your diary which you enclosed; they are delightful, but I have come to the conclusion that you are one of those who have the gift of "seeing only the *good side* of things." It is true that I know nothing about the children's home run by Mrs. Chertkovaya (though I'll find out about it at the first opportunity); I'm sure that everything there is just as you describe it, but at the same time there may be some drawbacks *that you preferred to take no notice of.* All this reveals your nature and I have an immense respect for you, precisely because of that trait of yours.

I also see that you yourself belong to the new type of individual (in the good sense)—an active person who wants to get things done. I am very pleased to have made your acquaintance, even if only through correspondence. I don't know where the doctors will send me this summer; I suppose it will be to Ems, where I have been the last two years, or it might be to Yessentuki in the Caucasus, in which case I may make a detour and stop over in Kharkov on my way back. I have been wanting to visit our southern provinces, which I've never seen, for a long time. Then, if God is willing and if you are prepared to do me the honor, we will meet personally.

You write that you have the impression that I risk "turning my capital into small change" in the *Diary*. Well, I have heard the same thought expressed by others here. But let me tell you this, *among other things:* I have come to the incontrovertible conclusion that a creative writer must have, besides his poetic vision, a thorough knowledge (historical background, as well as the current facts) of the *reality* he is trying to portray. In my view, among the Russians, only Count Lev Tolstoy fulfills this condition in a superlative way. Victor Hugo, whom I rate very highly as a novelist (the late F. Tyutchev even grew angry with me once because of this and said that my *Crime and Punishment* was a better novel than *Les misérables*), although he goes to unnecessary lengths at times in describing certain details, has made some amazing studies of things that, without him, would have remained unknown to the world. And that is why, in preparation for a very long novel I've decided to write, I felt it would be worthwhile to devote myself to a special study—not of reality in the strict sense, because I was already acquainted with that, but a study of specific aspects of current development. As I see it, one of the most important of contemporary problems is, for instance, the younger generation as well as the contemporary Russian family, which, I suspect, is very different from what it was only twenty years ago.

But there is much besides that. It is easy for a man of 53 to fall behind the new generation if he doesn't watch his step. The other day I met Goncharov and, when I asked him quite candidly whether he understood all aspects of life as it is today, he replied bluntly that there was much he has "ceased to understand." Of course, I am very well aware that, with his *immense intelligence,* he is not only capable of understanding but could even teach the teachers. But obviously, when it came to the particular meaning of my question (and he understood me before I had finished asking it), it was not that he was incapable of understanding it, rather that he preferred not to understand it. "My ideals are dear to me, as are the things I have come to appreciate so much in life," he added. "And it is with them that I want to spend the few years I have left to live; it would be tiresome for me to study these people"—he gestured toward the passing crowd on Nevsky Prospect—"because I feel I would be wasting my precious time on them." I don't know whether I've made myself clear, Khristina Danilovna, but I am somehow still attracted by the idea of writing something about which I have the fullest knowledge; and that is why, for a certain time, I intend to combine my research with the publication of *Diary of a Writer* so as not squander a multitude of impressions.

All this, of course, is an ideal! Would you believe, for instance, that I still do not have a clear conception of the form the *Diary* should have, and I am not sure that I'll ever find a suitable form, so that the *Diary* might continue for another two years, or it could be a failure. I have, for instance, something like 10–15 themes (not less than that) whenever I sit down to write. But the themes that I like best I reluctantly put aside for later, because they would take up too much space and generate too much heat (the Kroneberg affair, for instance), the issue would suffer because, with just a few articles it would lack variety. And so I end up writing on things other than those I would have liked to write about.

On the other hand, I was rather naive in thinking that this could be a *genuine* diary. A genuine diary is a virtual impossibility; mine is only a semblance, for public consumption. I come across facts and gather many impressions that intrigue me, but how can I write about them? Sometimes it is plainly impossible. For example, for three months now I have been receiving a great number of letters from all over, signed and anonymous, all of them sympathetic. Some of these letters are quite extraordinary and highly original and they represent every conceivable shade of *opinion* in existence today. I would like to write an article on this *widest possible* range of opinions, which merge into a general salutation to me—specifically, about the impression left by these letters (without mentioning any names) and also about a thought that has more and more preoccupied me: "where is our *common ground*, which are the points on which we, people of different opinions, can all agree?" But after having given that article a lot of thought, I suddenly realized that I could not write it *with absolute sincerity*. And if there were no sincerity, would there be any point in writing it at all? Besides, it would lack intensity.

Two days ago, in the morning, two girls about 20 years old suddenly came in to see me unheralded and said: "We have wanted to meet you ever since Lent. People laughed at us and assured us that you wouldn't receive us and that, even if you did, you wouldn't tell us anything. But we thought we would try anyway and so we've come, Miss So-and-so and Miss So-and-so." My wife received them at first and then I went out to them. They told us that they were students at the Academy of Medicine, that there were as many as 500 women there already, and that they had entered the Academy "to get a higher education and be useful to society later." I had never met this type of new girl before (although I know a great many of the old *nihilist women* from personal acquaintance and have made a thorough study of them). Believe me, I have seldom spent a more pleasurable time than the two hours in the company of these two girls. What simplicity, what naturalness, what freshness of feeling, what purity of heart and mind—the most *genuine concern* and the most sincere gaiety!

Through them, I have of course met many others like them and I must say that they have made a strong and glowing impression on me. But how would I put it into words? With all the sincerity and enthusiasm I feel for young people, I wouldn't know how to describe it. It's all so subjective. And this being the case, what then are the impressions I could set down? Yesterday I learned to my surprise that a young man who is still a student (exactly where, I cannot say) and who had once been pointed out to me, while visiting the house of friends, chanced to step into the room of the family's private tutor and, seeing a *forbidden book* on his desk, reported this to the head of the household, who dismissed the tutor on the spot. When, sometime later, the young man was in the house of other acquaintances, and someone pointed out to him that he had *acted despicably,* he just *did not understand.* So there you have the other side of the coin. But how should I handle it? It is both an individual case and, at the same time, not simply that. What is particularly characteristic here, as people have told me, is a way of thinking and a mentality that resulted in the fact that *he did not understand,* and something interesting could be said about that.

But I have got carried away and, besides, I am very bad at writing letters. Please forgive my handwriting—I have the grippe, a headache, and today I have a speck in my eye, so I can hardly see the letters as I write. Allow me to shake your hand and do me the honor of considering me as one who has a profound respect for you. Please accept my assurances to this effect,

Your servant,

F. Dostoyevsky.

---

109. Khristina Danilovna Alchevskaya (1843–1918) was an important figure in public education. She was principal of the Kharkov Sunday School and introduced a number of innovations, including the publication *What People Should Read* (Chto chitat narodu), which carried annotated lists of books for the general reader and became extremely popular. She had earlier written an enthusiastic letter to Dostoyevsky, inspired by the first issue of *Diary of a Writer,* which devoted much attention to children. With the letter to which this is a response, she enclosed a passage from her own diary, telling of a visit to the children's home that had been founded in 1871 by the wealthy philanthropist Ye. I. Chertkovaya, in which some forty children were fed and clothed free and were taught to read.

Although Dostoyevsky writes that he is "a man of 53," he was actually 54; he often made a mistake about the date of his birth.

Dostoyevsky did in fact devote considerable space to the Kroneberg affair in the *Diary of a Writer* for February 1876. It was a widely discussed case, recently tried in St. Petersburg, in which a man had been accused of flogging his seven-year-old daughter but had been acquitted by the jury; Dostoyevsky held it to be a monstrous miscarriage of justice, for which he blamed the subtly deceitful arguments of the defense lawyer, V. D. Spasovich (see Letter 86).

110.   To V. A. ALEKSEYEV
[Petersburg, June 7, 1876]

Dear Sir:

Forgive me for not answering your letter of June 3 until today, but I have not been well as the result of an epileptic attack.

You pose a complex question, so much so that it requires a long answer. The matter in itself is quite clear. There are three colossal, universal ideas blended together in the devil's Temptation of Christ; and now 18 centuries have gone by and there is nothing more difficult, i.e., more complex, than these ideas, and they have not been worked out even yet.

"Stones and bread" means the social question of the day, a question of *environment*. There is no prophecy here, it has always been this way. "Rather than going to the downtrodden beggars, who, suffering from starvation and oppression, look more like wild beasts than human beings, rather than going to the hungry and preaching abstention from sins and humility and chastity—would it not be better to *feed* them first? That would be more humane. Others before You have come to preach, but You are the Son of God, the whole world has been waiting for You with impatience; act then, as One superior to all in intelligence and justice, give them all food, *sustain* them, give them a social organization that will ensure them bread and order forevermore—and only then, ask them to account for their sins. Then, if they will sin, they will be ungrateful, but now, if they sin they do so out of hunger. It is a sin to call them to account.

"You are the Son of God and are therefore omnipotent. Here, you see these stones, they are legion. You have only to will it and the stones shall be turned into loaves of bread.

"Order things, then, so that henceforth the earth will produce without toil, give people the wisdom or show them the order that will guarantee their welfare. Surely you do not doubt that the vices and miseries that afflict man have come from cold, hunger, and poverty and from the impossible struggle for existence.["]

This is the first idea that the spirit of evil held up to Christ. You must agree that it is one that is quite difficult to deal with. Contemporary *socialism*, both in Europe and here at home, eliminates Christ from everything and is concerned, above all, with *bread*, it calls in science and asserts that the sole cause of all human miseries is *poverty*, the struggle for existence, the "corrupting environment."

To that Christ answered, "Man does not live by bread alone"—i.e., he gave expression to the axiom that man is spiritual in origin. The idea of the devil could apply only to man as a beast. But Christ knew that bread alone does not bring life to man. And if, beside bread, man is not possessed of a spiritual life, an ideal of Beauty, he will languish and die, go insane, kill himself, or abandon himself to pagan fantasies. And since Christ carried the ideal of Beauty in Himself and in His Word, He decided that it was better to inculcate in the soul of man the ideal of Beauty; bearing it in their souls, all men would become brothers and then, of course, they would work for one another and would all be rich. Whereas, if they are given bread, they will become enemies to one another out of sheer boredom.

But what if they are given both Beauty and Bread at the same time? Then man would be deprived of *labor,* of *individuality,* of the opportunity to *sacrifice his goods for the sake of his neighbor*—in a word, he would be deprived of life as such, the ideal of life. And therefore, it is best to do only one thing: to proclaim the spiritual ideal.

The proof that this is precisely the meaning of that short passage in the Gospels, and not merely that Christ was hungry and the Devil advised him to pick up a stone and will that it become bread—the proof lies precisely in Christ's answer, revealing the mystery of human nature: "Man does not live by bread alone (i.e., merely as an animal)."

If the question had been simply one of satisfying Christ's hunger, would there have been any reason to broach the subject of man's spiritual nature in general? Besides, Christ did not have to wait for the Devil's advice on how to obtain bread. He could have obtained it before if He had chosen to. By the way, remember Darwin's and other contemporary theories about man's descent from the ape. Without going into any theories, Christ declares directly that, besides belonging to the animal world, man also belongs to the spiritual world. Well then, it does not really matter what man's origins are (the Bible does not explain how God molded him out of clay or carved him out of a stone), but it does say that *God breathed life into him* (but what is bad is that by sinning man can once again turn into a beast).

Your obedient servant,
F. Dostoyevsky

Pisareva studied and rubbed elbows with today's youth, who have no interest in religion and dream of socialism, i.e., of a world order in which there will be bread above all and the bread will be distributed equally and there will be no private property. According to my observations, these very socialists, awaiting a social order in which there will be no individual responsibility, meanwhile love money tremendously and attach even excessive value to it, precisely because of the idea they have of it.

---

110. V. A. Alekseyev (1828–1884) was a soloist in the Marinsky Theater orchestra. His letter to Dostoyevsky was provoked by the discussion, in the May 1876

issue of *Diary of a Writer,* of the suicide of a midwife named Pisareva. In her suicide note, Pisareva had left detailed instructions concerning the small sum of money she was leaving behind, and Dostoyevsky was struck by the fact that in her last moments she could devote so much attention to money. He saw in this "the last echo of the main prejudice of the entire life of today's youth, who dream of 'stones being turned into bread.'" Alekseyev recognized the biblical phrase and had written Dostoyevsky to ask what he meant by its use.

111. To P. P. Pototsky
[Petersburg, Tuesday, June 10, 1876]

You write that I attack a certain narrow circle of women of that type. You are mistaken: I am not attacking anyone and when I spoke of Pisareva I didn't at all say [an illegible word] as you imagine. You are also mistaken when you say it is a "narrow circle"—it is a wide one, and the further things go the wider it grows.

It embraces all those persons who are looking for something above the average and outside the daily routine, who want to lead a *spiritual* life and participate in the affairs of mankind, who are prepared to act and to serve others. But when they leave their homes, they fall among groups of people who assure them that there is no such thing as a spiritual life, that spiritual life is a fairy tale and not something real; and that there is no such thing as generosity, either, but only the struggle for existence.

Pisareva asked, then: "What am I to do?" "Be a midwife," they answered her. "At least that way you'll be useful to society." She believed them and studied to become a midwife. They were long years of study, without any spiritual food whatever. She would have liked to find out about things, to broaden her horizons, her mind, to acquire some education—but, instead of that, without any sort of education they pushed her directly into a difficult trade. Being a person with a heart, there was no doubt that she would over-exert herself and wear herself out. "I would like to see the beauty of mankind and of the world, and show my own generosity," she thought to herself sometimes—but meanwhile, everywhere there was only the struggle for existence! Finally she is struck by an idea: they had told her that there was no such thing as generosity and that, if she wished to be useful, she should become a midwife. But if there's no generosity, *there is no need to be useful, either.* Useful to whom, anyway? And complete disillusionment follows.

You write that I should search out the underlying reasons and stop attacking these women. I repeat—I am not attacking them; and, as to the reasons—I have just pointed them out to you. I will add one more: the lack of education, the inadequate upbringing in the family from early childhood, and for all the generous impulses one might have, a sore lack of intellectual development [several lines missing] there was no incentive [an illegible word].

I don't know how old you are. There are many things in your letter that I don't understand at all. There is nothing that surprises me very much, I simply regret it.

But I have some advice for you: be careful about alluding too superficially to a case such as Pisareva's. You would do better to give it a lot of thought and then perhaps you would understand that if you tell a person that there is no such thing as generosity but only the elemental struggle for existence (egoism), it amounts to depriving a person of individuality and *freedom*. And those are things that a human being will always renounce with difficulty and in despair. On the whole, though, I like what you wrote me. The only thing I would advise you (and I have the right to do so) is that you write more legibly.

I am leaving Petersburg today for a month, and that, of course, will bring an end to our correspondence.

Your well-wisher,
Dostoyevsky.

---

111. Pavel Platonovich Pototsky was a cadet at the Mikhailov Artillery Academy. His letter, too, was occasioned by Dostoyevsky's reference to Pisareva's suicide in *Diary of a Writer*. "Listen," he had written, "why should you attack Pisareva like that? Why should you be so sorry for her? . . . is this state of mind really so surprising in some women at the present time? Do you find that there is a wide circle of such women . . .? In that case, why don't you direct your barbs at the causes rather than at the consequences?"

112.   To A. G. DOSTOYEVSKAYA
Berlin, Wednesday, July 7/19 [1876]

My dear friend Anechka,

I got to Berlin this morning at six-thirty and stopped at the Britisch-Hotel Unter den Linden. But I wonder where you are at this moment—probably still in Novgorod? I was terribly worried about you throughout the trip, Anya. Mainly because, all these last days, you had hardly any sleep and were rushing around and doing enough work for four, and now you again have the moving to do. I won't cease worrying now until I get a letter from you (and when will that be?), and that will spoil everything for me, as I know from experience, despite the diversions during the trip and the fuss that goes with it.

For my part, I had quite a comfortable and uneventful journey, and I managed to get some sleep during the forty-eight hours in the train. It wasn't very roomy, though, in either the Russian or the German train, on the contrary, it was packed, but the people were quite bearable. It was only as we were nearing Eydtkuhnen that a Yid attached himself to me. He had

423

boarded the train in Vilnius and was, so to say, a Yid of the upper class, rich, with two sons in Petersburg—one a doctor, the other a lawyer. He kept spitting outrageously and without let-up in the compartment, discharging whole pools of spittle. While indulging in this charming habit, he installed himself in front of me and proceeded to tell me at tremendous length that he was on his way to Karlsbad to undergo treatment for his hemorrhoids, explaining what kind of hemorrhoids he was suffering from, when exactly it had healed over and what his lumps were like, and so on and so forth, and I was forced to listen to all that just out of politeness, but there was no way I could escape, and so he went on tormenting me for about four hours.

In Eydtkuhnen I changed 100 rubles and they promptly gave me 265 marks plus some change, whereas in Petersburg I was lucky to get 262 marks. I was very sorry that the rest of my money was stowed away and that I couldn't convert it all into marks then and there. Then the train left. My companions now were all Germans, very polite and friendly people, all of them merchants and all talking constantly of money and interest, and though I just cannot imagine who they thought I was, they all looked after me and treated me with great consideration. It was they who made it possible for me to get some sleep by arranging the cushions of the seat so as to make me comfortable, etc. One of them, a young German from Petersburg, kept telling the rest of them that his papa did business in Petersburg, that he is received in the high society of the capital, that he had been on a bear-hunting party with the highest society, and he kept imitating the way a bear gets up on its hind legs and roars, how he himself fired at the beast and wounded it, and how the wounded bear ran off, ran to the railway tracks and ran alongside a train that was streaking toward Moscow, and died only after covering more than 7 versts. This German Khlestakov looked highly respectable and apparently spoke with competence about the geschefts and interest, for the rest of the Germans (and one of them in particular) were, it seems, experts in these matters and very solid people. But in both the Russian and the German trains, the only things they talked about were geschefts and interest, the prices of articles and merchandise, the happy materialistic life with camellias and officers, and never about anything else. No culture, no loftier preoccupations—nothing! I have absolutely no idea who there is today still capable of reading anything and how it is possible that the *Diary of a Writer* is still bought by several thousand people. Nevertheless, these Germans are a considerate and friendly people, so long as they don't try our patience too hard, and then, of course, it is impossible not to scold them.

In Bromberg, at one A.M., the conductor announced that we were stopping for 8 minutes. Since this was a Schnellzug, 8 minutes means three. I rushed to you know where for one minute and had just managed to find it when I heard two bells, started rushing back (it seemed awfully far), and then I suddenly heard the conductor slamming the car doors closed. I ran with all my strength and made it, but I could not find my car as I could not read its number—163—in the darkness. The conductor had already moved on further, a whistle blew, and they were about to leave. Suddenly I hear someone calling out of an open window, about two cars away: "Pst, pst, hier, hier!" Must be someone of our crowd, I thought, they had seen me and they were calling me. I ran over and looked: a German stuck his head out of the window—a complete stranger. Nevertheless, I cried out: "Ist das hier?" He answered: "Was hier." What the hell! I decided to run further along, but the German shouted: "Hören sie, hören sie, was suchen sie?" "A, der Teufel mein wagen! 163, ist das hier?" "O, nein das ist nicht hier . . ."—So why were you calling me, you blockhead! And then the train started to move, and then, lo and behold, there comes my car! I opened the door on the fly, my friends gave me a hand and I managed to jump in; otherwise, I would have been left behind. This is the second time in my life that this has happened to me on that line. Do you remember when we asked a German in Dresden where the Gemälde-Galerie was?

Then an extremely rich and respectable-looking German started vomiting and he vomited all the way to Berlin. Out of the window, it goes without saying. All of us, six people, tried to be helpful and everyone offered some advice. One suggested that he should drink as much beer *as possible,* and so, at the first stop he leaped out and filled himself with beer. It didn't help. I advised him to try some brandy. "Brandy!" the man cried out, "that is just what I was thinking myself!" He jumped out at the next stop and had a drink. The advice continued and reached the point where someone recommended that he eat a piece of marzipan (from Eydtkuhnen on, it is sold at the stations) and he ate a piece. Finally, the German Khlestakov suggested he try champagne, but by that time we were already getting close to Berlin and the fellow said that, as soon as he got to his hotel in Berlin, he would certainly order some champagne. During the night it started to rain and we entered boring Berlin in a drenching rain, which is still continuing. Nevertheless, I must go to the post office because I don't know how much postage to put on the letter. I'm leaving for Ems at 10 o'clock tonight.

My darling Anya, kiss the sweet children and especially Lyoshenka. I feel especially sorry for him. I am so sad not to be able to walk around Berlin for a bit but instead have to stay in the hotel. I see that I should have bought a knee rug because the nights are cold. Don't forget to send me Prokhorovna's address and let me know what you have decided about the overcoat. Please forgive me, my darling, for all the inconveniences I caused you. I am sorry about the 500 rubles I am spending for the Ems trip. The only thing that consoles me is that the 500 rubles may bring me 5000 if I get my health back. My sweet one, I am so longing to kiss you. Kiss Lilya and Fedya, Lilya especially and Fedya, too. Speak to them of me, and to Fedya a bit more. I will miss you all so much. I hope you'll take it easy now and get your strength back, my angel.

I kiss you many times, as many times *as on the eve of my departure.* Remember me.

I am all yours and the children's,
F. Dostoyevsky.

P.S. Write about everything, including the details and the trifles. I won't write again until the day after tomorrow, when I will already have seen Ort and have managed to rent an apartment. Your,

Dost.

---

112. Anna Grigorevna had gone to Petersburg both to attend to some publishing business and to see Dostoyevsky off to Ems, and he presumed that she had stopped in Novgorod on her way back to Staraya Russa.

113. To A. G. Dostoyevskaya
Ems, Thursday, July 15/27, 1876

My dear friend Anya,

I got your 2nd letter yesterday, the tiny note of July 9, and, without waiting for the time we agreed on, I hasten to answer you. The fact is that your letter left a painful impression on me. I see that it won't be an easy thing for you to get your health back, but why do you say that you'll have to take only 15 baths? But maybe the menstruation won't last 10 days and, with a change of air and different living conditions, it will revert to normal. And besides, even if it lasts for 10 days, that would still leave you a good month for the baths. Are you taking them only every other day? Can't you take them every day? Ah, my angel, it is my fervent wish that, after this year of childbirth, nursing, and work on the *Diary,* your health will finally be restored in [Staraya] Russa. Ah, my love, my heart aches for you. I have been thinking here about how you worked and suffered—and what reward do you get for it? If only we could have gotten more money out of it, but we didn't, and the only thing we can hope for is something next year, but that is just pie in the sky. Anya, I am so much in love with you that I cannot think of anything else but you. I dream about the coming winter: your health will be restored in Russa and, after we move to Petersburg, I have decided you won't do any more shorthand or copying for me, and if we get enough subscribers, you *absolutely* must hire someone to help you, Nikiforova, for instance. But I will explain my ideas on the subject to you in greater detail when we are together again.

I am happy about the children so long as they are well. Take loving care of Lesha. I am so longing to see Fedya. Don't neglect Lilya and, if you can, start, little by little, teaching her to read. I believe she has your character, Anya, she will grow up into a kind, intelligent, and honest person and, at the same time, be *generous-minded;* but Fedya has my character, my straight-forward simplicity. That is the only quality I can boast of, although I am aware that privately you may have laughed at that simplicity of mine more than once. Isn't that so, Anya? But then, you are permitted everything because you are my lord and sovereign master, and it is my happiness to submit to you. This is not to say that I don't reserve something for myself or that I can get rid of my whims or of my hypochondria, but you have never fully realized, Anya, how much love I have for you despite all that, and now it is as if I had gathered new forces and had started loving you anew as I never loved you before. Wait, my angel, I will devote myself to you yet and perhaps you will see that there is some good in me yet.

I have hardly anything to tell you about myself. I am dying of boredom here, but the real problem is that *you are not with me.* So far my cure isn't going well at all. My nerves are in a very bad state, I have throat spasms, a decidedly rare occurrence during the past few years, except when I was under extreme nervous tension. Yesterday and the day before I felt as though I were going to have an attack, i.e., it was as if something were seizing my whole soul, which is the sensation I have during the last moment before an attack when it happens while I am awake. The prospect of an attack frightens me because I don't know what will become of the *Diary,* which I haven't started working on yet. Indeed, will I be able to write anything at all, feeling as weak and overwrought as I do. I do go out for walks, though, and eat with good appetite, but I don't get much sleep, not more than three or four hours a night, because I sweat so much. I sweat terribly during the day, too, and this is not because it is so hot. I am sure it is a reaction to the waters, and, who knows, perhaps this time, the waters may be of no help to me, because to have a salutary effect, they must be taken when the nerves are completely relaxed. But during the nights when I lie there drenched in sweat, I have a nasty, dry cough. Though we are having some splendid weather, not a day goes by when it doesn't pour for hours, and suddenly there will be a whirlwind, in the literal sense of the word. Two days ago we had a terrible thunderstorm. With these squalls, it is awfully easy for one who is constantly perspiring to catch cold.

As I am preparing to resume writing, I have been rereading my old notes in my notebooks and I have also reread all the correspondence I brought here with me. I have taken out a library card (a miserable library) and borrowed a Zolà [*sic*], because I have badly neglected European literature during the past few years. But just imagine: I can hardly read it, it's such an abomination. And to think that, in Russia, Zolà is proclaimed as the great luminary of realism.

As for my life here, they feed me poorly and I can't say that it is very peaceful, either: The guests are terribly ill-mannered, they stamp on the stairs, they bang their doors, they shout loudly. I don't know what Ort will say when I see him. All he cares about really is to get through a visit as quickly as possible, and he never examines a patient thoroughly except at the 1st visit, and even during that first visit, he only does so out of propriety and because he doesn't want to scare off the patient with his lack of interest from the very start. But who knows, perhaps I'll get well; if only my nerves calm down a little, the treatment will go all right. But it would certainly have done me a lot of good if we had come here together, i.e., if only that had been possible. *Without you* I cannot stay for long—that's certain. When I was leaving, although I knew in advance how painful it would be for me, I was by and large glad to go because I hoped that my departure would make things *easier* for you, because I had inflicted too much of both boredom and work on you, so that you could *rest from me* and refresh your spirits. But now, your postscriptum gave me a sudden surprise. And those 4 lines are written in such a hasty and sprawling script, as if your hand were trembling with emotion. That means that you met *him* at the very last moment, on Saturday morning. And you add: "I'll tell you more about it later"—which means that I have to wait until Sunday! But, in the meantime, Anka, I am simply afraid. My dear and only friend, though I know that a husband who does not conceal *his fear* in such circumstances places himself in a ridiculous position in his wife's eyes, I am stupid enough not to hide it: I am afraid, really afraid. When you wrote, laughing your sweet laughter (which I love so much), "be jealous," you achieved your goal. I am indeed jealous, Anya! I am just like Fedya and I cannot hide my first reaction from you. I told you, my sweet: "Have a good time, play with whomever you wish," but [a word heavily crossed out] *I allowed* you to do so only because I love you impossibly. Your rich, charming, and luxuriant nature (heart and mind), combined with your *generosity,* such as is not to be found in other women, has wilted and flagged in my company, in ennui and work and I could *allow,** relying on the generosity, the conscience, and, above all, the intelligence of my Anka [ten lines crossed out].

The gay and fascinating [eleven lines crossed out]. My sweet, my love, I write all this and [sixteen lines crossed out, of which only the following can be deciphered:] I still hope, although it torments me so much. You write that you love me and miss me, but you wrote that before you met him, before that postscriptum! Anechka, although you . . ., but think of me, *don't hurt*

---

*A whole line crossed out here, evidently by Anna Grigorevna—Eds.

me too much, otherwise I will lose my friend in you. Anyway, you won't tell me everything, that's for sure. I repeat—it's all in your power.

Anka, my idol, my sweet, my honest [illegible word]. Don't forget me. And that you are my idol and my god—that's a fact. I adore every atom of your body and of your soul and I kiss all of you, *all,* because all of it is *mine, mine!* Farewell—but when will we see each other again? Write me all the details (although I know you will hide all that from me). What dress were you wearing? I go down on my knees before you and I kiss each of your feet endlessly. I imagine doing that every minute and I delight in it. Anka, my god, don't hurt me so.

I bless and kiss the children. Please talk to them about me, Anya! Once more, I kiss you and I kiss you every minute and I even kissed that 2nd letter of yours about 50 times.

All yours,
F. Dostoyevsky.

---

113. The postscript to Anna Grigorevna's letter of July 9 reads: "My dear! Whom do you think I met on the last day? Him!!! Guess who and be jealous! Details in the next letter."

114.   To A. G. Dostoyevskaya
[Ems] Saturday, July 24/August 5, 1876

Anechka, my priceless wife,

I kiss you passionately for your angelic letter of July 18. But, my dearest joy, where did you get the idea that you were just a "golden mean"? You are a rare woman and, more than that, you are superior to all others. You yourself do not have the faintest idea of your own capabilities. You not only run the whole house and take care of all my business affairs, but you also manage your fussy and troublesome family, starting with me and all the way down to Lesha. But even in attending to my business, you are wasting your talents on minor things. You stay up nights supervising the sales and the "office" of the *Diary,* even though, so far, the returns can only be counted in kopeks and who knows if they will ever amount to anything substantial? But all of this is but a trifle for you. If you were made a queen and given a whole kingdom to rule over, I can assure you that you would rule it better than anyone else— that is how much intelligence, common sense, heart, and efficiency you possess. At the end of your letter you ask how I can love "such an old and plain woman" as you. Well, that is just a downright lie. For me you are an enchantment and there is no one else like you. And any man of feeling and discernment would agree with me if he took a good look at you, and that is why I feel so jealous sometimes. You have no idea how much enchantment there is in your eyes and in your smile and how fascinating you can be when you become animated in conversation. The whole trouble is that you see so little of people, for otherwise you yourself would be surprised at your triumphs. This is, of course, to my advantage, although, Anka, my tsarina and the mistress of my soul, I would sacrifice everything and even suffer fits of jealousy if you decided that you would like to get out and have a good time. I would be so happy at the thought that you were enjoying yourself. And if I did feel jealous, I would avenge myself with love. Believe me, Anka, whenever you dress up even a bit to go out, just the least little bit, you can't imagine how much younger-looking and striking you suddenly become! It often surprised even me. The trouble is that you stay at home working all the time and so sometimes you are simply careless.

No, Anka, I repeat, this winter you must order yourself some clothes and start getting out to see people, whether with me or without me. You must enjoy yourself for the pleasure it will give me. There should be less work to do and we must definitely make some other arrangements for the *Diary;* we will do it gradually, but as soon as possible. And, finally, how can you be surprised that I should love you as a husband and a man? Why, who ever made me feel as good as you have, who else ever succeeded in merging into one body and soul with me? And we do share all our secrets on *that score.* Is it any wonder, then, that I adore every atom of you and kiss *the whole of you,* never becoming satiated, as it actually happens? Why, you yourself have no idea what an angel of a wife you are in this respect! But I'll prove to you all the things I say as soon as I get back. Even assuming that I am a passionate man, do you really think that another man (even a passionate one) could love a woman so insatiably, as I have proved to you a thousand times already? Actually, all those past proofs of love were nothing; when I get back to you this time, I may very well eat you up! (No one else will read this letter and you must never show it to anyone.)

And now, let me talk business. Your mother has left, you are alone, but you write nothing about the nanny. I gather, therefore, there is no nanny. So what kind of a peaceful life are you having? I won't stop worrying until you write me that you have found a nanny. I am glad that you are taking the baths. Sweet little Leshka, I will be so happy when I see him. Write me about Fedya, too. Ah, dear Lilka! If only we could make some money, Anka!

You write in your letter what you so often tell me—that we are strange people who have lived together for ten years but love each other even more than before. But I predict that if we live together for 20 years, you will still write: "what strange people we are, we have lived together for 20 years and we love each other even more than before." I can guarantee that, at least as far as my own feelings go, but I cannot guarantee that I will live another 10 years. However, my health is good, although I don't know whether the cure will be successful. My nerves are incomparably steadier, and I have to walk twice as far as I had to before in order to tire myself out. Well, it seems that the cure may be successful, after all.

I have met here one Baron Gan, an artillery general, with whom I used to sit under the bell at Simonov's in Petersburg. He told me that Fryorikh told him in Berlin that he was *incurable* but that (last year) he went to see the Wunderfrau in Munich (you have probably heard of her—she treats people with all sorts of diseases with her secret method and *cures them all,* and people come to her from all over the world, and the German doctors do not dare to raise a word of protest, because she has cured absolutely incurable patients), and that she helped him *considerably,* so that now he feels fine. Still, he is drinking Krenchen here just as I am. It wouldn't be a bad idea if I went to Munich next year—better yet, the two of us (you for your anemia), especially since she charges next to nothing. Her whole treatment doesn't last more than 10 days, so that, in case of failure, we could always come here and take a Krenchen cure. This, of course, would make sense only if I were firmly convinced that the 500 rubles we spent on the trip would be returned tenfold.

At any rate, for the moment, both my cure and my state of health seem to be progressing as well as anyone could hope for.

But the real trouble, Anka, is with the *Diary.* That *Diary!* I have just sat down to write it and see in every way that I am hopelessly behind. I have about 12 days left here to write it in, but what days they are! Would you believe me if I told you that I simply have no time! I get up at 6, get dressed, and at 7 go to take the waters. I come back home at 9, have my breakfast and rest until 10 (because I continue taking my exercise). At 10, I spend half an hour on my preparations and then I write until 12; between 12 and 1, I again take some exercise, as prescribed. At 1 o'clock I have lunch, and I am not allowed to start working immediately after lunch and, besides, I usually spend that time writing letters (and that's why you mustn't be angry with me, Anka, if from now on I write you only short letters). At 4 o'clock, I have to go to the spring again, and I don't get back home until 6. That's when I have to do some recopying, but at 7 I have to get up and do some strenuous exercise! At 8, tea, and at 10, to bed.

So essentially I have just 2 hours for writing and 1½ hours for recopying. It's terrible, terrible! How can I write under these circumstances? It is nothing like the writing I do during the night at home! And besides, the *Diary* is turning out to be such rubbish, such dribble, and, as luck would have it, this particular issue must be put out as elegantly as possible, for otherwise— kaput! In brief, Anka, I am in a state of melancholy, literary melancholy. And on top of it all, I am melancholy for you and the children, wondering if something may have happened to you. I now know that I cannot rid myself of that idea.

I expect to leave here August 7, Anya. I figure that will enable me to work and do some writing for about another 9 days after I get back to Staraya Russa. That would be fine. My angel, I am at your feet, I kiss and adore you.

I kiss you passionately, the whole, whole of you. I kiss the children. Tell them that their papa will soon be back. Ah, my sweet, I pray to God to guard you all! And may God send you, Anka, a little better health. You write that you have no books, but my dear, there is a lending library and you could take out a card. Don't begrudge yourself a few kopeks.

All yours, your worshiper and your husband who is in love with you,

F. Dostoyevsky.

P.S. Anka, my joy, remember what you promised me yourself . . . [several words crossed out] *everything, everything* . . . You must keep your word my [one word crossed out]. This is very, very important. Do you hear me? *Do you understand*? [One line crossed out.]

I kiss the five toes of your foot.

Kiss the children.

---

114. The letter from Anna Grigorevna to which this is a response had been equally passionate and self-deprecating. She had written:

> I am such an ordinary woman, a golden mean, a person with petty whims and demands. . . . And now, suddenly, I find myself loved by the most magnanimous, noble, pure, honorable, and saintly of men! You have no idea, Fedya, how proud I am when I think of your love and how highly I value it. I have always told you that you are my sun, that you are on top of the mountain while I lie at the foot of it. . . . I do not just love and respect you, I actually *adore* and *worship* you.

The "bell at Simonov's" refers to the compressed-air treatments Dostoyevsky had been taking.

115.   To K. I. Maslennikov
[Petersburg] November 5, 1876

Dear Sir, much respected K.I.M.,

I am afraid that I am late in answering you and that, having inquired once or twice, you won't return to Isakov's store again for the letter.

First of all, let me thank you for your flattering opinion of my article and, second, for your kind opinion of me personally. I myself had been intending to pay a visit to Kornilova, although I hardly expected to be of any help to her. But your letter spurred me to action.

I went immediately to see Prosecutor Fuchs. When he heard of my wish to see Kornilova and of the petition to His Highness for a pardon for her, he replied that it was all quite feasible and asked me to come to his office the next day, and in the meantime he would find out more about it. The next day he sent an order to the prison warden authorizing me to pay Kornilova *sev-*

eral visits, while he himself ever so obligingly promised *to be of every possible assistance* to me in the future. The main point, however, is that it is *impossible* to file the petition at this juncture because, two days ago, Kornilova's defense lawyer submitted an appeal of the sentence to the Senate. Therefore, the case is still pending, and it is only in the event that the Senate denies the appeal that the period for a petition to the imperial authority begins.

Since it was too late for me to go to the prison that day, I went there the next day. My idea (and it was approved by the prosecutor) was first to ascertain whether Kornilova still wished to be pardoned, i.e., whether she wanted to go back to her husband, etc. I saw her in the prison hospital: she had had the baby there only 5 days before. I must admit to you, I was extremely surprised by the results of our meeting: it turned out that I had guessed *almost* everything exactly right in my article. Her husband comes to see her, they cry together, and he even wanted to bring the little girl, "but they won't let her out of the children's home," as Kornilova told me sadly. There is, however, a difference from my picture of the situation, albeit not a major one: he is a genuine peasant, although he goes around in a frock coat and is employed as a ladler in the establishment where government paper money is made at a salary of 30 rubles a month. And that's about the only difference.

I spoke with Kornilova for half an hour without anyone else present. She is a *very* likable woman. At first I merely told her in a general way that I wanted to help her. She quickly came to trust me, undoubtedly because she felt that the prosecutor wouldn't have authorized me to come to see her on some *trivial* matter. She has a rather strong and clear mind, but it is at the same time very Russian, simple and even naive. She used to be a seamstress and, even after her marriage, she took in work and earned some money. She has a very young face and is not bad-looking. There is, in her expression, a beautiful, serene, spiritual quality, but she obviously belongs to the simple and cheerful type of woman. She is quite calm now, but she says that she's "very bored" and wishes "they'd make up their minds soon." Avoiding any mention of her *pregnancy*, I asked her how she could have done it. She answered briefly, in a moving tone of voice: "I don't know myself, it was as if some stranger's will had entered me." And she said another curious thing: "I got dressed, and though I didn't intend to go to the police station, *I just went out* into the street, and I don't know myself how I got to the police station."

To my question whether she would like to return to her husband, she replied: "Oh, yes," and began to cry! Then she added with deep feeling: "My husband comes to see me and weeps over what has happened to me," trying thus to show me "what a good man he is." She cried very bitterly when she spoke of the testimony of the prison officer against her, that from the very beginning of her marriage she had hated both her husband and her step-daughter: "That's not true, I couldn't have told him anything like that." "Life with my husband became bitter in the end, I kept crying all the time, and he kept scolding me." And, on the morning of the crime, he beat her.

I didn't conceal from her the possibility of a petition to His Highness, in case the appeal failed. She listened to me very attentively and cheered up noticeably: "You have given me new heart," she said. "I was feeling so miserable before!"

I inquired discreetly whether she needed anything. She understood me and said very simply, without sounding in the least offended, that quite frankly she had everything, including money, and that there was nothing she really needed. Her newborn daughter lay on the bed nearby. As I was about to take my leave, I walked over to have a look at the baby, and admired it. She was very pleased and, immediately thereafter, when I was saying good-bye to her, she volunteered this information: "She was christened yester-day—we named her Yekaterina."

I left her and went to see Assistant Supervisor Anna Petrovna Boreisha, who praised Kornilova effusively: "How simple she has become, how intelligent and gentle." She related that when she first arrived at the prison a few months ago, she was another woman entirely, "insolent and rude, abusing her husband—she behaved as though she were half insane." But after a short while in the prison she started to become quite another person. The remarkable thing is that for some time now she has been uneasy and apprehensive "that her husband might marry someone else" (she imagines that he may have done so already). Before they sentenced her, he seldom came to see her. Another interesting point: Anna Petrovna assured me that "her husband is not at all worthy of her, that he is dim-witted and heartless, and that Kornilova apparently sent for him twice before he *eventually* came to see her." However, Kornilova insisted again and again on the fact that her husband comes to see her and that *he weeps over her fate,* in other words, she was trying to convince me of "what a good man he is," etc.

It is, of course, impossible to give you the complete picture in a few words, and there are things that escape me. I am convinced more than ever that it was all due to her sickness, and although *I do not have hard facts* to go on, my meeting with her tends to bear out my opinion.

And so there's no point in thinking about a petition before the decision on the appeal is rendered, and I don't know when that will be. But then, if the appeal is rejected (which is the most likely possibility), I will draft the petition for her. The prosecutor has promised me his cooperation. So have you, and so it would seem that there is *a hope* for her future. In Jerusalem, there was a font, Bethesda, but the water in it acquired healing properties only when the angel came down from Heaven and stirred it. A cripple complained to Christ that he had been waiting by the font for a long time, but that there was no *man* around to dip him into the font when the water was stirred. From the tenor of your letter, I sense that you would like to be such a *man* to our patient. Don't miss the moment when the water is stirred. God will reward you for it, and I, too, will do what I can right up to the end. And in the meantime, allow me to assure you of my feelings of utmost esteem,

Yours,

F. Dostoyevsky.

---

115. Kornilova had thrown her six-year-old stepdaughter out of a fourth-floor window—though somehow the child was not hurt. Dostoyevsky had written about it in *Diary of a Writer;* first he suggested that the crime was so "strange" that there must be more to it than met the eye, and later he argued that it could be attributed to the fact that Kornilova was in the fourth month of her first pregnancy—"a time when a woman is subject to all sorts of strange influences and impressions to which her spirit submits in a peculiar and helpless way." He also imagined the scene in the prison, with Kornilova's husband "coming to visit her with his little daughter, the victim of the crime," and all of them crying together over what had happened.

The addressee, K. I. Maslennikov, was an official in the department of the Ministry of Justice that processed petitions for pardon (his chief was A. F. Koni), and he had written to Dostoyevsky offering his assistance. He had signed his letter with his initials "K.I.M." and had asked Dostoyevsky to address his answer to Isakov's bookstore.

116.   To A. A. Romanov
[Petersburg, November 16, 1876]

Your Imperial Highness, Most Gracious Sovereign:

I have started this year the monthly publication, *Diary of a Writer.* Despite my great desire, I did not dare present it to Your Imperial Highness, as I had the honor of doing with one of my earlier works. But when I embarked on this new undertaking, I was not certain myself that I would not discontinue it at the very beginning, because I lacked the strength and the health necessary for urgent and regular work. It was for this reason that I did not dare to present to Your Imperial Highness a work that was still so indefinite.

The present great forces at work molding Russia's history have lifted the heart and spirit of the Russian people with unfathomable power to a height at which many heretofore incomprehensible things have become understandable and have lighted up in our consciousness *the sacredness of the Russian idea* more brightly than it has ever been lighted before. And I could not fail to give heartfelt expression to everything that had begun and sprung up on our soil and among our just and magnificent people. There are, in my *Diary,* a few words that burst from my heart, ardently and sincerely—that, I remember—and although I have not yet completed one year of publication, I have been envisaging and dreaming for a long time of the happiness that would be mine to present my humble efforts to Your Imperial Highness.

So please forgive me, Your Most Gracious Majesty, for my boldness, do not judge too harshly one whose love for you is limitless, and allow me to send you every month from now on each new issue of the *Diary of a Writer.*

It is with a feeling of reverence and esteem that I take the liberty of calling myself a grateful and faithful servant of Your Imperial Highness,
Fyodor Dostoyevsky.

116. Dostoyevsky's draft of this letter was even more servile in tone than the final version. Toward the end, for example, he had written that the "slightest attention" from the future tsar, "if I had the happiness to attract it to me, would constitute the greatest honor and the greatest joy for me."

117.   To A. G. KOVNER
Petersburg, February 14, 1877.

Dear Sir, Mr. A. Kovner!

I have been long in answering you because I am a sick man and have all I can do just to put together my monthly publication. Moreover, I *am compelled* to answer several dozen letters every month. And finally, I have a family and other affairs and obligations. I have absolutely no time for myself and it is quite impossible for me to enter into a long correspondence—especially with you.

Rarely have I read anything more intelligent than your first letter to me (your 2nd letter is something special). I fully believe everything you say about yourself. You express yourself on the subject of the crime you once committed so clearly and (to me at least) so intelligibly, that I, without knowing your case *in detail,* look on it, at least for the moment, just as you do.

You pass judgment on my novels. There's no point, of course, in my saying anything to you about that, but I was pleased that you singled out *The Idiot* as being the best of them all. Can you imagine that I have heard the same opinion expressed 50 times, if not more. People continue to buy the book every year and there is, in fact, a growing demand for it. I have brought up the subject of *The Idiot* because all those who have told me they considered it my best novel have something special in their mental make-up, which has always struck me and appealed to me. And if you have that same mental quality, so much the better *for me.* Provided, of course, that you were sincere. But even assuming you were insincere . . .

But let us leave that. I hope you will not become discouraged. You have resumed your literary work—that is a good sign. As for helping you to place your writing somewhere, I don't really know what to say. I can only speak about it to Nekrasov and Saltykov at *Notes of the Fa.*—and I will certainly do so even *before reading your work,* but I do not put any great hope even in that. Although they are very kindly disposed toward me, on one occasion last year they rejected a manuscript that had been written by someone I recommended to them and that I delivered to them in person; they rejected it, in fact, without even opening the envelope, on the grounds that they could never publish anything by *such* a person, regardless of what he wrote, and that their magazine had a standard to uphold . . . And so I left empty-handed. But I'll talk to them about you, emphasizing that if my late brother were still around and publishing his magazine *Time,* either your comedy or your novella would certainly have been published in that magazine, if it was only the least bit compatible with its policy, even though you had served time in a penitentiary.

N.B. I do not quite like the two lines of your letter in which you say that you feel no remorse for the act you perpetrated in the bank. There is something higher than the dictates of reason and contingent circumstances of every description, something to which everyone must submit (i.e., again, something somewhat like a *standard*). Perhaps a man of your intelligence will not be offended at the frankness of my remark, even though it is quite *uncalled for.* First of all, I myself am no better than you or anyone else (and I am not being falsely modest in saying that, because why should I say it if I didn't mean it?) and, in the 2nd place, if I vindicate you in my own way in my heart (just as I invite you to vindicate me), it is better, after all, if I vindicate you than if you do so yourself. I don't know if this is clear. (N.B. By the way, a little parallel: a Christian, i.e., a real, noble, and ideal Christian, says: "I must share my goods with my lesser brother and serve him in every way I can.["] But a Communard says: "Yes, you must share your goods with me, who am poor and not your equal, and you must serve me." The Christian is right and the Communard is wrong. It is quite possible, however, that you will now find what I have been trying to say even less comprehensible.)

And now, on the subject of the Jews. I cannot go into a subject like that too deeply in a letter, *especially when writing to you,* as I said before. You are so intelligent that we wouldn't be able to resolve such a controversial problem even in a hundred letters, and we would just exhaust ourselves. Let me tell you that I have received observations of a similar kind from other Jews before. Recently, for instance, I received an ideally noble letter from a Jewish woman, who signed her name, which also contained bitter reproaches. I expect I will write a few lines about these reproaches from Jews in the February installment of the *Diary* (which I haven't started writing as yet, having been sick until now after a recent attack of epilepsy, a sickness with which I am afflicted). But let me tell you now that I am not an enemy of the Jews at all and never have been. But as you say, its 40-century existence proves that this tribe has exceptional vitality, which could not help, during the course of its history, taking the form of various Status in Statu. And there is no doubt that the most pronounced case of Status in Statu is that of our Russian Jews. And if that is so, how can they fail to find themselves, even if only *partially,* at variance with the indigenous population—the Russian tribe? You point to the Jewish intelligentsia, but then you are also a member of that intelligentsia and just look how you hate the Russians, and specifically only *because you are a Jew,* although a cultivated one.

Your 2nd letter contains a few lines on the moral and religious conscience of the 60-million-strong Russian people. These are words of terrible hatred—yes, hatred—because, being an intelligent man, you ought to understand yourself that you are not the least bit competent to judge this matter (i.e., the question of to what extent and how intensely a Russian man of the people is a Christian). I would never make any such pronouncement about Jews as you make about Russians. During the 50 years of my life, I have found that Jews, whether good or bad, won't even sit down at the same table with a Russian, while a Russian feels no hesitation about sitting down with a Jew. So who hates whom? Who is intolerant toward whom? And what sort of an idea is it that the Jews are a nation of the insulted and injured? On the contrary, it is the Russians who have been humiliated by the Jews in every respect, because the Jews, besides enjoying almost complete equality of rights (they can even be officers, which, in Russia, is everything), have their own rights besides, their own law, their own statute, their own status quo that is protected by the *Russian* laws themselves.

But let's leave it at that, the subject is a long one. I have not been an enemy of the Jews. I have Jewish acquaintances. There are Jewish women who come to me now for advice on all sorts of subjects, and they read the *Diary of a Writer,* and although they are touchy, as all Jews are, when it comes to things Jewish, they bear me no enmity, on the contrary, they come to see me.

On the Kornilova affair, I will say only that you know nothing about it and therefore are not competent to talk about it, either. But what a cynic you are. With a view such as yours of man's heart and his actions, the only thing left to do is to wallow in materialistic pleasures . . .

You have been sentenced to serve 4 years in the penal battalions. Doesn't that mean hard labor? If that's the case, I am worried about you. You will just have to stick it out without allowing yourself to become debased. But where will you find the strength if you have such an opinion about people? I will not discuss with you your ideas about God and immortality. These arguments (i.e., all those you use) have been known to me—I swear—since I was 20 years old! Please don't be angry with me if I say that I was amazed at how elementary they were. Undoubtedly it is because it's the first time you've given any thought to these matters. Or am I mistaken?

438

But I really do not know you at all, despite your letter. Your letter (the first) is a good one and is fascinating. From the bottom of my heart I want to believe that you are completely sincere. But even if you are not sincere, it doesn't make any difference, because in this particular instance a lack of sincerity is a very complex and profound thing in itself. Please believe in the complete sincerity with which I shake the hand you offer me. But raise yourself spiritually and give shape to your ideal. Why, you have been seeking it all this time, haven't you?

> With profound respect,
> Yours, Fyodor Dostoyevsky

---

117. Arkady Grigorevich Kovner (1842–1909) was a Russian-Jewish writer who had published two books in Hebrew criticizing narrow "nationalistic" views among Jews; later, he wrote a regular column in the *Voice,* in which he engaged in polemics with the *Citizen* during the time that Dostoyevsky was its editor. He then went to work for a bank, but was convicted of embezzling a large sum of money. In his first letter to Dostoyevsky, a very long one written from prison, he told the story of his life, expressed his admiration for Dostoyevsky's novels, and said he was "determined to broach one question that has me completely baffled. I am referring to your hatred for the 'Yid,' which manifests itself in almost every issue of your *Diary.*" (Dostoyevsky customarily referred to Jews, in his letters and in his journalistic writings, by the pejorative term "Zhid," though in this letter he uses the more formal and respectful term "Yevrei," or "Hebrew.") Dostoyevsky responded not only with this letter but also in an article in the *Diary of a Writer.* In addition to the two letters mentioned here, Kovner wrote four others, which, as far as is known, were not answered.

118.   To A. F. GERASIMOVA
S.-Petersburg, March 7, 1877

Dear Madam, Mrs. Gerasimova:

Your letter has caused me great torment, because I have been unable to answer it for such a long time. What will you think of me? You may, perhaps, in your depressed state, take my silence as an affront.

I want you to know that I am up to my neck in work. Besides the urgent work on my *Diary,* I am overwhelmed by correspondence. Several letters like yours arrive every day (literally), and they cannot be answered in two lines. I have suffered *three* epileptic fits; for many years now I have not had attacks of such violence and in such close succession. After an attack I am so broken physically and mentally that, for two or three days, I am quite incapable of working, writing, or even reading. And now that you know this, kindly forgive me for this tardy reply.

I could not possibly have thought, in any case, that your letter was either *childish* or *stupid,* as you put it. More than anything, it reflects a general mood and there are now very many young girls who are suffering like you. But I will not write you at length on that subject; rather, I shall express a few basic thoughts of mine, both on the question generally and concerning you particularly. I suppose that to advise you to calm down and, remaining in your parents' house, to try to find some intellectual occupation (to get yourself trained in some field, such as education, etc.) would be quite useless, for you wouldn't listen to me. But why in the world are you in such a hurry and where are you rushing to? You are in a hurry to be *useful,* and yet, fired by the zeal such as you have (I assume that it is sincere), you could, provided that you take your time and equip yourself with the proper education, really prepare yourself for a role that would be *a hundred times* more useful than the benighted and insignificant occupation of nurse, midwife, or doctor. You are anxious to enroll in the local medical courses. I very strongly advise you against it. They wouldn't give you anything in the way of an education; in fact, it would be even worse than that. And what good would it do if you did become a midwife or a doctor one day? You can always acquire such a specialty later on if you absolutely wish to, but wouldn't it be better to set your aims higher now and get yourself a higher education? Just look at all our specialists (including even our university professors). Why do they disgrace (instead of benefiting!) their work and profession? The reason is that most of our specialists are people who are *profoundly uneducated.* It is not as in Europe, where you meet men like Humboldt, Claude Bernard, and others with a universal view, who have a vast education and a *knowledge* that is not confined to their specialty alone. In Russia, however, even men of vast talent are essentially uneducated and know very little outside their own sphere. A man like Sechenov, for example, has no understanding of his adversaries (the philosophers) and is thus more likely to do harm than good with his scientific conclusions. And the majority of our university students, both male and female, are people without any education whatever. So how can they possibly be useful to mankind! All that interests them is to find a job quickly and draw a salary.

Thanks to the efforts of some *influential* people, *university courses* for women have been organized at a school on Vasilevsky Island, here in Petersburg. And now, many of these influential people are putting pressure on the government to confer upon those graduating from these courses certain rights, *as far as possible* the same as those conferred on men holding university diplomas, i.e., the possibility of obtaining certain positions and pursuing certain careers, etc. I have spoken of you to a very influential lady, precisely one of those who are trying to establish the courses for women *on an equal basis.* She was very responsive and promised me that, if it were possible for you to move to Petersburg, she would get you into that establishment in the near future, although you might have to wait a little while. Believe me, here you would at least broaden and deepen your education and, possibly, you might even obtain the *rights* that the sponsors of the courses are petitioning for. Then, upon graduation, you could choose a specialty or go directly to work upon passing the examinations.

I was not able to make out from your letter what the situation is in your parents' home and I'm not sure what you mean by the phrase *run away from my father,* for I do not understand why your father would object and would not allow you to pursue your education in those university courses on Vasilevsky Island? It is not the Medical Academy, it is not preparing you to become a midwife, which quite understandably might alarm him, as it would alarm me, too, if it were my own daughter (because I would want my daughter to raise the level of her education and of her socially useful work, rather than *lower* it). Besides, as a last resort, your father could always get some information on these courses from one of the sponsors, perhaps from the very lady whom I approached about you (a person of noble heart who is dedicated to the performance of good deeds). She is Anna Pavlovna Filosofova, the wife of State Secretary Filosofov. For my part, at least, I can promise you full support from her. She is deeply and sincerely sympathetic toward all young people, particularly women who are seeking to obtain an education.

It is obviously impossible for a person of your temperament and outlook to be a merchant's wife. But to be a good wife and especially a mother—this is the highest fulfillment of a woman's destiny. You will readily understand that I can say nothing to you about the young man you mention. You describe him as fainthearted—but, if he sympathizes with you and is prepared to help you in any way he can, he can hardly be fainthearted. Actually, though, I have no way of knowing. The most important thing is that he should be a kind and honorable man. And if, in addition, he *really* is kind and honorable, it could be that spiritually he is your superior, rather than you his. But since you also write that you are not in love with him, there is *nothing further* to say. Nothing can justify ruining one's life. If you don't love him, *don't marry* him. If you wish, you may write me again. The lady I have mentioned (keep her name secret—although you may give it to your father if absolutely necessary) will also help you. Please forgive me now if you find that my letter falls short of what you may have expected, but then, you ask me a great many questions and they are not easy to answer.

All yours,
F. Dostoyevsky.

---

118. This letter from Gerasimova (of whom nothing else is known) was one of many that Dostoyevsky began to receive, especially from young people, seeking his advice. She had written that she wanted to become a doctor. Her father strenuously objected; a young man who "fully sympathizes with my ideas and promises me com-

plete freedom" had proposed to her, but she did not love him, and yet she also rejected the prospect of ending up "as the wife of some fat merchant," bearing him children every year and becoming "a sort of cook and nanny." And so, she asked, "Tell me, what am I to do?"

Ivan Mikhailovich Sechenov (1829–1905) was a physiologist who also wrote on general philosophical problems. He had been graduated from the same army engineering school as Dostoyevsky, four years after him.

The Bestuzhev Institute of Higher Education for Women had been in operation for several years on Vasilevsky Island. Anna Pavlovna Filosofova (1837–1912) was one of its founders.

119. To S. Ye. Lure
Petersburg, April 17, 1877

Much esteemed and ever so kind Sofya Yefimovna,

I am still not well, still terribly busy, and I'm thoroughly worn out. After I had got out the issue, I thought I would take a rest and answer all my letters (yours first of all). But so many new letters arrived, demanding urgent replies for the most varied and pressing reasons, and so many new people came around to see me, some of whom were so strange that I had all I could do to get rid of them, that it consumed all of my time (and sapped my health). And it is only now that I have been able to snatch a few minutes to answer you. First of all, thank you for feeling so attached to me. Secondly, I hope I didn't cause you any harm among your friends by publishing the story about Hindenburg just as you had related it in your letter. I started having misgivings about that only recently. While I was writing the issue and having it printed, I was thinking only about you, but now I am also thinking about your whole circle. Please let me know if I have in any way wronged you or caused you displeasure, and if I have—please forgive me.

Your letter is very curious, but the main thing is that you ask me what to do about the disagreement with your family, especially in connection with your examination. I am inclined to this view: Don't be too hard on your parents and don't disregard their wishes too rashly. You won't change their opinion in any case, and you cannot very well deal harshly with them and tear at their hearts, because, after all, they are your father and mother.

If you love those who are in misfortune and you wish to serve mankind, you should bear in mind that the greatest misfortune is for good, kind, generous people to *fail to understand* or cease to understand, because of their environment or the life they have led, certain ideas, and for them to come into open conflict with those whom they want to love and to make happy. This happens most often between parents and children. Obviously, you are not expected to sacrifice your individuality and all your dearest convictions, but you must nevertheless be understanding and sympathetic toward them *to the utmost*. That is a real act of love for mankind, and one needn't go far to seek an opportunity to perform an act of love for mankind, since it is usually in our homes, before our eyes. I know nothing of your present relations, but couldn't you, to begin with, be gentler with them, and then promise them something, although *not right away*, explaining that you are still young and that you feel you must remain single for at least another year. As for your studies and your exams, I am sure you could arrive at a more congenial arrangement (and one more favorable to you) if you did overcome the bitterness in the relations with your family and drew closer to them. But you absolutely must promise them something or other. In a year's time, much water will have flowed under the bridge.

By the way, concerning what you tell me about the 12- and 30-thousand ruble dowries, I can only say that I didn't quite understand the reason for your anger with your fiancé. It seems to me that he was merely trying to tell you, in the simplest and most graphic way, that he loves you more than money because, although he could if he wanted marry another girl with a dowry of 30,000 rubles, he would rather marry you with only 12 thousand rubles, since it is not the money that he loves but you yourself. This is what I gather from your letter, but there may be something else to it that I am not aware of. You ask, "What would he say if I didn't have even 12,000?" My guess is that he would say just the same thing, i.e., "I want this girl, even without a dowry, because I love her and not her dowry." After all, it isn't his fault that there is a 12,000-ruble dowry to go with you, is it? But the really important side of the question is not this, but rather whether you love him and feel close to him in your way of thinking. If you do not, then, of course, you shouldn't marry him, although remember that, at your age, it is very difficult to judge people without making mistakes.

Concerning Victor Hugo, I believe I mentioned him to you, but I see now how young you are, when you compare him to Goethe and Shakespeare. I am myself very fond of *Les misérables*, which came out at the same time as my *Crime and Punishment* (rather it appeared 2 years earlier). Our great poet, the late F. I. Tyutchev, and many others, at the time, found *Crime and Punishment* incomparably superior to *Les misérables*. But I argued with them and tried to prove to them that *Les misérables* was superior to my epic, and I argued in all sincerity, and I still hold to this view today, despite the contrary opinion of all our connoisseurs. However, my liking for *Les misérables* does not prevent me from seeing its great defects. The character of Valjean is splendidly drawn and the book contains very many distinctive and beautiful passages. I wrote about this last year in my *Diary*. But on the other hand, his lovers are so ridiculous, they are such French bourgeois in the most despicable sense! How ridiculous are the endless chatter and the rhetorical passages of the novel. But most ridiculous of all are his republicans, who are inflated and false characters. His rogues come off much better; wherever these fallen people come through with authenticity we feel

Victor Hugo's humanity, love, and generosity, and it is admirable that you noticed and appreciated it. I was particularly delighted that you appreciated the character of l'abbé Meriel [sic].

You wrote me some anecdotes about your local cranks. I, too, could tell you a few anecdotes about all the cranks who occasionally come to see me, and I am sure that there are things that would surprise you.

Don't be sad, gather your strength for a while, and then you can think of coming to Petersburg again or to Moscow (where there are also possibilities for study). I am sure you will succeed, because you have character.

I will be leaving Petersburg for the country in the middle of May, but perhaps you could write me before then. I will let you know my address later (the summer address, that is).

Your sincerely devoted,
F. Dostoyevsky.

---

119. Sofya Yefimovna Lure was another of Dostoyevsky's correspondents who wrote to him for advice; she sent him at least nine letters and also visited him on several occasions. In the letter to which this is a reply, she had written not only that she had misgivings concerning her fiancé but also that her parents would not allow her to take the examinations for university entrance and that, in secret from her parents, she was teaching at a school for paupers. In a previous letter, she had given a description of the funeral of a much-admired Dr. Hindenburg, which Dostoyevsky had reprinted almost verbatim in *Diary of a Writer* under the title, "The Funeral of Everyman" (Pokhorony obshchecheloveka).

120. To S. D. Yanovsky
Petersburg, December 17, 1877

My deeply esteemed and sincerely beloved Stepan Dmitriyevich:

I have reproduced exactly the salutation in your letter because nothing could be truer than that I have always esteemed you deeply and loved you sincerely. And whenever I think of the far distant past and recall my youth, your dear and loving countenance always rises up in my memory, and I feel that you were truly one of the few who loved me, with understanding and forgiveness, and to whom I was devoted simply and directly with all my heart and without ulterior motive. It is a fine thing that you now and then call on me to exchange some ideas and impressions, or, to describe it more aptly, to share our life's experience.

But let me pass on to business now. I am sending you Ap[ollon] Grigorev's book, which Strakhov has just published. I won't be sending you my *Diary* next year because I have decided to suspend its publication for a while (one year). There are many reasons for this: I am tired, my epilepsy has worsened (precisely because of the *Diary*), and, finally, I would like to be a bit freer next year, although it is quite unlikely that I will spend even as much as two months without working. I have been carrying a novel in my head and in my heart and it is begging me to give it expression. There are other reasons, too: I feel that to resume publication after an interval of a year would be just right, as I would like to try a new periodical publication, of which my *Diary* would be a part. Thus, I will actually expand the form of my activity, for the *Diary* itself has now taken on a form that cannot possibly be altered.

You wouldn't believe, my dear Stepan Dmitriyevich, how many expressions of sympathy I have received from the Russian people during these two years of publication. Encouraging letters, even expressions of the most sincere love, have come to me by the hundreds. Since October, when I announced the suspension of publication, letters have poured in daily from every corner of Russia, written by people from all (the most varied) classes of society, all telling me how sorry they are and begging me not to give up my enterprise. Embarrassment alone prevents me from trying to convey to you the extent of the sympathy that is being expressed to me by all. And I wish you knew how much I myself have learned from these letters from hundreds of Russians during these two years of publication.

But the most important thing I have learned is that there are in Russia incomparably more truly Russian people, with the true and virtuous Russian way of looking at things, free of distorted Petersburg intellectualism, than I could have imagined two years ago. So many more, indeed, that I couldn't have conceived it even in my most ardent wishes and fantasies. Believe me, my friend, many things in Russia are in no way as hopeless as they seemed to us before and, above all, there are many things to indicate a thirst for a new, righteous life, a profound faith in an impending change in our intelligentsia's way of thinking, an intelligentsia that has lost contact with the people and, indeed, does not understand them at all. You are angry with Krayevsky, but he is not an isolated case; they were all denigrating the people, they have laughed and they continue to laugh at its stirrings and to ridicule the clear and sacred manifestation of the people's will and the form in which it has expressed itself. That is why these gentlemen are vanishing from the scene; they have become outdated and played out. Those who fail to understand the people today must inevitably join the stockbrokers and the Yids, and this will be the final * of the representatives of our "progressive" thought. But a new order is coming. In our armies, *our* young men and *our* young women (the nurses) have shown something very different from what certain persons expected of and prophesied for them. So let us wait.

(As for Krayevsky, he is in the service of certain *persons* and, besides, he has been trying to gain distinction through eccentricity ever since the Serbian war, and having set out on this path, he can no longer retreat.)

* The word "final" is in Latin letters.—Eds.

I must say, though, that very little that makes sense can be gleaned even from our newspapers, except for the *Moscow Gazette* and its political editorials, which are very highly regarded abroad. The rest of the press is just catering to the feelings of the moment. In the hundreds of letters I have received during these two years, I have most of all been praised for my sincerity and the integrity of my thinking, which would indicate that these are the qualities which we are most lacking, qualities which people are thirsting for, but which they fail to find. We have few citizens among the representatives of the intelligentsia.

My wife sends you her sincere regards (we have three small children, two sons and a daughter). Of our old friends, I see most of all Maikov (he has a liver ailment and spends his summers abroad, taking the waters) and Poretsky, whom I meet now and then at the houses of common acquaintances. I will give them all your regards. How is your health? You don't write me much about it. I have a "catarrh of the respiratory system"—you see, I have even learned the official name of my sickness by heart. I have been going to Ems almost every summer. Please convey my gratitude to your Russian Circle of Vevey for their interest and sympathy. And now, good-bye, I kiss and embrace you.

> Yours, forever and unchangingly,
> Fyodor Dostoyevsky.

---

120. Apollon Grigorev's book was the first volume of his collected works.
The "new publication" that Dostoyevsky speaks of never materialized, but the novel he was carrying "in my head and in my heart" was *The Brothers Karamazov*.

121.   To N. L. OZMIDOV
[Petersburg, February 1878]

My dear and most kind Nikolai Lukich,

First of all, forgive me for being so intolerably late in answering you, owing to illness and all sorts of hindrances. Secondly, what answer can I offer and what insights can I give to the portentous and eternal question that you raise? And anyway, how can a question like that be dealt with in a few lines in a letter? Now, if we could discuss the problem for a few hours, that would be a different story, although, probably even then, nothing would come of it because words and arguments are perhaps the least effective devices for convincing unbelievers. Wouldn't it be more to the point, really, if you read somewhat more attentively the epistles of St. Paul? There is a great deal there directly concerning faith, and nothing can compare with it. It would be a good thing, too, if you read the whole of the Bible in [a Russian] translation. That book, read that way, leaves an amazing impression upon one, and whether you are a believer or not, you certainly are bound to agree that no other book like it exists or could exist in the world.

It is quite impossible to provide any insights into the problem. All I will say is this: every organism exists on earth in order to live and not to destroy itself. This has been scientifically established and science has adduced rather precisely the laws that bear out this axiom. Obviously, mankind as a whole is nothing but an organism, an organism that, beyond doubt, has its own laws of existence. Human reason is trying to discover what these laws are. Now, assume that there is no God or immortality of the soul (God and the immortality of the soul—it is all one and the same idea). Now tell me, why should I live righteously and do good deeds if I am to die entirely on earth? Without immortality, all I have to worry about is how to last out until the day when my time is up and, after that, to let everything go up in flames. And if that is so, why shouldn't I (as long as I can rely upon my cleverness and agility to avoid being caught by the law) cut another man's throat, rob and steal, or, if I am somehow reluctant to cut people's throats, why shouldn't I at least try to live at other people's expense, trying only to satisfy my own appetites? After all, I shall die, everyone else will die, and nothing will be left, anyway! Therefore, it appears that the organism of mankind is the only one not subject to the universal axiom and lives only to *destroy itself* rather than to feed and preserve itself. But what kind of society is that in which all its members are one another's enemies? That would lead to utter absurdity. Now, add to all this the *I* that is conscious of this state of affairs. But then, if the *I* is conscious of everything, i.e., of the world and its axiom, that *I* must be of a higher order than all that, or at least, it is not contained in this alone but, as it were, stands outside of it, above it all, judges it and is aware of it all. But if so, that implies that the *I* is not only not subject to the earthly axiom, to the earthly laws, but is beyond them and is subject to a higher law.

Where is this law? It is not on earth, where everything is finite and dies irrevocably and without resurrection. And does this not suggest that there is something to immortality of the soul? And if this were not so, would you yourself, Nikolai Lukich, worry about it, search for it, write letters about it? That shows that you cannot cope with your own *I*, you cannot fit it into the earthly order, but are looking for something else outside this world to which it must also belong. But whatever I write here, it will be to no avail. I cordially shake your hand as I take my leave of you. May these things keep worrying you and may you keep searching. Who knows, you may find the answer.

Your servant and sincere well-wisher,

F. Dostoyevsky

---

121. Nothing is known of the addressee, Nikolai Lukich Ozmidov, other than what he wrote in two letters to Dostoyevsky and in another to Anna Grigorevna. He

described himself as a farmer who read a great deal in his spare time and gave much thought to "the eternal questions" and to the establishment of a new educational system, for which he sought a foundation in either religion or science. He thus found himself "fluctuating between faith and disbelief." He had written to Dostoyevsky: "You are the only writer in whom I find indications and explanations of human peculiarities that practically no one else seems to see. . . ."

122. To V. V. MIKHAILOV

Petersburg, March 16, 1878

Much esteemed Vladimir Vasilevich, dear correspondent,

Your charming, warm, intelligent letter reached me on November 19 of last year, and today is March 16, 1878. I wonder whether you will be willing to forgive me for getting around to answering you only now? Although it is true that a few words in the December issue of my *Diary,* which came out in January, were addressed to you, that does not absolve me.

I am not really trying to justify myself but I can give you at least two reasons. The first is the painful and despondent state I was in until the very last number of the *Diary* came out. That is why I decided not to answer anyone until I had produced that last number. And after that, almost up till this very moment, I was dogged by increasingly poor health, epilepsy and then severe mental depression. So this is the first reason and I would like you, please, to believe it. The second reason is the terrible, unconquerable, unimaginable reluctance I have to write letters. Although I love receiving letters, I feel it almost impossible and even absurd to write letters myself: I am totally unable to express what I think in a letter. Sometimes I may write a letter and then suddenly I receive comments or objections to ideas that I am supposed to have expressed but which, in fact, could never even have occurred to me. If I end up in hell, I am sure that I will be condemned to write at least ten letters a day there. So this is the second reason and please believe it.

Your letter filled me with a terribly warm and friendly feeling for you. I receive very many friendly letters but I don't have very many correspondents like you. I feel in you a *kindred* person, and now, as my life is running out, a meeting with a *kindred* person fills me with joy and strengthens my hopes. It shows that there are people in Russia—and quite a few, at that—who are the life force of the country and who will save her if only they can join forces. And it is so that we can join forces that I am answering you and extending my hand to you in the fullness of my heart.

I have reread your letter three times and—I confess—I have also let someone else read it, and I will show it to someone else, too. I would like to explain your views and instill your spirit—your (genuine) Russian spirit—in some of the people around here. (N.B. I read your letter, by the way, to Apollon Nikolayevich Maikov, the poet; he was carried away and even kept your letter for a while himself. He and I are in agreement on very many points.)

I won't go into the details of your letter. There are many things happening here that I could tell you about, but I do not know how to write briefly and simply—I just don't know how to write letters. But if you ask me something specific, i.e., if you wish to have my specific opinion on some point or other, I promise I will answer you. But now, another matter: You would like, as you say in your letter, to write me again. I greatly appreciate that and *I am counting on it*. Among other things, I was very interested to learn from your letter that you like children, have spent much time with children, and see a lot of them even now. And so, I would like to ask a favor of you, my dear Vladimir Vasilevich: I have been planning, and will soon start writing, a long novel in which, among other things, a considerable part will be played by children, and specifically young children from the ages of about 7 to 15. There will be several portrayals of children. I am studying them now and have studied them all my life, and I love them and have children of my own. But the observations of a person like you (I know it) would be of great value to me. And so, write me what you yourself know *about children*—both about the Petersburg children who called you "uncle" and about the Yelizavetgrad children, *anything you can tell me about them*. (Various incidents, their habits, their answers, the words and sayings they use, their special traits, their family life, their beliefs, their evil deeds and innocence; nature and the teacher, Latin, etc., in short—whatever you know about them.) That would be of great help to me and I would be extremely grateful to you and I will await your letter anxiously. I expect to be in Petersburg until May 15, after which I'll probably be in Staraya Russa (with my children). Until May 15, I'll be at the same address as now.

I am sending you my photograph and I apologize to you once more. Although I was discourteous toward you, I like you very much indeed.

Good-bye, then, for now. Please believe in my warmest sincerity and in my most profound respect.

All yours,
Fyodor Dostoyevsky

---

122. Vladimir Vasilevich Mikhailov (1832–1895) was an educator who headed a boarding school for boys in Petersburg and later taught in a vocational school in Yelizavetgrad (now Kirovograd). The "few words" addressed to him in the December 1877 issue of *Diary of a Writer* were apparently merely an acknowledgment of a letter from him and a promise to answer.

The novel Dostoyevsky was planning, in which children were to play "a considerable part," was, of course, *The Brothers Karamazov*.

123.   To an Unknown Mother
Petersburg, March 27, 1878.

Dear Madam,

I am only now answering your letter of February 20, after a month's delay which was caused by sickness and lack of time and so I beg you not to be angry with me.

You ask me questions that would require treatises rather than a letter to answer, and indeed it would take a whole lifetime to give answers to questions like yours. And suppose I wrote you a 10-page letter but failed to make some particular point clear the way I could in a direct conversation, and you didn't understand me, didn't agree with me, and dismissed the entire 10 pages? Perhaps it is quite impossible for people who know nothing of each other to correspond on such topics. In my opinion, it is quite impossible and nothing but harm can come of it.

From your letter, I conclude that you are a good mother and that you are greatly preoccupied with your growing child. However, I cannot understand why you should need an answer to the questions you sent me. You worry about too many things and your concern is rather exaggerated. There are much simpler ways of handling these things. Why do you need to ask questions like "What is *good* and what is not?" Such questions concern only you, as they concern any *introspective* person, but what do they have to do with bringing up a child? Anyone who can grasp the *truth* would feel in his conscience what is right and what is not. Be kind, and let the child understand that you are kind (by himself, without any prompting) and let him keep in mind that you were kind to him, and then, you may be sure, you will have fulfilled your duty toward him for the rest of his life, because you will have taught him *directly* that kindness is good. Moreover, all his life, he will remember your example with great respect and, perhaps, with tenderness. And even if you were to do much that was wrong, or simply acted irresponsibly, unsoundly, or even ridiculously—there is *no doubt* that, sooner or later, he would forgive all your bad actions because of all the good things he would remember. I want you to know, too, that this is all you can possibly do for him. And yet it is more than enough. And his memory of the *good* features in his parents—i.e., of their kindness, truthfulness, honesty, compassion, absence of false pride and as far as possible of lying—all that will, sooner or later, mold your child into a different person. I can assure you of that. And don't go thinking that this is not enough: a tiny branch grafted to a huge tree is enough to change that tree's fruit.

Your child is 3 years old; acquaint him with the Gospels, teach him to believe in God, strictly, as prescribed by the Law. This is a sine qua non, because, without that, he cannot become a good man but will, at the best, turn into a *sufferer* and, at worst, into an indifferent *fat man,* or something even worse. There is no way of improving on Christ, believe me.

Now imagine that, having reached the age of 15 or 16, your child comes to you (from the school, for instance, where he may have made some undesirable friends) and asks you or his father this sort of question: "Why should I love you and why should I consider it my duty to love you?" If this should happen, believe me, no matter how skillful your arguments, they will be of no use, and there is no answer you can give him. So you must see to it that he *doesn't come* to you with such a question. And the only way to make sure of it is to see that he loves you directly and spontaneously, so that the question could never even occur to him—unless he somehow got contaminated by paradoxical ideas at school. But after all, he will have no trouble in differentiating a paradox from the truth, and all you will have to do in answer to his question will be to smile and continue to treat him kindly.

Besides, excessive and abnormal concern over one's child may get on his nerves and bore him; simply bore him, mutual affection notwithstanding, and so a sense of proportion is terribly important. In your case, it seems that it is this sense of proportion that is most lacking. Thus, you write as follows: "If I just lived for their sakes—for my husband and my son—I would be leading a selfish life, and do I have the right to live this way when there are other people around who need me?" What an idle and gratuitous thought! What is to stop you from living for other people just because you also happen to be a wife and mother? On the contrary, it is by living for those around you, by pouring out on them your kindness and *the promptings of your heart* that you will become a bright example for your child and become twice as dear to your husband. But the very fact that you ask that question indicates that you imagine that you must cling to your husband and child to the exclusion of the *rest of the world,* i.e., without any sense of proportion. Indeed, in that way all you will do is bore your child, even if he does love you. Note also that you may find your range of activities too narrow and that you may be longing for a vast, almost a worldwide range of action. The only question, though, is whether every person is entitled to such wishes. Believe me, being a good example within only a narrow range of action is extremely useful, because it influences scores and hundreds of people. A firm determination never to lie and to live righteously will make the people around you ashamed of their irresponsibility and make them change. And that in itself will be an accomplishment. There is an awful lot that can be achieved this way. You do not really have to drop everything and rush off to the Petersburg Medical Academy or flit from one course of lectures for women to another, *trying to solve your problems.* I see women like that every day and, I can tell you, they are a sorry lot! And even if they were originally good people, they gradually become bad. Seeing no activity around them, they begin to love people bookishly and abstractly—they love mankind but disdain the unfortunate individual; they are bored when they meet him and they avoid him.

I don't at all know how to answer your questions, because I don't even understand them. Of course, if the child is bad, the blame lies, at one and the same time, both with his natural evil inclinations (because a person certainly is born with them) and with those who brought him up and either did not know how, or were too lazy, to *overcome* his evil inclinations before it was too late and to channel them in the right direction (by setting a good example). And secondly, the child, like the adult, is influenced by the majority in the environment in which he finds himself, or falls completely under the influence of particular individuals. There is no question about it, and it all depends on the circumstances (but it is your duty to overcome these circumstances because you are a mother, but you must achieve this, not by sentimentality and insistent demonstrations of your love, but by setting a good tangible example). As to the question about work, I don't even wish to discuss it. Just instill the right feelings into your child and he will acquire a love of labor. But I have written enough as it is, I am tired now, although I have not said much, so that, of course, you won't really understand me.

Please be assured of my esteem.

Yours faithfully,
Fyodor Dostoyevsky

Peter the Great could have stayed quietly and peacefully in his Moscow palace living on 1 ½ million rubles of state income, but he nevertheless worked hard throughout his whole life. He *labored,* and he was always surprised that people could live without working.

124. TO A GROUP OF UNIVERSITY STUDENTS
Petersburg, April 18, 1878

Much esteemed gentlemen, student-correspondents:

Forgive me for not having answered you all this time; in addition to the fact that I haven't been feeling well, there were other circumstances that caused the delay. At first I wanted to answer you publicly in the press, but then it suddenly turned out that this was impossible *for reasons beyond my control,* at least it was impossible to answer you as fully as was necessary. On the other hand, I wondered, if I were to answer you simply by letter, what sort of answer I could give you. Your questions encompass *everything,* absolutely *everything* that touches on the present internal state of Russia; and so what could I do: write a whole book, an entire profession de foi . . . ?

So finally I decided to write this little letter at the risk of being misunderstood by you to a considerable degree, even though that would greatly displease me.

You write: "For us, the most important thing is to determine to what extent we, the students, are ourselves to blame. What conclusions about us can society and we ourselves draw from these events?"

And you go on to point out very subtly and correctly the essential characteristics of the attitude of the contemporary Russian press toward the young generation: "A kind of cautionary tone of condescending indulgence unmistakably prevails in our press" (i.e., toward you). That is very true: it is precisely cautionary, prepared in advance to fit every possible occasion, following a pattern that is well known and has become extremely stereotyped and worn-out.

And you write further: "Obviously, we have nothing to expect from these people who themselves expect nothing of us and who turn away from us after pronouncing their irrevocable verdict against the 'savage mob.'"

That is absolutely true—just as you say, they do *turn away* from you and they (at least most of them) are not the slightest bit concerned about you. But there are others, and they are not so rare, both in the press and in society, who are crushed by the thought that the young generation has drawn back *from the people* (that is first and foremost) and then, i.e., today, from society as well. Because that's how it is. The young generation lives in a daydream, immersed in abstract ideas and following alien teachings; it wishes to know nothing about Russia and yet itself is trying to teach Russia. And, finally, today it has fallen into the clutches—and there is *no doubt* about it—of some completely alien political party that doesn't give a damn about the young generation and uses it as material, as Panurge's flock, for its own alien and special aims. Do not try to deny this, gentlemen—that's the way it is.

You ask, gentlemen: "To what extent are we ourselves, the students, to blame?" Here is my answer: in my opinion, you are not to blame at all. You are only the children of that very "society" which you reject today and which is "false in every respect." But our student, when he tears himself away from it, when he leaves it, does not go to join the people but strays off somewhere abroad, into *Europeanism,* into the abstract realm of a "universal man" who has never existed. And in so doing, he also breaks with the people, despising and repudiating them, acting like the true son of that very society from which he has also been torn away. And this at a time when our entire salvation lies precisely in the people (but that is a long subject) . . . But then, the young generation cannot be strictly held responsible for breaking with the people. Before knowing what life is, how could it possibly have *reached out, in its thoughts, to the people!*

But now, to make things worse, the people have seen and taken note of the fact that Russia's young intellectuals have broken away from them, and what is worse still is the fact that, then and there, the people branded these young men as *students.* The people singled them out long ago—as far back as the early sixties and, since then, all this going *to the people* has evoked nothing but disgust in the people. "Little lords,"* the people call them (that is the term they use, I can vouch for it, that is how they refer to them). But, all the same, there is a mistake here on the people's part, too, because never before has Russia experienced a time when the young generation (as if sensing that Russia had reached some decisive juncture and was teetering on the edge of an abyss) was, in the overwhelming majority, more sincere, more pure of heart, more thirsting for truth and integrity, more prepared to sacrifice everything, including life, for the truth and the word of truth. This is truly Russia's great hope! I have felt this way for a long time and for a long time have been writing about it. And suddenly, what happens? The youth, thirsting for this word of truth, search for it God knows where, in astonishing places (and in this concurring once more with the rotten European Russian society from which they sprang), but not among the people, not in the land. Eventually, at some point, neither the young generation nor society will *recognize the people*. Instead of sharing the life of the people, the young generation, while knowing nothing about the people and, indeed, profoundly disdaining their basic institutions, such as religion, go to the people—not to learn from them, but to teach them, to teach them condescendingly, full of scorn toward them—a purely aristocratic, lordly undertaking! "Little lords," the people say of them—and rightly so.

It's a strange thing: at all times and places, everywhere in the world, democrats have been for the people; only in our country did our democratic Russian intellectuals join the aristocrats in an alliance against the people: they go to the people "in order to do good for them," while scorning all their basic institutions and traditions. And scorn does not lead to love!

Last winter, during the incident at Kazan Square, a group of young people desecrated a national shrine, smoking cigarettes in the cathedral and causing a public scandal. "Look here," I would have said to these fellows on Kazan Square (and indeed I did say so to a few of them straight to their faces), "if you do not believe in God, that's your business, but why do you have to insult the people by profaning their cathedral?" And on that occasion, the people once again called them "little lords," and what is even worse, labeled them "students," although there was a goodly number of some sorts of Jews and Armenians among them (it has been established that the demonstration was political, organized from the outside). So, since the Zasulich affair, the people once again have been calling the revolver-brandishing street mobs "students." This is bad, although there is no doubt that some students were indeed involved in the incident. It is bad because the people are already singling them out, and hatred and dissension have started to spread. And now you yourselves, gentlemen, refer to the people of Moscow as "butchers," just

---

* *Barchenki.*

as does the entire intellectual press. What's this all about? Aren't butchers people? They are people, real people, and Minin was a butcher, too. Indignation was aroused only because of the way the people reacted. But you should know, gentlemen, that when people are insulted, they are always going to react this way. The people are unpolished, they are peasants. In actual fact, it was all the result of a misunderstanding, but of an old misunderstanding, with much accumulated resentment (something that had gone unnoticed) between the people and society, i.e., its most militant and impulsive segment—the young generation. The whole affair turned out quite ugly and got unnecessarily out of hand, because nothing can ever be proved with one's fists. But that is how it has always and everywhere been with *the people,* all over the world. At their political meetings, the English people often make use of their fists against their opponents, and during the French Revolution, the people howled with joy and danced in front of the guillotine during the days when it was *in action.* All that, no doubt, is repulsive. But the fact is that the people (and I say the "people" and not just the "butchers," for nothing is to be gained by deluding ourselves with words) have risen up against the young generation and have already stigmatized them as students; but on the other hand, it is unfortunate (and conspicuously so) that the press, society, and the young generation have joined together in their refusal to recognize the people, claiming that what they see is not the people but the rabble.

Gentlemen, if there is something in what I say that you do not agree with, you will be better off if you do not lose your tempers. There are enough sad things without that as it is. In the rotting society there are lies on *all* sides. It cannot keep itself in hand. Only the people are strong and steadfast, but the hostility between society and the people has become something terrible during the past two years. While they were freeing the people from serfdom, our sentimentalists touchingly thought that the people would just spontaneously embrace their European lie, the enlightenment, as they called it. But it turned out the people could think for themselves and, above all, they began to be *consciously* aware of the mendacity of the upper stratum of Russian life. The events of the past two years have shed light on many things and have made the people even firmer. But the people can discern not only their enemies but their friends as well. Some sad, heartbreaking facts have appeared: the sincerest, most honest members of the young generation, seeking truth, would have gone to the people to alleviate their sufferings, but what happened? The people chase them away and fail to acknowledge their honest efforts. That is because the young generation has failed to recognize the people for what they are; they despise and deprecate the principles they believe in and offer them remedies that the people consider outrageous and senseless.

Here in Petersburg, we are in a frightful mess. Among the young, the law of the revolver prevails along with the conviction that the government is afraid of them. But the people, whom they continue to despise, still count for nothing for them, and they fail to notice that the people are at least not afraid of them and will never lose their heads. And what if further clashes take place? We are passing through a painful time, gentlemen!

Gentlemen, I have written *what I could*. At least I have given a straight, albeit incomplete, answer to your question: in my opinion the students are not to blame, indeed, never has the young generation been more sincere and honest (which is no small thing, but a great and remarkable historic fact). The trouble is, though, that the young generation has inherited the lies of two centuries of our history. Therefore, it is *beyond their strength* to analyze the event in all of its complexity, and they cannot be blamed, the more so since they found themselves directly involved (and now the injured party) in this affair. But although it is *beyond their strength,* the one or the ones who succeed in finding the true path, even today, will be blessed! The break with the environment must be much greater than, for instance, the break between today's society and tomorrow's, as the socialists see it. It must be greater because, in order to go to the people and remain with the people, one must, first of all, *learn not to despise them,* and that is something that is almost impossible for the upper stratum of our society in its relations with the people. Secondly, one must, for example, believe in God, and our Europeanism entirely excludes this (although in Europe they do believe in God).

I greet you, gentlemen, and, if you will allow me, I shake your hands. And if you wish to make me very happy, for God's sake, do not consider me as some sort of high-flown teacher or preacher. You have appealed to me to tell you the truth as I feel it in my heart and my conscience, and I have told you what I believe to be the truth, the truth as far as I am capable of grasping it. And after all, no one can do more than his strengths and abilities allow.

All yours, Fyodor Dostoyevsky

---

124. On April 3, 1878, about 150 university students from Moscow had gathered at the Kursk railroad station to meet a group of Kiev students who had been banished from the latter city and were being sent into internal exile. During the procession to a transit jail, a crowd of butchers and other shopkeepers assaulted the students, killing one of them and injuring others badly. Apparently, neither the police nor a military unit stationed nearby intervened. The incident provoked great controversy in the press—the right-wing *Moscow Gazette* called the attack "the answer of simple Russian people" to an earlier demonstration celebrating the acquittal of Vera Zasulich—and among the students themselves. (Zasulich had been accused of attempting to assassinate the military governor of St. Petersburg but had been acquitted by a jury.) One group of students, dissatisfied with the "commonplaces, loud phrases, and customary catchwords" they were hearing from both sides, wrote to Dostoyevsky, saying, "We are faced with a question to which neither the press nor

public opinion has provided a concrete answer . . . we could have expected you to resolve the issue if you had continued to publish your *Diary*." Three of the students—N. D. Dolgorukov, P. N. Milyukov, and F. Samarin—later became leaders of the Constitutional Democratic party.

Dostoyevsky may have felt it was impossible to answer the students "publicly in the press" because of the censorship.

Dostoyevsky's account of "the incident at Kazan Square" seems to be much exaggerated. On December 6, 1876, a group of students had tried to persuade a priest at Kazan Cathedral to have a prayer said for Nikolai Chernyshevsky, who was then under sentence of internal exile. Failing in this, they held a demonstration outside the cathedral. But no charge was made that they had smoked cigarettes inside the cathedral or had "desecrated" it in any other way.

Kuzma Minin (d. 1616) was a merchant of Nizhny Novgorod who, together with Prince Dmitry Mikhailovich Pozharsky, formed an army to drive the Poles from Moscow in 1612. The two men are regarded as national heroes.

By "the events of the past two years," Dostoyevsky is probably alluding to the campaign to help the Slavic peoples of the Balkan peninsula win freedom from Turkey, culminating in the Russo-Turkish War of 1877–1878.

125. To S. A. Yurev
Staraya Russa, July 11, 1878

Dear Sir, Sergei Andreyevich:

I received your letter the day before yesterday, July 9. I have known of and respected you ever since *Conversation* began publication with you as its editor. Since then, I have heard from several people that you have also spoken of me kindly. I would be extremely glad to make your acquaintance personally. In your letter you express the belief that I have preserved my opinion of you "despite the fact that we have not seen each other for such a long time." But have we, in fact, ever seen each other and become personally acquainted? You cannot imagine how often such reminders weigh heavily upon me. The thing is that, for twenty-five years now, I have been suffering from epilepsy, which I contracted in Siberia. This illness has gradually deprived me of the ability to remember faces and events, to such an extent that I have (literally) even forgotten all the themes and details of my novels, and, since some of them have never been reprinted since they were first published, I actually have no idea of what they are about. And so please do not be angry with me for having forgotten the time and circumstances of our acquaintance and of our subsequent meetings. This has often happened to me with other people. Please be so kind as to remind me, at your convenience, of the time and circumstances of our previous acquaintance.

As for my novel, here is the full truth in answer to your flattering invitation. The novel is under way and I am writing it now, but it is far from finished; indeed, it has barely begun. And it is always this way with me: I embark on a long novel in the middle of the summer (N.B.—the scope of my novels is 40–45 printer's sheets) and complete about half of it by New Year, when, as a rule, the first part of it appears in some magazine or other, starting with the January issue. After that, the novel is run in the magazine for the whole year, except for occasional interruptions, through the December issue, and I always finish it in the same year in which publication began. Thus far, there has never been an instance when a novel carried over into the next year.

When, after a long-standing collaboration with *Russian Messenger,* I published my novel *A Raw Youth* in Nekrasov's magazine, taking advantage of his offer despite the fact that *R[ussian] Messenger* was expecting to get the novel, I informed M. N. Katkov that I nevertheless still considered myself primarily a contributor to his publication. That is why, in connection with my currrent novel, I have already contacted Mikh[ail] Nikiforovich and have even taken an advance of 2000 rubles (as I have always taken in the past). Nevertheless, we haven't yet come to a final agreement about my novel for reasons that would be difficult to explain in detail in a letter but which, in essence, relate to outside circumstances and have no connection with the novel's literary value. The situation will be clarified only at the end of September or in October of this year, 1878.

Thus I will be in a position to give you a clear-cut answer to your offer to publish my novel in *Russian Thought* only in October, if you happen to be in Moscow at that time. By then, the question of where I will publish the novel will be definitely settled.

As for *Russian Thought,* I was sincerely delighted when I heard the news of its forthcoming appearance, remembering *Conversation,* and I shall always be flattered to serve it to the best of my abilities.

If you find it necessary to contact me for any reason, I will be here in Staraya Russa until August 25.

---

125. Sergei Andreyevich Yurev, who had been the editor of *Conversation,* was now to be the editor of a new magazine, *Russian Thought* (Russkaya duma), and he had written to Dostoyevsky to ask whether his "new novel, which, I understand, is almost finished," might be published in it. Actually, the magazine did not appear until 1880, and then under the title of *Russian Idea* (Russkaya mysl).

126.   To L. V. Grigorev
Staraya Russa, July 21, 1878

Dear Sir, Leonid Vasilevich:

I thank you for your warm and cordial letter of May 9. I was unable to answer you right away for various reasons: the death of my child, our departure for Staraya Russa for the summer, my trip to Moscow, and from Moscow to the Optina Hermitage in the company of Vladimir Solovyov (our young philosopher of whom you may have heard), then, on my return to Staraya Russa, a week of sickness, etc., etc.

I am very pleased for you (as for a human being in general), because you, a man of the [18]60s, not only do not feel that you are spent and finished but realize that you are full of vigor and recognize that you have the strength and the right to be a part of everything that is alive, contemporary, and vital, of everything that is pulsating with continuing life. Well, I, for one, feel just the same, although my sympathies do not lie at all with the 60s or even with the forties—as a matter of fact, I like the present years best, because something is actually being accomplished, unlike the past, which saw only crystal-ball gazing and idealizing. Indeed, it would be difficult for anyone to err more than a Russian does. Some time has elapsed now since the emancipation of the serfs, and what do we see? Scandalous practices in the rural administrations, and a deterioration of mores; floods of vodka, the rise of pauperism and the kulaks, i.e., the European proletariat and bourgeoisie, etc., etc. Isn't that the way it looks? Well, if you stop there, you will be surprised beyond measure, and you will immediately fall into error, because you will have overlooked the most important point. If it had not been for the 2 years of war we've had, no one would ever have guessed that along with all the bad traits that have certainly been acquired by the people in the course of these years, they have also acquired a political awareness, a clear understanding of the significance of Russia and her destiny (and even if it is not fully clear, it is becoming more and more *clarified*). To put it succinctly, the *supreme* idea has been grafted on and the graft has taken. And as long as we have supreme ideas or the germ of supreme ideas, the rest will take care of itself; everything can burn up and regenerate itself. But our liberals of the 60s are doing their best to bury the fact of the people's awareness and, in this instance, they join with the persecutors of the people, with those who despise them, with those who are still prone to regard the people merely as taxpaying units and nothing else.

They have exactly the same attitude when it comes to our young intellectuals. Just take the ugly facts at their face value and you will declare, as Ketcher did in Moscow, that *the young generation is rotting*. This is not true at all—the young generation is *seeking for truth* with all the boldness of the Russian heart and intelligence, the only trouble being that *they have lost their guides*. But that is a crucial problem for us and we still have time to talk about it. As to the facts, I am not worried about them—I have my own observations.

Perhaps you are bored in Anapa but, in my opinion, it is best for *the cause* that people of integrity and vitality do not concentrate in the urban centers of Russia as, for instance, the French have concentrated in Paris. Let each of them, as they spread all over Russia, store up the Russian spirit in all its variety and do their duty by spreading it further. For that is what Russia lives by.

I will be here, in Russa, until October. I am resting and am writing at present a novel, and I don't know yet what I will be working on in the winter. I will decide in October.

Those of my books that are on the market are:

The Devils—3.5 rubles, *The Idiot*—3.5 rubles, *Crime and Punishment*—3.5 rubles, *A Raw Youth*—3.5 rubles, *Notes from the House of the Dead*—2 rubles. Altogether, therefore, 16 rubles. However, I give my subscribers a 10 percent reduction, which means that the entire set would come to 14.40 rubles. Moreover, I pay for the postage myself.

With sincere respect, I shake your hand and remain

Your faithful servant,

F. Dostoyevsky

---

126. Very little is known about the addressee, Leonid Vasilevich Grigorev. He was one of many people who were moved to write to Dostoyevsky because of the views he expressed in *Diary of a Writer*. Judging from his letters (this is a response to the second one he wrote to Dostoyevsky), he had been living in the town of Anapa "among the people" for sixteen years.

The Dostoyevskys' third and last child, Aleksei, born August 10, 1875, had died, apparently of a sudden epileptic fit, on May 16, 1878. According to Anna Grigorevna, the child's death was one of the reasons Dostoyevsky visited the Optina Hermitage. While there, he spoke to the elder Father Amvrosii (Aleksandr Mikhailovich Grenkov, 1812–1891), who was famous for his asceticism and humility; he told him of the bereavement he and his wife had suffered, and the elder's words to him were, Anna Grigorevna later wrote, the words "that Zosima says to the bereaved mother in *The Brothers Karamazov*."

Vladimir Sergeyevich Solovyov (1853–1900), the son of Sergei Mikhailovich and the brother of Vsevolod, had already begun to earn a reputation as a conservative thinker and later became a well-known philosopher. Among his major works were *The Crisis of Western Philosophy* (Krizis zapadnoi filosofii, 1875), *The History and Future of Theocracy* (Istoriya i budushchnost teokratii, 1877), and *La Russie et l'église* (Russia and the Church, 1889). It has been suggested that he was a model for Alyosha Karamazov and that his ideas about religion and politics entered into the debate between Ivan Karamazov and the Grand Inquisitor.

Nikolai Khristoforovich Ketcher (1809–1886) was a physician, poet, and translator of German and English literature. In the 1860s he had a reputation as a rightist political thinker.

127.   To V. F. Putsykovich
Staraya Russa, August 29, 1878

Much esteemed Viktor Feofilovich,

I received your letter, for which I am very grateful, two weeks ago, and yet I haven't managed to answer it until now, although I wanted to do so every day. Even now, I'll be writing you only a few lines, just to assure you of my affection for you and to tell you that I have not failed to think of you now and then. You ask why I haven't written and why you haven't heard anything of me. But, to start with, there was no one but you to whom I could write and I didn't even know (until I got your letter) where you were. Besides, there is nothing much I can tell you. I am working on a novel now, but it is very hard going, and I am still only at the beginning of it and so I am very dissatisfied. The weather has been rather bad here and I have had two attacks—so there you have all my news. Moreover, I won't be in Petersburg for at least another month, i.e., around October. In the first place, it is better for my work for me to be here; in the second place, the air here is excellent; and in the third place, the weather has improved and it looks as if we're going to have a splendid fall.

But having said all this, I beg you, just the same, to write to me at least once from Petersburg when you get this letter, because I am sitting here in complete isolation, struggling along with just the newspapers, of which I am sick and tired. Thank you for sending me the news about Aksakov—I will write him without fail. You write that they never found Mezentsov's assassins and that it was certainly the work of a nihilist gang. How could it be otherwise? That is certainly the case. But what I would like to know is whether our country is going to snap out of its present stagnation and shake free of its old traditional routine! Your story about how you sent to Mezentsov the anonymous letter from the Odessa socialists who had threatened you with death for writing in opposition to socialism is superb in its originality. You had absolutely no reply and your letter sank into oblivion—and that's that! Incidentally, when will they finally realize how much the Yids (by my own observation) and perhaps the Poles are behind this nihilist business. There were a bunch of Yids involved in the Kazan Square incident, and then it was Yids in the Odessa incident. Odessa, the city of the Yids, is the center of our militant socialism. In Europe, it's the same situation: the Yids are terribly active in socialism, and I'm not speaking now about the Lassalles and the Karl Marxes. Understandably so: the Yid has everything to gain from every cataclysm and coup d'état, because it is he himself, status in statu, who constitutes his own community, which is unshakable and only gains from anything that serves to undermine non-Yid society.

The articles in our press about the assassination of Mezentsov are the height of stupidity. They sound as if they were written by liberal fathers who disagree with the excesses of their nihilist children because they have gone further than they did. And, although they say that the people have not been contaminated by socialism yet, none of them recognizes the importance of that fact, not a single one of them admires the people for it, but, on the contrary, they continue to spurn the people, are condescending toward them, and pride themselves on their Europeanism. If I were still putting out the *Diary,* I would do a piece on this subject.

I had no idea that Meshchersky was in Petersburg. If you see him, give him my heartfelt regards. Isn't he writing something? If he is working on a novel, let him write it with care, meticulously, not rush it posthaste. With a talent like his, he shouldn't be allowed to spoil his work with impunity. Is Konstantin Petrovich Pobedonostsev in Petersburg? Please convey my profound respects to him if you see him. And who is this N. Morskoi whose novel *The Aristocracy of the Arcade* is now being published in *New Times?* Is it Burenin, by any chance? It is an excellent piece, even though it is a caricature.

Good-bye then, dear fellow, I shake your hand.

Sincerely yours,
F. Dostoyevsky

P.S. My wife thanks you for remembering her and sends you her regards.

---

127. Nikolai Vladimirovich Mezentsov (1827–1878) was the head of the Third Section. He was stabbed to death on August 4, 1878, by a young revolutionary whom the police failed to capture. What Dostoyevsky scorns as the "Europeanism" in the reaction of the press probably refers to the pleas in even the right-wing newspapers for steps toward a constitutional regime.

Prince Meshchersky was working on a novel, *The Terrible Woman: A Sketch of Contemporary High Society* (Uzhasnaya zhenshchina: Sovremenny velikosvetsky etyud), which was published soon after this letter was written.

N. Morskoi was the pen name not of the critic, journalist, and writer Viktor Petrovich Burenin (1841–1926), as Dostoyevsky suggests, but of Nikolai Konstantinovich Lebedev (1846–1888), whose novels—including *The Aristocracy of the Arcade* (Aristokratiya Gostinogo Dvora)—seemed imitative of Dostoyevsky's in several respects.

128. PETITION BY RETIRED SECOND LIEUTENANT FYODOR
MIKHAILOVICH DOSTOYEVSKY
[Petersburg, March 1879]

The gracious grant of an ensign's commission in 1856, when I was serving as a noncommissioned officer in the 7th Siberian Battalion of the Line, which I had joined after serving out my sentence of four years at hard labor of the 2nd category at the Omsk fortress, restored to me my civic rights that I had forfeited by my participation in criminal propaganda in Petersburg in 1849. In my passport, issued to me in Semipalatinsk upon my resignation from the army on June 30, 1859, it is not stated that I am to be under police surveillance. Nevertheless, I am still under such surveillance, as I was told, in one instance, in the 3rd Special Section of His Majesty's Chancellery, to which I have always had to address a special request to obtain permission to travel abroad, and again, as recently as 1875, when, while spending the winter of 1874–1875 in Staraya Russa, I learned from the Staraya Russa police inspector himself that I was under his surveillance.

It has been 25 years since I was pardoned and my civic rights were restored to me. My opinions, both political and religious, have been expressed since then in hundreds of pages. I hope that these opinions are such that my political reliability cannot be considered suspect, and therefore I take the liberty of requesting that police surveillance over me be discontinued.

---

128. On March 10, one A. A. Kireyev had written to Dostoyevsky, telling him of a conversation he had had with the Minister of the Interior on the subject of freeing Dostoyevsky from police surveillance and suggesting that Dostoyevsky address a petition on that subject to the minister.

129.   To K. K. Romanov
[Petersburg] March 15, 1879

Your Imperial Majesty,

I am supremely aggrieved that it is utterly impossible for me to comply with your request and take advantage of your ever so flattering invitation.

Tomorrow, Friday, March 16, at 8 P.M., as luck would have it, I am scheduled to give a reading at a benefit of the Literary Fund.

The tickets were bought out by the public even before the announcement appeared in the press, and if anything prevented me from participating in the reading as advertised by the administrators of the fund, they, in the event of my failure to appear, would be obliged to refund the money to the public.

I repeat to you, Your Majesty, how terrible I feel about this. I was very much looking forward all this time to the invitation to be among you that was extended to me by his Imperial Highness Sergei Aleksandrovich, and I am grief-stricken by this unfortunate contretemps.

Please forgive me and do not think ill of me, may the expression of my fervent feelings find favor in your eyes, and please know me to be Your Majesty's eternally and infinitely devoted and humble and loyal servant.

Yours,
Fyodor Dostoyevsky

---

129. Grand Duke Konstantin Konstantinovich Romanov (1858–1915) wrote poetry and in 1889 was elected president of the Russian Academy of Sciences. Ac-

cording to Anna Grigorevna, Dostoyevsky subsequently was invited to dine with him frequently, and the two became quite friendly.

130.   To K. K. ROMANOV
[Petersburg] March 21, 1879

Your Imperial Majesty,

Tomorrow at 9:30 P.M., it will be my pleasure to be present at the convocation of Your Imperial Majesty.

Please know me to be Your Majesty's infinitely devoted and most faithful servant.

Fyodor Dostoyevsky

131.   To N. A. LYUBIMOV
Staraya Russa, May 10, 1879

Dear Sir, much esteemed Nikolai Alekseyevich,

I have sent to your name today, at the editorial office of R[*ussian*] *Messenger, two and a half printer's sheets* of text (minimum) of *The Brothers Karamazov* for the forthcoming May issue of *R.M.*

This is Book Five, entitled "*Pro* and *Contra*," but not all of it, only half. The 2nd half of this 5th book will be mailed to you (in good time) for your June issue, and will consist of *three* printer's sheets. I was forced to split this Book 5 of my novel between 2 numbers of *R.M.* for the following reasons: (1) Even if I had exerted every effort, I would, at best, have completed the whole thing by the end of May (I was too far behind because of the move to Staraya Russa and all the preparations it involved), which would have meant my not getting to see the proofs, and that is something I consider essential. (2) This Book Five is, in my opinion, the culminating point of the novel and it must be completed with special care.

As you will see from the text I have sent you, it deals with the theme of the ultimate blasphemy and with the central core of the destructive idea of our times, in Russia, among the young generation who have lost contact with reality; and in juxtaposition to blasphemy and anarchism is the refutation of them, which I am preparing now and which will find expression in the last words of the dying Elder Zosima, one of the characters of the novel. Since the difficulty of the task I have set myself is obvious, you will, I am sure, my dear Nikolai Alekseyevich, understand and forgive me for having preferred to extend it over 2 issues, rather than spoil the culminating chapter by excessive haste. On the whole, this chapter will be filled with action. But in the text I have sent you today, I draw only the character of one of the principal persons in the novel, as seen in the formulation of his fundamental beliefs. That body of beliefs is precisely what I recognize as the *Synthesis* of today's Russian anarchism. It is the denial, not of God, but of the significance of His creation. Socialism as a whole originated in and began with the denial of the concept of historical reality and has become a program of destruction and anarchy. The original anarchists were, in many instances, people of sincere convictions. My hero chooses an argument that, *in my opinion,* is irrefutable—the senselessness of children's suffering—and from it reaches the conclusion that all historical reality is an absurdity. I do not know whether I have carried it off well or not, but I do know that the personality of my hero couldn't be more realistic. (Many people reproached me for the implausibility of many of my characters in *The Devils,* but later, believe it or not, actual developments proved them all to be real, which goes to show that they had been correctly conceived. For instance, K. P. Pobedonostsev told me of two or three cases, among the anarchists who had been arrested, who strikingly resembled certain characters in *The Devils.*) Everything that my hero says in the text that has been sent to you is based on reality. All the stories about the children are actually true, they were reported in newspapers that I could refer you to, and there is nothing that I have invented. The general who set his dogs on a child—it's all fact, an actual event that was reported last winter in *Archives,* I think, and then reprinted in a number of other newspapers.

The blasphemy of my hero will be solemnly refuted in the next chapter (to appear in your June number), and I am working on it now in fear, awe, and reverence, since I consider my task (the crushing of anarchism) as a civic duty. Wish me luck, much esteemed Nikolai Alekseyevich.

I am awaiting the proofs with the greatest impatience. My address is: Staraya Russa, to F. M. Dostoyevsky.

I do not think that there is a single *unseemly* word in the text I have sent you. There is only that bit about the torturers who, to train a little girl of five not to soil her bed at night, smeared her with *her own excrement.* But I beg and beseech you not to delete that. It is taken from a current criminal trial. In all the newspapers (only 2 months ago—Mecklenburg, the mother, the *Voice*), they used the word "excrement." It cannot be softened, Nikolai Alekseyevich, it would be just deplorable if that had to be done! We are not writing for 10-year-old children. But I am quite sure that, even without my asking, you would keep my text intact.

One more small thing. The lackey Smerdyakov sings a lackey's song, which contains the following couplet:

The glorious crown,
As long as my beloved is well.

I did not invent that song, but rather I noted it down when I heard it in Moscow 40 years ago. It was composed by a group of merchant's clerks of the 3rd category and it became popular among lackeys. It has never been recorded by any anthologist and I am the first to use it.

The actual text of the couplet is, however:

The *Tsar's* crown,
As long as my beloved is well.

And so, if you find it at all possible, for heaven's sake restore the word "Tsar's" instead of "glorious," which I had substituted for it only to be on the safe side (the word "glorious" would pass on its own).

How is Mikhail Nikiforovich's health? Please convey my profoundest respect to him.

Kindly remember me to your wife.

And please be assured, much esteemed Nikolai Alekseyevich, of my very best feelings toward you.

Your obedient servant,
F. Dostoyevsky

P.S. Wouldn't it be possible to announce on the final page that the conclusion of Book Five, "Pro and Contra," will appear in the next issue, no. 6?

I will mail the text for the June number by June 10 (at the very latest) and possibly before that. This way, I will catch up with the schedule and will be sending you my material before the 10th of every month. I will then publish every month without interruption.

---

131. The story of the general who had set his dogs on a child appeared in *Russian Messenger* in 1877. A peasant boy had injured the foot of one of a nobleman's hounds, and as punishment the boy was ordered to run naked across the fields and the hounds were let loose after him. His mother tried to rescue him but was driven away; she lost her mind and died two days later.

Similarly, the story about the girl whose parents smeared her with her own excrement appeared in the *Voice* in 1879. Though they lived in Kharkov, the mother came from Mecklenburg, and at the trial (the child had also been beaten, deprived of food, and kept in unsanitary conditions), the prosecutor insisted that such treatment would never have happened among Russians. The *Voice*'s correspondent disagreed and recalled an incident of the maltreatment of a child that he had witnessed in Kirsanov. In *The Brothers Karamazov*, Dostoyevsky combined the two stories in Ivan's conversation with Alyosha (chapter 4, book 5, part 2).

Despite what Dostoyevsky says about the "lackey's song," a very similar song had been published in an anthology that appeared in Petersburg in 1817, though it made no reference to a crown. When Smerdyakov's verse appeared in the *Russian Messenger* (chapter 2, book 5, part 2), it contained Dostoyevsky's preferred wording, "The Tsar's crown" (Tsarskaya korona).

132. To K. P. POBEDONOSTSEV

Staraya Russa, May 19, 1879

Dear Sir, dear and much esteemed Konstantin Petrovich,

Although it is only May 19 today, my letter will not reach you before the 21st, and so I hasten to send you my best wishes for your saint's day. I recall, by the way, that exactly a year ago I came to see you in the morning, on this very day, but it seems as if it were only two or three weeks, at most a month ago—that is how impermissibly fast time goes by and is running out on us!

Here it is a month since I've been here, living quite alone with my family and seeing hardly anybody. The weather has been fine on the whole, the bird-cherry and the apple trees have shed their blossoms and the lilac is in full bloom. I have been sitting and working, but I haven't done too much. Still, I have sent off half of one *book* (2½ sheets) for the May issue of *R[ussian] M[essenger]*, but I am sitting waiting for the proofs and I don't know what will happen now. The thing is, the book in question, called "*Pro and Contra*," is the culminating point of my novel, and the theme of that book is blasphemy and the refutation of blasphemy. Well, I have finished and mailed off the blasphemy but will send the refutation only for the June issue. I have come to grips with the blasphemy, as I myself felt and understood it most keenly, i.e., precisely as it manifests itself now in Russia among (almost) our *entire* upper crust, and principally among the younger generation, i.e., the scientific and philosophical refutation of the existence of God having been already discarded, the present day *serious socialists* no longer bother with it (as they used to throughout the last century and the first half of the present one). Instead, they vehemently *deny* God's creation, God's world and *its significance*. It is only this that contemporary civilization finds nonsensical. Thus, I flatter myself with the hope that, even on such abstract grounds, I have not been unfaithful to realism. The refutation (not a direct one, i.e., not in a face-to-face argument) will come as the last words of the dying elder.

Many critics have reproached me for generally choosing, as it were, wrong themes for my novels, themes that are not realistic, etc.; but I feel, on the contrary, that there is nothing more realistic than precisely these themes . . .

I did send it off to them all right, but now and then the thought crops up—what if, for some reason or other, they suddenly decide not to publish it in *R.M.*?

But enough of that. If something hurts someone, he keeps on talking about it all the time.

I read the newspapers here but I cannot understand what is going on. They simply don't say much. Only yesterday I read in *New Times* a directive from the Ministry of Public Education that teachers were to refute socialism in the classroom (does this imply, then, that they should get into arguments with the students?). It is impossible to imagine anything more dangerous.

When I arrived here there was a lot of talk about an officer, Dubrovin, of the Wilmanstrand regiment, which is stationed here (he was hanged). They say he kept trying to act like a madman up till the very moment when they put the noose around his neck, although he didn't really have to put on an act, being really and beyond all doubt quite insane. But when we begin to try to form our opinions from an example that is held up before our eyes, we are surprised for the hundredth time by two things that simply refuse to change in our country. To be precise, if we were to consider Dubrovin's regiment by itself, on the one hand, and, on the other, Dubrovin himself, we would find a difference so great that they would appear like creatures from different planets. And yet, Dubrovin lived and acted in the firm belief that everyone and his entire regiment as well would suddenly become exactly like him and would share the selfsame views on this matter.

On the other hand, we say straight out: these are madmen. However, these madmen have their own logic, their own theories, their own code of behavior, even their own god—and all that could not be more solidly ingrained in them. No one pays any attention to that: it's all nonsense, they say, it's like nothing on earth and, therefore, must be just nonsense. We have no culture of our own (everyone else does), dear Konstantin Petrovich, and if we don't, it is through the fault of that nihilist Peter the Great. He pulled it up by the roots. And since man does not live by bread alone, our poor cultureless fellow is forced to invent something as fantastic and preposterous as possible, just as long as it does not resemble anything he knows (and so, although he has borrowed it all wholesale from European socialism, even there, he has managed to change it to the point where it no longer resembles anything at all).

And now I have filled four pages, and imagine, dear Konstantin Petrovich, I have written about just those things I didn't want to write about! But that cannot be helped now. I vigorously shake your hand and send you my most sincere wishes for all the best and for many, many happy returns. Now, the idea that you will receive what I have written here and read it pleases me.

If you were to write me even a few words, it would bolster my spirits tremendously. When I came to see you last winter, it was also to restore my spirits.

So, may God send you peace of mind—I know of nothing better that one could wish a man in our times.

My profound respects to your much-esteemed wife.

Your fully devoted and faithful servant,

F. Dostoyevsky

My address: Staraya Russa, to F. M. Dostoyevsky.

---

132. The directive from the Ministry of Public Education had warned of "the pernicious infection of harmful anarchist [rather than socialist] doctrines" and em-

phasized the duty of teachers "to strengthen in the pupils entrusted to them feelings of loyalty to the throne and respect for religion."

Lieutenant Vladimir Dmitriyevich Dubrovin (1855–1879) had been under police surveillance because he was suspected of having some connection with the assassination of Mezentsov (see Letter 127). When military police entered his apartment, he put up armed resistance, and when he was arrested and carried out of the house, he harangued the onlookers, urging them to kill "tsars and emperors." Even in jail, he continued to make inflammatory speeches, and at one point he tried to commit suicide. On the basis of medical testimony, the military court declared him sane and he was sentenced to death by hanging.

Dostoyevsky's remarks about culture and socialism in Europe and Russia seem to echo the thoughts that had been expressed by Gradovsky in two articles that had been published in *Russian Discourse* earlier in 1879.

133. To N. A. Lyubimov
Staraya Russa, June 11, 1879

Dear Sir, much esteemed Nikolai Alekseyevich:

Two days ago I sent off to the *Russian Messenger* the continuation of *The Karamazovs* for the June issue (the conclusion of chapter 5, "*Pro* and *Contra*"). This completes what "*the lips utter in pride and blasphemy.*" The modern *denier,* a rabid one, declares openly that he stands for what the devil advises, and claims that this will more certainly bring happiness to mankind than the teachings of Christ. To our Russian socialism, which is so stupid (but also dangerous, because the young generation is involved in it), the *lesson* must seem very forceful—one's daily bread, the Tower of Babel (i.e., the future reign of socialism), and the complete enslavement of freedom of conscience—that is what this desperate denier and atheist comes to! The difference is that our socialists (and you know very well that they do not consist only of the underground nihilist scum) knowingly act like Jesuits and liars, refusing to admit that their ideal is an ideal of the coercion of the human conscience and the reduction of mankind to the level of cattle, whereas my socialist (Ivan Karamazov) is a sincere man who openly admits that he agrees with the Grand Inquisitor's view of mankind and with the contention that belief in Christ assumes that man is a much nobler creature than he really is. So the question is asked point blank: "You, the would-be future saviors of mankind, do you despise man or do you respect him?"

And all this is supposedly done in the name of love for mankind. They are saying, in effect: "The commandments of Christ are stern and abstract and unbearable for the weak," and so, instead of the law of Freedom and Light, they impose on men, through bread, the law of chains and enslavement.

In the next book, there will be the death of Elder Zosima and his last conversations with his friends. This is not a sermon, but rather a sort of story, an account of an incident in his own life. If I can bring it off, I will have accomplished something useful: *I will force them to admit* that a pure and ideal Christian is not an abstraction but a tangible, real possibility that can be contemplated with our own eyes and that it is in Christianity alone that the salvation of the Russian land from all her afflictions lies. I pray God that I may succeed; it will be a stirring piece if only I am granted sufficient inspiration. But above all, the theme is one that would never even occur to any other contemporary writer or poet, and so, it is completely *original*. It is for this theme that the entire novel is being written, and I only hope that I will carry it off—that's what concerns me most now! I will send you some material for the *July* issue without fail, and by July 10 at the latest. I will do my utmost to keep this promise.

I received your letter, much esteemed Nikolai Alekseyevich, concerning the money you will be sending me, and I am waiting impatiently for the promised thousand rubles. I have almost no money left and I am rather reluctant to borrow any. And so, *I beg you most urgently* to send me the thousand rubles as soon as possible and, if you can, *without delay*, because I need it very badly.

Where is Mikhail Nikiforovich now, in Moscow or at his country estate? And how is his health? Please give him my warmest wishes and regards.

And now, if you have a little friendly feeling toward me (I believe you do, from our meetings and conversations), I wonder whether you wouldn't do me a *special* favor, my dear Nikolai Alekseyevich. In one of my letters, I casually mentioned Putsykovich, the former editor of *Citizen*. He wrote me that Mikhail Nikiforovich had promised to send him a monthly sum for his articles from Berlin. In the meantime (he writes me), he has reached the limits of extreme poverty in Berlin. He is really a very good man. He is now toying with the idea—quite a risky one to be sure, but really not a bad idea at all—of publishing *Citizen* in Berlin as a monthly magazine. He wants to try to start publishing on credit, because he does not even have enough money for food. The man will never write anything base and one more Russian periodical of the right opinion is a useful thing, even if it is published abroad. If there is any possibility of supporting him, even in the smallest way (literally), with some hundred or two hundred rubles, he would be able to get out his first number and then one could see how things go afterward. He is a man who could be influenced and guided. He anticipates that he will get some subscribers, although not too many at first.

What I would very much appreciate is for you to have a talk with Mikhail Nikiforovich about him and then tell me: what does he think of Putsykovich and is it true that Mikhail Nikiforovich promised to send him a certain monthly sum in Berlin (for his services as a correspondent)? Putsykovich, at

470

least, assured me that this was so in his letters to me. I shall await your answer on this. Please, my most kind Nikolai Alekseyevich, find a spare moment and drop me a line on the subject. I feel awfully sorry for Putsykovich and I am rather fond of him. He is in dire straits and has almost reached the point of despair.

And with that, I remain your respectful and devoted,

F. Dostoyevsky

P.S. My regards to your much esteemed wife.

Putsykovich's address is: Berlin, Dorotheen Strasse, 60, Wictor Putsyko-vitch [*sic*].

134.   To A. G. Dostoyevskaya
Hôtel d'Alger, Ems, July 30/August 11, 1879

My dear friend and incomparable little wife Anya,

I got your letter of the 24th yesterday, am writing you this today, the 30th, and it will go off tomorrow. By now, you must have received all my letters from Ems and know how things stand. But it is awful that it should take so many days to get an answer to one's letter—that is an excruciating thought. I kiss and hug you, I thank Lilechka for her little letter, and I congratulate Fedya on the fish. Tell him to catch three eels in time for my arrival and we will make a fish soup. I love them so, my little angels; and as for Your Grace, why, that just goes without saying. If we could only see each other soon. Here I feel so lonely and depressed that it really hurts. There's not a soul I know here—nothing but alien, foreign mugs. The mornings are foggy and cold. Krenchen has an irritant effect on me and it gives me such nightmares that I can hardly sleep at night. I am still having spells of coughing as before, but I am beginning to hope that perhaps, somehow, I will get some relief here. I have the impression that I can breathe a bit more easily, I can move around more, and the phlegm is a bit looser, although the cough persists.

I am also very worried about my work. I thought that living here in isolation, I could do a lot of work, but as it turns out, I can work for only 2 hours out of the 24, and that during the day, not at night. I get up at 6, I am at the spring at 7, and I return at 9 for coffee. Drinking my coffee and resting after it takes another hour, and before you know it, it's already *10 o'clock*. From 10 till 12 I work. At twelve, I leave for the post office and take a walk before lunch. At 1, I have lunch. From 2 to 4 in the afternoon, I either write letters (Putsykovich, for one, won't leave me in peace—he bombards me with his letters and he would like nothing better than to send me the proofs of his magazine to correct for him, as if that's all I had to do!) or go out to read the newspapers. From 4 to 5 : 30 I go to take the waters again. Then I go out for another walk at seven—that is compulsory. At 8 it is already dark, the candles are lit, I have my tea, and at 10 I go to bed. And so the day goes by. Then, on top of everything else, I have nightmares all night long, my nerves are shot, and I worry about my work. Ah, what a holiday it will be when, at last, I send the manuscript off to R[ussian] Messenger!

It goes without saying that nothing worth mentioning has happened to me here, except for the most insignificant incidents. For instance, I lost a shirt of mine (I don't think it was one of my better ones) and didn't realize it until yesterday. It was probably stolen when I was still at the Hôtel de France, but it is too late now to go over there to inquire. The day after I moved to the d'Alger from the Hôtel de France, I realized that I had left my trousers behind at the de France. I went over there and the flunkey looked embarrassed. It turned out that he had already put them well out of the way in his own trunk. I got my trousers back and took them with me, but I am sure that, besides the trousers, I had left my shirt behind as well. Here in the Hôtel d'Alger, there is no one who would have stolen it. The 2nd incident came when I bought myself an umbrella. The day before yesterday, on Saturday at noon, I started my gargling treatments. It is done in a room in which there are 50 stands for people who are gargling. I had put my umbrella in a corner and when I left, I forgot about it. ¼ of an hour later, I realized I had forgotten it and went back, but it was gone: someone had made off with it. It had rained that night and all morning that day, and I thought to myself: "Tomorrow is Sunday and the stores will be closed—what shall I do it if rains tomorrow." So I went and bought myself what looked like a really lousy umbrella—a silk one, of course—for 14 marks (6 rubles in our money). The shopkeeper (a miserable Yid) who sold it to me said to me: "Did you ask the police about your umbrella?" "Are there police at the casino?" "Yes, there's a post there." I hadn't even known about it. I went there, asked about it, and they gave me back my lost umbrella on the spot; it had been brought in quite some time ago. What a pity! I offered 2 marks to that scoundrel of a shopkeeper to take back his umbrella and give me back 12 marks, but he refused. A real shame, money is the only thing that counts . . . The third incident concerns my Yid neighbors in the Hôtel d'Alger. For four days I sat there and endured their chatter next door (a mother and son). They talk pages, whole volumes of talk, nonstop, without the slightest respite; and worst of all, it's more like squealing than shouting, like in a kagal,* or a prayer hall, completely oblivious to the fact that they're not the only people in the house. Although they are (rich) Russian Yids, they're from somewhere in the west-

---

* The Russian word *kagal* (derived from the Hebrew word *gahal*, a meeting) referred to the assembly of elders of the Jewish communities. It was also used figuratively with the pejorative meaning of a noisy and disorderly gathering.—Eds.

ern regions, from Kovno. Since it was already 10 o'clock and time to go to sleep, I yelled *as I was getting into bed:* "Ah, those damned Yids—will they ever let you sleep!" The next day the landlady *M-me Bach* looked in and told me that her Yids had complained that they had been offended by me, that I had called them Yids, and that they were checking out of their room. I told the landlady that I was going to leave myself, because her Yids were more than I could stand; you couldn't read, write, or even think straight. The landlady was terribly upset by my threatening to leave and said that she would rather get rid of the Yids, but she offered me a splendid suite upstairs that will be available in a week's time. I know that suite, it's really a nice one, and besides it's two thalers a week cheaper. I agreed, and even though the Yids haven't shut up and persist in their loud talk, still they've stopped yelling and for the moment things are bearable. Well, those are my adventures.

I have started twitching at night, and I'm very fearful of an attack.

Now about you. I gather that you are going to the Nil on the 6th. I don't want to bother and pester you, my sweet darling, but do take a couple of addressed envelopes and a sharpened pencil along with you and, whenever you come to a post office, drop me a note, even if it's only 3 lines in pencil. And take good care of the children. Take care of yourself, too, like the apple of my eye, do it *for me,* do you hear, Anka, for me and for me *alone.* So you are gadding about and going to balls, milady? For what purpose? Anka, my darling, stay healthy, my sweet, don't catch cold, take good care of yourself—we need you, the children and I.

I pray for you all, and while I am praying, all sorts of *strange* thoughts come to me. I cannot suppress them and they upset my nerves. Already I have an accumulation of the sort of secrets we usually tell each other on the very first day of my return after a long absence, right after dinner, like in the old days when we locked up to count our money. Anka, I am dying to hug you—not only in that sense, but in that sense too—I feel as if I were on fire. As for the B's—whatever that may be, forget about them completely, or at least don't dream about them, although I cannot control the dreams of my little wife [a few words heavily crossed out] may she remain my wife. I kiss you—first your little lips, then your little hands, then your little feet, then the whole of you. Kiss the children. Tell them that I want them to obey you, especially during your journey to the Nil. Look after them, my darling, I am terribly worried. I have almost another month to stay here—what a horror!

F. Dostoyevsky.

You may go to balls, milady, *provided you do not forget me.* My regards to all—to the priest and to Anna Vasilevna especially. And send me the 100 rubles. I will bring back with me whatever is left over. The ruble has again dropped on the exchange.

I expect to get your promised letter tomorrow.

Anya, my sweet, don't you dare lose weight—on the contrary, *put some on.* But above all—get healthier and healthier. Once again, I kiss the children.

---

134. The Nil Stoblensky Hermitage, founded in the middle of the sixteenth century, was located on an island in Lake Seliger, about 90 miles southeast of Staraya Russa.

Anna Vasilevna (Korvin-Krukovskaya) Jaclard was spending the summer in Staraya Russa with her family.

135.   To A. G. DOSTOYEVSKAYA
Ems, August 1/13, 1879

Anya, my sweet angel,

I have just received your letter of July 27. I expected it yesterday, but I had made a mistake in my calculations. My sweet darling, you write that the 25th was your name day. That surprised me no end because I never thought your name day was in the summer, particularly not in July! I know that your birthday is on August 30, but your name day has always been in February. And however hard I try to think, why, I cannot remember ever having celebrated your name day in July. Either it is you who have made a mistake or it is I who have no memory whatever. Yes, indeed, although I do love my Anka so infinitely, I seem to be quite incapable of ever remembering, once and for all, the dates of her birthday and her name day. And this time you even chided me: "And you didn't even think of congratulating me!" Of course I didn't, since I was sure that your name day was in February! I kiss your little hands and feet and *all* the rest of you and I beg you to forgive me. And having done that, I beg my sweet and dearest wife to accept my best wishes for the day of her saint, which I missed. I congratulate you from the bottom of my heart, Anka, and may God grant you life to celebrate your name day another 75 times, at the very least.

You keep writing about the Nil, and so I am answering your letter immediately in the hope that my letter will still be in time to reach you in Staraya Russa. But I have to confess that I write to you at least twice as much as you write to me. And you still write that I do not think about all of you as often as you do about me. But I'm not grumbling, I don't want to pester you, because writing letters is, I know, a chore, and I say this despite the fact that, even at night, I dream that I have received a letter from you—that is how much I thirst for some sort of news of you all. Thank Lyubochka for her charming little letter and Fedya for his good intention. It's terrible how much I love them. I am also extremely concerned about all of you—I mean, about what's happening to you—how you are and what you are doing. And, by the way, is Foma there, and is he spending the night at the house? You write that you don't sleep well at night: for goodness sake, Anka, get some sleep and sleep soundly, and why the need for such regularity? If you wake up at 12, then put them on the potty at 12, and if you wake up at 3, there is no need for you to wait until 4 to put them on the potty, do it at 3 instead. Otherwise, you will fray your nerves and, God forbid, lose weight; you promised me to try to put some on, at least *in certain parts,* but more about that below.

I am very glad that Lyubimov acted so promptly and was even nice enough to send a telegram, and I am glad that I wrote him such a polite letter, so that he cannot possibly be offended. So I see that, if it is 500 and 800, they have settled the accounts down to the very last line—that isn't bad at all.

I have had some quite unexpected expenses: This morning, at the spring, I dropped my magnificent crystal glass on the stone floor and it broke to pieces. I had paid 5 marks for it. I immediately bought another one for 4 marks, but that's a loss of nine marks already. Besides, it is a bad omen. I am still highly irritable because of the waters, I sleep very poorly, twitch at night; I am taking 4 glasses a day. I don't know what will happen later, but there has been no let-up in my coughing spells, and they are especially bad at night and when I get up. The mornings here are misty, but during the day it gets quite hot. There is no one I know here, and very few Russians in general. It is gloomy and boring. I have started writing now and, thus far, it is coming along fine.

One of these days, I will write a separate letter to Lilya and Fedya.

Give my regards to everybody back home and especially to Anna Vasilevna. I wonder whether Anna Ivanovna deserved to be given Mrs. Rokhel's flowers. There are so many flowers around here that they sell them by the armful. But I do not buy any, because there is is no one here to give them to, since my queen is far away. And who is my queen? You are. That's my verdict, for while staying in this place I've fallen in love with you more than you can possibly imagine. Now, something *extremely intimate:* My queen, my clever lady, writes to me that she is having the most seductive dreams [two lines heavily crossed out]. That filled me with enthusiasm and elation, because I myself think of my queen and mistress here not only at night, but also during the day—beyond measure, till it drives me crazy. Don't get the idea that I think only of that one aspect, no, no, that is not so, but in all honesty I must admit that I think of that aspect, too, until I am burning with desire. The letters you write me are rather dry, but suddenly up crops that phrase [ten and a half lines heavily crossed out] which she would not grasp at once, while remaining a clever girl and an angel, and so all that happened to the exclusive joy and admiration of her little husband, because her little husband particularly likes it when she is completely frank with him. And this is precisely what he values and what keeps him captivated. And so, suddenly the phrase: the most seductive dreams [six lines crossed out]. Allow me, milady [two lines crossed out] I kiss you desperately at this moment. But in order to decide about the dream [one and a half lines crossed out] the fact that the heart of my adored little wife—Anka, from this page alone, you can see what a state I am in. It is as if I were in delirium, I am afraid I will have an attack. I kiss your little hands, the backs and palms of them, and your feet, and all of you,

All yours,
F. Dostoyevsky.

I'll be writing to you according to what I learn from your letters about your trip to the Nil. And while you are there, what about saying a prayer for me? I am really much too sinful. Give my special regards to the priest.

Filosofova wrote to me here. From the Caucasus, she is going on to Pskov Province.

If at all possible, write me something while you are on the way. I kiss my angels Anya [evidently should have been "Lyuba"] and Fedya. Tell them that I beseech them to be obedient. During the journey, don't let Fedya play around the wheels of the carriage or near the horses. And I implore you, Anya, don't lose them somehow in the crowd!

---

135. Foma was apparently the caretaker of the Dostoyevskys' house in Staraya Russa. Anna Ivanovna was Maikov's wife, whom Dostoyevsky disliked. "Mrs. Rokhel" (actually, Röchl) was the wife of the doctor who was director of the spa in Staraya Russa.

136.   To L. F. Dostoyevskaya

Ems, August 7/19, 1879

Lilichka, my sweet angel,

I kiss you and bless you and love you very much. I thank you for writing me letters. I read them and kiss them, and every time I get one, I stop and think of you. I feel lonely without you here. There is no one I know, so that I stay silent all the time and I am afraid I'll forget how to talk. I am coming back home in about three weeks.

My sweet Lilya, you must listen to Mommy and not quarrel with Fedya. And you must both remember to do your lessons. I pray to God for all of you and beg Him to send you good health. Give my regards to the priest and kiss Fedya for me. Please obey Mommy and do not make her sad. Good-bye, my sweet Lilichka, I love you very much. Kiss Mommy for me,

Your papa,
F. Dostoyevsky.

476

137. To F. F. Dostoyevsky
Ems, August 7/19, 1879

My dear, sweet Fedya,

I kiss you and bless you and think of you often. How do you spend your time? What do you play at? If you go to the Nil Stoblensky, I want you to obey Mommy during the trip. And now, too, Fedichka, my dear boy, I want you to learn your lessons and obey your Mommy. Do not quarrel with Lilichka, and you must love each other just as I love both of you. Kiss Lilya and Mommy for me. Study your reading. There are many boys here who go to school—I see them practically every day—some of them are only five years old and are already at school. There are also boys here who go fishing in the river. Have you caught any fish, Fedya? I kiss and hug and bless you.

Your papa,

F. Dostoyevsky.

138. To N. A. Lyubimov
Ems, August 7/19, 1879

Dear Sir, much esteemed Nikolai Alekseyevich:

I hasten to send you herewith *Book Six* of *The Karamazovs, the whole of it,* to be published in the no. 8 (August) issue of *Russian Messenger.* I have called this 6th book "A Russian Monk," a bold and provocative title, for it will incite all the critics who dislike us to cry out: "Is this what a Russian monk is like? How dare one to put him on such a pedestal?" But so much the better if they cry out, don't you agree? (And I am certain that they won't be able to restrain themselves.) I am convinced that I have not sinned against reality: I have done justice not only to an ideal but also to reality.

I am not certain, though, that I have done it successfully. I myself feel that I have not been able to express $\frac{1}{10}$ of what I would have liked to. Nevertheless, I view this *Book Six* as the culminating point of the novel.

It goes without saying that many of the teachings of my Elder Zosima (or should I rather say, his way of expressing them) are inherent in his personality, i.e., in the manner in which his character is portrayed. And although I fully share the thoughts that he expresses, if I were to express them myself, *in my own name,* I would do so in another language and in another form. But he *could not* express himself in any other language or *in any other spirit* than the ones I have ascribed to him. Otherwise, I would have failed to create a live literary character. This is true, for example, of Zosima's discourses on what *is a monk,* or on *servants and masters,* or on whether *one can sit in judgment over another man,* etc. I modeled this character and figure on the ancient Russian monks and holy men: along with their profound humility they had limitless and naive hopes for Russia's future, for her moral and even political destiny. Didn't the metropolitans Sts. Sergius, Pyotr, and Aleksei always think of Russia in those terms?

I would be extremely grateful to you (*I implore* you), much esteemed Nikolai Alekseyevich, to entrust the proofs of this book to a reliable editor, since my absence prevents me from attending to them myself. I beg you to pay special attention to the proofreading of half-sheets *10 to 17* inclusive (the section headed "On the Holy Scriptures in the Life of Father Zosima"). This is an exalted and poetic chapter; the prototype is taken from certain teachings of Tikhon Zadonsky, and the ingenuousness of the narrative from the book of the wanderings of the monk Parfeny. Please take a look at it yourself, Nikolai Alekseyevich—be like a father to me! And after the proofs of the entire book have been gone over, please submit them to Mikhail Nikiforovich. I would very much like him to read them and say what he thinks, because I value his opinion very highly.

I hope you won't find anything that you will have to delete in this book or that you will have to correct editorially—not a single word, I assure you of that.

I would also be very much obliged if you would keep all the divisions into chapters and *subchapters* just as I have them. I have introduced into the novel something that is purported to be someone else's manuscript (the Note of Aleksei Karamazov) and it goes without saying that this manuscript has been divided up by Aleksei Karamazov in his own way. Here I will inject a NBene of protest: in the June issue, in the chapter "The Grand Inquisitor," you not only failed to respect my divisions, you even had 10 consecutive pages without *a single paragraph break*. This upset me a great deal and I am lodging a cordial complaint with you.

The next book, Book Seven, entitled "Grushenka," which will conclude Part Two of *The Karamazovs* this year, will be sent to you without fail from Staraya Russa around September 10. This Book Seven is meant for publication in the September and October numbers of *Russian Messenger*. This Book Seven will be only about 4 printer's sheets long, so that there will be only 2 printer's sheets for September at most. That cannot be helped, however, since Book Seven consists of two separate episodes, which are, as it were, two independent stories. But then, with the ending of Part Two, *the spirit and the meaning* of the novel is completely *fulfilled*. If it is not, it is I, the artist, who am to blame. As for Part Three of the novel (at most the same number of printer's sheets as Part One), I am postponing it, as I have already written you, until the coming year. It's my health, my health, that has interfered! Thus, Part Two will be, as it may seem, disproportionately long. But it just happened that way and cannot be helped.

I would like to tell you how very grateful I am to you for the favor you did me in sending the money to my wife in Staraya Russa as I asked you to. She has already written me to tell me that she has received it.

And now I will ask another favor of you, a bit in advance: Please do not forget, much esteemed Nikolai Alekseyevich, to see to it that the August number of R[ussian] Messenger is sent promptly to Staraya Russa! I expect to get home just around the time that it will be coming out.

Please accept the assurance of my profound and sincere respect,

Your faithful servant,

Fyodor Dostoyevsky.

Book Six, "The Russian Monk," which is being sent now, consists of a total of 53 half-sheets of letter-size paper.

---

138. St. Sergius (1314?–1392?) was the founder of the Troitse-Sergiyevskaya monastery at Zagorsk. Metropolitan Pyotr (d. 1326) supported the princes of Moscow in their struggle for the throne against the princes of Tver, and he became the first metropolitan to be installed in Moscow. Metropolitan Aleksei (d. 1378) played a similar role for Dmitry Donskoi in establishing Moscow as the center of resistance to the Tatars.

The monk Parfeny (d. 1868), of the Guslitsky Preobrazhensky monastery, was the author of A Tale of Wandering through Russia, Moldavia, Turkey, and the Holy Land (Skazaniye o stranstvii po Rossii, Moldavii, Turtsii, i Sv. Zemle, 1856).

139. To K. P. Pobedonostsev
Ems, August 9/21, 1879

Much esteemed Konstantin Petrovich,

I haven't answered until now your splendid letter addressed to me in Staraya Russa, because I had hoped to see you in person, if only briefly, on my way to Ems. But when I went to see you (in the Finnish church house), you were not in, although the doorman told me that you came there very often. I was very disappointed, because a talk with you is always heartening and buoys up my spirits and that is just what I needed most at that time. I was quite ill when I left for Ems. As a result of the bad weather, my chest condition (emphysema) took such a turn for the worse in Staraya Russa during the summer that I felt broken not only in body but in spirit, too. And to that must be added the hard work I had to do on The Karamazovs and, finally, the painful spectacle of what is going on and of the "Insane Asylum" of the Russian press and intelligentsia.

Here, I am in the third week of my cure without knowing what it will do for me, and meanwhile, the rate of exchange being what it is, this trip is costing me 700 rubles that could very well have been set aside for my family. As I sit here, I keep thinking that I will surely die soon, say in a year or two, and what then will become of the three most precious possessions I have after I am gone? And aside from that, I am in the gloomiest state of mind here: it is a narrow gorge, and granted that it is a very picturesque setting, but this is my 4th year here and I have come to hate every rock in sight, because it is hard for anyone to imagine how depressing these 4 visits have been for me. But my stay this time is the most horrible of all: teeming throngs of all sorts of riff-raff from all corners of Europe (very few Russians among them, and the few there are are strangers from Russia's borderlands) crammed into a narrow space (the gorge), not a soul I can talk to, and, above all, everything here is alien to me, completely alien—it is just too much. And I'll have to put up with this all the way to our September, i.e., 5 whole weeks . . . And mark you: literally half of the visitors here are Yids. Back in Berlin, where I saw Putsykovich on my way here, I remarked to him that, in my view, Germany, at any rate, Berlin, was being taken over by the Yids. And now I have found here, in an issue of *Moscow Gazette,* an excerpt from a pamphlet that has just appeared in Germany. This pamphlet, entitled *What Has the Jew To Do With It?*, is a Jew's answer to a German who dared to write that Germany was being completely taken over by the Jews in all respects. "It is not the Jews who are everywhere," the pamphlet claims, "it is the Germans." But even if the Jews are not everywhere, Jewish influence is omnipresent, because, the pamphlet claims, the Jewish spirit and the Jewish nationality are superior to the German and, in fact, have infected Germany with "*the spirit of profiteering realism,*" etc., etc. Thus, my view proved to be quite correct; both the Germans and the Jews themselves testify to it. But, apart from the profiteering realism, which is also making inroads on us in Russia, you would scarcely believe how everything here is dishonest, i.e., in trade, at least, etc. Today's German merchant not only cheats the foreigner (that would still be forgivable), but he literally *fleeces* him. When I tried to complain about it here, they told me laughingly that they treat everybody in the same way. Ah, why bother about them!

As soon as I arrived here, I got down to work, and, at last, the day before yesterday, I sent off to Moscow the installment due in August. It will come out on the 31st of August. This is Book Six of the novel and it is called "A Russian Monk." (N.B. It consists of some biographical data from the life of the elder Zosima and some of his teachings.) I expect lots of abuse from the critics; although I myself feel that I haven't given expression to even $\frac{1}{10}$ of what I wanted to say, I would still like to call your attention to this segment, my dear and much esteemed Konstantin Petrovich, because I am very eager to know what you think of it. I wrote this book for *the few,* and I consider it the culminating point of my work. By the way, I won't finish the novel this year; the 3rd and final part will have to wait until next year. But now, I am going to get down to my work again here.

In Berlin, I saw Putsykovich. Eventually somebody or other will help him out. He solemnly swore that he would bring out the promised issue of the *Citizen* in Berlin in three days, but to this day he has not got it out, and I don't think he ever will. One thing I have noticed about him is that he is a very lazy man who is quite incapable of hard work. As you know, I have tried to help him up till now, but now I feel he is hopeless. And yet he always manages to blame others for everything.

But here I have gone and written a whole letter, and it is about nothing but myself. Please forgive me for this, my dear and much esteemed Konstantin Petrovich. Your prisoners—Sakhalin, and what you wrote me about them—have racked my soul; it is something that touches me too closely, despite the interval of 25 years. But I will talk to you about it when we meet. And in the meantime, until our long-awaited and happy meeting, I remain your truly and ever devoted,

F. Dostoyevsky.

---

139. The "painful spectacle of what is going on" probably refers to the intensification of terrorist activity against the tsarist regime and the increasing number of trials that were being held in connection with it.

In the letter to which this is a response, Pobedonostsev had written of a voyage of 600 prisoners from Odessa to Sakhalin that he had helped to arrange. In order that it be "as much as possible a journey of solace," he had the prisoners escorted by priests, "an old doctor who loves his fellow men," and others; the Archbishop of Odessa saw the prisoners off and gave them some "touching" advice, and they sang a prayer in chorus.

140. To V. F. Putsykovich
Ems, August 14/26, 1879

Much esteemed Viktor Feofilovich,

I have received the *Citizen* and I thank you for sending it to me, but I am very surprised at you: Do you really imagine that the censors will allow it into Russia? And if they do not, what is the point of publishing it? After all, do you think there will be any subscribers if the issue cannot enter Russia? And how did you manage to roll up such a succession of blunders? I cannot imagine that the censorship would let through *personal insults* to well-known high officials or tolerate sneers directed at them. It was not permissible to write that Orlov had *gone a bit too far,* and even less so to say that Gorchakov and Shuvalov had been delighted to use other people's hands to do things they wouldn't do with their own at the Congress. And what you say about the sea bathing in Biarritz and Ostend. All those are personally offensive remarks. The expression, *She gave herself a spanking,* is also impossible, because after all it was the Emperor's wish. Look how the newspapers in Russia contrive to speak about it, under our censorship: I have read accusations in the *Moscow Gazette* about the Congress that are 10 times stronger than yours, and they manage without Biarritz, Ostend, other people's hands, and "she gave herself a spanking." I, at least, am absolutely certain that the censorship will never let it pass. I wonder how, after having edited a magazine for so many years, you can so completely lack a sense of what is possible and what is not. In 1877, before the war, Meshchersky wrote an anecdote about Gorchakov (without naming him) and the magazine was suspended for 3 months, or perhaps it was even 6. Do you really think they will allow it merely because you're publishing it abroad? So there go your subscriptions. And all that just for the sake of such nothings! All those broadsides, after all, add nothing to the meaning.

> You say the right word
> but the wrong way,

as the saying goes. And it is even more regrettable because the number is not bad at all and really could have attracted a number of subscribers. But enough for now, good-bye, I am late and must hurry off to the baths. Don't be angry: I am not lecturing you, I just had to get this off my chest, disappointed as I am to see a man spoiling his own work. Good-bye, I am leaving here in 2 weeks. Let me hear from you.

All yours,
F. Dostoyevsky.

---

140. The article that Dostoyevsky is criticizing was an attack on Russian diplomacy at the Congress of Berlin (June 13 to July 13, 1878), during which Russia lost the benefits it had gained in the Treaty of San Stefano ending the war with Turkey. Prince Aleksandr Mikhailovich Gorchakov (1798–1883), the Minister of Foreign Affairs, was widely accused of having succumbed to Bismarck's influence. Count Pyotr Andreyevich Shuvalov (1827–1889) was the Russian ambassador to Great Britain; Prince Nikolai Alekseyevich Orlov (1827–1885) was the Russian ambassador to France.

141. To A. G. Dostoyevskaya
Ems, August 16/28, 1879

I have just received your dear letter (of the 11th), my dear Anechka. I am now very sorry that I sent you my last impatient letter about the money. I swear to you that I was terribly worried, because by putting it off from one day to the next, you might suddenly have realized that it was already too late. Besides, I was under the impression that you were expecting me to return home much later than I was planning to. I will leave here (at least I will do my best to) definitely on the 29th (our style). Don't be angry with me. I've taken to brooding a great deal in my loneliness and I keep imagining all kinds of gloomy and unpleasant things happening. I feel so depressed that I cannot begin to describe it: I have even forgotten how to talk, and it actually surprises me when I catch myself saying a word aloud. For over three weeks now, I haven't heard my own voice.

You write that you sent me the 100 rubles "yesterday," which would mean on the 10th, but, although I have just now received your letter of the 11th, I haven't received the money yet. It's strange that it should be so late. But of course I will get it, perhaps tomorrow. You write me that I must be sparing with the money, and about the opera glasses. But I am being careful and I am keeping within my planned budget for everything except tobacco, on which I spend a bit more because I cannot find my usual brand here. But although my spending is strictly regulated, it is still hellishly high. I repeat that it is unlikely that I will have a single ruble left by the time I get back. Whenever I try to make calculations, I soon throw up my hands in despair— I'll be lucky if I can scrape through. As for the opera glasses, I am absolutely furious about them, because I was evidently duped and paid more than they are worth. But I wanted to buy them very badly. But then, in Russia there never were such swindling shopkeepers as there are now in Germany. It is the Yids again, the Yids have taken over everything, and they cheat like mad, and I mean cheat.

You write that you are very concerned about my health. As I told you before, I myself do not know what will come out of my treatment, although I am beginning to hope that it will do me some good. I am definitely gaining strength, I do feel that. My cough has subsided somewhat and is not so violent, but it is still there and I'll never get rid of it completely. Besides, it is so damp here that I keep catching cold and then for days on end I have a terrible tickling sensation in my throat. My breathing, however, is deeper and easier, and I do not get out of breath so much. Counting from tomorrow, exactly 12 days of the treatment remain, i.e., the last third.

Anyway, the state of my health will become clear in the fall and winter. But you know, Anya, you yourself write very little about your own health and that worries me a great deal. I want you to return to Petersburg after the summer in much better health. Your health is now much more important for the children than mine is. I think and worry about you a lot. I have read and reread in ecstasy your sweet words about your love for me. You write "love me" as though I had to be told to! It only sickens me to put certain things into words, and you could have seen as much for yourself, but, alas, you don't know how to see it. My husbandly rapture alone, so constant (indeed, it actually keeps growing every year), should mean something to you, but either you don't want to understand it or you are utterly incapable of understanding it, because of your lack of experience. Just show me any other marriage where that phenomenon is as strong as it is in our 12-year marriage. And my rapture and delight are inexhaustible. You may say that this is only the crudest aspect of it. No, it is not crude, and, as a matter of fact, all the rest is determined by it. But that, precisely, is something that you refuse to understand. To finish this tirade, I officially declare that I am thirsting to kiss every toe on your foot, and, you'll see, I will reach my goal. You write: "and what if somebody should read our letters?" Well, let them; let them envy us.

You write about the bad time you are going through because of the repairs being made on the house. What can you do about it—you asked for it yourself. But I see that the time is going by and I wonder what's happened about your trip to the Nil? Besides, I am still trembling at the thought of Mrs. Bergman's visit, which will cost you a lot of bother and be a tremendous strain on your nerves. I hope to God that everything works out for the best and pleasantly for you. Here, I keep thinking about our plans for the future and about that property I would like to buy. This has almost become an obsession with me, you know. I am so full of anxieties about the children and their future. I have got down to work on the novel and I am writing, but not very much because, if you can believe it, *I literally have no time.* I only hope that when I get back (on September 3rd or 4th) I will bring half of the September installment with me. I will have to get down to work on the other half the very next day without taking time off for a rest. And with all that, my work must be refined, elegant, and polished like a piece of jewelry. These are the most important chapters and should determine the readers' opinion of the novel. I am quite pleased with the installment I have sent them for August, although I anticipate (knowing them) that they will introduce many fatal errors into it.

But all that is in the future, and in the meantime I feel lonely here, and it is no ordinary loneliness but a morbid feeling, which could drive me out of my mind. I believe that lots of people are beginning to leave this place, although it is still appallingly crowded. There are awfully few Russians here, and none whom I know. It has been raining for the last three days.

Well now, how about Jaclard! He's all right, I'll tell you. He's just as he should be, a man who picks the flowers of joy, not like poor us, the frightened and the downtrodden! I was very interested in what you wrote about the staging of Krylov's fables. It sounds very good and quite charming.

I also admit that a trip to the Nil would be extremely instructive for the children and would leave them with something to remember for their whole lives. And of course the Nil is much better than the Bergman woman.

Thank dear little Lilya for her ever so sweet letter and tell Fedya that his letter is wonderful, that I just love it, and that I will keep it as long as I live. So good-bye, my angel, my golden treasure, my bright and beautiful wife. Yes, that's what you are—my beautiful one! And if I weren't restrained by what you say about censorship of the mail, God alone knows what I'd write you. *Nevertheless, I again kiss your feet.* [Two lines erased.] I kiss it continuously in my thoughts. And I also love your golden heart terribly, I revere and worship it. As for the nerves—that is something that can be cured, can't it? I kiss and bless the children and keep thinking of them. But enough for now.

Your eternal,

F. Dostoyevsky.

Are the children looking forward to my arrival? Do they mention me now and then? Teach Fedya to read. Is it possible that Lilichka is pale? I often look at their snapshots here.

I still do not get much sleep and continue having nightmares. Do look after your own health, Anya.

It suddenly occurs to me: Will this letter find you in Staraya Russa? And what if you decide to go off to the Nil? But I certainly do not object to that trip and only hope you can manage it without any special strain and worry.

I am afraid of catching cold on my long and hurried journey home and thus jeopardizing my cure. Once again, I kiss you (1000 times). Regards to all.

---

141. The "Bergman woman" was probably the wife of August A. Bergman, who had helped with the printing of *Epoch*, but it is not known why Dostoyevsky expected that her visit would be such a strain on Anna Grigorevna's nerves.

142.   To K. P. Pobedonostsev

Ems, August 25/September 6, 1879

Much esteemed and most worthy Konstantin Petrovich,

I have received your two letters and I thank you from the bottom of my heart for both of them, particularly for the first, in which you speak of my emotional state. You are perfectly, profoundly right and your thoughts have plainly buoyed me up. But I am sick in spirit and full of apprehension. Sitting here in sad and total isolation, I was bound to become depressed. Nevertheless, I ask you: Is it really possible to remain calm in our times? Why, you yourself, in your 2nd letter (and what is a letter?), point out all the intolerable things that are taking place. It so happens that, just now, I am still busy working on my novel (and I will finish it only next year!), but I am tormented by a desire to resume my *Diary* because there really are things that I have to say, just the things you would wish me to say, not sterile, commonplace polemics, but firm, fearless words. The main trouble is that now even those who have something to say are afraid. And what is it they are afraid of? Of a ghost, unquestionably. The "all-European" ideas in science and enlightenment stand despotically over everybody and no one dares to speak his mind. I understand only too well why Gradovsky's last few articles, in which he hailed the students as members of the intelligentsia, met with such huge success among our Europeans: it is precisely because he sees the cure for all the present horrors of the mess we are in in that same old Europe, and in Europe alone.

As for my literary status (I have never spoken to you about this), I consider it almost phenomenal that a man consistently writing against European principles, who compromised himself once and for all with *The Devils*, i.e., as an exponent of reaction and obscurantism, and a man who, notwithstanding the Europeanizers, their journals, newspapers, and literary critics, is, nevertheless, recognized by our youth, the very same youth who have been corrupted by the nihilist scum, etc. I have been informed of that from many quarters, both by individuals who have approached me and in collective declarations. They have told me that they look to me *alone* for a heartfelt and vibrant word and that they consider me alone their *guiding writer*. These statements by the young are well known to all our literati, to the pirates of the pen, and to the crooks of the publishing business, and they are flabbergasted by them—if it were not so, they wouldn't leave me alone to write so freely. They would tear me to pieces like a pack of dogs, but they are afraid, and in their bewilderment, they wait and see which way the wind will blow.

I've been reading that miserable *Voice* here—my God, how stupid, how sickeningly apathetic and quiescently petrified it is. Believe it or not, at times my rage turns to hilarity, for instance upon reading that 11-year-old thinker Yev[geny] Markov on women's rights. This is the acme of stupidity. You write that you did not like the issue of Putsykovich's publication. You are certainly right, but after all it is quite impossible even to say anything to the man, let alone give him advice, because he is very touchy and so sure of himself. Actually, all he cares about is circulation, but as for how he goes about all the rest, he is not to any great extent weighed down by scruples.

Your opinion of what you have read of *The Karamazovs* (about the force and vigor of the writing) flatters me greatly, but then, you also raise the *absolutely essential* question: That thus far I don't seem to have the answer to all these atheistic arguments, and an answer is indispensable. Yes, you have something there, and this is now my major worry and concern. For I attempt, as a matter of fact, to give the answer to this whole *negative side* in Book Six, "A Russian Monk," which will be coming out on August 31. And that's why I am trembling over it, wondering whether it will be an *adequate* answer. What makes it even more difficult is that the answer itself is not a direct one, not really a point-by-point refutation of the ideas formulated earlier (by the Grand Inquisitor and earlier), but only an indirect one. What is offered here is a world view that stands in direct opposition to the one that was previously presented, but again the opposition is not made point by point but, so to speak, in the form of an artistic picture. And that is just what worries me—i.e., will I be understood and will I even come close to my goal. And here, on top of everything else, there were certain artistic imperatives: I needed to draw a character who was both humble and sublime, whereas real life is full of the ridiculous and is only sublime in its inner meaning; and so, to satisfy the demands of art, I was also forced to touch upon some of the coarser aspects of existence when telling the life story of my monk. Then, there are also some of the monk's teachings, which people will inveigh against as being absurd because they are too exalted. I know very well that they are absurd in the everyday sense, but, in another, deeper sense, they seem quite appropriate. In any case, I am very uneasy and I would like very much to have your opinion, because I esteem and value your opinion very highly. I did write it with great love.

I see, however, that I have let myself go in telling you about my work. I shall be in Petersburg on September 1st or 2nd (hurrying to Staraya Russa to rejoin my family), and I will come by to see you (I cannot tell you in advance at what time it will be), and if I'm lucky enough to find you in we can have a moment together. Good-bye, then, my most kind and sincerely esteemed Konstantin Petrovich, may God send you many years of health—and no better wish is needed in our time, because people like you must go on living. From time to time, a silly and sinful thought crosses my mind: what would happen to *Russia* if we, the last of the Mohicans, should die? True, a second later I smile scornfully at the thought. Nevertheless, we must go on living and keep doing our duty. And are you not a man of duty? By the way: When I told Putsykovich about your letter in which you described the sending of the political prisoners to Sakhalin, he started badgering me to let him publish that passage in the *Citizen*. It goes without saying that I refused.

All yours,
F. Dostoyevsky.

---

142. In an article in the *Voice* in August 1879, Gradovsky had objected to the "going-to-the-people" movement and had advised students instead: "You can be useful to the people only by remaining yourselves, i.e., members of the Russian intelligentsia, only by gradually coming to swell the ranks of educated, reasonable, and moral Russian citizens."

Yevgeny Lvovich Markov (1835–1903) was a liberal writer and critic who contributed to many magazines and published popular travel sketches and novels.

143.   To N. A. Lyubimov
Staraya Russa, September 16, 1879

Dear Sir, much esteemed Nikolai Alekseyevich:

Under separate cover, I am sending to the offices of *R[ussian] Messenger Book Seven* of *Karamazovs*, consisting of 41 half-sheets, for publication in the September issue. This *Book* contains four chapters: three I am sending you now and the 4th I will send two days from now; it will be in your editorial office by the 20th. This 4th chapter will be only four printed pages long, but it is the most important, and it concludes the episode. I would have sent it along with the rest had not an epileptic attack forced me to put off my work for two days. But at least I am sending you 41 half-sheets (you should receive them on September 18), which you can begin setting right away, and the remaining 3 half-sheets (i.e., chapter 4), which I am holding on to for another two days, do not amount to a great deal of text and won't hold you up, provided, of course, you decide to publish the whole thing despite its being sent so late. And I can't tell you how much I want it to be published all as a single installment. All my hopes rest with you, much esteemed Nikolai Alekseyevich.

I am moving back to Petersburg on the 25th (to my old address). And that is why, once again, I cannot wait here for the proofs. I think the copy is quite legible. Please, much esteemed Nikolai Alekseyevich, tell the copy editor for me that I would be infinitely appreciative if he would see me through one more time. I thank him very much for the last number, too.

I beseech you, Nikolai Alekseyevich, not to have anything deleted from this Book. In fact, there isn't anything to delete—*everything is in order.* There is only one word that you may question—I say of the corpse that it started to *stink.* But then that word is uttered by Father Ferapont, who doesn't know how to talk any other way, and even if he could say *smell,* he wouldn't say it, but he would say *stink.* Please let it stand, *in the name of Christ!* There is nothing else. Unless, maybe, the business about the laxative. But that is written well and, besides, it is essential as an important accusation. The last chapter (which I will be sending you), "Cana of Galilee," is the most important chapter in Book Seven, and possibly in the entire novel. Now, with this installment, I have finished with the monastery. There will be nothing more about the monastery. The next Book (for your October number) will conclude this Part and then there will be the interruption which I notified you of before.

And now, please accept the assurance of my most sincere esteem.

Your most obedient servant,
Fyodor Dostoyevsky.

My Petersburg address: Kuznechny Lane, near St. Vladimir's Church, House No. 5, Apartment 10, Fyodor Mikhailovich Dostoyevsky.

One small Nota bene in case it may be needed: For God's sake, don't think for a minute that I would allow myself in my novel so much as to question the miraculous power of relics. I speak only of the relics of the dead monk Zosima, and that is quite a different matter. A commotion similar to the one I describe in the monastery occurred once in Mount Athos and was described briefly and with touching simplicity in "The Peregrinations of the Monk Parfeny."

Dostoyevsky.

P.S. Much esteemed Nikolai Alekseyevich, I beg you to be especially thorough when correcting the proofs concerning the legend of *the onion*. This is a jewel that I wrote down as it was told to me by a peasant woman, and certainly this is *the first time it has been written down*. At least, I never heard of it before myself.

Dostoyevsky.

---

143. In chapter 1, book 7, of *The Brothers Karamazov,* Father Ferapont, who had scoffed at the idea that the elder Zosima might be a saint, claims that he has been vindicated when the elder's body begins to smell from decay on the very day of his death, which Father Ferapont interprets to mean that Zosima was just an ordinary sinner, after all.

Dostoyevsky had earlier written to Lyubimov that book 8 would be the last installment he would send that year. In November, however, he wrote that "things have turned out differently"; he would be sending one more book, book 9, for publication in December. This book "cropped up . . . suddenly and unexpectedly" when he realized, "while consulting a prosecutor (with much legal experience)," that the preliminary investigation, "a very interesting and extremely deficient part of our legal process . . . was totally missing in my novel." In the event, he did not deliver this book until January 1880, anyway.

Again, Dostoyevsky errs when he says that he was the first to have transcribed the legend of the onion. Two versions of it, one of them quite close to Dostoyevsky's, appeared in A. N. Afanaseva's collection of Russian legends published in 1859.

144.   To Ye. N. Lebedeva
Petersburg, November 8, 1879

Dear Madam:

Old man Karamazov was killed by the servant Smerdyakov. All the details will be cleared up in the subsequent development of the novel. Ivan Fyodorovich participated in the murder only indirectly and remotely, only to the extent that he refrained (deliberately) from talking Smerdyakov out of it during their conversation before Ivan's departure for Moscow and from expressing clearly and categorically his disapproval of the contemplated crime (which Iv. F——ch clearly visualized and foresaw); thus he, *as it were, permitted* Smerdyakov to perpetrate it. The fact that Smerdyakov absolutely had to have that *permission* will also become clear later on. Dmitry Fyodorovich is completely innocent of his father's murder.

489

When Dmitry Karamazov jumped down from the fence and started wiping with his handkerchief the blood from the head of the old manservant he had wounded, his words "You've had it now, old man," etc., in themselves give a hint to the readers that he was *not* a parricide. If he had killed his father and 10 minutes later had killed Grigory also, he would hardly have climbed down from the fence to the wounded servant, unless perhaps to make sure that he had really killed the man who could be an important witness to the crime he had committed. But besides that, he seems to be full of compassion when he says, "You've had it, old man," etc. If he had killed his father, he would not have stood over the body of the servant with words of pity. It is not only the subject of a novel that is important to the reader, but also a certain understanding of the human soul (psychology), and every author has the right to expect this from his reader.

In any case I am flattered by your interest in my book.

Please accept the assurance of my most sincere respect,

Your faithful servant,

F. Dostoyevsky.

---

144. Dostoyevsky is here answering questions from a reader concerning chapter 4, book 8, of *The Brothers Karamazov,* in which Dmitry Karamazov restrains himself from killing his father but wounds the old servant Grigory. This chapter had been published in the October 1879 issue of the *Russian Messenger.*

145.   To N. M. DOSTOYEVSKY

[Petersburg] April 21 [1880]

My dear brother Nikolai Mikhailovich,

Thank you for your letter (which I just received today). It is already a whole year since we saw each other. I don't know what it means: Whether it is, on your part, a deliberate way of behaving, or something else. Meanwhile, our lives are nearing their end and are indeed so close to it that you won't have time to put into practice even the best ways of behaving. I always keep in mind that you are my brother, but there are many things about people that I have given up trying to understand.

We shall probably go somewhere or other soon after Holy Week. Besides, I have work to do, and yet my life is such a bustle, from which I can't extricate myself, that I can't even work.

My health is not so good. Anna Grigorevna is also feeling not quite well. She sends you her regards and thanks you for your good wishes.

The children, thank God, are in good health.

I wish you good health, too.

Yesterday I had to go out for some essential visits and I believe I caught a cold. I wish you good health from the bottom of my heart and shake your hand heartily. Happy Easter!

Your brother,
F. Dostoyevsky

---

145. The "bustle" in Dostoyevsky's life was probably due to the heavy schedule of public readings he was called upon to make for the benefit of various charitable organizations (see Letter 154).

146.   To K. P. POBEDONOSTSEV
Staraya Russa, May 19, 1880

Highly esteemed Konstantin Petrovich,

Following a tradition of several years, I cannot let May 21st go by without sending you sincere and heartfelt greetings on your name day, wishing you all the best and everything that you wish for yourself. Above all, may God grant you good health and then a full measure of success in your new endeavors. I am sending this to your old address in the hope that the post office will know your new address. Before leaving Petersburg (exactly one week ago), I firmly intended to come by to see you so as to say good-bye to you for the summer and to ask you for a word of guidance that I badly needed for a very special reason. But the hustle and bustle connected with my departure prevented me from doing so. And I certainly did not come to Russa to rest and relax: I have to go to Moscow for the unveiling of the Pushkin monument, and not only for myself but also as the representative of the Slav Philanthropic Society. And as I feared from the start, the way it looks I am not going to enjoy myself but, instead, may be in for a rather bad time, because this affair touches upon convictions that are very dear and vital to me. Even before I left Petersburg, I had vaguely heard that a certain clique was on the rampage in Moscow, trying to prevent certain views from being expressed at the ceremony and fearful that *some* people might come up with *reactionary* statements at the meetings of the [Society of] Friends of Russian Literature, the organizers of the festivities. I, however, have been expressly invited by the chairman of the Society and by the Society itself (by official invitation) to *speak* at the unveiling ceremony. Even the newspapers have reported rumors about all sorts of intrigues. I have prepared my speech on Pushkin, in the *ultimate* spirit of my (or, if I dare say so, *our*) convictions, and this is why I expect that there may be a certain amount of abuse. But I refuse to be intimidated and I am not afraid; I feel I must defend my beliefs and I will speak up fearlessly. There the professors are wooing Turgenev, who has definitely become a sort of personal enemy to me. (He has spread a piece of gossip through *Messenger of Europe* about an event of 35 years ago that never did happen.) But I cannot sing Pushkin's glory while pleading for "Verochka."

But why should I burden you, after all, with such petty gossip. However, the trouble is that it is not just ordinary gossip but a matter of great public importance, because Pushkin symbolizes the idea that all of us (just a handful of people at present) are serving, and this is something that has to be pointed out and explained, and this is just what they hate. There is also the possibility that they won't give me a chance to speak. But then I will have my speech published.

I shake your hand hard, highly esteemed Konstantin Petrovich. When I return from Moscow, I will get down to work and finish *The Karamazovs*, working throughout the whole summer. But I am not complaining, for I love this work. I have definitely decided to resume publication of the *Diary of a Writer*, next year. Then I will once again turn to you (as I did in the past) for guidance and advice, and I know implicitly that you will not fail me.

And in the meantime, accept the assurance of my most ardent loyalty,
Your most faithful servant,
F. Dostoyevsky.

My wife sends you her congratulations and has just reproached me for having forgotten to mention her in my letter.

---

146. Pobedonostsev had just been appointed supreme procurator of the Holy Synod.

The "piece of gossip" that had appeared in *Messenger of Europe* was a story by P. V. Annenkov that, after Belinsky had praised Dostoyevsky's novel *Poor Folk* in manuscript, Dostoyevsky had insisted that it be printed with "some special typographical arrangement, such as a border around each page," in order "to distinguish it" from the other material in the anthology in which it was published. The story was false. However, it is not altogether clear that it had been inspired by Turgenev. Nor is it clear what Dostoyevsky means by his allusion to "Verochka" (he puts the name in quotation marks himself).

147. To A. G. DOSTOYEVSKAYA
Loskutnaya Hotel, Tverskaya Avenue
Moscow
Sunday, May 25, 1880

My dear friend Anya,

Yesterday morning Lavrov, Nik[olai] Aksakov and Zverev, a lecturer at the university, made a formal call on me to pay their respects. That same morning I had to return the visit of each of them. It took up a lot of my time and meant a lot of running around. Then I went to Yurev's. He received me enthusiastically, with embraces and all. He told me that they plan to request permission to hold the unveiling of the monument in the fall—in October, rather than in June or July, as suggested, apparently, by the authorities; but then the inauguration ceremony would be a sham, since no one would come. I could not find out anything from Yurev about the actual situation because he is a rather disorganized man, a sort of modernized version of Repetilov, but with an element of shrewdness. (There is no doubt, though, that there have been all sorts of intrigues.) Among other things, I mentioned my article, whereupon, all of a sudden, Yurev says to me: "I didn't ask you for an article!" (i.e., for his magazine). But I remember very clearly that he did in his letters. The trouble is that this Repetilov is sly: he does not feel like accepting my article now and paying for it: "Keep it for the fall, for the fall, give it to us then, don't give it to anyone but us, we have priority, remember, and that will give you time to put the finishing touches on it" (as though he already knew that the article was still in need of polishing). I, of course, immediately stopped talking about the article and gave him only a very vague promise for the fall. I didn't like that one bit.

After leaving him, I went to Novikova's and was very cordially received. Then I went to pay a few other calls and then went to Katkov's; I didn't find either Katkov or Lyubimov in. Then I made the round of the booksellers. Two of them (including Kashkin) had moved to new quarters. They all promised to let me have something on Monday. I wonder whether they will keep their promises. However, I will go to see them again on Monday and will try to get the new addresses by then. Then I went to Iv[an] S. Aksakov's. He is still in town but I didn't find him at home, he was at the bank. After that I returned to the hotel and had my dinner. Then at 7 o'clock I drove over to Katkov's. Both Katkov and Lyubimov were there; they welcomed me very warmly and I had a talk with Lyubimov about the delivery of *The Karamazovs*. They insist on June. (I will have to work like hell when I get back.) Then I mentioned the article and Katkov tried to convince me to give it to him, i.e., for the fall. Infuriated as I was with Yurev, I *almost* promised it to him. So that now if *Russian Thought* decides they want my article, I'll make them pay handsomely for it, and if they won't pay my price I will give it to Katkov (and by that time I could expand the article).

From Katkov's (where I spilled my tea on myself and got all wet), I went to Varya's. She was at home and, although it was almost 10 o'clock by then, we went together to pay a visit to Yelena Pavlovna. Varya had just received a letter for me from our brother Andrei (concerning the documents on the estate). I kept the letter. It turned out that Yelena Pavlovna had moved to another apartment and that she has given up renting rooms. So we went to her new apartment and found, visiting her there, Masha and Nina Ivanova (with whom Yelena Pavlovna has made up) and Khmyrov. The Ivanovs are leaving for Darovoye in three days and Khmyrov is going there too, because his wife is staying there now with Vera Mikhailovna. We sat there for an hour or so. On returning to the hotel, I found a letter that Nik. Aksakov and Lavrov had personally delivered. They invite me to dinner on the 25th (i.e., today) and they will come and pick me up at 5 o'clock. It is organized by the staff of *Russian Thought,* but other people will be there as well. From what Yurev said (when I saw him), I gather there will be from 15 to 30 people. I have the impression that the dinner is being given in honor of my visit to Moscow, i.e., that I am the guest of honor, and that it will be in some restaurant. (All these young Moscow literati are so eager to make my acquaintance.) It's three o'clock now; in 2 hours they will come to pick me up, but I am still hesitating about what to wear—frock coat or tails.

Well, so now you have my complete report. I didn't ask Katkov for money, but I told Lyubimov that I might need some during the summer, to which he said that if I needed any, all I would have to do would be to ask him and he would have it sent to wherever I told him. Tomorrow I will have to make the rounds of the booksellers, stop by Yelena Pavlovna's to see whether there's a letter from you, pay a visit to Mashenka, who is very anxious to see me, etc. The day after tomorrow, on Tuesday the 27th, I will leave for Russa, but I am not sure yet whether I will take the morning or the midday train. I am afraid, though, that they won't give me a chance to attend to my business tomorrow: Yurev kept screaming that he "must talk and talk and talk with me," and all that. Actually, it all bores me very much and my nerves are on edge. I don't expect I'll write you again unless something very special should happen. Good-bye, darling, I kiss you warmly as well as the children. Kiss Lilya and Fedya for me many times. I love you all very much.

Your,
F. Dostoyevsky.

May 25, 2 P.M.

Post-Scriptum

My dear Anya, yesterday I had already unsealed the envelope that was ready to be mailed in order to add a postscript. This morning, Ivan Serg[eyevich] Aksakov came to the hotel and implored me to remain for the unveiling ceremonies because they are expected to take place before the 5th. He said that I could not leave, that I had no *right* to leave, that I exert great influence on Moscow, on the youth in general and on the university students in particular, that my departure would jeopardize the triumph of our fundamental ideas, that after he had heard the outline of my speech at the dinner last night, he became utterly convinced that it was my duty to speak and so on and so forth. He also pointed out to me that, being a delegate from the Slav Philanthropic Society, I couldn't leave, since all the other delegates had decided to stay on because of the rumor that the unveiling ceremonies were to take place soon.

After he left, Yurev (at whose house I am having dinner tonight) dropped in and said the same thing. Today (the 25th), Dolgoruky left for Petersburg and *he gave his word* to send a telegram from Petersburg about the exact day of the unveiling of the monument. They expect to receive the telegram no later than Wednesday the 28th and *possibly even tomorrow.* This is what I have decided: to wait for the telegram and if the unveiling is really to take place between June 1st and 5th, I will remain. If it is to take place later, I will leave for Russa on the 28th or 29th. And that's what I told Yurev.

What worries me most is that I have not been able to locate Zolotaryov. Yurev promised to find out where he is and let me know today. Then I will be able to leave, even though I am a delegate of the Slav Philanthropic Society, because I will have arranged with Zolotaryov to represent us at the ceremonies (by the way, we must pay for the wreaths for the monument out of our own pockets, and a wreath costs 50 rubles!). At one point Yurev started pestering me to let him publish my article in *Russian Thought.* So I told him everything, i.e., that I had *almost promised* it to Katkov. He became very upset and distressed, apologized, and claimed that I had misunderstood him, that it was a quid pro quo; and when I hinted that I charged money for my work, he exclaimed that Lavrov had told him to pay me anything I asked, i.e., even 400 or 500 rubles.

I also told Yurev that the reason I had *almost* promised the article to Katkov was to obtain a delay in publishing *The Karamazovs,* which could be explained (to the public) by the fact that the Pushkin article was appearing in place of *The Karamazovs.* But if I now give that piece to R[ussian] *Thought,* it will look as if I asked Katkov for the delay so that I could work for his enemy Yurev. (So imagine the position I am in! But it's Yurev's own fault.) Katkov will be offended. Still, Katkov would not pay 100 rubles (why, he's giving me only 300 rubles [per printer's sheet] for *The Karamazovs,* and for an article he surely wouldn't pay even 300 rubles), and that extra hundred and fifty rubles from Yurev would pay for the additional time I am spending here until the unveiling of the monument. In short, there is no end of troubles and complications. I don't know what is going to happen, but for the moment I've decided to stay here until the 28th. Therefore, unless the unveiling of the monument is scheduled for before the 5th, I will be back in Russa on the 29th or 30th (having done my best before then to place my article somewhere or other).

I want to hear something from you immediately (I repeat my request again). Will I really not get a single line from you while I am here? *Write immediately* to the addresses I mentioned yesterday in my letter (which you will receive together with this P. Scriptum). If you prefer, send me a telegram.

Yurev said that today many people came to see him to protest: Why hadn't he let them know about yesterday's dinner party? There were even 4 students who came seeking admittance to the dinner.

By the way, I had visits from Sukhomlinov (he is in town), Gattsuk, Viskovatov and others.

I am off to the booksellers now. Good-bye. Once again I kiss you all.

All yours,

F. Dostoyevsky.

Yurev had already got hold of Iv. Aksakov's article on Pushkin. That is probably why he was trying to dodge the issue the day before yesterday. But after hearing at the dinner what I had to say about Pushkin, he probably decided that he *must* have my article, too. Turgenev has also written an article on Pushkin.

---

147. The unveiling of the monument to Pushkin, which was planned as a major literary event, had been scheduled for the end of May. However, Mariya Aleksandrovna, the wife of Tsar Alexander II, died on May 22, and the tsar ordered that the unveiling be postponed "until some other time." It was then rescheduled for June 4, but was postponed again and finally took place on June 6.

Vukol Mikhailovich Lavrov (1852–1912) was a journalist and translator of Polish works. He was the editor of *Russian Thought* for twenty-five years, beginning in 1880.

Nikolai Petrovich Aksakov (1848–1909) was a theologian and historian and a contributor to several contemporary journals. Nikolai Andreyevich Zverev (1850–1917) was a professor of philosophy and the history of law at Moscow University; he later became deputy minister of public education and then head of the Chief Administration for Press Affairs.

Repetilov is a character in Aleksandr Sergeyevich Griboyedov's play *Woe from Wit* (Gore ot uma, 1825).

Olga Alekseyevna (Kireyeva) Novikova (1840–1921) was a journalist who had been the London correspondent for *Moscow Gazette* and had written several books, in both English and Russian, about the two countries and their relationships.

The Ivan Aksakov mentioned in the second paragraph of the letter was a bank director. The Ivan Aksakov mentioned in the postscript was a leading Slavophile writer (see the note to Letter 50).

Yelena Pavlovna Ivanova was a relative by marriage of Dostoyevsky's sister Vera Mikhailovna. Masha and Nina were Vera Mikhailovna's daughters. Dmitry Nikolayevich Khmyrov (1847–1926) was a teacher of mathematics and the husband of another of Vera Mikhailovna's daughters, Sonya.

Prince Dolgoruky (Dolgorukov) was the governor general of Moscow.

Dostoyevsky refers to Yurev as Katkov's enemy because of the polemics that had recently broken out between their respective journals, *Russian Thought* and *Moscow Gazette*.

Dostoyevsky need not have worried about the expenses of his stay in Moscow.

Soon after this letter was written, he learned that all his expenses were being paid by the city of Moscow as its guest.

Mikhail Ivanovich Sukhomlinov (1828–1901) was the author of an eight-volume history of the Russian Academy of Sciences and of other works on Russian science and literature. Aleksei Alekseyevich Gattsuk (1832–1891) was the editor of the *Weekly Illustrated Supplement to the Religious Calendar* (Yezhenedelnoye illyustrirovannoye prilozheniye k Krestnomu kalendaryu), which is mentioned in chapter 9, book 11, of *The Brothers Karamazov*. Pavel Aleksandrovich Viskovatov (1842–1906) was a professor of Russian literature at Derpt University.

148.   To A. G. DOSTOYEVSKAYA
Hotel Loskutnaya, Room 33
Tverskaya Avenue, Moscow
May 25–26, 1880.

My dear friend Anya,

Here's another letter for you (I'm writing this at about 2 A.M.). It may not reach you before I get home (for I still plan to leave here on Tuesday, the 27th), but I am writing *just in case* because circumstances may make it necessary for me to stay here for a little while longer. But let me proceed in the proper order. Today, the 25th, at 5 o'clock, Lavrov and Nik[olai] Aksakov came for me and took me in their own carriage to the Hermitage. They were wearing frock coats and I went in a frock coat, too, although, as it turned out, the dinner was indeed being given in my honor. There were already 22 people waiting for us at the Hermitage—literary figures, professors, scholars. In a *solemn* welcoming speech, Yurev started by saying that many more people were eager to attend the dinner and that if it had been postponed by only a single day, several hundred persons would have been present; but they had organized the party too hastily and now they were afraid that, when many other people learned about it, they would reproach them for not having been invited. Among the guests, there were 4 university professors, one high-school principal, Polivanov (a friend of the Pushkin family), Ivan Sergeyevich Aksakov, Nikolai Aksakov, Nikolai Rubinstein (from Moscow), etc., etc.

The dinner was a very lavish affair. A whole room had been reserved (which must have cost quite a bit of money). They brought in filets of smoked sturgeon that were 1½ arshins long, one-and-a-half-arshin-long boiled sterlets, turtle soup, wild strawberries, quail, some marvelous asparagus, ice cream, the most exquisite wines, and rivers of champagne. 6 speeches were made in my honor (with the speakers standing up to deliver them), some of them very long. Those who spoke were Yurev, both Aksakovs, 3 of the professors, and Nikolai Rubinstein. During the dinner two telegrams of greeting arrived, one of them from a preeminent professor who had had to leave

Moscow at the last moment; it spoke of my "tremendous" importance in literature as an artist of "universal sensitivity," as a polemicist, and as a Russian. After that there was an endless succession of toasts with everyone getting up and coming over to clink glasses with me. I will tell you more details when I see you. It was all in an atmosphere of great enthusiasm. I answered them all with a quite successful speech, which produced a great effect, and then switched to the subject of Pushkin. It made a powerful impression.

Now I must tell you about an annoying and complicated matter. A delegation from the Society of Friends of Russian Literature went to see Prince Dolgorukov today, and he told them that the unveiling of the monument would take place sometime between June 1st and 5th, without giving them the exact date, however. And they seemed to be delighted with this decision: This way, they say, the literary figures and delegations will not leave Moscow and, although there will be no music and no theatrical performances, there will still be meetings of the Friends of Literature, with speeches and dinners. When I said that I was planning to leave on the 27th, a determined roar of protest went up: "We just won't let you go!" Polivanov (who is on the committee for the inauguration of the monument), Yurev, and Aksakov declared publicly that all Moscow was buying tickets to attend the meetings and that all the ticket buyers (to the meetings of the Friends of Russian Literature) were inquiring, as they bought the tickets (and inquiring repeatedly beforehand): *will Dostoyevsky be reading?* But since they couldn't be told at which particular meeting I would speak—whether it would be at the first or the 2nd one—everyone then started buying tickets for both meetings. "All of Moscow will be sad and furious if you leave," they all told me. I tried to get out of it by saying that I had to get on with writing *The Karamazovs,* which unleashed a clamor seriously suggesting that a delegation be sent to Katkov to ask him to give me a postponement. Then I tried to argue that you and the children would be worried if I were to stay away for so long, and so they offered (and they were not joking) not only to send you a telegram but even to send a delegation to Staraya Russa to beg for your permission for me to stay here. I then told them that I would decide tomorrow, i.e., on Monday the 26th.

Now I am sitting here in great difficulty and anxiety: On the one hand, the strengthening of my influence not only in Petersburg but also in Moscow is very important to me; on the other hand, staying here would mean separation from all of you, difficulties with *The Karamazovs,* expenses, etc. Finally, although my "Word" on Pushkin will definitely be published now, the question is where, because on Saturday I almost promised it to Katkov, which would make the Friends and Yurev very sad indeed. But if I were to give the speech to them, it would infuriate Katkov.

For the moment I am sticking to my decision to leave, if not on the 27th, then on the 28th or 29th, when Dolgoruky will at last give us the *exact* date of the unveiling. I may have to wait until then. But then again Dolgorukov speaks *in his own name* and has not received as yet any specific instructions from Petersburg as to the exact *date* (and, as a matter of fact, I understand he is going to Petersburg himself for a few days). So, suppose I decide to stay here until June 5 and there discover that a higher order has again postponed the inauguration until June 10 or 15, am I then to go on waiting or what? Tomorrow I will tell Yurev that I am leaving on the 27th, but that if I should stay on here, it will be only because of some precise and compelling circumstances.

In any case, I am now in a state of tremendous anxiety. I stopped over at Yelena Pavlovna's after the dinner to see if there was any mail, but there was *nothing from you*. Of course, it is still a bit early for a letter from Russa to get here, but is it possible that there will be nothing from you tomorrow, either? Yelena Pavlovna and I then went over to see Mashenka Ivanova and I told her that I had had dinner with Rubinstein and she was very excited about it. At any rate, as soon as you get this letter, answer me right away without bothering about whether I may have left Moscow by then or not, since, if it misses me here, Yelena Pavlovna will send it back unsealed to Russa. And so answer me at once without fail. Here is the exact address of Yelena Pavlovna's: *Voskresene Parish, Ostozhenka Street, Dmitriyevskaya's House, for F. M. Dostoyevsky.* If you want to send me a telegram, you can send it either to Yelena Pavlovna's or directly to me at the Loskutnaya Hotel, Tverskaya Avenue—either way I will certainly get it (but for letters, you'd better address them to Yelena Pavlovna's).

NB I was elected a member of the Society of the Friends of Russian Literature already a year ago, but the former secretary, Bessonov, out of neglect failed to notify me of it and they have now apologized to me. I hug you hard, my dear, and I kiss the children. At night I have strange, portentous dreams.

All yours,
F. Dostoyevsky

Yes, that speech of mine was really good. Once again I hug you. Kiss the children for me and talk to them about their papa.

All yours,
F. Dostoyevsky.

P.S. I think, after all, I will insist and leave on the 27th. It is true, though, that in that case it won't be appropriate to have the speech published, because it will no longer be of interest as a speech but will be just an article. And it will have to be reworked.

---

148. Lev Ivanovich Polivanov (1838–1898) was principal of the highly regarded Polivanov High School in Moscow and acting secretary of the Society of Friends of

Russian Literature from 1878 to 1880. He apparently had an important role in arranging the ceremonies for the unveiling of the Pushkin monument.

Nikolai Grigorevich Rubinstein (1835–1881), younger brother of Anton, was director of the Moscow Conservatory of Music.

149.   To A. G. Dostoyevskaya
Loskutnaya Hotel, Room 33
Moscow
May 28–29 [1880]
2 A.M.

My dear Anya,

The only news I have is that Dolgorukov's telegram arrived today announcing that the unveiling of the monument is to take place on the 4th. This time it is official. Therefore, I can leave Moscow on the 8th, or even the 7th, and you may be sure that I won't lose any time. But remain here I *must*, and I have decided to do so. The main thing is that I am needed here, not just by the Friends of Russian Literature, but by our whole party and the whole idea for which we have been struggling for 30 years now. For the hostile party (Turgenev, Kovalevsky, and almost the entire university) is determined to play down the importance of Pushkin as the man who gave expression to the Russian national identity, by denying the very existence of that identity. To oppose them, our side has only Ivan Serg. Aksakov (Yurev and the rest carry no weight), but Ivan Aksakov is out of date and Moscow has had its fill of him. But Moscow has never seen me or heard me speak and I am now the main focus of interest. My voice will carry weight and our side will prevail. I have struggled for this all my life, and so it would be quite unthinkable for me to flee now from the battlefield. And when Katkov himself—who is no Slavophile—says, "You must not leave, it is impossible for you to leave," then obviously *I must not* leave.

At noon today, while I was still asleep, Yurev came to my room with that telegram. He sat around while I was getting dressed, and at that moment I was informed that two ladies had come to see me. I hadn't finished dressing, so I sent to find out who they were. The fellow returned with a note that a Mrs. Ilina wanted to obtain my permission to publish a book containing selections from my writings suitable for children and to publish a book for young readers. What do you think of that! Why, we should have thought of that ourselves long ago and published a book like that for *children*—it would certainly sell and might bring us a profit of 2000 rubles. And now this woman is asking me to make her a present of these 2000 rubles. What impudence! Yurev at once went to tell her that I was not at all prepared to grant her the permission and that I could not receive her (he went because it was he himself who had thoughtlessly suggested to her that she come and see me). No sooner had he left than Varvara Mikhailovna arrived, and before she was even inside the room, Viskovatov appeared behind her. Seeing that I had visitors, Varya left in a great hurry. Yurev came back and told me that the second lady visitor had come on her own; she did not tell him her name and said only that she had come to express her infinite esteem, amazement, and gratitude for what I had given her by my books, etc. Having said that, she departed and I never saw her. I had some tea served to my guests and then Grigorovich came in. We sat there for a couple of hours in my room until Yurev and Viskovatov left, but Grigorovich stayed on, apparently with no intention of leaving. He started telling me all kinds of stories accumulated during the past thirty years, reminiscing about the past and all that. Half of the things he told me were, of course, sheer fabrication but some of it was actually quite interesting. Then, when it was almost 5 o'clock, he announced that he did not wish to part from me and started begging me to go and have dinner with him. So I went with him, again to the Moscow Inn, where we had a very leisurely dinner, during which he talked the whole time. Suddenly Averkiyev and his wife came in. Averkiyev sat down with us and Dona Anna declared that she would come by and see me (I really need her!). It turned out that two of Pushkin's nephews, Pavlishchev and Pushkin, and some other fellow were having dinner at a nearby table. Pavlishchev also came over and said that he'd come by to see me. In short, it's just like it was in Petersburg, they won't leave me in peace.

After dinner, Grigorovich started trying to convince me to drive with him through the park "to get some fresh air," but I refused, parted with him, returned to my hotel on foot and 10 minutes later drove off to Yelena Pavlovna's to see if there was any mail. But there was no letter for me; only the Ivanova girls were there. Mashenka is leaving tomorrow. I sat around until 11 o'clock, then returned to the hotel to have some tea and to write you a letter. That's my whole report.

It's very bad that our letters take as long as three or four days to reach their destination. Since I informed you I was coming back and you are expecting me on the 28th, you won't be writing me again, of course, and now imagine the time it will take before you receive my yesterday's and today's letters about the change in my plans! I am afraid you'll find it all bewildering and start worrying.

But that cannot be helped. It's awful, though, that I may have nothing from you for perhaps another 2 days, because I miss you very badly. I feel very sad here despite all the guests and all the dinners. Ah, Anya, what a shame it is that we couldn't have arranged (of course, it was plainly impossible) for you to come along with me! I have heard that even Maikov has changed his mind and decided to come. I still have a lot of running around to do here: I have to report to City Hall and register there as a delegate (exactly when, I still don't know) in order to get a pass to the ceremonies.

They are renting the windows of the houses around the square at 50 rubles a window. All around the square they are setting up wooden stands for the public, with seats also going at exorbitant prices. What worries me also is that it may be a rainy day and I might catch cold. I won't be speaking at the dinner on the opening day. I believe that my speech is scheduled for the 2nd day, at the meeting of the Friends. They are also thinking of replacing the theatrical performance by readings from Pushkin by prominent literary figures (Turgenev, me, Yurev). (They have asked me to read the scene of the monk-chronicler and the monologue of the miser in "The Covetous Knight." Furthermore, Yurev, I, and Viskovatov will each read one poem on Pushkin's death: Yurev will read Guber's, Viskovatov—Lermontov's, and I—Tyutchev's.)

Time is running out and people prevent me from doing what I have to do. I haven't yet managed to go to pick up the money at the Central Store or at the Morozovs. I haven't been to Chayev's and I must pay a visit to Varya. I would also like very much to meet Nikolai, the bishop of Japan, and Aleksei, the vicar of Moscow—they are very interesting men. I don't sleep well and am constantly haunted by nightmares. I am afraid I might catch cold on the opening day and cough during my reading.

I'll be waiting now for a letter from you with great impatience. How are the children? My God, how anxious I am to see them! Are you feeling well? Are you in good spirits, or are you cross? It is painful for me to be away from all of you. Well, good-bye. I won't go to Yel[ena] Pavlovna's tomorrow; she has promised to forward any letter that arrives. I hug you all very hard and I bless the children.

All yours,
F. Dostoyevsky.

P.S. If anything should happen, wire me at the Loskutnaya Hotel. And address the letters to the hotel, too. Do you get my letters all right? It would be a disaster if some letter got lost!

Zolotaryov hasn't arrived yet.

---

149. By "our party," Dostoyevsky means the Slavophiles, and "the whole idea" refers to the view that the Russian people were the bearers of true Christianity.

Maksim Maksimovich Kovalevsky (1851–1916) was a sociologist and a historian of the law and one of the leading figures in the liberal movement.

Dmitry Vasilevich Grigorovich was one of the four representatives of the Literary Fund at the Pushkin festivities.

"Dona [Dostoyevsky presumably means "Donna"] Anna" is a sarcastic reference to Averkiyev's wife, a former actress, whom Dostoyevsky disliked.

Lev Nikolayevich Pavlishchev (1834–1915) was a son of Pushkin's sister and the author of a book of reminiscences about his uncle. Anatoly Lvovich Pushkin was a son of Pushkin's brother Lev Sergeyevich.

The "monk-chronicler" is Pimen in Pushkin's *Boris Godunov*. Dostoyevsky did read this passage at the festivities, but not the scene from "The Covetous Knight" (Skupoi rytsar, 1832) or Tyutchev's poem. Instead, without his knowledge and somewhat to his annoyance, he was "assigned" to read two of Pushkin's poems: "The Tale of the She-Bear" (Skazka o mededikhe, published posthumously in 1855) and "The Prophet" (Prorok, 1826).

Eduard Ivanovich Guber (1814–1847), in addition to his poem on Pushkin's death, had published a translation of part 1 of Goethe's *Faust;* in 1847, he had written a critical review of Dostoyevsky's early work.

Mikhail Yurevich Lermontov (1814–1841) was a poet and novelist. His "Death of a Poet" (Smert poeta, 1837) brought him immediate fame; it accused the Petersburg court society of responsibility for Pushkin's death and led to Lermontov's arrest and imprisonment (though he was pardoned a year later). He was also the author of a classic Russian novel, *A Hero of Our Time* (Geroi nashego vremeni, 1840). Like Pushkin, he was killed in a duel.

Morozov was one of several Moscow book dealers with whom Dostoyevsky had business relations in connection with the publication of his works.

Nikolai Aleksandrovich Chayev was acting chairman of the Society of Friends of Russian Literature from 1878 to 1884.

Nikolai, the bishop of Japan, was Ivan Dmitriyevich Kasatkin (1836–1912); his "Letters from Japan" were published over many years in the *Moscow Gazette*. Aleksei, the vicar of Moscow, was Aleksandr Fyodorovich Platonov (1828–1890), professor of canon law at the Moscow Theological Academy and author of many books and articles on theological subjects. Dostoyevsky did visit the two men a few days later, and he wrote to Anna Grigorevna: "They said that they felt greatly honored by my visit and were very happy to meet me. They have read my books. That shows that they appreciate it when they find someone who is on God's side."

150.   To A. G. Dostoyevskaya
Loskutnaya Hotel, Room 33
Moscow
June 7, 1880
Midnight

My sweet, precious darling Anya,

I'm writing this in haste. The unveiling of the monument took place yesterday. How can I possibly describe it to you? Why, 20 pages wouldn't be enough, and I really haven't a minute to spare. It's already 3 nights that I've had only 5 hours sleep, and tonight it'll be the same.

After the unveiling, there was a dinner with speeches, followed by the readings, with music, at the literary evening in the Hall of Nobility. I read the Pimen scene. Even though it was an impossible choice (for surely one cannot very well shout Pimen across a whole hall) and the reading took place in a hall with the worst possible acoustics, I was told it was superb, although the audience had difficulty in hearing me. I was given a tremendous reception. For a long time they wouldn't let me start reading, everyone kept cheering, and after the reading they called me back 3 times. But Turgenev, who read miserably, was called back more times than I was. Backstage (a huge dark space) I noticed as many as a hundred young people who yelled frantically when Turgenev came on stage. It occurred to me right away that they were members of a claque, installed there by Kovalevsky. That is exactly what they turned out to be: At this morning's session, because of this claque, Ivan Aksakov refused to make his speech after Turgenev (who in his speech had belittled Pushkin by refusing to acknowledge him as our national poet). Aksakov explained to me that the claque had been organized long in advance and brought in deliberately by Kovalevsky (they were all his students and the whole lot of them were Westernizers) to make Turgenev appear to be the leader of their movement and at the same time to humiliate us if we tried to say anything against them.

Nevertheless, the reception given to me yesterday was quite amazing, although it was only those sitting in the front rows that applauded. In addition to that, crowds of men and women came backstage to shake my hand. As I walked across the hall during intermission, a host of people, youths and graybeards and ladies, rushed toward me exclaiming, "You're our prophet. We've become better people since we read *The Karamazovs*." (In brief, I realized how tremendously important *The Karamazovs* is.) Today, as I was leaving the morning session at which I hadn't spoken, the same thing happened. On my way downstairs to pick up my coat in the cloakroom, men, women, etc., kept stopping me. In the evening, during the dinner, two ladies brought me flowers. I knew some of these women by name—Tretyakova, Golokhvastova, Moshnina, and others. I'll pay a visit to Tretyakova (the wife of the owner of the art gallery) the day after tomorrow.

Today we had the second literary dinner, attended by a couple of hundred people. The young people met me when I arrived, paid homage to me, looked after me, and made frenzied speeches to me—and all this before dinner. During the dinner many people spoke and proposed toasts. I didn't want to speak, but toward the end of the dinner, people leaped up from their seats and forced me to say something. I said only a few words and they were met by a roar of enthusiasm—literally a roar. Then, already in another room, a great crowd clustered around me and we talked long and passionately (over coffee and cigars). And when, around 9:30, I got up to go home (2-thirds of the guests were still there), they cheered me, and even those who didn't sympathize with me were forced to join in willy-nilly. Then the whole crowd streamed down the stairs after me and, hatless and coatless, made their way into the street and installed me in my cab. And then, all of a sudden, they rushed up to kiss my hands, not just one but scores of them, and not only the young but old graybeards, too. No, Turgenev has only his claque, but my people have genuine enthusiasm. Maikov witnessed all this; he must have been surprised. Several people I didn't know came over to me and whispered that a whole plot was being hatched against Aksakov and me at tomorrow morning's reading. Tomorrow is the 8th, my most crucial day: In the morning I'll give my speech and in the evening I have to read twice—"The She-Bear" and "The Prophet." I'm determined to read "The Prophet" well. Wish me luck.

There's a lot of noise and excitement around here. Last night, at the dinner in the City Hall, Katkov risked delivering a long speech, which nevertheless produced an effect on at least part of the audience. Outwardly, Kovalevsky is very friendly with me and in one toast mentioned my name, among others. Turgenev, too. Annenkov tried to thrust himself upon me, but I turned away. Look, Anya, here I'm writing to you when I still haven't put the final touches on my speech. On the 9th, I have those visits to make and must make up my mind whom to give my speech to. Everything hinges on the effect it will produce. I've been here a long time, spent a fair amount of money, but then I've laid the foundations of our future. I must give the speech a final going over and get my clothes ready for tomorrow.

Tomorrow is my big day. I'm afraid I won't get enough sleep. I'm afraid I may have an attack.

The Central Store won't pay up, it's hopeless. Good-bye, darling. I embrace you and kiss the children. I'll probably leave on the 10th and be home late on the 11th. Prepare yourself. I hug you all hard and bless you.

Your forever faithful,
F. Dostoyevsky

NB. This letter will probably be my last from here.

---

150. Olga Andreyevna Golokhvastova (d. 1894) was the author of several plays and novels. She and her husband, Pavel Dmitriyevich, a historian and literary critic, were close to the Slavophiles.

Despite his fears, Dostoyevsky did not suffer an epileptic attack while in Moscow.

151.   To A. G. DOSTOYEVSKAYA
Hotel Loskutnaya, Room 33
Moscow
June 8, 1880
8 P.M.

My dear Anya,

I mailed off today the letter I wrote you yesterday, the 7th, but now I can't resist sending you these few lines as well, although I am completely exhausted, both morally and physically. So it is quite possible that you'll receive this letter at the same time as the other. This morning I read my speech at the meeting of the Friends [of Russian Literature]. The auditorium was packed. No, Anya, you'll never be able to imagine, to conceive the effect that speech produced! My successes in Petersburg were nothing compared to this—just plain *nothing!* When I appeared on the stage, the auditorium thundered with applause and for a very, very long time I wasn't given a chance to begin. I bowed and made signs, begging them to let me read—but to no avail: elation, enthusiasm (all because of *The Karamazovs!*). At last I began reading. At every page, sometimes at every sentence, I was interrupted by bursts of applause. I read in a loud voice, with fire. Everything I wrote about Tatyana was received with enthusiasm. (This is a great victory for our idea over 25 years of delusions!) And when, at the end, I proclaimed the *universal oneness* of mankind, the hall seemed to go into hysterics, and when I finished, there was—I won't call it a roar—it was a howl of elation. People in the audience who had never met before, wept, sobbed, embraced each other, *and swore to become better, not to hate each other any more but to love one another.* The order of the meeting was shattered. Everyone rushed up to me on the stage: grandes dames, girl students, state secretaries, male students—they all hugged and kissed me. All the members of our Society who were on the stage hugged me, kissed me, and all of them, to a man, literally cried in their elation. They kept calling me back for half an hour, waving their handkerchiefs. Suddenly—to give you an idea of what went on—two old men I'd never seen before came up to me: "For 20 years we have been enemies, have never spoken to each other, but now we've embraced and made up. It is you who have reconciled us. You're our saint, you're our prophet!" "Prophet, prophet!" people were shouting in the crowd.

Turgenev, for whom I had put in a good word in my speech, rushed up to me and embraced me with tears in his eyes. Annenkov darted toward me, shook my hand, and kissed my shoulder. "You're a genius, you're more than a genius!" the two of them kept saying. Aksakov (Ivan) came running onto the stage and declared to the audience that my speech *wasn't simply a speech but a historic event!* Clouds had been hanging over the horizon but now the word of Dostoyevsky had scattered them and brightened everything, like the rising sun. From now on, an era of brotherhood would reign and there would be an end to strife. Yes, yes! they all shouted and again embraced each other and again shed tears. The meeting broke up. I hurried backstage, trying to escape, but they forced their way in behind me, all of them, especially the women. They kissed my hands, they wouldn't leave me alone. The students pushed forward. One of them, in tears, fell down on the floor in front of me in hysterics and lost consciousness. It was a complete, total victory! Yurev (the chairman) rang his bell and declared that the Society of the Friends of Russian Literature had unanimously elected me as an *honorary* member. More screams and shouts.

After almost an hour's interruption, the meeting was resumed. No one seemed to want to speak. Aksakov got up and declared that he was not going to read his speech because everything had been said and settled by the great words of our genius—Dostoyevsky. However, we all prevailed upon him to deliver his speech. While he was delivering it, a plot was being hatched. I was beginning to feel very weak and wanted to leave but they kept me by force. At that hour of the day, they managed to buy a most expensive laurel wreath, 2 arshins in diameter, and at the end of the session, a throng of women (more than a hundred of them) stormed the stage and crowned me with the wreath in front of the whole audience: "This is for the Russian woman, of whom you said so many good things!" Everyone wept, and again there was enthusiasm. Mayor Tretyakov thanked me in the name of the City of Moscow.

You will agree, Anya, that it was worthwhile staying here: these are the foundations of the future, the foundations of *everything,* even if I were to die.

When I got back to the hotel, I found your letter about the foal, but you write so unfeelingly about my staying on. In an hour, I'll go and give my reading at the 2nd literary celebration. I'll read "The Prophet." Tomorrow— the visits. I'll leave here the day after tomorrow, the 10th, and be back home on the 11th—*unless something very important detains me here*. I must place my article. But with whom? They'll all be trying to grab it now. It's terrible. Good-bye, my precious, desirable, priceless one. I kiss your little feet. I embrace the children, bless them and kiss them. I kiss the foal. I bless you all. My head is out of order, my hands and legs are trembling. Good-bye, until very soon.

Yours all and entirely,
Dostoyevsky

---

151. The "good word" that Dostoyevsky had included in his speech about Turgenev was to make a favorable comparison between the portrayal of Tatyana, the heroine of Pushkin's *Eugene Onegin,* and that of Liza in Turgenev's *Nest of Gentlefolk.* Turgenev, in later comments, while admitting that Dostoyevsky's speech had been "clever, brilliant, and cunningly calculated" and that he himself had "fallen under its spell," nevertheless said that "it was based entirely on false premises that flatter Russian vanity" and insisted that "these gentlemen of the Slavophile party haven't swallowed us yet."

Shortly after Dostoyevsky delivered his speech, Katkov sent him a telegram saying it was "accepted enthusiastically" for publication, and it appeared in the *Moscow Gazette* on June 13.

152.   To N. A. LYUBIMOV

Staraya Russa, August 10, 1880

Dear Sir, highly esteemed Nikolai Alekseyevich:

At the same time as this letter, I am sending off the installment of *The Karamazovs* for the August issue of *R[ussian] Messenger*. This is the conclusion of "Book Eleven," consisting of 72 half-sheets of regular-size writing paper, i.e., exactly 3½ printer's sheets.

I beg you urgently to send me the proofs in good time. I won't hold them up a minute more than I have to.

The twelfth and last book of *The Karamazovs* will reach your office *without fail* around the 10th or the 12th of next month (September). It will also be three or 3½ printer's sheets long, not more. That will leave the *Epilogue* of the novel, 1½ printer's sheets—for publication in the October number.

Now, concerning the installment I am sending you:

I personally am quite satisfied with chapters 6, 7, and 8. I am not sure, however, highly esteemed Nikolai Alekseyevich, how you will feel about chapter 9. Perhaps you will find it a bit too peculiar! But I assure you, I was not just trying to be original. I feel, however, duty-bound to tell you that I checked with doctors (several of them) long ago and they confirm that not only nightmares but also hallucinations are possible before bouts of "white fever." My hero, of course, has hallucinations, too, but he confuses them with his nightmares. It is a question here not only of a physical (pathological) phenomenon, in which a person begins to lose, at times, the ability to distinguish between the real and the imaginary (something that happens to everyone at least once in his life), but also of a psychological trait that is in keeping with the character of my hero: Although he denies the reality of the apparition, as soon as the apparition vanishes, he insists that it was real. *Suffering as he is from his inability to believe, he at the same time wishes (unconsciously) that the apparition should not be just a figment of his imagination, but something that was actually there.*

But why am I telling you all this? You will judge for yourself when you read it, highly esteemed Nikolai Alekseyevich. You must, however, forgive me my *devil:* It is only a minor devil and not Satan with his "singed wings."

I don't think that the chapter is too boring, although it is a little long. Nor do I think that it contains anything that the censors will find objectionable, except perhaps for such words as "the *hysterical shrieks* of the cherubs." I beseech you to let that stand! Remember, it is the *devil* who says it and that is the only way he can say it. If, however, you decide it is absolutely impossible, then, please replace *hysterical shrieks* with *joyful cries.* But couldn't we leave *shrieks?* Otherwise, it will be too prosaic and the tone will not be right.

I don't think that my devil does anything that the censor could object to.

As for the two anecdotes about the *confessionals,* they may be a bit flippant but they are certainly in no way obscene. They don't even begin to compare with the things Mephistopheles pours out in both parts of *Faust.*

I believe that the 10th and last chapter contains an adequate explanation of Ivan's mental state and therefore of his nightmare in chapter 9. And let me repeat—I have checked the medical facts with doctors.

Although I myself think that chapter 9 *could have been omitted,* for some reason or other I *greatly enjoyed* writing it and I don't at all wish to disavow it.

My hero suffers a frenzied bout of white fever just when he is testifying at the trial (but that will come only later, in Book Twelve).

And so I have expressed to you all my doubts, highly esteemed Nikolai Alekseyevich. I shall be waiting most impatiently for the proofs.

How are things with you and are you still at your summer house? Have you been blessed with good weather? We have been having marvelous weather here, touch wood, while in Petersburg, which seems so near, it has been raining. As long as I am here, my health improves, despite my work.

I am looking forward to the pleasure of sending you my *Diary of a Writer,* which is coming out on August 12 in Petersburg—this will be the only number for this year.

My most sincere regards to your wife.

Please be so good as to convey my profound respects to Mikhail Nikiforovich.

I enclose the receipt for the one thousand rubles and I thank you for the speedy satisfaction of my request.

I beseech you to send me the August issue of *R. Messenger* in Staraya Russa. I have received the July issue and am very grateful to you for it.

Please accept the assurance of my most profound respect and unwavering loyalty,

Your faithful servant,
F. Dostoyevsky.

---

152. The publishers complied with Dostoyevsky's plea: In chapter 9 of book 11, the words "hysterical shrieks" (istericheskiye vvizgi) were used, rather than "joyful cries" (radostnyye kriki).

153. To N. L. OZMIDOV
Staraya Russa, August 18, 1880

Dear Sir, Nikolai Lukich:

I have read your letter very carefully, but what answer can I give to it? As you very intelligently remark in your letter, it is impossible to describe everything in a letter. I would even go so far as to say that it is impossible to give a satisfactory description of anything in a letter, beyond the most general outline. As for coming here to see me to seek my advice, I think that that, too, would be quite pointless, because I do not consider myself particularly qualified to answer your questions. You write that, up till now, you have not allowed your daughter to read any literary works for fear of stirring her imagination. Well, I wouldn't quite agree with that. Imagination is an inherent force in every human being and is particularly strong in children, in whom it becomes developed very early, before other faculties, and it demands to be satisfied. By refusing to satisfy it, you risk either killing it altogether or, on the contrary, you may cause it to develop excessively (which is harmful) by allowing it to thrive on its own innate strength. Such a strain would only drain the child's spiritual side prematurely. And exposure to *the beautiful* is exactly what is needed in childhood. When I was 10 years old, I saw a performance of Schiller's *The Robbers* in Moscow, with Mochalov acting in it, and, I assure you, the very strong impression it made on me affected my spiritual development very favorably. At the age of 12, while spending my summer holidays in the countryside, I read the whole of Walter Scott, and although it may have stirred my imagination and my impressionability, I feel that I made proper use of it, did not guide it in the wrong direction, and, when the many beautiful and lofty impressions I gathered from that reading were carried over into my life, they formed a great force in my heart with which to combat temptations and corrupting passions.

I would recommend that you give your daughter Walter Scott to read now, especially since he is quite forgotten in Russia today and by the time she is on her own she won't find the occasion or the need to acquaint herself with that great writer. So hasten to acquaint her with him while she is still at home with you, because Walter Scott is of great educational value. And let her also read Dickens—everything he has written, without exception. Acquaint her also with the literature of past centuries (*Don Quixote* and even *Gil Blas*). It would be best to start with poetry. She must read all of Pushkin, poetry as well as prose. The same goes for Gogol. Turgenev, Goncharov—if you wish. As for my works, I doubt that everything I have written would be appropriate for her. It would be good if she read in full Schlosser's history and Solovyov's history of Russia. She shouldn't neglect Karamzin. For the time being, don't give her Kostomarov. The conquests of Peru and of Mexico by Prescott are indispensable. In general, historical works are of tremendous educational importance. She must read all of Lev Tolstoy's works. Shakespeare, Schiller, Goethe—they are all available in excellent Russian translations. Well, that should do for the time being. But you will see yourself, as the years go by, that there are quite a few more things you could add to this list! Newspaper writings ought to be avoided, at least for the time being. I am not sure whehter you will be satisfied with my advice. I have written on the basis of my views and *experience*. I will be delighted if you find all this helpful. I don't feel that a meeting between us at this time is at all necessary, especially since I happen to be particularly busy just now. And I repeat again, I do not at all consider myself to be such an authority in this matter. The number of the *Diary* has been sent to you. It costs, including postage, only 35 kopeks, so that I consider I owe you 65 kopeks.

Your sincerely devoted,
F. Dostoyevsky.

---

153. Pavel Stepanovich Mochalov (1800–1848) was a famous Russian actor.

Friedrich Schlosser (1776–1861) was a German historian whose works had been translated into Russian.

For Dostoyevsky's reaction when he first read Prescott's works, see Letter 16.

154.   To P. Ye. Guseva
Petersburg
Kuznechny Lane
near St. Vladimir's Church
House No. 5, Apartment 10
October 15, 1880

Much esteemed Pelageya Yegorovna:

Instead of making such bitter reproaches, you might have assumed, at least for a second, that something had happened and that circumstances had prevented me from answering you. My family and I spent the whole summer in Staraya Russa (a mineral spa) and I have been back in Petersburg for only 5 days. Your first letter of July, the one addressed to *Messenger of Europe,* took an exceedingly long time to reach me, until the end of August. And anyway, what could I possibly have done, sitting in Staraya Russa, to influence the editorial board of *Little Flame,* a periodical I am not acquainted with and have not the least wish to be acquainted with? As for why I did not answer your letter, you won't believe the reason: The reason is that, if there is a man serving a sentence at hard labor, it is I. I did serve 4 years at hard labor in Siberia, but my life and work there was [*sic*] more bearable than it is now. From June 15 to October 1, I wrote as many as 20 printer's sheets of a novel and got out my *Diary of a Writer,* another three sheets. And moreover, I can't write off the top of my head, I must write artistically. I owe that to God, to poetry, to my reputation as a writer, and, literally, to the entire Russian reading public, which is waiting for the ending of my work. And that is why I sat and wrote literally day and night. From August right up until today, I haven't answered a single letter. Writing letters is torture for

511

me, but people keep bombarding me with letters and requests. Would you believe that I do not have time to read a single book or even a newspaper? I do not even have time to talk to my children. And I don't talk to them. And my health is worse than anything you can imagine. A catarrh of the respiratory passages has developed into emphysema, an incurable disease (suffocation, insufficient air), and my days are numbered. Owing to the pressure of work, my epilepsy has also become more acute. You are at least in good health and you ought to have pity for those who are not. If you are complaining about your health, you are not, after all, suffering from a fatal illness, and may God allow you to enjoy many years of good health, but—well, please forgive me.

As for your second letter, which is dated September and is full of reproaches, I received it only a few days ago, in Petersburg. My mail was still being sent to St[araya] Russa and was not being forwarded from there, because I had (inadvertently, of course), left incorrect instructions. And so now I have received dozens of letters at one time.

I have no connection with *Little Flame* nor, for that matter, do I have any connections with any editorial houses at all. Almost all of them are my enemies, although I don't know why. My own position is such that I cannot make the rounds of the editorial houses. I cannot go today to talk to people who yesterday said terrible things about me. That is literally impossible for me. I will, however, do my best to get your manuscript back from *Little Flame*. But where can I place it? Every scoundrel whom I might ask to publish your novel will look at me as if I were someone begging him for a tremendous favor. On the other hand, before I do anything, I would have to take a look at your manuscript myself, but I literally don't have a minute to attend to my own most pressing and sacred duties: I have neglected everything, abandoned everything, and I'm not speaking of myself. It is night now, after 6 A.M., the town is beginning to wake up, but I haven't gone to bed yet. And the doctors tell me that I must avoid overexertion, that I must sleep at night and not sit for 10 or 12 hours bent over my desk. Why do I write at night? Because no sooner do I wake up at 1 P.M. than my bell starts ringing without letup: one comes asking me for one favor, another for another favor, a third makes demands on me, and a fourth demands insistently that I solve some sort of "accursed" unsolvable problem for him, warning me that, if I don't do it, he will shoot himself (although I may never have set eyes on him before). Finally, there are all sorts of delegations—university students, male and female, high-school students, individuals from various charitable organizations—asking me to read at their evenings. And when am I supposed to think, to work, to read, to live.

I will send someone to the editorial office of *Little Flame* and I will insist that they return the manuscript. But as for reading it and placing it, I have no idea when or how I could possibly do anything about it. *For I literally cannot*, having neither the time *nor the right connections*. Perhaps you think that I don't want to go to see these people because I am too proud? But for pity's sake, how could I go to Stasyulevich or to the *Voice* or to *Rumor* or to any place where they abuse me in the vilest way. And if I brought them a manuscript that later happened not to be a success, they would say: Dostoyevsky hoodwinked us, we trusted him because he is an authority, but he duped us in order to get some money out of us. The press will get hold of it, spread it around, set people's tongues wagging. You don't know what the literary world is like.

Don't be surprised that I should say things like this. I am very tired and my nerves are painfully upset. I would say the same thing to anybody else— male or female! Do you realize that I have dozens of manuscripts lying around that have come by mail from complete strangers who want me to read them and send them to magazines with my recommendation: "You must know all the editors," they say! But when, then, am I supposed to live and do my own work? And what a fine thing it would be for me to haunt the editorial offices. If everybody has told you that your novel is too long and drawn out, then of course there must be something wrong with it. I absolutely have no idea what I will do. If I do anything, I will let you know. I don't know when that will be. If you find all of this too vague, ask someone else to handle it for you. For anyone else I wouldn't have lifted a finger: I am doing this for you in memory of Ems. I remember you only *too* well. I did read your letter (the first one), *indeed I read it*. But don't write me about that in letters. With a friendly handshake, I remain all yours,

F. Dostoyevsky.

[Added in the margin:] The entire literary world, without exception, is hostile to me—*only* the readers of Russia love me.

---

154. Pelageya Yegorovna Guseva was a little-known writer who had published some poems and stories under the pen name of A. Shumova. She had met Dostoyevsky in Ems in the summer of 1875.

Messenger of Europe was a liberal magazine. Stasyulevich was its publisher and editor. *Little Flame* (Ogonyok) was a weekly magazine of literature, science, and art, edited by N. P. Alovert from 1879 to 1883. It was regarded as a refuge for unsuccessful writers. *Rumor* (Molva) was a daily newspaper of politics, economics, and literature. All of these publications, as well as the *Voice*, had criticized *The Brothers Karamazov* and Dostoyevsky's speech at the Pushkin ceremony.

155.   To A. F. Blagonravov
Petersburg, December 19, 1880

Dear Sir, Aleksandr Fyodorovich:

I thank you for your letter. You correctly conclude that I see the root of evil in unbelief, but that a person who rejects his national identity rejects his faith at the same time. This is precisely the case with us, since our whole national identity is based on Christianity. The words "peasant," "Christian Orthodox Russia"—these are our primary foundations. For us, a Russian who rejects his national identity (and there are many such) must be either an atheist or a man indifferent to religion. Conversely, one who is an unbeliever or is indifferent cannot and will never understand either the Russian people or Russian national identity. The most important question now is how to convince our intelligentsia of this fact. Try to bring up the subject and they will either eat you alive or brand you as a traitor. But a traitor to whom? To them—i.e., to something wafting in the air, something that it is even difficult to think up a name for, because they themselves are not in a position to think of a name for themselves. Or a traitor to the people? No, I would rather be with the people, because there is much more to hope for from them than from the Russian intelligentsia, which rejects the people and is not even intelligent.

But a new intelligentsia is arising that strives to be with the people. And the first sign of an indissoluble link with the people is respect and love for what the people as a whole respect and love more than anything else in the world—i.e., their God and their faith.

This new, developing Russian intelligentsia seems to be raising its head just now. And it seems that it is just now that it is needed for our cause, and it is itself beginning to become aware of it.

It is because I preach God and national identity that they are trying with all their might to rub me off the face of the earth. Because of that chapter in *The Karamazovs* (about the hallucination) which you, a doctor, found so satisfactory, some have already tried to brand me a reactionary, a fanatic, a man who has "written himself out of his mind." And they naively imagine that everybody will chime in with them: "What? Dostoyevsky has come to writing about the devil now! Ah, what a vulgar man he is, and how uncouth!" But I don't think they've succeeded! I want to thank you, especially in your capacity as a doctor, for telling me that my description of that man's psychic sickness is correct. The opinion of an expert is an important support for me, and you will agree that that man (Ivan Karamazov) could, under the given circumstances, have had no other hallucination than the one he had. I intend to give a critical analysis of that chapter myself in some future number of the *Diary*.

514

And with that, please accept the assurance of my most sincere and best feelings,

Yours very faithfully,
Fyodor Dostoyevsky.

---

155. Aleksandr Fyodorovich Blagonravov was a provincial physician.

156.   To Ye. N. Geiden
Petersburg, January 28, 1881

On the 26th an artery burst in my lungs, precipitating an influx of blood into my lungs. After the first seizure there was a second one in the evening, accompanied by a tremendous loss of blood and choking. By 12:15 A.M. Fyod[or] Mikh[ailovich] was fully convinced that he was dying; he confessed and took communion. Little by little his breathing improved, the bleeding slowed down. But inasmuch as the burst blood vessel has not healed, the bleeding has not stopped.

---

156. Countess Yelizaveta Nikolayevna Geiden (née Zubova) was chairwoman of the Society of St. George, a charitable organization, and a friend and correspondent of Dostoyevsky's during the 1870s.

This letter was dictated by Dostoyevsky to Anna Grigorevna between 5 and 6 A.M. on the day of his death.

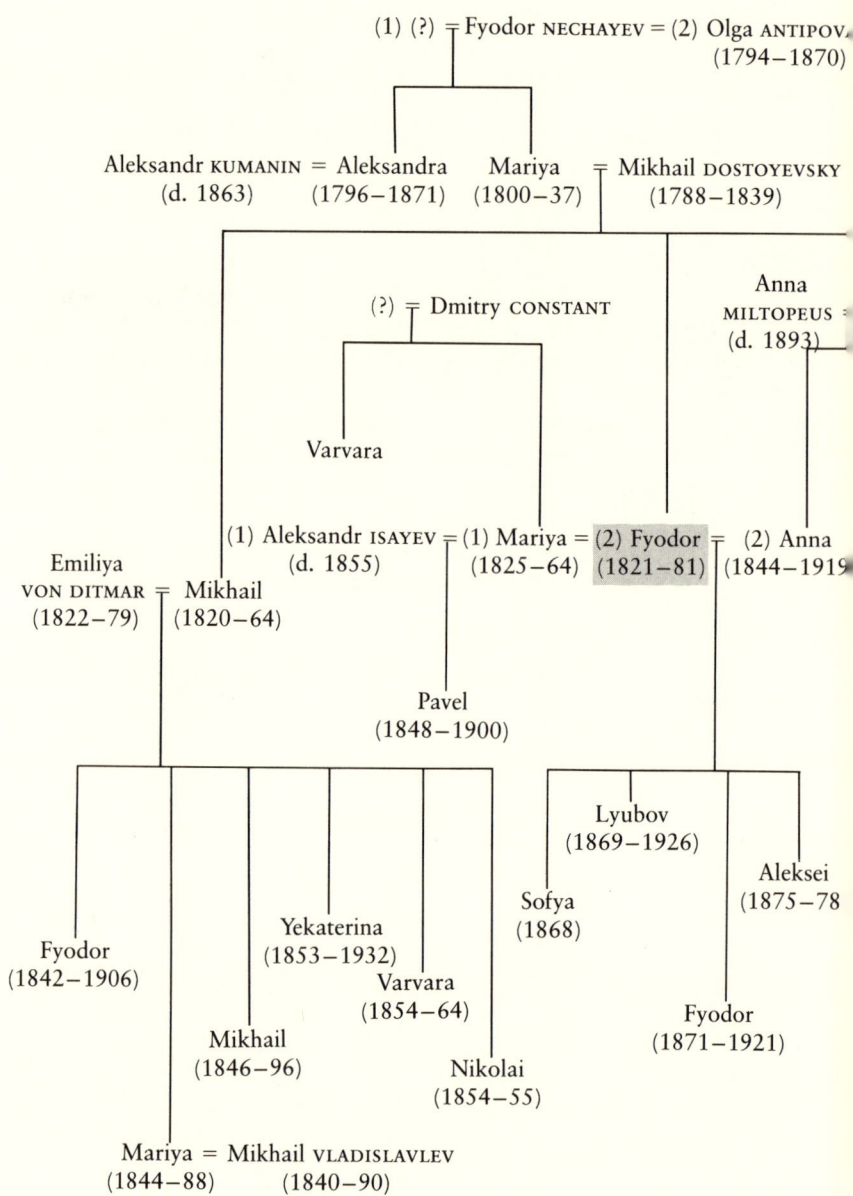

(1) (?) ⊤ Fyodor NECHAYEV = (2) Olga ANTIPOV
(1794–1870)

Aleksandr KUMANIN = Aleksandra   Mariya   ⊤ Mikhail DOSTOYEVSKY
(d. 1863)   (1796–1871)   (1800–37)   (1788–1839)

Anna
MILTOPEUS
(d. 1893)

(?) ⊤ Dmitry CONSTANT

Varvara

(1) Aleksandr ISAYEV ⊤ (1) Mariya = (2) Fyodor ⊤ (2) Anna
(d. 1855)   (1825–64)   (1821–81)   (1844–1919)

Emiliya
VON DITMAR ⊤ Mikhail
(1822–79)   (1820–64)

Pavel
(1848–1900)

Lyubov
(1869–1926)

Aleksei
(1875–78)

Sofya
(1868)

Fyodor
(1842–1906)

Yekaterina
(1853–1932)

Varvara
(1854–64)

Fyodor
(1871–1921)

Mikhail
(1846–96)

Nikolai
(1854–55)

Mariya = Mikhail VLADISLAVLEV
(1844–88)   (1840–90)

516

GENEALOGY

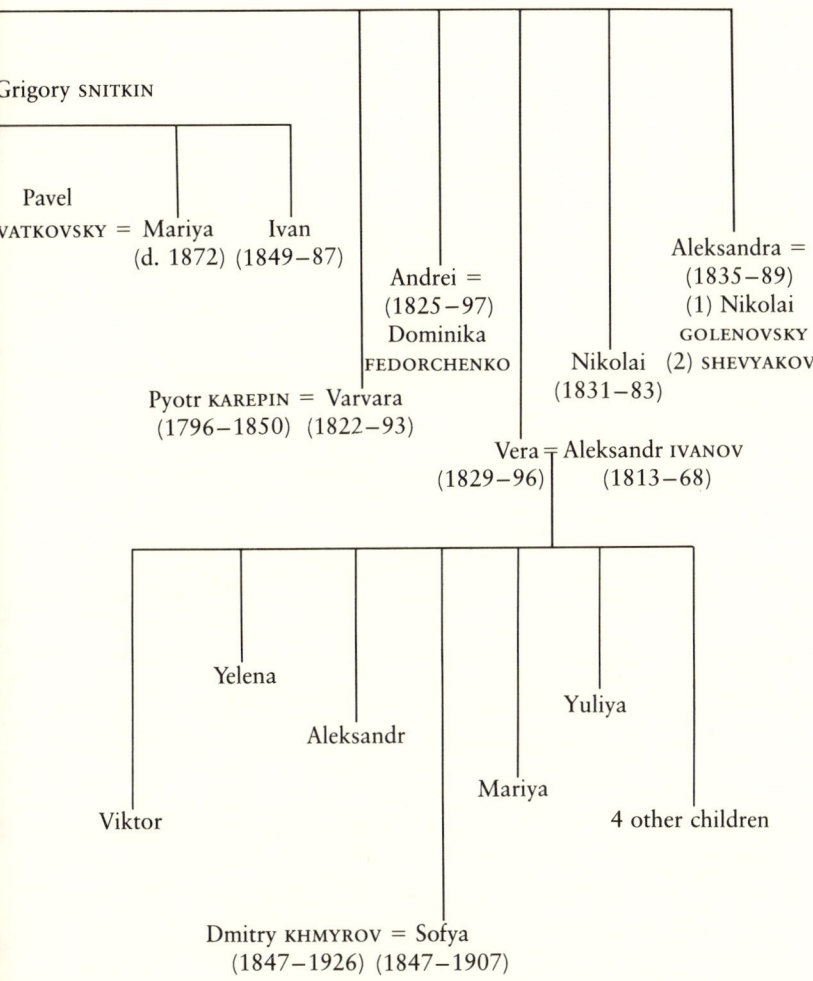

Grigory SNITKIN

Pavel
VATKOVSKY = Mariya   Ivan
(d. 1872) (1849–87)

Pyotr KAREPIN = Varvara
(1796–1850) (1822–93)

Andrei =
(1825–97)
Dominika
FEDORCHENKO

Aleksandra =
(1835–89)
(1) Nikolai
GOLENOVSKY
Nikolai   (2) SHEVYAKOV
(1831–83)

Nikolai
(1831–83)

Vera ⊤ Aleksandr IVANOV
(1829–96)   (1813–68)

Yelena

Aleksandr

Viktor

Mariya

Yuliya

4 other children

Dmitry KHMYROV = Sofya
(1847–1926) (1847–1907)

517

BIOGRAPHICAL SKETCHES OF FAMILY MEMBERS AND FREQUENTLY MENTIONED PERSONS

ANDRYUSHA   Dostoyevsky, Andrei Mikhailovich.

ANKA, ANNA GRIGOREVNA, ANYA, ANYUSHKA   Dostoyevskaya, Anna Grigorevna.

BELINSKY, VISSARION GRIGOREVICH (1811–1848)   One of Russia's most important literary critics, who was the first to recognize Dostoyevsky's genius and exercised a strong influence on his ideological evolution. Dostoyevsky's own relation to the heritage of Belinsky was ambiguous and complex, and shifted back and forth between profound admiration and vituperative resentment several times during his life.

CONSTANT, VARVARA DMITRIYEVNA   Sister of Dostoyevsky's first wife.

DOSTOYEVSKAYA, ALEKSANDRA MIKHAILOVNA   (1835–1889)   The youngest of Dostoyevsky's brothers and sisters, and the one with whom his relations were coolest. In 1854, she married Nikolai Ivanovich Golenovsky; after his death, she married Vladimir Shevyakov.

DOSTOYEVSKAYA, ANNA GRIGOREVNA (1844–1919)   Dostoyevsky's second wife. They met in October 1866, when she went to work for him as a stenographer. Dostoyevsky described the beginning of their relationship thus:

> My stenographer . . . turned out to be a young and quite comely girl of twenty, from a good family, who had finished secondary school with distinction and was extraordinarily self-possessed and good-natured. The two of us worked wonderfully together. As the novel [*The Gambler,* which he was dictating to her] neared completion, I became aware that my stenographer sincerely loved me, although she had never

said so much as a word about it, and I myself was coming to like her more and more. As I had found life terribly dull and oppressive since my brother's death, I proposed to her.

They were married in 1867. Not only *The Gambler* but also the second half of *Crime and Punishment* (on which he was working at the same time) and all his later works passed through her hands, and the opportunity to dictate changed his whole method of working. Anna Grigorevna was intelligent and efficient, had great energy and practical abilities, and often helped in negotiations with creditors and publishers. Her critical opinion was highly valued by Dostoyevsky, and he sometimes rewrote whole passages on the basis of her comments. Their marriage was a happy one and endured until his death. Afterward, Anna Grigorevna wrote a book about their life together; edited several collections of his works and published an index to them; founded the Dostoyevsky School at Staraya Russa; and organized a "Dostoyevsky Room" at the Pushkin Library in Moscow.

Dostoyevskaya, Emiliya Fyodorovna (1822–1879)   Wife of Dostoyevsky's brother Mikhail (née von Ditmar).

Dostoyevskaya, Lyubov Fyodorovna (1869–1926)   Dostoyevsky's second child. She wrote a book of short stories as well as a book about her father.

Dostoyevskaya, Mariya Dmitriyevna (1825–1864)   Dostoyevsky's first wife (née Constant). They met while Dostoyevsky was in Semipalatinsk, and her education and sensitivity made her stand out in that provincial town. When her first husband, Aleksandr Ivanovich Isayev, died in 1855, Dostoyevsky was eager to marry her; but she delayed, apparently hinting that she might marry someone else. They did marry early in 1857, but the marriage ran into difficulties almost from the start. Despite their mutual unhappiness, they remained strongly attached, even devoted, to each other until her death, and Dostoyevsky always spoke of her as a noble spirit, a "knight in female clothing." Dostoyevsky's troubled love affair with her was transposed into his first post-Siberian novel, *The Insulted and Injured,* and she also furnished inspiration for the character of Katerina Ivanovna, the tubercular wife of the drunkard Marmeladov in *Crime and Punishment.*

Dostoyevskaya, Mariya Fyodorovna (1800–1837)   Dostoyevsky's mother. She came from an old merchant family (née Nechayeva) and was evidently intelligent and possessed of artistic and musical talent. In the stern family atmosphere created by her husband, she was protector and comforter, and she was adored by her children. She died of tuberculosis.

DOSTOYEVSKAYA, MARIYA MIKHAILOVNA (1844–1888)   Second-born child of Dostoyevsky's brother Mikhail; a talented pianist. She married Mikhail Ivanovich Vladislavlev (1840–1890), who had been a contributor to the Dostoyevsky brothers' magazines and later became a professor of philosophy at Petersburg University.

DOSTOYEVSKAYA, SONYA FYODOROVNA (1868)   Dostoyevsky's first child. She died when three months old.

DOSTOYEVSKAYA, VARVARA MIKHAILOVNA (1822–1893)   The eldest of Dostoyevsky's sisters. At the age of seventeen, she married Pyotr Andreyevich Karepin, who was then a forty-four-year-old widower.

DOSTOYEVSKAYA, VARVARA MIKHAILOVNA (1854–1864)   Fifth child of Dostoyevsky's brother Mikhail.

DOSTOYEVSKAYA, VERA MIKHAILOVNA (1829–1896)   A younger sister of Dostoyevsky's and apparently his favorite. In 1846, she married Aleksandr Pavlovich Ivanov.

DOSTOYEVSKAYA, YEKATERINA MIKHAILOVNA (1853–1932)   Fourth child of Dostoyevsky's brother Mikhail. She married Vyacheslav A. Manassein (1841–1901), a doctor, scholar, and public figure, and publisher of the magazine *The Physician* (Vrach).

DOSTOYEVSKY, ALEKSEI FYODOROVICH (1875–1878)   Dostoyevsky's fourth child.

DOSTOYEVSKY, ANDREI MIKHAILOVICH (1825–1897)   A younger brother of Dostoyevsky's; trained as a civil engineer. He did not play a major role in Dostoyevsky's life, but he did leave copious notes covering the lives of all the members of the family.

DOSTOYEVSKY, FYODOR FYODOROVICH (1871–1921)   Dostoyevsky's third child. Those who knew him have described him as weak and colorless, and he apparently was supported by his mother for most of his life.

DOSTOYEVSKY, FYODOR MIKHAILOVICH (1842–1906)   Oldest child of Dostoyevsky's brother Mikhail; Dostoyevsky's godchild. A talented musician and pianist, he studied under Nikolai Rubinstein and became director of the Saratov Music School.

DOSTOYEVSKY, MIKHAIL ANDREYEVICH (1788–1839)   Dostoyevsky's father. He was born into a clerical family and studied at a seminary, but later entered the Moscow Academy of Medicine and Surgery. In 1812, he was appointed to a military hospital. He remained with the army until 1820, when he received an appointment in the female outpatient department of the Charity Hospital in Moscow, where Dostoyevsky was born. He retired in 1837 to the family estate in Darovoye, and he died there, probably murdered by his own serfs.

DOSTOYEVSKY, MIKHAIL MIKHAILOVICH (1820–1864)   Dostoyevsky's older brother. The two brothers were very close from their early years, and they became especially close when they worked together in publishing the magazines *Time* and *Epoch*. Mikhail published several literary works of his own, but, faced with the need to support a large family, he became proprietor of a cigarette factory. Upon his death, Dostoyevsky struggled to pay off the debts left from their various enterprises.

DOSTOYEVSKY, MIKHAIL MIKHAILOVICH (1846–1896)   Son of Dostoyevsky's brother Mikhail. A sickly man and an alcoholic, he died in a poorhouse or, according to some reports, in an insane asylum.

DOSTOYEVSKY, NIKOLAI MIKHAILOVICH (1831–1883)   Dostoyevsky's youngest brother. He was trained as a civil engineer but was an alcoholic and poverty-stricken for most of his life. Dostoyevsky frequently came to his aid.

DOSTOYEVSKY, NIKOLAI MIKHAILOVICH (1854–1855)   Last-born child of Dostoyevsky's brother Mikhail.

EMILIYA   Dostoyevskaya, Emiliya Fyodorovna.

FEDINKA, FEDYA   Dostoyevsky, Fyodor Mikhailovich (son of Dostoyevsky's brother Mikhail), and Dostoyevsky, Fyodor Fyodorovich.

GOGOL, NIKOLAI VASILEVICH (1809–1852)   A major Russian writer, toward whom—as toward several others—Dostoyevsky had ambivalent feelings. In *Diary of a Writer,* Dostoyevsky tells of gatherings of his friends at which they read Gogol aloud to each other, "sometimes all night," and he speaks of Gogol's *Dead Souls* and *Marriage* as "profound creations." But he also says that, "in those sections where he ceases to be an artist and begins merely to reason, [he] is simply weak." It is generally believed that the character of Foma Opiskin in *Village of Stepanchikovo* is a caricature of Gogol.

GOLENOVSKY, NIKOLAI (d. 1872)   Husband of Dostoyevsky's sister Aleksandra; an army colonel stationed at the Pavlovsky Officers' School in Petersburg.

ISAYEV, PAVEL ALEKSANDROVICH (1848–1900)   Dostoyevsky's stepson, the son of Mariya Dmitriyevna Isayeva and her first husband. Dostoyevsky was at first quite fond of him and assumed responsibility for him after Mariya Dmitriyevna's death. Afterward, however, Dostoyevsky became increasingly irritated with his behavior, accusing him of laziness, vanity, and rudeness. In the last years of Dostoyevsky's life, he had very little contact with Pavel.

ISAYEVA, MARIYA DMITRIYEVNA   Dostoyevskaya, Mariya Dmitriyevna.

IVANOV, ALEKSANDR PAVLOVICH (1813–1868)   Husband of Dostoyevsky's sister Vera; a physician and a teacher of physics at the Konstantinovsky Surveyors' Institute in Moscow. Dostoyevsky was very fond of him and held him in high esteem.

IVANOVA, SOFYA (SONYA) ALEKSANDROVNA (1847–1907)   Daughter of Dostoyevsky's sister Vera; married a schoolteacher, D. I. Khmyrov. Dostoyevsky felt very warmly toward her, had great respect for her intelligence and character, and wrote her at length about his literary plans, his family, and his financial preoccupations. He and Anna Grigorevna named their first child after her. However, sometime after 1871, there was a disagreement between them, perhaps over financial matters, and they drifted apart.

KAREPIN, PYOTR ANDREYEVICH (1796–1850)   Husband of Dostoyevsky's sister Varvara. After the death of Dostoyevsky's father, Karepin was named trustee of the estate and thus became the family "guardian."

KATKOV, MIKHAIL NIKIFOROVICH (1818–1887)   Publisher of the influential newspaper *Moscow Gazette* and then founder (1856) of the important magazine *Russian Messenger,* which published such writers as Tolstoy, Saltykov-Shchedrin, Pleshcheyev, Turgenev, Ostrovsky, and Ogaryov, as well as Dostoyevsky (*Crime and Punishment, The Idiot, The Devils,* and *The Brothers Karamazov*). Though relatively liberal at first, Katkov became more and more conservative during the later part of his life.

KOLECHKA, KOLYA   Dostoyevsky, Nikolai Mikhailovich.

Krayevsky, Andrei Aleksandrovich (1810–1889)   Publisher and editor, from 1839 on, of *Notes of the Fatherland,* a magazine in which several of Dostoyevsky's works first appeared. Dostoyevsky was constantly in debt to him, received payments from him in driblets, and was angered by the obligation to deliver fixed amounts to him by fixed deadlines. In 1865, when Dostoyevsky was in difficult financial circumstances, he offered the idea for a novel called *The Drunkards* (an early version of *Crime and Punishment*) to Krayevsky, but they could not agree on terms.

Kumanina, Aleksandra Fyodorovna (1796–1871)   Sister of Dostoyevsky's mother. In 1813, she married Aleksandr Alekseyevich Kumanin. They were Dostoyevsky's wealthiest relatives, and arguments over their estate plagued the family for many years.

Lyosha   Dostoyevsky, Aleksei Fyodorovich.

Lyuba, Lyulya   Dostoyevskaya, Lyubov Fyodorovna.

Maikov, Apollon Nikolayevich (1821–1897)   A poet and a close friend of Dostoyevsky's. Both Apollon and his younger brother Valerian (also a friend of Dostoyevsky's) were connected to the Petrashevsky circle. The views of Apollon and Dostoyevsky were quite close; while Dostoyevsky was abroad from 1867 to 1871, the two men carried on a very active correspondence, and Maikov often gave Dostoyevsky moral and material support. However, during the second half of the 1870s, there was a cooling in their relationship, perhaps as a result of changes in Dostoyevsky's views.

Masenka, Mashenka   Dostoyevskaya, Mariya Mikhailovna.

Misha   Dostoyevsky, Mikhail Mikhailovich.

Nekrasov, Nikolai Alekseyevich (1821–1877)   Poet, novelist, and publisher, with whom Dostoyevsky had close relationships—ranging from the warmest to the most hostile—for more than thirty years. Nekrasov was one of the first to express admiration for *Poor Folk,* which was published in his almanac *Petersburg Miscellany,* and his own poetry was later published in *Time.* On the other hand, Nekrasov offended Dostoyevsky by offering unacceptable conditions for the publication of *The Village of Stepanchikovo* in his magazine *Contemporary,* though he subsequently published other work of Dostoyevsky's both in *Contemporary* and in *Notes of the Fatherland,* which he edited later. The night that Nekrasov died, according to an article that Dostoyevsky wrote in *Diary of a Writer,* he reread much of what Nekrasov had written, and "my whole life passed rapidly before me."

NIKOLAI, NIKOLYA   Dostoyevsky, Nikolai Mikhailovich.

PASHA, PASHECHKA, PAVEL   Isayev, Pavel Aleksandrovich.

SASHA, SASHENKA, SASHUROCHKA   Dostoyevskaya, Aleksandra Mikhailovna.

SNITKINA, ANNA GRIGOREVNA   Dostoyevskaya, Anna Grigorevna.

SONECHKA, SONYA   Ivanova, Sofya Aleksandrovna.

STRAKHOV, NIKOLAI NIKOLAYEVICH (1828–1896)   Educated as a zoologist, but best known as a writer, critic, and philosopher. He had a close relationship with Dostoyevsky for many years, but they later became estranged both personally and philosophically. Strakhov wrote the first biography of Dostoyevsky, which included the first publication of many of his letters.

TURGENEV, IVAN SERGEYEVICH (1818–1883)   One of the major writers among Dostoyevsky's contemporaries. His relationship with Dostoyevsky was quite friendly at times; but the two men came increasingly into both personal and literary conflict, and in 1867 they broke off altogether. Turgenev was unlike Dostoyevsky in many ways: he was well-born, an admirer of European culture, a pessimist and a skeptic—and a universally recognized artist for most of his life. Despite their differences and their clashes, Dostoyevsky always admired several of Turgenev's novels.

VARINKA, VARYA   Dostoyevskaya, Varvara Mikhailovna.

VARVARA DMITRIYEVNA   Constant, Varvara Dmitriyevna.

VERINKA, VEROCHKA   Dostoyevskaya, Vera Mikhailovna.

VLADISLAVLEVA, MARIYA MIKHAILOVNA   Dostoyevskaya, Mariya Mikhailovna.

WRANGEL, BARON ALEKSANDR YEGOROVICH (1833–?)   Close friend of Dostoyevsky's for many years. Trained as a lawyer, he was appointed district attorney in Semipalatinsk in 1854, and there he befriended Dostoyevsky and won his admittance to social circles. From 1857 to 1859, he participated in archeological expeditions in the Far East, and he then served in diplomatic positions in Copenhagen and other European cities. His friendship with Dostoyevsky continued after the latter's return from Siberia, but they drifted apart in the early 1860s. After his retirement, Wrangel wrote a book of reminiscences about Dostoyevsky.

General Index

in, 274; liberal, 188n; new, 25; radical, 243, 244; recognition for writers, 303; Romanticism, 3, 9n, 12n, 20; Westernization, 199n, 254, 277, 278–279n, 295n, 346n, 504

living quarters, 37, 42; addresses, 24, 37, 42, 127, 218, 232; problems with, 377–379, 473; search for, 155, 396, 397, 407

Longinov, M. N., 384n; letter to, 383

Lure, S. Ye., 444n; letter to, 442

Lvov, F. N., 64, 65n

Lyubinov, N. A., 233n, 237, 475; letters to, 232, 233, 235, 464, 469, 477, 487, 489n; money from, 234n; visit to, 493

Maikov, Apollon, xiv, xv, 43n, 52, 82, 112, 145, 147, 148, 267n, 278–279n, 287n, 302, 306n, 324, 373, 501, 505, 524; godfather to children, 280, 323; hope of help from, 94, 96, 257, 316; judgments by, 150, 301n, 302n, 325; letters to, 83, 248, 260, 272, 279, 293, 295, 306, 315, 329, 342, 346; poetry of, 85, 87–88, 88n, 99n, 274, 279n, 285, 372, 389, 449; rift with, 368; "Council of Clermont," 85, 88n; "Council of Constance," 308, 310. See also Song of Igor's Campaign, The

Maikov, N. A., 52, 54, 55n

Maikov, Valerian, 42, 43n, 52, 55n, 84, 152n

Maikova, Y. P., 52, 54, 55n, 84

Malherbe, François de, 20, 21n

Markov, Y. L., 486, 487n

marriage, first, xiii, 4, 113, 520; D on, 113, 115, 119; importance of, 98; plans for, 78, 79, 111; unhappiness in, 167, 207, 520

marriage, second, xiv, 243; plans for, 237, 239n; proposal, 169, 235; success of, xvi, 243, 367, 520

Maslennikov, K. I., 435n; letter to, 432

Medem, N. V., 172n; letter to, 171

Merkurov family, 6, 7n, 7, 8, 12

Meshchersky, Prince V. P., 367, 374n, 374–375, 378, 387, 389–390, 462, 462n; disagreements with, 385–386, 386–387n, 393n; letter to, 385; work for, 371; "Letters from a Pretty Woman," 386, 386n, 387n

Mezentsov, N. V., 461–462, 462n, 469n

Mikhailov, V. V., 449n; letter to, 448

Milan, 296–297

Miller, O. F., 384n, 388, 392n

Milyukov, A. P., 134, 135n, 145, 150, 191, 199n, 235n

Milyukov, P. N., xvi

Minayev, D. D., 150, 152n

Minin, Kuzma, 455, 457n

Moller, Y. A., 126, 127–128n, 137

Mombelli, N. A., 64, 65n

monasteries, 155, 162n, 332, 334, 368, 459, 460n, 476, 485

Moscow: honorary dinner in, 494, 496, 497–498; plans to visit, 323–324, 371; Pushkin monument in, 491, 493, 494–495, 498–500, 499n; Slavic Congress in, 298, 301n; trips to, 237, 238n, 492–507

Moscow Gazette: 221n, 267n, 273, 287n, 411n, 456n; interest in, 265, 270, 323, 481; views on, 228, 230n, 344, 446; writing for, 507n

mystères du palais des czars, Les, 299, 301n

Nabakov, I. A., 64, 66n, 84

Nadein, M. P., 388, 392n

Napoleon III, 16, 21n, 284, 338, 345n

Nechayev, S. G., 244, 328n, 340, 342n, 369–370

Nekrasov, N. A., 30–32, 32n, 35, 39, 40, 138n, 144–145, 147, 163, 437, 524–525; publishing with, 149–150, 367–368, 398n, 404; rift with, 42

newspapers, 267n, 273; concern about, 344, 479; evaluation of, 344, 446,

Wrangel, Baron A. Y., 70, 72, 78–79, 163, **526**; correspondence with, xiv, 99–100n, 147, 156; description of, 75–76, 81–82, 84–85; friendship with, 104–105; help from, xiii, 4, 100, 168–169, 221n; letters to, 89, 103, 109, 205, 224; loans from, 74, 75n, 78, 80–81

writing: constant, 38, 224, 231–232, 235, 257, 260, 288, 292n, 293, 300, 322; and deadlines, 125, 136, 168, 169, 224, 333; delays, 327–328; desire for, 77, 370; fear of cuts in, 412, 465, 478, 488; ideas for, 34, 38, 52, 256, 329, 371, 445; material for, 249, 260–261; need for opinions on, 139, 141, 142, 164, 273, 372, 478, 480, 487; payment for, 127, 133–134, 141–142, 145, 185–186, 223, 305, 306, 317, 404n, 405n; plans for, 119, 120, 129, 145, 210, 211, 331, 417–418; problems with, 25, 86, 118, 233n, 398, 405–406, 431; process, 133, 141, 352; and revising, 27–28, 232–233, 233n. *See also* literary career; work

Yakushkin, Y. I., 82, **83n**; help from, 117; letter to, 117

Yanovsky, Dr. S. D., 52, **55n**, 167, 169–170, 170n, 267, 333; friendship with, 444; letter to, 444

Yastrzhembsky, I.-F. L., 57, 58, 64, **65n**

Yeliseyev, G. Z., 187, **188n**, 274, 278n

Yerzhinsky, O., 191, **193n**

Yid, use of term, 423, 424, 439n, 445, 461, 472, 473, 480, 483

youth, Russian, 453–456, 459, 485, 487n. *See also* students

Yurev, S. A., **458n**, 492–496, 496n, 497, 498, 499, 501, 502; letter to, 457

Zadonsky, Tikhon, 332, **334n**, 341, 478

Zarubin, P. A., 195, **199n**

Zasulich affair, 454, 456–457n

zemstvo organizations, 259n, 274, 278n, 284, 287n

Zhdan-Pushkin, I. V., 123, **124n**, 152

Zhukovsky, V. A., 9n

Zola, Émile, 427–428

Zotov, R. M., 12, **12n**

Zverev, N. A., 492, 493, **496n**

INDEX OF WORKS BY DOSTOYEVSKY